Praise for *Head First HTML and CSS*

"*Head First HTML and CSS* is a thoroughly modern introduction to forward-looking practices in web page markup and presentation. It correctly anticipates readers' puzzlements and handles them just in time. The highly graphic and incremental approach precisely mimics the best way to learn this stuff: make a small change and see it in the browser to understand what each new item means."

> — **Danny Goodman, author of *Dynamic HTML: The Definitive Guide***

"Eric Freeman and Elisabeth Robson clearly know their stuff. As the Internet becomes more complex, inspired construction of web pages becomes increasingly critical. Elegant design is at the core of every chapter here, each concept conveyed with equal doses of pragmatism and wit."

> — **Ken Goldstein, Executive Vice President and Managing Director, Disney Online**

"The Web would be a much better place if every HTML author started off by reading this book."

> — **L. David Baron, Technical Lead, Layout and CSS, Mozilla Corporation**
> *http://dbaron.org/*

"I've been writing HTML and CSS for 10 years now, and what used to be a long trial-and-error learning process has now been reduced neatly into an engaging paperback. HTML used to be something you could just hack away at until things looked okay on screen, but with the advent of web standards and the movement toward accessibility, sloppy coding practice is not acceptable anymore…from a business standpoint or a social responsibility standpoint. *Head First HTML and CSS* teaches you how to do things right from the beginning without making the whole process seem overwhelming. HTML, when properly explained, is no more complicated than plain English, and the authors do an excellent job of keeping every concept at eye level."

> — **Mike Davidson, President and CEO, Newsvine, Inc.**

"The information covered in this book is the same material the pros know, but taught in an educational and humorous manner that doesn't ever make you think the material is impossible to learn or you are out of your element."

> — **Christopher Schmitt, author of *The CSS Cookbook* and *Professional CSS*, schmitt@christopher.org**

"Oh, great. You made an HTML book simple enough a CEO can understand it. What will you do next? Accounting simple enough my developer can understand it? Next thing you know, we'll be collaborating as a team or something."

> — **Janice Fraser, CEO, Adaptive Path**

More Praise for *Head First HTML and CSS*

"I *heart* *Head First HTML and CSS*—it teaches you everything you need to learn in a 'fun coated' format!"

— **Sally Applin, UI designer and fine artist, *http://sally.com***

"This book has humor and charm, but most importantly, it has heart. I know that sounds ridiculous to say about a technical book, but I really sense that at its core, this book (or at least its authors) really care that the reader learns the material. This comes across in the style, the language, and the techniques. Learning—real understanding and comprehension—on the part of the reader is clearly topmost in the minds of the authors. And thank you, thank you, thank you, for the book's strong and sensible advocacy of standards compliance. It's great to see an entry-level book, that I think will be widely read and studied, campaign so eloquently and persuasively on behalf of the value of standards compliance in web page code. I even found in here a few great arguments I had not thought of—ones I can remember and use when I am asked (as I still am)—'what's the deal with compliance and why should we care?' I'll have more ammo now! I also liked that the book sprinkles in some basics about the mechanics of actually getting a web page live—FTP, web server basics, file structures, etc."

— **Robert Neer, Director of Product Development, Movies.com**

"*Head First HTML and CSS* is a most entertaining book for learning how to build a great web page. It not only covers everything you need to know about HTML and CSS, it also excels in explaining everything in layman's terms with a lot of great examples. I found the book truly enjoyable to read, and I learned something new!"

— **Newton Lee, Editor-in-Chief, ACM Computers in Entertainment**
   http://www.acmcie.org

"My wife stole the book. She's never done any web design, so she needed a book like *Head First HTML and CSS* to take her from beginning to end. She now has a list of websites she wants to build—for our son's class, our family…If I'm lucky, I'll get the book back when she's done."

— **David Kaminsky, Master Inventor, IBM**

"Beware. If you're someone who reads at night before falling asleep, you'll have to restrict *Head First HTML and CSS* to daytime reading. This book wakes up your brain."

— **Pauline McNamara, Center for New Technologies and Education,
   Fribourg University, Switzerland**

Praise for other books by Eric Freeman and Elisabeth Robson

"From the awesome *Head First Java* folks, this book uses every conceivable trick to help you understand and remember. Not just loads of pictures: pictures of humans, which tend to interest other humans. Surprises everywhere. Stories, because humans love narrative. (Stories about things like pizza and chocolate. Need we say more?) Plus, it's darned funny."

> — **Bill Camarda, READ ONLY**

"This book's admirable clarity, humor, and substantial doses of clever make it the sort of book that helps even nonprogrammers think well about problem solving."

> — **Cory Doctorow, co-editor of Boing Boing**
>   **and author of *Down and Out in the Magic Kingdom***
>   **and *Someone Comes to Town, Someone Leaves Town***

"I feel like a thousand pounds of books have just been lifted off of my head."

> — **Ward Cunningham, inventor of the wiki**
>   **and founder of the Hillside Group**

"This book is close to perfect, because of the way it combines expertise and readability. It speaks with authority and it reads beautifully. It's one of the very few software books I've ever read that strikes me as indispensable. (I'd put maybe 10 books in this category, at the outside.)"

> — **David Gelernter, professor of computer science,**
>   **Yale University, and author of *Mirror Worlds* and *Machine Beauty***

"A nosedive into the realm of patterns, a land where complex things become simple, but where simple things can also become complex. I can think of no better tour guides than these authors."

> — **Miko Matsumura, industry analyst, The Middleware Company**
>   **former Chief Java Evangelist, Sun Microsystems**

"I laughed, I cried, it moved me."

> — **Daniel Steinberg, Editor-in-Chief, java.net**

"Just the right tone for the geeked-out, casual-cool guru coder in all of us. The right reference for practical development strategies—gets my brain going without having to slog through a bunch of tired, stale professor-speak."

> — **Travis Kalanick, founder of Scour and Red Swoosh,**
>   **member of the MIT TR100**

"I literally love this book. In fact, I kissed this book in front of my wife."

> — **Satish Kumar**

Other O'Reilly books by Eric Freeman and Elisabeth Robson

Head First Design Patterns

Head First HTML with CSS & XHTML (first edition)

Head First HTML5 Programming

Other related books from O'Reilly

HTML5: Up and Running

HTML5 Canvas

HTML5: The Missing Manual

HTML5 Geolocation

HTML5 Graphics with SVG and CSS3

HTML5 Forms

HTML5 Media

Other books in O'Reilly's *Head First* series

Head First C#

Head First Java

Head First Object-Oriented Analysis & Design (OOA&D)

Head First Servlets and JSP

Head First SQL

Head First Software Development

Head First JavaScript

Head First Ajax

Head First Rails

Head First PHP & MySQL

Head First Web Design

Head First Networking

Head First iPhone and iPad Development

Head First jQuery

Head First
HTML and CSS

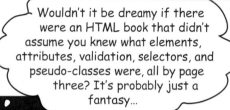

Wouldn't it be dreamy if there were an HTML book that didn't assume you knew what elements, attributes, validation, selectors, and pseudo-classes were, all by page three? It's probably just a fantasy...

Elisabeth Robson
Eric Freeman

O'REILLY®

Beijing • Cambridge • Farnham • Köln • Sebastopol • Tokyo

Head First HTML and CSS

by Elisabeth Robson and Eric Freeman

Printed in Canada.

Published by O'Reilly Media, Inc., 1005 Gravenstein Highway North, Sebastopol, CA 95472.

O'Reilly Media books may be purchased for educational, business, or sales promotional use. Online editions are also available for most titles (*http://my.safaribooksonline.com*). For more information, contact our corporate/institutional sales department: (800) 998-9938 or *corporate@oreilly.com*.

Series Creators:	Kathy Sierra, Bert Bates
Editor:	Brett McLaughlin (first edition), Mike Hendrickson (second edition)
Cover Designer:	Karen Montgomery
HTML Wranglers:	Elisabeth Robson, Eric Freeman
Production Editor:	Kristen Borg
Indexer:	Ron Strauss
Proofreader:	Rachel Monaghan
Page Viewer:	Oliver

Printing History:

December 2005: First Edition.

September 2012: Second Edition.

Nutshell Handbook, the Nutshell Handbook logo, and the O'Reilly logo are registered trademarks of O'Reilly Media, Inc. The *Head First* series designations, *Head First HTML and CSS*, and related trade dress are trademarks of O'Reilly Media, Inc.

Many of the designations used by manufacturers and sellers to distinguish their products are claimed as trademarks. Where those designations appear in this book, and O'Reilly Media, Inc., was aware of a trademark claim, the designations have been printed in caps or initial caps.

While every precaution has been taken in the preparation of this book, the publisher and the authors assume no responsibility for errors or omissions, or for damages resulting from the use of the information contained herein.

In other words, if you use anything in *Head First HTML and CSS* to, say, run a nuclear power plant, you're on your own. We do, however, encourage you to visit the Head First Lounge.

No elements or properties were harmed in the making of this book.

Thanks to Clemens Orth for the use of his photo, "applestore.jpg", which appears in Chapter 5.

ISBN: 978-0-596-15990-0

[TI]

Browser wars? You'll find out in Chapter 6.

To the W3C, for saving us from the browser wars and for their brilliance in separating structure (HTML) from presentation (CSS)…

And for making HTML and CSS complex enough that people need a book to learn it.

Authors of Head First HTML and CSS

Eric Freeman

Elisabeth Robson

Eric is described by Head First series co-creator Kathy Sierra as "one of those rare individuals fluent in the language, practice, and culture of multiple domains from hipster hacker, corporate VP, engineer, think tank."

Professionally, Eric recently ended nearly a decade as a media company executive—having held the position of CTO of Disney Online and Disney.com at the Walt Disney Company. Eric is now devoting his time to WickedlySmart, a startup he co-created with Elisabeth.

By training, Eric is a computer scientist, having studied with industry luminary David Gelernter during his Ph.D. work at Yale University. His dissertation is credited as the seminal work in alternatives to the desktop metaphor, and also as the first implementation of activity streams, a concept he and Dr. Gelernter developed.

In his spare time, Eric is deeply involved with music; you'll find Eric's latest project, a collaboration with ambient music pioneer Steve Roach, available on the iPhone App Store under the name Immersion Station.

Eric lives with his wife and young daughter on Bainbridge Island. His daughter is a frequent vistor to Eric's studio, where she loves to turn the knobs of his synths and audio effects.

Write to Eric at eric@wickedlysmart.com or visit his site at http://ericfreeman.com.

Elisabeth is a software engineer, writer, and trainer. She has been passionate about technology since her days as a student at Yale University, where she earned a master's of science in computer science and designed a concurrent, visual programming language and software architecture.

Elisabeth's been involved with the Internet since the early days; she co-created the award-winning website, the Ada Project, one of the first websites designed to help women in computer science find career and mentorship information online.

She's currently co-founder of WickedlySmart, an online education experience centered on web technologies, where she creates books, articles, videos and more. Previously, as Director of Special Projects at O'Reilly Media, Elisabeth produced in-person workshops and online courses on a variety of technical topics and developed her passion for creating learning experiences to help people understand technology. Prior to her work with O'Reilly, Elisabeth spent time spreading fairy dust at the Walt Disney Company, where she led research and development efforts in digital media.

When not in front of her computer, you'll find Elisabeth hiking, cycling or kayaking in the great outdoors, with her camera nearby, or cooking vegetarian meals.

You can send her email at beth@wickedlysmart.com or visit her blog at http://elisabethrobson.com.

Table of Contents (summary)

Table of Contents (the real thing)

Intro

Your brain on HTML and CSS. Here *you* are trying to *learn* something, while here your *brain* is doing you a favor by making sure the learning doesn't *stick*. Your brain's thinking, "Better leave room for more important things, like which wild animals to avoid and whether naked snowboarding is a bad idea." So how *do* you trick your brain into thinking that your life depends on knowing HTML and CSS?

getting to know html

1 The Language of the Web

The only thing that is standing between you and getting yourself on the Web is learning to speak the lingo: HyperText Markup Language, or HTML for short. So, get ready for some language lessons. After this chapter, not only are you going to understand some basic **elements** of HTML, but you'll also be able to speak HTML with a little **style.** Heck, by the end of this book, you'll be talking HTML like you grew up in Webville.

No pressure, but thousands of people are going to visit this web page when you're finished. It not only needs to be correct, it's gotta look great, too!

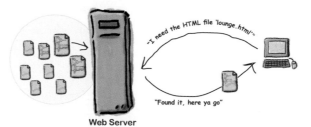

Web Server

going further with hypertext

2

Meeting the "HT" in HTML

Did someone say "hypertext?" What's that? Oh, only the entire basis of the Web. In Chapter 1 we kicked the tires of HTML and found it to be a nice markup language (the "ML" in HTML) for describing the structure of web pages. Now we're going to check out the "HT" in HTML, hypertext, which will let us break free of a single page and link to other pages. Along the way we're going to meet a powerful new element, the <a> element, and learn how being "relative" is a groovy thing. So, fasten your seat belts—you're about to learn some hypertext.

building blocks

Web Page Construction

3

I was told I'd actually be creating web pages in this book?

You've certainly learned a lot already: tags, elements, links, paths...but it's all for nothing if you don't create some killer web pages with that knowledge. In this chapter we're going to ramp up construction: you're going to take a web page from conception to blueprint, pour the foundation, build it, and even put on some finishing touches. All you need is your hard hat and your toolbelt, as we'll be adding some new tools and giving you some insider knowledge that would make Tim "The Toolman" Taylor proud.

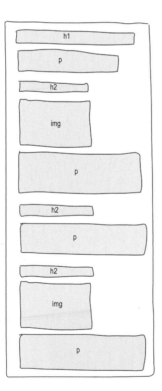

getting connected

A Trip to Webville

4

Web pages are a dish best served on the Internet. So far
you've only created HTML pages that live on your own computer. You've also
only linked to pages that are on your own computer. We're about to change all
that. In this chapter we'll encourage you to get those web pages on the Internet
where all your friends, fans, and customers can actually see them. We'll also
reveal the mysteries of linking to other pages by cracking the code of the h, t, t, p,
:, /, /, w, w, w. So, gather your belongings; our next stop is Webville.

adding images to your pages

Meeting the Media

5

Smile and say "cheese." Actually, smile and say "gif," "jpg," or "png"—these are going to be your choices when "developing pictures" for the Web. In this chapter you're going to learn all about adding your first media type to your pages: images. Got some digital photos you need to get online? No problem. Got a logo you need to get on your page? Got it covered. But before we get into all that, don't you still need to be formally introduced to the <img> element? So sorry, we weren't being rude; we just never saw the "right opening." To make up for it, here's an entire chapter devoted to <img>. By the end of the chapter you're going to know all the ins and outs of how to use the <img> element and its attributes. You're also going to see exactly how this little element causes the browser to do extra work to retrieve and display your images.

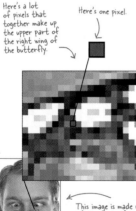

Here's a lot of pixels that together make up the upper part of the right wing of the butterfly.

Here's one pixel.

This image is made up of thousands of pixels when it's displayed on a computer screen.

standards and all that jazz

6 Serious HTML

What else is there to know about HTML? You're well on your way to mastering HTML. In fact, isn't it about time we move on to CSS and learn how to make all this bland markup look fabulous? Before we do, we need to make sure your HTML is really ready for the big leagues. Don't get us wrong, you've been writing first-class HTML all along, but there are just a few extra things you need to do to make it "industry standard" HTML. It's also time you think about making sure you're using the latest and greatest HTML standard, otherwise known as HTML5. By doing so, you'll ensure that your pages play well with the latest i-Device, and that they'll display more uniformly across all browsers (at least the ones you'd care about). You'll also have pages that load faster, pages that are guaranteed to play well with CSS, and pages that are ready to move into the future as the standards grow. Get ready, this is the chapter where you move from web tinkerer to web professional.

getting started with CSS

7 Adding a Little Style

I was told there'd be CSS in this book. So far you've been concentrating on learning HTML to create the structure of your web pages. But as you can see, the browser's idea of style leaves a lot to be desired. Sure, we could call the fashion police, but we don't need to. With CSS, you're going to completely control the presentation of your pages, often without even changing your HTML. Could it really be so easy? Well, you *are* going to have to learn a new language; after all, Webville is a bilingual town. After reading this chapter's guide to learning the language of CSS, you're going to be able to stand on *either* side of Main Street and hold a conversation.

Five-Minute Mystery

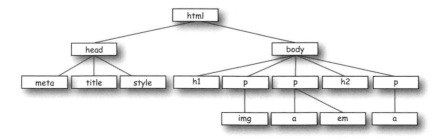

styling with fonts and colors

Expanding Your Vocabulary

8

Your CSS language lessons are coming along nicely. You already have the basics of CSS down, and you know how to create CSS rules to select and specify the style of an element. Now it's time to build your vocabulary, and that means picking up some new properties and learning what they can do for you. In this chapter we're going to work through some of the most common properties that affect the display of text. To do that, you'll need to learn a few things about fonts and color. You're going to see you don't have to be stuck with the fonts everyone else uses, or the clunky sizes and styles the browser uses as the defaults for paragraphs and headings. You're also going to see there is a lot more to color than meets the eye.

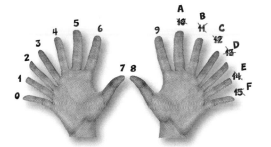

the box model

Getting Intimate with Elements

9

To do advanced web construction, you really need to know your building materials. In this chapter we're going to take a close look at our building materials: the HTML elements. We're going to put block and inline elements right under the microscope and see what they're made of. You'll see how you can control just about every aspect of how an element is constructed with CSS. But we don't stop there—you'll also see how you can give elements unique identities. And, if that weren't enough, you're going to learn when and why you might want to use multiple stylesheets. So, turn the page and start getting intimate with elements.

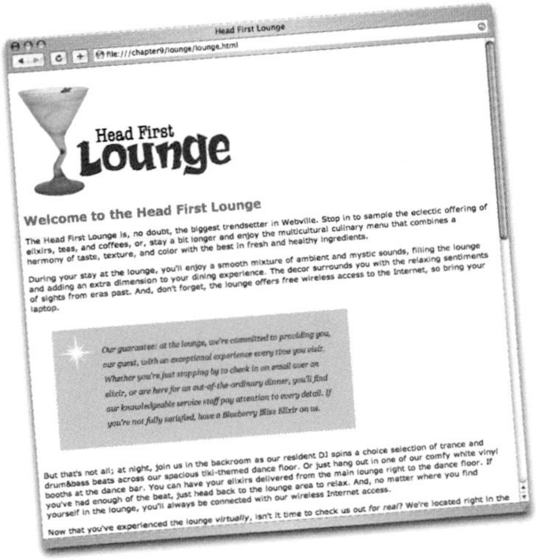

divs and spans

Advanced Web Construction

10

It's time to get ready for heavy construction. In this chapter we're going to roll out two new HTML elements: <div> and <span>. These are no simple "two by fours"; these are full-blown steel beams. With <div> and <span>, you're going to build some serious supporting structures, and once you've got those structures in place, you're going to be able to style them all in new and powerful ways. Now, we couldn't help but notice that your CSS toolbelt is really starting to fill up, so it's time to show you a few shortcuts that will make specifying all these properties a lot easier. And we've also got some special guests in this chapter, the *pseudo-classes*, which are going to allow you to create some very interesting selectors. (If you're thinking that "pseudo-classes" would make a great name for your next band, too late; we beat you to it.)

Weekly Elixir Specials

Lemon Breeze

The ultimate healthy drink, this elixir combines herbal botanicals, minerals, and vitamins with a twist of lemon into a smooth citrus wonder that will keep your immune system going all day and all night.

Chai Chiller

Not your traditional chai, this elixir mixes maté with chai spices and adds an extra chocolate kick for a caffeinated taste sensation on ice.

Black Brain Brew

Want to boost your memory? Try our Black Brain Brew elixir, made with black oolong tea and just a touch of espresso. Your brain will thank you for the boost.

Join us any evening for these and all our wonderful elixirs.

layout and positioning

Arranging Elements

11

It's time to teach your HTML elements new tricks. We're not going to let those HTML elements just sit there anymore—it's about time they get up and help us create some pages with real *layouts*. How? Well, you've got a good feel for the <div> and <span> structural elements and you know all about how the box model works, right? So, now it's time to use all that knowledge to craft some real designs. No, we're not just talking about more background and font colors—we're talking about full-blown professional designs using multicolumn layouts. This is the chapter where everything you've learned comes together.

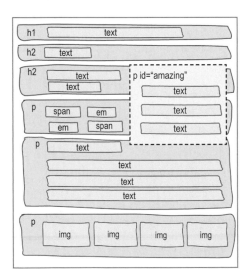

html5 markup

Modern HTML

12

So, we're sure you've heard the hype around HTML5. And, given how far along you are in this book, you're probably wondering if you made the right purchase. Now, one thing to be clear about, up front, is that everything you've learned in this book has been HTML, and more specifically has met the HTML5 standard. But there are some new aspects of HTML markup that were added with the HTML5 standard that we haven't covered yet, and that's what we're going to do in this chapter. Most of those additions are evolutionary, and you're going to find you are quite comfortable with them given all the hard work you've already done in this book. There's some revolutionary stuff too (like video), and we'll talk about that in this chapter as well. So, let's dive in and take a look at these new additions!

tables and more lists

Getting Tabular

13

If it walks like a table and talks like a table... There comes a time in life when we have to deal with the dreaded *tabular data*. Whether you need to create a page representing your company's inventory over the last year or a catalog of your vinylmation collection (don't worry, we won't tell), you know you need to do it in HTML, but how? Well, have we got a deal for you: order now, and in a single chapter we'll reveal the secrets that will allow you to put your very own data right inside HTML tables. But there's more: with every order we'll throw in our exclusive guide to styling HTML tables. And, if you act now, as a special bonus, we'll throw in our guide to styling HTML lists. Don't hesitate; call now!

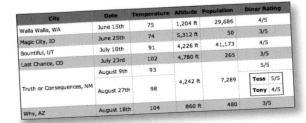

html forms

Getting Interactive

14

So far all your web communication has been one-way: from your page to your visitors. Golly, wouldn't it be nice if your visitors could talk back? That's where HTML forms come in: once you enable your pages with forms (along with a little help from a web server), your pages are going to be able to gather customer feedback, take an online order, get the next move in an online game, or collect the votes in a "hot or not" contest. In this chapter you're going to meet a whole team of HTML elements that work together to create web forms. You'll also learn a bit about what goes on behind the scenes in the server to support forms, and we'll even talk about keeping those forms stylish.

15

appendix: leftovers
The Top Ten Topics (We Didn't Cover)

We covered a lot of ground, and you're almost finished with this book. We'll miss you, but before we let you go, we wouldn't feel right about sending you out into the world without a little more preparation. We can't possibly fit everything you'll need to know into this relatively short chapter. Actually, we *did* originally include everything you need to know about HTML and CSS (not already covered by the other chapters), by reducing the type point size to .00004. It all fit, but nobody could read it. So, we threw most of it away, and kept the best bits for this Top Ten appendix.

 **Index**

Intro

In this section, we answer the burning question:
"So, why DID they put that in an HTML book?"

Who is this book for?

If you can answer "yes" to all of these:

 1 Do you have access to a computer with a **web browser** and a **text editor**?

 If you have access to any computer manufactured in the last decade, the answer is yes.

 2 Do you want to **learn, understand,** and **remember** how to **create** web pages using the best techniques and the most recent standards?

 3 Do you prefer **stimulating dinner-party conversation** to **dry, dull, academic lectures?**

this book is for you.

Who should probably back away from this book?

If you can answer "yes" to any one of these:

1 **Are you <u>completely</u> new to computers?**

(You don't need to be advanced, but you should understand folders and files, simple text editing applications, and how to use a web browser.)

2 Are you a kick-butt web developer looking for a *reference* book?

3 Are you **afraid to try something different**? Would you rather have a root canal than mix stripes with plaid? Do you believe that a technical book can't be serious if HTML tags are anthropomorphized?

this book is not for you.

[Note from marketing: this book is for anyone with a credit card.]

We know what you're thinking.

"How can this be a serious book?"

"What's with all the graphics?"

"Can I actually learn it this way?"

And we know what your brain is thinking.

Your brain craves novelty. It's always searching, scanning, *waiting* for something unusual. It was built that way, and it helps you stay alive.

Today, you're less likely to be a tiger snack. But your brain's still looking. You just never know.

So what does your brain do with all the routine, ordinary, normal things you encounter? Everything it *can* to stop them from interfering with the brain's *real* job—recording things that *matter*. It doesn't bother saving the boring things; they never make it past the "this is obviously not important" filter.

How does your brain *know* what's important? Suppose you're out for a day hike and a tiger jumps in front of you—what happens inside your head and body?

Neurons fire. Emotions crank up. *Chemicals surge.*

And that's how your brain knows…

This must be important! Don't forget it!

But imagine you're at home, or in a library. It's a safe, warm, tiger-free zone. You're studying. Getting ready for an exam. Or trying to learn some tough technical topic your boss thinks will take a week, 10 days at the most.

Just one problem. Your brain's trying to do you a big favor. It's trying to make sure that this *obviously* non-important content doesn't clutter up scarce resources. Resources that are better spent storing the really *big* things. Like tigers. Like the danger of fire. Like how you should never again snowboard in shorts.

And there's no simple way to tell your brain, "Hey brain, thank you very much, but no matter how dull this book is, and how little I'm registering on the emotional Richter scale right now, I really *do* want you to keep this stuff around."

Your brain thinks THIS is important.

Great. Only 637 more dull, dry, boring pages.

Your brain thinks THIS isn't worth saving.

We think of a "Head First" reader as a <u>learner</u>.

So what does it take to *learn* something? First, you have to *get* it, then make sure you don't *forget* it. It's not about pushing facts into your head. Based on the latest research in cognitive science, neurobiology, and educational psychology, *learning* takes a lot more than text on a page. We know what turns your brain on.

Some of the Head First learning principles:

Make it visual. Images are far more memorable than words alone, and make learning much more effective (up to 89% improvement in recall and transfer studies). It also makes things more understandable. **Put the words within or near the graphics** they relate to, rather than on the bottom or on another page, and learners will be up to *twice* as likely to solve problems related to the content.

Browsers make requests for HTML pages or other resources, like images.

Web Server   "Found it, here ya go"

It really sucks to forget your <body> element.

Use a conversational and personalized style. In recent studies, students performed up to 40% better on post-learning tests if the content spoke directly to the reader, using a first-person, conversational style rather than taking a formal tone. Tell stories instead of lecturing. Use casual language. Don't take yourself too seriously. Which would *you* pay more attention to: a stimulating dinner-party companion, or a lecture?

Does it make sense to create a bathtub class for my style, or just to style the whole bathroom?

Get the learner to think more deeply. In other words, unless you actively flex your neurons, nothing much happens in your head. A reader has to be motivated, engaged, curious, and inspired to solve problems, draw conclusions, and generate new knowledge. And for that, you need challenges, exercises, and thought-provoking questions, and activities that involve both sides of the brain, and multiple senses.

The head element is where you put things about your page.

Get—and keep—the reader's attention. We've all had the "I really want to learn this, but I can't stay awake past page one" experience. Your brain pays attention to things that are out of the ordinary, interesting, strange, eye-catching, unexpected. Learning a new, tough, technical topic doesn't have to be boring. Your brain will learn much more quickly if it's not.

Touch their emotions. We now know that your ability to remember something is largely dependent on its emotional content. You remember what you *care* about. You remember when you *feel* something. No, we're not talking heart-wrenching stories about a boy and his dog. We're talking emotions like surprise, curiosity, fun, "what the...?", and the feeling of "I rule!" that comes when you solve a puzzle, learn something everybody else thinks is hard, or realize you know something that "I'm more technical than thou" Bob from engineering *doesn't*.

Metacognition: thinking about thinking

If you really want to learn, and you want to learn more quickly and more deeply, pay attention to how you pay attention. Think about how you think. Learn how you learn.

Most of us did not take courses on metacognition or learning theory when we were growing up. We were *expected* to learn, but rarely *taught* how to learn.

I wonder how I can trick my brain into remembering this stuff...

But we assume that if you're holding this book, you really want to learn how to create web pages. And you probably don't want to spend a lot of time. And you want to *remember* what you read, and be able to apply it. And for that, you've got to *understand* it. To get the most from this book, or *any* book or learning experience, take responsibility for your brain. Your brain on *this* content.

The trick is to get your brain to see the new material you're learning as Really Important. Crucial to your well-being. As important as a tiger. Otherwise, you're in for a constant battle, with your brain doing its best to keep the new content from sticking.

So how *DO* you get your brain to think HTML & CSS are as important as a tiger?

There's the slow, tedious way, or the faster, more effective way. The slow way is about sheer repetition. You obviously know that you *are* able to learn and remember even the dullest of topics, if you keep pounding on the same thing. With enough repetition, your brain says, "This doesn't *feel* important to him, but he keeps looking at the same thing *over* and *over* and *over*, so I suppose it must be."

The faster way is to do **anything that increases brain activity,** especially different *types* of brain activity. The things on the previous page are a big part of the solution, and they're all things that have been proven to help your brain work in your favor. For example, studies show that putting words *within* the pictures they describe (as opposed to somewhere else in the page, like a caption or in the body text) causes your brain to try to make sense of how the words and picture relate, and this causes more neurons to fire. More neurons firing = more chances for your brain to *get* that this is something worth paying attention to, and possibly recording.

A conversational style helps because people tend to pay more attention when they perceive that they're in a conversation, since they're expected to follow along and hold up their end. The amazing thing is, your brain doesn't necessarily *care* that the "conversation" is between you and a book! On the other hand, if the writing style is formal and dry, your brain perceives it the same way you experience being lectured to while sitting in a roomful of passive attendees. No need to stay awake.

But pictures and conversational style are just the beginning.

Here's what WE did:

We used *pictures*, because your brain is tuned for visuals, not text. As far as your brain's concerned, a picture really *is* worth 1,024 words. And when text and pictures work together, we embedded the text *in* the pictures because your brain works more effectively when the text is *within* the thing the text refers to, as opposed to in a caption or buried in the text somewhere.

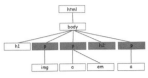

We used *redundancy*, saying the same thing in *different* ways and with different media types, and *multiple senses*, to increase the chance that the content gets coded into more than one area of your brain.

We used concepts and pictures in *unexpected* ways because your brain is tuned for novelty, and we used pictures and ideas with at least *some emotional content*, because your brain is tuned to pay attention to the biochemistry of emotions. That which causes you to *feel* something is more likely to be remembered, even if that feeling is nothing more than a little **humor**, **surprise**, or **interest.**

Be the Browser

We used a personalized, **conversational style**, because your brain is tuned to pay more attention when it believes you're in a conversation than if it thinks you're passively listening to a presentation. Your brain does this even when you're *reading*.

We included more than 100 **activities**, because your brain is tuned to learn and remember more when you **do** things than when you *read* about things. And we made the exercises challenging-yet-doable, because that's what most *people* prefer.

BULLET POINTS

We used **multiple learning styles**, because *you* might prefer step-by-step procedures, while someone else wants to understand the big picture first, while someone else just wants to see a code example. But regardless of your own learning preference, *everyone* benefits from seeing the same content represented in multiple ways.

We include content for **both sides of your brain**, because the more of your brain you engage, the more likely you are to learn and remember, and the longer you can stay focused. Since working one side of the brain often means giving the other side a chance to rest, you can be more productive at learning for a longer period of time.

Puzzles

And we included **stories** and exercises that present **more than one point of view,** because your brain is tuned to learn more deeply when it's forced to make evaluations and judgments.

We included **challenges**, with exercises, and by asking **questions** that don't always have a straight answer, because your brain is tuned to learn and remember when it has to *work* at something. Think about it—you can't get your *body* in shape just by *watching* people at the gym. But we did our best to make sure that when you're working hard, it's on the *right* things. That **you're not spending one extra dendrite** processing a hard-to-understand example, or parsing difficult, jargon-laden, or overly terse text.

We used **people**. In stories, examples, pictures, etc., because, well, because *you're* a person. And your brain pays more attention to *people* than it does to *things*.

We used an **80/20** approach. We assume that if you're going to be a kick-butt web developer, this won't be your only book. So we don't talk about *everything*. Just the stuff you'll actually *need*.

Here's what YOU can do to bend your brain into submission

So, we did our part. The rest is up to you. These tips are a starting point; listen to your brain and figure out what works for you and what doesn't. Try new things.

Cut this out and stick it on your refrigerator.

- -

① Slow down. The more you understand, the less you have to memorize.

Don't just *read*. Stop and think. When the book asks you a question, don't just skip to the answer. Imagine that someone really *is* asking the question. The more deeply you force your brain to think, the better chance you have of learning and remembering.

② Do the exercises. Write your own notes.

We put them in, but if we did them for you, that would be like having someone else do your workouts for you. And don't just *look* at the exercises. **Use a pencil.** There's plenty of evidence that physical activity *while* learning can increase the learning.

③ Read the "There Are No Dumb Questions."

That means all of them. They're not optional sidebars—*they're part of the core content!* Don't skip them.

④ Make this the last thing you read before bed. Or at least the last *challenging* thing.

Part of the learning (especially the transfer to long-term memory) happens *after* you put the book down. Your brain needs time on its own, to do more processing. If you put in something new during that processing time, some of what you just learned will be lost.

⑤ Drink water. Lots of it.

Your brain works best in a nice bath of fluid. Dehydration (which can happen before you ever feel thirsty) decreases cognitive function.

⑥ Talk about it. Out loud.

Speaking activates a different part of the brain. If you're trying to understand something, or increase your chance of remembering it later, say it out loud. Better still, try to explain it out loud to someone else. You'll learn more quickly, and you might uncover ideas you hadn't known were there when you were reading about it.

⑦ Listen to your brain.

Pay attention to whether your brain is getting overloaded. If you find yourself starting to skim the surface or forget what you just read, it's time for a break. Once you go past a certain point, you won't learn faster by trying to shove more in, and you might even hurt the process.

⑧ *Feel* something!

Your brain needs to know that this *matters*. Get involved with the stories. Make up your own captions for the photos. Groaning over a bad joke is *still* better than feeling nothing at all.

⑨ *Create* something!

Apply this to something new you're designing, or rework an older project. Just do *something* to get some experience beyond the exercises and activities in this book. All you need is a pencil and a problem to solve…a problem that might benefit from using HTML and CSS.

Read me

This is a learning experience, not a reference book. We deliberately stripped out everything that might get in the way of learning whatever it is we're working on at that point in the book. And the first time through, you need to begin at the beginning, because the book makes assumptions about what you've already seen and learned.

We begin by teaching basic HTML, then standards-based HTML5.

To write standards-based HTML, there are a lot of technical details you need to understand that aren't helpful when you're trying to learn the basics of HTML. Our approach is to have you learn the basic concepts of HTML first (without worrying about these details), and then, when you have a solid understanding of HTML, teach you to write standards-compliant HTML (the most recent version of which is HTML5). This has the added benefit that the technical details are more meaningful after you've already learned the basics.

It's also important that you be writing compliant HTML when you start using CSS, so we make a point of getting you to standards-based HTML before you begin any serious work with CSS.

We don't cover every single HTML element or attribute or CSS property ever created.

There are a *lot* of HTML elements, *a lot* of attributes, and *a lot* of CSS properties. Sure, they're all interesting, but our goal was to write a book that weighs less than the person reading it, so we don't cover them all here. Our focus is on the core HTML elements and CSS properties that *matter* to you, the beginner, and making sure that you really, truly, deeply understand how and when to use them. In any case, once you're done with *Head First HTML and CSS*, you'll be able to pick up any reference book and get up to speed quickly on all the elements and properties we left out.

This book advocates a clean separation between the structure of your pages and the presentation of your pages.

Today, serious web pages use HTML to structure their content, and CSS for style and presentation. Nineties-era pages often used a different model, one where HTML was used for both structure and style. This book teaches you to use HTML for structure and CSS for style; we see no reason to teach you outdated bad habits.

We encourage you to use more than one browser with this book.

While we teach you to write HTML and CSS that are based on standards, you'll still (and probably always) encounter minor differences in the way web browsers display pages. So, we encourage you to pick at least two modern browsers and test your pages using them. This will give you experience in seeing the differences among browsers and in creating pages that work well in a variety of them.

We often use tag names for element names.

Rather than saying "the a element," or "the 'a' element," we use a tag name, like "the <a> element." While this may not be technically correct (because <a> is an opening tag, not a full-blown element), it does make the text more readable, and we usually follow the name with the word "element" to avoid confusion.

The activities are NOT optional.

The exercises and activities are not add-ons; they're part of the core content of the book. Some of them are to help with memory, some are for understanding, and some will help you apply what you've learned. ***Don't skip the exercises.*** The crossword puzzles are the only things you don't *have* to do, but they're good for giving your brain a chance to think about the words in a different context.

The redundancy is intentional and important.

One distinct difference in a Head First book is that we want you to *really* get it. And we want you to finish the book remembering what you've learned. Most reference books don't have retention and recall as a goal, but this book is about *learning*, so you'll see some of the same concepts come up more than once.

The examples are as lean as possible.

Our readers tell us that it's frustrating to wade through 200 lines of an example looking for the two lines they need to understand. Most examples in this book are shown within the smallest possible context, so that the part you're trying to learn is clear and simple. Don't expect all of the examples to be robust, or even complete—they are written specifically for learning, and aren't always fully functional.

We've placed all the example files on the Web so you can download them. You'll find them at `http://wickedlysmart.com/hfhtmlcss/`.

The Brain Power exercises don't have answers.

For some of them, there is no right answer, and for others, part of the learning experience of the Brain Power activities is for you to decide if and when your answers are right. In some of the Brain Power exercises, you will find hints to point you in the right direction.

Tech reviewers (first edition)

Louise Barr

Joe Konior

Valentin Crettaz

Corey McGlone

Barney Marispini

Fearless leader of the Extreme Review Team

Eiffel Tower

Marcus Green

Ike Van Atta

Pauline McNamara

Pauline gets the "kick-ass reviewer" award.

Johannes de Jong

David O'Meara

Our reviewers:

We're extremely grateful for our technical review team. **Johannes de Jong** organized and led the whole effort, acted as "series dad," and made it all work smoothly. **Pauline McNamara**, "co-manager" of the effort, held things together and was the first to point out when our examples were a little more "baby boomer" than hip. The whole team proved how much we needed their technical expertise and attention to detail. **Valentin Crettaz**, **Barney Marispini**, **Marcus Green**, **Ike Van Atta**, **David O'Meara**, **Joe Konior**, and **Corey McGlone** left no stone unturned in their review and the book is much better for it. You guys rock! And further thanks to **Corey** and **Pauline** for never letting us slide on our often too formal (or we should just say it, incorrect) punctuation. A shout-out to JavaRanch as well for hosting the whole thing.

A big thanks to **Louise Barr**, our token web designer, who kept us honest on our designs and on our use of HTML and CSS (although you'll have to blame us for the actual designs).

Acknowledgments (first edition)*

Esteemed Reviewer
David Powers

Even more technical review:

We're also extremely grateful to our esteemed technical reviewer **David Powers**. We have a real love/hate relationship with David because he made us work so hard, but the result was *oh so worth it*. The truth be told, based on David's comments, we made significant changes to this book and it is technically twice the book it was before. Thank you, David.

At O'Reilly:

Our biggest thanks to our editor, **Brett McLaughlin**, who cleared the path for this book, removed every obstacle to its completion, and sacrificed family time to get it done. Brett also did hard editing time on this book (not an easy task for a Head First title). Thanks, Brett; this book wouldn't have happened without you.

Don't let the sweater fool you—this guy is hardcore (technically of course).

Brett McLaughlin

Our sincerest thanks to the whole O'Reilly team: **Greg Corrin, Glenn Bisignani, Tony Artuso,** and **Kyle Hart** all led the way on marketing and we appreciate their out-of-the-box approach. Thanks to **Ellie Volkhausen** for her inspired cover design that continues to serve us well, and to **Karen Montgomery** for stepping in and bringing life to this book's cover. Thank you, as always, to **Colleen Gorman** for her hardcore copyedit (and for keeping it all fun). And we couldn't have pulled off a color book like this without **Sue Willing** and **Claire Cloutier**.

No Head First acknowledgment would be complete without thanking **Mike Loukides** for shaping the Head First concept into a series, and to **Tim O'Reilly** for always being there and his continued support. Finally, thanks to **Mike Hendrickson** for bringing us into the Head First family and having the faith to let us run with it.

Kathy Sierra and Bert Bates:

Last, and anything but least, to **Kathy Sierra** and **Bert Bates**, our partners in crime and the BRAINS who created the series. Thanks, guys, for trusting us *even more* with your baby. We hope once again we've done it justice. The three-day jam session was the highlight of writing the book, we hope to repeat it soon. Oh, and next time around, can you give LTJ a call and tell him he's just going to have to make a trip back to Seattle?

Bert Bates

Kathy Sierra

Hard at work researching Head First Parelli

Kara

*The large number of acknowledgments is because we're testing the theory that everyone mentioned in a book acknowledgment will buy at least one copy, probably more, what with relatives and everything. If you'd like to be in the acknowledgment of our *next* book, and you have a large family, write to us.

Tech reviewers (second edition)

We couldn't sleep at night without knowing that our high-powered HTML & CSS reviewer, **David Powers**, has scoured this book for inaccuracies. Truth is, so many years had passed since the first edition that we had to hire a private detective to locate him (it's a long story, but he was finally located in his underground HTML & CSS lair and research lab). Anyway, more seriously, while all the technical faults in this book sit solely with the authors (that's us), we can assure you in every case David tried to make sure we did things right. Once again, David was instrumental in the writing of this book.

We're extremely grateful for everyone on our technical review team. **Joe Konior** joined us once again for this edition, along with **Dawn Griffiths** (co-author of *Head First C*), and **Shelley Powers** (an HTML & CSS "power"house who has been writing about the Web for years). Once again, you all rock! Your feedback was amazingly thorough, detailed, and helpful. Thank you.

David Powers

Less pink, more HTML & CSS power!

Dawn Griffiths

Joe Konior

Acknowledgments (second edition)

Our biggest thanks to our chief editor, **Mike Hendrickson**, who made this book happen in every way (other than actually writing it) , was there for us the entire journey, and more importantly (the biggest thing any editor can do) totally trusted us to get it done! Thanks, Mike; none of our books would have happened without you. You've been our champion for well over a decade and we love you for it!

Of course it takes a village to publish a book, and behind the scenes a talented and friendly group at O'Reilly made it all happen. Our sincerest thanks to the whole O'Reilly team: **Kristen Borg** (production editor extraordinaire); the brilliant **Rachel Monaghan** (proofreader); **Ron Strauss** for his meticulous index; **Rebecca Demarest** for illustration help; **Karen Montgomery**, ace cover designer; and last but definitely not least, **Louise Barr**, who always helps our pages look better.

Mike Hendrickson

Lou Barr

Safari® Books Online

Safari® Books Online is an on-demand digital library that lets you easily search over 7,500 technology and creative reference books and videos to find the answers you need quickly.

With a subscription, you can read any page and watch any video from our library online. Read books on your cell phone and mobile devices. Access new titles before they are available for print, and get exclusive access to manuscripts in development and post feedback for the authors. Copy and paste code samples, organize your favorites, download chapters, bookmark key sections, create notes, print out pages, and benefit from tons of other time-saving features.

O'Reilly Media has uploaded this book to the Safari Books Online service. To have full digital access to this book and others on similar topics from O'Reilly and other publishers, sign up for free at *http://my.safaribooksonline.com*.

1 getting to know HTML

The Language of the Web

Not so fast...to get to know me, you've got to speak the **universal language**. You know, HTML and CSS.

The only thing that is standing between you and getting yourself on the Web is learning to speak the lingo: HyperText Markup Language, or HTML for short. So, get ready for some language lessons. After this chapter, not only are you going to understand some basic **elements** of HTML, but you'll also be able to speak HTML with a little **style**. Heck, by the end of this book you'll be talking HTML like you grew up in Webville.

The Web
~~Video~~ killed the radio star

Want to get an idea out there? Sell something? Just need a creative outlet? Turn to the Web—we don't need to tell you it has become the universal form of communication. Even better, it's a form of communication **YOU** can participate in.

But if you really want to use the Web effectively, you've got to know a few things about **HTML**—not to mention, a few things about how the Web works too. Let's take a look from 30,000 feet:

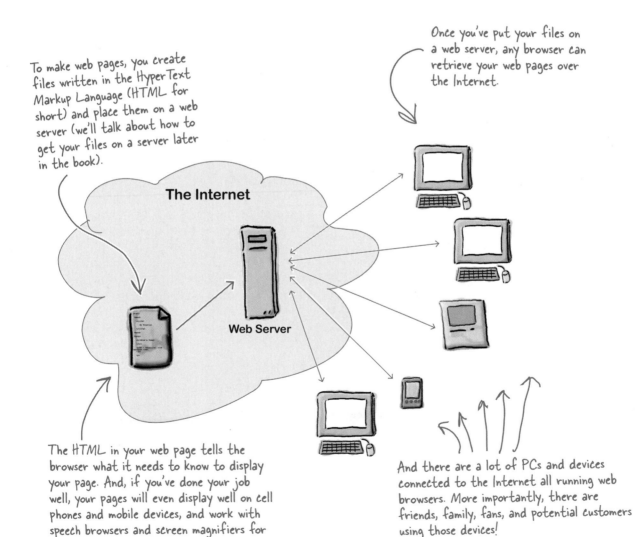

Once you've put your files on a web server, any browser can retrieve your web pages over the Internet.

To make web pages, you create files written in the HyperText Markup Language (HTML for short) and place them on a web server (we'll talk about how to get your files on a server later in the book).

The Internet

Web Server

The HTML in your web page tells the browser what it needs to know to display your page. And, if you've done your job well, your pages will even display well on cell phones and mobile devices, and work with speech browsers and screen magnifiers for the visually impaired.

And there are a lot of PCs and devices connected to the Internet all running web browsers. More importantly, there are friends, family, fans, and potential customers using those devices!

What does the web <u>server</u> do?

Web servers have a full-time job on the Internet, tirelessly waiting for requests from web browsers. What kinds of requests? Requests for web pages, images, sounds, or maybe even a video. When a server gets a request for any of these resources, the server finds the resource, and then sends it back to the browser.

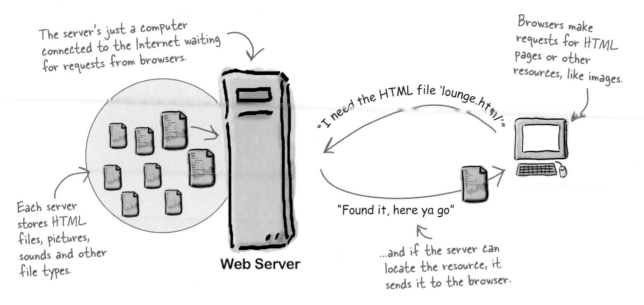

The server's just a computer connected to the Internet waiting for requests from browsers.

Browsers make requests for HTML pages or other resources, like images.

"I need the HTML file 'lounge.html'"

Each server stores HTML files, pictures, sounds and other file types.

Web Server

"Found it, here ya go"

...and if the server can locate the resource, it sends it to the browser.

What does the web <u>browser</u> do?

You already know how a browser works: you're surfing around the Web and you click on a link to visit a page. That click causes your browser to request an HTML page from a web server, retrieve it, and display the page in your browser window.

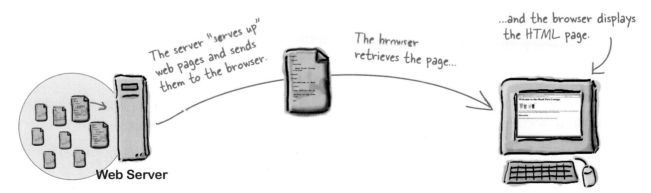

The server "serves up" web pages and sends them to the browser.

The browser retrieves the page...

...and the browser displays the HTML page.

Web Server

But how does the browser know how to display a page? That's where HTML comes in. HTML tells the browser all about the content and structure of the page. Let's see how that works…

What you write (the HTML)

So, you know HTML is the key to getting a browser to display your pages, but what exactly does HTML look like? And what does it do?

Let's have a look at a little HTML…imagine you're going to create a web page to advertise the *Head First Lounge*, a local hangout with some good tunes, refreshing elixirs, and wireless access. Here's what you'd write in HTML:

```
<html>
  <head>
    <title>Head First Lounge</title>   Ⓐ
  </head>
  <body>
    <h1>Welcome to the Head First Lounge</h1>   Ⓑ
    <img src="drinks.gif">   Ⓒ
    <p>
Ⓓ     Join us any evening for refreshing elixirs,
       conversation and maybe a game or
       two of <em>Dance Dance Revolution</em>.   Ⓔ
       Wireless access is always provided;
       BYOWS (Bring your own web server).
    </p>
    <h2>Directions</h2>   Ⓕ
    <p>
Ⓖ     You'll find us right in the center of
       downtown Webville. Come join us!
    </p>
  </body>
</html>
```

We don't expect you to know HTML yet.

At this point you should just be getting a feel for what HTML looks like; we're going to cover everything in detail in a bit. For now, study the HTML and see how it gets represented in the browser on the next page. Be sure to pay careful attention to each letter annotation and how and where it is displayed in the browser.

What the browser creates

When the browser reads your HTML, it interprets all the *tags* that surround your text. Tags are just words or characters in angle brackets, like <head>, <p>, <h1>, and so on. The tags tell the browser about the *structure and meaning* of your text. So rather than just giving the browser a bunch of text, with HTML you can use tags to tell the browser what text is in a heading, what text is a paragraph, what text needs to be emphasized, or even where images need to be placed.

Let's check out how the browser interprets the tags in the Head First Lounge:

Notice how each tag in the HTML maps to what the browser displays.

there are no Dumb Questions

Q: So HTML is just a bunch of tags that I put around my text?

A: For starters. Remember that HTML stands for HyperText Markup Language, so HTML gives you a way to "mark up" your text with tags that tell the browser how your text is structured. But there is also the HyperText aspect of HTML, which we'll talk about a little later in the book.

Q: How does the browser decide how to display the HTML?

A: HTML tells your browser about the structure of your document: where the headings are, where the paragraphs are, what text needs emphasis, and so on. Given this information, browsers have built-in default rules for how to display each of these elements.

But you don't have to settle for the default settings. You can add your own style and formatting rules with CSS that determine font, colors, size, and a lot of other characteristics of your page. We'll get back to CSS later in the chapter.

Q: The HTML for the Head First Lounge has all kinds of indentation and spacing, and yet I don't see that when it is displayed in the browser. How come?

A: Correct, and good catch. Browsers ignore tabs, returns, and most spaces in HTML documents. Instead, they rely on your markup to determine where line and paragraph breaks occur.

So why did we insert our own formatting if the browser is just going to ignore it? To help us more easily read the document when we're editing the HTML. As your

HTML documents become more complicated, you'll find a few spaces, returns, and tabs here and there really help to improve the readability of the HTML.

Q: So there are two levels of headings, <h1> and a subheading <h2>?

A: Actually there are six, <h1> through <h6>, which the browser typically displays in successively smaller font sizes. Unless you are creating a complex and large document, you typically won't use headings beyond <h3>.

Q: Why do I need the <html> tag? Isn't it obvious this is an HTML document?

A: The <html> tag tells the browser your document is actually HTML. While some browsers will forgive you if you omit it, some won't, and as we move toward "industrial-strength HTML" later in the book, you'll see it is quite important to include this tag.

Q: What makes a file an HTML file?

A: An HTML file is a simple text file. Unlike a word processing file, there is no special formatting embedded in it. By convention, we add an ".html" to the end of the filename to give the operating system a better idea of what the file is. But, as you've seen, what really matters is what we put inside the file.

Q: Everyone is talking about HTML5. Are we using it? If so, why aren't we saying "HTML-FIVE" instead of "HTML"?

A: You're learning about HTML, and HTML5 just happens to be the latest version of HTML. HTML5 has had a lot of attention recently, and that's because it simplifies

many of the ways we write HTML and enables some new functionality, which we're going to cover in this book. It also provides some advanced features through its JavaScript application programming interfaces (APIs), and those are covered in Head First HTML5 Programming.

Q: Markup seems silly. What-you-see-is-what-you-get applications have been around since, what, the '70s? Why isn't the Web based on a format like Microsoft Word or a similar application?

A: The Web is created out of text files without any special formatting characters. This enables any browser in any part of the world to retrieve a web page and understand its contents. There are WYSIWYG applications out there like Dreamweaver, and they work great. But in this book we're going to take it down to the bare metal, and start with text. Then you're in good shape to understand what your Dreamweaver application is doing behind the scenes.

Q: Is there any way to put comments to myself in HTML?

A: Yes, if you place your comments in between <!-- and --> the browser will totally ignore them. Say you wanted to write a comment "Here's the beginning of the lounge content." You'd do that like this:

```
<!-- Here's the beginning of
the lounge content -->
```

Notice that you can put comments on multiple lines. Keep in mind anything you put between the "<!--" and the "-->", even HTML, will be ignored by the browser.

Sharpen your pencil ——————————

You're closer to learning HTML than you think…

Here's the HTML for the Head First Lounge again. Take a look at the tags and see if you can guess what they tell the browser about the content. Write your answers in the space on the right; we've already done the first couple for you.

```
<html>
  <head>
    <title>Head First Lounge</title>
  </head>
  <body>
    <h1>Welcome to the Head First Lounge</h1>
    <img src="drinks.gif">
    <p>
        Join us any evening for refreshing elixirs,
        conversation and maybe a game or
        two of <em>Dance Dance Revolution</em>.
        Wireless access is always provided;
        BYOWS (Bring your own web server).
    </p>
    <h2>Directions</h2>
    <p>
        You'll find us right in the center of
        downtown Webville. Come join us!
    </p>
  </body>
</html>
```

Tells the browser this is the start of HTML.

Starts the page "head" (more about this later)

Tells the browser the title of the page is "Head First Lounge"

Starts the page "body"

Heading of the section

Places an image in the page

Begins a paragraph

Puts emphasis on "Dance Dance Revolution"

Closes the paragraph

Starts & closes a subheading

Begins another paragraph

Ends another paragraph

Closes the body of the page

Tells the browser this is the end of the HTML

Sharpen your pencil
Solution

```
<html>                                              Tells the browser this is the start of HTML.

   <head>                                           Starts the page "head".

      <title>Head First Lounge</title>              Gives the page a title.

   </head>                                           End of the head.

   <body>                                            Start of the body of page.

      <h1>Welcome to the Head First Lounge</h1>     Tells browser that "Welcome to..." is a heading.

      <img src="drinks.gif">                         Places the image "drinks.gif" here.

      <p>                                            Start of a paragraph.

         Join us any evening for refreshing elixirs,

         conversation and maybe a game or

         two of <em>Dance Dance Revolution</em>.    Puts emphasis on Dance Dance Revolution.

         Wireless access is always provided;

         BYOWS (Bring your own web server).

      </p>                                           End of paragraph.

      <h2>Directions</h2>                            Tells the browser that "Directions" is a
                                                     subheading.

      <p>                                            Start of another paragraph.

         You'll find us right in the center of

         downtown Webville. Come join us!

      </p>                                           End of paragraph.

   </body>                                           End of the body.

</html>                                              Tells the browser this is the end of
                                                     the HTML.
```

Your big break at Starbuzz Coffee

Starbuzz Coffee has made a name for itself as the fastest growing coffee shop around. If you've seen one on your local corner, look across the street—you'll see another one.

In fact, they've grown so quickly, they haven't even managed to put up a web page yet…and therein lies your big break: By chance, while buying your Starbuzz Chai Tea, you run into the Starbuzz CEO…

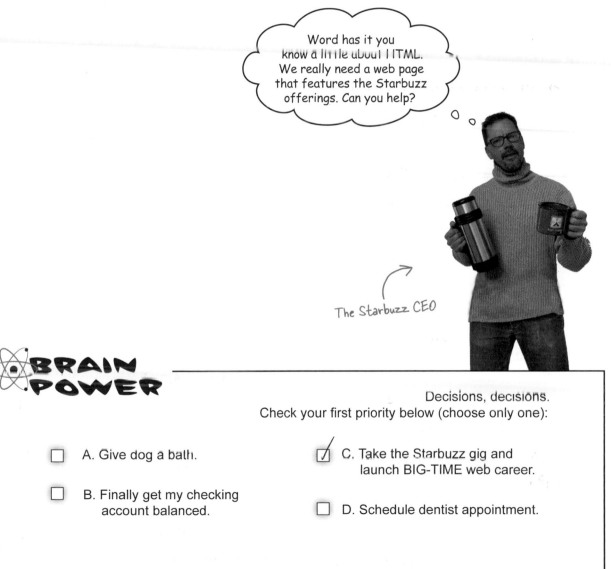

> Word has it you know a little about HTML. We really need a web page that features the Starbuzz offerings. Can you help?

The Starbuzz CEO

BRAIN POWER

Decisions, decisions.
Check your first priority below (choose only one):

- [ ] A. Give dog a bath.

- [ ] B. Finally get my checking account balanced.

- [✓] C. Take the Starbuzz gig and launch BIG-TIME web career.

- [ ] D. Schedule dentist appointment.

Wonderful! We're so glad you'll be helping us. * Here's what we need on our first page...

The CEO scribbles something on a napkin and hands it to you...

Title of the page
Heading

Add heading called Menu

Coffee Starbuzz Coffee Starbuzz Coffee Starbuzz

Thanks for giving us a hand! On the web page we just need something simple (see below) that includes the beverage names, prices, and descriptions.

House Blend, $1.49   Sub heading
A smooth, mild blend of coffees from Mexico, Bolivia <p>
and Guatemala.

Mocha Cafe Latte, $2.35   Subheading
Espresso, steamed milk and chocolate syrup. <p>

Cappuccino, $1.89   Subheading
A mixture of espresso, steamed milk and foam. <p>

Chai Tea, $1.85   Subheading
A spicy drink made with black tea, spices, milk and honey. <p>

Place emphasis on prices

Sharpen your pencil

Take a look at the napkin. Can you determine the *structure* of it? In other words, are there obvious headings? Paragraphs? Is it missing anything like a title?

Go ahead and mark up the napkin (using your pencil) with any structure you see, and add anything that is missing.

You'll find our answers at the end of Chapter 1.

* If by chance you chose option A, B, or D on the previous page, we recommend you donate this book to a good library, use it as kindling this winter, or what the heck, go ahead and sell it on Amazon and make some cash.

Creating the Starbuzz web page

Of course, the only problem with all this is that you haven't actually created any web pages yet. But that's why you decided to dive head first into HTML, right?

No worries, here's what you're going to do on the next few pages:

 Create an HTML file using your favorite text editor.

 Type in the menu the Starbuzz CEO wrote on the napkin.

❸ **Save the file as "index.html".**

❹ **Open the file "index.html" in your favorite browser, step back, and watch the magic happen.**

No pressure, but thousands of people are going to visit this web page when you're finished. It not only needs to be correct, it's gotta look great, too!

Creating an HTML file (Mac)

All HTML files are text files. To create a text file, you
need an application that allows you to create plain text
without throwing in a lot of fancy formatting and special
characters. You just need plain, pure text.

We'll use TextEdit on the Mac in this book; however, if
you prefer another text editor, that should work fine as
well. And, if you're running Windows, you'll want to skip
ahead a couple of pages to the Windows instructions.

Step one:

Navigate to your **Applications** folder

The TextEdit application is in the *Applications*
folder. The easiest way to get there is to
choose New Finder Window from the Finder's
File menu and then look for the Application
directly in your shortcuts. When you've found
it, click on Applications.

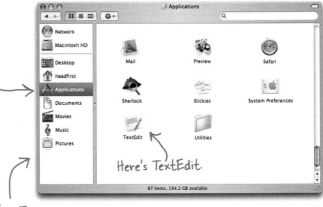

Step two:

Locate and run **TextEdit**

You'll probably have lots of applications listed
in your *Applications* folder, so scroll down until
you see TextEdit. To run the application,
double-click on the TextEdit icon.

Your Finder
shortcuts

Here's TextEdit.

Step three (optional):

Keep **TextEdit** in your **Dock**

If you want to make your life easier,
click and hold on the TextEdit icon in
the Dock (this icon appears once the
application is running). When it displays
a pop-up menu, choose Options, then
"Keep in Dock." That way, the TextEdit
icon will always appear in your Dock
and you won't have to hunt it down in
the *Applications* folder every time you
need to use it.

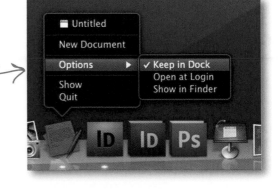

Step four:

Change your TextEdit **Preferences**

By default, TextEdit is in "rich text" mode, which means it will add its own formatting and special characters to your file when you save it—not what you want. So, you'll need to change your TextEdit Preferences so that TextEdit saves your work as a pure text file. To do this, first choose the Preferences menu item from the TextEdit menu.

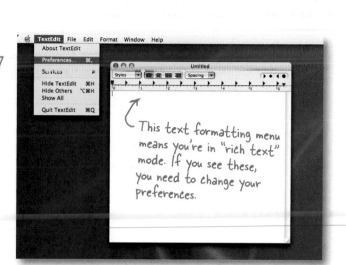

This text formatting menu means you're in "rich text" mode. If you see these, you need to change your preferences.

Step five:

Set Preferences for **Plain text**

Once you see the Preferences dialog box, there are three things you need to do.

First, choose "Plain text" as the default editor mode in the New Document tab.

In the "Open and Save" tab, make sure "Ignore rich text commands in HTML files" is checked.

Last, make sure that the "Add .txt extension to plain text files" is **un**checked.

That's it; to close the dialog box, click on the red button in the top-left corner.

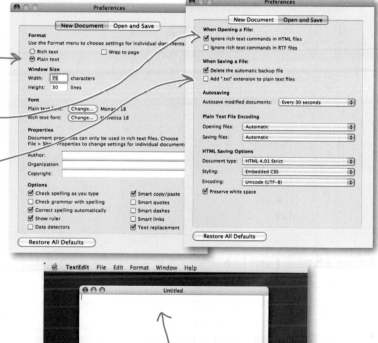

Step six:

Quit and **restart**

Now quit out of TextEdit by choosing Quit from the TextEdit menu, and then restart the application. This time, you'll see a window with no fancy text formatting menus at the top. You're now ready to create some HTML.

See, the formatting menu is gone: that means we're in text mode.

Creating an HTML file (Windows)

Or another version of Windows

If you're reading this page you must be a Windows 7 user. If you're not, you might want to skip a couple of pages ahead. Or, if you just want to sit in the back and not ask questions, we're okay with that too.

To create HTML files in Windows 7, we're going to use Notepad—it ships with every copy of Windows, the price is right, and it's easy to use. If you've got your own favorite editor that runs on Windows 7, that's fine too; just make sure you can create a plain-text file with an ".html" extension.

If you're using another version of Windows, you'll find Notepad there as well.

Assuming you're using Notepad, here's how you're going to create your first HTML file.

Step one:

Open the **Start** menu and navigate to Notepad.

You'll find the Notepad application in *Accessories*. The easiest way to get there is to click on the Start menu, then on All Programs, then Accessories. You'll see Notepad listed there.

Step two:

Open **Notepad**.

Once you've located Notepad in the *Accessories* folder, go ahead and click on it. You'll see a blank window ready for you to start typing HTML.

But recommended

Step three (optional):

Don't hide extensions of well-known file types.

By default, Windows File Explorer hides the file extensions of well-known file types. For example, a file named "Irule.html" will be shown in the Explorer as "Irule" without its ".html" extension.

It's much less confusing if Windows shows you these extensions, so let's change your folder options so you can see them.

First, open Folder Options by clicking the Start button, clicking Control Panel, clicking "Appearance and Personalization," and then clicking Folder Options.

Next, in the View tab, under "Advanced settings," scroll down until you see "Hide extensions for known file types" and *uncheck* this option.

That's it. Click on the OK button to save the preference and you'll now see the file extensions in the Explorer.

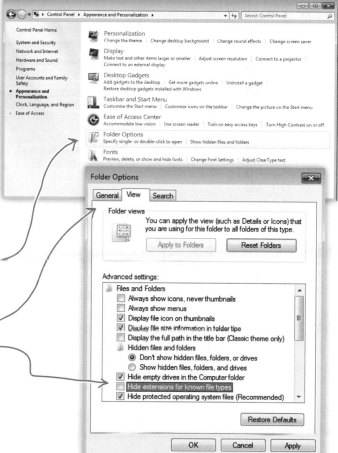

there are no
Dumb Questions

Q: **Why am I using a simple text editor? Aren't there powerful tools like Dreamweaver and Expression Web for creating web pages?**

A: You're reading this book because you want to understand the true technologies used for web pages, right? Now those are all great tools, but they do a lot of the work for you, and until you are a master of HTML and CSS, you want to learn this stuff without a big tool getting in your way.

Once you're a master, however, these tools do provide some nice features like syntax checking and previews. At that point, when you view the "code" window, you'll understand everything in it, and you'll find that changes to the raw HTML and CSS are often a lot faster than going through a user interface. You'll also find that as standards change, these tools aren't always updated right away and may not support the most recent standards until their next release cycle. Since you'll know how to change the HTML and CSS without the tool, you'll be able to keep up with the latest and greatest all the time.

There are many more fully featured editors that include great features like clips (for automatically inserting bits of HTML you write often), preview (for previewing directly in the editor before you test in the browser), syntax coloring (so tags are a different color from content), and much more. Once you get the hang of writing basic HTML and CSS in a simple editor, it may be worth checking out one of the fancier editors, such as Coda, TextMate, CoffeeCup, or Aptana Studio. There are many out there to choose from (both free and not).

Q: **I get the editor, but what browser am I supposed to be using? There are so many— Internet Explorer, Chrome, Firefox, Opera, Safari—what's the deal?**

A: The simple answer: use whatever browser you like. HTML and CSS are industry standards, which means that all browsers try to support HTML and CSS in the same way (just make sure you are using the newest version of the browser for the best support).

The complex answer: in reality there are slight differences in the way browsers handle your pages. If you've got users who will be accessing your pages in a variety of browsers, then always test your web page in several different browsers. Some pages will look exactly the same; some won't. The more advanced you become with HTML and CSS, the more these slight differences may matter to you, and we'll get into some of these subtleties throughout the book.

Any of the major browsers—Internet Explorer, Chrome, Firefox, Opera, and Safari—will work for most examples (except where noted); they are all modern browsers with great HTML and CSS support. And as a web developer, you'll be expected to test your code in more than one browser, so we encourage you to download and get familiar with at least two!

Q: **I'm creating these files on my own computer—how am I going to view these on the Web?**

A: That's one great thing about HTML: you can create files and test them on your own computer and then later publish them on the Web. Right now, we're going to worry about how to create the files and what goes in them. We'll come back to getting them on the Web a bit later.

Meanwhile, back at Starbuzz Coffee...

Okay, now that you know the basics of creating a plain-text file, you just need to get some content into your text editor, save it, and then load it into your browser.

Start by typing in the beverages straight from the CEO's napkin; these beverages are the content for your page. You'll be adding some HTML markup to give the content some structure in a bit, but for now, just get the basic content typed in. While you're at it, go ahead and add "Starbuzz Coffee Beverages" at the top of the file.

Type in the info from the napkin like this.

Untitled - Notepad

File   Edit   Format   View   Help

```
Starbuzz Coffee Beverages

House Blend, $1.49
A smooth, mild blend of coffees from Mexico, Bolivia and Guatemala.

Mocha Cafe Latte, $2.35
Espresso, steamed milk and chocolate syrup.

Cappuccino, $1.89
A mixture of espresso, steamed milk and foam.

Chai Tea, $1.85
A spicy drink made with black tea, spices, milk and honey.|
```

Windows

Untitled.txt

```
Starbuzz Coffee Beverages

House Blend, $1.49
A smooth, mild blend of coffees from Mexico, Bolivia and Guatemala.

Mocha Cafe Latte, $2.35
Espresso, steamed milk and chocolate syrup.

Cappuccino, $1.89
A mixture of espresso, steamed milk and foam.

Chai Tea, $1.85
A spicy drink made with black tea, spices, milk and honey.
```

Mac

Saving your work

Once you've typed in the beverages from the CEO's napkin, you're going to save your work in a file called "index.html". Before you do that, you'll want to create a folder named "starbuzz" to hold the site's files.

To get this all started, choose Save from the File menu and you'll see a Save As dialog box. Then, here's what you need to do:

① First, create a "starbuzz" folder for all your Starbuzz-related files. You can do this with the New Folder button.

Click here to create a new folder.

Windows

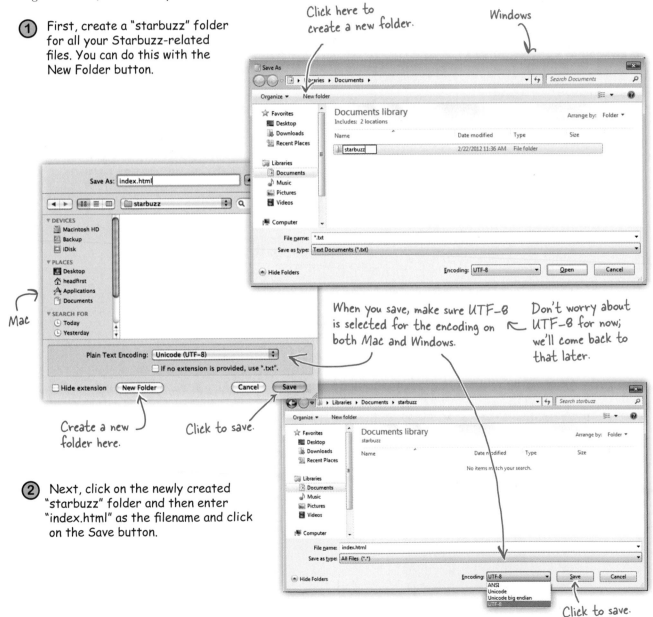

Mac

When you save, make sure UTF-8 is selected for the encoding on both Mac and Windows.

Don't worry about UTF-8 for now; we'll come back to that later.

Create a new folder here.

Click to save.

② Next, click on the newly created "starbuzz" folder and then enter "index.html" as the filename and click on the Save button.

Click to save.

Opening your web page in a browser

Are you ready to open your first web page? Using your favorite browser, choose "Open File…" (or "Open…" using Windows 7 and Internet Explorer) from the File menu and navigate to your "index.html" file. Select it and click Open.

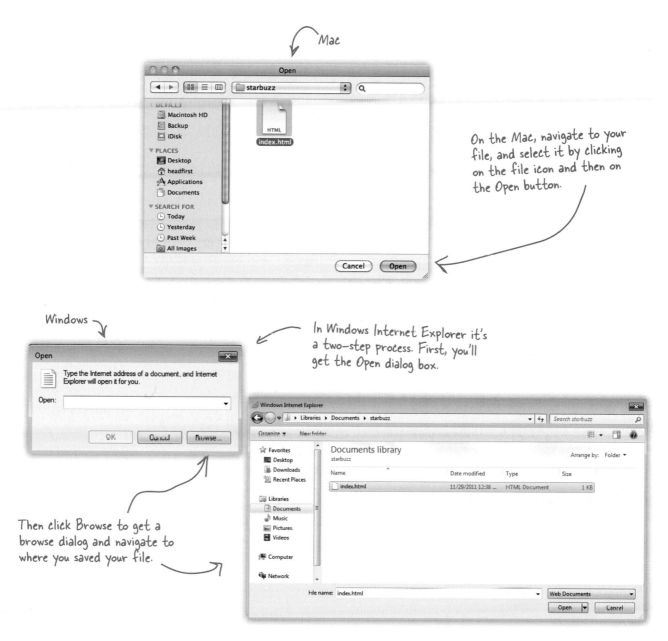

Mac

On the Mac, navigate to your file, and select it by clicking on the file icon and then on the Open button.

Windows

In Windows Internet Explorer it's a two-step process. First, you'll get the Open dialog box.

Then click Browse to get a browse dialog and navigate to where you saved your file.

Take your page for a test drive

Success! You've got the page loaded in the browser, although the results are a little…uh…unsatisfying. But that's just because all you've done so far is go through the mechanics of creating a page and viewing it in the browser. And so far, you've only typed in the *content* of the web page. That's where HTML comes in. HTML gives you a way to tell the browser about the *structure* of your page. What's structure? As you've already seen, it is a way of marking up your text so that the browser knows what's a heading, what text is in a paragraph, what text is a subheading, and so on. Once the browser knows a little about the structure, it can display your page in a more meaningful and readable manner.

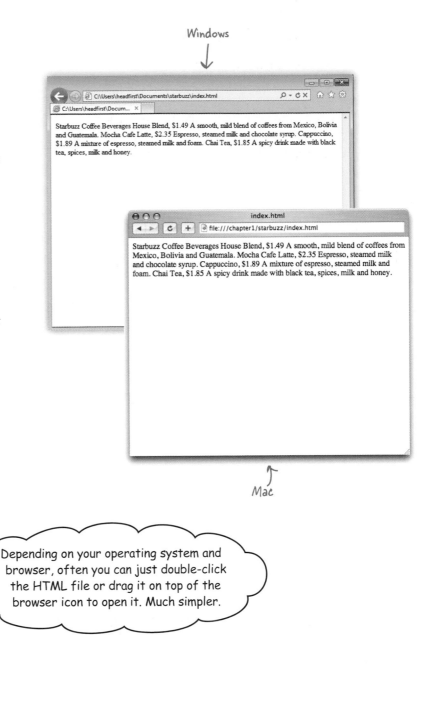

Windows

Starbuzz Coffee Beverages House Blend, $1.49 A smooth, mild blend of coffees from Mexico, Bolivia and Guatemala. Mocha Cafe Latte, $2.35 Espresso, steamed milk and chocolate syrup. Cappuccino, $1.89 A mixture of espresso, steamed milk and foam. Chai Tea, $1.85 A spicy drink made with black tea, spices, milk and honey.

index.html

Starbuzz Coffee Beverages House Blend, $1.49 A smooth, mild blend of coffees from Mexico, Bolivia and Guatemala. Mocha Cafe Latte, $2.35 Espresso, steamed milk and chocolate syrup. Cappuccino, $1.89 A mixture of espresso, steamed milk and foam. Chai Tea, $1.85 A spicy drink made with black tea, spices, milk and honey.

Mac

Depending on your operating system and browser, often you can just double-click the HTML file or drag it on top of the browser icon to open it. Much simpler.

Markup Magnets

So, let's add that structure…

Your job is to add structure to the text from the Starbuzz napkin. Use the fridge magnets at the bottom of the page to mark up the text so that you've indicated which parts are headings, subheadings and paragraph text. We've already done a few to get you started. You won't need all the magnets below to complete the job; some will be left over.

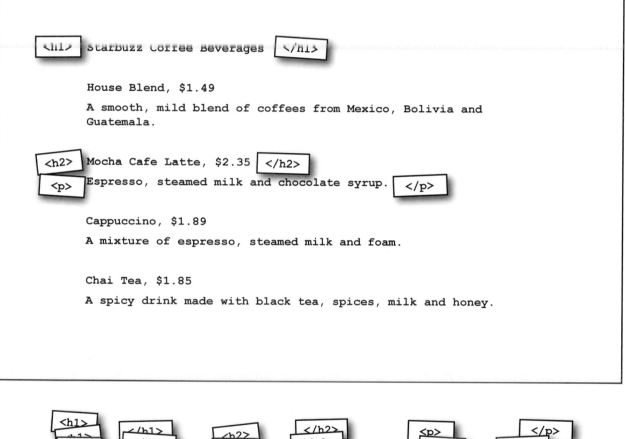

`<h1>` Starbuzz Coffee Beverages `</h1>`

House Blend, $1.49

A smooth, mild blend of coffees from Mexico, Bolivia and Guatemala.

`<h2>` Mocha Cafe Latte, $2.35 `</h2>`
`<p>` Espresso, steamed milk and chocolate syrup. `</p>`

Cappuccino, $1.89

A mixture of espresso, steamed milk and foam.

Chai Tea, $1.85

A spicy drink made with black tea, spices, milk and honey.

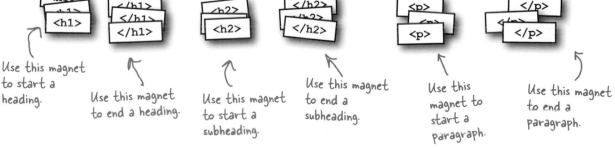

`<h1>` `<h1>` `<h1>`
Use this magnet to start a heading.

`</h1>` `</h1>` `</h1>`
Use this magnet to end a heading.

`<h2>` `<h2>`
Use this magnet to start a subheading.

`</h2>` `</h2>` `</h2>`
Use this magnet to end a subheading.

`<p>` `<p>` `<p>`
Use this magnet to start a paragraph.

`</p>` `</p>` `</p>`
Use this magnet to end a paragraph.

Congratulations, you've just written your first HTML!

They might have looked like fridge magnets, but you were really *marking up* your text with HTML. Only, as you know, we usually refer to the magnets as *tags*. Check out the markup below and compare it to your magnets on the previous page.

> Use the <h1> and </h1> tags to mark headings. All the text in between is the actual content of the heading.

<h1>Starbuzz Coffee Beverages**</h1>**

<h2>House Blend, $1.49**</h2>**
<p>A smooth, mild blend of coffees from Mexico, Bolivia and Guatemala.**</p>**

> The <h2> and </h2> tags go around a subheading. Think of an <h2> heading as a subheading of an <h1> heading.

<h2>Mocha Cafe Latte, $2.35**</h2>**
<p>Espresso, steamed milk and chocolate syrup.**</p>**

> The <p> and </p> tags go around a block of text that is a paragraph. That can be one or many sentences.

<h2>Cappuccino, $1.89**</h2>**
<p>A mixture of espresso, steamed milk and foam.**</p>**

<h2>Chai Tea, $1.85**</h2>**
<p>A spicy drink made with black tea, spices, milk and honey.**</p>**

> Notice that you don't have to put matching tags on the same line. You can put as much content as you like between them.

Are we there yet?

You have an HTML file with markup—does that make a web page? Almost.
You've already seen the `<html>`, `<head>`, `<title>`, and `<body>` tags, and
we just need to add those to make this a first-class HTML page…

First, surround your HTML
with <html> & </html>
tags. This tells the browser
the content of the file is
HTML.

Next add <head> and </head> tags. The
head contains information about your web
page, like its title. For now, think about it
this way: the head allows you to tell the
browser things <u>about</u> the web page.

Go ahead and put a title
inside the head. The title
usually appears at the top
of the browser window.

```
<html>
```

```
<head>

        <title>Starbuzz Coffee</title>
</head>
```

The head consists of the <head>
& </head> tags and everything
in between.

```
<body>
        <h1>Starbuzz Coffee Beverages</h1>
        <h2>House Blend, $1.49</h2>
        <p>A smooth, mild blend of coffees from Mexico,
                Bolivia and Guatemala.</p>

        <h2>Mocha Cafe Latte, $2.35</h2>
        <p>Espresso, steamed milk and chocolate syrup.</p>

        <h2>Cappuccino, $1.89</h2>
        <p>A mixture of espresso, steamed milk and foam.</p>

        <h2>Chai Tea, $1.85</h2>
        <p>A spicy drink made with black tea, spices,
                milk and honey.</p>
</body>
```

```
</html>
```

The body consists
of the <body>
& </body> tags
and everything in
between.

The body contains all the content and
structure of your web page—the parts of
the web page that you <u>see</u> in your browser.

Keep your head
and body separate
when writing HTML.

Another test drive

Go ahead and change your "index.html" file by adding in the <head>, </head>, <title>, </title>, <body> and </body> tags. Once you've done that, save your changes and reload the file into your browser.

Notice that the title, which you specified in the <head> element, shows up here.

You can reload the index.html file by selecting the Open File menu item again, or by using your browser's reload button.

Now things look a bit better. The browser has interpreted your tags and created a display for the page that is not only more structured, but also more readable.

○ ○ ○   Starbuzz Coffee

◄ ►   C   +   file:///chapter1/starbuzz/index.html

Starbuzz Coffee Beverages

House Blend, $1.49

A smooth, mild blend of coffees from Mexico, Bolivia and Guatemala.

Mocha Cafe Latte, $2.35

Espresso, steamed milk and chocolate syrup.

Cappuccino, $1.89

A mixture of espresso, steamed milk and foam.

Chai Tea, $1.85

A spicy drink made with black tea, spices, milk and honey.

Sweet!

Tags dissected

Okay, you've seen a bit of markup, so let's zoom in and take a look at how tags really work.

You usually put tags around some piece of content. Here we're using tags to tell the browser that our content, "Starbuzz Coffee Beverages," is a top-level heading (that is, heading level one).

This is the closing tag that ends the heading; in this case the </h1> tag is ending an <h1> heading. You know it's a closing tag because it comes after the content, and it's got a "/" before the "h1". All closing tags have a "/" in them.

Here's the opening tag that begins the heading.

```
<h1> Starbuzz Coffee Beverages </h1>
```

Tags consist of the tag name surrounded by angle brackets; that is, the < and > characters.

The whole shebang is called an element. In this case, we can call it the <h1> element. An element consists of the enclosing tags and the content in between.

We call an opening tag and its closing tag matching tags.

To tell the browser about the structure of your page, use pairs of tags around your content.

Remember:

Element = Opening Tag + Content + Closing Tag

there are no
Dumb Questions

Q: So matching tags don't have to be on the same line?

A: No; remember the browser doesn't really care about tabs, returns, and most spaces. So, your tags can start and end anywhere on the same line, or they can start and end on different lines. Just make sure you start with an opening tag, like <h2>, and end with a closing tag, like </h2>.

Q: Why do the closing tags have that extra "/"?

A: That "/" in the closing tag is to help both you and the browser know where a particular piece of structured content ends. Otherwise, the closing tags would look just like the opening tags, right?

Q: I've noticed the HTML in some pages doesn't always match opening tags with closing tags.

A: Well, the tags are supposed to match. In general, browsers do a pretty good job of figuring out what you mean if you write incorrect HTML. But, as you're going to see, these days there are big benefits to writing totally correct HTML. If you're worried you'll never be able to write perfect HTML, don't be; there are plenty of tools to verify your code before you put it on a web server so the whole world can see it. For now, just get in the habit of always matching your opening tags with closing tags.

Q: Well, what about that <img src="drinks.gif"> tag in the lounge example? Did you forget the closing tag?

A: Wow, sharp eye. There are some elements that use a shorthand notation with only one tag. Keep that in the back of your mind for now, and we'll come back to it in a later chapter.

Q: An element is an opening tag + content + closing tag, but can't you have tags inside other tags? Like the <head> and <body> are inside an <html> tag?

A: Yes, HTML tags are often "nested" like that. If you think about it, it's natural for an HTML page to have a body, which contains a paragraph, and so on. So many HTML elements have other HTML elements between their tags. We'll take a good look at this kind of thing in later chapters, but for now just get your mind noticing how the elements relate to each other in a page.

BRAIN
POWER

Tags can be a little more interesting than what you've seen so far. Here's the paragraph tag with a little extra added to it. What do you think this does?

```
<p id="houseblend">A smooth, mild
blend of coffees from Mexico, Bolivia
and Guatemala.</p>
```

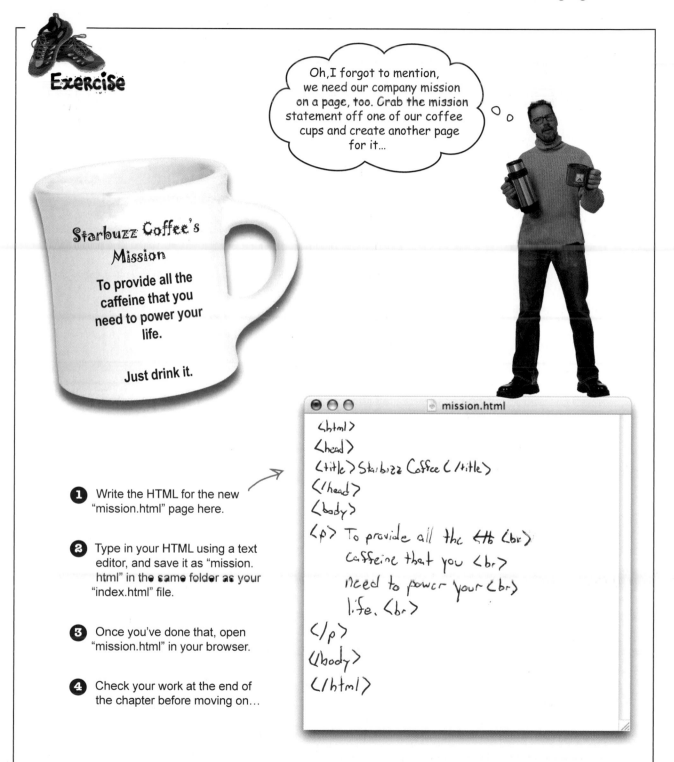

Exercise

Oh, I forgot to mention, we need our company mission on a page, too. Grab the mission statement off one of our coffee cups and create another page for it...

Starbuzz Coffee's Mission

To provide all the caffeine that you need to power your life.

Just drink it.

❶ Write the HTML for the new "mission.html" page here.

❷ Type in your HTML using a text editor, and save it as "mission. html" in the same folder as your "index.html" file.

❸ Once you've done that, open "mission.html" in your browser.

❹ Check your work at the end of the chapter before moving on...

```
mission.html

<html>
<head>
<title> Starbuzz Coffee </title>
</head>
<body>
<p> To provide all the <ttb <br>
    caffeine that you <br>
    need to power your <br>
    life. <br>
</p>
</body>
</html>
```

Okay, it looks like you're getting somewhere. You've got the main page and the mission page all set. But don't forget the CEO said the site needs to look great too. Don't you think it needs a little style?

Right. We have the structure down, so now we're going to concentrate on its presentation.

You already know that HTML gives you a way to describe the structure of the content in your files. When the browser displays your HTML, it uses its own built-in default style to present this structure. But relying on the browser for style obviously isn't going to win you any "designer of the month" awards.

That's where CSS comes in. CSS gives you a way to describe how your content should be presented. Let's get our feet wet by creating some CSS that makes the Starbuzz page look a little more presentable (and launch your web career in the process).

CSS is an abbreviation for Cascading Style Sheets. We'll get into what that all means later, but for now just know that CSS gives you a way to tell the browser how elements in your page should look.

Meet the style element

To add style, you add a new (say it with us) E-L-E-M-E-N-T
to your page—the `<style>` element. Let's go back to the
main Starbuzz page and add some style. Check it out…

The `<style>` element is placed inside the head of your HTML.

Just like other elements, the `<style>` element has an opening tag, `<style>`, and a closing tag, `</style>`.

The `<style>` tag also has an (optional) attribute, called type, which tells the browser the kind of style you're using. Because you're going to use CSS, you can specify the "text/css" type.

And here's where you're going to define the styles for the page.

```
<html>
    <head>
        <title>Starbuzz Coffee</title>
        <style type="text/css">


        </style>
    </head>
    <body>
        <h1>Starbuzz Coffee Beverages</h1>

        <h2>House Blend, $1.49</h2>
        <p>A smooth, mild blend of coffees from Mexico, Bolivia and
        Guatemala.</p>

        <h2>Mocha Caffe Latte, $2.35</h2>
        <p>Espresso, steamed milk and chocolate syrup.</p>

        <h2>Cappuccino, $1.89</h2>
        <p>A mixture of espresso, steamed milk and milk foam.</p>

        <h2>Chai Tea, $1.85</h2>
        <p>A spicy drink made with black tea, spices, milk and honey.</p>
    </body>
</html>
```

there are no Dumb Questions

Q: An element can have an "attribute"? What does that mean?

A: Attributes give you a way to provide additional information about an element. Like, if you have a `<style>` element, the attribute allows you to say exactly what kind of style you're talking about. You'll be seeing a lot more attributes for various elements; just remember they give you some extra info about the element.

Q: Why do I have to specify the type of the style ("text/css") as an attribute of the style? Are there other kinds of style?

A: At one time the designers of HTML thought there would be other styles, but as it turns out we've all come to our senses since then and you can just use `<style>` without an attribute—all the browsers will know you mean CSS. We're disappointed; we were holding our breath for the `<style type="50sKitsch">` style. Oh well.

Giving Starbuzz some style...

Now that you've got a `<style>` element in the HTML head, all you need to do is supply some CSS to give the page a little pizzazz. Below you'll find some CSS already "baked" for you. Whenever you see the 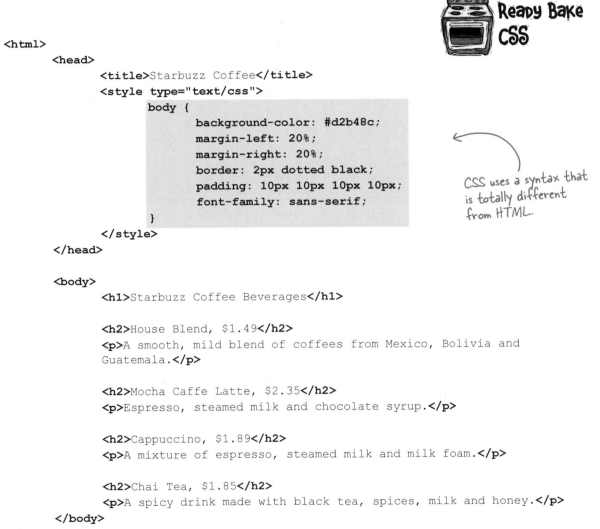 logo, you're seeing HTML and CSS that you should type in as-is. *Trust us.* You'll learn how the markup works later, after you've seen what it can do.

So, take a look at the CSS and then add it to your "index.html" file. Once you've got it typed in, save your file.

Ready Bake CSS

```
<html>
    <head>
        <title>Starbuzz Coffee</title>
        <style type="text/css">
            body {
                background-color: #d2b48c;
                margin-left: 20%;
                margin-right: 20%;
                border: 2px dotted black;
                padding: 10px 10px 10px 10px;
                font-family: sans-serif;

            }
        </style>
    </head>

    <body>
        <h1>Starbuzz Coffee Beverages</h1>

        <h2>House Blend, $1.49</h2>
        <p>A smooth, mild blend of coffees from Mexico, Bolivia and
        Guatemala.</p>

        <h2>Mocha Caffe Latte, $2.35</h2>
        <p>Espresso, steamed milk and chocolate syrup.</p>

        <h2>Cappuccino, $1.89</h2>
        <p>A mixture of espresso, steamed milk and milk foam.</p>

        <h2>Chai Tea, $1.85</h2>
        <p>A spicy drink made with black tea, spices, milk and honey.</p>
    </body>
</html>
```

CSS uses a syntax that is totally different from HTML.

Cruisin' with style...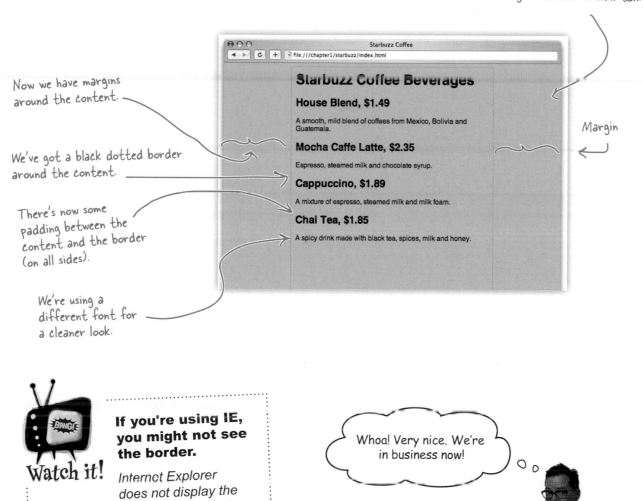

It's time for another test drive, so reload your "index.html" file again.
This time, you'll see the Starbuzz web page has a whole new look.

Background color is now tan.

Now we have margins around the content.

We've got a black dotted border around the content.

There's now some padding between the content and the border (on all sides).

We're using a different font for a cleaner look.

Margin

Starbuzz Coffee Beverages

House Blend, $1.49

A smooth, mild blend of coffees from Mexico, Bolivia and Guatemala.

Mocha Caffe Latte, $2.35

Espresso, steamed milk and chocolate syrup.

Cappuccino, $1.89

A mixture of espresso, steamed milk and milk foam.

Chai Tea, $1.85

A spicy drink made with black tea, spices, milk and honey.

Watch it!

If you're using IE, you might not see the border. *Internet Explorer does not display the border around the body correctly. Try loading the page in Firefox, Chrome or Safari to see the border.*

Whoa! Very nice. We're in business now!

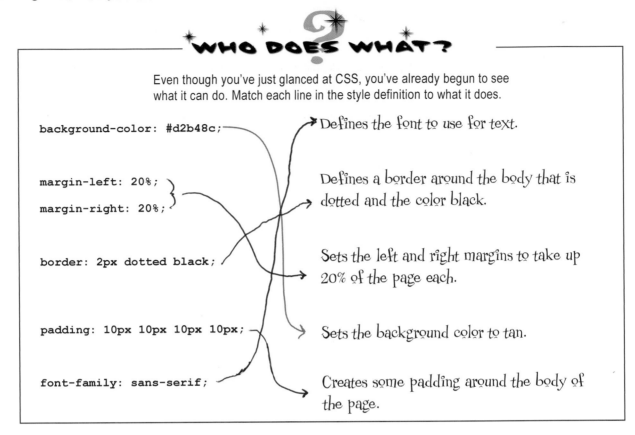

WHO DOES WHAT?

Even though you've just glanced at CSS, you've already begun to see what it can do. Match each line in the style definition to what it does.

`background-color: #d2b48c;` → Defines the font to use for text.

`margin-left: 20%;`
`margin-right: 20%;` → Defines a border around the body that is dotted and the color black.

`border: 2px dotted black;` → Sets the left and right margins to take up 20% of the page each.

`padding: 10px 10px 10px 10px;` → Sets the background color to tan.

`font-family: sans-serif;` → Creates some padding around the body of the page.

there are no Dumb Questions

Q: CSS looks like a totally different language than HTML. Why have two languages? That's just more for me to learn, right?

A: You are quite right that HTML and CSS are completely different languages, but that is because they have very different jobs. Just like you wouldn't use English to balance your checkbook, or math to write a poem, you don't use CSS to create structure or HTML to create style because that's not what they were designed for. While this does mean you need to learn two languages, you'll discover that because each language is good at what it does, this is actually easier than if you had to use one language to do both jobs.

Q: #d2b48c doesn't look like a color. How is #d2b48c the color "tan"?

A: There are a few different ways to specify colors with CSS. The most popular is called a "hex code," which is what #d2b48c is. This really is a tan color. For now, just go with it, and we'll be showing you exactly how #d2b48c is a color a little later.

Q: Why is there a "body" in front of the CSS rules? What does that mean?

A: The "body" in the CSS means that all the CSS between the "{" and "}" applies to content within the HTML <body> element. So when you set the font to sans-serif, you're saying that the default font within the body of your page should be sans-serif.

We'll go into a lot more detail about how CSS works shortly, so keep reading. Soon, you'll see that you can be a lot more specific about how you apply these rules, and by doing so, you can create some pretty cool designs.

Exercise

Now that you've put a little style in the Starbuzz "index.html" page, go ahead and update your "mission.html" page to have the same style.

1 Write the HTML for the "mission.html" page below, and then add the new CSS.

2 Update your "mission.html" file to include the new CSS.

3 Once you've done that, reload "mission.html" in your browser.

4 Make sure your mission page looks like ours at the end of the chapter.

```
mission.html

<html>
  <head>
  <title> Starbuzz Coffee </title>
  <style>
      body {
          background-color: #d2b48c;
          margin-left: 20%;
          margin-right: 20%;
          border: 2px dotted black;
          padding: 10px 10px 10px 10px;
          font-family: sans-serif;
      }
  </style>
  </head>
  <body>
      <p> To provide all the caffeine that you need to power
          your life </p>
      <p> Just drink it </p>
  </body>
</html>
```

Fireside Chats

Tonight's talk: **HTML and CSS on content and style**

HTML	**CSS**
Greetings, CSS; I'm glad you're here because I've been wanting to clear up some confusion about us.	
	Really? What kind of confusion?
Lots of people think that my tags tell the browsers how to *display* the content. It's just not true! I'm all about *structure*, not presentation.	
	Heck yeah—I don't want people giving you credit for my work!
Well, you can see how some people might get confused; after all, it's possible to use HTML without CSS and still get a decent-looking page.	
	"Decent" might be overstating it a bit, don't you think? I mean, the way most browsers display straight HTML looks kinda crappy. People need to learn how powerful CSS is and how easily I can give their web pages great style.
Hey, I'm pretty powerful too. Having your content structured is much more important than having it look good. Style is so superficial; it's the structure of the content that matters.	
	Get real! Without me, web pages would be pretty damn boring. Not only that, but take away the ability to style pages and no one is going to take your pages seriously. Everything is going to look clumsy and unprofessional.
Whoa, what an ego! Well, I guess I shouldn't expect anything else from you—you're just trying to make a fashion statement with all that style you keep talking about.	

HTML

CSS

Fashion statement? Good design and layout can have a huge effect on how readable and usable pages are. And you should be happy that my flexible style rules allow designers to do all kinds of interesting things with your elements without messing up your structure.

Right. In fact, we're totally different languages, which is good because I wouldn't want any of your style designers messing with my structure elements.

Don't worry, we're living in separate universes.

Yeah, that is obvious to me any time I look at CSS—talk about an alien language.

Yeah, like HTML can be called a language? Who has ever seen such a clunky thing with all those tags?

Millions of web writers would disagree with you. I've got a nice clean syntax that fits right in with the content.

Just take a look at CSS; it's so elegant and simple, no goofy angle brackets <around> <everything>. <See> <I> <can><talk> <just><like><Mr.><HTML><,><look><at> <me><!>

Hey, ever heard of closing tags?

Just notice that no matter where you go, I've got you surrounded by <style> tags. Good luck escaping!

Ha! I'll show you…because, guess what? I *can* escape…

Stay tuned!

> Not only is this one fine cup of House Blend, but now we've got a web page to tell all our customers about our coffees. Excellent work. I've got some bigger ideas for the future; in the meantime, can you start thinking about how we are going to get these pages on the Internet so other people can see them?

BULLET POINTS

- HTML and CSS are the languages we use to create web pages.

- Web servers store and serve web pages, which are created from HTML and CSS. Browsers retrieve pages and render their content based on the HTML and CSS.

- HTML is an abbreviation for HyperText Markup Language and is used to structure your web page.

- CSS is an abbreviation for Cascading Style Sheets, and is used to control the presentation of your HTML.

- Using HTML, we mark up content with tags to provide structure. We call matching tags, and their enclosed content, elements.

- An element is composed of three parts: an opening tag, content, and a closing tag. There are a few elements, like <img>, that are an exception to this rule.

- Opening tags can have attributes. We've seen one already: type.

- Closing tags have a "/" after the left angle bracket, in front of the tag name, to distinguish them as closing tags.

- Your pages should always have an <html> element along with a <head> element and a <body> element.

- Information about the web page goes into the <head> element.

- What you put into the <body> element is what you see in the browser.

- Most whitespace (tabs, returns, spaces) is ignored by the browser, but you can use it to make your HTML more readable (to you).

- You can add CSS to an HTML web page by putting the CSS rules inside the <style> element. The <style> element should always be inside the <head> element.

- You specify the style characteristics of the elements in your HTML using CSS.

HTMLcross

It's time to sit back and give your left brain something to do. It's your standard crossword; all of the solution words are from this chapter.

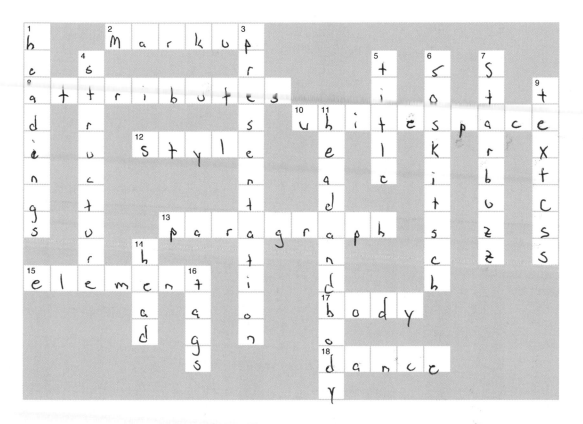

Across

2. The "M" in HTML.
8. Tags can have these to provide additional information.
10. Browsers ignore this.
12. You define presentation through this element.
13. Purpose of <p> element.
15. Two tags and content.
17. What you see in your page.
18. We emphasized Dance _____ Revolution.

Down

1. There are six of these.
3. CSS is used when you need to control this.
4. You mark up content to provide this.
5. Appears at the top of the browser for each page.
6. Style we wish we could have had.
7. Company that launched your web career.
9. Only type of style available. text CSS (knew it was CSS)
11. Always separate these in HTML.
14. About your web page.
16. Opening and closing.

Sharpen your pencil Solution

Go ahead and mark up the napkin (using your pencil) with any structure you see, and add anything that is missing.

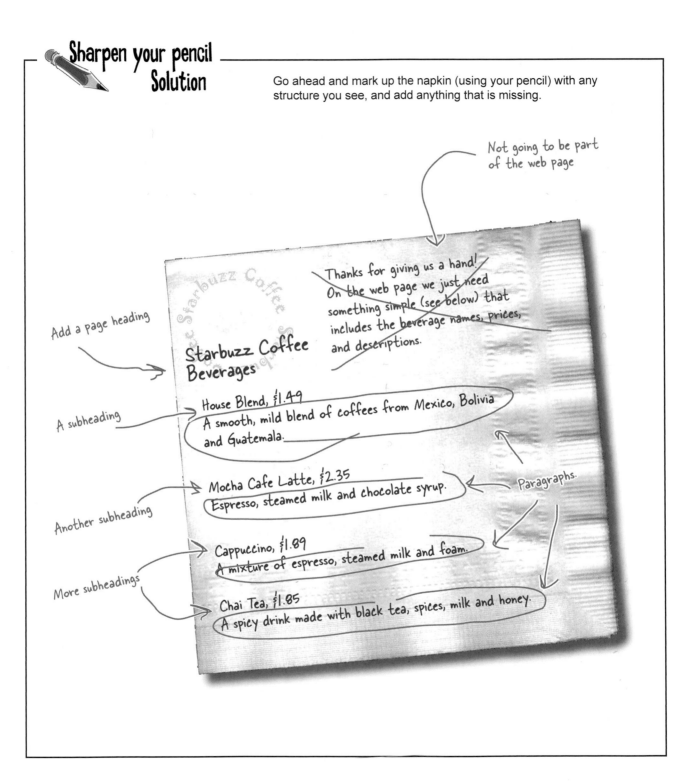

Not going to be part of the web page

Thanks for giving us a hand! On the web page we just need something simple (see below) that includes the beverage names, prices, and descriptions.

Add a page heading

Starbuzz Coffee Beverages

A subheading

House Blend, $1.49
A smooth, mild blend of coffees from Mexico, Bolivia and Guatemala.

Another subheading

Mocha Cafe Latte, $2.35
Espresso, steamed milk and chocolate syrup.

Paragraphs.

More subheadings

Cappuccino, $1.89
A mixture of espresso, steamed milk and foam.

Chai Tea, $1.85
A spicy drink made with black tea, spices, milk and honey.

Markup Magnets Solution

Your job was to add some structure to the text from the Starbuzz napkin. Use the fridge magnets at the bottom of the page to mark up the text so that you've indicated which parts are headings, subheadings, and paragraph text. Here's our solution.

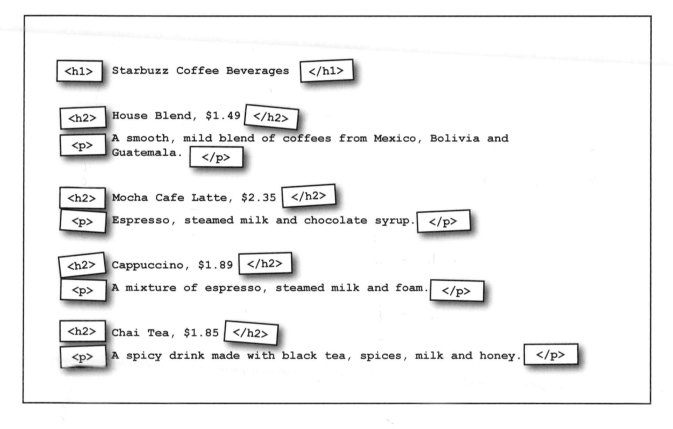

```
<h1>  Starbuzz Coffee Beverages  </h1>

<h2>  House Blend, $1.49  </h2>
<p>   A smooth, mild blend of coffees from Mexico, Bolivia and
      Guatemala.  </p>

<h2>  Mocha Cafe Latte, $2.35  </h2>
<p>   Espresso, steamed milk and chocolate syrup.  </p>

<h2>  Cappuccino, $1.89  </h2>
<p>   A mixture of espresso, steamed milk and foam.  </p>

<h2>  Chai Tea, $1.85  </h2>
<p>   A spicy drink made with black tea, spices, milk and honey.  </p>
```

```
<h1>
<h1>    </h1>
        </h1>
```

Leftover magnets

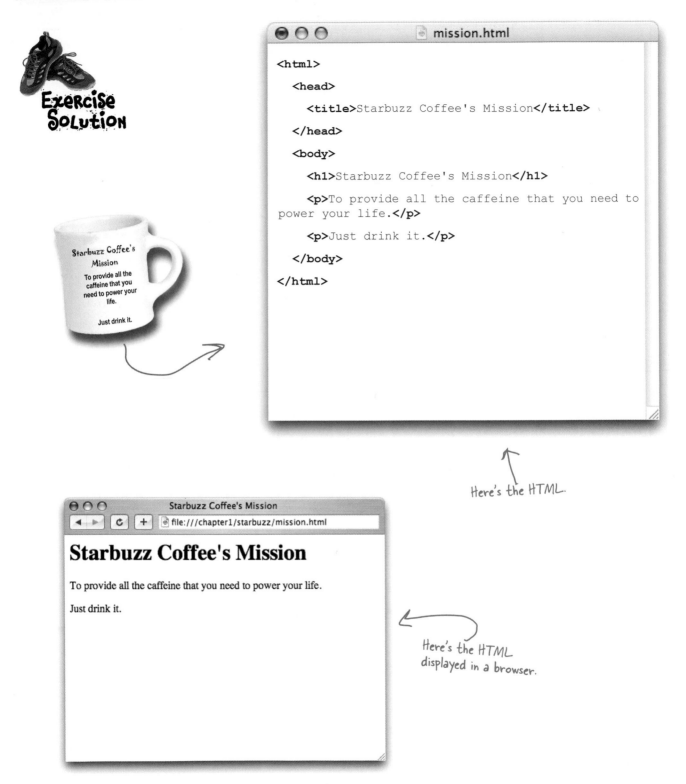

Exercise Solution

mission.html

```html
<html>
  <head>
    <title>Starbuzz Coffee's Mission</title>
  </head>
  <body>
    <h1>Starbuzz Coffee's Mission</h1>
    <p>To provide all the caffeine that you need to
power your life.</p>
    <p>Just drink it.</p>
  </body>
</html>
```

Here's the HTML.

Starbuzz Coffee's Mission

file:///chapter1/starbuzz/mission.html

Starbuzz Coffee's Mission

To provide all the caffeine that you need to power your life.

Just drink it.

Here's the HTML
displayed in a browser.

Exercise Solution

Here's the CSS in the mission page.

```
                          mission.html
<html>
   <head>
      <title>Starbuzz Coffee's Mission</title>
      <style type="text/css">
         body {
            background-color: #d2b48c;
            margin-left: 20%;
            margin-right: 20%;
            border: 2px dotted black;
            padding: 10px 10px 10px 10px;
            font-family: sans-serif;
         }
      </style>
   </head>
   <body>
      <h1>Starbuzz Coffee's Mission</h1>
      <p>To provide all the caffeine that you need to power
your life.</p>
      <p>Just drink it.</p>
   </body>
</html>
```

Now, the style matches the main Starbuzz page.

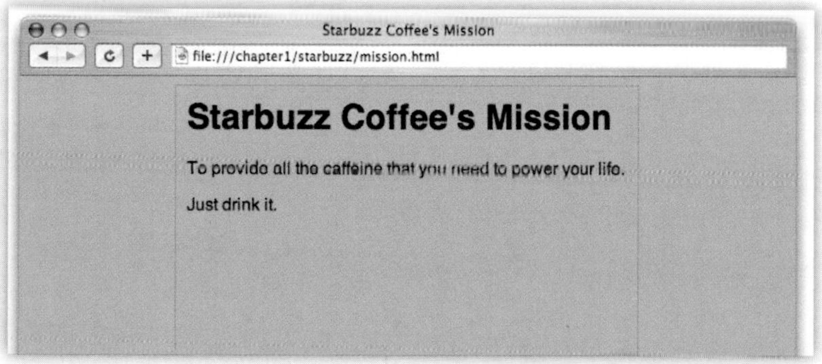

Starbuzz Coffee's Mission

file:///chapter1/starbuzz/mission.html

Starbuzz Coffee's Mission

To provide all the caffeine that you need to power your life.

Just drink it.

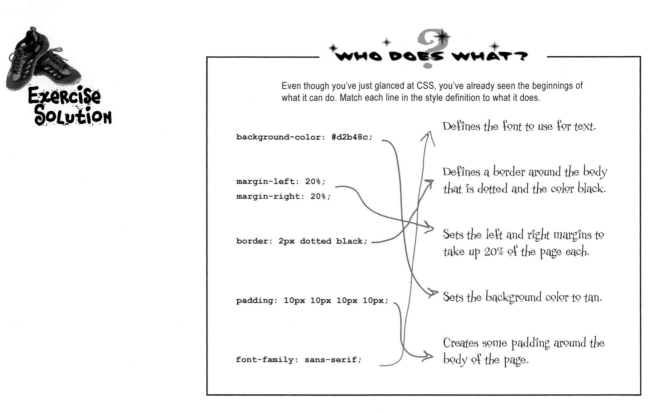

Exercise Solution

WHO DOES WHAT?

Even though you've just glanced at CSS, you've already seen the beginnings of what it can do. Match each line in the style definition to what it does.

`background-color: #d2b48c;` — Defines the font to use for text.

`margin-left: 20%;`
`margin-right: 20%;` — Defines a border around the body that is dotted and the color black.

`border: 2px dotted black;` — Sets the left and right margins to take up 20% of the page each.

`padding: 10px 10px 10px 10px;` — Sets the background color to tan.

`font-family: sans-serif;` — Creates some padding around the body of the page.

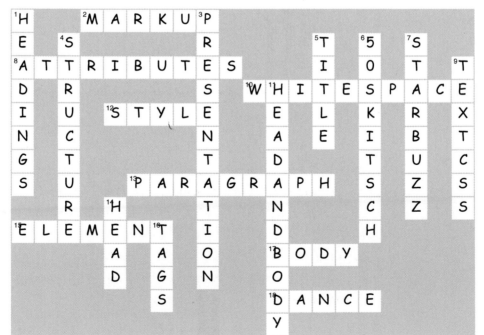

2 going further with hypertext
Meeting the "HT" in HTML

Did someone say "hypertext?" What's that? Oh, only the entire basis of the Web. In Chapter 1 we kicked the tires of HTML and found it to be a nice markup language (the "ML" in HTML) for describing the structure of web pages. Now we're going to check out the "HT" in HTML, hypertext, which will let us break free of a single page and link to other pages. Along the way we're going to meet a powerful new element, the <a> element, and learn how being "relative" is a groovy thing. So, fasten your seat belts—you're about to learn some hypertext.

Head First Lounge, *new and improved*

Remember the Head First Lounge? Great site, but wouldn't it be nice if customers could view a list of the refreshing elixirs? Even better, we should give customers some real driving directions so they can find the place.

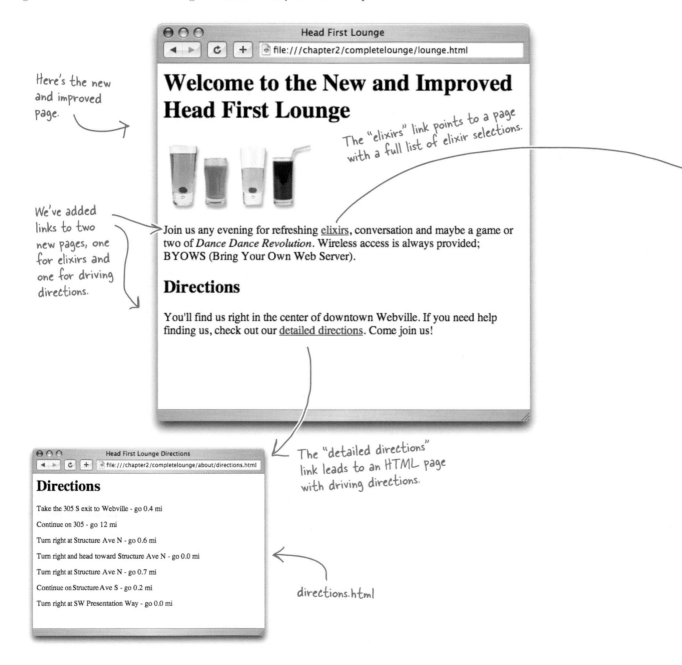

Here's the new and improved page.

The "elixirs" link points to a page with a full list of elixir selections.

We've added links to two new pages, one for elixirs and one for driving directions.

The "detailed directions" link leads to an HTML page with driving directions.

directions.html

Head First Lounge Elixirs

file:///chapter2/completelounge/beverages/elixir.html

Our Elixirs

Green Tea Cooler

Chock full of vitamins and minerals, this elixir combines the healthful benefits of green tea with a twist of chamomile blossoms and ginger root.

Raspberry Ice Concentration

Combining raspberry juice with lemon grass, citrus peel and rosehips, this icy drink will make your mind feel clear and crisp.

Blueberry Bliss Elixir

Blueberries and cherry essence mixed into a base of elderflower herb tea will put you in a relaxed state of bliss in no time.

Cranberry Antioxidant Blast

Wake up to the flavors of cranberry and hibiscus in this vitamin C rich elixir.

A page listing some refreshing and healthy drinks. Feel free to grab one before going on.

elixir.html

Creating the new and improved lounge in three steps...

Let's rework the original Head First Lounge page so it links to the two new pages.

1 The first step is easy because we've already created the "directions.html" and "elixir.html" files for you. You'll find them in the source files for the book, which are available at http://wickedlysmart.com/hfhtmlcss. Ready Bake

2 Next you're going to edit the "lounge.html" file and add in the HTML needed to link to "directions.html" and "elixir.html".

3 Last, you'll give the pages a test drive and try out your new links. When you get back, we'll sit down and look at how it all works.

Flip the page and let's get started...

Creating the new lounge

① Grab the source files

Go ahead and grab the source files from http://wickedlysmart.com/hfhtmlcss. Once you've downloaded them, look under the folder "chapter2/lounge" and you'll find "lounge.html", "elixir.html", and "directions.html" (and a bunch of image files).

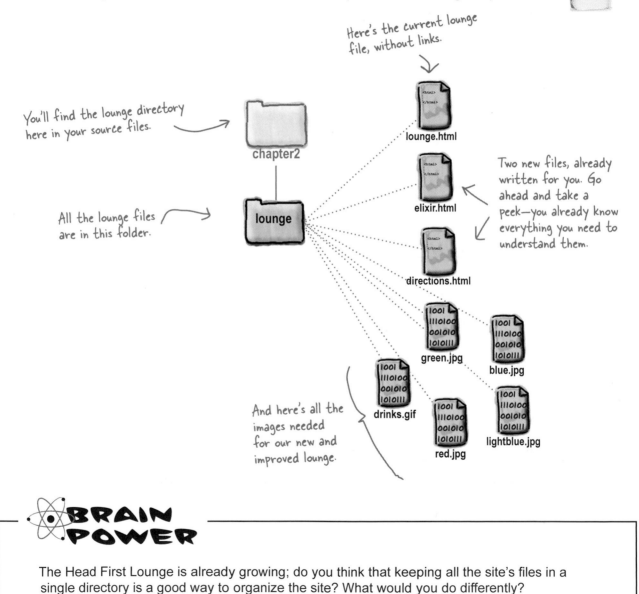

Here's the current lounge file, without links.

lounge.html

You'll find the lounge directory here in your source files.

chapter2

All the lounge files are in this folder.

lounge

elixir.html

Two new files, already written for you. Go ahead and take a peek—you already know everything you need to understand them.

directions.html

green.jpg

blue.jpg

And here's all the images needed for our new and improved lounge.

drinks.gif

red.jpg

lightblue.jpg

⚛ BRAIN POWER

The Head First Lounge is already growing; do you think that keeping all the site's files in a single directory is a good way to organize the site? What would you do differently?

---

② Edit lounge.html

Open "lounge.html" in your editor. Add the new text and HTML that is highlighted below.
Go ahead and type this in; we'll come back and see how it all works on the next page.

```
<html>
  <head>
    <title>Head First Lounge</title>
  </head>
  <body>
    <h1>Welcome to the New and Improved Head First Lounge</h1>
    <img src="drinks.gif">
    <p>
      Join us any evening for
      refreshing <a href="elixir.html">elixirs</a>,
      conversation and maybe a game or two of
      <em>Dance Dance Revolution</em>.
      Wireless access is always provided;
      BYOWS (Bring your own web server).
    </p>
    <h2>Directions</h2>
    <p>
      You'll find us right in the center of downtown Webville.
      If you need help finding us, check out
      our <a href="directions.html">detailed directions</a>.
      Come join us!
    </p>
  </body>
</html>
```

Let's add "New and Improved" to the heading.

Here's where we add the HTML for the link to the elixirs.

To create links, we use the <a> element; we'll take a look at how this element works in just a sec...

We need to add some text here to point customers to the new directions.

And here's where we add the link to the directions, again using an <a> element.

③ Save lounge.html and give it a test drive.

When you're finished with the changes, save the file "lounge.html" and open it in
your browser. Here are a few things to try:

 Click on the elixir link and the new elixir page will display.

 Click on the browser's back button and "lounge.html"
should be displayed again.

 Click on the directions link and the new directions page
will display.

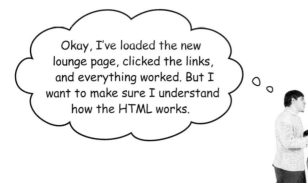

Okay, I've loaded the new lounge page, clicked the links, and everything worked. But I want to make sure I understand how the HTML works.

Behind the Scenes

What did we do?

① Let's step through creating the HTML links. First, we need to put the text we want for the link in an `<a>` element, like this:

`<a>elixirs</a>`   `<a>driving directions</a>`

The `<a>` element is used to create a link to another page.

The content of the `<a>` element is the link text. In the browser, the link text appears with an underline to indicate you can click on it.

② Now that we have text for the link, we need to add some HTML to tell the browser where the link points to:

For this link, the browser will display the text "elixirs" that, when clicked, will take the user to the "elixir.html" page.

`<a href="elixir.html">elixirs</a>`

The href attribute is how you specify the destination of the link.

And for this link, the browser will display a "driving directions" link that, when clicked, will take the user to the "directions.html" page.

`<a href="directions.html">driving directions</a>`

What does the browser do?

Behind
the Scenes

(1) First, as the browser renders the page, if it encounters an `<a>` element, it takes the content of the element and displays it as a clickable link.

```
<a href="elixir.html">elixirs</a>
```

Both "elixirs" and "detailed directions" are between the opening and closing `<a>` tags, so they end up being clickable text in the web page.

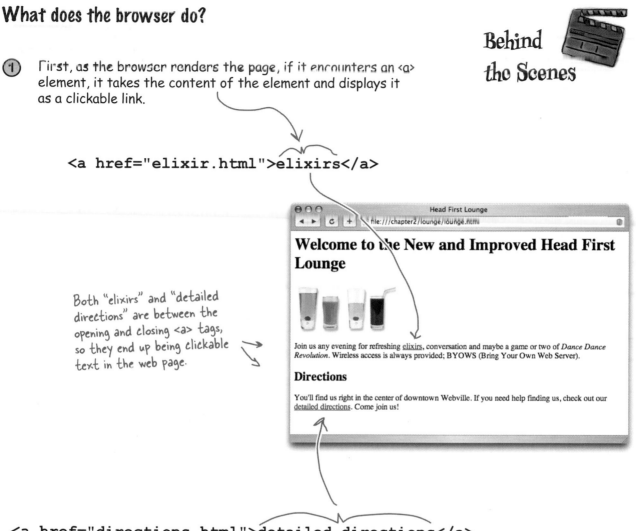

```
<a href="directions.html">detailed directions</a>
```

Use the `<a>` element to create a hypertext link to another web page.
The content of the `<a>` element becomes clickable in the web page.
The href attribute tells the browser the destination of the link.

Behind
the Scenes

② Next, when a user clicks on a link, the browser uses the "href" attribute to determine the page the link points to.

The user clicks on either the "elixirs" link or...

...on "detailed directions".

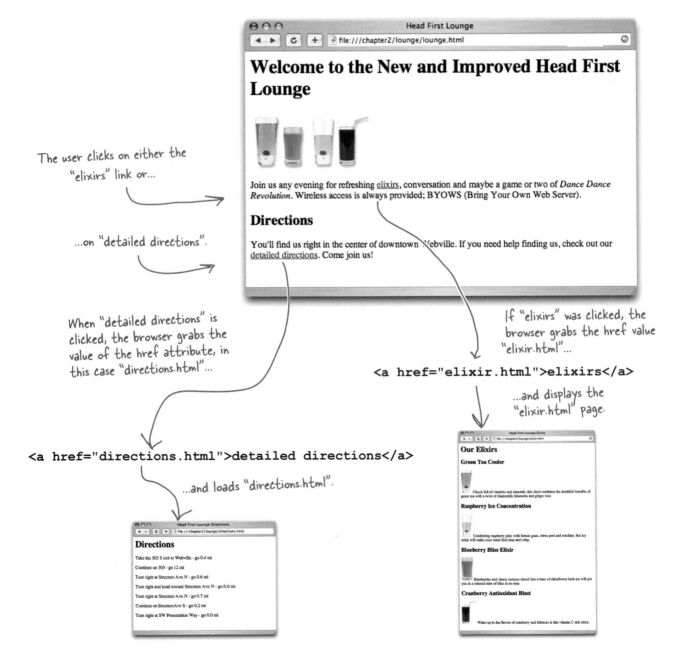

When "detailed directions" is clicked, the browser grabs the value of the href attribute, in this case "directions.html"...

If "elixirs" was clicked, the browser grabs the href value "elixir.html"...

`<a href="elixir.html">elixirs</a>`

...and displays the "elixir.html" page.

`<a href="directions.html">detailed directions</a>`

...and loads "directions.html".

Understanding attributes

Attributes give you a way to specify additional information about an element. While we haven't looked at attributes in detail, you've already seen a few examples of them:

The type attribute specifies which style language we're using, in this case CSS.

```
<style type="text/css">
```

The href attribute tells us the destination of a hyperlink.

```
<a href="irule.html">
```

```
<img src="sweetphoto.gif">
```

The src attribute specifies the filename of the picture an img tag displays.

Let's cook up an example to give you an even better feel for how attributes work:

What if <car> were an element?

If <car> were an element, then you'd naturally want to write some markup like this:

```
<car>My Red Mini</car>
```

With no attributes, all we can supply is a descriptive name for the car.

But this <car> element only gives a descriptive name for your car—it doesn't tell us the make, precise model, whether it is a convertible, or a zillion other details we might want to know. So, if <car> were really an element, we might use attributes like this:

But with attributes, we can customize the element with all kinds of information.

```
<car make="Mini" model="Cooper" convertible="no">My Red Mini</car>
```

Better, right? Now this markup tells us a lot more information in an easy-to-write, convenient form.

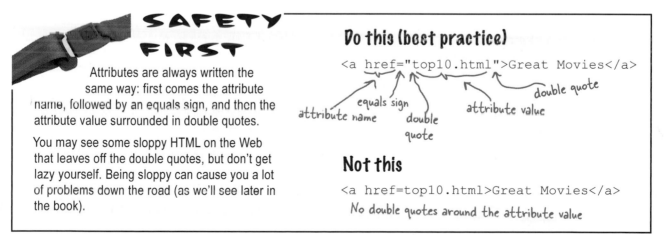

SAFETY FIRST

Attributes are always written the same way: first comes the attribute name, followed by an equals sign, and then the attribute value surrounded in double quotes.

You may see some sloppy HTML on the Web that leaves off the double quotes, but don't get lazy yourself. Being sloppy can cause you a lot of problems down the road (as we'll see later in the book).

Do this (best practice)

```
<a href="top10.html">Great Movies</a>
```

attribute name equals sign double quote attribute value double quote

Not this

```
<a href=top10.html>Great Movies</a>
```

No double quotes around the attribute value

Q: **Can I just make up new attributes for an HTML element?**

A: Web browsers only know about a predefined set of attributes for each element. If you just made up attributes, then browsers wouldn't know what to do with them, and as you'll see later in the book, doing this will very likely get you into trouble. When a browser recognizes an element or an attribute, we like to say that it "supports" that element or attribute. You should only use attributes that you know are supported.

That said, for programming web applications (the subject of *Head First HTML5 Programming*), HTML5 now supports custom data attributes that allow you to make up custom names for new attributes.

Q: **Who decides what is "supported"?**

A: There are standards committees that worry about the elements and attributes of HTML. These committees are made up of people ~~with nothing better to do~~ who generously give their time and energy to make sure there's a common HTML roadmap that all organizations can use to implement their browsers.

Q: **How do I know what attributes and elements are supported? Or can all attributes be applied to any element?**

A: Only certain attributes can be used with a given element. Think about it this way: you wouldn't use an attribute "convertible" with the element <toaster>, would you? So, you only want to use attributes that make sense and are supported by the element.

You're going to be learning which attributes are supported by which elements as you make your way through the book. After you've finished the book, there are lots of great references you can use to refresh your memory, such as *HTML & XHTML: The Definitive Guide* (O'Reilly).

The "href" attribute is pronounced "h - ref"...

...rhymes with "space chef".

Attributes Exposed

This week's interview:
Confessions of the href attribute

Head First: Welcome, href. It's certainly a pleasure to interview as big an attribute as you.

href: Thanks. It's good to be here and get away from all the linking; it can wear an attribute out. Every time someone clicks on a link, guess who gets to tell the browser where to go next? That would be me.

Head First: We're glad you could work us into your busy schedule. Why don't you take us back to the beginning…What does it mean to be an attribute?

href: Sure. Well, attributes are used to customize an element. It's easy to wrap some <a> tags around a piece of content, like "Sign up now!"—we do it like this: <a>Sign up now!</a>—but without me, the href attribute, you have no way to tell the <a> element the destination of the link.

Head First: Got it so far…

href: …but with an attribute you can provide additional information about the element. In my case, that's where the link points to: <a href="signup.html">Sign up now!</a>. This says that the <a> element, which is labeled "Sign up now!", links to the "signup.html" page. Now, there are lots of other attributes in the world, but I'm the one you use with the <a> element to tell it where it points to.

Head First: Nice. Now, I have to ask, and I hope you aren't offended, but what is with the name? href? What's with that?

href: It's an old Internet family name. It means "hypertext reference," but all my friends just call me "href" for short.

Head First: Which is?

href: A hypertext reference is just another name for a resource that is on the Internet or your computer. Usually the resource is a web page, but I can also point to PDF documents…all kinds of things.

Head First: Interesting. All our readers have seen so far are links to their own pages; how do we link to other pages and resources on the Web?

href: Hey, I gotta get back to work, the whole Web is getting gunked up without me. Besides, isn't it your job to teach them this stuff?

Head First: Okay, okay, yes, we're getting to that in a bit…thanks for joining us, href.

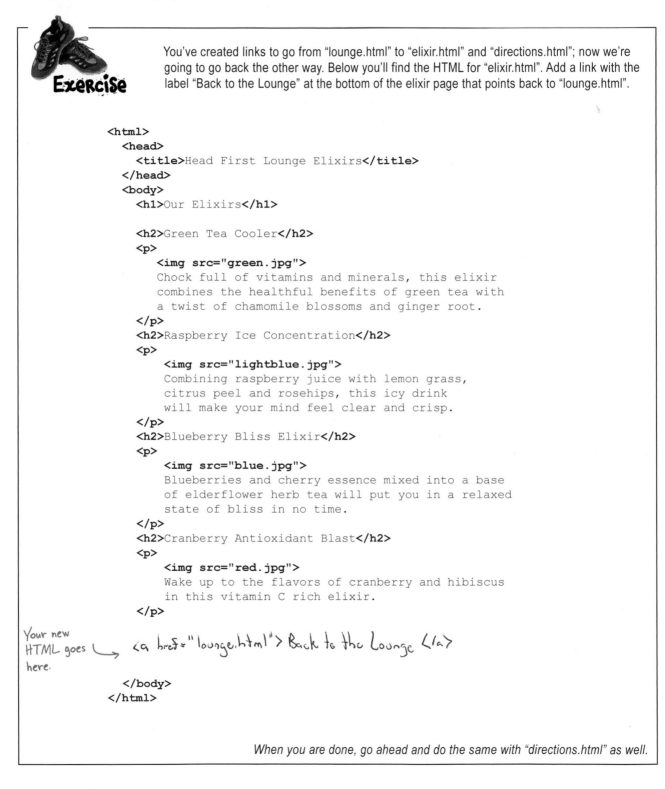

You've created links to go from "lounge.html" to "elixir.html" and "directions.html"; now we're going to go back the other way. Below you'll find the HTML for "elixir.html". Add a link with the label "Back to the Lounge" at the bottom of the elixir page that points back to "lounge.html".

```html
<html>
  <head>
    <title>Head First Lounge Elixirs</title>
  </head>
  <body>
    <h1>Our Elixirs</h1>

    <h2>Green Tea Cooler</h2>
    <p>
      <img src="green.jpg">
      Chock full of vitamins and minerals, this elixir
      combines the healthful benefits of green tea with
      a twist of chamomile blossoms and ginger root.
    </p>
    <h2>Raspberry Ice Concentration</h2>
    <p>
      <img src="lightblue.jpg">
      Combining raspberry juice with lemon grass,
      citrus peel and rosehips, this icy drink
      will make your mind feel clear and crisp.
    </p>
    <h2>Blueberry Bliss Elixir</h2>
    <p>
      <img src="blue.jpg">
      Blueberries and cherry essence mixed into a base
      of elderflower herb tea will put you in a relaxed
      state of bliss in no time.
    </p>
    <h2>Cranberry Antioxidant Blast</h2>
    <p>
      <img src="red.jpg">
      Wake up to the flavors of cranberry and hibiscus
      in this vitamin C rich elixir.
    </p>
```

Your new HTML goes here. → `<a href="lounge.html"> Back to the Lounge </a>`

```html
  </body>
</html>
```

When you are done, go ahead and do the same with "directions.html" as well.

CONSTRUCTION ZONE BEGINS

We need some help constructing and deconstructing <a> elements. Given your new knowledge of the <a> element, we're hoping you can help. In each row below, you'll find some combination of the label, destination, and the complete <a> element. Fill in any information that is missing. The first row is done for you.

Label	Destination	What you write in HTML
Hot or Not?	hot.html	`<a href="hot.html">Hot or Not?</a>`
Resume	cv.html	`<a href="cv.html"> Resume </a>`
Eye Candy	candy.html	`<a href="candy.html">Eye Candy</a>`
See my mini	mini-cooper.html	`<a href="mini-cooper.html"> See my mini </a>`
let's play	millionaire.html	`<a href="millionaire.html"> let's play </a>`

there are no Dumb Questions

Q: I've seen many pages where I can click on an image rather than text. Can I use the <a> element for that?

A: Yes, if you put an <img> element between the <a> tags, then your image will be clickable just like text. We're not going to talk about images in depth for a few chapters, but they work just fine as links.

Q: So I can put anything between the <a> tags and it will be clickable? Like, say, a paragraph?

A: You can indeed put a <p> element inside an <a> element to link an entire paragraph. You'll mostly be using text and images (or both) within the <a> element, but if you need to link a <p> or a <h1> element, you can. What tags will go inside other tags is a whole other topic, but don't worry; we'll get there soon enough.

> Your work on the Head First Lounge has really paid off. With those enticing elixirs and directions, lots of people are frequenting the place and visiting the website. Now we've got plans for expanding the lounge's online content in all sorts of directions.

Getting organized

Before you start creating more HTML pages, it's time to get things organized. So far, we've been putting all our files and images in one folder. You'll find that even for modestly sized websites, things are much more manageable if you organize your web pages, graphics, and other resources into a set of folders. Here's what we've got now:

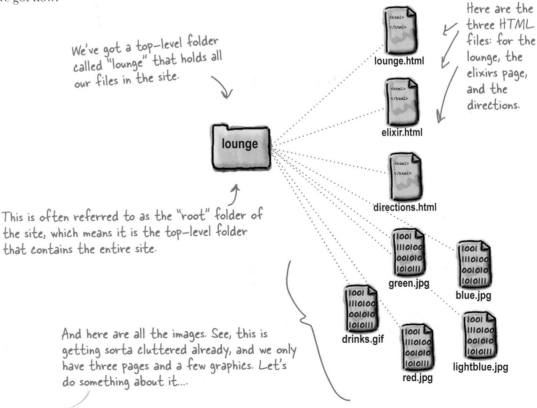

We've got a top-level folder called "lounge" that holds all our files in the site.

This is often referred to as the "root" folder of the site, which means it is the top-level folder that contains the entire site.

Here are the three HTML files: for the lounge, the elixirs page, and the directions.

lounge.html

elixir.html

directions.html

green.jpg

blue.jpg

drinks.gif

red.jpg

lightblue.jpg

And here are all the images. See, this is getting sorta cluttered already, and we only have three pages and a few graphics. Let's do something about it....

Organizing the lounge...

Let's give the lounge site some meaningful organization now. Keep in mind there are lots of ways to organize any site; we're going to start simple and create a couple of folders for pages. We'll also group all those images into one place.

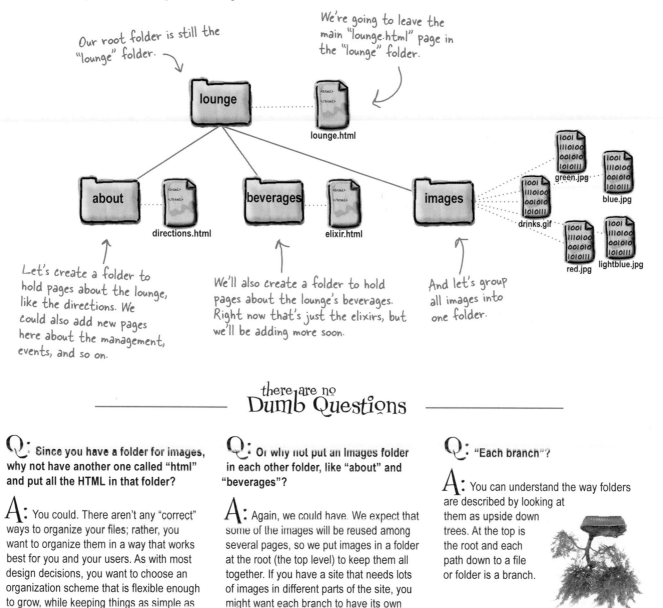

Our root folder is still the "lounge" folder.

We're going to leave the main "lounge.html" page in the "lounge" folder.

Let's create a folder to hold pages about the lounge, like the directions. We could also add new pages here about the management, events, and so on.

We'll also create a folder to hold pages about the lounge's beverages. Right now that's just the elixirs, but we'll be adding more soon.

And let's group all images into one folder.

there are no Dumb Questions

Q: Since you have a folder for images, why not have another one called "html" and put all the HTML in that folder?

A: You could. There aren't any "correct" ways to organize your files; rather, you want to organize them in a way that works best for you and your users. As with most design decisions, you want to choose an organization scheme that is flexible enough to grow, while keeping things as simple as you can.

Q: Or why not put an images folder in each other folder, like "about" and "beverages"?

A: Again, we could have. We expect that some of the images will be reused among several pages, so we put images in a folder at the root (the top level) to keep them all together. If you have a site that needs lots of images in different parts of the site, you might want each branch to have its own image folder.

Q: "Each branch"?

A: You can understand the way folders are described by looking at them as upside down trees. At the top is the root and each path down to a file or folder is a branch.

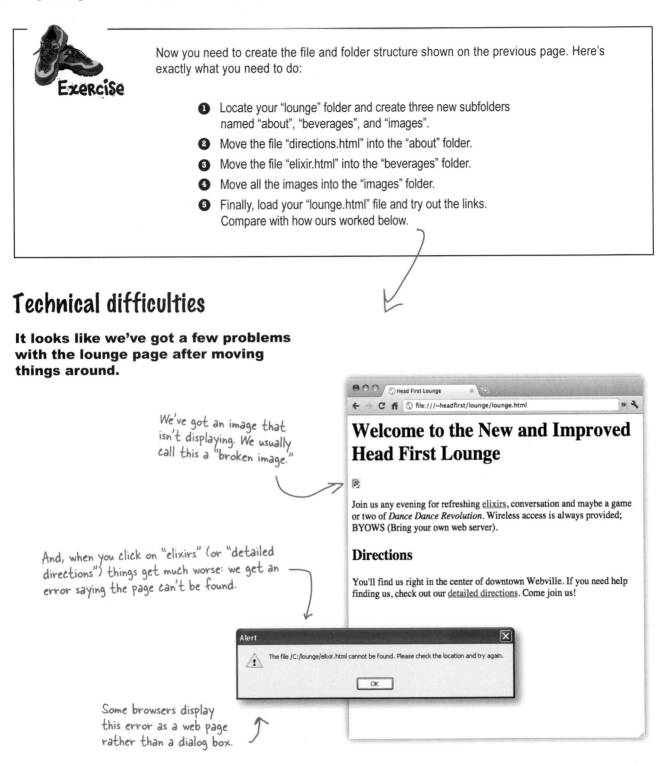

Now you need to create the file and folder structure shown on the previous page. Here's exactly what you need to do:

Exercise

❶ Locate your "lounge" folder and create three new subfolders named "about", "beverages", and "images".

❷ Move the file "directions.html" into the "about" folder.

❸ Move the file "elixir.html" into the "beverages" folder.

❹ Move all the images into the "images" folder.

❺ Finally, load your "lounge.html" file and try out the links. Compare with how ours worked below.

Technical difficulties

It looks like we've got a few problems with the lounge page after moving things around.

We've got an image that isn't displaying. We usually call this a "broken image."

And, when you click on "elixirs" (or "detailed directions") things get much worse: we get an error saying the page can't be found.

Some browsers display this error as a web page rather than a dialog box.

Head First Lounge

file:///~headfirst/lounge/lounge.html

Welcome to the New and Improved Head First Lounge

Join us any evening for refreshing elixirs, conversation and maybe a game or two of *Dance Dance Revolution*. Wireless access is always provided; BYOWS (Bring your own web server).

Directions

You'll find us right in the center of downtown Webville. If you need help finding us, check out our detailed directions. Come join us!

Alert

⚠ The file /C:/lounge/elixir.html cannot be found. Please check the location and try again.

OK

I think the problem is that the browser thinks the files are still in the same folder as "lounge.html". We need to change the links so they point to the files in their new folders.

Right. We need to tell the browser the new location of the pages.

So far you've used href values that point to pages in the *same folder*. Sites are usually a little more complicated, though, and you need to be able to point to pages that are in *other folders*.

To do that, you trace the path from your page to the destination file. That might mean going down a folder or two, or up a folder or two, but either way we end up with a *relative path* that we can put in the href.

Planning your paths...

What do you do when you're planning that vacation in the family truckster? You get out a map and start at your current location, and then trace a path to the destination. The directions themselves are *relative* to your location—if you were in another city, they'd be different directions, right?

Okay, you'd really go to Google Maps, but work with us here!

To figure out a relative path for your links, it's the same deal: you start from the page that has the link, and then you trace a path through your folders until you find the file you need to point to.

There are other kinds of paths too. We'll get to those in later chapters.

Let's work through a couple of relative paths (and fix the lounge at the same time).

Linking down into a subfolder

① Linking from "lounge.html" to "elixir.html".

We need to fix the "elixirs" link in the "lounge.html" page. Here's what the <a> element looks like now:

```
<a href="elixir.html">elixirs</a>
```

Right now we're just using the filename "elixir.html", which tells the browser to look in the same folder as "lounge.html".

② Identify the source and the destination.

When we reorganized the lounge, we left "lounge.html" in the "lounge" folder, and we put "elixir.html" in the "beverages" folder, which is a subfolder of "lounge".

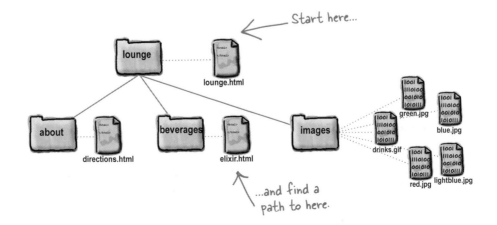

Start here...

...and find a path to here.

③ **Trace a path from the source to the destination.**

Let's trace the path. To get from the "lounge.html" file to "elixir.html", we need to go into the "beverages" folder first, and then we'll find "elixir.html" in that folder.

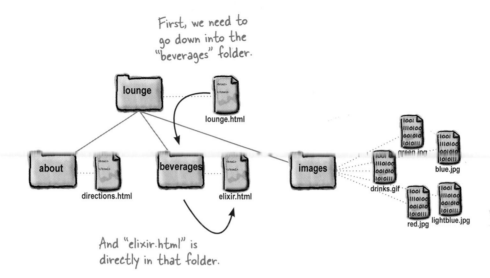

First, we need to go down into the "beverages" folder.

And "elixir.html" is directly in that folder.

④ **Create an href to represent the path we traced.**

Now that we know the path, we need to get it into a format the browser understands. Here's how you write the path:

First, we go into the beverages folder.

Separate all parts of the path with a "/".

Finally, we have the filename.

beverages / elixir.html

Putting it all together...

<a href="beverages/elixir.html">elixirs**</a>**

We put the relative path into the href value. Now when the link is clicked, the browser will look for the "elixir.html" file in the "beverages" folder.

Sharpen your pencil

Your turn: trace the relative path from "lounge.html" to "directions.html". When you've discovered it, complete the <a> element below. Check your answer in the back of the chapter, and then go ahead and change both <a> elements in "lounge.html."

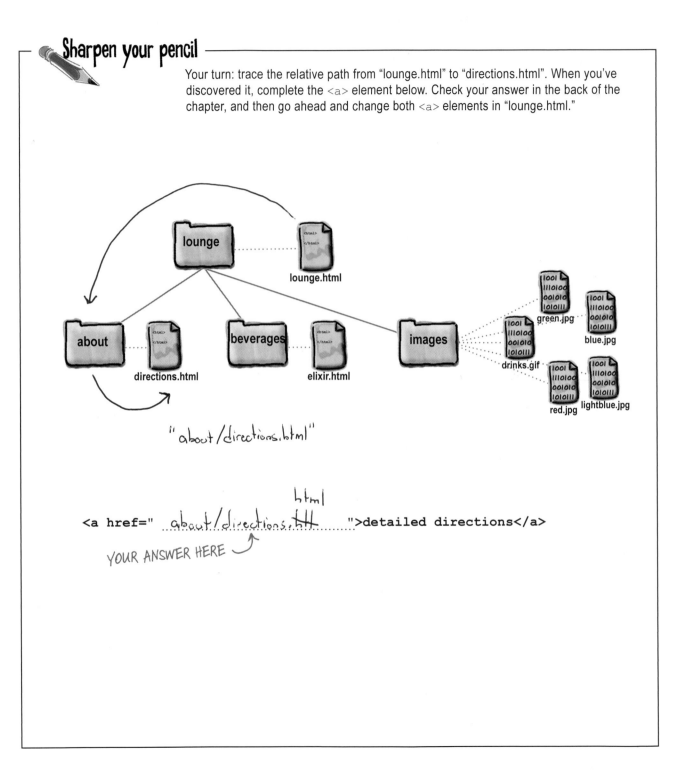

"about/directions.html"

```
                         html
<a href="  about/directions.ht|     ">detailed directions</a>
      YOUR ANSWER HERE
```

Going the other way; linking up into a "parent" folder

(1) Linking from "directions.html" to "lounge.html".

Now we need to fix those "Back to the Lounge" links. Here's what the `<a>` element looks like in the "directions.html" file:

```
<a href="lounge.html">Back to the Lounge</a>
```

Right now, we're just using the filename "lounge.html", which tells the browser to look in the same folder as "directions.html". That's not going to work.

(2) Identify the source and the destination.

Let's take a look at the source and destination. The source is now the "directions.html" file, which is down in the "about" folder. The destination is the "lounge.html" file that sits above the "about" folder, where "directions.html" is located.

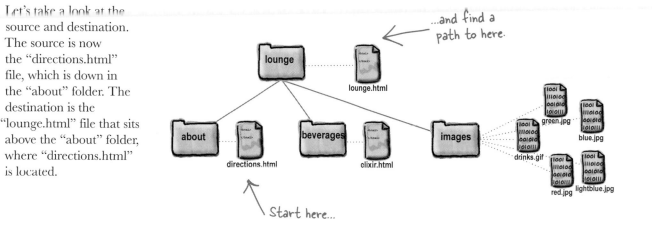

...and find a path to here.

Start here...

(3) Trace a path from the source to the destination.

Let's trace the path. To get from the "directions.html" file to "lounge.html", we need to go up one folder into the "lounge" folder, and then we'll find "lounge.html" in that folder.

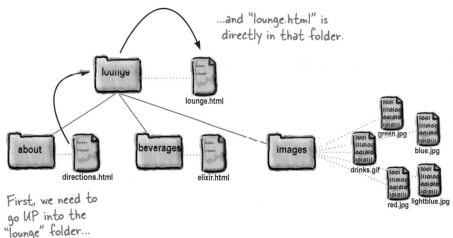

...and "lounge.html" is directly in that folder.

First, we need to go UP into the "lounge" folder...

④ Create an href to represent the path we traced.

We're almost there. Now that you know the path, you need to get it into a format the browser understands. Let's work through this:

First, you need to go up one folder. How do you do that? With a "..". That's right, two periods. Go with it, we'll explain in a sec.

Separate all parts of the path with a "/".

Finally, you have the filename.

```
../ lounge.html
```

Pronounce ".." as "dot dot".

Putting it all together...

```
<a href="../lounge.html">Back to the Lounge</a>
```

Now when you click on the link, the browser will look for the "lounge.html" file in the folder above.

Dot dot
~~Up~~, down,
housewares,
lingerie?

<h1 style="text-align:center">there are no
Dumb Questions</h1>

Q: What's a parent folder? If I have a folder "apples" inside a folder "fruit", is "fruit" the parent of "apples"?

A: Exactly. Folders (you might have heard these called directories) are often described in terms of family relationships. For instance, using your example, "fruit" is the parent of "apples", and "apples" is the child of "fruit". If you had another folder "pears" that was a child of "fruit", it would be a sibling of "apples." Just think of a family tree.

Q: Okay, parent makes sense, but what is ".."?

A: When you need to tell the browser that the file you're linking to is in the parent folder, you use ".." to mean "move UP to the parent folder." In other words, it's browser-speak for parent.

In our example, we wanted to link from "directions.html", which is in the "about" folder, to "lounge.html", which is in the "lounge" folder, the parent of "about". So we had to tell the browser to look UP one folder, and ".." is the way we tell the browser to go UP.

Q: What do you do if you need to go up two folders instead of just one?

A: You can use ".." for each parent folder you want to go up. Each time you use ".." you're going up by one parent folder. So, if you want to go up two folders, you'd type "../..". You still have to separate each part with the "/", so don't forget to do that (the browser won't know what "...." means!).

Q: Once I'm up two folders, how do I tell the browser where to find the file?

A: You combine the "../.." with the filename. So, if you're linking to a file called "fruit.html" in a folder that's two folders up, you'd write "../../fruit.html". You might expect that we'd call "../.." the "grandparent" folder, but we don't usually talk about them that way, and instead say, "the parent of the parent folder," or "../.." for short.

Q: Is there a limit to how far up I can go?

A: You can go up until you're at the root of your website. In our example, the root was the "lounge" folder. So, you could only go up as far as "lounge".

Q: What about in the other direction—is there a limit to how many folders I can go down?

A: Well, you can only go down as many folders as you have created. If you create folders that are 10 deep, then you can write a path that takes you down 10 folders. But we don't recommend that—when you have that many folder levels, it probably means your website organization is too complicated!

In addition, some browsers impose a limit on the number of characters you can have in a path. The spec advises caution above 255 characters, although modern browsers support longer lengths. If you have a large site, however, it's something to be aware of.

Q: My operating system uses "\" as a separator; shouldn't I be using that instead of "/"?

A: No; in web pages you always use "/" (forward slash). Don't use "\" (backslash). Various operating systems use different file separators (for instance, Windows uses "\" instead of "/") but when it comes to the Web, we pick a common separator and all stick to it. So, whether you're using Mac, Windows, Linux, or something else, always use "/" in the paths in your HTML.

Your turn: trace the relative path from "elixir.html" to "lounge.html" from the "Back to the Lounge" link. How does it differ from the same link in the "directions.html" file?

Answer: It doesn't; it is exactly the same.

Fixing those broken images...

You've almost got the lounge back in working order; all you need to do now is fix those images that aren't displaying.

We haven't looked at the `<img>` element in detail yet (we will in a couple of chapters), but all you need to know for now is that the `<img>` element's `src` attribute takes a relative path, just like the `href` attribute.

Here's the image element from the "lounge.html" file:

`<img src="drinks.gif">`

Here's the relative path, which tells the browser where the image is located. We specify this just like we do with the href attribute in the `<a>` element.

Hey, it's nice you fixed all those links, but didn't you forget something? All our images are broken! Don't leave us hanging—we've got a business to run.

Finding the path from "lounge.html" to "drinks.gif"

To find the path, we need to go from the "lounge.html" file to where the images are located, in the "images" folder.

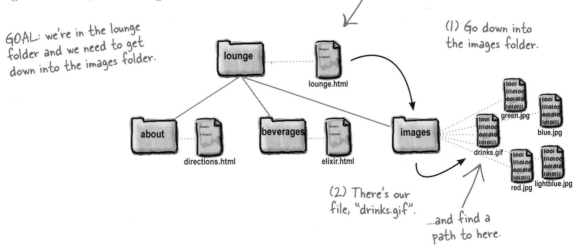

GOAL: we're in the lounge folder and we need to get down into the images folder.

Start here...

(1) Go down into the images folder.

(2) There's our file, "drinks.gif".

...and find a path to here.

green.jpg

blue.jpg

red.jpg lightblue.jpg

drinks.gif

lounge

lounge.html

about directions.html

beverages elixir.html

images

So when we put (1) and (2) together, our path looks like "images/drinks.gif", or:

`<img src="images/drinks.gif">`

Finding the path from "elixir.html" to "red.jpg"

The elixirs page contains images of several drinks: "red.jpg", "green.jpg", "blue.jpg", and so on. Let's figure out the path to "red.jpg" and then the rest will have a similar path because they are all in the same folder:

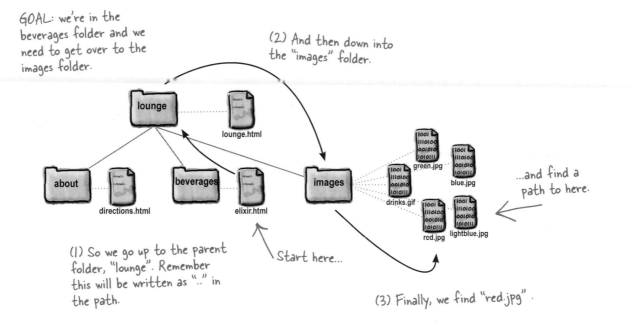

GOAL: we're in the beverages folder and we need to get over to the images folder.

(2) And then down into the "images" folder.

...and find a path to here.

(1) So we go up to the parent folder, "lounge". Remember this will be written as ".." in the path.

Start here...

(3) Finally, we find "red.jpg".

So putting (1), (2), and (3) together, we get:

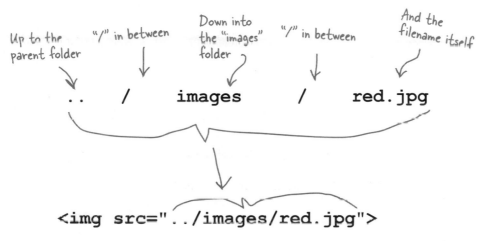

Up to the parent folder

"/" in between

Down into the "images" folder

"/" in between

And the filename itself

`.. / images / red.jpg`

`<img src="../images/red.jpg">`

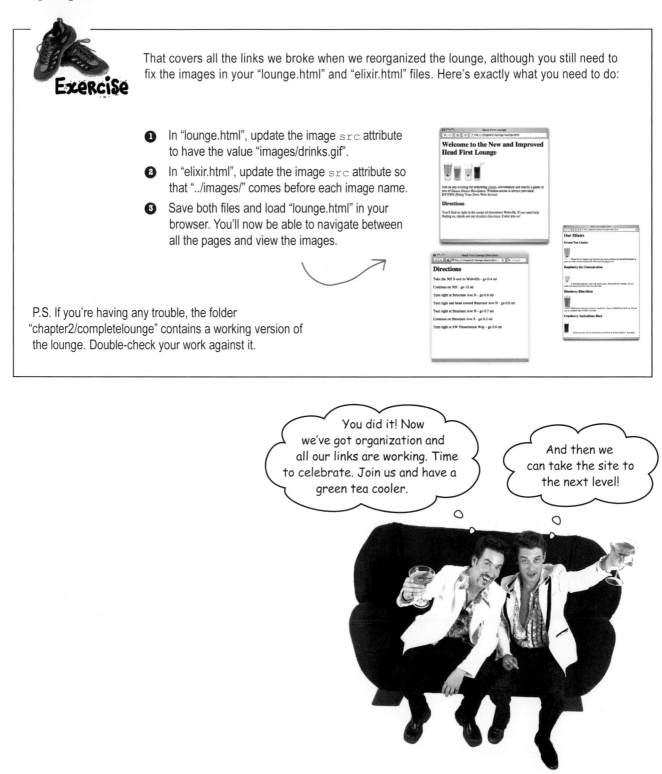

Exercise

That covers all the links we broke when we reorganized the lounge, although you still need to fix the images in your "lounge.html" and "elixir.html" files. Here's exactly what you need to do:

1 In "lounge.html", update the image `src` attribute to have the value "images/drinks.gif".

2 In "elixir.html", update the image `src` attribute so that "../images/" comes before each image name.

3 Save both files and load "lounge.html" in your browser. You'll now be able to navigate between all the pages and view the images.

P.S. If you're having any trouble, the folder "chapter2/completelounge" contains a working version of the lounge. Double-check your work against it.

You did it! Now we've got organization and all our links are working. Time to celebrate. Join us and have a green tea cooler.

And then we can take the site to the next level!

BULLET POINTS

- When you want to link from one page to another, use the <a> element.

- The href attribute of the <a> element specifies the destination of the link.

- The content of the <a> element is the label for the link. The label is what you see on the web page. By default, it's underlined to indicate you can click on it.

- You can use words or an image as the label for a link.

- When you click on a link, the browser loads the web page that's specified in the href attribute.

- You can link to files in the same folder, or files in other folders.

- A relative path is a link that points to other files on your website relative to the web page you're linking from. Just like on a map, the destination is relative to the starting point.

- Use ".." to link to a file that's one folder above the file you're linking from.

- ".." means "parent folder."

- Remember to separate the parts of your path with the "/" (forward slash) character.

- When your path to an image is incorrect, you'll see a broken image on your web page.

- Don't use spaces in the names you choose for files and folders for your website.

- It's a good idea to organize your website files early on in the process of building your site, so you don't have to change a bunch of paths later when the website grows.

- There are many ways to organize a website; how you do it is up to you.

The Relativity Grand Challenge

Here's your chance to put your relativity skills to the test. We've got a website for the top 100 albums in a folder named "music". In this folder you'll find HTML files, other folders, and images. Your challenge is to find the relative paths we need so we can link from our web pages to other web pages and files.

On this page, you'll see the website structure; on the next page, you'll find the tasks to test your skills. For each source file and destination file, it's your job to make the correct relative path. If you succeed, you will truly be champion of relative paths.

Good luck!

Feel free to draw right on this website picture to figure out the paths.

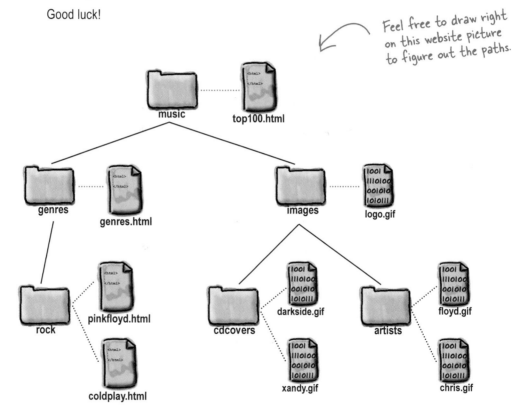

It's time for the competition to begin.

Ready...set...write!

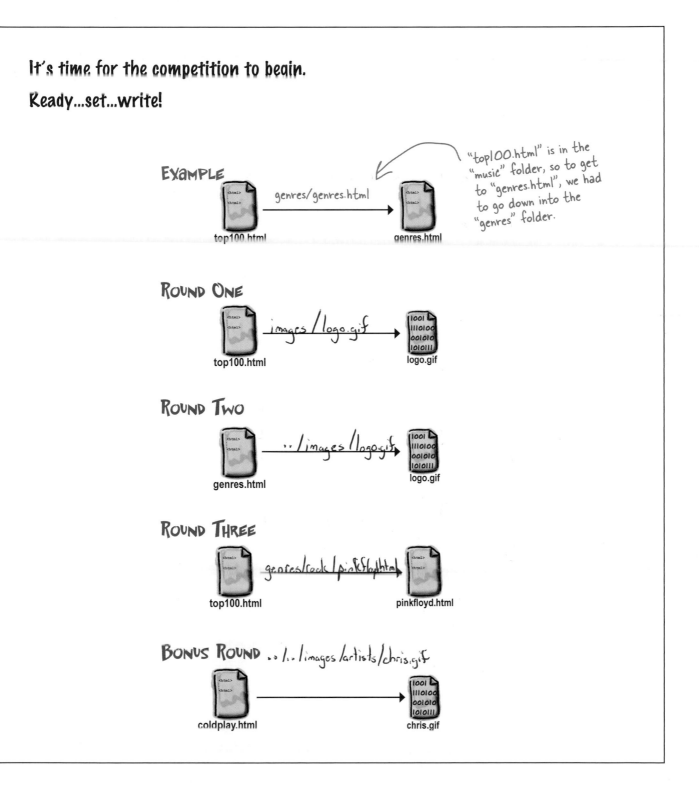

EXAMPLE

genres/genres.html

top100.html → genres.html

"top100.html" is in the "music" folder, so to get to "genres.html", we had to go down into the "genres" folder.

ROUND ONE

images / logo.gif

top100.html → logo.gif

ROUND TWO

.. / images / logo.gif

genres.html → logo.gif

ROUND THREE

genres/rock/pinkfloyd.html

top100.html → pinkfloyd.html

BONUS ROUND   .. / .. / images / artists / chris.gif

coldplay.html → chris.gif

HTMLcross

How does a crossword help you learn HTML? Well, all the words are HTML-related and from this chapter. In addition, the clues provide the mental twist and turns that will help you burn alternative routes to HTML right into your brain!

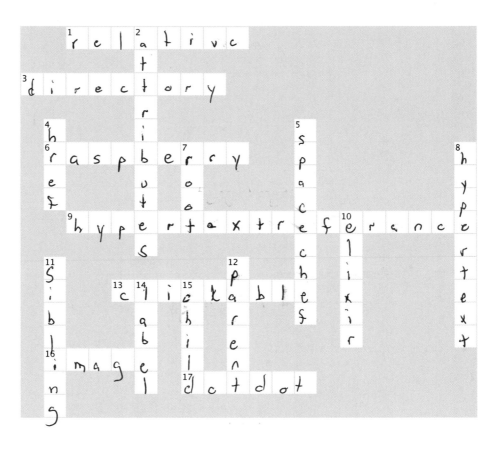

Across

1. "../myfiles/index.html" is this kind of link.
3. Another name for a folder.
6. Flavor of blue drink.
9. What href stands for.
13. Everything between the <a> and </a> is this.
16. Can go in an <a> element, just like text.
17. Pronounced "..".

Down

2. href and src are two of these.
4. Hardest-working attribute on the Web.
5. Rhymes with href.
7. Top folder of your site.
8. The "HT" in HTML.
10. Healthy drink.
11. A folder at the same level.
12. Use .. to reach this kind of directory.
14. Text between the <a> tags acts as a _____.
15. A subfolder is also called this.

You needed to add a link with the label "Back to the Lounge" at the bottom of the elixir page that points back to "lounge.html". Here's our solution.

Exercise Solution

```html
<html>
  <head>
    <title>Head First Lounge Elixirs</title>
  </head>
  <body>
    <h1>Our Elixirs</h1>

    <h2>Green Tea Cooler</h2>
    <p>
            <img src="green.jpg">
            Chock full of vitamins and mi
            combines the healthful benefi
            a twist of chamomile blossoms
    </p>
    <h2>Raspberry Ice Concentration</h2>
    <p>
            <img src="lightblue.jpg">
            Combining raspberry juice wit
            citrus peel and rosehips, thi
            will make your mind feel clea
    </p>
    <h2>Blueberry Bliss Elixir</h2>
    <p>
            <img src="blue.jpg">
            Blueberries and cherry essence mixed into a base
            of elderflower herb tea will put you in a relaxed
            state of bliss in no time.
    </p>
    <h2>Cranberry Antioxidant Blast</h2>
    <p>
            <img src="red.jpg">
            Wake up to the flavors of cranberry and hibiscus
            in this vitamin C rich elixir.
    </p>
    <p>
        <a href="lounge.html">Back to the Lounge</a>
    </p>
  </body>
</html>
```

Here's the new <a> element pointing back to the lounge.

We put the link inside its own paragraph to keep things tidy. We'll talk more about this in the next chapter.

Exercise solutions

Label	Destination	Element
Hot or Not?	hot.html	`<a href="hot.html">Hot or Not?</a>`
Resume	cv.html	`<a href="cv.html">Resume</a>`
Eye Candy	candy.html	`<a href="` candy.html `">Eye Candy</a>`
See my mini	mini-cooper.html	`<a href="mini-cooper.html">See my mini</a>`
let's play	millionaire.html	`<a href="millionaire.html">` let's play `</a>`

```
  1 R E L 2 A T I V E
          T
3 D I R E C T O R Y
          R
  4 H     I                    5 S
  6 R A S P B E 7 R R Y        P              8 H
  E       U     O             A              Y
  F       T     O             C              P
        9 H Y P E R T E X T R E F 10 E R E N C E
          S                   C    L          R
  11 S               12 P     H    I          T
  I     13 C 14 L 15 C K A B L E   X          E
  B       A   H   R           F    I          X
  L       B   I   E                R          T
  16 I M A G E   L
  N       L   17 D O T D O T
  G
```

Sharpen your pencil
Solution

Trace the relative path from "lounge.html" to "directions.html". When you've discovered it, complete the <a> element below.

Here's the solution. Did you change both <a> elements in "lounge.html"?

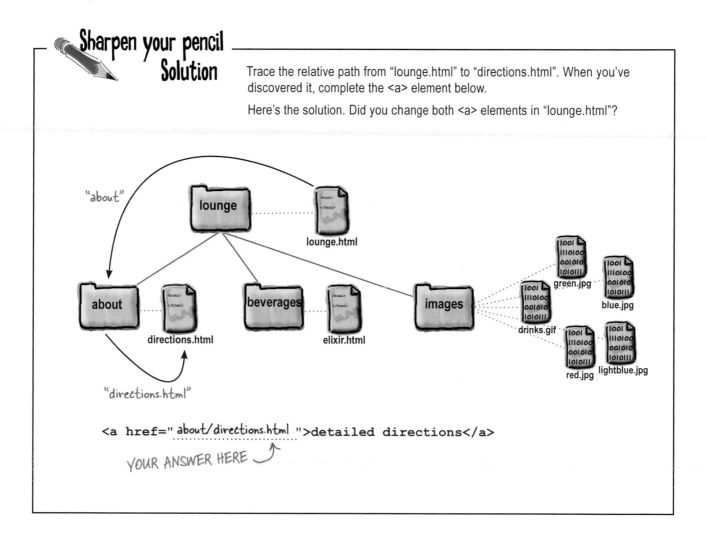

```
<a href=" about/directions.html ">detailed directions</a>
```

YOUR ANSWER HERE

 # The Relativity Grand Challenge Solution

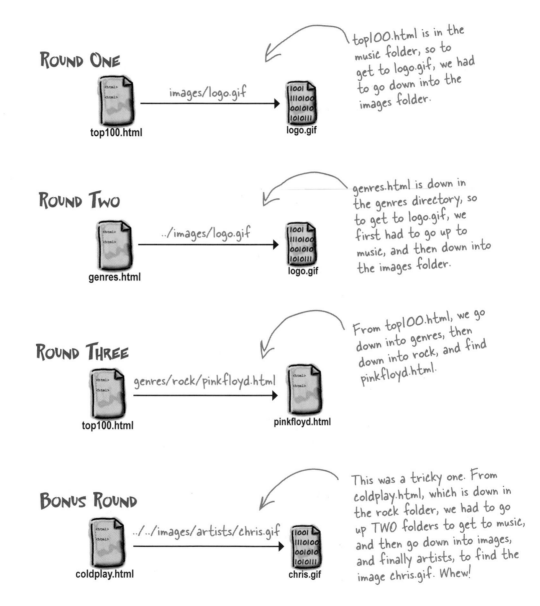

ROUND ONE

top100.html → images/logo.gif → logo.gif

top100.html is in the music folder, so to get to logo.gif, we had to go down into the images folder.

ROUND TWO

genres.html → ../images/logo.gif → logo.gif

genres.html is down in the genres directory, so to get to logo.gif, we first had to go up to music, and then down into the images folder.

ROUND THREE

top100.html → genres/rock/pinkfloyd.html → pinkfloyd.html

From top100.html, we go down into genres, then down into rock, and find pinkfloyd.html.

BONUS ROUND

coldplay.html → ../../images/artists/chris.gif → chris.gif

This was a tricky one. From coldplay.html, which is down in the rock folder, we had to go up TWO folders to get to music, and then go down into images, and finally artists, to find the image chris.gif. Whew!

3 building blocks

Web Page Construction

> We better find some hard hats, Betty. It's a real construction zone around here, and these web pages are going up fast!

I was told I'd actually be creating web pages in this book?

You've certainly learned a lot already: tags, elements, links, paths...but it's all for nothing if you don't create some killer web pages with that knowledge. In this chapter we're going to ramp up construction: you're going to take a web page from conception to blueprint, pour the foundation, build it, and even put on some finishing touches. All you need is your hard hat and your toolbelt, as we'll be adding some new tools and giving you some insider knowledge that would make Tim "The Toolman" Taylor proud.

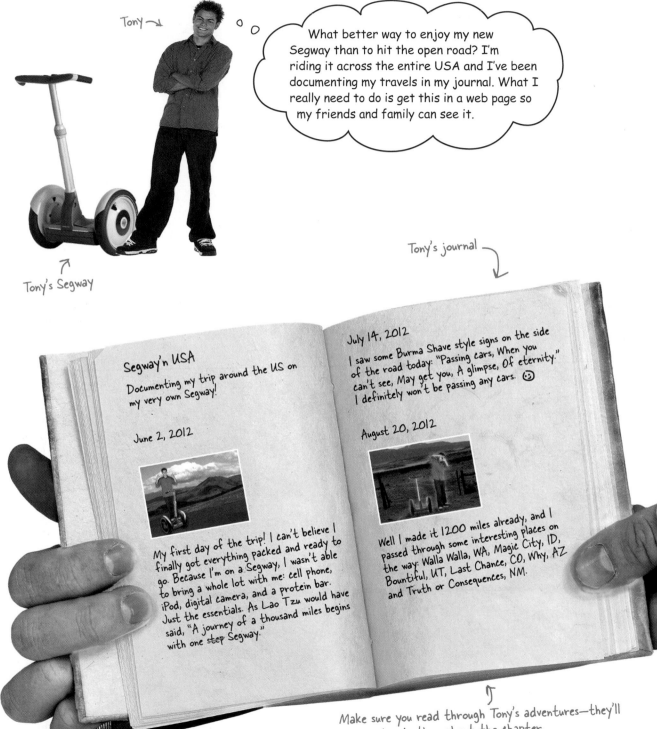

Tony →

What better way to enjoy my new Segway than to hit the open road? I'm riding it across the entire USA and I've been documenting my travels in my journal. What I really need to do is get this in a web page so my friends and family can see it.

↑
Tony's Segway

Tony's journal →

Segway'n USA

Documenting my trip around the US on my very own Segway!

June 2, 2012

My first day of the trip! I can't believe I finally got everything packed and ready to go. Because I'm on a Segway, I wasn't able to bring a whole lot with me: cell phone, iPod, digital camera, and a protein bar. Just the essentials. As Lao Tzu would have said, "A journey of a thousand miles begins with one step Segway."

July 14, 2012

I saw some Burma Shave style signs on the side of the road today: "Passing cars, When you can't see, May get you, A glimpse, Of eternity." I definitely won't be passing any cars. ☺

August 20, 2012

Well I made it 1200 miles already, and I passed through some interesting places on the way: Walla Walla, WA, Magic City, ID, Bountiful, UT, Last Chance, CO, Why, AZ and Truth or Consequences, NM.

↰
Make sure you read through Tony's adventures—they'll come in handy throughout the chapter.

From journal to website, at 12 mph

← The Segway's ^top speed.
recommended

Tony's got his hands full driving across the United States on his Segway. Why don't you give him a hand and create a web page for him?

Here's what you're going to do:

 1 First, you're going to create a rough sketch of the journal that is the basis for your page design.

2 Next, you'll use the basic building blocks of HTML (`<h1>`, `<h2>`, `<h3>`, `<p>`, and so on) to translate your sketch into an outline (or blueprint) for the HTML page.

3 Once you have the outline, then you're going to translate it into real HTML.

4 Finally, with the basic page done, you'll add some enhancements and meet some new HTML elements along the way.

 ## Sharpen your pencil

STOP! Do this exercise before turning the page.

Take a close look at Tony's journal and think about how you'd present the same information in a web page.

Draw a picture of that page on the right. No need to get too fancy; you're just creating a rough sketch. Assume all his journal entries will be on one page.

Things to think about:

- Think of the page in terms of large structural elements: headings, paragraphs, images, and so on.

- Are there ways his journal might be changed to be more appropriate for the Web?

Your sketch goes here. →

> Segway's USA
> List of dates
> ⸽
>
> Date
>
> [Img] (If any)
>
> Description
>
> Quote from day (If any)
>
> Top of page
> ⸽
>
> Top of page

Documenting my trip around the US on my very own Segway

The rough design sketch

Tony's journal looks a lot like a web page; all we need to do to create the design sketch is to get all his entries on one page and map out the general organization. It looks like, for each day that Tony creates an entry, he has a date heading, an optional picture, and a description of what happened that day. Let's look at the sketch…

Tony gave his journal a title, "Segway'n USA," so let's get that right at the top as a heading.

He also gave his journal a description. We'll capture that here as a small paragraph at the top.

Each day, Tony creates an entry that includes the date, usually a picture, and a description of the day's adventures. So, that's a heading, an image, and another paragraph of text.

Sometimes he doesn't include a picture. In this entry, he just has a heading (the date) and a description of the day's events.

The third entry should look just like the first one: a heading, an image, and a paragraph.

Unlike Tony's paper journal, our page length isn't limited, so we can fit many entries on one web page. His friends and family can just use the scroll bar to scroll through his entries…

However, notice that we reversed the order of the journal entries from newest to oldest. That way, the most recent entries appear at the top where users can see them without scrolling.

Segway'n USA
Documenting my trip around the US on my very own Segway!

August 20, 2012

Well I made it 1200 miles already, and I passed through some interesting places on the way: Walla Walla, WA, Magic City, ID, Bountiful, UT, Last Chance, CO, Why, AZ and Truth or Consequences, NM.

July 14, 2012
I saw some Burma Shave style signs on the side of the road today: "Passing cars, When you can't see, May get you, A glimpse, Of eternity." I definitely won't be passing any cars.

June 2, 2012

My first day of the trip! I can't believe finally got everything packed and ready to go. Because I'm on a Segway, I wasn't able to bring a whole lot with me: cell phone, iPod, digital camera, and a protein bar. Just the essentials. As Lao Tzu would have said, "A journey of a thousand miles begins with one Segway."

From a sketch to an outline

Now that you've got a sketch of the page, you can take each section and draw something that looks more like an outline or blueprint for the HTML page…

Here we've taken each area of the sketch and created a corresponding block in our blueprint.

All you need to do now is figure out which HTML element maps to each content area, and then you can start writing the HTML.

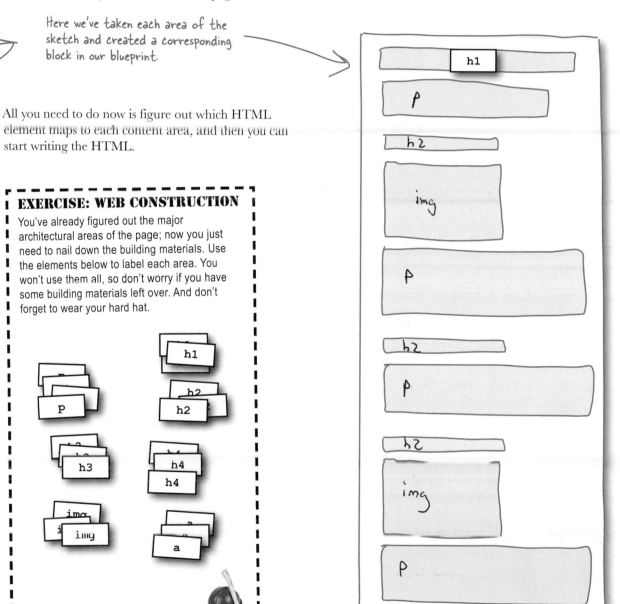

EXERCISE: WEB CONSTRUCTION

You've already figured out the major architectural areas of the page; now you just need to nail down the building materials. Use the elements below to label each area. You won't use them all, so don't worry if you have some building materials left over. And don't forget to wear your hard hat.

From the outline to a web page

You're almost there. You've created an outline of Tony's web page. Now all you need to do is create the corresponding HTML to represent the page and fill in Tony's text.

Before you begin, remember that every web page needs to start with the `<html>` element and include the `<head>` and `<body>` elements.

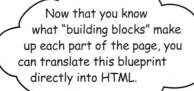

Now that you know what "building blocks" make up each part of the page, you can translate this blueprint directly into HTML.

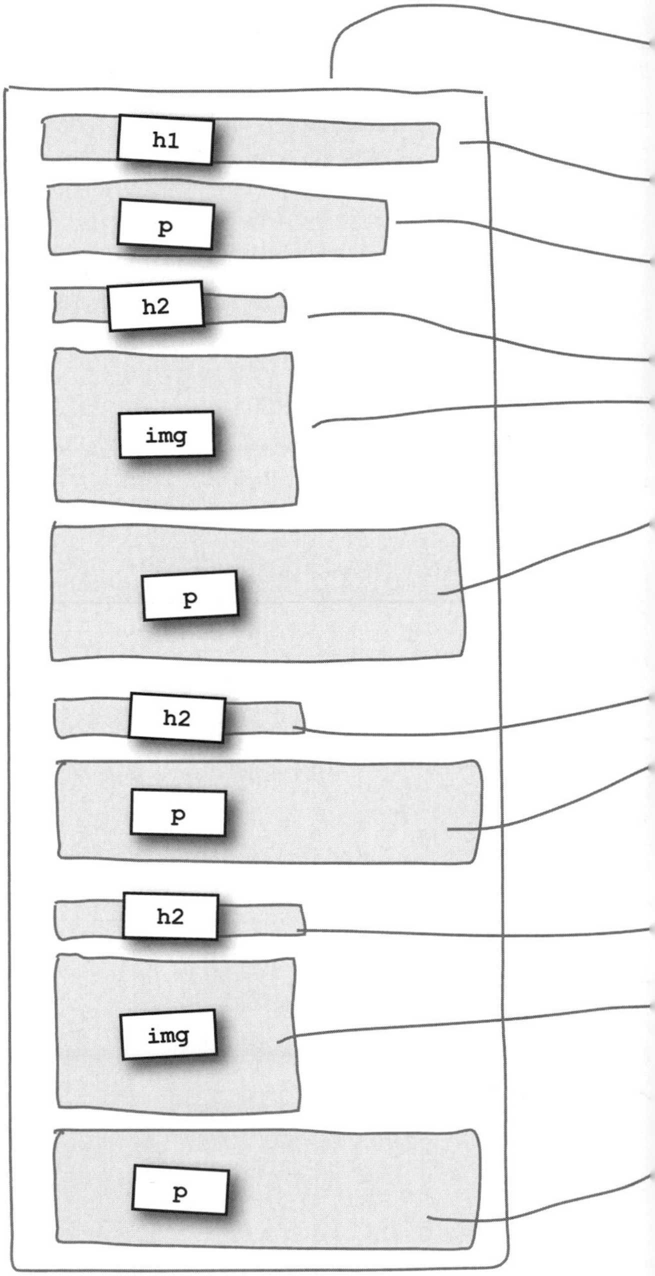

h1

p

h2

img

p

h2

p

h2

img

p

Don't forget, you always need the <html>, <head>, <title>, and <body> elements.

We're using the title of the journal as the title of the web page.

```html
<html>
  <head>
    <title>My Trip Around the USA on a Segway</title>
  </head>
  <body>

    <h1>Segway'n USA</h1>
    <p>
        Documenting my trip around the US on my very own Segway!
    </p>

    <h2>August 20, 2012</h2>
    <img src="images/segway2.jpg">
    <p>
        Well I made it 1200 miles already, and I passed
        through some interesting places on the way: Walla Walla,
        WA, Magic City, ID, Bountiful, UT, Last Chance, CO,
        Why, AZ and Truth or Consequences, NM.
    </p>

    <h2>July 14, 2012</h2>
    <p>
        I saw some Burma Shave style signs on the side of the
        road today: "Passing cars, When you can't see, May get
        you, A glimpse, Of eternity." I definitely won't be passing
        any cars.
    </p>

    <h2>June 2, 2012</h2>
    <img src="images/segway1.jpg">
    <p>
        My first day of the trip! I can't believe I finally got
        everything packed and ready to go. Because I'm on a Segway,
        I wasn't able to bring a whole lot with me: cell phone, iPod,
        digital camera, and a protein bar. Just the essentials. As
        Lao Tzu would have said, "A journey of a thousand miles begins
        with one Segway."
    </p>

  </body>
</html>
```

Here's the heading and description of Tony's journal.

heading
image
description

Here's Tony's most recent entry.

Here's his second entry, which doesn't have an image.

And at the bottom, Tony's first entry, with the image "segway1.jpg".

Last, but not least, don't forget to close your <body> and <html> elements.

Go ahead and type this in. Save your file to the "chapter3/journal" folder as "journal.html". You'll find the images "segway1.jpg" and "segway2.jpg" already in the "images" folder. When you're done, give this page a test drive.

Test driving Tony's web page

My Trip Around the USA on a Segway

`file:///chapter3/journal/journal.html`   Google

Segway'n USA

Documenting my trip around the US on my very own Segway!

August 20, 2012

Well I made it 1200 miles already, and I passed through some interesting places on the way: Walla Walla, WA, Magic City, ID, Bountiful, UT, Last Chance, CO, Why, AZ and Truth or Consequences, NM

July 14, 2012

I saw some Burma Shave style signs on the side of the road today: Passing cars, When you can't see, May get you, A glimpse, Of eternity. I definitely won't be passing any cars.

June 2, 2012

My first day of the trip! I can't believe I finally got everything packed and ready to go. Because I'm on a Segway, I wasn't able to bring a whole lot with me: cellphone, iPod, digital camera, and a protein bar. Just the essentials. As Lao Tzu would have said, "A journey of a thousand miles begins with one Segway."

Look how well this page has come together. You've put everything in Tony's journal into a readable and well-structured web page.

Fantastic! This looks great; I can't wait to add more entries to my page.

Tony's calling in from the road...

Adding some new elements

You have the basic elements of HTML down. You've gone from a hand-written journal to an online version in just a few steps using the basic HTML elements `<p>`, `<h1>`, `<h2>`, and `<img>`.

Now we're going to s-t-r-e-t-c-h your brain a little and add a few more common elements. Let's take another look at Tony's journal and see where we can spruce things up a bit…

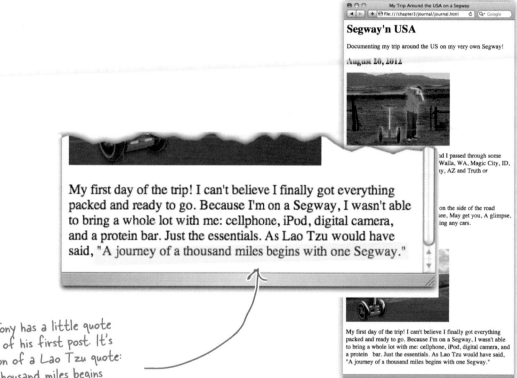

Check this out: Tony has a little quote stuck at the end of his first post. It's his remixed version of a Lao Tzu quote: "A journey of a thousand miles begins with one Segway."

HTML has an element, `<q>`, for just that kind of thing. Let's take a look on the next page…

Meet the <q> element

Got a short quote in your HTML? The <q> element is just what you need. Here's a little test HTML to show you how it works:

```html
<html>
  <head>
    <title>Quote Test Drive</title>
  </head>
  <body>
    <p>
      You never know when you'll need a good quote, how
      about <q>To be or not to be</q>, or <q>Wherever you go, there you are</q>.
    </p>
  </body>
</html>
```

We've got two quotes in this HTML...

We surround each quote with a <q> opening tag and a </q> closing tag. Notice that we don't put our own double-quote characters around the quotes.

And test drive

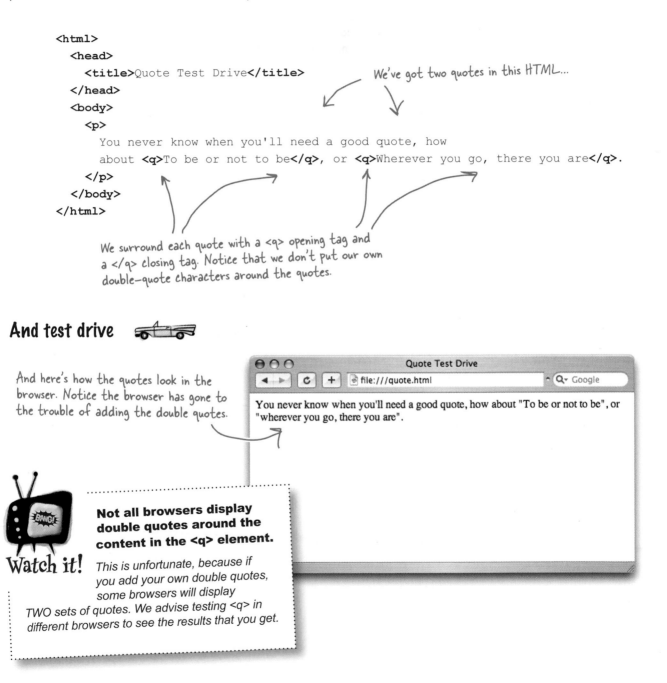

And here's how the quotes look in the browser. Notice the browser has gone to the trouble of adding the double quotes.

Quote Test Drive

file:///quote.html

You never know when you'll need a good quote, how about "To be or not to be", or "wherever you go, there you are".

Watch it!

Not all browsers display double quotes around the content in the <q> element.

This is unfortunate, because if you add your own double quotes, some browsers will display TWO sets of quotes. We advise testing <q> in different browsers to see the results that you get.

Wait a sec...you removed the double quotes and substituted a <q> element, which just displays double quotes? Am I supposed to be impressed? Are you trying to make things more complicated?

No. We're trying to make things more **structured** and **meaningful**.

There are lots of reasons people use double quotes in text, but when we use <q>, that means something specific—it means the text of an *actual quote* (in Tony's case, a "remixed" quote).

See! Using double quotes doesn't make something an actual quote.

In other words, what we've done is to add more meaning by marking up the quote. Before we added the <q> element, the browser just knew it had a paragraph of text with a few double-quote characters in it. Now, because we're using the <q> element, the browser *knows* that some of that text is a real quote.

So what? Well, now that the browser knows this is a quote, it can display it in the best way possible. Some browsers will display double quotes around the text and some won't; and in instances where browsers are using non-English languages, other methods might be used. And don't forget mobile devices, like cell phones, or audio HTML browsers and screen readers for the visually impaired. It's also useful in other situations, such as a search engine that scours the Web looking for web pages with quotes. Structure and meaning in your pages are Good Things.

One of the best reasons (as you'll see when we get back to presentation and CSS later in the book) is that you'll be able to style quotes to look just the way you want. Suppose you want quoted text to be displayed in italics and colored gray? If you've used the <q> element to structure the quoted content in your web pages, you'll be able to do just that.

Exercise

Here's Tony's journal. Go ahead and rework his Lao Tzu quote to use the <q> element. After you've done it on paper, make the changes in your "journal.html" file and give it a test drive. You'll find the solution in the back of the chapter.

```html
<html>
  <head>
    <title>Segway'n USA</title>
  </head>
  <body>

    <h1>Segway'n USA</h1>
    <p>
        Documenting my trip around the US on my very own Segway!
    </p>

    <h2>August 20, 2012</h2>
    <img src="images/segway2.jpg">
    <p>
      Well I made it 1200 miles already, and I passed
      through some interesting places on the way: Walla Walla,
      WA, Magic City, ID, Bountiful, UT, Last Chance, CO,
      Why, AZ and Truth or Consequences, NM.
    </p>

    <h2>July 14, 2012</h2>
    <p>
      I saw some Burma Shave style signs on the side of the
      road today: "Passing cars, When you can't see, May get
      you, A glimpse, Of eternity." I definitely won't be passing
      any cars.
    </p>

    <h2>June 2, 2012</h2>
    <img src="images/segway1.jpg">
    <p>
      My first day of the trip! I can't believe I finally got
      everything packed and ready to go. Because I'm on a Segway,
      I wasn't able to bring a whole lot with me: cell phone, iPod,
      digital camera, and a protein bar. Just the essentials. As
      Lao Tzu would have said, "A journey of a thousand miles begins
      with one Segway."
    </p>
  </body>
</html>
```

The Case of the Elements Separated at Birth

Identical twins were born in Webville a number of years ago, and by a freak accident involving an Internet router malfunction, the twins were separated shortly after birth. Both grew up without knowledge of the other, and only through another set of freak circumstances did they later meet and discover their identity, which they decided to keep secret.

Five-Minute Mystery

After the discovery, they quickly learned that they shared a surprising number of things in common. Both were married to wives named Citation. They also both had a love for quotations. The first twin, the `<q>` element, loved short, pithy quotes, while the second, `<blockquote>`, loved longer quotes, often memorizing complete passages from books or poems.

Being identical twins, they bore a strong resemblance to each other, and so they decided to put together an evil scheme whereby they might stand in for each other now and then. They first tested this on their wives (the details of which we won't go into), and they passed with flying colors—their wives had no idea (or at least pretended not to).

Next they wanted to test their switching scheme in the workplace where, as another coincidence, they both performed the same job: marking up quotes in HTML documents. So, on the chosen day, the brothers went to the other's workplace fully confident they'd pull off their evil plan (after all, if their wives couldn't tell, how could their bosses?), and that's when things turned bad. Within 10 minutes of starting the work day, the brothers had both been found to be imposters and the standards authorities were immediately alerted.

How were the twins caught in the act?
Keep reading for more clues…

Looooong quotes

Now that you know how to do short quotes, let's tackle long ones. Tony's given us a long quote with the Burma Shave jingle.

In his journal, Tony just put the Burma Shave quote right inside his paragraph, but wouldn't it be better if we pulled this quote out into a "block" of its own, like this:

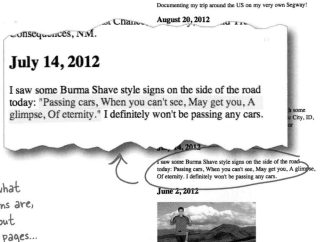

> I saw some Burma Shave style signs on the side of the road today:
>
> > Passing cars,
> > When you can't see,
> > May get you,
> > A glimpse,
> > Of eternity.
>
> I definitely won't be passing any cars.

If you don't know what "Burma Shave" slogans are, we'll tell you all about them in just a few pages...

That's where the `<blockquote>` element comes in. Unlike the `<q>` element, which is meant for short quotes that are part of an existing paragraph, the `<blockquote>` element is meant for longer quotes that need to be displayed on their own.

> It's important to use the right tool for the job, and the `<blockquote>` element is perfect for this job.

Adding a <blockquote>

Let's get a <blockquote> into Tony's online journal.

1 Open your "journal.html" file and locate the July 14th entry. Rework the paragraph to look like this:

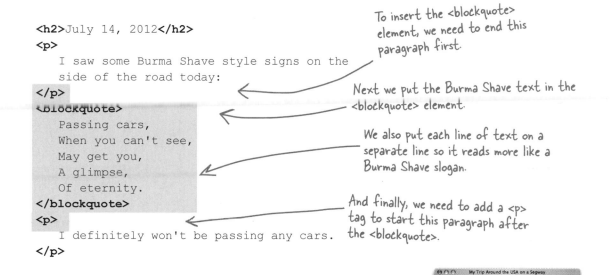

```
<h2>July 14, 2012</h2>
<p>
    I saw some Burma Shave style signs on the
    side of the road today:
</p>
<blockquote>
    Passing cars,
    When you can't see,
    May get you,
    A glimpse,
    Of eternity.
</blockquote>
<p>
    I definitely won't be passing any cars.
</p>
```

To insert the <blockquote> element, we need to end this paragraph first.

Next we put the Burma Shave text in the <blockquote> element.

We also put each line of text on a separate line so it reads more like a Burma Shave slogan.

And finally, we need to add a <p> tag to start this paragraph after the <blockquote>.

2 Time for another test drive. Open "journal.html" in your browser and take a look at the results of your work:

<blockquote> creates a separate block (like <p> does), plus it indents the text a bit to make it look more like a quote. Just what we wanted...

But our quote isn't looking quite like we wanted because all the lines are running together. We really wanted them on different lines. Hmmm. Let's come back to that in a bit...

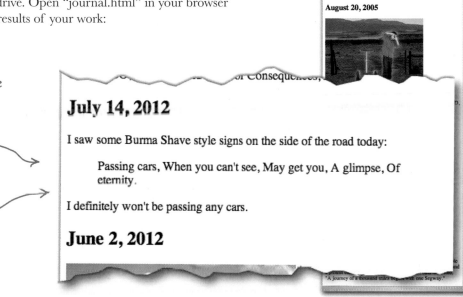

there are no
Dumb Questions

Q: So let me see if I have this right: I use <q> when I just want to have some quote in with the rest of my paragraph, and I use <blockquote> when I have a quote that I want to break out on its own in my web page?

A: You've got it. In general you'll use <blockquote> if you want to quote something that was a paragraph or more, while you can use <q> anytime you just want to throw in a quote as part of your running text.

Q: Multiple paragraphs in a block quote? How do I do that?

A: Easy. Just put paragraph elements inside your <blockquote>, one for each paragraph. Do try this at home.

Q: How do I know what my quotes or block quotes will look like in other browsers? It sounds like they may handle it differently.

A: Yes. Welcome to the World Wide Web. You don't really know what your quotes will look like without trying them out in different browsers. Some browsers use double quotes, some use italics, and some use nothing at all. The only way to really determine how they'll look is to style them yourself, and we'll certainly be doing that later.

Q: I get that the <blockquote> element breaks its text out into a little block of its own and indents it, so why isn't the <blockquote> inside the paragraph, just like the <q> element is?

A: Because the <blockquote> really is like a new paragraph. Think about this as if you were typing it into a word processor. When you finish one paragraph, you hit the Return key twice and start a new paragraph. To type a block quote, you'd do the same thing and indent the quote. Put this in the back of your mind for a moment; it's an important point and we're going to come back to it in a sec.

Also, remember that the indenting is just the way some browsers display a <blockquote>. Some browsers might not use indentation for <blockquote>. So, don't rely on a <blockquote> to look the same in all browsers.

Q: Can I combine quote elements? For instance, could I use the <q> element inside the <blockquote> element?

A: Sure. Just like you can put a <q> element inside the <p> element, you can put <q> inside <blockquote>. You might do this if you're quoting someone who quoted someone else. But a <blockquote> inside a <q> doesn't really make sense, does it?

Q: You said that we can style these elements with CSS, so if I want to make the text in my <q> element italics and gray, I can do that with CSS. But couldn't I just use the <em> element to italicize my quotes?

A: Well, you could, but it wouldn't be the right way to do it, because you'd be using the <em> element for its effect on the display rather than because you're really writing emphasized text. If the person you were quoting really did emphasize a word, or you want to add emphasis to make a strong point about the quote, then go right ahead and use the <em> element inside your quote. But don't do it simply for the italics. There are easier and better ways to get the look you want for your elements with CSS.

Solved: The Case of the Elements Separated at Birth

How were the identical quote twins found to be imposters so quickly?

As you've no doubt guessed by now, <q> and <blockquote> were discovered as soon as they went to work and began to mark up text. <q>'s normally unobtrusive little quotes were popping out into blocks of their own, while <blockquote>'s quotes were suddenly being lost inside regular paragraphs of text. In follow-up interviews with the victims of the pranks, one editor complained, "I lost an entire page of liner quotes thanks to these wackos." After being reprimanded and sent back to their respective jobs, <blockquote> and <q> fessed up to their wives, who immediately left town together in a T-Bird convertible. But that's a whole 'nother story (it didn't end well).

Five-Minute Mystery Solved

The _real_ truth behind the <q> and <blockquote> mystery

Okay, it's time to stop the charade: <blockquote> and <q> are actually different types of elements. The <blockquote> element is a *block* element and the <q> element is an *inline* element. What's the difference? Block elements are always displayed as if they have a linebreak before and after them, while inline elements appear "in line" within the flow of the text in your page.

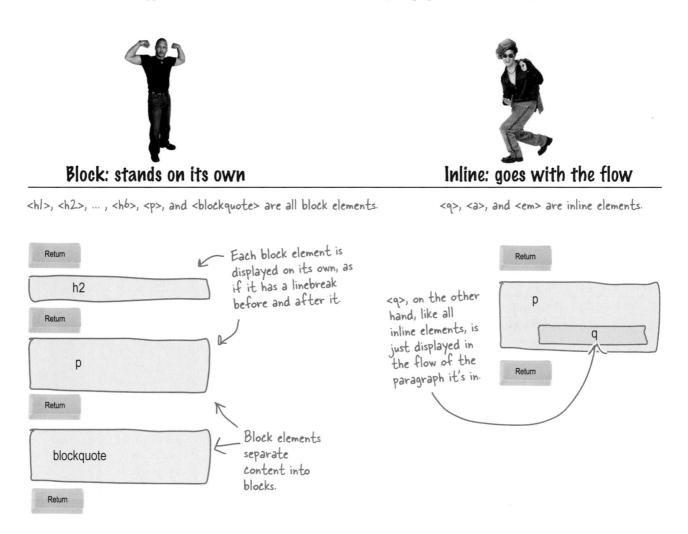

Block: stands on its own

<hl>, <h2>, … , <h6>, <p>, and <blockquote> are all block elements.

Inline: goes with the flow

<q>, <a>, and <em> are inline elements.

Each block element is displayed on its own, as if it has a linebreak before and after it.

<q>, on the other hand, like all inline elements, is just displayed in the flow of the paragraph it's in.

Block elements separate content into blocks.

Remember: block elements stand on their own; inline elements go with the flow.

Once again, this all sounds great, but why is all this talk of linebreaks, blocks, and inline elements useful? Can we get back to web pages?

Don't underestimate the power of knowing how HTML works. You're soon going to see that the way you combine elements in a page has a lot to do with whether elements are displayed as block or inline. We'll get to all that.

In the meantime, you can also think about block versus inline this way: block elements are often used as the major building blocks of your web page, while inline elements usually mark up small pieces of content. When you're designing a page, you typically start with the bigger chunks (the block elements) and then add in the inline elements as you refine the page.

The real payoff is going to come when we get to controlling the presentation of HTML with CSS. If you know the difference between inline and block, you're going to be sipping martinis while everyone else is still trying to get their layout right.

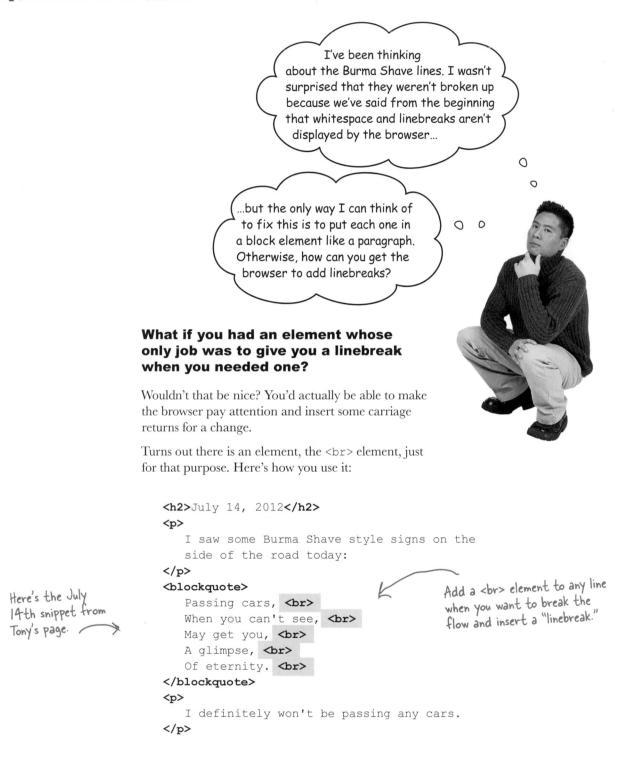

I've been thinking about the Burma Shave lines. I wasn't surprised that they weren't broken up because we've said from the beginning that whitespace and linebreaks aren't displayed by the browser...

...but the only way I can think of to fix this is to put each one in a block element like a paragraph. Otherwise, how can you get the browser to add linebreaks?

What if you had an element whose only job was to give you a linebreak when you needed one?

Wouldn't that be nice? You'd actually be able to make the browser pay attention and insert some carriage returns for a change.

Turns out there is an element, the <br> element, just for that purpose. Here's how you use it:

```
<h2>July 14, 2012</h2>
<p>
    I saw some Burma Shave style signs on the
    side of the road today:
</p>
<blockquote>
    Passing cars, <br>
    When you can't see, <br>
    May get you, <br>
    A glimpse, <br>
    Of eternity. <br>
</blockquote>
<p>
    I definitely won't be passing any cars.
</p>
```

Here's the July 14th snippet from Tony's page.

Add a <br> element to any line when you want to break the flow and insert a "linebreak."

Go ahead and add the <br> elements to Tony's journal. After you make the changes, save the file, and give it a test drive.

Exorcise

Here's what the changes should look like. Now it reads like a Burma Shave slogan should read!

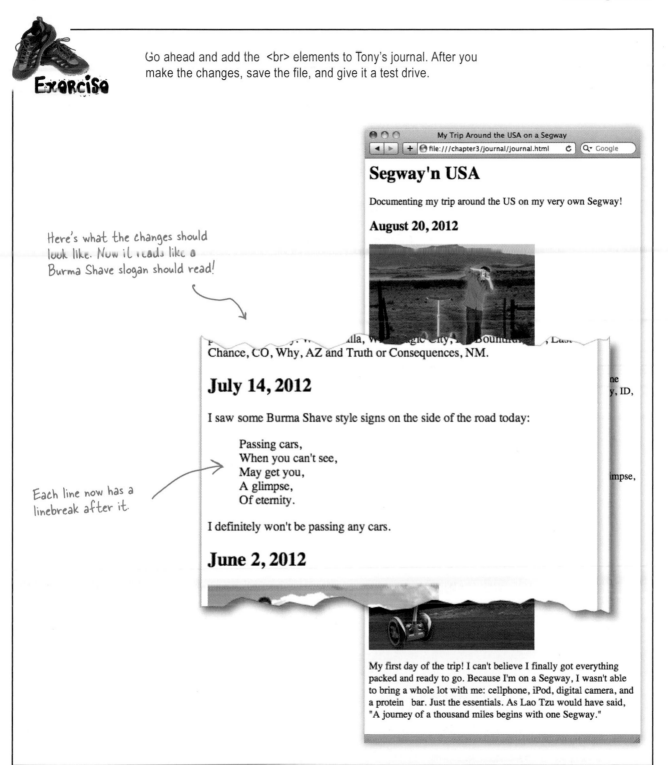

Segway'n USA

Documenting my trip around the US on my very own Segway!

August 20, 2012

...lla, W... ...gic City, ...Boundar... ...Last Chance, CO, Why, AZ and Truth or Consequences, NM.

July 14, 2012

I saw some Burma Shave style signs on the side of the road today:

Passing cars,
When you can't see,
May get you,
A glimpse,
Of eternity.

Each line now has a linebreak after it.

I definitely won't be passing any cars.

June 2, 2012

My first day of the trip! I can't believe I finally got everything packed and ready to go. Because I'm on a Segway, I wasn't able to bring a whole lot with me: cellphone, iPod, digital camera, and a protein bar. Just the essentials. As Lao Tzu would have said, "A journey of a thousand miles begins with one Segway."

> In Chapter 1 we said that an element is an *opening tag* + *content* + *closing tag*. So how is <br> an element? It doesn't have any content, and it doesn't even have a closing tag.

Exactly. It doesn't have any content.

The <br> element is an element that doesn't have any content. Why? Because it's just meant to be a linebreak, nothing else. So, when an element doesn't have any real content by design, we just use a shorthand to represent the element and it ends up looking like <br>. After all, if we didn't have this shorthand, you'd be writing
</br> every time you needed a linebreak, and how much sense does that make?

 isn't the only element like this; there are others, and we have a name for them: *void elements*. In fact, we've already seen another void element, the <img> element. We'll be coming back to look at the <img> element in detail in a couple chapters.

They used to be called "empty elements," which apparently made too much sense, so they renamed them to void. Personally, we still like empty.

Keep in mind, the reason for the shorthand isn't laziness so much as it is efficiency. It's more efficient to represent void elements this way (efficient in typing, in the number of characters that end up in a page, and so on). In fact, after reading HTML for a while, you'll find that it is easier on your eyes too.

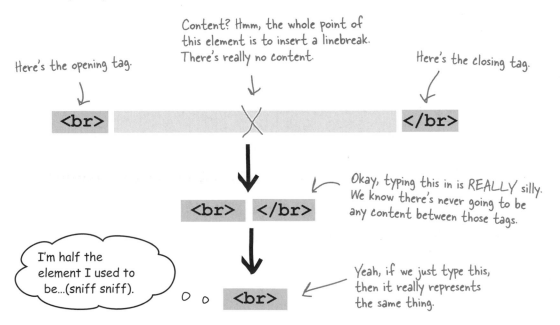

Here's the opening tag.

Content? Hmm, the whole point of this element is to insert a linebreak. There's really no content.

Here's the closing tag.

**
** ✗ **</br>**

Okay, typing this in is REALLY silly. We know there's never going to be any content between those tags.

**
** **</br>**

> I'm half the element I used to be...(sniff sniff).

**
**

Yeah, if we just type this, then it really represents the same thing.

there are no
Dumb Questions

Q: So, the only purpose of <br> is to insert a linebreak?

A: Right; the only place the browser typically inserts breaks in your content is when you start a new block element (like <p>, <h1>, and so on). If you want to insert a linebreak into your text, then you use the <br> element.

Q: Why is <br> called an "void" element?

A: Because it has no content, as in element = opening tag + content + closing tag. So, it's void because there's no content and no closing tag. Think like the "void of space"; there's nothing there, it's empty.

Q: I still don't get it. Explain why the <br> element is "void"?

A: Think about an element like <h1> (or <p> or <a>). The whole point of the element is to mark up some content, like:

```
<h1>Don't wait, order now</h1>
```

With the <br> element, the point is just to insert a linebreak into your HTML. There is no content you are trying to mark up. We don't need all the extra brackets and markup, so we just shorten it into a more convenient form. If you're thinking "void" is kind of a weird name, you're right: it comes from computer science and means "no value."

Q: Are there any other void elements? I think <img> must be a void element, too, right?

A: Yes, there are a couple of them. You've already seen us use the <img> element, and we'll be getting to the details of this element soon.

Q: Can I make any element void? For instance, if I have a link, and don't want to give it any content, can I just write <a href="mypage.html"> instead?

A: No, There are two types of elements in the world: normal elements, like <p>, <h1>, and <a>, and void elements, like <br> and <img>. You don't switch back and forth between the two. For instance, if you just typed <a href="mypage.html">, that's an opening tag without content or a closing tag (not good). If you write <a href="mypage.html"></a>, that's an empty element and is perfectly fine, but isn't very useful in your page!

Q: I've seen pages not with <br>, but with <br />. What does that mean?

A: It means exactly the same thing. The syntax used in <br /> is a more strict syntax that works with XHTML. Whenever you see <br />, just think <br>, and unless you're planning on writing pages compliant with XHTML (see the appendix for more information on XHTML), you should just use <br> in your HTML.

Elements that don't have any content by design are called void elements. When you need to use a void element, like <br> or <img>, you only use an opening tag. This is a convenient shorthand that reduces the amount of markup in your HTML.

Meanwhile, back at Tony's site...

You've come a long way already in this chapter: you've designed and created Tony's site, you've met a few new elements, and you've learned a few things about elements that most people creating pages on the Web don't even know (like block and inline elements, which are really going to come in handy in later chapters).

But you're not done yet. We can take Tony's site from good to great by looking for a few more opportunities to add some markup.

Like what? How about lists? Check this out:

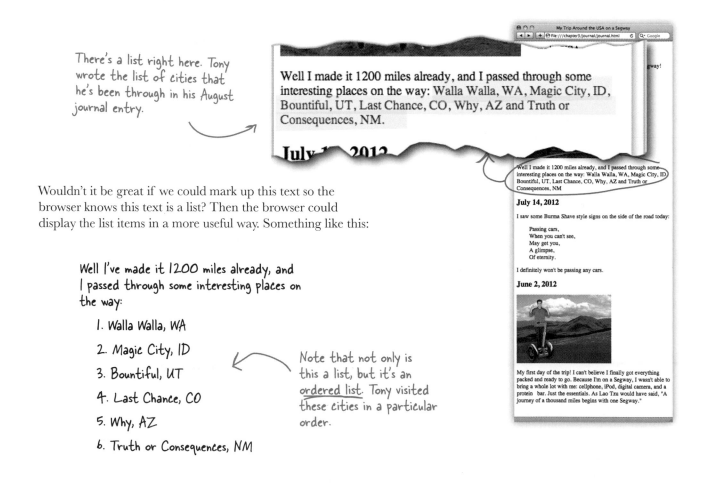

There's a list right here. Tony wrote the list of cities that he's been through in his August journal entry.

Wouldn't it be great if we could mark up this text so the browser knows this text is a list? Then the browser could display the list items in a more useful way. Something like this:

Well I've made it 1200 miles already, and I passed through some interesting places on the way:

1. Walla Walla, WA
2. Magic City, ID
3. Bountiful, UT
4. Last Chance, CO
5. Why, AZ
6. Truth or Consequences, NM

Note that not only is this a list, but it's an ordered list. Tony visited these cities in a particular order.

Of course, you <u>could</u> use the \<p\> element to make a list...

It wouldn't be hard to make a list using the \<p\> element. It would end up looking something like this:

```
<p>
1. Red Segway
</p>
<p>
2. Blue Segway
</p>
```

← Top two preferred colors for Segway.

But there are lots of reasons <u>not</u> to.

You should be sensing a common theme by now. You always want to choose the HTML element that is closest in meaning to the structure of your content. If this is a list, let's use a list element. Doing so gives the browser and you (as you'll see later in the book) the most power and flexibility to display the content in a useful manner.

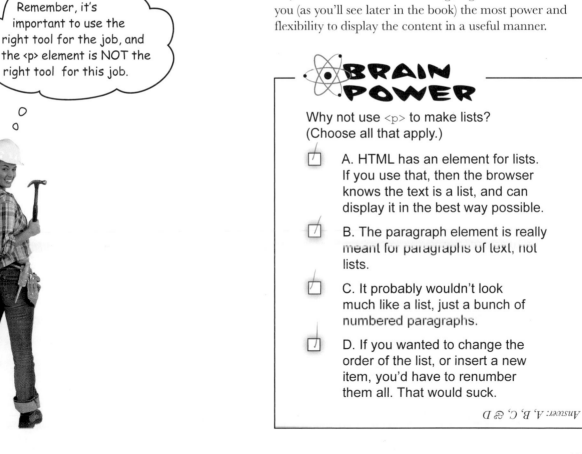

Remember, it's important to use the right tool for the job, and the \<p\> element is NOT the right tool for this job.

✺BRAIN POWER

Why not use \<p\> to make lists? (Choose all that apply.)

☑ A. HTML has an element for lists. If you use that, then the browser knows the text is a list, and can display it in the best way possible.

☑ B. The paragraph element is really meant for paragraphs of text, not lists.

☑ C. It probably wouldn't look much like a list, just a bunch of numbered paragraphs.

☑ D. If you wanted to change the order of the list, or insert a new item, you'd have to renumber them all. That would suck.

Answer: A, B, C, & D

Constructing HTML lists in two easy steps

Creating an HTML list requires two elements that, when used together, form the list. The first element is used to mark up each *list item*. The second determines what kind of list you're creating: *ordered* or *unordered*.

Let's step through creating Tony's list of cities in HTML.

Step one:

Put each list item in an <li> element.

To create a list, you put each list item in its own `<li>` element, which means enclosing the content in an opening `<li>` tag and a closing `</li>` tag. As with any other HTML element, the content between the tags can be as short or as long as you like and broken over multiple lines.

We're just showing a fragment of the HTML from Tony's journal here.

Locate this HTML in your "journal.html" file and keep up with the changes as we make them.

```
<h2>August 20, 2012</h2>
     <img src="images/segway2.jpg">
<p>
Well I've made it 1200 miles already, and I passed
through some interesting places on the way:

</p>
```

First, move the list items outside of the paragraph. The list is going to stand on its own.

```
<li>Walla Walla, WA</li>
<li>Magic City, ID</li>
<li>Bountiful, UT</li>
<li>Last Chance, CO</li>
<li>Why, AZ</li>
<li>Truth or Consequences, NM</li>
```

...and then enclose each list item with an <li>, </li> set of tags.

 Each of these <li> elements will become an item in the list.

```
<h2>July 14, 2012</h2>
<p>
I saw some Burma Shave style signs on the side of
the road today:
</p>
```

Step two:

Enclose your list items with either the <ol> or <ul> element.

If you use an <ol> element to enclose your list items, then the items will be displayed as an ordered list; if you use <ul>, the list will be displayed as an unordered list. Here's how you enclose your items in an <ol> element.

Again, we're just showing a fragment of the HTML from Tony's journal here.

```
<h2>August 20, 2012</h2>
    <img src="images/segway2.jpg">
<p>
Well I've made it 1200 miles already, and I passed
through some interesting places on the way:
</p>
<ol>
    <li>Walla Walla, WA</li>
    <li>Magic City, ID</li>
    <li>Bountiful, UT</li>
    <li>Last Chance, CO</li>
    <li>Why, AZ</li>
    <li>Truth or Consequences, NM</li>
</ol>
<h2>July 14, 2012</h2>
<p>
I saw some Burma Shave style signs on the side of
the road today:
</p>
```

We want this to be an ordered list, because Tony visited the cities in a specific order. So we use an <ol> opening tag.

All the list items sit in the middle of the <ol> element and become its content.

And here we close the <ol> element.

BRAIN POWER

Is <ol> a block element or inline? What about <li>?

No since they break at the beginning and end of the element

Make It Stick

unordered **l**ist = ul

ordered **l**ist = ol

list **i**tem = li

🚗 Taking a test drive through the cities

Make sure you've added all the HTML for the list, reload your "journal.html" file and you should see something like this:

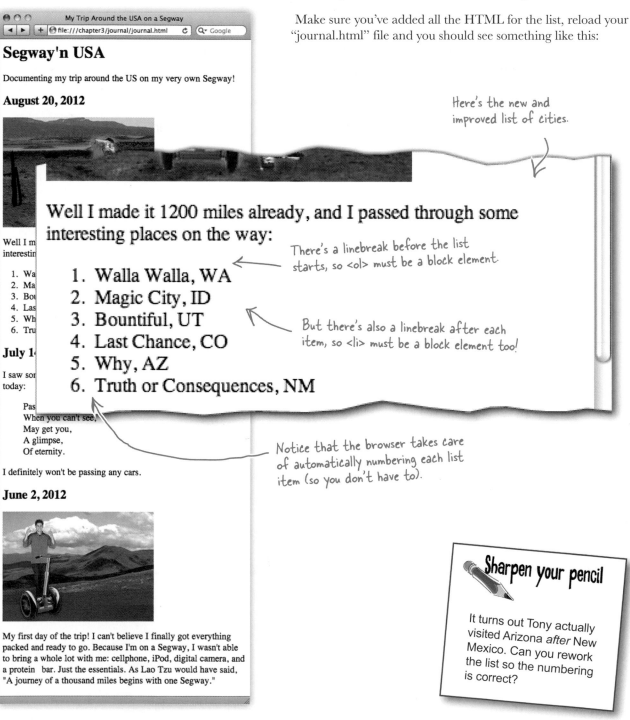

Here's the new and improved list of cities.

Segway'n USA

Documenting my trip around the US on my very own Segway!

August 20, 2012

Well I made it 1200 miles already, and I passed through some interesting places on the way:

There's a linebreak before the list starts, so <ol> must be a block element.

1. Walla Walla, WA
2. Magic City, ID
3. Bountiful, UT
4. Last Chance, CO
5. Why, AZ
6. Truth or Consequences, NM

But there's also a linebreak after each item, so <li> must be a block element too!

Notice that the browser takes care of automatically numbering each list item (so you don't have to).

July 14

I saw sor... today:

Pas...
When you can't see,
May get you,
A glimpse,
Of eternity.

I definitely won't be passing any cars.

June 2, 2012

My first day of the trip! I can't believe I finally got everything packed and ready to go. Because I'm on a Segway, I wasn't able to bring a whole lot with me: cellphone, iPod, digital camera, and a protein bar. Just the essentials. As Lao Tzu would have said, "A journey of a thousand miles begins with one Segway."

Sharpen your pencil

It turns out Tony actually visited Arizona *after* New Mexico. Can you rework the list so the numbering is correct?

Exercise

Here's another list from Tony's journal: cell phone, iPod, digital camera, and a protein bar. You'll find it in his June 2nd entry. This is an *unordered* list of items.

The HTML for this entry is typed below. Go ahead and add the HTML to change the items into an HTML unordered list (remember, you use `<ul>` for unordered lists). We've already reformatted some of the text for you.

When you've finished, check your answers in the back of the chapter. Then make these changes in your "journal.html" file and test.

```
<h2>June 2, 2012</h2>
<img src="segway1.jpg">
<p>
    My first day of the trip! I can't believe I finally got
    everything packed and ready to go. Because I'm on a Segway,
    I wasn't able to bring a whole lot with me:


        cell phone
        iPod
        digital camera
        and a protein bar


    Just the essentials. As
    Lao Tzu would have said, <q>A journey of a
    thousand miles begins with one Segway.</q>
</p>
```

there are no
Dumb Questions

Q: Do I always have to use <ol> and <li> together?

A: Yes, you should always use <ol> and <li> together (or <ul> and <li>). Neither one of these elements really makes sense without the other. Remember, a list is really a group of items: the <li> element is used to identify each item, and the <ol> element is used to group them together.

Q: Can I put text or other elements inside an <ol> or <ul> element?

A: No, the <ol> and <ul> elements are designed to work only with the <li> element.

Q: What about unordered lists? Can I make the bullet look different?

A: Yes. But hold that thought. We'll come back to that when we're talking about CSS and presentation.

Q: What if I wanted to put a list inside a list? Can I do that?

A: Yes, you sure can. Make the content of any <li> either <ol> or <ul>, and you'll have a list within a list (what we call a *nested list*).

```
<ol>
    <li>Charge Segway</li>       Nested list
    <li>Pack for trip
        <ul>                          Here's the
            <li>cell phone</li>       <li>. It
            <li>iPod</li>             encloses
            <li>digital camera</li>   the nested
            <li>a protein bar</li>    list.
        </ul>
    </li>
    <li>Call mom</li>
</ol>
```

Q: I think I basically understand how block elements and inline elements are displayed by the browser, but I'm totally confused about what elements can go inside other elements, or, as you say, what can be "nested" inside of what.

A: That's one of the hardest things to get straight with HTML. This is something you're going to be learning for a few chapters, and we'll show you a few ways to make sure you can keep the relationships straight. But we're going to back up and talk about nesting a little more first. In fact, since you brought it up, we'll do that next.

Q: So HTML has ordered and unordered lists. Are there any other list types?

A: Actually, there is another type: definition lists. A definition list looks like this:

Each item in the list has a term, <dt>, and a description, <dd>.

```
<dl>
    <dt>Burma Shave Signs</dt>
    <dd>Road signs common in the U.S. in
the 1920s and 1930s advertising shaving
products.</dd>
    <dt>Route 66</dt>
    <dd>Most famous road in the U.S. highway
system.</dd>
</dl>
```

Type this in and give it a try.

Q: Burma Shave?

A: Burma Shave was a company that made brushless shaving cream in the early part of the 20th century. They began advertising their product using roadside signs in 1925, and these signs proved to be very popular (if somewhat distracting for drivers).

The signs were grouped in bunches of four, five, or six, each with one line from the slogan. At one point, there were 7,000 of these signs on roadsides throughout the United States. Most are gone now, but there are still a few left, here and there.

Putting one element inside another is called "nesting"

When we put one element inside another element, we call that *nesting*. We say, "the <p> element is nested inside the <body> element." At this point, you've already seen lots of elements nested inside other elements. You've put a <body> element inside an <html> element, a <p> element inside a <body> element, a <q> element inside a <p> element, and so on. You've also put a <head> element inside the <html> element, and a <title> element inside the <head>. That's the way HTML pages get constructed.

The more you learn about HTML, the more important having this nesting in your brain becomes. But no worries—before long you'll naturally think about elements this way.

<q> nested inside <p>, nested inside <body>, nested inside <html>.

To understand the nesting relationships, draw a picture

Drawing the nesting of elements in a web page is kind of like drawing a family tree. At the top you've got the great-grandparents, and then all their children and grandchildren below. Here's an example...

```
<html>
  <head>
    <title>Musings</title>
  </head>
  <body>
    <p>
      To quote Buckaroo,
      <q>The only reason
        for time is so
        that everything
        doesn't happen
        at once.</q>
    </p>
  </body>
</html>
```

Simple web page

Let's translate this into a diagram, where each element becomes a box, and each line connects the element to another element that is nested within it.

<html> is always the element at the root of the tree.

<html> has two nested elements: <head> and <body>. You can call them both "children" of <html>.

<body> is nested within the <html> element, so we say <body> is the "child" of <html>.

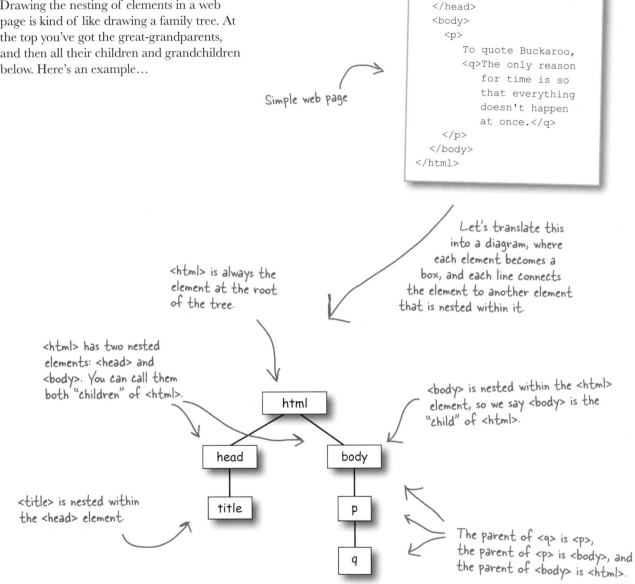

<title> is nested within the <head> element.

The parent of <q> is <p>, the parent of <p> is <body>, and the parent of <body> is <html>.

Using nesting to make sure your tags match

Your first payoff for understanding how elements are nested is that you can avoid mismatching your tags. (And there's gonna be more payoff later; just wait.)

What does "mismatching your tags" mean and how could that happen? Take a look at this example:

`<p>I'm so going to tweet <em>this</em></p>`

Here's how this HTML looks; `<em>` is nested inside `<p>`.

```
p
|
em
```

SAFETY FIRST

Properly nest your elements

So far, so good, but it's also easy to get sloppy and write some HTML that looks more like this:

`<p>I'm so going to tweet <em>this</p></em>`

WRONG: the `<p>` tag ends before the `<em>` tag! The `<em>` element is supposed to be inside the `<p>` element.

Given what you now know about nesting, you know the `<em>` element needs to be nested fully within, or contained in, the `<p>` element.

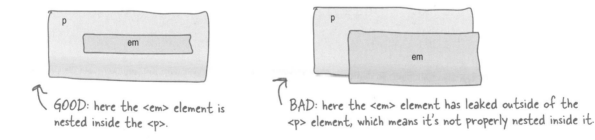

GOOD: here the `<em>` element is nested inside the `<p>`.

BAD: here the `<em>` element has leaked outside of the `<p>` element, which means it's not properly nested inside it.

So what?

It's okay to mess up your nesting if you like playing Russian roulette. If you write HTML without properly nesting your elements, your pages may work on some browsers but not on others. By keeping nesting in mind, you can avoid mismatching your tags and be sure that your HTML will work in all browsers. This is going to become even more important as we get more into "industrial strength HTML" in later chapters.

BE the Browser

Below, you'll find an HTML file with some mismatched tags in it. Your job is to play like you're the browser and locate all the errors. After you've done the exercise, look at the end of the chapter to see if you caught all the errors.

```
<html>
<head>
    <title>Top 100</title>
<body>
<h1>Top 100
<h2>Dark Side of the Moon</h2>
<h3>Pink Floyd</h3>
<p>
    There's no dark side of the moon; matter of fact <q>it's all dark.
</p></q>
<ul>
    <li>Speak to Me / Breathe</li>
    <li>On The Run</li>
    <li>Time</li>
    <li>The Great Gig in The Sky</li>
    <li>Money</li>
    <li>Us And Them</em>
    <li>Any Colour You Like</li>
    <li>Brain Damage</li>
    <li>Eclipse</li>
</ul>
</p>
<h2>XandY</h3>
<h3>Coldplay</h2>
<ol>
    <li>Square One
    <li>What If?
    <li>White Shadows
    <li>Fix You
    <li>Talk
    <li>XandY
    <li>Speed of Sound
    <li>A Message
    <li>Low
    <li>Hardest Part
    <li>Swallowed In The Sea
    <li>Twisted Logic
</ul>
</body>
</head>
```

Who am I?

A bunch of HTML elements, in full costume, are playing a party game, "Who am I?" They'll give you a clue—you try to guess who they are based on what they say. Assume they always tell the truth about themselves. Fill in the blanks to the right to identify the attendees. Also, for each attendee, write down whether or not the element is inline or block.

Tonight's attendees:

Any of the charming HTML elements you've seen so far just might show up!

Clue	Name	Inline or block?
I'm the #1 heading.	h1	block
I'm all ready to link to another page.	a	inline
Emphasize text with me.	em	inline
I'm a list, but I don't have my affairs in order.	ul	block
I'm a real linebreaker.	br	inline
I'm an item that lives inside a list.	li	block
I keep my list items in order.	ol	block
I'm all about image.	img	inline
Quote inside a paragraph with me.	q	inline
Use me to quote text that stands on its own.	blockquote	block

I was just creating a web page explaining everything I was learning from this book, and I wanted to mention the <html> element inside my page. Isn't that going to mess up the nesting? Do I need to put double quotes around it or something?

You're right, that can cause problems.

Because browsers use < and > to begin and end tags, using them in the content of your HTML can cause problems. But HTML gives you an easy way to specify these and other special characters using a simple abbreviation called a *character entity*. Here's how it works: for any character that is considered "special" or that you'd like to use in your web page, but that may not be a typeable character in your editor (like a copyright symbol), you just look up the abbreviation and then type it into your HTML. For example, the > character's abbreviation is `&gt;` and the < character's is `&lt;`.

So, say you wanted to type "The <html> element rocks." in your page. Using the character entities, you'd type this instead:

```
The &lt;html&gt; element rocks.
```

Another important special character you should know about is the & (ampersand) character. If you'd like to have an & in your HTML content, use the character entity `&amp;` instead of the & character itself.

So what about the copyright symbol (that's ©)? And all those other symbols and foreign characters? You can look up common ones at this URL:

```
http://www.w3schools.com/tags/ref_entities.asp
```

or, for a more exhaustive list, use this URL:

```
http://www.unicode.org/charts/
```

there are no
Dumb Questions

Q: Wow, I never knew the browser could display so many different characters. There are a ton of different characters and languages at the www.unicode.org site.

A: Be careful. Your browser will only display all these characters if your computer or device has the appropriate fonts installed. So, while you can probably count on the basic entities from the www.w3schools.com page to be available on any browser, there is no guarantee that you can display all these entities. But, assuming you know something about your users, you should have a good idea of what kind of foreign language characters are going to be common on their machine.

Q: You said that & is special and I need to use the entity & in its place, but to type in any entity I have to use a &. So for, say, the > entity, do I need to type &gt;?

A: No, no! The reason & is special is precisely because it is the first character of any entity. So, it's perfectly fine to use & in your entity names, just not by itself.

Just remember to use & anytime you type in an entity, and if you really need an & in your content, use & instead.

Q: When I looked up the entities at the www.w3cschools.com, I noticed that each entity has a number too. What do I use that for?

A: You can use either the number, like &#100 or the name of an entity in your HTML (they do the same thing). However, not all entities have names, so in those cases your only choice is to use the number.

Crack the Location Challenge

Dr. Evel, in his quest for world domination, has put up a private web page to be used by his evil henchmen. You've just received a snippet of intercepted HTML that may contain a clue to his whereabouts. Given your expert knowledge of HTML, you've been asked to crack the code and discover his location. Here's a bit of the text from his home page:

```
There's going to be an evil henchman meetup
next month at my underground lair in
&#208;&epsilon;&tau;&#114;&ouml;&igrave;&tau;.
Come join us.
```

Hint: visit http://www.w3schools.com/tags/ref_entities.asp
and/or type in the HTML and see what your browser displays.

<em>
Use this element to mark up text you'd say in a different voice, like if you are emphasizing a point.

<strong>
Use this element to mark up text you want emphasized with extra strength.

<pre>
Use this element for formatted text when you want the browser to show your text exactly as you typed it.

Whenever you want to make a link, you'll need the <a> element.

<a>

<time>
This element tells the browser that the content is a date or time, or both.

A void element for making linebreaks.

**
**

Use this element for short quotes...you know, like "to be or not to be," or "No matter where you go, there you are."

<q>

<ul>
Need to display a list? Say, a list of ingredients in a recipe or a to-do list? Use the <ul> element.

This is an element for including an image, like a photo, in your page.

<img>

<p>
Just give me a paragraph, please.

<ol>
If you need an ordered list instead, use the <ol> element.

This is for lengthy quotations—something that you want to highlight as a longer passage, say, from a book.

The code element is used for displaying code from a computer program.

<li> is for items in lists, like chocolate, hot chocolate, chocolate syrup...

<code>

<li>

<blockquote>

Here are a bunch of elements you already know, and a few you don't.

Remember, half the fun of HTML is experimenting! So make some files of your own and try these out.

Rockin' page. It's perfect for my trip and it really does a good job of providing an online version of my journal. You've got the HTML well organized too, so I should be able to add new material myself. So, when can we actually get this off your computer and onto the Web?

BULLET POINTS

- Plan the structure of your web pages before you start typing in the content. Start with a sketch, then create an outline, and finally write the HTML.

- Plan your page starting with the large, block elements, and then refine with inline elements.

- Remember, whenever possible, use elements to tell the browser what your content means.

- Always use the element that most closely matches the meaning of your content. For example, never use a paragraph when you need a list.

- <p>, <blockquote>, <ol>, <ul>, and <li> are all block elements. They stand on their own and are displayed (by default) with a linebreak above and below the content within them.

- <q> and <em> are inline elements. The content in these elements flows in line with the rest of the content in the containing element.

- Use the <br> element when you need to insert your own linebreaks.

-
 is a "void" element.

- Void elements have no content.

- A void element consists of only one tag.

- An "empty" element has no content. But it does have both opening and closing tags.

- A nested element is an element contained completely within another element. If your elements are nested properly, all your tags will match correctly.

- You make an HTML list using two elements in combination. use <ol> with <li> for an ordered list; use <ul> with <li> for an unordered list.

- When the browser displays an ordered list, it creates the numbers for the list so you don't have to.

- You can build nested lists within lists by putting <ol> or <ul> elements inside your <li> elements.

- Use character entities for special characters in your HTML content.

HTMLcross

It's time to give your right brain a break and put that left brain to work: all the words are HTML-related and from this chapter.

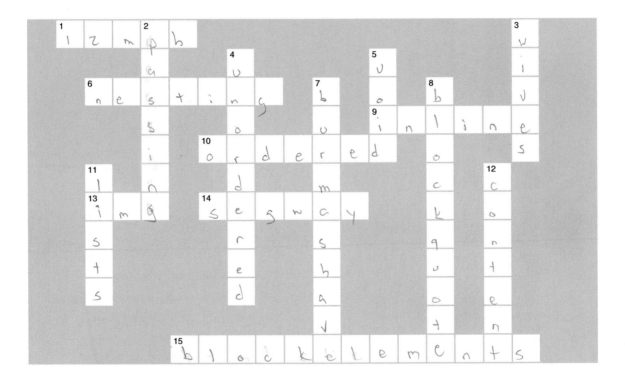

Across

1. Max speed of a Segway.
6. Putting one element inside another is called this.
9. <q> is this type of element.
10. Use <ol> for these kinds of lists
13. Another void element.
14. Tony's transportation.
15. Major building blocks of your pages.

Down

2. Tony won't be doing any of this
3. Left together in a T-bird.
4. Use <ul> for these kinds of lists
5. Element without content.
7. Famous catchy road signs.
8. Block element for quotes.
11. Requires two elements.
12. Void elements have none.

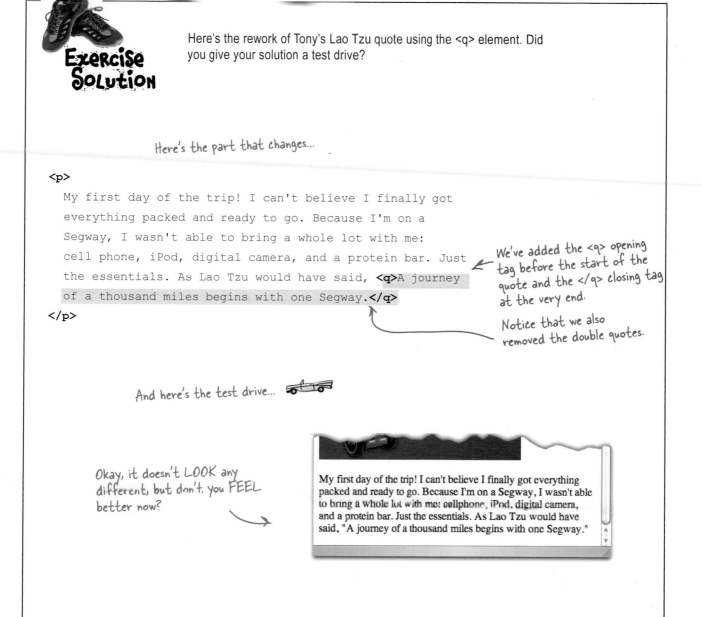

Here's the rework of Tony's Lao Tzu quote using the <q> element. Did you give your solution a test drive?

Here's the part that changes...

```
<p>
    My first day of the trip! I can't believe I finally got
    everything packed and ready to go. Because I'm on a
    Segway, I wasn't able to bring a whole lot with me:
    cell phone, iPod, digital camera, and a protein bar. Just
    the essentials. As Lao Tzu would have said, <q>A journey
    of a thousand miles begins with one Segway.</q>
</p>
```

We've added the <q> opening tag before the start of the quote and the </q> closing tag at the very end.

Notice that we also removed the double quotes.

And here's the test drive...

Okay, it doesn't LOOK any different, but don't you FEEL better now?

My first day of the trip! I can't believe I finally got everything packed and ready to go. Because I'm on a Segway, I wasn't able to bring a whole lot with me: cellphone, iPod, digital camera, and a protein bar. Just the essentials. As Lao Tzu would have said, "A journey of a thousand miles begins with one Segway."

Here's another list from Tony's journal: cell phone, iPod, digital camera, and a protein bar. You'll find it in his June 2 entry. This is an *unordered* list of items.

Make these changes in your "journal.html" file, too. Does it look like you expected?

```
<h2>June 2, 2012</h2>
<img src="segway1.jpg">
<p>
    My first day of the trip! I can't believe I finally got
    everything packed and ready to go. Because I'm on a Segway,
    I wasn't able to bring a whole lot with me:
</p>
<ul>
        <li>cell phone</li>
        <li>iPod</li>
        <li>digital camera</li>
        <li>and a protein bar</li>
</ul>
<p>
    Just the essentials. As
    Lao Tzu would have said, <q>A journey of a
    thousand miles begins with one Segway.</q>
</p>
```

First, end the previous paragraph.

Start the unordered list.

Put each item into an <li> element.

End the unordered list.

And we need to start a new paragraph.

BE the Browser
Solution

```
<html>
<head>
    <title>Top 100</title>                          ⟵ Missing </head> closing tag
<body>
<h1>Top 100                          ⟵ Missing </hl> closing tag
<h2>Dark Side of the Moon</h2>
<h3>Pink Floyd</h3>
<p>
    There's no dark side of the moon; matter of fact <q>it's all dark.
</p></q>                                    ⟵ <p> and <q> are not nested
<ul>                                          properly: the </p> tag should
    <li>Speak to Me / Breathe</li>            come after the </q> tag.
    <li>On The Run</li>
    <li>Time</li>
    <li>The Great Gig in The Sky</li>
    <li>Money</li>                            ⟵ We have a closing </em> where we
    <li>Us And Them</em>                        should have a closing </li> tag.
    <li>Any Colour You Like</li>
    <li>Brain Damage</li>
    <li>Eclipse</li>
</ul>                          ⟵ Here's a closing </p> that doesn't
</p>                             match any opening <p> tag.
<h2>XandY</h3>                 ⟵ We mixed up the closing </h2> and </h3> tags on these headings.
<h3>Coldplay</h2>
<ol>                          ⟵ We started an <ol> list, but it's
    <li>Square One               matched with a closing </ul> tag.
    <li>What If?
    <li>White Shadows
    <li>Fix You
    <li>Talk                   ⟵ We're missing all our
    <li>XandY                    closing </li> tags.
    <li>Speed of Sound
    <li>A Message
    <li>Low
    <li>Hardest Part
    <li>Swallowed In The Sea
    <li>Twisted Logic
</ul>          ⟵ This doesn't match the opening <ol> tag at the start of the list above.
</body>
</head>       ⟵ Here's our missing </head> tag, but we're missing a closing </html> tag.
```

Exercise Solution

Who am I?

A bunch of HTML elements, in full costume, are playing a party game "Who am I?" They gave you a clue—you tried to guess who they were based on what they said.

Tonight's attendees:

Quite a few of the charming HTML elements you've seen so far showed up for the party!

	Name	Inline or block?	
I'm the #1 heading.	h1	block	
I'm all ready to link to another page.	a	hmm...	Hmm, it looks like an inline, BUT <a> can wrap block elements, not just text. So, depending on the context, <a> can be either inline or block.
Emphasize text with me.	em	inline	
I'm a list, but I don't have my affairs in order.	ul	block	
I'm a real linebreaker.	br	hmm...	Stumped? is in limbo land between block and inline. It does create a linebreak, but doesn't break a bit of text into two separate blocks, like if you had two <p> elements.
I'm an item that lives inside a list.	li	block	
I keep my list items in order.	ol	block	
I'm all about image.	img	inline	We haven't talked about this in detail yet, but, yes, <img> is inline. Give it some thought and we'll come back to this in Chapter 5.
Quote inside a paragraph with me.	q	inline	
Use me to quote text that stands on its own.	blockquote	block	

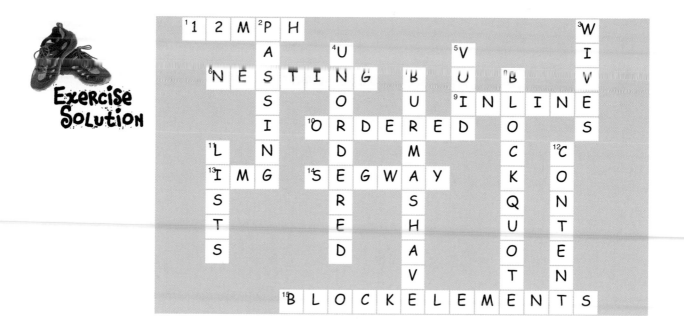

Exercise Solution

¹1	2	M	²P	H											³W
			A		⁴U			⁵V							I
⁶N	E	S	T	I	N	G	⁷B	U		⁸B					V
			S		O		U		⁹I	N	L	I	N	E	E
			I		¹⁰O	R	D	E	R	E	D				S
¹¹L			N		U		M		C			¹²C			
¹³I	M	G		¹⁴S	E	G	W	A	Y		K	O			
S				R			A			Q	N				
T				E			S			U	T				
S				D			H			O	E				
							A			T	N				
							V								
		¹⁵B	L	O	C	K	E	L	E	M	E	N	T	S	

Crack the Location Challenge

You could have looked up each entity or typed them in. In either case, the answer looks like Detroit!

```
There's going to be an evil henchman meetup
next month at my underground lair in
&#208;&epsilon;&tau;&#114;&ouml;&igrave;
&tau;. Come join us.
```

evel.html

There's going to be an evil henchman meetup next month at my underground lair in Ðετröìτ. Come join us.

4 getting connected

A Trip to Webville

We're going to Webville! We're leaving our dusty ol' local filesystem behind for good.

Web pages are a dish best served on the Internet.

So far you've only created HTML pages that live on your own computer. You've also only linked to pages that are on your own computer. We're about to change all that. In this chapter we'll encourage you to get those web pages on the Internet where all your friends, fans, and customers can actually see them. We'll also reveal the mysteries of linking to other pages by cracking the code of the h, t, t, p, :, /, /, w, w, w. So, gather your belongings; our next stop is Webville.

WARNING: once you get to Webville, you may never come back. Send us a postcard.

> Remember me from way back in Chapter 1? You were going to get the Starbuzz website online so our customers could actually see it.

Getting Starbuzz (or yourself) onto the Web

You're closer to getting Starbuzz—or even better, your own site—on the Web than you might think. All you need to do is find a "web hosting company" (we'll call this a "hosting company" from now on) to host your pages on their servers, and then copy your pages from your computer to one of those servers.

Of course it helps to understand how your local folders are going to "map" to the server's folders, and once you put your pages on the server, how you point a browser to them. But we'll get to all that. For now, let's talk about getting you on the Web. Here's what you're going to need to do:

1 **Find yourself an hosting company.**

2 **Choose a name for your site (like www.starbuzzcoffee.com).**

3 **Find a way to get your files from your computer to a server at the hosting company (there are a few ways).**

4 **Point your friends, family, and fans to your new site and let the fun begin.**

We're going to take you through each of these steps, and even if you're not going to set up a website online *right now*, follow along because you'll learn some important things you'll need to know later. So, get ready for a quick detour from HTML...

A Web Detour

Finding a hosting company

To get your pages on the Web, you need a server that actually lives on the Web *full-time*. Your best bet is to find a hosting company and let them worry about the details of keeping a server running. No worries, though; finding a hosting company is fairly straightforward and inexpensive.

Which company? Well, we'd *love* to sign you up for web hosting at **Head First Hip Web Hosting, Inc.**, but that doesn't really exist. So, you're going to have to do a little homework on your own. While finding a company to host your pages isn't difficult, it's kind of like choosing a cable TV company: there are lots of options and plans. You really have to shop around for the best deals and for the service that works for you.

The good news is that you should be able to get started for almost nothing out of your pocket, and you can always upgrade later if you need additional features. While we can't suggest a particular provider, we can tell you a few things to look for in a provider, and we also list a few of the more popular providers at:

`http://wickedlysmart.com/hosting-providers/`

> Note from marketing: if a hosting company writes a big enough check, we can!

Relax

You don't have to got your pages on the Web to finish this book.

While it's a lot more fun if your pages are actually *on the Web*, you can finish the rest of this book by working on your own computer.

In either case, follow along for the next few pages so you know how everything fits together.

One-minute hosting guide

We can't tell you everything you need to know about getting a hosting company (after all, this book is about HTML and CSS), but we're going to give you a good push in the right direction. Here are some features to think about while you're shopping.

- *Technical support:* Does the hosting company have a good system for handling your technical questions? The better ones will answer your questions quickly either over the phone or via email.

- *Data transfer:* This is a measure of the amount of pages and data the hosting company will let you send to your visitors during a given month. Most hosting companies offer reasonable amounts of data transfer for small sites in their most basic plans. If you're creating a site that you expect will have lots of visitors, you may want to carefully look into this.

- *Backups:* Does the hosting company regularly make a backup of your pages and data that can be recovered in the event that the server has a hardware failure?

- *Domain names:* Does the hosting company include a domain name in its pricing? More about these on the next page.

- *Reliability:* Most hosting companies report keeping websites up 99% of the time or better.

- *Goodies:* Does your package include other goodies such as email addresses, forums, or support for scripting languages (something that may become important to you in the future)?

HELLO, my ^domain name is...

Even if you've never heard of a *domain name*, you've seen and used a zillion of them; you know…google.com, facebook.com, amazon.com, disney.com, and maybe a few you wouldn't want us to mention.

So what is a domain name? Just a unique name that is used to locate your site. Here's an example:

This part is the domain name.

www.starbuzzcoffee.com

This part is the name of a specific server IN the domain.

There are different domain "endings" for different purposes: .com, .org, .gov, .edu; and also for different countries: .co.uk, .co.jp, and so on. When choosing a domain, pick the one that best fits you.

After years of struggling, we finally have our very own domain name.

There are a couple of reasons you should care about domain names. If you want a unique name for your site, you're going to need your own domain name. Domain names are also used to link your pages to other websites (we'll get to that in a few pages).

There is one other thing you should know. Domain names are controlled by a centralized authority (ICANN) to make sure that only one person at a time uses a domain name. Also (you knew it was coming), you pay a small annual registration fee to keep your domain name.

How can you get a domain name?

The easy answer is to let your hosting company worry about it. They'll often throw in your domain name registration with one of their package deals. However, there are hundreds of companies that would be glad to help—you can find a list of them at:

http://www.internic.net/regist.html

As with finding a hosting company, we're afraid we'll have to leave you to find and register your own domain name. You'll probably find that going through your hosting company is the easiest way to get that done.

there are no
Dumb Questions

Q: Why is it called a "domain name" rather than a "website name"?

A: Because they are different things. If you look at www.starbuzzcoffee.com, that's a website name, but only the "starbuzzcoffee.com" part is the domain name. You could also create other websites that use the same domain name, like corporate.starbuzzcoffee.com or employees.starbuzzcoffee.com. So the domain name is something you can use for a lot of websites.

Q: If I were going to get the domain name for Starbuzz, wouldn't I want to get the name www.starbuzzcoffee.com? Everyone seems to use websites with the www at the front.

A: Again, don't confuse a domain name with a website name: starbuzzcoffee.com is a domain name, while www.starbuzzcoffee.com is the name of a website. Buying a domain is like buying a piece of land; let's say, 100mainstreet.com. On that land, you can build as many websites as you like, for example: home.100mainstreet.com, toolshed.100mainstreet.com, and outhouse.100mainstreet.com. So www.starbuzzcoffee.com is just one website in the starbuzzcoffee.com domain.

Q: What's so great about a domain name anyway? Do I really need one? My hosting company says I can just use their name, www.dirtcheaphosting.com?

A: If that meets your needs, there is nothing wrong with using their name. But (and it's a big but) here's the disadvantage: should you ever want to choose another hosting company, or should that hosting company go out of business, then everyone who knows your site will no longer be able to easily find it. If, on the other hand, you have a domain name, you can just take that with you to your new hosting company (and your users will never even know you've switched).

Q: If domain names are unique, that means someone might already have mine. How can I find out?

A: Good question. Most companies that provide registration services for domain names allow you to search to see if a name is taken (kind of like searching for vanity license plates). You'll find a list of these companies at http://www.internic.net/regist.html.

Here's an exercise you really need to go off and do on your own. We'd love to personally help, but there's only so much you can ask of book authors (and feeding the cat while you're on vacation is probably out too).

DO try this at home

It's time to seek out a hosting company and grab a domain name for your site. Remember, you can visit Wickedly Smart for some suggestions and resources. Also remember that you can complete the book without doing this (even though you really should!).

My Web Hosting Company: ....

My Domain Name: ....

CONTENTS:
HTML and Images

LOCATION:
Root folder

A Web Detour

Moving in

Congratulations! You've got your hosting company lined up, you've found a domain name, and you've got a server all ready for your web pages. (Even if you don't, keep following along because this is important stuff.)

Now what? Well, it's time to move in, of course. So, take that For Sale sign down and gather up all those files; we're going to get them moved to the new server. Like any move, the goal is to get things moved from, say, the kitchen of your old place to the kitchen of your new place. On the Web, we're just worried about getting things from your own root folder to the root folder on the web server. Let's get back to Starbuzz and step through how we do this. Here's what things look like now:

Here's the root folder for Starbuzz

starbuzz

```
<html>
</html>
```
index.html

Remember your Starbuzz pages? There are two: the main page (index.html) and the page that contains the mission statement (mission.html).

```
<html>
</html>
```
mission.html

Here's the new web server. The hosting company has already created a root folder for you, which is where all your pages are going to go.

starbuzz

Your computer, where the Starbuzz pages currently live

Here's the new website name. We're using the starbuzzcoffee.com domain (since we beat you to it, you'll have to use your own domain name instead).

www.starbuzzcoffee.com

A Web Detour

there are no
Dumb Questions

Q: Wait a sec, what's the "root folder" again?

A: Up until now, the root folder has just been the top-level folder for your pages. On the web server, the root folder becomes even more important because anything inside the root folder is going to be accessible on the Web.

Q: My hosting company seems to have called my root folder "mydomain_com". Is that a problem?

A: Not at all. Hosting companies call root folders lots of different things. The important thing is that you know where your root folder is located on the server, and that you can copy your files to it (we'll get to that in a sec).

Q: So let me make sure I understand. We've been putting all our pages for the site in one folder, which we call the root folder. Now we're going to copy all that over to the server's root folder?

A: Exactly. You're going to take all the pages on your own computer, and put them all inside your site's root folder on the hosting company server.

Q: What about subfolders, like the "images" folder? Do I copy those too?

A: Yes, you're basically going to replicate all the pages, files, and folders in your own root folder onto the server. So if you've got an "images" folder on your computer, you'll have one on the server too.

Getting your files to the root folder

You're now one step away from getting Starbuzz Coffee on the Web: you've identified the root folder on your hosting company's server and all you need to do is copy your pages over to that folder. But how do you transfer files to a web server? There are a variety of ways, but most hosting companies support a method of file transfer called FTP, which stands for File Transfer Protocol. You'll find a number of applications out there that will allow you to transfer your files via FTP; we'll take a look at how that works on the next page.

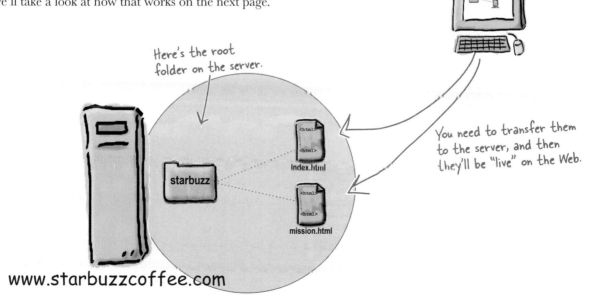

The files are sitting on your computer.

Here's the root folder on the server.

You need to transfer them to the server, and then they'll be "live" on the Web.

www.starbuzzcoffee.com

A Web Detour

As much FTP as you can possibly fit in two pages

Seriously, this really is an HTML and CSS book, but we didn't want to leave you up a creek without a paddle. So, here's a very quick guide to using FTP to get your files on the Web. Keep in mind your hosting company might have a few suggestions for the best way to transfer your files to their servers (and since you are paying them, get their help). After the next few pages, we're off our detour and back to HTML and CSS until we reach the end of the book (we promise).

We'll assume you've found an FTP application. Some are command-line driven, some have complete graphical interfaces, and some are even built into applications like Dreamweaver and Expression Web. They all use the same commands, but with some applications you type them in yourself, while in others you use a graphical interface. Here's how FTP works from 10,000 feet:

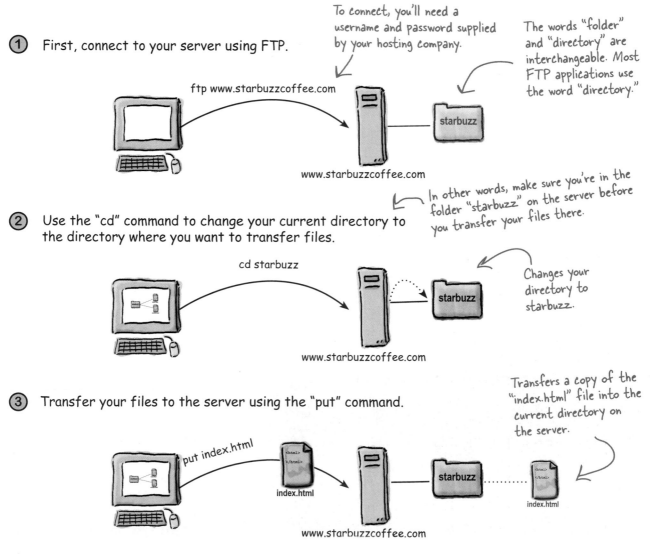

① First, connect to your server using FTP.

To connect, you'll need a username and password supplied by your hosting company.

The words "folder" and "directory" are interchangeable. Most FTP applications use the word "directory."

ftp www.starbuzzcoffee.com

starbuzz

www.starbuzzcoffee.com

In other words, make sure you're in the folder "starbuzz" on the server before you transfer your files there.

② Use the "cd" command to change your current directory to the directory where you want to transfer files.

cd starbuzz

starbuzz

Changes your directory to starbuzz.

www.starbuzzcoffee.com

Transfers a copy of the "index.html" file into the current directory on the server.

③ Transfer your files to the server using the "put" command.

put index.html

index.html

starbuzz

index.html

www.starbuzzcoffee.com

④ You can also make a new directory on the server with the "mkdir" command.

This is just like making a new folder, only you're doing it on the server, not your own computer.

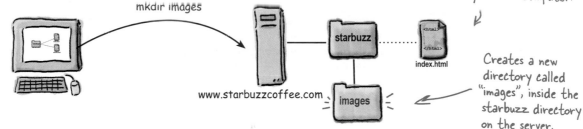

mkdir images

www.starbuzzcoffee.com

Creates a new directory called "images", inside the starbuzz directory on the server.

⑤ You can retrieve files too, with the "get" command.

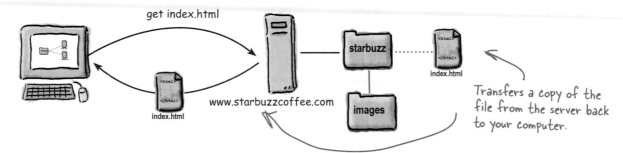

get index.html

www.starbuzzcoffee.com

index.html

Transfers a copy of the file from the server back to your computer.

Let's put all that together. Here's an example of FTP being used from a command-line application:

Most FTP applications come with much friendlier graphical interfaces, so feel free to skip right over this if you're using one of those.

```
File Edit  Window Help  Jam
%ftp www.starbuzzcoffee.com
Connected to www.starbuzzcoffee.com
Name: headfirst
Password:******
230 User headfirst logged in.
ftp> dir
drwx------  4096 Sep  5 15:07 starbuzz
ftp> cd starbuzz
CWD command successful
ftp> put index.html
Transfer complete.
ftp> dir
-rw-------  1022 Sep  5 15:07 index.html
ftp> mkdir images
Directory successfully created
ftp> cd images
CWD command successful
ftp> bye
```

Connect and log in.

Get a directory of what is there.

One directory called starbuzz

Change to the starbuzz directory.

Transfer index.html there.

Look at the directory; there's index.html.

Make a directory for images, and then quit using the bye command.

FTP commands

Whether you're typing in FTP commands on the command line, or using an FTP application with a graphical interface, the commands or operations you can perform are pretty much the same.

- *dir:* get a listing of the current directory.

- *cd:* change to another directory. ".." means up one directory here, too.

- *pwd:* display the current directory you're in.

- *put <filename>:* transfers the specified filename to the server.

- *get <filename>:* retrieves the specified filename from the server, back to your computer.

there are no
Dumb Questions

Q: My hosting company told me to use SFTP, not FTP. What's the difference?

A: SFTP, or Secure File Transfer Protocol, is a more secure version of FTP, but works mostly the same way. Just make sure your FTP application supports SFTP before you make a purchase.

Q: So do I edit my files on my computer and then transfer them each time I want to update my site?

A: Yes, for small sites, that is normally the way you do things. Use your computer to test your changes and make sure things are working the way you want before transferring your files to the server. For larger websites, organizations often create a test site and a live site so that they can preview changes on the test site before they are moved to the live site.

If you're using a tool like Dreamweaver or Coda, these tools will allow you to test your changes on your own computer, and then when you save your files, they are automatically transferred to the website.

Q: Can I edit my files directly on the web server?

A: That usually isn't a good idea because your visitors will see all your changes and errors before you have time to preview and fix them.

That said, some hosting companies will allow you to log into the server and make changes on the server. To do that, you usually need to know your way around a DOS or Linux command prompt, depending on what kind of operating system your server is running.

Popular FTP applications

Here are a few of the most popular FTP applications for Mac and Windows:

For Mac OS X:

- Fetch (http://fetchsoftworks.com/) is one of the most popular FTP applications for Mac. $

- Transmit (http://www.panic.com/transmit/). $

- Cyberduck (http://cyberduck.ch/). FREE

For Windows:

- Smart FTP (http://www.smartftp.com/download/). $

- WS_FTP (http://www.wsftple.com/). FREE for the basic version, $ for the Pro version

- Cyberduck (http://cyberduck.ch/). FREE

Most FTP applications have a trial version you can download to try before you buy.

DO try this at home

It's another homework assignment for you (check each item as you do it):

☐ Make sure you know where your root folder is on the server at your hosting company.

☐ Figure out the best way (and the best tool to use) to transfer files from your computer to the server.

☐ For now, go ahead and transfer the Starbuzz "index.html" and "mission.html" files to the root folder of the server.

End of Web Detour

Back to business...

That's the end of the detour, and we're back on the web superhighway. At this point, you should have the two Starbuzz pages, "index.html" and "mission.html", sitting under your root folder on a server (or if not, you're at least following along).

After all this work, wouldn't it be satisfying to make your browser retrieve those pages over the Internet and display them for you? Let's figure out the right address to type into your browser…

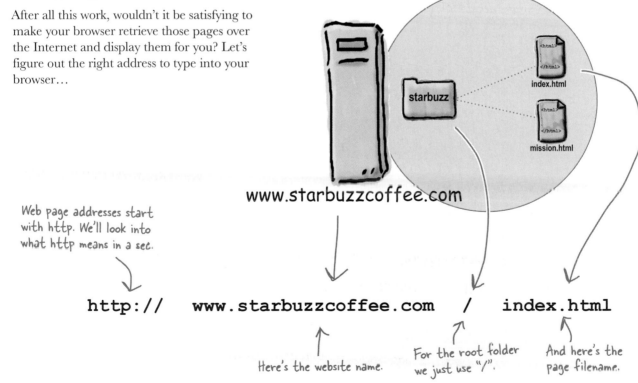

www.starbuzzcoffee.com

Web page addresses start with http. We'll look into what http means in a sec.

http://   www.starbuzzcoffee.com   /   index.html

Here's the website name.

For the root folder we just use "/".

And here's the page filename.

Mainstreet, USA URL

You've probably heard the familiar "h" "t" "t" "p" "colon" "slash" "slash" a zillion times, but what does it mean? First of all, the web addresses you type into the browser are called *URLs* or Uniform Resource Locators.

If it were up to us, we would have called them "web addresses," but no one asked, so we're stuck with Uniform Resource Locators. Here's how to decipher a URL:

`http://www.starbuzzcoffee.com/index.html`

The first part of the URL tells you the <u>protocol</u> that needs to be used to retrieve the resource.

The second part is the website name. At this point, you know all about that.

And the third part is the <u>absolute path</u> to the resource from the root folder.

To locate anything on the Web, as long as you know the server that hosts it, and an *absolute path* to the resource, you can create a URL and most likely get a web browser to retrieve it for you using some *protocol*—usually HTTP.

> **A Uniform Resource Locator (URL) is a global address that can be used to locate anything on the Web, including HTML pages, audio, video, and many other forms of web content.**
>
> **In addition to specifying the location of the resource, a URL also names the <u>protocol</u> that you can use to retrieve that resource.**

Come on down to
http://www.earlsautos.com

$100

What is HTTP?

HTTP is also known as the *HyperText Transfer Protocol.* In other words, it's an agreed-upon method (a protocol) for transferring hypertext documents around the Web. While "hypertext documents" are usually just HTML pages, the protocol can also be used to transfer images, or any other file that a web page might need.

HTTP is a simple request and response protocol. Here's how it works:

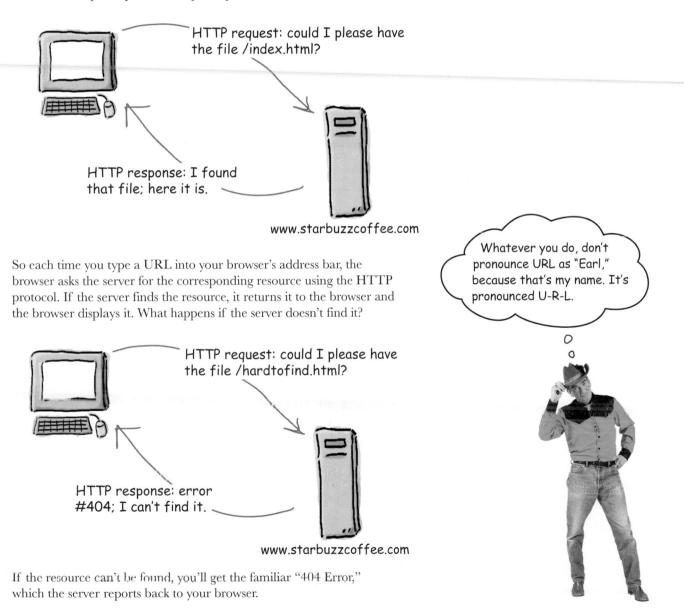

HTTP request: could I please have the file /index.html?

HTTP response: I found that file; here it is.

www.starbuzzcoffee.com

So each time you type a URL into your browser's address bar, the browser asks the server for the corresponding resource using the HTTP protocol. If the server finds the resource, it returns it to the browser and the browser displays it. What happens if the server doesn't find it?

HTTP request: could I please have the file /hardtofind.html?

HTTP response: error #404; I can't find it.

www.starbuzzcoffee.com

Whatever you do, don't pronounce URL as "Earl," because that's my name. It's pronounced U-R-L.

If the resource can't be found, you'll get the familiar "404 Error," which the server reports back to your browser.

What's an absolute path?

The last time we talked about paths, we were writing HTML to make links with the <a> element. The path we're going to look at now is the absolute path part of a URL, the last part that comes after the protocol (http) and the website name (www.starbuzzcoffee.com).

An absolute path tells the server how to get from your root folder to a particular page or file. Take Earl's Autos site, for example. Say you want to look in Earl's inventory to see if your new Mini Cooper has come in. To do that, you'll need to figure out the absolute path to the file "inventory.html" that is in the "new" folder. All you have to do is trace through the folders, starting at the root, to get to the "new" folder where his "inventory.html" file is located. The path is made up of all the folders you go through to get there.

So, that looks like root (we represent root with a "/"), "cars", "new", and finally, the file itself, "inventory.html". Here's how you put that all together:

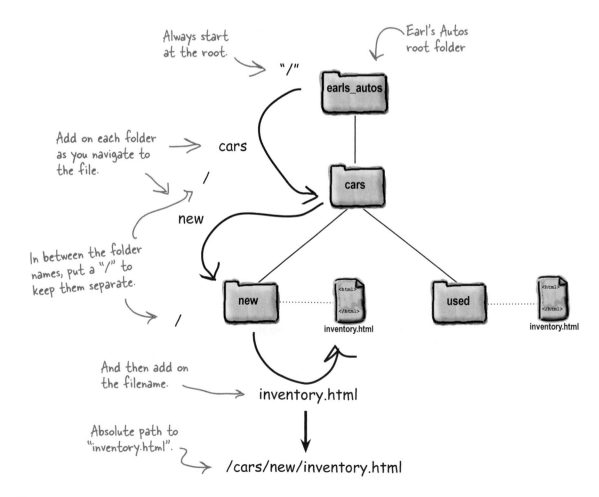

Always start at the root.

Earl's Autos root folder

"/"

earls_autos

Add on each folder as you navigate to the file.

cars

/

new

cars

In between the folder names, put a "/" to keep them separate.

/

new

inventory.html

used

inventory.html

And then add on the filename.

inventory.html

Absolute path to "inventory.html".

/cars/new/inventory.html

there are no Dumb Questions

Q: What is important about the absolute path?

A: The absolute path is what a server needs to locate the file you are requesting. If the server didn't have an absolute path, it wouldn't know where to look.

Q: I feel like I understand the pieces (protocols, servers, websites, and absolute paths), but I'm having trouble connecting them.

A: If you add all those things together, you have a URL, and with a URL you can ask a browser to retrieve a page (or other kinds of resources) from the Web. How? The protocol part tells the browser the method it should use to retrieve the resource (in most cases, this is HTTP). The website part (which consists of the server name and the domain name) tells the browser which computer on the Internet to get the resource from. And the absolute path tells the server what page you're after.

Q: We learned to put relative paths in the href attribute of our <a> elements. How can the server find those links if they aren't absolute?

A: Wow, great question. When you click on a link that is relative, behind the scenes the browser creates an absolute path out of that relative path and the path of the page that you click on. So, all the web server ever sees are absolute paths, thanks to your browser.

Q: Would it help the browser if I put absolute paths in my HTML?

A: Ah, another good question, but hold that thought—we'll get back to that in a sec.

Sharpen your pencil

You've waited long enough. It's time to give your new URL a spin. Before you do, fill in the blanks below and then type in the URL (like you haven't already). If you're having any problems, this is the time to work with your hosting company to get things sorted out. If you haven't set up an hosting company, fill in the blanks for www.starbuzzcoffee.com, and type the URL into your browser anyway.

http :// www.starbuzzcoffee.org /

protocol   **website name**   **absolute path**

I'd like my visitors to be able to type "http://www.starbuzzcoffee.com" and not have to type the "index.html". Is there a way to do that?

Remember, when we're talking about web servers or FTP, we usually use the term "directory" instead of "folder." But they're really the same thing.

Yes, there is. One thing we haven't talked about is what happens if a browser asks for a directory rather than a file from a web server. For instance, a browser might ask for:

http://www.starbuzzcoffee.com/images/

The images directory in the root directory

or

http://www.starbuzzcoffee.com/

The root directory itself

When a web server receives a request like this, it tries to locate a *default* file in that directory. Typically a default file is called "index.html" or "default.htm" and if the server finds one of these files, it returns the file to the browser to display.

So, to return a file by default from your root directory (or any other directory), just name the file "index.html" or "default.htm".

But you need to find out what your hosting company wants you to name your default file, because it depends on the type of server they use.

But I asked about "http://www.starbuzzcoffee.com", which looks a little different. It doesn't have the ending "/".

Oops, you sure did. When a server receives a request like yours without the trailing "/" and there is a directory with that name, then the server will add a trailing slash for you. So if the server gets a request for:

http://www.starbuzzcoffee.com

it will change it to:

http://www.starbuzzcoffee.com/

which will cause the server to look for a default file, and in the end it will return the file as if you'd originally typed:

http://www.starbuzzcoffee.com/index.html

How default pages work

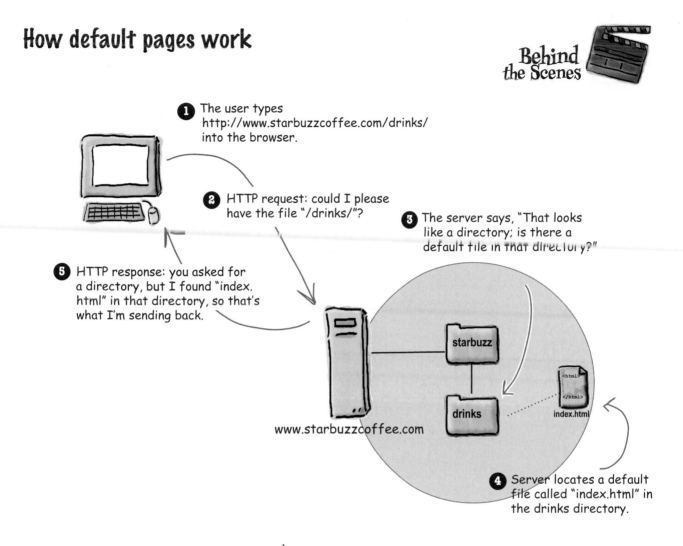

1 The user types
http://www.starbuzzcoffee.com/drinks/
into the browser.

2 HTTP request: could I please
have the file "/drinks/"?

3 The server says, "That looks
like a directory; is there a
default file in that directory?"

5 HTTP response: you asked for
a directory, but I found "index.
html" in that directory, so that's
what I'm sending back.

www.starbuzzcoffee.com

starbuzz

drinks

index.html

4 Server locates a default
file called "index.html" in
the drinks directory.

there are no
Dumb Questions

Q: **So anyone who comes to my site
with the URL http://www.mysite.com is
going to see my "index.html" page?**

A: Right. Or, possibly "default.htm"
depending on which kind of web server your
hosting company is using. (Note that "default.
htm" usually has no "l" on the end. This is a
Microsoft web server oddity.)

There are other possible default filenames,
like "index.php", that come into play if you
start writing scripts to generate your pages.
That's way beyond this book, but that doesn't
mean you won't be doing it in the future.

Q: **So when I'm giving someone my
URL, is it better to include the
"index.html" part or not?**

A: Not. It's always better to leave it off.
What if, in the future, you change to another
web server and it uses another default file
name like "default.htm"? Or you start writing
scripts and use the name "index.php"? Then
the URL you originally gave out would no
longer be valid.

Earl needs a little help with his URLs

Earl may know Earl, but he doesn't know U-R-L. He needs a little help figuring out the URL for each of the files below, labeled A, B, C, D, and E. On the right, write in the URL needed to retrieve each corresponding file from www.earlsautos.com.

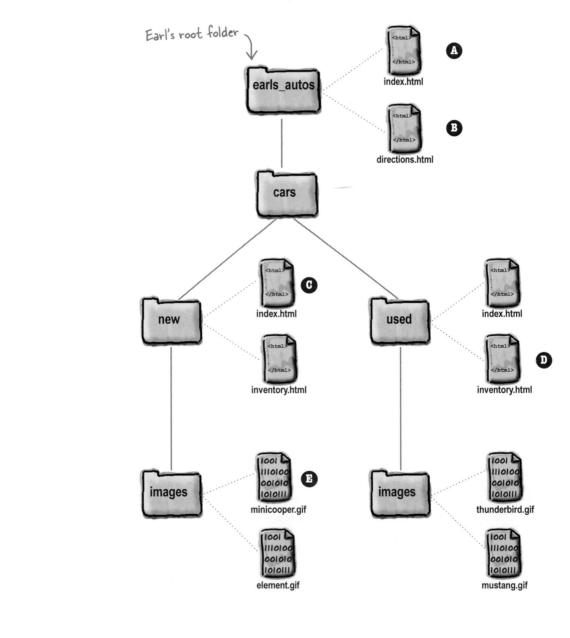

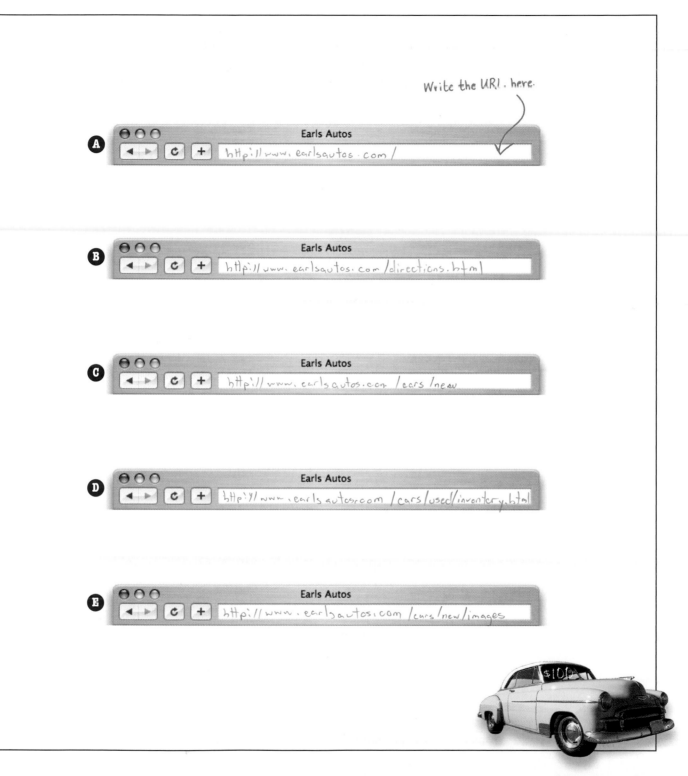

Write the URL here.

A — Earls Autos — http://www.earlsautos.com/

B — Earls Autos — http://www.earlsautos.com/directions.html

C — Earls Autos — http://www.earlsautos.com/cars/new

D — Earls Autos — http://www.earlsautos.com/cars/used/inventory.html

E — Earls Autos — http://www.earlsautos.com/cars/new/images

How do we link to other websites?

URLs aren't just for typing into browsers; you can use them right in your HTML. And, of course, right on cue, the Starbuzz CEO has a new task for you: make a link from the main Starbuzz page over to the caffeine information at `http://wickedlysmart.com/buzz`. As you can probably guess, we're going to throw that URL right into an <a> element. Here's how:

```
<a href="http://wickedlysmart.com/buzz">Caffeine Buzz</a>
```

An everyday, normal, garden–variety <a> element.

We've put a URL in the href. Clicking on the label "Caffeine Buzz" will retrieve a page from wickedlysmart.com/buzz

That's all there is to it. To link to any resource on the Web, all you need is its Uniform Resource Locator, which goes in the <a> element as the value of the `href` attribute. Let's go ahead and add this in the Starbuzz "index.html" page.

Linking to Caffeine Buzz

Open your Starbuzz "index.html" file in the "chapter4/starbuzz" folder, and scan down to the bottom. Let's add two new links: a relative link to the mission statement in "mission.html", and a link to Caffeine Buzz. Make the changes below, then save and load your "index.html" file in your browser. Click on the link and enjoy the Caffeine Buzz.

```html
<html>
    <head>
        <title>Starbuzz Coffee</title>
        <style type="text/css">
                body {
                        background-color: #d2b48c;
                        margin-left: 20%;
                        margin-right: 20%;
                        border: 2px dotted black;
                        padding: 10px 10px 10px 10px;
                        font-family: sans-serif;
                }
        </style>
    </head>

    <body>
        <h1>Starbuzz Coffee Beverages</h1>
        <h2>House Blend, $1.49</h2>
        <p>A smooth, mild blend of coffees from Mexico,
            Bolivia and Guatemala.</p>

        <h2>Mocha Cafe Latte, $2.35</h2>
        <p>Espresso, steamed milk and chocolate syrup.</p>

        <h2>Cappuccino, $1.89</h2>
        <p>A mixture of espresso, steamed milk and foam.</p>

        <h2>Chai Tea, $1.85</h2>
        <p>A spicy drink made with black tea, spices,
            milk and honey.
        </p>
        <p>
            <a href="mission.html">Read about our Mission</a>.
            <br>
            Read the <a href="http://wickedlysmart.com/buzz">Caffeine Buzz</a>.
        </p>
    </body>
</html>
```

Here's the link to the "mission.html" file. This uses a relative path to link to "mission.html".

We added a <br> to put the links on two different lines.

And we've added some structure here by grouping the links and text into a paragraph.

Here's where we've added the link to the wickedlysmart.com/buzz page.

And now for the test drive...

Here's the page with the new link, just as we planned.

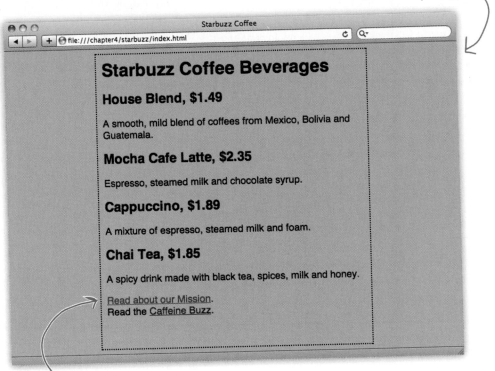

Starbuzz Coffee Beverages

House Blend, $1.49

A smooth, mild blend of coffees from Mexico, Bolivia and Guatemala.

Mocha Cafe Latte, $2.35

Espresso, steamed milk and chocolate syrup.

Cappuccino, $1.89

A mixture of espresso, steamed milk and foam.

Chai Tea, $1.85

A spicy drink made with black tea, spices, milk and honey.

Read about our Mission.
Read the Caffeine Buzz.

Here's the new link. Notice, we only linked the words "Caffeine Buzz," so it looks a little different from the other link.

And when you click on the link, your browser will make an HTTP request to wickedlysmart.com/buzz and then display the result.

there are no
Dumb Questions

At Caffeine Buzz, we use relative links to other pages on our site, and URLs to link offsite, like www.caffeineanonymous.com.

Q: It seems like there are two ways to link to pages now: relative paths and URLs.

A: Relative paths can only be used to link to pages within the same website, while URLs are typically used to link to other websites.

Q: Wouldn't it be easier if I just stuck with URLs for links to my own pages and outside pages? That would work, wouldn't it?

A: Sure, it would work, but there's a couple of reasons you don't want to go there. One problem is that URLs are hard to manage when you have a lot of them in a web page: they're long, difficult to edit, and they make HTML more difficult to read (for you, the page author).

Also, if you have a site with nothing but URLs that link to local pages and you move the site or change its name, you have to go change all those URLs to reflect the new location. If you use relative paths, as long as your pages stay in the same set of folders—because the links are all relative—you don't have to make any changes to your <a> element href attributes.

So, use relative links to link to your own pages in the same site, and URLs to link to pages at other sites.

Q: Haven't we seen one other protocol? I kept seeing "file:///" before we started using a web server.

A: Yes; good catch. The file protocol is used when the browser is reading files right off your computer. For example, the file URL, "file:///chapter4/starbuzz/index.html", tells the browser that the file "index.html" is located at the path "/chapter4/starbuzz/". This path may look different depending on your operating system and browser.

One important thing to notice in case you try to type in a file URL is that the file URL has three slashes, not two, like HTTP. Remember it this way: if you take an HTTP URL and delete the website name you'll have three slashes, too.

Q: Are there other protocols?

A: Yes, many browsers can support retrieval of pages with the FTP protocol, and there is a mail protocol that can send data via email. HTTP is the protocol you'll be using most of the time.

Q: I've seen URLs that look like this: http://www.mydomain.com:8000/index.html. Why is there a ":8000" in there?

A: The ":8000" is an optional "port" that you can put in an HTTP URL. Think of a port like this: the website name is like an address, and the port is like a mailbox number at an address (say, in an apartment complex). Normally everything on the Web is delivered to a default port (which is 80), but sometimes web servers are configured to receive requests at a different port (like 8000). You'll most likely see this on test servers. Regular web servers almost always accept requests on port 80. If you don't specify a port, it defaults to 80.

The Case of Relatives and Absolutes

PlanetRobots, Inc., faced with the task of developing a website for each of its two company divisions—PlanetRobot Home and PlanetRobot Garden—decided to contract with two firms to get the work done. RadWebDesign, a seemingly experienced firm, took on the Home division's website and proceeded to write the site's internal links using only URLs (after all, they're more complicated, so they must be better). A less experienced, but well-schooled firm, CorrectWebDesign, was tasked with PlanetRobot's Garden site, and used relative paths for links between all the pages within the site.

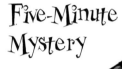

Just as both projects neared completion, PlanetRobots called with an urgent message: "We've been sued for trademark infringement, so we're changing our domain name to RobotsRUs. Our new web server is going to be `www.robotsrus.com`." CorrectWebDesign made a couple of small changes that took all of five minutes and was ready for the site's unveiling at the RobotsRUs corporate headquarters. RadWebDesign, on the other hand, worked until 4 a.m. to fix their pages but luckily completed the work just in time for the unveiling. However, during a demo at the unveiling, the horror of horrors occurred: as the team leader for RadWebDesign demonstrated the site, he clicked on a link that resulted in a "404—Page Not Found" error. Displeased, the CEO of RobotsRUs suggested that RadWebDesign might want to consider changing their name to BadWebDesign and asked CorrectWebDesign if they were available to consult on fixing the Home site.

What happened? **How did RadWebDesign flub things up so badly when all that changed was the name of the web server?**

Web page fit and finish

Can you say "web career"? You've certainly delivered everything the Starbuzz CEO has asked for, and you've now got a high-profile website under your belt (and in your portfolio).

But you're not going to stop there. You want your websites to have that professional "fit and finish" that makes good sites into great ones. You're going to see lots of ways to give your sites that extra "polish" in the rest of this book, but let's start here with a way to improve your links.

Improving accessibility by adding a title to your links

Wouldn't it be nice if there were a way to get more information about the link you're about to click on? This is especially important for the visually impaired using screen readers because they often don't want the entire URL spoken to them: ("h" "t" "t" p ":" "slash" "slash" "w" "w" "w" "dot"), and yet the link's label usually only gives a limited description, like "Caffeine Buzz."

The <a> element has an attribute called title just for this purpose. Some people are confused by this attribute name because there's an *element* named <title> that goes in the <head>. They have the same name because they are related—it is often suggested that the value of the title attribute be the same as value of the <title> element of the web page you are linking to. But that isn't a requirement and often it makes more sense to provide your own, more relevant description in the title attribute.

Here's how you add a title attribute to the <a> element:

```
Read the <a href="http://wickedlysmart.com/buzz"
        title="Read all about caffeine on the Buzz">Caffeine Buzz</a>
```

The title element has a value that is a textual description of the page you are linking to.

Exercise

Now that we've got a title attribute, let's see how your visitors would make use of it. Different browsers make different use of the title, but many display a tool tip. Add the changes above to your "index.html" file and reload the page to see how it works in your browser.

The title test drive...

For most browsers, the title is displayed as a tool tip when you pass the mouse over a link. Remember that browsers for the visually impaired may read the link title aloud to a visitor.

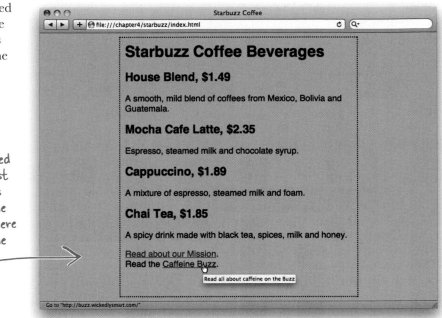

The title is displayed as a tool tip in most browsers. Just pass your mouse over the link and hold it there a second to see the tool tip.

The Head First Guide to Better Links

Here are a few tips to keep in mind to further improve the fit and finish of your links:

♦ Keep your link labels concise. Don't make entire sentences or large pieces of text into links. In general, keep them to a few words. Provide additional information in the title attribute.

♦ Keep your link labels meaningful. Never use link labels like "click here" or "this page." Users tend to scan pages for links first, and then read pages second. So, providing meaningful links improves the usability of your page. Test your page by reading just the links on it; do they make sense? Or do you need to read the text around them?

♦ Avoid placing links right next to each other; users have trouble distinguishing between links that are placed closely together.

Open your Starbuzz "index.html" file and add a title to the link to "mission.html" with the text "Read more about Starbuzz Coffee's important mission." Notice that we didn't make the mission link's label as concise as it should be. Shorten the link label to "our Mission." Check the back of the chapter for the answer, and test your changes.

Great job on the links. I'd really like for people to link directly to the coffee section of the Buzz site. Is that possible?

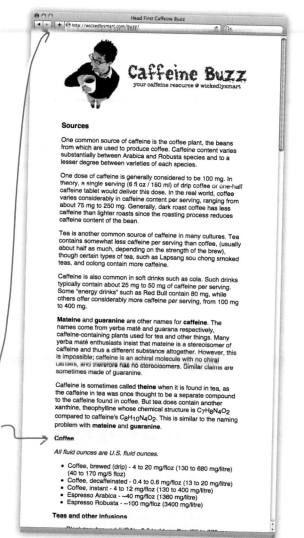

Linking into a page

So far, whenever you've linked to another page, the page loads and your browser displays it from the top.

But the CEO's asking you to *link into* a particular spot in the page: the Coffee section.

Sound impossible? Come on, this is Head First—we've got the technology. How? Well, we haven't told you everything about the <a> element yet. Turns out the <a> element can team up with the id attribute to take you straight to a specific point in a page.

Using the id attribute to create a destination for <a>

We haven't talked about the id attribute yet; it's an important attribute with special properties, and we'll get into more detail about other special properties of id later in the book. For now, think of it as a way of uniquely identifying an element. One special property that elements with ids get is that you can link to them. Let's see how to use the id attribute to create a destination in a page for <a>.

① Find the location in the page where you'd like to create a landing spot. This can be any text on the page, but often is just a heading.

② Choose an identifier name for the destination, like "coffee" or "summary" or "bio," and insert an id attribute into the opening tag of the element.

Let's give it a try. Say you want to provide a way to link to the Chai Tea item on the Starbuzz page. Here's what it looks like now:

Here's the snippet from "index.html" with the Chai heading and description.

```
<h2>Chai Tea, $1.85</h2>

<p>A spicy drink made with black tea, spices, milk
and honey.</p>
```

Following the two steps above, we get this:

Add the id to the opening tag of the heading.

And we'll give this destination the identifier "chai".

It's important that your id be __unique__. That is, the "chai" id must be the only "chai" id in the page!

```
<h2 id="chai">Chai Tea, $1.85</h2>

<p>A spicy drink made with black tea, spices, milk and
honey.</p>
```

By giving it an id, you've made a destination out of the Chai Tea heading in the "index.html" page.

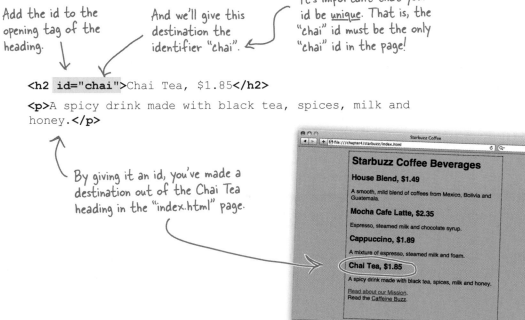

How to link to elements with ids

You already know how to link to pages using either relative links or URLs. In either case, to link to a specific destination in a page, just add a # on the end of your link, followed by the destination identifier. So if you wanted to link from any Starbuzz Coffee web page to the "chai" destination heading, you'd write your <a> element link this:

```
<a href="index.html#chai">See Chai Tea</a>
```

Unfortunately, linking to Chai Tea isn't very impressive because the whole page is small enough that it easily fits in the browser. Let's link to the Coffee section of http://wickedlysmart.com/buzz instead. Here's what you're going to do:

 The main benefit of specific destinations is to link to locations in long files so your visitors don't have to scroll through the file looking for the right section.

1 Figure out the id of the Coffee heading.

2 Alter the existing <a> element in the Starbuzz Coffee "index.html" file to point to the destination heading.

3 Reload your "index.html" page and test out the link.

Finding the destination heading

To find the destination heading, you're going to have to look at the wickedlysmart.com/buzz page and view their HTML. How? Almost all browsers have a "View Source" option. So, visit the page and when it is fully loaded, choose the "View Source" option, and you'll see the markup for the page.

In most browsers, you can right-click to "View Source."

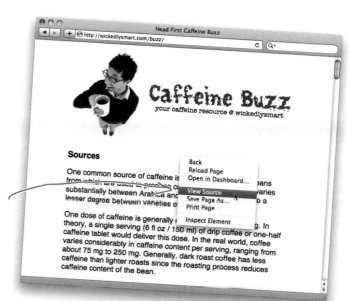

Now that you've got your hands on their HTML...

Scroll down until you see the Coffee section; it looks like this:

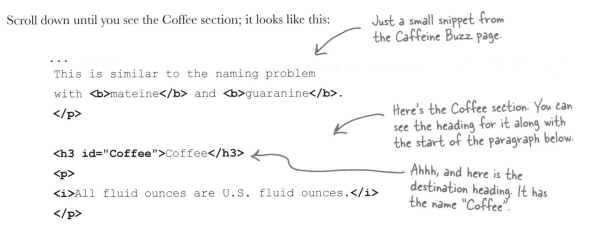

```
...
This is similar to the naming problem
with <b>mateine</b> and <b>guaranine</b>.
</p>


<h3 id="Coffee">Coffee</h3>
<p>
<i>All fluid ounces are U.S. fluid ounces.</i>
</p>
```

Just a small snippet from the Caffeine Buzz page.

Here's the Coffee section. You can see the heading for it along with the start of the paragraph below.

Ahhh, and here is the destination heading. It has the name "Coffee".

Reworking the link in "index.html"

Now all you need to do is revisit the link to Caffeine Buzz and add on the destination anchor name, like this:

This is a snippet from the Starbuzz "index.html" file.

The default file at wickedlysmart.com/buzz is index.html. So, we'll add that to the URL so we can use it with the destination id.

Add # along with the destination id to your href.

```
Read the <a href="http://wickedlysmart.com/buzz/index.html#Coffee"
          title="Read all about caffeine on the Buzz">Caffeine Buzz</a>
```

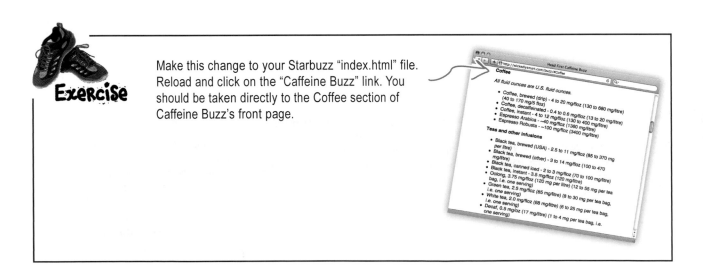

Exercise

Make this change to your Starbuzz "index.html" file. Reload and click on the "Caffeine Buzz" link. You should be taken directly to the Coffee section of Caffeine Buzz's front page.

there are no
Dumb Questions

Q: When I have two attributes in an element, is the order important? For example, should the title attribute always come after the href?

A: The order of attributes is not important in any element (if it were, we'd all have headaches 24/7). So, use any ordering you like.

Q: How would I create a tool tip for an element that's not an <a>?

A: You can add the title attribute to any element, so if you want a tool tip on, say, a heading, you can add a title attribute to your <h1> opening tag just like we did with <a>. There are a few elements that use the title attribute for more than just a tool tip, but the tool tip is its most common purpose.

Q: Can I add an id attribute to any element?

A: Yes, you can. You could link into the middle of a paragraph by adding an id to an <em> element, for instance. It's unlikely that you'll often need to do that, but you can do it if you want.

Q: Could I link to a link by adding an id attribute to an <a> element in the destination?

A: Yes!

Q: I noticed in the id names, you used "chai" with all lowercase letters and Caffeine Buzz used "Coffee" with an uppercase "C". Does it matter?

A: You can use any combination of upper- and lowercase characters in your id attributes. Just make sure you are consistent and always use the same upper- and lowercase letters in your hrefs and destination id (which is why it is often easier to make these names entirely lowercase every time). If you aren't consistent, don't expect your links to work correctly on every browser. The most important thing about the id name you choose is that it must be unique in your page.

Q: Can I put a link to a destination from within the same document?

A: Sure. In fact, it is common to define a destination "top" at the top of a page (say, on the top heading of the page) and have a link at the bottom of the page reading "Back to top." It is also common in long documents to have a table of contents for the entire page. For instance, to link to the "top" destination heading in the same page, you would write <a href="#top">Back to top</a>.

Q: Why did we need to add the "/index.html" to the Buzz URL in order to create a link to the destination heading? Couldn't we have just written: http://wickedlysmart.com/buzz#Coffee?

A: No, that won't always work because the browser adds that trailing slash on the end of the URL for you, which could end up replacing the id reference. You could, however, have written: http://wickedlysmart.com/buzz/#Coffee, which will produce the same results as the link we created using "index.html". This will come in handy if you don't know if the default file is named "index.html".

Q: If a web page doesn't provide a destination and I still need to link to a specific part of the page, how can I?

A: You can't. If there is no destination (in other words, no element with an id), then you can't direct the browser to go to a specific location in a web page. You might try to contact the page author and ask them to add one (even better, tell them how!).

Q: Can I have a destination id like "Jedi Mindtrick" or does an id have to be only one word?

A: To work consistently with the most browsers, always start your id with a letter (A–Z or a–z) and follow it with any letter, digit, hyphen, underscore, colon, or period. So, while you can't use a space and have a name like "Jedi Mindtrick", that isn't much of a restriction because you can always have "Jedi-Mindtrick", "Jedi_Mindtrick", "JediMindtrick", and so on.

Q: How can I tell others what destinations they can link to?

A: There is no established way of doing this, and in fact, "View Source" remains the oldest and best technique for discovering the destinations you can link to.

Q: Do I always use just words as the content of an <a> element?

A: No. The <a> element has always been able to create links from words and images (inline content), and has recently been updated (in HTML5) so that you can create links from block elements, like <p> and <blockquote> too! So <a> can be used to create links from all kinds of things.

Five-Minute Mystery Solved

The Case of Relatives and Absolutes

So, how did RadWebDesign flub up the demo? Well, because they used URLs for their `hrefs` instead of relative links, they had to edit and change every single link from `http://www.planetrobots.com` to `http://www.robotsrus.com`. Can you say error-prone? At 3:00 a.m., someone yawned and accidentally typed `http://www.robotsru.com` (and as fate has it, that was the same link that the CEO clicked on at the demo).

Oops... someone forgot an "s" on the end of the name.

CorrectWebDesign, on the other hand, used relative paths for all internal links. For example, the link from the company's mission statement to the products page, `<a href="../products.html">`, works whether the site is called PlanetRobots or RobotsRUs. So, all CorrectWebDesign had to do was update the company name on a few pages.

So RadWebDesign left the demo sleep-deprived and with a little egg on their face, while CorrectWebDesign left the meeting with even more business. But the story doesn't end there. It turns out that RadWebDesign dropped by a little coffeehouse/bookstore after the demo and, determined not to be outdone, picked up a certain book on HTML and CSS. What happened? Join us in a few chapters for "The Case of Brute Force Versus Style."

> Awesome job linking to the Buzz site...I know I keep asking for changes, but really, this is the last one. Can you make the Buzz site come up in a separate window when I click on the link? I don't want the Starbuzz page to go away.

Linking to a new window

We have another new requirement from the Starbuzz CEO (there are *always* new requirements for websites). What he wants is this: when you click on the "Caffeine Buzz" link in the Starbuzz Coffee page, the Starbuzz Coffee page shouldn't go away. Instead, a whole new window should open up with the Caffeine Buzz page in it, like this:

Here's the main Starbuzz Coffee page.

When the Caffeine Buzz window pops open, it will open over the top of the Starbuzz page, but the Starbuzz page will still be there.

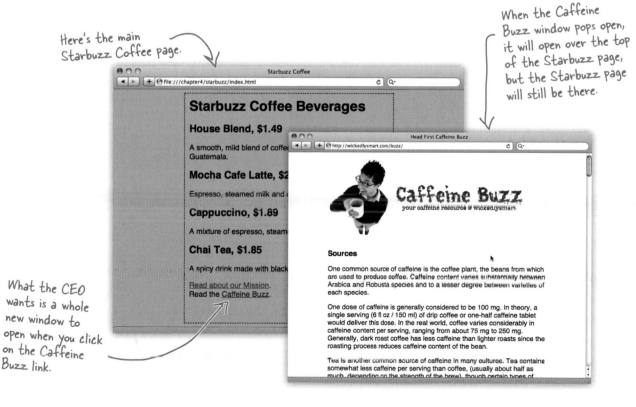

What the CEO wants is a whole new window to open when you click on the Caffeine Buzz link.

Opening a new window using target

To open a page in a new window, you need to tell the browser the name of the window in which to open it. If you don't tell the browser a specific window to use, the browser just opens the page in the *same* window. You can tell the browser to use a *different* window by adding a `target` attribute to the `<a>` element. The value of the `target` attribute tells the browser the "target window" for the page. If you use "_blank" for the target, the browser will *always* open a new window to display the page. Let's take a closer look:

```
<a target="_blank" href="http://wickedlysmart.com/buzz"
   title="Read all about caffeine on the Buzz">Caffeine Buzz</a>
```

The target attribute tells the browser where to open the web page that is at the link in the href attribute. If there is no target, then the browser opens the link in the same window. If the target is "_blank", then the browser opens the link in a new window.

Exercise

Open your Starbuzz "index. html" file. Add the `target` attribute to the `<a>` tag that links to the Caffeine Buzz page. Now give it a try—did you get a new window?

BRAIN POWER

Can you think of some advantages and some disadvantages to using the target attribute to open a page in a new window?

there are no
Dumb Questions

Q: I'm getting a new tab instead of a new window. Am I doing something wrong?

A: No, you're not. Most browsers now have a default setting to open new windows in a tab, rather than a whole new browser window, because that's what users seem to prefer. But a new tab and a new window are really the same thing; it's just that the tab shares the same window border as your original window. If you want to force a whole new window, most browsers have a way to do this through the preferences settings.

Q: What if I have more than one `<a>` element with a target? If there's already a "_blank" new window open, will it open in the window that's already open? Or will it open in a new "_blank" window?

A: If you give the name "_blank" to the targets in all your `<a>` elements, then each link will open in a new blank window. However, this is a good question because it brings up an important point: you don't actually have to name your target "_blank". If you give it another name, say, "coffee", then all links with the target name "coffee" will open in the same window. The reason is that when you give your target a specific name, like "coffee", you are really naming the new window that will be used to display the page at the link. "_blank" is a special case that tells the browser to *always* use a new window.

The Target Attribute Exposed

This week's interview:
Using target considered bad?

Head First: Hello, Target! We're so glad you could join us.

Target: I'm glad to be here. It's nice to know you're still interested in hearing about me.

Head First: Why do you say that?

Target: Well, to be honest, I'm not as popular as I used to be.

Head First: Why do you think that is?

Target: I think it's because users want to be in control of when a window opens. They don't always like new windows popping open at unexpected times.

Head First: Well, it can be very confusing—we've had complaints from people who end up with so many windows on their screens, they can't find the original page.

Target: But it's not like it's difficult to get rid of the windows…just click on the little close button. What's so hard about that?!

Head First: True, but if users don't know a new window has opened, then they can get confused. Sometimes the new window completely covers the old window and it's hard to tell what's happening.

Target: Well, browsers are getting better at this kind of thing.

Head First: How so?

Target: Browsers often open external pages in a new tab, within the same browser window, rather than opening them in a brand-new window.

Head First: Ah, yes, that would help because it will be a lot less confusing to see a new tab open, which the user can visit whenever they want. Unlike opening a new window, it isn't so disorienting.

Head First: How does this help with screen readers though?

Target: You mean browsers used by the visually impaired?

Head First: Right. Some screen readers play a sound when a new window opens, but others just ignore the new window completely, or else they jump right to the new window immediately. Either way, it's gotta be confusing for someone who can't see what's going on. I have no idea how they are handling tabs.

Target: [Sigh] Yeah, we just aren't there yet in terms of providing good tools that meet everyone's needs, especially the visually impaired. That said, we seem to need to have the ability to take the user to pages outside our own site, and many sites do that by opening another window (or tab, if the browser supports it).

Head First: Yup. We need you, but we need to get better about not confusing the user.

Target: I'm hoping the web standard and browser teams will make all this better.

Head First: I guess for now we're just going to have to remember to use you when it's appropriate, but to keep in mind those people who might be visually impaired and not overuse you.

Target: You got it. You've helped ease my burden a bit here; thanks for helping me get the word out!

Head First: Any time, Target!

HTMLcross

Here are some mind benders for your left brain.

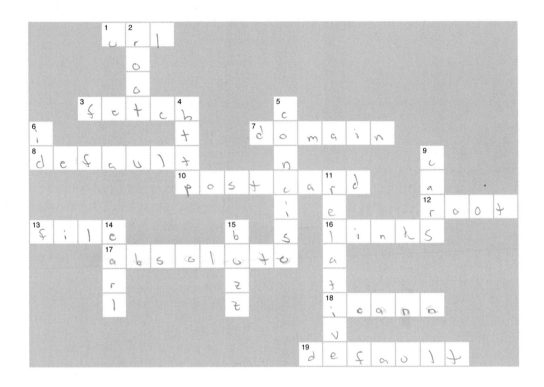

Across

1. Web address to a resource.
3. A Mac FTP application.
7. Unique name on the Web.
8. The file you get when you ask for a directory.
10. What are you supposed to send back from Webville?
12. Top directory of your website.
13. Protocol we've been using up until this chapter.
16. People can scan these rather than reading text.
17. Path from the root.
18. Controls domain names.
19. The file you get when you ask for a directory.

Down

2. Top directory of your website.
4. Request/response protocol.
5. Keep your link labels _____.
6. Attribute used to make an element into a destination.
9. Earl sold these.
11. Always use these kinds of links when linking to pages on the same server.
14. Wrong way to pronounce URL.
15. Informative caffeine site.

BULLET POINTS

- Typically the best way to get on the Web is to find a hosting company to host your web pages.

- A domain name is a unique name, like amazon.com or starbuzzcoffee.com, that is used to identify a site.

- A hosting company can create one or more web servers in your domain. Servers are often named "www".

- The File Transfer Protocol (FTP) is a common means of transferring your web pages and content to a server.

- FTP applications, like Fetch for Mac or WS_FTP for Windows, can make using FTP easier by providing a graphical user interface.

- A URL is a Uniform Resource Locator, or web address, that can be used to identify any resource on the Web.

- A typical URL consists of a protocol, a website name, and an absolute path to the resource.

- HTTP is a request and response protocol used to transfer web pages between a web server and your browser.

- The file protocol is used by the browser to read pages from your computer.

- An absolute path is the path from the root folder to a file.

- "index.html" and "default.htm" are examples of default pages. If you specify a directory without a filename, the web server will look for a default page to return to the browser.

- You can use relative paths or URLs in your <a> element's href attribute to link to other web pages. For other pages in your site, it's best to use relative paths, and use URLs for external links.

- Use the id attribute to create a destination in a page. Use # followed by a destination id to link to that location in a page.

- To help accessibility, use the title attribute to provide a description of the link in <a> elements.

- Use the target attribute to open a link in another browser window. Don't forget that the target attribute can be problematic for users on a variety of devices and alternative browsers.

Wait, wait! Before you go, we need our logo on the web page! Hello? Oh, I guess they've already gone on to Chapter 5...

Sharpen your pencil Solution

You've waited long enough. It's time to give your new URL a spin. Before you do, fill in the blanks below and then type in the URL (like you haven't already). If you're having any problems, this is the time to work with your hosting company to get things sorted out. If you haven't set up an hosting company, fill in the blanks for www. starbuzzcoffee.com, and type the URL into your browser anyway.

<u>http</u>   <u>://</u>   <u>www.starbuzzcoffee.com</u>   <u>/index.html</u>

protocol   website name   absolute path

Your website name here.

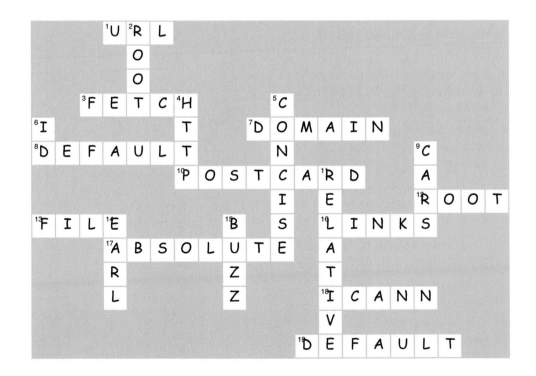

Earl needs a little help with his URLs

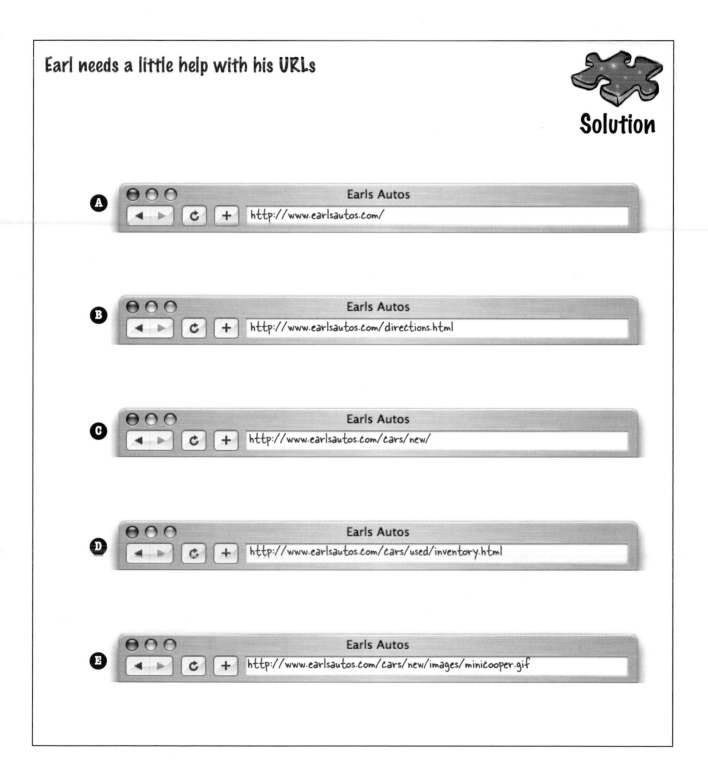

Solution

A
Earls Autos
http://www.earlsautos.com/

B
Earls Autos
http://www.earlsautos.com/directions.html

C
Earls Autos
http://www.earlsautos.com/cars/new/

D
Earls Autos
http://www.earlsautos.com/cars/used/inventory.html

E
Earls Autos
http://www.earlsautos.com/cars/new/images/minicooper.gif

Exercise Solution

Add a title to the link to "mission.html" with the text "Read more about Starbuzz Coffee's important mission." Notice that we didn't make the mission link's label as concise as it should be. Shorten the link label to "our Mission". Here's the solution; did you test your changes?

```html
<html>
    <head>
        <title>Starbuzz Coffee</title>
        <style type="text/css">
            body {
                    background-color: #d2b48c;
                    margin-left: 20%;
                    margin-right: 20%;
                    border: 1px dotted gray;
                    padding: 10px 10px 10px 10px;
                    font-family: sans-serif;
            }
        </style>
    </head>
    <body>
        <h1>Starbuzz Coffee Beverages</h1>
        <h2>House Blend, $1.49</h2>
        <p>A smooth, mild blend of coffees from Mexico,
           Bolivia and Guatemala.</p>

        <h2>Mocha Cafe Latte, $2.35</h2>
        <p>Espresso, steamed milk and chocolate syrup.</p>

        <h2>Cappuccino, $1.89</h2>
        <p>A mixture of espresso, steamed milk and foam.</p>

        <h2>Chai Tea, $1.85</h2>
        <p>A spicy drink made with black tea, spices,
           milk and honey.
        </p>
        <p>
            Read about <a href="mission.html"
title="Read more about Starbuzz Coffee's important mission">our Mission</a>.
            <br>
            Read the <a href="http://wickedlysmart.com/buzz"
                  title="Read all about caffeine on the Buzz">Caffeine Buzz</a>.
        </p>
    </body>
</html>
```

Add a title attribute to the mission link.

Move the "Read about" outside the <a> element.

5 adding images to your pages

Meeting the Media

Smile and say "cheese." Actually, smile and say "gif," "jpg," or "png"—these are going to be your choices when "developing pictures" for the Web. In this chapter you're going to learn all about adding your first media type to your pages: images. Got some digital photos you need to get online? No problem. Got a logo you need to get on your page? Got it covered. But before we get into all that, don't you still need to be formally introduced to the <img> element? So sorry, we weren't being rude; we just never saw the "right opening." To make up for it, here's an entire chapter devoted to <img>. By the end of the chapter you're going to know all the ins and outs of how to use the <img> element and its attributes. You're also going to see exactly how this little element causes the browser to do extra work to retrieve and display your images.

How the browser works with images

Browsers handle `<img>` elements a little differently than other elements. Take an element like an `<h1>` or a `<p>`. When the browser sees these tags in a page, all it needs to do is display them. Pretty simple. But when a browser sees an `<img>` element, something very different happens: the browser has to retrieve the image before it can be displayed in a page.

The best way to understand this is to look at an example. Let's take a quick look back at the elixirs page from the Head First Lounge, which has four `<img>` elements:

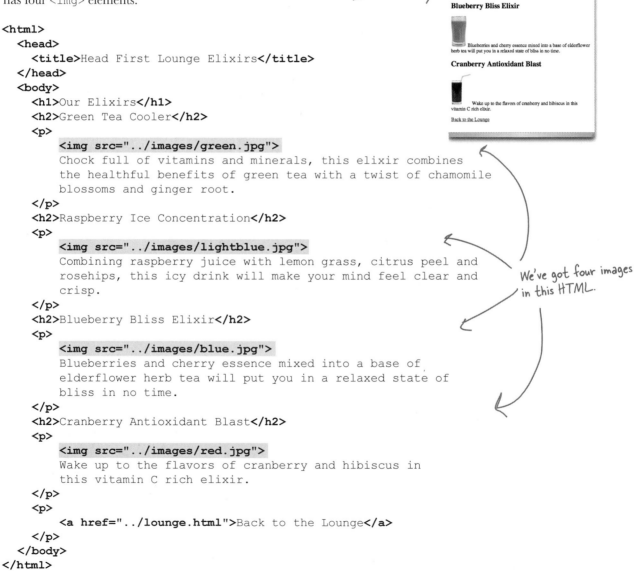

We've got four images in this HTML.

```
<html>
  <head>
    <title>Head First Lounge Elixirs</title>
  </head>
  <body>
    <h1>Our Elixirs</h1>
    <h2>Green Tea Cooler</h2>
    <p>
        <img src="../images/green.jpg">
        Chock full of vitamins and minerals, this elixir combines
        the healthful benefits of green tea with a twist of chamomile
        blossoms and ginger root.
    </p>
    <h2>Raspberry Ice Concentration</h2>
    <p>
        <img src="../images/lightblue.jpg">
        Combining raspberry juice with lemon grass, citrus peel and
        rosehips, this icy drink will make your mind feel clear and
        crisp.
    </p>
    <h2>Blueberry Bliss Elixir</h2>
    <p>
        <img src="../images/blue.jpg">
        Blueberries and cherry essence mixed into a base of
        elderflower herb tea will put you in a relaxed state of
        bliss in no time.
    </p>
    <h2>Cranberry Antioxidant Blast</h2>
    <p>
        <img src="../images/red.jpg">
        Wake up to the flavors of cranberry and hibiscus in
        this vitamin C rich elixir.
    </p>
    <p>
        <a href="../lounge.html">Back to the Lounge</a>
    </p>
  </body>
</html>
```

Now let's take a look behind the scenes and step through how the browser retrieves and displays this page when it is requested from `http://wickedlysmart.com/lounge/`:

Behind the Scenes

① First, the browser retrieves the file "elixir.html" from the server.

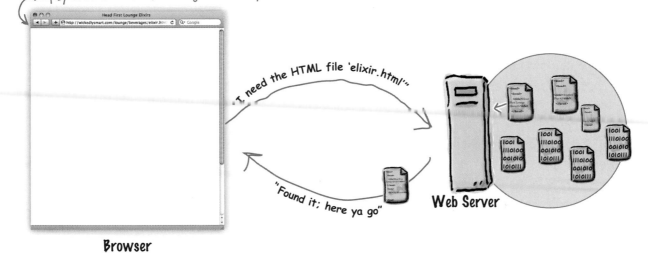

Empty browser window; nothing retrieved yet.

"I need the HTML file 'elixir.html'"

"Found it; here ya go"

Web Server

Browser

---

② Next the browser reads the "elixir.html" file, displays it, and sees it has four images to retrieve. So, it needs to get each one from the web server, starting with "green.jpg".

The HTML page is retrieved, but the browser still needs to get the images.

Our Elixirs

Green Tea Cooler

Chock full of vitamins and minerals, this elixir combines the healthful benefits of green tea with a twist of chamomile blossoms and ginger root.

Raspberry Ice Concentration

Combining raspberry juice with lemon grass, citrus peel and rosehips, this icy drink will make your mind feel clear and crisp.

Blueberry Bliss Elixir

Blueberries and cherry essence mixed into a base of elderflower herb tea will put you in a relaxed state of bliss in no time.

Browser

"Oh, it looks like I need green.jpg, too."

"Found it; here ya go"

Web Server

③ Having just retrieved "green.jpg", the browser displays it and then moves on to the next image: "lightblue.jpg".

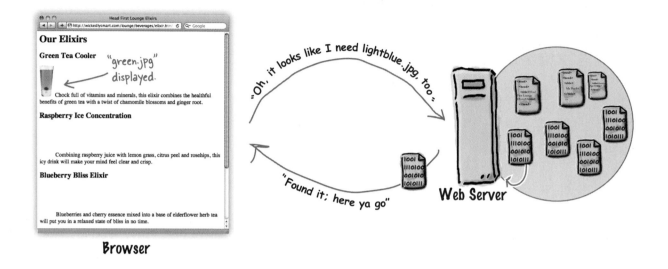

④ Now the browser has retrieved "lightblue.jpg", so it displays that image and then moves on to the next image, "blue.jpg". This process continues for each image in the page.

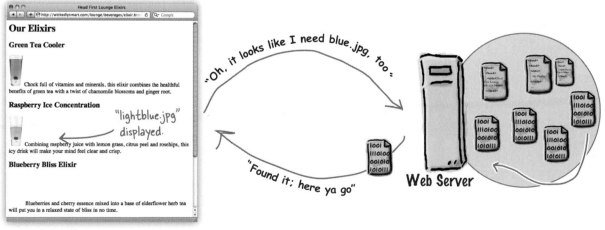

How images work

Images are just images, right? Well, actually there are a zillion formats for images out there in the world, all with their own strengths and weaknesses. But luckily, only three of those formats are commonly used on the Web: JPEG, PNG, and GIF. The only tricky part is deciding which to use when.

So, what are the differences among JPEG, PNG, and GIF?

Use JPEG for photos and complex graphics

Use PNG or GIF for images with solid colors, logos, and geometric shapes.

Works best for continuous tone images, like photographs.

Can represent images with up to 16 million different colors.

Is a "lossy" format because to reduce the file size, it throws away some information about the image.

Does not support transparency.

Files are smaller for more efficient web pages.

No support for animation.

PNG works best for images with a few solid colors, and images with lines, like logos, clip art, and small text in images.

PNG can represent images with millions of different colors. PNG comes in three flavors: PNG-8, PNG-24, and PNG-32, depending on how many colors you need to represent.

PNG compresses the file to reduce its size, but doesn't throw anything way. So, it is a "lossless" format.

Allows colors to be set to "transparent" so that anything underneath the image will show through.

Files tend to be larger than their JPEG equivalents, but can be smaller or larger than GIF depending on the number of colors used.

Like PNG, GIF works best for images with a few solid colors, and images with lines, like logos, clip art, and small text in images.

GIF can represent images with up to 256 different colors.

GIF is also a "lossless" format.

GIF also supports transparency, but allows only one color to be set to "transparent."

Files tend to be larger than their JPEG equivalents.

Supports animation.

Would the real image format please stand up?

This week's interview: Image formats mix it up

Head First: Well, hello everyone. I think this might be the first time we've interviewed three interviewees at once!

JPEG: Hey there, and hey to GIF and PNG.

GIF: I'm not sure why I have to share the interview couch with these other bozos. Everyone knows GIF is the original image format of the Web.

JPEG: Ha! As soon as you get good at representing complex images, like photos, maybe then people will take you seriously again, but I'm not sure how you're going to do that with only 256 colors.

Head First: PNG, help us out here? You've been kind of quiet so far…

PNG: Yeah, it's easy to be quiet when you're #1. I can represent complex images like JPEG and I'm also lossless like GIF. Truly the best of both worlds.

Head First: Lossless?

PNG: Right; when you store an image in a lossless format, you don't lose any of the information, or detail, in the image.

GIF: Me too! I'm lossless too, you know.

Head First: Well, why would anyone want a lossy format?

JPEG: There's always a tradeoff. Sometimes what you want is a fairly small file you can download fast, but that has great quality. We don't always need perfect quality. People are very happy with JPEG images.

PNG: Sure, sure, but have you ever looked at lines, logos, small text, solid colors? They don't look so great with JPEG.

Head First: Wait a sec, JPEG raises an interesting issue. So GIF and PNG, are your file sizes large?

PNG: I'll admit my file sizes can be on the large size sometimes, but I provide three formats so you can right-size your images: PNG-8, PNG-24, and PNG-32.

GIF: Sounds like complexity to me—more things for your users to remember.

PNG: Well, GIF, wouldn't the world be nice if we could fit all images into 256 colors? But we can't.

GIF: Hey, for line drawings, figures, that kind of thing, it's often very easy to fit images into 8 bits, and for that I look great.

JPEG: Ha, when is the last time you saw a photo stored in GIF? People have figured out your downsides, GIF.

GIF: Did I mention I can be transparent? You can take parts of me, and anything behind me shows right through.

PNG: You can't compete with me on that one, GIF. I can set any number of colors to transparent; you are limited to one color.

GIF: One color or many, who cares? One is all you need.

PNG: Not if you want to have anti-aliased transparent areas in your image!

GIF: Huh?

PNG: Yeah, you know, because I allow more than one color to be transparent, so you can have nice soft edges around the transparent areas.

Head First: That sounds like a nice feature. Can you do that, JPEG?

JPEG: No, but I'm not too worried about it; there aren't many photos you'd want to do that to. That's for logos.

PNG: Hmmm, I'm seeing my transparency used all over the Web.

Head First: Well, I'll have to think twice before doing a three-person interview again, but it sounds to me like GIF and PNG, you're great for logos and text images; JPEG, you're great for photos; and PNG, you come in handy if we want transparency as well as lots of colors. Bye!

PNG, JPEG, GIF: Wait, no, hold on!!!

WHICH IMAGE FORMAT?

Congratulations: you've been elected "Grand Image Format Chooser" of the day. For each image below, choose the format that would best represent it for the Web.

JPEG   or   PNG   or   GIF

Image	JPEG	PNG	GIF
(man drinking)	☑	☐	☐
CAUTION WATCH OUT FOR HOT CHOCOLATE	☐	☑	☐
(chef cooking)	☑	☐	☐
(couple)	☐	☐	☑
(bonsai tree)	☑	☐	☐

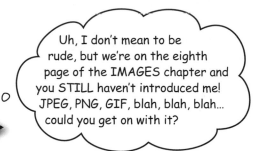

And now for the formal introduction: meet the <img> element.

We've held off on the introductions long enough. As you can see, there's more to dealing with images than just the HTML markup. Anyway, enough of that for now...it's time to meet the <img> element.

Let's start by taking a closer look at the element (although you've probably already picked up on most of how <img> works by now):

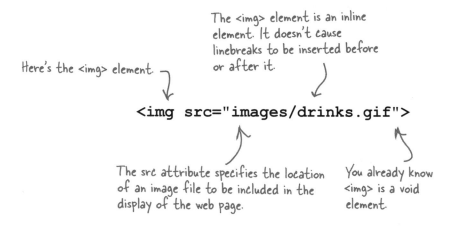

Here's the <img> element.

The <img> element is an inline element. It doesn't cause linebreaks to be inserted before or after it.

```
<img src="images/drinks.gif">
```

The src attribute specifies the location of an image file to be included in the display of the web page.

You already know <img> is a void element.

So, is that it? Not quite. There are a couple of attributes you'll want to know about. And of course you'll also want to know how to use the <img> element to reference images on the Web that aren't on your own site. But really, you already know the basics of using the <img> element.

Let's work through a few of the finer points of using the <img> element, and then put all this knowledge to work.

<img>: it's not just relative links anymore

The `src` attribute can be used for more than just relative links; you can also put a URL in your `src` attribute. Images are stored on web servers right alongside HTML pages, so every image on the Web has its own URL, just like web pages do.

You'll generally want to use a URL for an image if you're pointing to an image at a *different* website (remember, for links and images on the *same* site, it's better to use relative paths).

Here's how you link to an image using a URL:

```
<img src="http://www.starbuzzcoffee.com/images/corporate/ceo.jpg">
```

To include an image using its URL, just put the whole URL of the image in the src attribute.

The URL is the path to the image, so the filename at the end is always the filename of an image. There's no such thing as a default image like there is for web pages.

Sharpen your pencil

Here's a "Sharpen your pencil" that is actually about pencils (oh, and images too). This exercise involves a bit of trivia: *Given a typical, brand-new pencil, if you drew one continuous line with it, using the entire pencil up, how long would the line be?*

What's that got to do with images? To find the answer, you're going to have to write some HTML. The answer to this trivia is contained in the image that is at the URL http://wickedlysmart.com/hfhtmlcss/trivia/pencil.png. Your job is to add an image to this HTML and retrieve the answer:

```
<html>
    <head>
        <title>Sharpen your pencil trivia</title>
    </head>
    <body>
        <p>How long a line can you draw with the typical pencil?</p>
        <p>
        <img src="http://www.wickedlysmart.com/htmlcss/trivia/pencil.png">
        </p>
    </body>
</html>
```

Put your image element here.

there are no
Dumb Questions

Q: So the <img> element is quite simple—it just provides a way to specify the location of the image that needs to be displayed in the page?

A: Yes, that about sums it up. We'll talk about a couple of attributes you can add to the element. Later, you'll see a number of ways to use CSS to change the visual style of an image.

But there's a lot to know about the images themselves. What are the different image formats for? When should I use one over the other? How big should they be? How do I prepare images for use in a web page?

Q: We've learned that void elements are elements without content or a closing tag. We've also learned that the <img> element is void. But doesn't it have content (the image)?

A: Well, to be more precise, a void element is an element that doesn't have any content in the HTML page to put the opening and closing tags around. True, an image is content, but the <img> element refers to the image. The image isn't part of the HTML page itself. Instead, the image replaces the <img> element when the browser displays the page. And remember, HTML pages are purely text, so the image could never be directly part of the page. It's always a separate thing.

Q: Back to the example of a web page loading with images...when I load a web page, I don't see the images loading one after the other. Why?

A: Browsers often retrieve the images *concurrently*. That is, the browser makes requests for multiple images at the same time. Given the speed of computers and networks, this all happens fast enough that you usually see a page display along with its images.

Q: If I see an image on a web page, how do I determine its URL so that I can link to it?

A: Most browsers allow you to right-click on an image, which brings up a contextual menu with some choices. In these choices, you should see "Copy Image Address" or "Copy Image Link," which will place the URL in your clipboard. Another way to find the URL is to right-click and choose "Open Image in New Window," which will open the image in a browser window. Then you can get the URL of the image from the browser's address bar. A last option is to use your browser's View Source menu option and look through the HTML. Keep in mind, though, you might find a relative link to the image, so you'll have to "reconstruct" the URL using the website domain name and the path of the image.

Q: What makes a JPEG photo better than a GIF or PNG photo, or a GIF or PNG logo better than a JPEG logo?

A: "Better" is usually defined as some combination of image quality and file size. A JPEG photo will usually be much smaller than an equivalent-quality PNG or GIF, while a PNG or GIF logo will usually look better, and may have a smaller file size than in JPEG format.

Q: How do I choose between GIF and PNG? It seems like they are very similar.

A: PNG is the latest newcomer in graphic formats, and an interesting one because it can support both photos as well as logos. It also has more advanced transparency features than GIF. PNG is supported by all major browsers now, which wasn't true just a few years ago.

To choose between GIF and PNG, there are a few things to consider. First, PNG has slightly better compression than GIF, so for an image with the same number of colors (i.e., up to 256), your PNG file may be smaller. If you need more colors than GIF can offer, and JPEG isn't an option (for instance, you need transparency), PNG is definitely the way to go. However, if you need animation, then you should go with GIF because GIF is the only widely supported format that supports animation.

Always provide an alternative

One thing you can be sure of on the Web is that you never know exactly which browsers and devices will be used to view your pages. Visitors are likely to show up with mobile devices, screen readers for the visually impaired, browsers that are running over very slow Internet connections (and may retrieve only the text, not the images, of a site), cell phones, Internet-enabled T-shirts...Who knows?

But in the middle of all this uncertainty, *you can be prepared*. Even if a browser can't display the images on your page, there is an alternative. You can give the visitor some indication of what information is in the image using the `<img>` element's `alt` attribute. Here's how it works:

```
<img src="http://wickedlysmart.com/hfhtmlcss/trivia/pencil.png"
     alt="The typical new pencil can draw a line 35 miles long.">
```

The alt attribute requires a bit of text that describes the image.

If the image can't be displayed, then this text is used in its place. It's like if you were reading the web page over the phone to someone, the alt text is what you'd say in place of the image.

Exercise

In this exercise you're going to see how your browser handles the alt attribute when you have a broken image. The theory goes that if an image can't be found, the alt attribute is displayed instead. But not all browsers implement this, so your results may vary. Here's what you need to do:

1 Take your HTML from the previous exercise.

2 Update the image element to include the `alt` attribute "The typical new pencil can draw a line 35 miles long."

3 Change the image name of "pencil.png" to "broken.png". This image doesn't actually exist, so you'll get a broken image.

4 Reload the page in your browser.

5 Finally, download a couple of other browsers and give this a try. Did you get different results?

For instance, you could try Firefox (http://www.mozilla.org/) or Opera (http://www.opera.com/).

Look at the end of the chapter to see our results...

Sizing up your images

There's one last attribute of the `<img>` element you should know about—actually, they're a pair of attributes: `width` and `height`. You can use these attributes to tell the browser, up front, the size of an image in your page.

Here's how you use `width` and `height`:

```
<img src="images/drinks.gif" width="48" height="100">
```

The width attribute tells the browser how wide the image should appear in the page.

The height attribute tells the browser how tall the image should appear in the page.

Both width and height are specified using the number of pixels. If you're not familiar with pixels, we'll go into what they are in a little more detail later in this chapter. You can add width and height attributes to any image; if you don't, the browser will automatically determine the size of the image before displaying it in the page.

there are no Dumb Questions

Q: Why would I ever use these attributes if the browser just figures it out anyway?

A: On many browsers, if you supply the width and height in your HTML, then the browser can get a head start laying out the page before displaying it. If you don't, the browser often has to readjust the page layout after it knows the size of an image. Remember, the browser downloads images after it downloads the HTML file and begins to display the page. The browser can't know the size of the images before it downloads them unless you tell it.

You can also supply width and height values that are larger or smaller than the size of the image and the browser will scale the image to fit those dimensions. Many people do this when they need to display an existing image at a size that is larger or smaller than its original dimensions. As you'll see later, however, there are many reasons not to use width and height for this purpose.

Q: Do I have to use these attributes in pairs? Can I just specify a width or a height?

A: You can, but if you're going to go to the trouble to tell the browser one dimension, supplying the second dimension is about the same amount of work (and there isn't a lot to be gained by supplying just a width or a height unless you're scaling the image to a particular width or height).

Q: We've said many times that we are supposed to use HTML for structure, and not for presentation. These feel like presentation attributes. Am I wrong?

A: It depends on how you are using these attributes. If you're setting the image width and height to the correct dimensions, then it is really just informational. However, if you are using the width and height to resize the image in the browser, then you are using these attributes for presentation. In that case, it's probably better to consider using CSS to achieve the same result.

Creating the ultimate fan site: myPod

iPod owners love their iPods, and they take them everywhere. Imagine creating a new site called "myPod" to display pictures of your friends and their iPods from their favorite locations, all around the world.

What do you need to get started? Just some knowledge of HTML, some images, and a love for your iPod.

We've already written some of the HTML for this site, but we haven't added the images yet—that's where you come in. But before you get to the images, let's get things set up; look for the "chapter5" folder in the sample source for the book. There you'll find a folder named "mypod". Open the "mypod" folder, and here's what you'll see inside:

iPhones are fine too!

My iPod in Seattle! You can see the Space Needle. You can't see the 628 coffee shops.

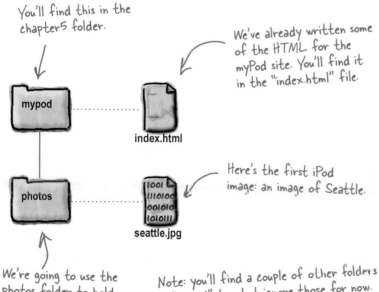

You'll find this in the chapter5 folder.

We've already written some of the HTML for the myPod site. You'll find it in the "index.html" file.

index.html

Here's the first iPod image: an image of Seattle.

seattle.jpg

We're going to use the photos folder to hold the images for the site.

Note: you'll find a couple of other folders in "mypod" too, but ignore those for now.

Check out myPod's "index.html" file

Open up the file "index.html", and you'll see work has already begun on myPod. Here's the HTML so far:

```
<html>
   <head>
      <title>myPod</title>
      <style type="text/css">
         body { background-color: #eaf3da;}
      </style>
   </head>
   <body>

      <h1>Welcome to myPod</h1>
      <p>
         Welcome to the place to show off your iPod, wherever you might be.
         Wanna join the fun? All you need is any iPod from the early classic
         iPod to the latest iPod Nano, the smallest iPod Shuffle to the largest
         iPod Video, and a digital camera. Just take a snapshot of your iPod in
         your favorite location and we'll be glad to post it on myPod. So, what
         are you waiting for?
      </p>

      <h2>Seattle, Washington</h2>
      <p>
         Me and my iPod in Seattle! You can see the
         Space Needle. You can't see the 628 coffee shops.
      </p>

   </body>
</html>
```

*We threw in some **Ready Bake CSS** here. Just type this in for now. All it does is give the page a light green background. We'll be getting to CSS in a few chapters, promise!*

This HTML should look familiar, as we're using the basic building blocks: <h1>, <h2>, and <p>.

And here's how it looks in the browser. Not bad, but we need images.

Sharpen your pencil

As you can see, a lot of the HTML is already written to get myPod up and running. All you need to do is add an <img> element for each photo you want to include. There's one photo so far, "seattle_video.jpg", so go ahead and add an element to place that image in the page below. When you've finished, load the page in your browser and check out the view of Seattle.

We need an image right here.

This is where you need to place the first photo.

```
<html>
   <head>
      <title>myPod</title>
      <style type="text/css">
         body { background-color: #eaf3da;}
      </style>
   </head>
   <body>

      <h1>Welcome to myPod</h1>
      <p>
         Welcome to the place to show off your iPod, wherever you might be.
         Wanna join the fun? All you need is any iPod from, the early classic
         iPod to the latest iPod Nano, the smallest iPod Shuffle to the largest
         iPod Video, and a digital camera. Just take a snapshot of your iPod in
         your favorite location and we'll be glad to post it on myPod. So, what
         are you waiting for?
      </p>

      <h2>Seattle, Washington</h2>
      <p>
         Me and my iPod in Seattle! You can see the
         Space Needle. You can't see the 628 coffee shops.
      </p>

      <p>
         <img src="photos/seattle.jpg">        Your <img> element is
                                               going to go right here.
      </p>

   </body>
</html>
```

Whoa! The image is way too large

Well, the image is right there where it should be, but that is one *large* image. Then again, most of the images that come from digital cameras these days are that large (or larger). Should we just leave the image like it is and let visitors use the scroll bar? You're going to see there are a couple of reasons why that's a bad idea.

Let's take a look at the image and the browser and see just how bad this situation is…

Watch it!

If the image fits nicely in your browser window, then your browser may have an "auto image resize" option turned on. More on this in just a sec…

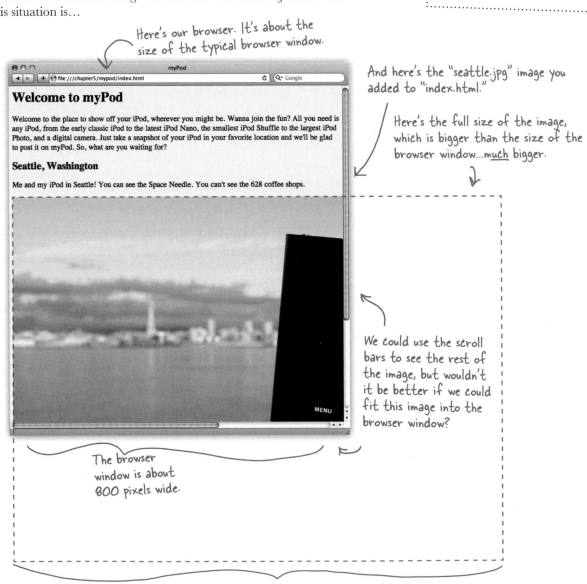

Here's our browser. It's about the size of the typical browser window.

And here's the "seattle.jpg" image you added to "index.html."

Here's the full size of the image, which is bigger than the size of the browser window…much bigger.

We could use the scroll bars to see the rest of the image, but wouldn't it be better if we could fit this image into the browser window?

The browser window is about 800 pixels wide.

The image is 1,200 pixels wide.

there are no
Dumb Questions

Q: What's wrong with having the user just use the scroll bar to see the image?

A: In general, web pages with large images are hard to use. Not only can your visitors not see the entire image at once, but also using scroll bars is cumbersome. Large images also require more data to be transferred between the server and your browser, which takes a lot of time and may result in your page being very slow to display, particularly for users on dial-up or other slow connections.

Q: Why can't I just use the width and height attributes to resize the images on the page?

A: Because the browser still has to retrieve the entire large image before it scales it down to fit your page.

Q: You said the browser window is 800 pixels wide; what exactly does that mean?

A: Your computer's display is made up of millions of dots called pixels. If you look very closely at your display, you'll see them:

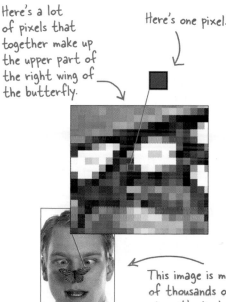

Here's a lot of pixels that together make up the upper part of the right wing of the butterfly.

Here's one pixel.

This image is made up of thousands of pixels when it's displayed on a computer screen.

And while screen sizes and resolutions tend to vary (some people have small monitors, some large), most people typically set their browsers to somewhere between 800 and 1,280 pixels wide. So, around 800 pixels is a good rule of thumb for the maximum width of your images (and your web pages too, but we'll get to that in a later chapter).

Q: How do the number of pixels relate to the size of the image on the screen?

A: A good rule of thumb is 96 pixels to every inch, although with today's high resolution monitors and retinal displays, it can go higher. We used to use a standard of 72 pixels per inch (ppi), but to handle modern displays, the concept of a CSS pixel has been created. The CSS pixel is 1/96 of an inch (96 ppi). So for a 3" wide × 3" high image, you'd use 96 (pixels) × 3 (inches) = 288 × 288 pixels.

Q: Well, how large should I make my images then?

A: In general, you want to keep the width of your image to less than 800 pixels wide. Of course, you may want your images to be significantly smaller (or somewhat larger) depending on what you're using the image for. What if the image is a logo for your page? You probably want that small, but still readable. After all, you don't need a logo the width of the entire web page. Logos tend to run between 100 and 200 pixels wide. So, ultimately, the answer to your question depends on the design of your page. For photos—which you usually do want to view as large as possible—you may want to have a page of small thumbnail images that load quickly, and then allow the user to click on each thumbnail to see a larger version of the image. We'll get to all that shortly.

Q: I think my browser automatically resized the image of Seattle, because it fits perfectly in the window. Why did my browser do this?

A: Some browsers have a feature that resizes any image that doesn't fit within the width of your browser. But many browsers don't do this, so you don't want to rely on it. Even if every browser did have this feature, you'd still be transferring a lot more data than necessary between the server and browser, which would make your page slow to load and less usable. And keep in mind that an increasing number of people are viewing web pages on mobile devices, and large images will impact data usage on these devices.

Resize the image to fit in the browser

Let's fix up this image so it fits the browser page better. Right now, this image is 1,200 pixels wide by 800 pixels tall (you'll see how to determine that in a sec). Because we want the width of the image to be less than 800 pixels, we need to decide on a width that would fit our myPod web page nicely. The whole point of myPod is viewing photos of iPods in their surroundings, so we probably want to have reasonably large images. If we reduce this image size by one-half to 600 pixels wide by 400 pixels high, that will still take up most of the browser width, while still allowing for a little space on the sides. Sound good? Let's get this image resized…

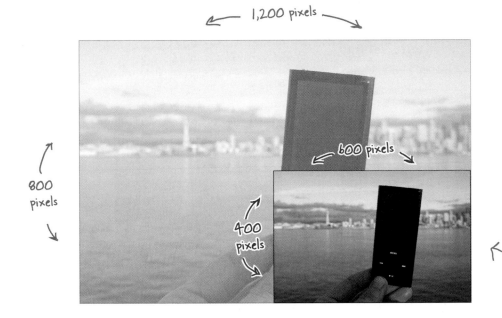

We need to resize the image so that it's still reasonably large, but is less than 800 pixels wide. 600 seems like a nice width that happens to be one-half the current size.

Here's what you're going to do:

1 **Open the image using a photo editing application.**

2 **Reduce the image size by one-half (to 600 pixels by 400 pixels).**

3 **Save the image as "seattle_video_med.jpg".**

Before we get started, which photo editing application are we going to use to resize the image? I have Photoshop Elements. Will that work?

Good question—there are lots of photo editing applications on the market (some freely available), which are all quite similar. We're going to use Adobe's Photoshop Elements to resize the images, because it is one of the most popular photo editing applications, and is available on both Windows and the Macintosh. If you own another photo editing application, you should have no problem following along and translating each editing task to your own application.

If you don't yet have a photo editing application, you might first check to see if there was one included with your operating system. If you have a Mac, you can use iPhoto to edit your photos. If you're a Windows user, you might find Microsoft's Digital Image Suite on your computer already. If you still don't have an editing application available to you, follow along and for each step, you can use the HTML and images included in the example folders.

If you don't have Adobe Photoshop Elements, but you'd like to follow along for the rest of the chapter with it, you can download it and try it out free for 30 days. The URL to download it is: http://www.adobe.com/go/tryphotoshop_elements.

Open the image

First, start your photo editing application and open the "seattle_video.jpg" image. In Photoshop Elements, you'll want to choose the "Open…" menu option under the File menu, which will open the Open dialog box. You're going to use this to navigate to the image "seattle_video.jpg" in the "chapter5/mypod/photos" folder.

Here's the Open dialog box. Use this dialog to navigate to the "seattle_video.jpg" image.

As you navigate through folders, you'll see a preview of the images in those folders here.

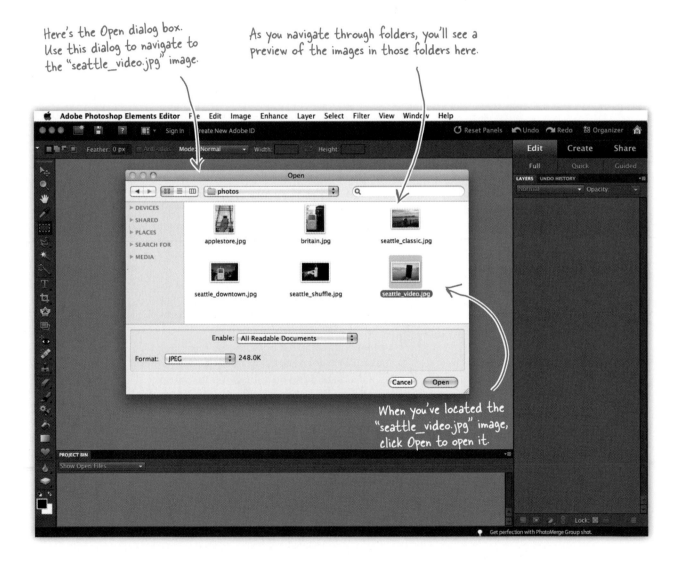

When you've located the "seattle_video.jpg" image, click Open to open it.

Resizing the image

Now that "seattle_video.jpg" is open, we're going to use the "Save for Web" dialog to both resize the image and save it. To get to that dialog box, just choose the "Save for Web" menu option from the File menu.

Here's the "seattle_video.jpg" image in Photoshop Elements.

To resize the image, choose "Save for Web" from the File menu.

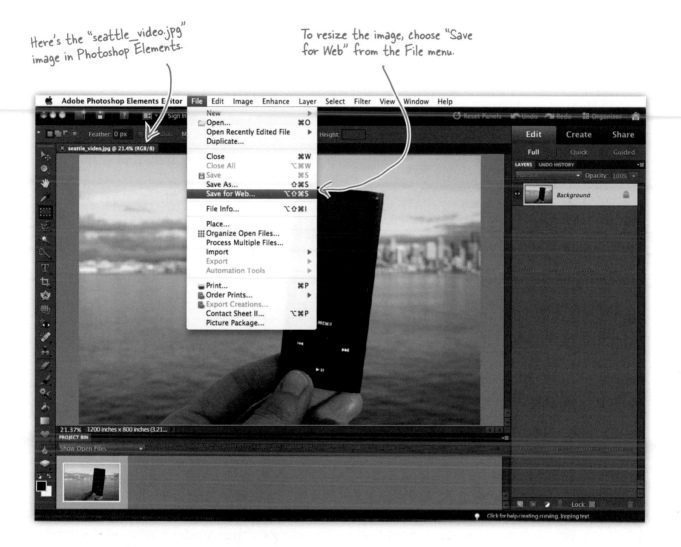

Resizing the image, continued...

After you've selected the "Save for Web" menu option, you should see the dialog box below; let's get acquainted with it before we use it.

This dialog lets you do all kinds of interesting things. For now, we're going to focus on how to use it to resize and save images in JPEG format for web pages.

Here's where you choose the format to save your file. Currently it's set to save as GIF; we're going to change this to JPEG in a couple of pages...

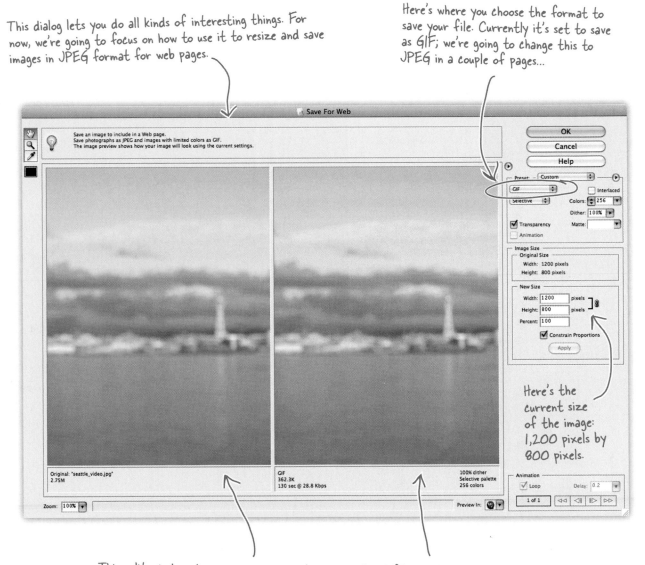

Here's the current size of the image: 1,200 pixels by 800 pixels.

This split window shows you your original image on the left, and the image in the format you're saving it for the Web on the right. Currently this is showing GIF format; we'll be changing this to JPEG in an upcoming step.

As you can see, there's a lot of functionality built into this dialog. Let's put it to good use. To resize the image, you need to change the width to 600 pixels and the height to 400 pixels. Then you need to save the image in JPEG format. Let's start with the resize…

(1) Change the image size here to a width of 600 and a height of 400. If you have Constrain Proportions checked, then all you have to do is type the new width, 600, and Elements will change the height to 400 for you.

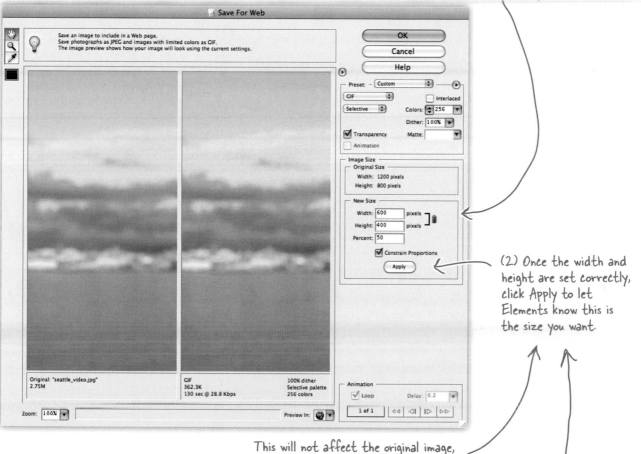

(2) Once the width and height are set correctly, click Apply to let Elements know this is the size you want.

This will not affect the original image, just the file you're going to save.

You must click Apply to reduce the image size; otherwise, the image will be saved at its original width and height.

You've resized—now save

Now you just need to save the image in the correct format (JPEG). To do that, you need to choose JPEG format and set the quality to Medium. We'll talk more about quality in a sec.

(1) Now that the image size is set, you just need to choose the format for the image. Currently it's set to save as GIF; change this to JPEG like we've done here.

(2) Set the quality to Medium.

(3) That's it; click OK and go to the next page.

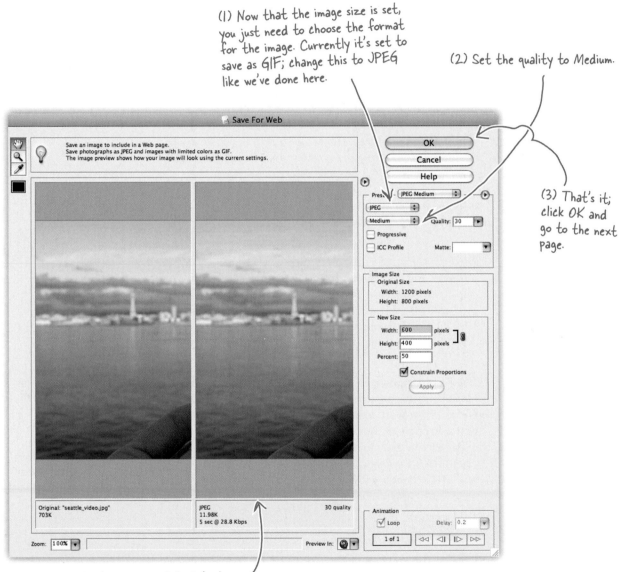

Notice that when you clicked Apply in the previous step, the image was resized and redisplayed.

Save the image

After you click OK, you'll get a Save dialog. Save the image as "seattle_video_med.jpg" so you don't overwrite the original photo.

Change the filename to seattle_video_med.jpg.

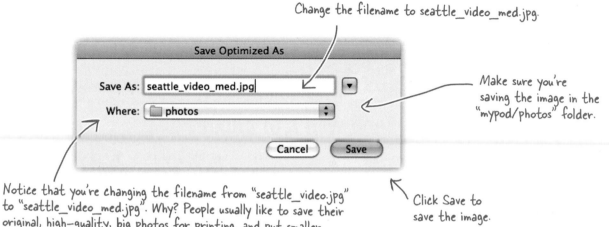

Make sure you're saving the image in the "mypod/photos" folder.

Click Save to save the image.

Notice that you're changing the filename from "seattle_video.jpg" to "seattle_video_med.jpg". Why? People usually like to save their original, high-quality, big photos for printing, and put smaller versions on the Web. If you saved this as "seattle_video.jpg", you'd be losing the original photo!

there are no Dumb Questions

Q: Can you say more about the quality setting in "Save for Web"?

A: The JPEG format allows you to specify the level of image quality you need. The lower the quality, the smaller the file size. If you look at the preview pane in the "Save for Web" dialog, you can see both the quality and file size change as you change the quality settings.

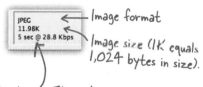

Image format

Image size (1K equals 1,024 bytes in size).

Photoshop Elements even tells you how long it would take to transfer over a dial-up modem to a browser.

The best way to get a feel for quality settings and the various image formats is to experiment with them on your own images. You'll soon figure out what quality levels are needed for your image and the type of web page you're developing. You'll also get to know when to use JPEG versus other formats.

Q: What is the number 30 next to the Quality label in the JPEG Options dialog box?

A: The number 30 is what Photoshop Elements considers Medium quality. JPEG actually uses a scale of 1–100%, and Low, Medium, High, etc. are just preset values that many photo editing applications use.

Q: Couldn't I just use the <img> element's width and height attributes to resize my image instead?

A: You could use the width and height attributes to resize an image, but that's not a good idea. Why? Because if you do that, you're still downloading the full-size image, and making the browser do the work to resize the image (just like when you have the auto resize option on in browsers that support that feature). The width and height attributes are really there to help the browser figure out how much space to reserve for the image; if you use them, they should match the actual width and height of the image.

Fixing up the myPod HTML

Once you've saved the image, you can close Photoshop Elements. Now all you need to do is change the myPod "index.html" page to include the new version of the photo, "seattle_video_med.jpg". Here's a snippet of the "index.html" file, showing only the parts you need to change.

```html
<html>
    <head>
        <title>myPod</title>
        <style type="text/css">
            body { background-color: #eaf3da;}
        </style>
    </head>
    <body>
        .
        .
        .
        <h2>Seattle, Washington</h2>
        <p>
            Me and my iPod in Seattle! You can see the
            Space Needle. You can't see the 628 coffee shops.
        </p>

        <p>
            <img src="photos/seattle_video_med.jpg" alt="My iPod in Seattle, WA">
        </p>

    </body>
</html>
```

The rest of the HTML goes here. You've already got it in your "index.html" file.

All you need to do is change the filename in the <img> element to the name of the image you just made: "seattle_video_med.jpg".

And now for the test drive...

Go ahead and make the changes, save them, and reload "index.html" in your browser. Things should look much better. Now the image is sized just right to give your visitors a good view—without overwhelming them with a large photo.

Now the image fits nicely in the browser window. And it's a smaller file size too, which will help the page load more quickly.

WHICH IMAGE FORMAT?

Your task this time: open the file "chapter5/testimage/eye.jpg" in Photoshop Elements. Open the "Save for Web" dialog and fill in the blanks below by choosing each quality setting for JPEG (Low, Medium, High, etc.), as well as PNG-24 and GIF. You'll find this information in the preview pane below the image. Once you've finished, determine which setting makes the most sense for this image.

JPEG
11.98K
5 sec @ 28.8 Kbps

Format
Size of image
Time to transfer over dial-up modem

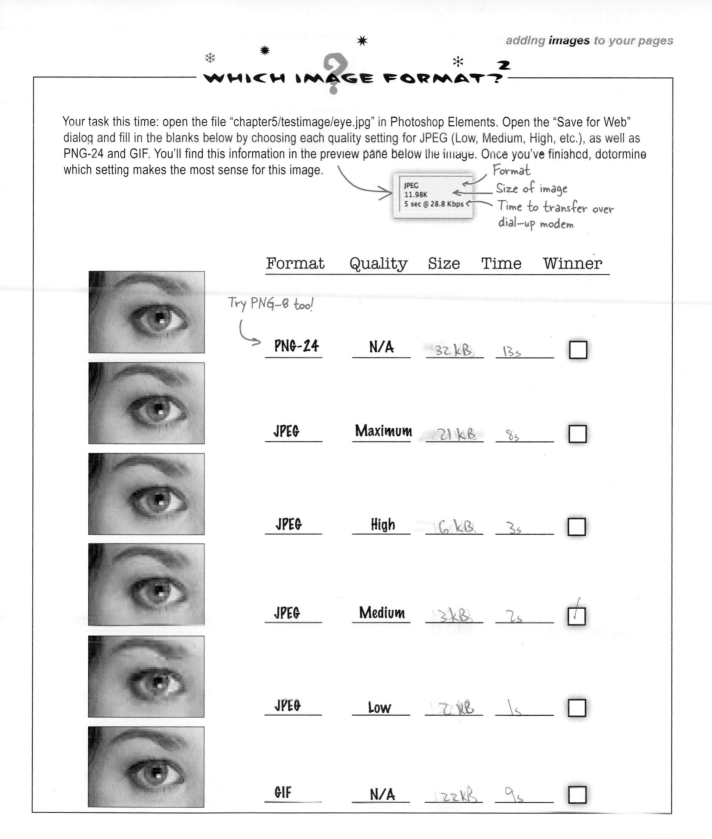

Format	Quality	Size	Time	Winner
PNG-24	N/A	32 KB	13s	☐
JPEG	Maximum	21 KB	8s	☐
JPEG	High	6 KB	3s	☐
JPEG	Medium	13 KB	2s	☑
JPEG	Low	7 KB	1s	☐
GIF	N/A	122 KB	9s	☐

Try PNG-8 too!

More photos for myPod

A new batch of photos has arrived for myPod: three more from Seattle and a few from a friend in Britain. The photos have already been resized to less than 800 pixels wide. Add the `<img>` elements for them (you'll find the images already in the photos folder):

```html
<html>
    <head>
        <title>myPod</title>
        <style type="text/css">
            body { background-color: #eaf3da;}
        </style>
    </head>
    <body>
        <h1>Welcome to myPod</h1>
        <p>
            Welcome to the place to show off your iPod, wherever you might be.
            Wanna join the fun? All you need is any iPod, from the early classic
            iPod to the latest iPod Nano, the smallest iPod Shuffle to the largest
            iPod Video, and a digital camera. Just take a snapshot of your iPod in
            your favorite location and we'll be glad to post it on myPod. So, what
            are you waiting for?
        </p>

        <h2>Seattle, Washington</h2>
        <p>
            Me and my iPod in Seattle! You can see the
            Space Needle. You can't see the 628 coffee shops.
        </p>

        <p>
            <img src="photos/seattle_video_med.jpg" alt="My video iPod in Seattle, WA">
            <img src="photos/seattle_classic.jpg" alt="A classic iPod in Seattle, WA">
            <img src="photos/seattle_shuffle.jpg" alt="An iPod Shuffle in Seattle, WA">
            <img src="photos/seattle_downtown.jpg" alt="An iPod in downtown Seattle, WA">
        </p>

        <h2>Birmingham, England</h2>
        <p>
            Here are some iPod photos around Birmingham. We've obviously got some
            passionate folks over here who love their iPods. Check out the classic
            red British telephone box!
        </p>

        <p>
            <img src="photos/britain.jpg" alt="An iPod in Birmingham at a telephone box">
            <img src="photos/applestore.jpg" alt="An iPod at the Birmingham Apple store">
        </p>
    </body>
</html>
```

Feel free to add some of your own photos here as well. Just remember to resize them first.

Let's keep all the Seattle photos together.

Same with the Birmingham photos...

Taking myPod for another test drive

At this point we don't need to tell you to reload the page
in your browser; we're sure you're way ahead of us. Wow,
what a difference a few images make, don't you think?
This page is starting to look downright interesting.

But that doesn't mean you're there yet. While you've got a
great set of images on the page, and even though you've
already resized them, the images are still quite large. Not
only is the page going to load more and more slowly as
you add more images, but also the user has to do a lot
of scrolling to see them all. Wouldn't it be better if users
could see a small "thumbnail" image for each photo, and
then click on the thumbnail to see the larger image?

*Here's what
the whole page
looks like now,
with all the
images.*

*And here's what the page
looks like now, close up.*

Reworking the site to use thumbnails

You're now going to make this page more usable by substituting a smaller image (which we call a *thumbnail*) for each photo, and then you'll create a link from that thumbnail to each of the larger photos. Here's how you're going to do this, one step at a time:

1 Create a new directory for the thumbnails.

2 Resize each photo to 150 by 100 pixels and save it in a "thumbnail" folder.

3 Set the `src` of each `<img>` element in "index.html" to the thumbnail version of the photo.

4 Add a link from each thumbnail to a new page containing the larger photo.

Create a new directory for thumbnails

To keep things organized, create a separate folder for the thumbnail images. Otherwise, you'll end up with a folder of larger images and small thumbnails all lumped together, which could get quite cluttered after you've added a significant number of photos.

Create a folder called "thumbnails" under the "mypod" folder. If you're working from the book example files, you'll find this folder already in there.

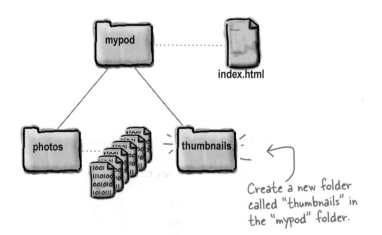

Create a new folder called "thumbnails" in the "mypod" folder.

Create the thumbnails

You've got a place to put your thumbnails, so let's create them. Start by opening "seattle_video_med.jpg" with your photo editing application. You're going to resize it to 150 by 100 pixels using the same method you used to create the 600 by 400 version:

In Photoshop Elements, choose the "Save for Web" menu option.

Then change the width to 150 and the height to 100 and click Apply.

Don't forget to change the format to JPEG, Medium quality.

Finally, click OK.

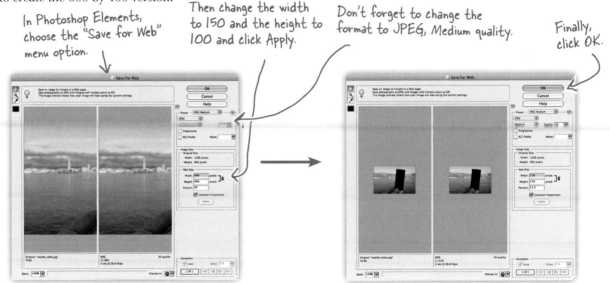

With the image resized, choose OK and save it as the same name but *in the thumbnail folder*. **Be careful**: if you save it to the "photos" folder, you'll be replacing the larger image.

Now, repeat this for each photo in your "photos" folder.

If you're working with the example files, you'll find the thumbnails already in the "thumbnails" folder, so you don't have to do every one (after all, you're learning HTML, not batch photo processing).

> What about the photos from Birmingham—they are taller than they are wide. Does 150x100 make sense?

Good catch. Because these images are taller than they are wide, we have two choices: we can switch the dimensions and make them 100 by 150, or we can crop each image and make a 150-by-100-pixel thumbnail from it. We're going to make ours 100 by 150; feel free to crop them and create 150-by-100-pixel images if you'd like to explore how to do that in your photo editing application.

Rework the HTML to use the thumbnails

Now you just need to change the HTML so that the `<img>` elements get their images from the "thumbnails" folder rather than the "photos" folder. And because you're currently using relative paths like "photos/seattle_video_med.jpg", that's going to be simple: for each `<img>` element, all you need to do is change the folder from "photos" to "thumbnails".

```html
<html>
    <head>
        <title>myPod</title>
        <style type="text/css">
            body { background-color: #eaf3da;}
        </style>
    </head>
    <body>
        <h1>Welcome to myPod</h1>
        <p>
            Welcome to the place to show off your iPod, wherever you might be.
            Wanna join the fun? All you need is any iPod, from the early classic
            iPod to the latest iPod Nano, the smallest iPod Shuffle to the largest
            iPod Video, and a digital camera. Just take a snapshot of your iPod in
            your favorite location and we'll be glad to post it on myPod. So, what
            are you waiting for?
        </p>

        <h2>Seattle, Washington</h2>
        <p>
            Me and my iPod in Seattle! You can see the
            Space Needle. You can't see the 628 coffee shops.
        </p>

        <p>
            <img src="thumbnails/seattle_video_med.jpg" alt="My video iPod in Seattle, WA">
            <img src="thumbnails/seattle_classic.jpg" alt="A classic iPod in Seattle, WA">
            <img src="thumbnails/seattle_shuffle.jpg" alt="An iPod Shuffle in Seattle, WA">
            <img src="thumbnails/seattle_downtown.jpg" alt="An iPod in downtown Seattle, WA">
        </p>

        <h2>Birmingham, England</h2>
        <p>
            Here are some iPod photos around Birmingham. We've obviously got some
            passionate folks over here who love their iPods. Check out the classic
            red British telephone box!
        </p>

        <p>
            <img src="thumbnails/britain.jpg" alt="An iPod in Birmingham at a telephone box">
            <img src="thumbnails/applestore.jpg" alt="An iPod at the Birmingham Apple store">
        </p>
    </body>
</html>
```

All you need to do is change the folder from "photos" to "thumbnails".

Take myPod for another test drive

Ahhh…much better. Visitors can see all the available pictures at a glance. They can also tell which photos go with each city more easily. Now we need to find a way to link from each thumbnail to the corresponding large image.

Wait a sec, don't you think you're pulling a fast one? The images used to be on top of each other; now they're side by side.

Right, but remember the <img> element is an <u>inline</u> element.

In other words, we didn't "pull anything." Because <img> is displayed as an inline element, it doesn't cause linebreaks to be inserted before and after the element is displayed. So, if there are several images together in your HTML, the browser will fit them side by side if the browser window is wide enough.

The reason the larger photos weren't side by side is because the browser didn't have room to display them next to each other. Instead, it displayed them on top of each other. A browser always displays vertical space before and after a block element, and if you look back at the screenshots, you'll see the images are right on top of each other with no space in between. That's another sign <img> is an inline element.

Turning the thumbnails into links

You're almost there. Now you just need to create a link from each thumbnail image to its larger version. Here's how this is going to work:

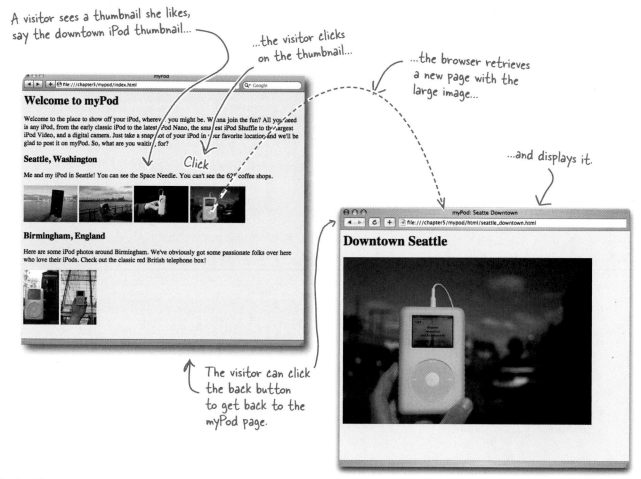

A visitor sees a thumbnail she likes, say the downtown iPod thumbnail...

...the visitor clicks on the thumbnail...

...the browser retrieves a new page with the large image...

...and displays it.

Click

The visitor can click the back button to get back to the myPod page.

To do this you need two things:

1. **A page to display each photo along with a heading that describes its content.**

2. **A link from each thumbnail in "index.html" to its corresponding photo page.**

Let's create the pages first, and then we'll come back and finish off the links.

Create individual pages for the photos

First, create a new folder called "html" to hold these individual pages, just below the "mypod" folder:

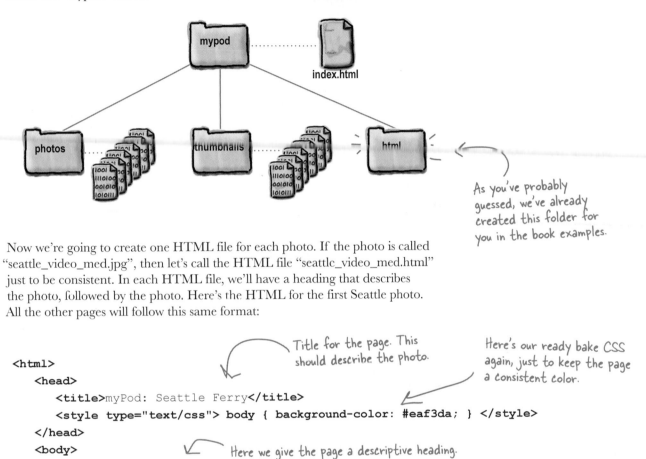

As you've probably guessed, we've already created this folder for you in the book examples.

Now we're going to create one HTML file for each photo. If the photo is called "seattle_video_med.jpg", then let's call the HTML file "seattlc_video_med.html" just to be consistent. In each HTML file, we'll have a heading that describes the photo, followed by the photo. Here's the HTML for the first Seattle photo. All the other pages will follow this same format:

Title for the page. This should describe the photo.

Here's our ready bake CSS again, just to keep the page a consistent color.

```
<html>
    <head>
        <title>myPod: Seattle Ferry</title>
        <style type="text/css"> body { background-color: #eaf3da; } </style>
    </head>
    <body>
        <h1>Seattle Ferry</h1>
        <p>
            <img src="../photos/seattle_video_med.jpg" alt="A video iPod on the ferry">
        </p>
    </body>
</html>
```

Here we give the page a descriptive heading.

Here's the <img> element that points to the large "seattle_video_med.jpg" photo. Let's also give the image a descriptive alt attribute.

Notice that we need to use ".." in the relative path because the "html" folder is a sibling of the "photos" folder, so we have to go up one folder and then down into "photos" when using relative links.

Exercise

If you look in the "html" folder in the chapter example files, you'll find all of the single photo pages already there, except one—the page for "seattle_downtown.jpg". Create a page called "seattle_downtown.html" in the "html" folder, and test it out. Get this working before you move on. You'll find the answer in the back of the chapter if you have any problems.

So, how do I make links out of images?

You've got your large photos, your smaller thumbnails, and even a set of HTML pages for displaying individual photos. Now you need to put it all together and get those thumbnails in "index.html" linked to the pages in the "html" folder. But how?

To link an image, you put the <img> element inside an <a> element, like this:

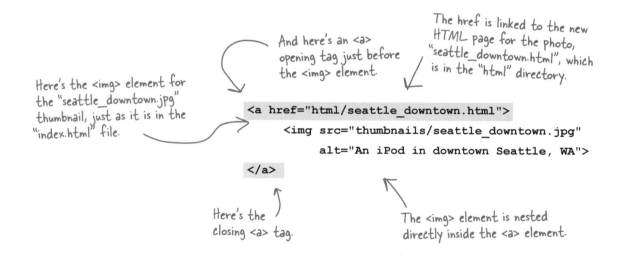

Here's the <img> element for the "seattle_downtown.jpg" thumbnail, just as it is in the "index.html" file.

And here's an <a> opening tag just before the <img> element.

The href is linked to the new HTML page for the photo, "seattle_downtown.html", which is in the "html" directory.

```
<a href="html/seattle_downtown.html">
        <img src="thumbnails/seattle_downtown.jpg"
             alt="An iPod in downtown Seattle, WA">
</a>
```

Here's the closing <a> tag.

The <img> element is nested directly inside the <a> element.

Once you've placed the <img> element into an <a> element, the browser treats the image as a clickable link. When you click the image, the browser will retrieve the page in the href.

Add the image links to "index.html"

This is the last step. You just need to wrap <a> elements around each thumbnail's <img> element in your "index.html" file. Remember, the href of each <a> element should link to the page containing the large version of the image in the "html" folder. Make sure that your links, thumbnails, and pages all match up correctly.

Here's the complete "index.html" file. All you need to do is add the HTML marked in gray.

```html
<html>
    <head>
        <title>myPod</title>
        <style type="text/css">
            body { background-color: #eaf3da;}
        </style>
    </head>
    <body>

        <h1>Welcome to myPod</h1>
        <p>
            Welcome to the place to show off your iPod, wherever you might be.
            Wanna join the fun? All you need is any iPod, from the early classic
            iPod to the latest iPod Nano, the smallest iPod Shuffle to the largest
            iPod Video, and a digital camera. Just take a snapshot of your iPod in
            your favorite location and we'll be glad to post it on myPod. So, what
            are you waiting for?
        </p>


        <h2>Seattle, Washington</h2>
        <p>
            Me and my iPod in Seattle! You can see the
            Space Needle. You can't see the 628 coffee shops.
        </p>


        <p>
        <a href="html/seattle_video_med.html">
            <img src="thumbnails/seattle_video_med.jpg" alt="My video iPod in Seattle, WA">
        </a>
        <a href="html/seattle_classic.html">
            <img src="thumbnails/seattle_classic.jpg" alt="A classic iPod in Seattle, WA">
        </a>
        <a href="html/seattle_shuffle.html">
            <img src="thumbnails/seattle_shuffle.jpg" alt="A iPod Shuffle in Seattle, WA">
        </a>
```

```
<a href="html/seattle_downtown.html">
    <img src="thumbnails/seattle_downtown.jpg" alt="An iPod in downtown Seattle, WA">
</a>
</p>


<h2>Birmingham, England</h2>
<p>
    Here are some iPod photos around Birmingham. We've obviously got some
    passionate folks over here who love their iPods. Check out the classic
    red British telephone box!
</p>


<p>
<a href="html/britain.html">
   <img src="thumbnails/britain.jpg" alt="An iPod in Birmingham at a telephone box">
</a>
<a href="html/applestore.html">
    <img src="thumbnails/applestore.jpg" alt="An iPod at the Birmingham Apple store">
</a>
    </p>
  </body>
</html>
```

For each thumbnail image, wrap an <a> element around it.
Just be careful to get the right href in each link!

Add these <a> elements to your "index.html" file.
Save, load into your browser, and check out myPod!

there are no Dumb Questions

Q: When we put an <a> element around text, we get an underline. Why don't we get something equivalent with images?

A: Actually, Internet Explorer puts a border around an image to show it is linked. (Our browser, Safari, doesn't do that.) If your browser puts a border around or a line under your linked images, and you don't like it, hold on a few more chapters and you'll learn how to change that with CSS. Also notice that when you pass your mouse over an image, your cursor will change to indicate you can click on the linked image. In most cases your users will know an image is linked by context and by the mouse cursor, even if there's no border.

Q: Can't we just link to the JPEG image directly without all those HTML pages? I thought the browser was smart enough to display images by themselves.

A: You're right; you could link directly to the image, like this: <a href="photos/seattle_downtown.jpg"> ... </a>. If you did that and clicked on the link, the browser would display the image by itself on a blank page. In general, though, linking directly to an image is considered bad form, because you usually want to provide some context for the images you are displaying.

The myPod web page is looking awesome! I think you should add a logo to the page—that would add a great finishing touch.

Great idea. In fact, we've got a myPod logo all ready to go.

Take another look in the folder "chapter5/mypod", and you'll find a folder called "logo". In that folder you'll find a file called "mypod.psd". The ".psd" means that the file has been saved in the Photoshop format, a common format for image editing software. But Photoshop format files are meant for processing digital images, not for web pages, so we'll have to do some work to get a "web ready" image from it.

Many photo editing applications understand .psd files, so even if you don't have Photoshop Elements, follow along for the next few pages. If your application can't open the ".psd" file, you'll find the images from each step in the "logo" folder.

Open the myPod logo

Let's check out the myPod logo: open up the file "mypod.psd" in the "chapter5/mypod/logo" folder in Photoshop Elements:

You'll find the "logo" folder in the "chapter5/mypod" folder.

If your photo editing application won't open the file, follow along anyway—the same principles apply for other formats as well.

A closer look...

Nice logo; it's got some typography combined with two circles, one gray and one white (obviously inspired by the click-wheel controls on the classic iPod).

But what is that checkered pattern in the background? That's the way most photo editing applications show you areas that are transparent. Keep all that in mind as we choose a graphic format for the logo…

Whenever you see this checkered pattern, that indicates a transparent area in the image.

What format should we use?

You already know that we have a couple of options in deciding how to save this image: we could use JPEG, PNG, or GIF. This logo uses only three colors, text, and some geometric shapes. From what you've learned about the two formats, you're probably leaning toward PNG or GIF. Either would be fine; the PNG might be a slightly smaller file at the same quality, so we'll go with PNG. And, because we only have three colors, we'll be safe using PNG-8 which allows only 256 colors, so using this format will reduce the file size even more.

So, go ahead and choose the "Save for Web" option under the File menu, and then choose PNG-8 in the format drop-down. You'll see we have a few more options. Let's take a look…

Remember, use this pull-down menu to set the format. We're going to set the format to PNG-8 to save the logo.

Here's where Photoshop Elements shows you the number of colors being used to save the PNG. It's already set to the maximum for PNG-8, 256. We'll leave it there.

When you set the format to PNG, this Transparency checkbox appears. By default, it's checked. Do we want a transparent background?

Also note the Matte option. This is related to transparency, as you'll see in a sec.

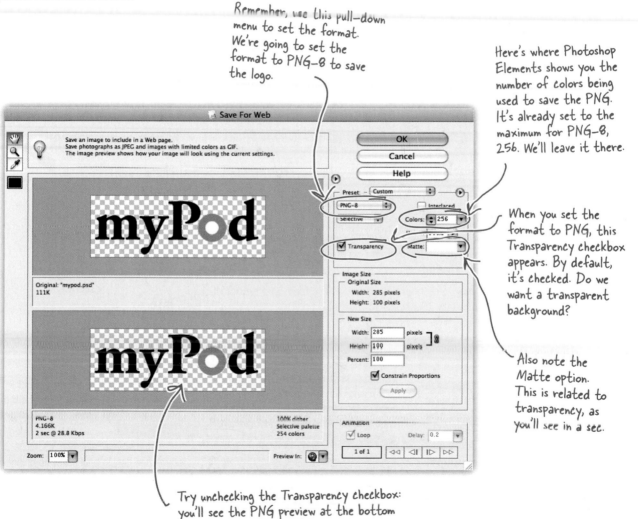

Try unchecking the Transparency checkbox: you'll see the PNG preview at the bottom change to a white background.

To be transparent, or not to be transparent? That is the question...

The myPod logo is going to be placed on a light green background, so you might think that transparency is going to be a good thing, right? Well, let's compare how the logo looks using a few options in the "Save for Web" dialog:

Here's the logo saved in three different ways and displayed on a web page with a green background.

myPod

myPod

myPod

Without transparency, things look pretty bad. Clearly, a white background isn't going to work on a green web page. (It might, however, work just fine on a white web page).

Here's what we get if we check Transparency and save. Better... but what's that white "halo" around the letters in the logo?

The halos happen because the photo editing application creates a "matte" to soften the text's edges against the background color. When it did that for this logo, however, it assumed it was softening the edges against a <u>white</u> background.

Ah, now we're talking; this looks great. For this version, we told Photoshop Elements to create the matte around the text using a <u>green</u> background. How? We'll show you next.

Save the transparent PNG

You know you want a transparent PNG version of the logo, and you also know we'll need to use a matte to prevent the halos around the text. Let's check out the PNG panel of the "Save for Web" dialog.

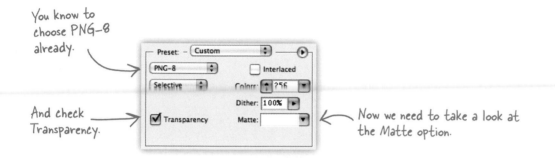

You know to choose PNG-8 already.

And check Transparency.

Now we need to take a look at the Matte option.

The Matte option allows you to select the color for the matte around the text. And we want that to be the color of the web page background.

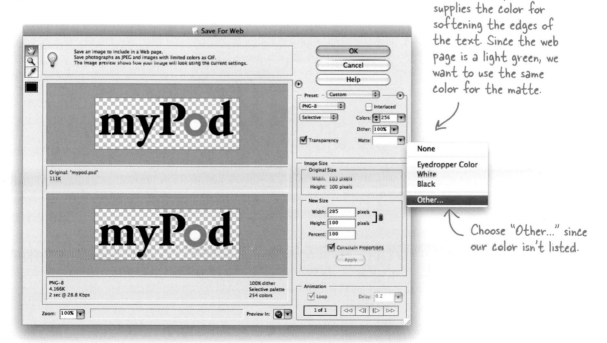

The Matte option supplies the color for softening the edges of the text. Since the web page is a light green, we want to use the same color for the matte.

Choose "Other..." since our color isn't listed.

Wait, what *is* the color of the web page background?

Remember that **Ready Bake CSS** in the myPod "index.html" file? That CSS is what sets the background color of the page to light green. And that's where we can get the color:

```
<style type="text/css">
    body { background-color: #eaf3da; }
</style>
```

Here's the background color right here.

What? You can't tell that's light green? For now, take our word for it; we'll come back to this in a few chapters and explain all about colors.

Set the matte color

When you click on the Matte pull-down menu and choose the "Other…" menu option, Photoshop Elements will bring up the Color Picker dialog.

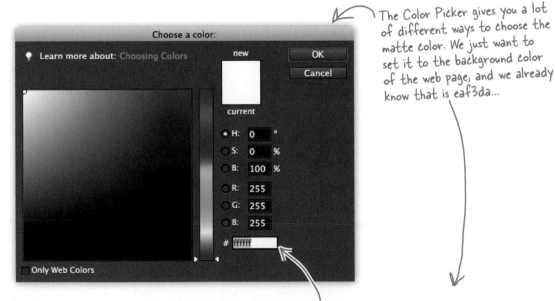

The Color Picker gives you a lot of different ways to choose the matte color. We just want to set it to the background color of the web page, and we already know that is eaf3da…

…which is going to go right here.

Set the matte color, continued

Go ahead and enter the color, "eaf3da", into the "Color Picker" dialog box. You'll see the color change to the background color of the myPod page.

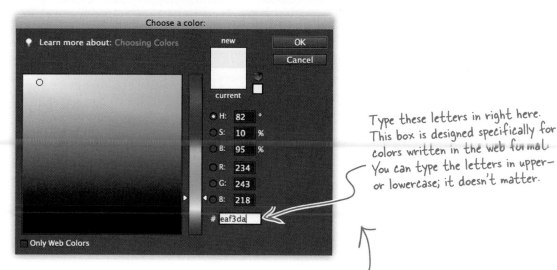

Type these letters in right here. This box is designed specifically for colors written in the web format. You can type the letters in upper- or lowercase; it doesn't matter.

Once you've typed the color into the Color Picker, click OK and it will apply the change to the logo.

Check out the logo with a matte

Now take a close look at the logo again in the preview pane. You'll see Photoshop Elements has added a light green matte around the hard edges, which will give the myPod logo text a softer, more polished look when the logo is in the web page.

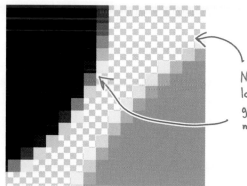

Now, when you look close up at the logo, you'll see the matte matches the green color in the background of the myPod web page.

Save the logo

Okay you've made all the adjustments you need to in the "Save for Web" dialog, so go ahead and click OK to save the image as "mypod.png".

> **Save Optimized As**
>
> Save As: mypod.png
>
> Where: 📁 logo
>
> Cancel   Save

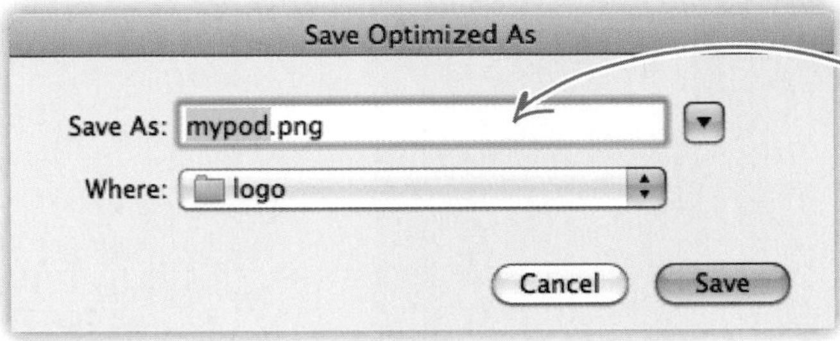

Elements will automatically change the extension of your filename to ".png". Save the image as "mypod.png" in the "logo" folder.

Add the logo to the myPod web page

Now all you need to do is add the logo to the myPod web page. We'll add it to the top so it appears above the website description and iPod images. That way, it's the first thing your visitors see when they come to your myPod page.

```html
<html>
   <head>
      <title>myPod</title>
      <style type="text/css">
         body { background-color: #eaf3da;}
      </style>
   </head>
   <body>
      <p>
         <img src="logo/mypod.png" alt="myPod Logo">
      </p>

      <h1>Welcome to myPod</h1>
         .
         .
         .
   </body>
</html>
```

Add the logo image at the top of the myPod web page. Remember to use the correct relative path for the logo, in the "logo" folder, and add an alt attribute that describes the image.

Rest of "index.html" HTML here...

And now for the final test drive

Let's test this puppy! Reload the web page in the browser
and see how your myPod transparent PNG logo works.

And it works—all that hard work paid off. You have a great-looking logo on your myPod web page.

Excellent work. The logo looks great. You've got a kick-ass myPod website here!

there are no Dumb Questions

Q: **Do I really need to know all this stuff about image formats to write good web pages?**

A: No. You can build great web pages without any images. However, images are a big part of the Web, so some knowledge of how images work can really help. Sometimes just an image or two makes the difference between a good page and a great one. There's a lot to know about images, but it's easy to learn as you go.

Q: **Why does the text need its edges softened?**

A: Check out the two versions of the myPod logo below:

myPod
myPod

You'll see the top version has very hard, jagged edges and is less readable. This is the way text is displayed by default on a computer screen. The second version has had its edges softened using a technique called *anti-aliasing*. Words that are anti-aliased on a computer screen are more readable and more pleasant to the eye.

Q: **So where does the matte come in?**

A: The process of anti-aliasing softens the edges relative to the background color. If you put the bottom version of the logo (from the previous Q&A) against a colored background, you'd see it has white edges in it. The Matte option in Photoshop Elements allows you to specify the color of the background that the text will be placed on, so when the text is softened it is done so against that color.

Q: **Does this technique just work for text?**

A: No, it works for any lines in your graphics that might result in "jaggies." Check out the circle in the myPod logo; it was matted too.

Q: **Why can't I just make the logo background color solid and match the color to the web page?**

A: You could do that too, but there is one disadvantage: if there are other things in your web page that are showing through the transparency, then they won't be seen with the solid color version. You haven't seen any examples of this yet, but when we get into CSS, you will.

Q: **What if I change my background color after I make the matted version?**

A: A slight variation in your background color probably wouldn't be noticeable; however, if you change the color dramatically, you'll have to recreate the PNG with a new matte color.

If you're placing a transparent image in your web page, make sure the matte color of the image matches the background color of your web page.

You can use **PNG** or **GIF** format for your transparent image.

BULLET POINTS

- Use the <img> element to place images in your web page.

- Browsers treat <img> elements a little differently than other HTML elements; after reading the HTML page, the browser retrieves each image from the web server and displays it.

- If you have more than a couple of large images on a web page, you can make your web page more usable and faster to download by creating thumbnails—small images that the user can click on to see the large version of the image.

- The <img> element is an inline element, which means that the browser doesn't put a linebreak before or after an image.

- The src attribute is how you specify the location of the image file. You can include images from your own site using a relative path in the src attribute, or images from other sites using a URL.

- The alt attribute of an <img> element is a meaningful description of the image. It is displayed in some browsers if the image can't be located, and is used by screen readers to describe the image for the visually impaired.

- A width of less than 800 pixels is a good rule of thumb for the size of photo images in a web page. Most photo images that are created by digital cameras are too large for web pages, so you'll need to resize them.

- Photoshop Elements is one of many photo editing applications you can use to resize your images. You can also use one of many free online tools to resize images. Just search for "free online image editor."

- Images that are too large for the browser make web pages difficult to use and slow to download and display.

- JPEG, PNG, and GIF are the three formats for images that are widely supported by web browsers.

- The JPEG format is best for photographs and other complex images.

- The GIF or PNG format is best for logos and other simple graphics with solid colors, lines, or text.

- JPEG images can be compressed at a variety of different qualities, so you can choose the best balance of quality and file size for your needs.

- The GIF and PNG image formats allow you to make an image with a transparent background. If you put an image with a transparent background in a web page, what's behind the image, such as the background color of the page, will show through the transparent parts of the image.

- GIF and PNG are lossless formats, which means the file sizes are likely to be larger than JPEG.

- PNG has better transparency control than GIF, and allows many more colors than GIF, which is limited to 256.

- PNG has three different size options: PNG-24 (supports millions of colors), PNG-16 (supports thousands of colors), and PNG-8 (supports 256 colors), depending on your needs.

- In Photoshop Elements, use the Matte color menu in the "Save for Web" dialog to choose the right color for softening the edges of your transparent PNG or GIF image.

- Images can be used as links to other web pages. To create a link from an image, use the <img> element as the content of an <a> element, and put the link in the href attribute of the <a> element.

HTMLcross

It's time to give your right brain another break and put that left brain to work. All these words are HTML-related and from this chapter.

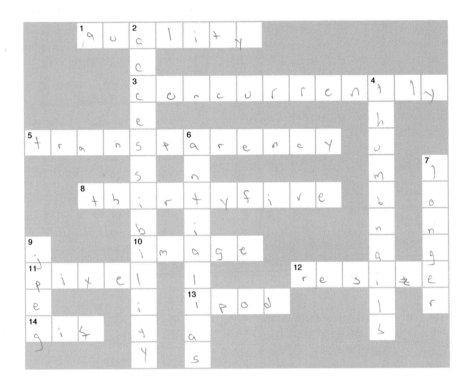

Across

1. With JPEG, you can control this.
3. Most web browsers retrieve images this way.
5. PNG and GIF have it, JPEG doesn't.
8. Miles you can draw with a pencil.
10. Web server makes a request for each one of these.
11. Smallest element on a screen.
12. You used Photoshop Elements to do this to images.
13. Lovable MP3 player.
14. Better for solid colors, lines, and small text.

Down

2. The alt attribute improves this.
4. Small images on a page.
6. Technique for softening edges of text.
7. The larger the image, the _____ it takes to transfer it.
9. Better for photos with continuous tones.

WHICH IMAGE FORMAT?
SOLUTION

Congratulations: you've been elected "Grand Image Format Chooser" of the day. For each image below, choose the format that would best represent it for the Web.

JPEG or PNG or GIF

A photo with lots of continuous shades of gray.

☑ ☐ ☐

Only a couple of colors with some text; definitely a PNG or GIF. No transparency? PNG might yield a smaller file.

☐ ☑ ☑

A photo with lots of colors; definitely a JPEG or PNG; and if you want a transparent background, go with PNG.

☑ ☑ ☐

Just a simple black and white icon; a PNG or GIF. If you need transparency, you might want anti-aliasing on the edges, and PNG would be better for that.

☐ ☑ ☑

This image is borderline. It has lots of continuous colors (JPEG), but is also slightly geometric (GIF) and you may want to use this in a way that requires transparency (PNG).

☑ ☑ ☑

Sharpen your pencil
Solution

Here's a "Sharpen your pencil" that is actually about pencils (oh, and images too). This exercise involves a bit of trivia: *Given a typical, brand-new pencil, if you drew one continuous line with it, using the entire pencil up, how long would the line be?*

What's that got to do with images? To find the answer, you had to write some HTML. The answer to this trivia is contained in the image that is at the URL: http://wickedlysmart.com/hfhtmlcss/trivia/pencil.png. Your job was to add an image to this HTML and retrieve the answer. Here's our solution.

```html
<html>
    <head>
        <title>Sharpen your pencil trivia</title>
    </head>
    <body>
        <p>How long a line can you draw with the typical pencil?</p>
        <p>
            <img src="http://wickedlysmart.com/hfhtmlcss/trivia/pencil.png">
        </p>
    </body>
</html>
```

If you put the image here, you can see the answer when you load the page.

How long a line can you draw with the typical pencil?

The typical new pencil can draw a line 35 miles long.

Source: http://www.papermate.com

EXERCISE SOLUTION

Here are the results of having a broken image in a few different browsers. In most cases, the browser is able to use the extra alt attribute information to improve what is displayed. Why do we care? After all, this is an error in a web page; we should just fix it, right? Well, in the real world, things are often not ideal; sometimes things break, Internet connections go bad in the middle of a page load, or visually impaired users need to hear what is in the image, because they can't see it.

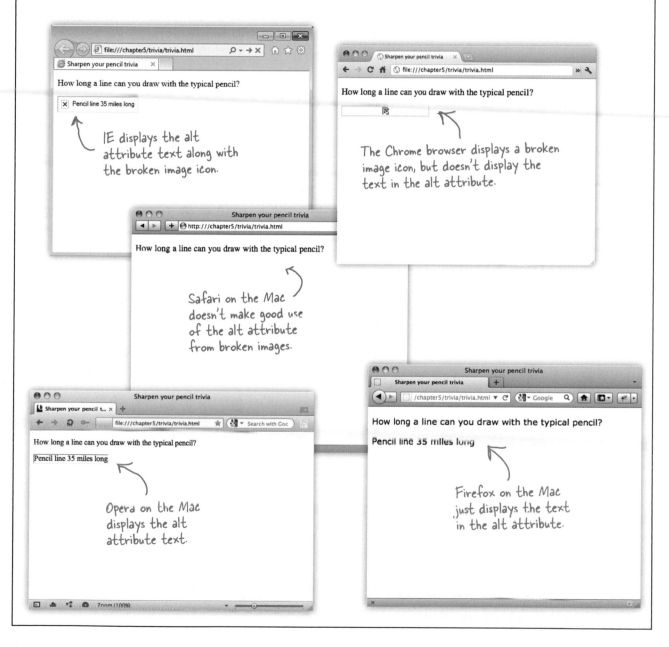

IE displays the alt attribute text along with the broken image icon.

The Chrome browser displays a broken image icon, but doesn't display the text in the alt attribute.

Safari on the Mac doesn't make good use of the alt attribute from broken images.

Opera on the Mac displays the alt attribute text.

Firefox on the Mac just displays the text in the alt attribute.

WHICH IMAGE FORMAT?²
SOLUTION

Your task this time: open the file "chapter5/testimage/eye.jpg" in Photoshop Elements. Open the "Save for Web" dialog and fill in the blanks below by choosing each quality setting for JPEG (Low, Medium, High, etc.), and also try PNG-24 and GIF. You'll find this information in the preview pane below the image. Once you've finished, determine which setting makes the most sense for this image.

Note that your numbers may differ depending on the version of software you are using.

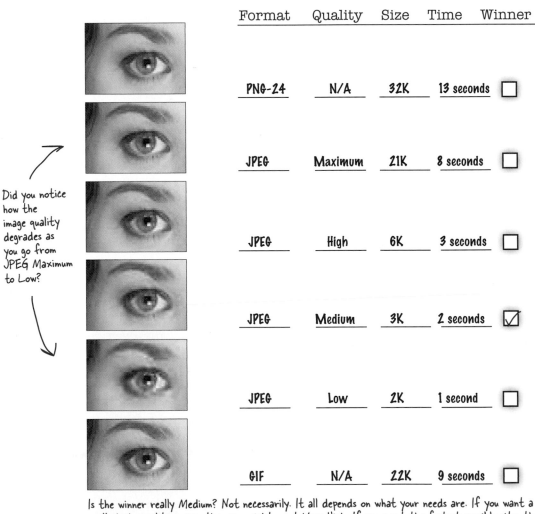

Did you notice how the image quality degrades as you go from JPEG Maximum to Low?

Format	Quality	Size	Time	Winner
PNG-24	N/A	32K	13 seconds	☐
JPEG	Maximum	21K	8 seconds	☐
JPEG	High	6K	3 seconds	☐
JPEG	Medium	3K	2 seconds	☑
JPEG	Low	2K	1 second	☐
GIF	N/A	22K	9 seconds	☐

Is the winner really Medium? Not necessarily. It all depends on what your needs are. If you want a really high-quality image, then you might want Very High. If you want the fastest possible site, then try Low. We've chosen Medium because it is a nice tradeoff in size versus the quality of the image. You may think Low is good enough, or that it's worth bumping the quality up to High. So, it's all very subjective. One thing is for sure, however: PNG and GIF don't work very well for this image (which should not be a surprise).

Exercise Solution

If you look in the "html" folder with the chapter examples, you'll find all of the single photo pages already there, except one: the page for "seattle_downtown.jpg". Create a page called "seattle_downtown.html" in the "html" folder, and test it out. Get this working before you move on,

Here's the answer:

Here's the HTML; this file should be called "seattle_downtown.html".

```html
<html>
    <head>
        <title>myPod: Seattle Downtown</title>
        <style type="text/css"> body { background-color: #eaf3da; } </style>
    </head>
    <body>
        <h1>Downtown Seattle</h1>
        <p>
        <img src="../photos/seattle_downtown.jpg" alt="An iPod in downtown Seattle, WA">
        </p>
    </body>
</html>
```

This file should go in the "html" folder under "mypod".

Here's the test drive.

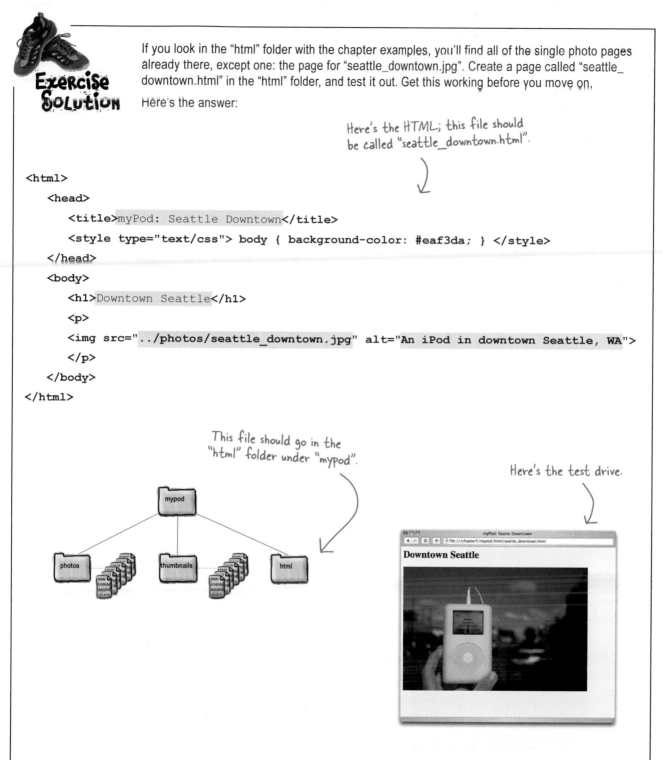

HTMLcross Solution

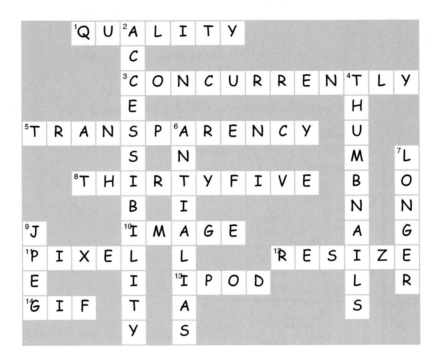

The completed crossword puzzle reads:

- 1 Across: QUALITY
- 2 Down: ACCESSIBLE
- 3 Across: CONCURRENTLY
- 4 Down: THUMBNAIL
- 5 Across: TRANSPARENCY
- 6 Down: ANTIALIAS
- 7 Down: LONGER
- 8 Across: THIRTYFIVE
- 9 Down: J
- 10 Across: IMAGE
- 11 Across: PIXEL
- 12 Across: RESIZE
- 13 Across: IPOD
- 14 Across: GIF

![Sharpen your pencil] **Sharpen your pencil Solution**

Here's how you add the image "seattle.jpg" to the file "index.html".

```
<h2>Seattle, Washington</h2>
<p>
    Me and my iPod in Seattle! You can see rain clouds and the
    Space Needle.  You can't see the 628 coffee shops.
</p>
<p>
    <img src="photos/seattle.jpg" alt="My iPod in Seattle, WA">
</p>
```

Getting Serious with HTML

What else is there to know about HTML? You're well on your way to mastering HTML. In fact, isn't it about time we move on to CSS and learn how to make all this bland markup look fabulous? Before we do, we need to make sure your HTML is really ready for the big leagues. Don't get us wrong, you've been writing first class HTML all along, but there are just a few extra things you need to do to make it "industry standard" HTML. It's also time you think about making sure you're using the latest and greatest HTML standard, otherwise known as HTML5. By doing so, you'll ensure they'll display more uniformly across all browsers (at least the ones you'd care about), not to mention, they'll play well with the latest i-Devices (pick your favorite). You'll also have pages that load faster, pages that are guaranteed to play well with CSS, and pages that are ready to move into the future as the standards grow. Get ready, this is the chapter where you move from web tinkerer to web professional.

Hey guys, the boss just sent an email. Before we add CSS to the Head First Lounge, he wants us to make sure our HTML is ready for prime time.

Jim

Frank

Joe

Jim: Ready for prime time?

Frank: Yeah, you know, make sure it's totally legit and ready for HTML5.

Jim: Our HTML is just fine…here, look at it in the browser. It looks beautiful.

Joe: Yeah, that's what I think…he's just trying to give us another thing to do.

Frank: Actually guys, I hate to admit it, but I think the boss is right on this one.

Jim, Joe: Huh?

Frank: Up until now we've pretty much ignored the fact that there are standards for this stuff. Not to mention there are different versions of HTML, like HTML 4.01, and now, HTML5. Are we doing everything we need to make sure we've got HTML5 covered?

Joe: Come on, this is just going to mean even more work. We've already got enough to do. Really, the page looks fine; I've even tested it on some of the newer devices.

Frank: That may be, but what I'm saying is that I think this will help us do less work in the future.

Joe: Oh yeah? How so?

Frank: Well, if we make sure our HTML is up-to-date with current standards, we won't have to make as many changes down the road. We should also make sure everything else is correct; you know, our syntax and all that. There are so many different browsers and versions of those browsers that if we're making mistakes in our HTML, then all bets are off in terms of how our pages will look in different browsers. And when we start adding presentation to HTML with CSS, the differences will get even more dramatic if our HTML isn't up to snuff.

Joe: So, by making sure we're adhering to the "standard," we'll have a lot fewer problems with our pages displaying incorrectly for our customers?

Frank: Right.

Jim: If it reduces the number of 3 a.m. calls I get, then that sounds like a good idea to me.

Joe: All right, how do we start? Don't we adhere to the standards now? What's wrong with our HTML?

Frank: Maybe nothing, but the boss wants to be current with HTML5, so we need to figure out which version of HTML we're using and if it's not HTML5, what we need to do to get there. And, when we're done, life should be much easier when we start using CSS.

Browsers all do a pretty good job of consistently displaying your pages when you write correct HTML, but when you make mistakes or do nonstandard things in your HTML, pages are often displayed differently from one browser to another. Why do you think that is the case?

A Brief History of HTML

HTML 1.0–2.0

These were the early days; you could fit everything there was to know about HTML into the back of your car. Pages weren't pretty, but at least they were hypertext enabled. No one cared much about presentation, and just about everyone on the Web had their very own "home page." Even a count of the number of pencils, paperclips, and Post-it notes on your desk was considered "web content" back then (you think we're kidding).

HTML 3

The long, cold days of the "Browser Wars." Netscape and Microsoft were duking it out for control of the world. After all, he who controls the browser controls the universe, right?

At the center of the fallout was the web developer. During the wars, an arms race emerged as each browser company kept adding their own proprietary extensions in order to stay ahead. Who could keep up? And not only that, back in those days, you had to often write two separate web pages: one for the Netscape browser and one for Internet Explorer. Not good.

HTML 4

Ahhh…the end of the Browser Wars and, to our rescue, the World Wide Web Consortium (nickname: W3C). Their plan: to bring order to the universe by creating the ONE HTML "standard" to rule them all.

The key to their plan? Separate HTML's structure and presentation into two languages—a language for structure (HTML) and a language for presentation (CSS)—and convince the browser makers it was in their best interest to adopt these standards.

But did their plan work?

Uh, almost…with a few changes (see HTML 4.01).

1989　　**1991**　　**1995**　　**1998**

Starting with this chapter, our goal is to write proper HTML5. As always, the world keeps moving, so we'll also talk about where things are going.

HTML 4.01

XHTML 1.0

HTML5

The good life: HTML 4.01 entered the scene in 1999, and was the "must have" version of HTML for the next decade.

4.01 wasn't really a big change from 4.0; just a few fixes were needed here and there. But compared to the early days of HTML (when we all had to walk barefoot in six feet of snow, uphill both ways), HTML 4.01 allowed us all to sleep well at night knowing that almost all browsers (at least the ones anyone would care about) were going to display our content just fine.

Just as we were all getting comfortable, a shiny object distracted everyone. That shiny object was XML. In fact, it really distracted HTML, and the two got hitched in a shotgun marriage that resulted in XHTML 1.0.

XHTML promised to end all the woes of the Web with its adherence to strictness and new way of doing things.

The only problem was, most people ended up hating XHTML. They didn't want a new way to write web pages, they just wanted to improve what they already had with HTML 4.01. Web developers were far more interested in HTML's flexibility than XHTML's strictness. And, more and more, these developers wanted to spend their time creating web pages that felt more like applications than documents (more on web apps later)…

Of course, with no support from the community, the marriage didn't end well and was replaced by new version of HTML named HTML5. With its support for most of the HTML 4.01 standard, and new features that reflect the way the Web has grown, HTML5 is what developers were looking for. And, with features like support for blog-like elements, new video and graphic capabilities, and a whole new set of capabilties aimed at building web applications, HTML5 was destined to become the standard.

To be honest, the divorce of HTML and XML took a lot of people by surprise, leading to confusion about what HTML5 actually *is* for a while. But that's all been sorted out, so read on to find out what HTML5 means to you, and how you can join in the fun.

1999	2001	2009	2012	????

And what will happen in the future? Will we all be going to work in flying cars and swallowing nutrition pills for dinner? Keep reading to find out.

The Browser Exposed

**This week's interview:
Why do you care so much about
which HTML version I'm using?**

Head First: We're glad to have you here, Browser. As you know, "HTML versions" have become a popular issue. What's the deal with that? You're a web browser, after all. I give you HTML and you display it the best you can.

Browser: Being a browser is tough…there are a lot of web pages out there, and many are written with old versions of HTML or with mistakes in their markup. Like you said, my job is to try to display every single one of those pages, no matter what.

Head First: So what's the big deal? You seem to be doing a pretty good job of it.

Browser: In some cases, sure, but have you ever looked at your pages on a lot of different browsers? When you are using old or incorrect markup, your page may look great on one browser, but not so great on another.

Head First: Really? Why is that? Don't you all do the same thing?

Browser: We do a great job of doing the same thing, *when we're displaying correct and up-to-date pages*. Like I said, when you venture into pages that aren't written well, then things get a lot dicier. Here's why: all of us browsers have the HTML specification to tell us how to display correct HTML, but when it comes to incorrect HTML, we just wing it. So, you might get very different behaviors on different browsers.

Head First: Ahh. So, what's the solution to this mess? We definitely want our pages to look good.

Browser: Easy. Tell me up front which version of HTML you're using. You'd be surprised how many pages don't even do that. And make sure your page doesn't contain any errors; you know, mismatched markup tags, that kind of thing.

Head First: How do we tell you which version we're using? Especially now that we're all moving on to HTML5.

Browser: Well, HTML5 is actually making things a little simpler.

Head First: Really? How is a new version of HTML helping? I would have thought yet another version would just make things even more difficult.

Browser: It's true that any new version of a language causes growing pains as everyone tries to catch up with the latest standard. But HTML5 simplifies the way you tell me the kind of HTML you're using. The HTML5 standard is also documenting many of the errors that can occur in web pages, so that all the browsers can be more consistent about how they handle those errors.

Head First: Oh, so does that mean we don't have to worry about making errors when we're writing our HTML?

Browser: No! Just because we can handle errors better doesn't mean you can be sloppy. You still want your page to be consistent with the standard and written without errors. If you don't, you might get inconsistent results across browsers, and let's not forget the browsers on mobile devices, too.

Head First: Back to how we tell you what version we're using?

Browser: Yeah, that used to be a total pain in the…

Head First: Uh, watch it, this is a PG-rated audience, and we're running out of time, quickly!

Browser: Okay, you can tell me all about the version of HTML you're using with a **doctype**. It's a little bit of "markup" you can use that goes at the very top of your HTML file. So, given we're out of time, go check it out!

HTML Archaeology

We did some digging and found some old HTML 4.01 and XHTML 1.1 pages. These pages use a doctype, at the very top of the HTML file, to tell the browser which version of HTML they're using. We've snipped out a couple of doctypes for you to look at. Check them out below...

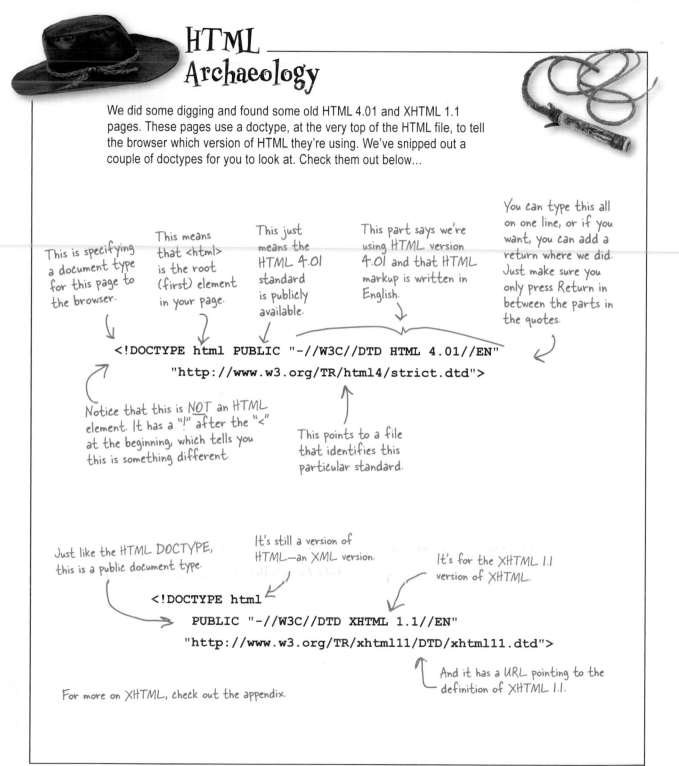

This is specifying a document type for this page to the browser.

This means that <html> is the root (first) element in your page.

This just means the HTML 4.01 standard is publicly available.

This part says we're using HTML version 4.01 and that HTML markup is written in English.

You can type this all on one line, or if you want, you can add a return where we did. Just make sure you only press Return in between the parts in the quotes.

```
<!DOCTYPE html PUBLIC "-//W3C//DTD HTML 4.01//EN"
        "http://www.w3.org/TR/html4/strict.dtd">
```

Notice that this is NOT an HTML element. It has a "!" after the "<" at the beginning, which tells you this is something different.

This points to a file that identifies this particular standard.

Just like the HTML DOCTYPE, this is a public document type.

It's still a version of HTML—an XML version.

It's for the XHTML 1.1 version of XHTML.

```
<!DOCTYPE html
    PUBLIC "-//W3C//DTD XHTML 1.1//EN"
    "http://www.w3.org/TR/xhtml11/DTD/xhtml11.dtd">
```

And it has a URL pointing to the definition of XHTML 1.1.

For more on XHTML, check out the appendix.

Sharpen your pencil

Rather than tell you the doctype definition for HTML5, we thought you might want to have fun working it out on your own. Take another look at the HTML 4.01 doctype definition below:

Remember, this is the doctype for "html".

And this means this standard is publicly available.

This part says we're using HTML version 4.01 and that this markup is written in ENglish.

```
<!DOCTYPE html PUBLIC "-//W3C//DTD HTML 4.01//EN"
         "http://www.w3.org/TR/html4/strict.dtd">
```

This points to a file that identifies this standard.

Remember, the doctype definition belongs at the top of your HTML file and tells the browser the type of your document—in this case, HTML 4.01. By using a doctype, the browser is able to be more precise in the way it interprets and renders your pages.

So, using your deductive powers, what do you think the doctype definition for HTML5 looks like? Write it here (you can refer back to your answer when we cover this on the next page, and no peeking at the answer!):

```
<!DOCTYPE html PUBLIC "-//W3C//DTD HTML 4.01//EN"
        "http://www.w3.org/TR/html5/strict.dtd">

<!doctype html>
```

Your answer goes here.

The new, and improved, HTML5 doctype

Okay, get ready for it. Here's the HTML5 doctype:

```
<!doctype html>
```

↑ And it's really simple!

← It's just one line; don't miss it.

How close was your answer in the Sharpen Your Pencil? This is much simpler, wouldn't you say? And, wow, you might even be able to remember it without having to look it up everytime you need a doctype.

← Our sympathies to those who had the old doctype tattooed on their palms to remember it.

Wait, isn't this supposed to tell the browser the version? Where's the version number? Is that a typo?

Good point. No, it's not a typo, and let's step through why: you know the doctype used to be a complicated mess full of version numbers and ugly syntax. But with the arrival of HTML5, the doctype was simplified so that now all we have to do is tell the browser we're using "html"; no more worrying about specific version numbers or languages or pointing to a standard.

How can that be? How can we just specify "html" without the rest? Doesn't the browser *need* that other information? Well, as it turns out, when the browser sees:

```
<!doctype html>
```

it assumes you're using standard HTML. No more getting all hung up on version numbers or where the standard is located; in fact, the HTML standard has become a "living standard," meaning that it will continue to grow and morph as needed, but without fixed version numbers. Now, you're probably thinking, "What exactly does a *living standard* mean? How is that going to work?" You'll see, on the next page…

HTML, the new "living standard"

You heard us right…rather than continue to crank out version 6, 7, 8 of HTML, the standards guys (and gals) have turned the specification into a living standard that will document the technology as it evolves. So, no more version numbers. And you can stop calling it HTML5 because it's just "HTML" from here on out.

Now, you're probably wondering how this is going to work in practice. After all, if the spec is continually changing, what does that mean for the poor browsers? Not to mention, for you, the web developer? One key to this working is *backwards compatibility*. Backwards compatibility means that we can keep adding new stuff to HTML, and the browsers will (eventually) support this new stuff, but they'll also keep supporting the old stuff. So the HTML pages you're writing today will keep working, even after new features have been added later.

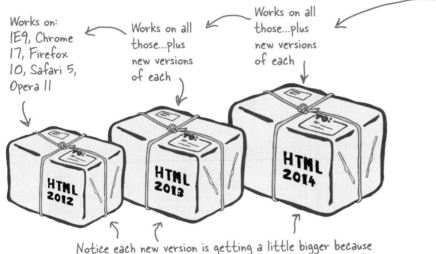

Works on:
IE9, Chrome 17, Firefox 10, Safari 5, Opera 11

Works on all those…plus new versions of each

Works on all those…plus new versions of each

Works on all those… plus fancy new browsers we haven't even thought of yet!

Notice each new version is getting a little bigger because new stuff is being added, but the old stuff still works!

Your HTML from today still works because the old stuff is still supported.

there are no Dumb Questions

Q: So what happens if the spec changes tomorrow? What do I do?

A: If you're writing solid HTML today and the spec changes tomorrow to incorporate a new element, then you can just keep on doing what you're doing. It's up to you whether you want to use that new element or not.

If the spec changes something you're already doing, like the way an element or attribute works, then browsers are supposed to continue to support the old way you're using it as well as the new way. That's what "backwards compatibility" means. Now, it is obviously a good thing if existing features are changed as little as possible, and if you, as a web developer, keep up-to-date on the spec and change your pages as the spec changes, but the idea is that your HTML will continue to work as the spec changes.

Q: What exactly is a spec, anyway?

A: The specification is the document that specifies what the HTML standard is; that is, what elements and attributes are in HTML, and more. This document is maintained by the World Wide Web Consortium (W3C, for short), but anyone can contribute to it and have a say in how the standard is developed.

> Okay, I think we've got it now. Let's get that doctype in the lounge files and update these pages to HTML5.

Adding the document type definition

Enough talk, let's get that doctype in the HTML.

Here's the doctype line. Just add it as the very first thing in the "lounge.html" file.

You can write DOCTYPE or doctype. Both work.

```html
<!doctype html>
<html>
  <head>
    <title>Head First Lounge</title>
  </head>
  <body>
    <h1>Welcome to the New and Improved Head First Lounge</h1>
        <img src="drinks.gif">
    <p>
        Join us any evening for refreshing
        <a href="elixir.html">elixirs</a>, conversation and
        maybe a game or two of <em>Dance Dance Revolution</em>.
        Wireless access is always provided; BYOWS (Bring
        your own web server).
    </p>
    <h2>Directions</h2>
    <p>
        You'll find us right in the center of downtown
        Webville. If you need help finding us, check out our
        <a href="directions.html">detailed directions</a>.
        Come join us!
    </p>
  </body>
</html>
```

The doctype test drive

Make the changes to your "lounge.html" file in the "chapter6/lounge" folder and then load the page in your browser.

Wow, no difference. Well, we didn't really expect any because all the doctype does is let the browser know for sure you're using HTML5.

Exercise

Add a **doctype** to the "directions.html" and "elixir.html" file as well. Go ahead and give them a good test. Just like "lounge.html", you won't see any fireworks (but you might sleep a bit better tonight).

HTML5 Exposed

This week's interview:
What's the big deal about HTML5?

Head First: HTML5, you're the "latest and greatest" version of HTML that everyone's yammering on about, but our readers want to know what's so great about you.

HTML5: First off, I've got a bunch of new elements and some new attributes too.

Head First: We don't seem to be using any of those yet, are we?

HTML5: All the elements you're using are part of my standard now, so you're using HTML5 elements. But no, you're not using any of the *new* ones yet…

Head First: Why not? Shouldn't we be using all the newest elements as soon as possible?

HTML5: Not necessarily. Remember (from Chapter 3): always use the right element for the job! And my newest elements have specific jobs. Some of them are for adding more structure and meaning to your page. Like my new `<article>` element, which is specifically for things like blog posts and news articles.

Head First: We could have used that in Chapter 3 for Tony's blog, right?

HTML5: That's true…I'm sure you'll add it later on.

Head First: I'm sure our readers are wondering, since they're learning HTML in this book, if they need to go learn HTML5 instead?

HTML5: No! HTML5 is just the next evolutionary step, everything they've learned is exactly the same in HTML5. HTML5 just adds some new stuff. In fact, we should stop saying "HTML5." I'm just the latest version of HTML, so call me HTML. Saying HTML5 at this point is just confusing.

Head First: Wait, after all the hype around HTML5, are you really suggesting we do away with your name?

HTML5: I am. You already know I'm a living standard and version numbers are dead. Well, I'm a living standard for HTML, not HTML5.

Head First: Got it. Our readers really should just continue learning HTML5—uhh sorry, HTML—and everything they've learned so far has been relevant. Not to mention all the new stuff ahead that they'll be learning is the latest and greatest HTML technology.

HTML5: Exactly.

Head First: I have to ask, though, I heard some of your new stuff is for building web apps. How does that relate?

HTML5: The biggest thing is that I'm not just for making web *pages* anymore; I'm designed for making full-blown web *applications*.

Head First: What's the difference?

HTML5: Web pages are mostly static pages. You'll have some images and a bunch of links, and a few nice effects here and there, like on the menus, but for the most part pages are for *reading*. Web applications, on the other hand, are for *interacting* with, *doing* stuff with. Like the applications on your desktop, only with web applications, you're doing stuff on the Web.

Head First: Can you give me an example?

HTML5: Social media apps, mapping apps, games…the list is endless.

Head First: We couldn't do that stuff before HTML5?

HTML5: Well, you could do some of it, but a lot of the features required to build those kinds of applications are being standardized for the first time with me. Before, if they existed at all, they were somewhat haphazard.

Head First: I don't think we're going to be building any apps in this book, though.

HTML5: No, but check out *Head First HTML5 Programming*. That book is all about building web applications with me!

Head First: We will! Thanks for being here, HTML5.

Okay, that wasn't bad; now we're telling the browser we're standard HTML.

Jim: Yeah, really easy. But also a little anticlimactic…we put this doctype at the top of our file to tell the browser our page is HTML, but so what? Nothing really changes.

Frank: Right, nothing you can see changes, but it does communicate to the browser that we're using standard HTML. And the browser can use that information to its (and our) advantage. Plus, the boss wanted us to be writing totally legit HTML, and for that we need the doctype.

Jim: Okay, is that it, then? Are we now writing industry standard HTML?

Frank: As far as I know, but this is where it gets interesting. The one thing that can trip us up now is errors we might have introduced into the page. Say we forgot a closing tag? Or had a typo in a tag name?

Jim: Oh right, well, wouldn't we know it if we did?

Frank: Not necessarily; the browser is pretty good at winging it when it sees errors.

Jim: How about I get the guys together, and we do a review of the entire page?

Frank: You may not need to…there are tools out there to help validate the page.

Jim: Validate?

Frank: Right, to go through the page and make sure all the markup is valid. Make sure we're keeping to the standard. It's a bit like a spell checker for HTML.

Jim: Sounds like a good idea. Where do we get these tools?

Frank: The standards guys over at the W3C have a validator, and it's free.

Jim: Great, let's do it.

Meet the W3C validator

Let's check out the W3C validator and have it validate our
lounge files. To follow along, just point your browser to
`http://validator.w3.org.`

The W3C validator is located at http://validator.w3.org.

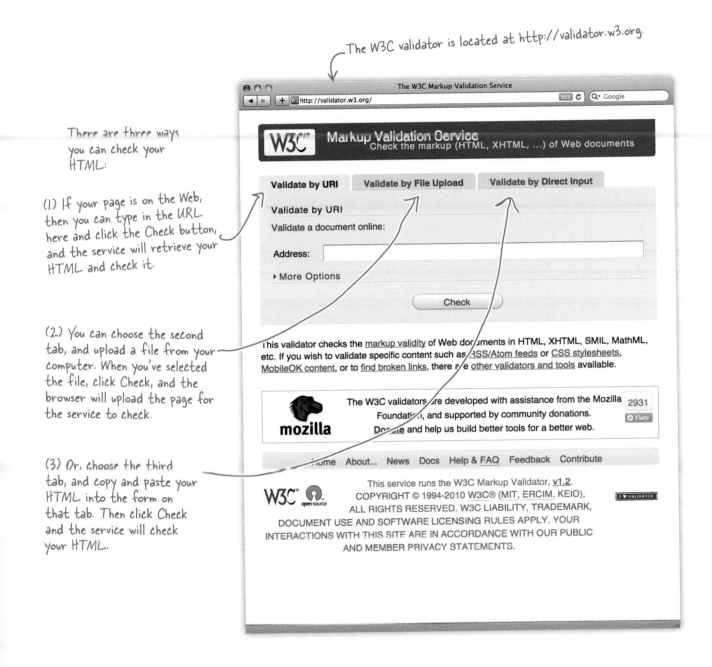

There are three ways
you can check your
HTML:

(1) If your page is on the Web,
then you can type in the URL
here and click the Check button,
and the service will retrieve your
HTML and check it.

(2) You can choose the second
tab, and upload a file from your
computer. When you've selected
the file, click Check, and the
browser will upload the page for
the service to check.

(3) Or, choose the third
tab, and copy and paste your
HTML into the form on
that tab. Then click Check
and the service will check
your HTML.

Validating the Head First Lounge

We're going to use the third tab, "Validate by Direct Input" to validate the "lounge.html" file. That means we need to copy and paste the HTML from "lounge.html" into the form on that tab; keep following along and give it a try…

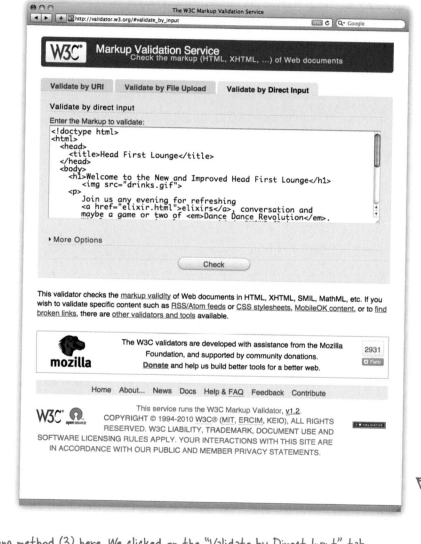

We're using method (3) here. We clicked on the "Validate by Direct Input" tab and pasted the code for "lounge.html", which now has the doctype for HTML5 at the top, into the form. We're ready for the big moment…will the web page validate? Bets anyone? Click Check (and turn the page) to find out…

Feel free to use method (1) or (2) if it's more convenient.

Houston, we have a problem...

That red on the page can't be good. It doesn't look
like the page validated. We'd better take a look…

We failed the
validation.
It looks like
there is one
error.

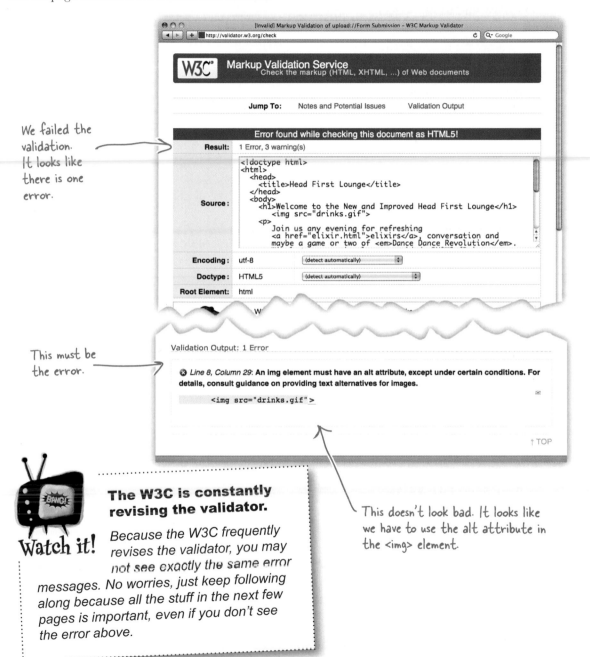

This must be
the error.

This doesn't look bad. It looks like
we have to use the alt attribute in
the <img> element.

Fixing that error

Okay, this looks pretty simple to fix. You just need to add an
`alt` attribute to your `<img>` elements in HTML5. Go ahead
and open "lounge.html", make the change, save, and then
let's try to validate again.

```
<!doctype html>
<html>
  <head>
    <title>Head First Lounge</title>
  </head>
  <body>
    <h1>Welcome to the New and Improved Head First Lounge</h1>
      <img src="drinks.gif" alt="Drinks">
    <p>
        Join us any evening for refreshing
        <a href="elixir.html">elixirs</a>, conversation and
        maybe a game or two of <em>Dance Dance Revolution</em>.
        Wireless access is always provided; BYOWS (Bring
        your own web server).
    </p>
    <h2>Directions</h2>
    <p>
        You'll find us right in the center of downtown
        Webville. If you need help finding us, check out our
        <a href="directions.html">detailed directions</a>.
        Come join us!
    </p>
  </body>
</html>
```

*You know the alt attribute;
add it into the <img> element.*

BRAIN POWER

Why do you think the alt attribute is required in HTML5?

We're almost there...

Success! We have a green bar on the page; that must be good. But there are three warnings. That sounds like we've still got a few things to take care of. Let's take a look:

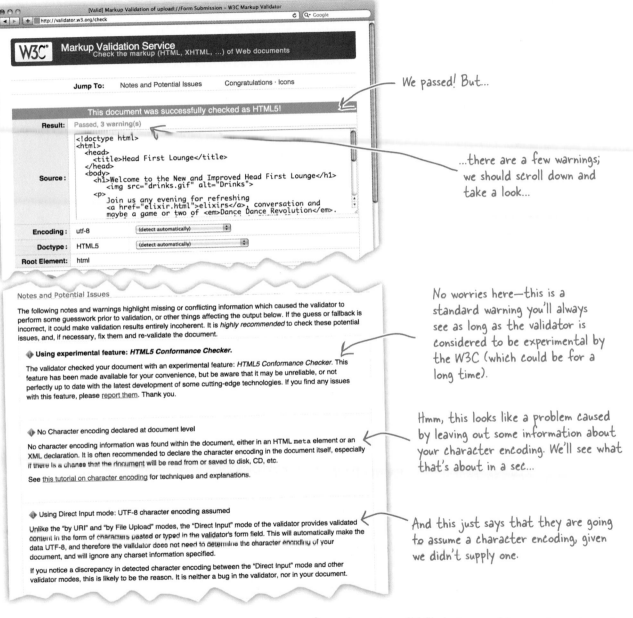

We passed! But...

...there are a few warnings; we should scroll down and take a look...

No worries here—this is a standard warning you'll always see as long as the validator is considered to be experimental by the W3C (which could be for a long time).

Hmm, this looks like a problem caused by leaving out some information about your character encoding. We'll see what that's about in a sec...

And this just says that they are going to assume a character encoding, given we didn't supply one.

So, we've got a valid file in terms of how we've written the HTML, but it looks like we need to do something about our "character encoding." Let's take a look at what that means...

See, we're getting this warning message that the validator can't find a character encoding.

> ⓘ No Character encoding declared at document level
>
> No character encoding information was found within the document, either in an HTML `meta` element or an XML declaration. It is often recommended to declare the character encoding in the document itself, especially if there is a chance that the document will be read from or saved to disk, CD, etc.

Frank: The character encoding tells the browser what kind of characters are being used in the page. For instance, pages can be written using encodings for English, Chinese, Arabic, and lots of other types of characters.

Jim: What's so hard about figuring out how to display a character? If there's an "a" in the file, then the browser should display an "a". Right?

Frank: Well, what if you're using Chinese in your pages? It's an entirely different "alphabet" and it has a heck of a lot more than 26 A–Z characters.

Jim: Oh. Good point...but shouldn't the browser be able to tell the difference? Those other languages look nothing like English.

Frank: No, the browser is just reading data. It can try to guess what kind of character encoding to use, but what if it's wrong? This can lead not only to pages being displayed wrong, but also potential exploits from hackers. The character encoding takes the guesswork out of it.

Jim: We've had the site up for a long time. Why is this an issue now?

Frank: Because the validator is saying "Hey, if I'm going to validate your page, you'd better tell me up front what characters you're going to use!" And think about it, we'd want to do that for the browsers out there anyway. Don't stress, we just need to add one more line to our HTML, called a `<meta>` tag. I should have thought of this sooner.

Jim: Got any other surprises for us? I really thought our web page would validate after we put the document type definition in our file...

Frank: I sure hope there are no more surprises! Let's get the `<meta>` tag in there and find out.

Adding a <meta> tag to specify the character encoding

Character encodings give us a way to represent all the letters, numbers and other symbols in our language on the computer. You might know of some of these encodings, like ASCII or even Morse code, and there are many other encodings out there. Luckily, the world has now standardized on the Unicode character encoding. With Unicode, we can represent all languages with one type of encoding. But, given there are other encodings out there, we still need to tell the browser we're using Unicode (or another encoding of your choice). To specify Unicode for your web pages, you'll need a <meta> tag in your HTML that looks like this:

"meta" means we're going to tell the browser something about the page...

The charset attribute is where we specify the character encoding.

The value of the charset attribute is the type of character encoding we're using.

```
<meta charset="utf-8">
```

Just like other HTML tags, the <meta> tag has attributes.

"utf-8" is an encoding in the Unicode family of encodings (one of several). "utf-8" is the version we use for web pages.

there are no Dumb Questions

Q: Doctypes, <meta> tags...ugh, do I need to really do all this to write web pages?

A: Specifying a doctype and character encoding with a <meta> tag are kind of like taxes: you gotta do them to be compliant. Look at it this way: you already understand them more than 98% of the web page writing population, which is great. But at the end of the day, everyone just puts the doctype and <meta> tag in their HTML and moves on with life. So make sure you've got them in your HTML, and then go do something much more fun.

Q: utf-8?

A: Work with us here. It's like WD-40; you don't worry about why it's called that, you just use it. As we said, utf-8 (also written sometimes as UTF-8) is part of the Unicode encoding family. The *u* in utf-8 means Unicode. Unicode is a character set supported across many commonly used software applications and operating systems, and is the encoding of choice for the Web, because it

supports all languages, and multilingual documents (documents that use more than one language). It's also compatible with ASCII, which was a common encoding for English-only documents. If you're interested in learning more about Unicode or character encodings in general, check out the information on character encoding at http://www.w3.org/International/O-charset.html.

Q: I've also seen <meta> tags that look like this: <meta http equiv="Content-Type" content="text/html;charset=utf-8" >. Do I need to use this instead sometimes?

A: No. That is the format for the <meta> tag in HTML 4.01 and earlier. In HTML5, you can just write <meta charset="utf-8">.

Q: Is this why you had us save our files using utf-8 for the encoding way back in Chapter 1?

A: Yes. You want the encoding of the file you're serving to the browser to match the encoding you specify in the <meta> tag.

Making the validator (and more than a few browsers) happy with a <meta> tag...

The <meta> tag belongs in the <head> element (remember that the <head> contains information *about* your page). Go ahead and add the <meta> tag line right into your HTML. Let's first add it to the "lounge.html" file:

```
<!doctype html>
<html>
  <head>
    <meta charset="utf-8">
    <title>Head First Lounge</title>
  </head>
  <body>
    <h1>Welcome to the New and Improved Head First Lounge</h1>
      <img src="drinks.gif" alt="Drinks">
    <p>
        Join us any evening for refreshing
        <a href="elixir.html">elixirs</a>, conversation and
        maybe a game or two of <em>Dance Dance Revolution</em>.
        Wireless access is always provided; BYOWS (Bring
        your own web server).
    </p>
    <h2>Directions</h2>
    <p>
        You'll find us right in the center of downtown
        Webville. If you need help finding us, check out our
        <a href="directions.html">detailed directions</a>.
        Come join us!
    </p>
  </body>
</html>
```

Here's the <meta> tag. We've added it to the <head> element above the <title> element.

Add this line above any other elements in the <head> element.

Want to place another bet? Is this going to validate? First, make the changes to your "lounge.html" file, save it, and reload it into your browser. Once again, *you* won't notice any change, but the *browser* will. Now let's see if it validates…

Third time's the charm?

This time, we picked the second tab (validate by file upload). You can choose whichever method works best for you. If you want to try the upload method, then upload your "lounge.html" HTML file to the W3C validator web page at `http://validator.w3.org`. Once you've done that, click the Check button…

"Successfully checked as HTML5"! Love the green!

We still have one warning…but we don't need to worry about it (see below).

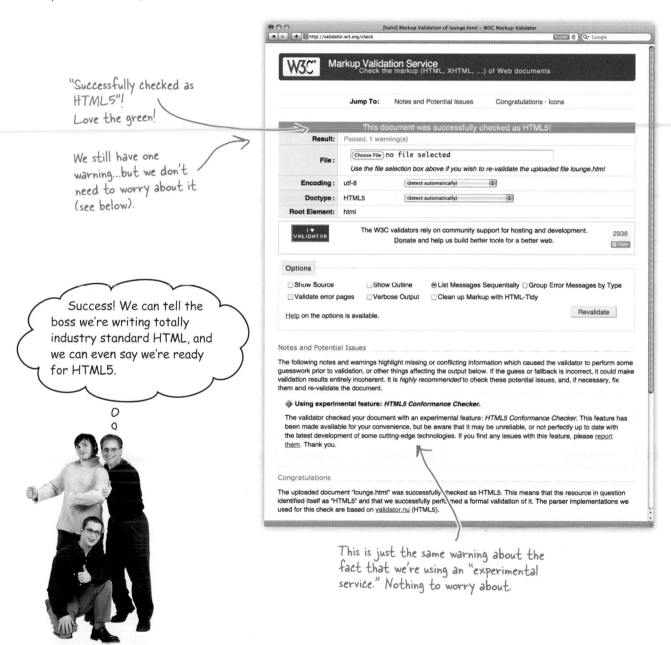

Success! We can tell the boss we're writing totally industry standard HTML, and we can even say we're ready for HTML5.

This is just the same warning about the fact that we're using an "experimental service." Nothing to worry about.

there are no
Dumb Questions

Q: The validator says it is experimental for HTML5. What does that mean?

A: The message "Using experimental feature: HTML5 Conformance Checker" in the validator means that the validator is checking your HTML according to the HTML5 standard, but because the HTML5 standard isn't final (and still has new features being added), the validator is prone to change, so the results you get when you validate your page aren't set in stone. That means, as a conscientious developer, it's in your best interest to stay up-to-date on the HTML standard, and check your pages fairly regularly.

Q: What have we really achieved in this chapter? My page still looks the same.

A: In this chapter we've tweaked your page slightly so that it is compliant with the HTML specification. What good is that? The closer you are to the spec, the more likely that your page is going to perform well in the real world. If you're producing a professional web page, you want it to be written using the industry standard, and that's what we've done in this chapter by adding a doctype, setting a character encoding, and cleaning up an oversight (the alt attribute) in the HTML.

Q: Why do we need that alt attribute anyway?

A: For two great reasons. First, if your image is broken for some reason (say, your image server goes down, or your connection is really slow), the alt attribute will (in most browsers) show the alt text you've specified in place of the image. Second, for vision-impaired users who are using a screen reader to read the page, the screen reader will read the alt text to the user, which helps them understand the page better.

Q: What if I tell the browser I'm using HTML5, and I'm not?

A: The browser will figure out that you're not really writing HTML5 and use the error handling capabilities it has to try to do the right thing. And then you're back to the problem of having the various browsers handle your page in different ways. The only way you can get predictable results is to tell the browser you're using HTML5 and to actually do so, properly.

Q: We talked a little about HTML5, but I want make sure I'm clear: is there any difference between the HTML we're writing and HTML5?

A: We're using standard HTML, which is HTML5. Now, HTML5 introduced some new markup (which we'll be seeing soon enough) as well as support for writing web applications (which we won't be doing in this book), but HTML5 is HTML, and everything you've been writing is HTML5 "compliant." So, sorry for the terminology, but going forward everything is just HTML, including all the new features provided by the HTML5 specification.

The good news is that everything you've learned is all ready for HTML5, and in fact you see how little you actually had to do to go from an "informal HTML" page to a professional HTML page. That said, you might want to tell your boss you're already using HTML5 just for bonus points toward your next raise.

Q: What's the big deal with HTML5 compared to HTML 4.01 anyway?

A: The big deal about HTML5 is threefold. First, there are some new elements and attributes in HTML5 that are pretty cool (like the <video> element), and others that will help you write better pages (we'll be getting to those later in the book).

Second, there are many new features that allow web developers to create web *applications* with HTML5. Web applications are web pages that behave more like applications (like the ones you're used to using on your laptop or mobile device) than static web pages. If you're interested in creating web applications, then after you're all done with this book (cue shameless plug), you should check out *Head First HTML5 Programming* (O'Reilly).

Finally, the HTML5 specification is a lot more robust than the specifications for the previous versions of HTML. Remember how we said that the specification is now documenting common errors that web developers make? And helping browsers to know how to handle those errors? That means that web pages with errors on them don't cause the havoc they used to, which is a good thing for users.

All in all, HTML5 is a big improvement over HTML 4.01, and well worth learning. We'll get you up to speed quickly over the next few chapters.

Your turn. Add the <meta> tag to "directions.html" and "elixir.html". Try validating them; do they validate? If not, fix them so that they do.

Use this space for notes about your
validating experience!

Time to play a little game with the validator. Take the code you just successfully validated as HTML5 (on page 241), and remove the doctype. That's right—remove it, just to see what happens when you validate. Go ahead and submit this version of the file to the validator and see what happens. Make notes below about the errors you get.

```html
<!doctype html>    ← Remove the doctype!
<html>
  <head>
    <meta charset="utf-8">
    <title>Head First Lounge</title>
  </head>
  <body>
    <h1>Welcome to the New and Improved Head First Lounge</h1>
      <img src="drinks.gif" alt="Drinks">
    <p>
      Join us any evening for refreshing
      <a href="elixir.html">elixirs</a>, conversation and
      maybe a game or two of <em>Dance Dance Revolution</em>.
      Wireless access is always provided; BYOWS (Bring
      your own web server).
    </p>
    <h2>Directions</h2>
    <p>
      You'll find us right in the center of downtown
      Webville. If you need help finding us, check out our
      <a href="directions.html">detailed directions</a>.
      Come join us!
    </p>
  </body>
</html>
```

1 Error stating doctype is missing

Your notes here. How many
errors did you get?

What does this tell you about the type of
your HTML if you don't include a doctype?

Calling all HTML professionals, grab the handbook...

Welcome to the elite set of HTML crafters, those who know how to create professional pages. There's a lot to remember, so the City of Webville prepared a handy guide to creating industry standard pages. This guide is meant for you—someone who is new to Webville. It isn't an exhaustive reference, but rather focuses on the more important best practices in building your pages. And you'll definitely be adding to the knowledge in this guide as you get to know your way around Webville in coming chapters. But for now, take one—they're FREE.

Webville Guide to HTML

In this handy guide, we've boiled down writing well-formed HTML pages into a common sense set of guidelines. Check them out:

Always begin with the <doctype>.

Always start each page with a doctype. This will get you off on the right foot with browsers, and with the validator too.

Use `<!docytype html>` at all times, unless you really are writing HTML 4.01 or XHTML.

The `<html>` element: don't leave home without it.

Following the doctype, the `<html>` element must always be the top, or root, element of your web page. So, after the doctype, the `<html>` tag will start your page and the `</html>` tag should end it, with everything else in your page nested inside.

Remember to use both your `<head>` and your `<body>` for better HTML.

Only the `<head>` and `<body>` elements can go directly inside your `<html>` element. This means that every other element must go either inside the `<head>` or the `<body>` element. No exceptions!

Feed your `<head>` the right character encoding.

Include a `<meta charset="utf-8">` tag in your `<head>`. The browser will thank you, and so will your users when they're reading comments on your blog from users around the world.

Webville Guide to HTML, continued

In this handy guide, we've boiled down writing well-formed HTML pages into a common sense set of guidelines. Check them out:

What's a `<head>` without a `<title>`?

Always give your `<head>` element a `<title>` element. It's the law. Failure to do so will result in HTML that isn't compliant. The `<head>` element is the only place you should put your `<title>`, `<meta>`, and `<style>` elements.

Be careful about nesting certain elements.

Within the guidelines we've provided here, the nesting rules are fairly flexible. But there are a couple of cases that don't make sense. Never nest an `<a>` element inside another `<a>` element because that would be too confusing for our visitors. Also, void elements like `<img>` provide no way to nest other inline elements within them.

Check your attributes!

Some element attributes are required, and some are optional. For instance, the `<img>` element wouldn't make much sense without a src attribute, and now you know the alt attribute is required too. Get familiar with the required and optional attributes of each element as you learn it.

HTML Archaeology

Throughout this book you've been using elements and attributes that are all part of the current HTML standard. So, you haven't had much opportunity to see the phased-out elements and attributes. Most of those elements actually got phased out in HTML 4.01, but they may still be hanging around in old web pages, so it doesn't hurt to know a little about these legacy elements. We did some digging and found an HTML 3.2 page that contains some elements and attributes that are no longer part of the standard, as well as a couple of common mistakes that are not recommended in modern HTML.

```
<html>
<head>
    <title>Webville Forecast</title>
</head>

<body bgcolor="tan" text="black">

    <p>
        The weather report says lots of rain and wind in store for
        <font face="arial">Webville</font> today, so be sure to
        stay inside if you can.
    </p>

    <ul>
        <li>Tuesday: Rain and 60 degrees.
        <li>Wednesday: Rain and 62 degrees.
    </ul>

    <p align=right>
      Bring your umbrella!

    <center><font size="small">This page brought to you buy Lou's
        Diner, a Webville institution for over 50 years.
    </font></center>

</body>
</html>
```

Here are some attributes that controlled presentation. bgcolor sets the background color of the page, and text sets the color of the body text.

Font changes were made with the <font> element and its face attribute.

You could get away without some closing tags, like </li> and </p>. You sometimes still can, but it is not recommended!!

Missing quotes around attribute values. Quotes are always recommended now, and required for attributes with multiple values.

Here were two ways to align text. Right-align a paragraph, or center a piece of text.

Text size was controlled with the <font> element, using the size attribute.

BE the Validator

Below, you'll find an HTML file. Your job is to play like you're the validator and locate ALL the errors. After you've done the exercise, look at the end of the chapter to see if you caught them all.

Use the validator to check your work once you're done (or if you need hints).

Missing `<!DOCTYPE html>`

```
<html>
<head>
    <meta charset="utf-9">
</head>
<body>
    <img src="chamberofcommerce.gif">
    <h1>Tips for Enjoying Your Visit in Webville
    <p>
        Here are a few tips to help you better enjoy your stay in Webville.
    </p>
    <ul>
        <li>Always dress in layers and keep an html around your
            head and body.</li>
        <li>Get plenty of rest while you're here, sleep helps all
            those rules sink in.</li>
        <li>Don't miss the work of our local artists right downtown
            in the CSS gallery. </li>
    </ul>
    </p>
    <p>
        Having problems? You can always find answers at
        <a href="http://wickedlysmart.com"><em>WickedlySmart</em></a>.
        Still got problems? Relax, Webville's a friendly place, just ask someone
        for help. And, as a local used to say:
    </p>
    <em><p>
        Don't worry. As long as you hit that wire with the connecting hook
        at precisely 88mph the instant the lightning strikes the tower…
        everything will be fine.
    </em></p>
</body>
</html>
```

Missing `<title>`

should be utf-8

Need alt in case image can't load

`</h1>` closing tag missing

`</li>` Missing closing tag

Closing tags not matching up

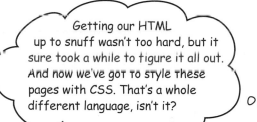

Getting our HTML up to snuff wasn't too hard, but it sure took a while to figure it all out. And now we've got to style these pages with CSS. That's a whole different language, isn't it?

BULLET POINTS

- HTML5 is the current HTML standard.

- The World Wide Web Consortium (W3C) is the standards organization that defines what standard HTML is.

- The document type definition (doctype) is used to tell the browser the version of HTML you're using.

- The HTML standard is now a "living standard," which means that the standard will change to incorporate new features and updates.

- The <meta> tag in the <head> element tells the browser additional information about a web page, such as the content type and character encoding.

- The charset attribute of the <meta> tag tells the browser the character encoding that is used for the web page.

- Most web pages use the utf-8 encoding for HTML files, and for the <meta> tag charset attribute.

- The alt attribute is required for the <img> element.

- The W3C validator is a free online service that checks pages for compliance with standards.

- Use the validator to ensure that your HTML is well formed and that your elements and attributes meet the standard.

- By adhering to the standard, your pages will display more quickly and with fewer display differences between browsers, and your CSS will work better.

HTMLcross

It's been a heck of a chapter. Go ahead and grab a cup of your favorite beverage, sit back, and strengthen those neural connections by doing this crossword. All the answers come from the chapter.

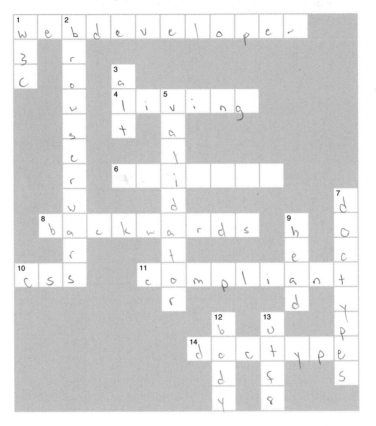

Across

1. Victim of the browser wars.
4. The HTML standard is a _____ standard.
6. Required in the <head> element.
8. Web standards makers have promised future HTML will be _____ compatible with older HTML.
10. The boss wanted to standardize before adding _____ to the Lounge pages.
11. When your HTML meets the standard, it is this.
14. Definition that tells the browser and validator what kind of document you're creating.

Down

1. Standards organization that supplies the validator.
2. Microsoft versus Netscape.
3. <img> attribute required in standard HTML.
5. This service will check your HTML for compliance with the standard.
7. The older _____ were much more complicated compared to the newest one.
9. Where you put information about the page.
12. Where you put web page content.
13. The most common encoding for web pages.

BE the Validator Solution

Below, you'll find an HTML file. Your job is to play like you're the validator and locate ALL the errors. Here's the solution.

Missing doctype

```
<html>
<head>
    meta charset="utf-9">
</head>
<body>
    <img src="chamberofcommerce.gif">
    <h1>Tips for Enjoying Your Visit in Webville
    <p>
        Here are a few tips to help you better enjoy your stay in Webville.
    </p>
    <ul>
        <li>Always dress in layers and keep an html around your
            head and body.</li>
        <li>Get plenty of rest while you're here, sleep helps all
            those rules sink in.</li>
        <li>Don't miss the work of our local artists right downtown
            in the CSS gallery.
    </ul>
    </p>
    <p>
        Having problems? You can always find answers at
        <a href="http://wickedlysmart.com"><em>WickedlySmart</em></a>.
        Still got problems? Relax, Webville's a friendly place, just ask someone
        for help. And, as a local used to say:
    </p>
    <em><p>
        Don't worry. As long as you hit that wire with the connecting hook
        at precisely 88mph the instant the lightning strikes the tower…
        everything will be fine.
    </em></p>
</body>
</html>
```

Should be "utf-8" instead of "utf-9" (which doesn't exist!)

<title> should be in the <head>.

No alt attribute

Missing </h1> tag. This will cause problems with the <p> element below.

Missing </li> tag. This will still validate, but it's not recommended!

Extra </p> that doesn't match a <p>

<em> and <p> tags are switched.

HTMLCross Solution

Exercise Solution

Your turn. Add the strict doctype and the <meta> tag to "directions.html" and "elixir.html". Try validating them—do they validate? If not, fix them so that they do.

Solution: To validate "elixir.html", you'll have to add the alt attribute to each of your <img> elements.

Exercise

Time to play a little game with the validator. Take the code you just successfully validated as HTML5 (on page 241), and remove the doctype. That's right—remove it, just to see what happens when you validate. Go ahead and submit this version of the file to the validator and see what happens. Make notes below about the errors you get.

```
<!doctype html>    ⟵ Remove the doctype!
<html>
  <head>
    <meta charset="utf-8">
    <title>Head First Lounge</title>
  </head>
  <body>
    <h1>Welcome to the New and Improved Head First Lounge</h1>
      <img src="drinks.gif" alt="Drinks">
    <p>
      Join us any evening for refreshing
      <a href="elixir.html">elixirs</a>, conversation and
      maybe a game or two of <em>Dance Dance Revolution</em>.
      Wireless access is always provided; BYOWS (Bring
      your own web server).
    </p>
    <h2>Directions</h2>
    <p>
      You'll find us right in the center of downtown
      Webville. If you need help finding us, check out our
      <a href="directions.html">detailed directions</a>.
      Come join us!
    </p>
  </body>
</html>
```

We get three errors and four warnings if we try to validate without the doctype. The validator assumes we're writing HTML 4.01 Transitional (which was a version of HTML 4.01 designed to use while you were "transitioning" to XHTML). The validator really doesn't like that there's no doctype, and complains a couple of times about that. It also complains about the <meta charset="utf-8">, because before HTML5, charset was not a valid attribute of the <meta> tag. You can get the idea that using a doctype makes both the validator, and the browsers, happier campers.

Your notes here. How many ⟋ errors did you get?

7 getting started with CSS

Adding a Little Style

Don't get me wrong, the hair, the hat—it all looks great. But don't you think he'd like it if you spent a little more time adding some style to your HTML?

I was told there'd be CSS in this book. So far you've been concentrating on learning HTML to create the structure of your web pages. But as you can see, the browser's idea of style leaves a lot to be desired. Sure, we could call the fashion police, but we don't need to. With CSS, you're going to completely control the presentation of your pages, often without even changing your HTML. Could it really be so easy? Well, you *are* going to have to learn a new language; after all, Webville is a bilingual town. After reading this chapter's guide to learning the language of CSS, you're going to be able to stand on *either* side of Main Street and hold a conversation.

You're not in Kansas anymore

You've been a good sport learning about markup and structure and validation and proper syntax and nesting and compliance, but now you get to really start *having some fun* by styling your pages. But no worries, all those HTML push-ups you've been doing aren't going to waste. In fact, you're going to see that a solid understanding of HTML is crucial to learning (and using) CSS. And learning CSS is just what we're going to do over the next several chapters.

Just to tease you a bit, on these two pages we've sprinkled a few of the designs you're going to work with in the rest of the book. Quite a difference from the pages you've been creating so far, isn't it? So, what do you need to do to create them? Learn the language of CSS, of course.

Let's get started…

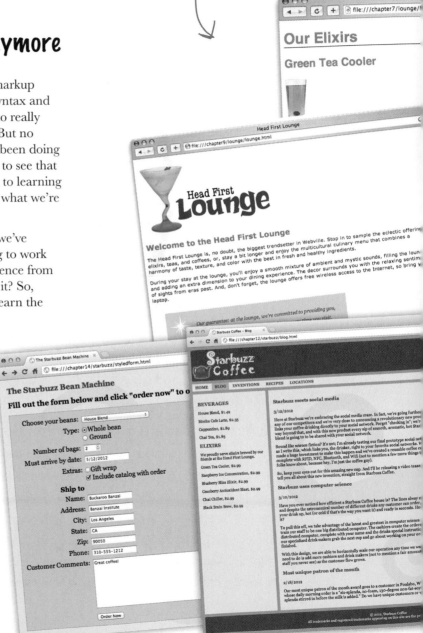

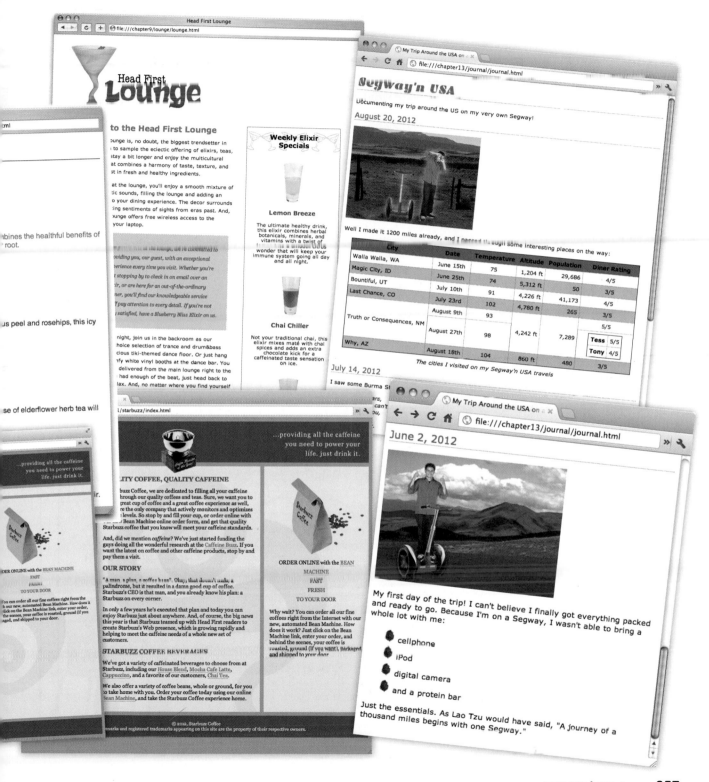

Overheard on Webville's "Trading Spaces"

Not up on the latest reality TV? No problem, here's a recap: take two neighbors, two homes, and $1,000. The two neighbors switch homes, and using the $1,000, totally redesign a room or two in 48 hours. Let's listen in…

…and this bathroom needs some serious help!

```
bathroom {
    tile: 1in white;
    drapes: pink;
}
```

Okay, let's get some design in this place…

```
bedroom {
    drapes: blue;
    carpet: wool shag;
}
```

Of course, in the Webville edition of the show, everyone talks about design in CSS. If you're having trouble understanding them, here's a little translation tip: each statement in CSS consists of a location (like bedroom), a property in that location (like drapes or carpet), and a style to apply to that property (like the color blue, or 1 inch tiles).

Using CSS with HTML

We're sure CSS has a bright future in the home design category, but let's get back to HTML. HTML doesn't have rooms, but it does have elements, and those elements are going to be the locations that we're styling. Want to paint the walls of your <p> elements red? No problem; only paragraphs don't have walls, so you're going to have to settle for the paragraph's `background-color` property instead. Here's how you do that:

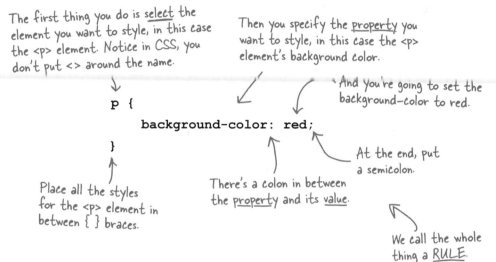

The first thing you do is select the element you want to style, in this case the <p> element. Notice in CSS, you don't put <> around the name.

Then you specify the property you want to style, in this case the <p> element's background color.

And you're going to set the background-color to red.

```
p {
    background-color: red;
}
```

Place all the styles for the <p> element in between { } braces.

There's a colon in between the property and its value.

At the end, put a semicolon.

We call the whole thing a RULE.

You could also write the rule like this:

```
p { background-color: red; }
```

Here, all we've done is remove the linebreaks. As with HTML, you can format your CSS pretty much as you like. For longer rules, you'll usually want to add some linebreaks and indenting to make the CSS more readable (for you).

Wanna add more style?

You can add as many properties and values as you like in each CSS rule. Say you wanted to put a border around your paragraphs, too. Here's how you do that:

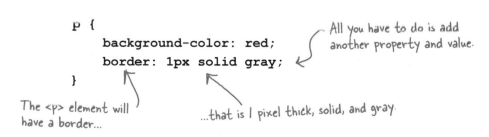

```
p {
    background-color: red;
    border: 1px solid gray;
}
```

All you have to do is add another property and value.

The <p> element will have a border...

...that is 1 pixel thick, solid, and gray.

there are no
Dumb Questions

Q: Does every <p> element have the same style? Or can I, say, make two paragraphs different colors?

A: The CSS rules we've used so far define the style for all paragraphs, but CSS is very expressive: it can be used to specify styles in lots of different ways, for lots of different elements—even subsets of elements. You'll see how to make paragraphs two different colors later in this chapter.

Q: How do I know what properties I can set on an element?

A: Well, there are lots of properties that can be set on elements, certainly more than you'd want to memorize, in any case. You're going to get quite familiar with the more common properties in the next few chapters. You'll probably also want to find a good CSS reference. There are plenty of references online, and O'Reilly's *CSS Pocket Reference* is a great little book.

Q: Remind me why I'm defining all this style in a separate language, rather than in HTML. Since the elements are written in HTML, wouldn't it be easier just to write style in HTML, too?

A: You're going to start to see some big advantages to using CSS in the next few chapters. But here's a quick answer: CSS really is better suited for specifying style information than HTML. Using just a small bit of CSS, you can create fairly large effects on the style of your HTML. You're also going to see that CSS is a much better way to handle styles for multiple pages. You'll see how that works later in this chapter.

Say you have an <em> element inside a paragraph. If you change the background color of the paragraph, do you think you also have to change the background of the <em> element so it matches the background color of the paragraph?

Getting CSS into your HTML

You know a little about CSS syntax now. You know how to select an element and then write a rule with properties and values inside it. But you still need to get this CSS into some HTML. First, we need some HTML to put it in. In the next few chapters, we're going to revisit our old friends—Starbuzz, and Tony and his Segway journal—and make things a little more stylish. But who do you think is dying to have their site styled first? Of course, the Head First Lounge guys. So, here's the HTML for the Head First Lounge main page. Remember, in the last chapter we fixed things up a little and made it proper HTML (would you have expected any less of us?). Now, we're adding some style tags, the easiest way to get style into your pages.

But not necessarily the best way. We'll come back to this later in the chapter and see another way.

```html
<!doctype html>
<html>
  <head>
    <meta charset="utf-8">
    <title>Head First Lounge</title>

    <style>


    </style>

  </head>
  <body>
    <h1>Welcome to the Head First Lounge</h1>
    <p>
        <img src="images/drinks.gif" alt="Drinks">
    </p>
    <p>
        Join us any evening for refreshing
        <a href="beverages/elixir.html">elixirs</a>,
        conversation and maybe a game or two of
        <em>Dance Dance Revolution</em>.
        Wireless access is always provided;
        BYOWS (Bring your own web server).
    </p>
    <h2>Directions</h2>
    <p>
        You'll find us right in the center of downtown
        Webville. If you need help finding us, check out our
        <a href="about/directions.html">detailed directions</a>.
        Come join us!
    </p>
  </body>
</html>
```

Here's what we're interested in: the <style> element.

To add CSS style directly to your HTML, add opening and closing style tags in the <head> element.

And your CSS rules are going to go right in here.

Adding style to the lounge

Now that you've got the `<style>` element in your HTML, you're going to add some style to the lounge to get a feel for writing CSS. This design probably won't win you any "design awards," but you gotta start somewhere.

The first thing we're going to do is change the color (something to match those red lounge couches) of the text in the paragraphs. To do that, we'll use the CSS `color` property like this:

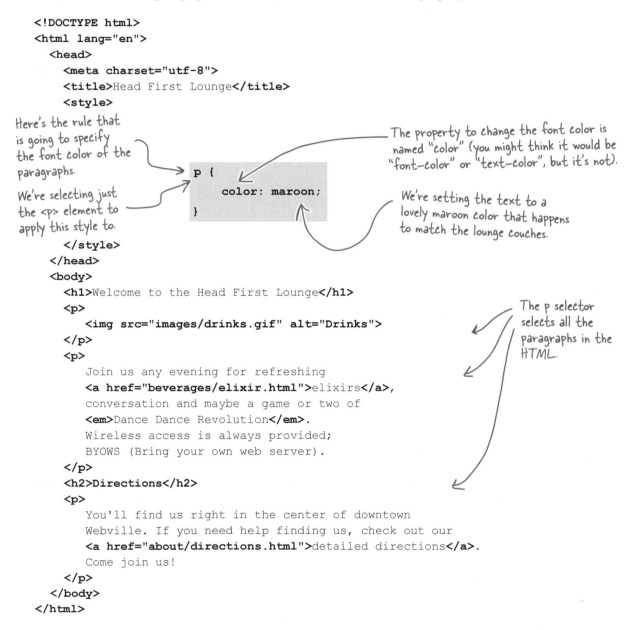

Here's the rule that is going to specify the font color of the paragraphs.

We're selecting just the `<p>` element to apply this style to.

The property to change the font color is named "color" (you might think it would be "font-color" or "text-color", but it's not).

We're setting the text to a lovely maroon color that happens to match the lounge couches.

The p selector selects all the paragraphs in the HTML.

```
<!DOCTYPE html>
<html lang="en">
  <head>
    <meta charset="utf-8">
    <title>Head First Lounge</title>
    <style>

    p {
          color: maroon;
    }

    </style>
  </head>
  <body>
    <h1>Welcome to the Head First Lounge</h1>
    <p>
        <img src="images/drinks.gif" alt="Drinks">
    </p>
    <p>
        Join us any evening for refreshing
        <a href="beverages/elixir.html">elixirs</a>,
        conversation and maybe a game or two of
        <em>Dance Dance Revolution</em>.
        Wireless access is always provided;
        BYOWS (Bring your own web server).
    </p>
    <h2>Directions</h2>
    <p>
        You'll find us right in the center of downtown
        Webville. If you need help finding us, check out our
        <a href="about/directions.html">detailed directions</a>.
        Come join us!
    </p>
  </body>
</html>
```

Cruising with style: the test drive

Go ahead and make all the changes from the last couple of pages to your "lounge.html" file in the "chapter7/lounge" folder, save, and reload the page in your browser. You'll see that the paragraph text color has changed to maroon:

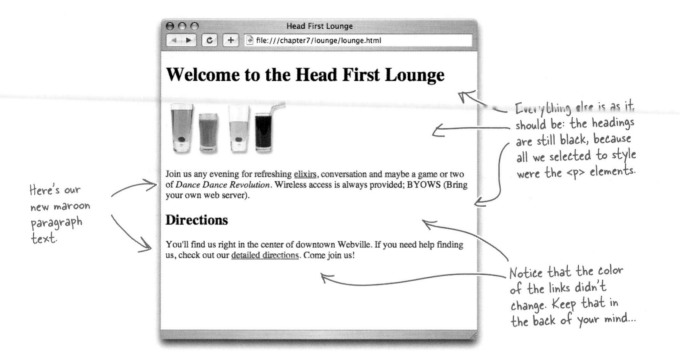

Here's our new maroon paragraph text.

Everything else is as it should be: the headings are still black, because all we selected to style were the <p> elements.

Notice that the color of the links didn't change. Keep that in the back of your mind...

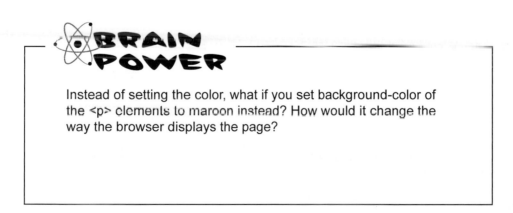

Instead of setting the color, what if you set background-color of the <p> elements to maroon instead? How would it change the way the browser displays the page?

Style the heading

Now let's give those headings some style. How about changing the font a bit? Let's change both the type of font, and also the color of the heading fonts:

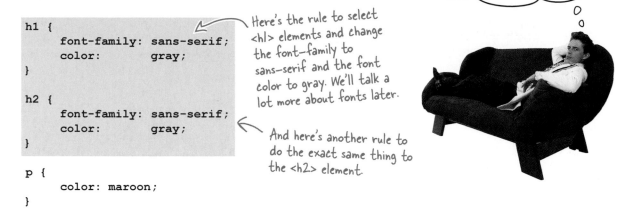

```
h1 {
    font-family: sans-serif;
    color:      gray;
}

h2 {
    font-family: sans-serif;
    color:      gray;
}

p {
    color: maroon;
}
```

Here's the rule to select <h1> elements and change the font-family to sans-serif and the font color to gray. We'll talk a lot more about fonts later.

And here's another rule to do the exact same thing to the <h2> element.

How about a different font for the lounge headings? Make them really stand out. I'm seeing big, clean, gray...

Actually, because these rules are *exactly* the same, we can combine them, like this:

```
h1, h2 {
    font-family: sans-serif;
    color:      gray;
}

p {
    color: maroon;
}
```

To write a rule for more than one element, just put commas between the selectors, like "h1, h2".

Test drive...

Add this new CSS to your "lounge.html" file and reload. You'll see that with one rule, you've selected both the <h1> and <h2> headings.

Both of the headings on the page are now styled with a sans-serif font and colored gray.

Head First Lounge

file:///chapter7/lounge/lounge.html

Welcome to the Head First Lounge

Join us any evening for refreshing elixirs, conversation and maybe a game or two of *Dance Dance Revolution*. Wireless access is always provided; BYOWS (Bring your own web server).

Directions

You'll find us right in the center of downtown Webville. If you need help finding us, check out our detailed directions. Come join us!

Let's put a line under the welcome message too

Let's touch up the welcome heading a bit more. How about a line under it? That should set the main heading apart visually and add a nice touch. Here's the property we'll use to do that:

```
border-bottom: 1px solid black;
```

This property controls how the border under an element looks.

We're going to style the bottom border so that it is a 1-pixel-thick, solid black line.

The trouble is, if we add this property and value to the combined h1, h2 rule in our CSS, we'll end up with borders on both our headings:

```
h1, h2 {
    font-family:    sans-serif;
    color:          gray;
    border-bottom: 1px solid black;
}

p {
    color: maroon;
}
```

Here we're adding a property to change the bottom border for both the <h1> and <h2> elements.

If we do this...

...we get bottom borders on both our headings. Not what we want.

So, how can we set the bottom border on just the <h1> element, without affecting the <h2> element? Do we have to split up the rules again? Turn the page to find out…

○ ○ ○   Head First Lounge

◀ ▶ C +   file:///chapter7/lounge/lounge.html

Welcome to the Head First Lounge

Join us any evening for refreshing <u>elixirs</u>, conversation and maybe a game or two of *Dance Dance Revolution*. Wireless access is always provided; BYOWS (Bring your own web server).

Directions

You'll find us right in the center of downtown Webville. If you need help finding us, check out our <u>detailed directions</u>. Come join us!

We have the technology: specifying a second rule, just for the <h1>

We don't have to split up the `h1,` `h2` rule, we just need to add another rule that is only for `h1` and add the border style to it.

```css
h1, h2 {
    font-family:      sans-serif;
    color:            gray;
}

h1 {
    border-bottom:  1px solid black;
}

p {
    color: maroon;
}
```

The first rule stays the same. We're still going to use a combined rule for the font-family and color for both <h1> and <h2>.

But now we're adding a second rule that adds another property just to <h1>: the border-bottom property.

Another test drive...

Change your CSS and reload the page. You'll see that the new rule added a black border to the bottom of the main heading, which gives us a nice underline on the heading and really makes it stand out.

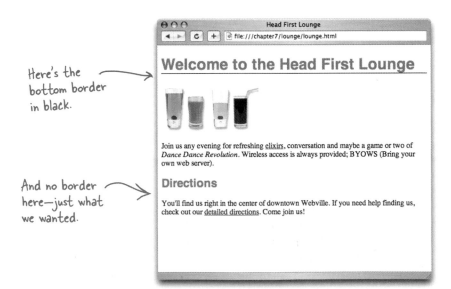

Here's the bottom border in black.

And no border here—just what we wanted.

Q: So how does that work when you have more than one rule for an element?

A: You can have as many rules as you want for an element. Each rule adds to the style information of the rule before it. In general, you try to group together all the common styles between elements, like we did with <h1> and <h2>, and then any style that is specific to an element, you write in another rule, like we did with the border-bottom style for the main heading.

Q: What's the advantage of that approach? Isn't it better to organize each element separately, so you know exactly what styles it has?

A: Not at all. If you combine common styles together, then if they change, you only have to change them in one rule. If you break them up, then there are many rules you have to change, which is error-prone.

Q: Why do we use a bottom border to underline text? Isn't there an underline style for text?

A: Good question. There is an underline style for text and we could use that instead. However, the two styles have slightly different effects on the page: if you use border-bottom, then the line will extend to the edge of the page. An underline is only shown under the text itself. The property to set text underline is called text-decoration and has a value of "underline" for underlined text. Give it a try and check out the differences.

So, how do selectors really work?

You've seen how to select an element to style it, like this:

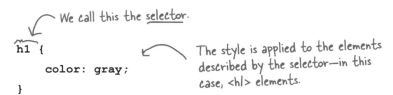

We call this the <u>selector</u>.

```
h1 {
       color: gray;
}
```

The style is applied to the elements described by the selector—in this case, <h1> elements.

Or how to select more than one element, like this:

Another selector. The style is applied to <h1> and <h2> elements

```
h1, h2 {
       color: gray;
}
```

You're going to see that CSS allows you to specify all kinds of selectors that determine which elements your styles are applied to. Knowing how to use these selectors is the first step in mastering CSS, and to do that you need to understand the organization of the HTML that you're styling. After all, how can you select elements for styling if you don't have a good mental picture of what elements are in the HTML, and how they relate to one another?

So, let's get that picture of the lounge HTML in your head, and then we'll dive back into selectors.

Markup Magnets

Remember drawing the hierarchy diagram of HTML elements in Chapter 3? You're going to do that again for the Lounge's main page. Below, you'll find all the element magnets you need to complete the diagram. Using the Lounge's HTML (on the right), complete the tree below. We've done a couple for you already. You'll find the answer in the back of the chapter.

Like this

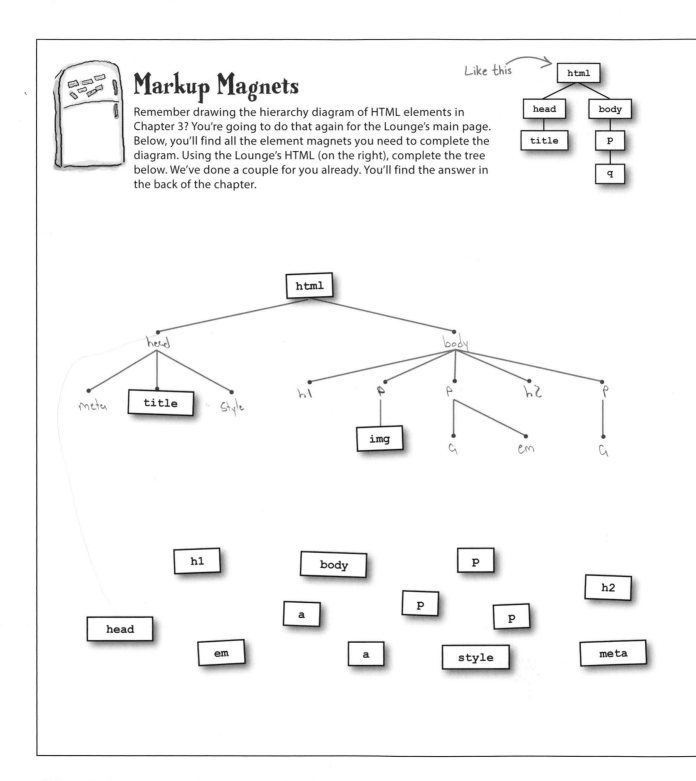

```
<!doctype html>
<html>
  <head>
    <meta charset="utf-8">
    <title>Head First Lounge</title>
    <style>
        h1, h2 {
                font-family:   sans-serif;
                color:         gray;
        }
        h1 {
                border-bottom: 1px solid black;
        }
        p {
                color: maroon;
        }
    </style>
  </head>
  <body>
    <h1>Welcome to the Head First Lounge</h1>
    <p>
        <img src="images/drinks.gif" alt="Drinks">
    </p>
    <p>
        Join us any evening for refreshing
        <a href="beverages/elixir.html">elixirs</a>,
        conversation and maybe a game or two
        of <em>Dance Dance Revolution</em>.
        Wireless access is always provided;
        BYOWS (Bring your own web server).
    </p>
    <h2>Directions</h2>
    <p>
        You'll find us right in the center of downtown
        Webville. If you need help finding us, check out our
        <a href="about/directions.html">detailed directions</a>.
        Come join us!
    </p>
  </body>
</html>
```

The Head First Lounge HTML

Seeing selectors visually

Let's take some selectors and see how they map to the tree you just created. Here's how this "h1" selector maps to the graph:

```
h1 {
    font-family: sans-serif;
}
```

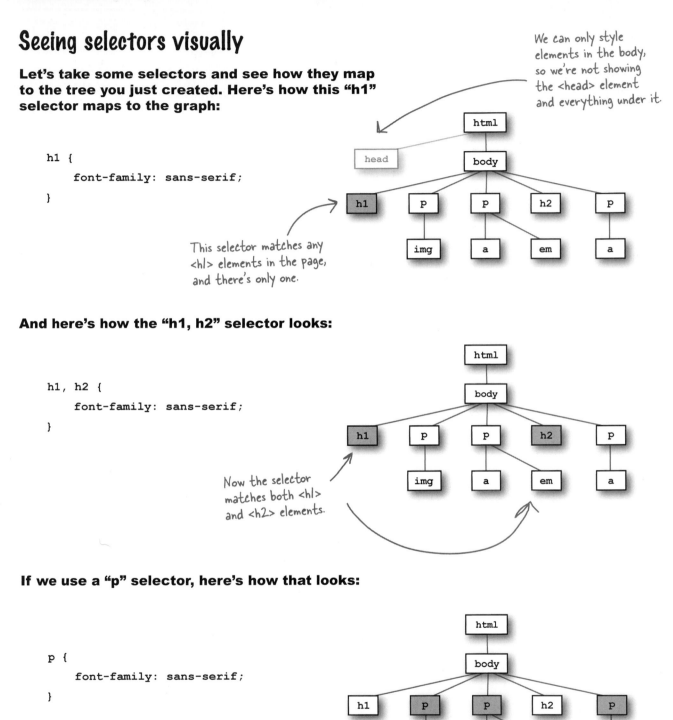

We can only style elements in the body, so we're not showing the <head> element and everything under it.

This selector matches any <h1> elements in the page, and there's only one.

And here's how the "h1, h2" selector looks:

```
h1, h2 {
    font-family: sans-serif;
}
```

Now the selector matches both <h1> and <h2> elements.

If we use a "p" selector, here's how that looks:

```
p {
    font-family: sans-serif;
}
```

This selector matches all the <p> elements in the tree.

Sharpen your pencil

Color in the elements that are **selected** by these selectors:

```
p, h2 {
    font-family: sans-serif;
}
```

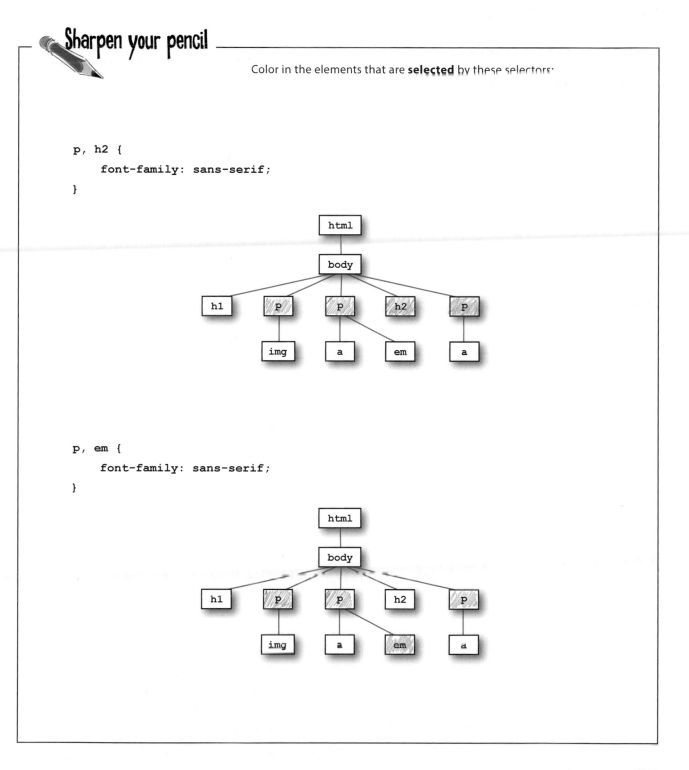

```
p, em {
    font-family: sans-serif;
}
```

The Case of Brute Force Versus Style

When we last left RadWebDesign in Chapter 4, they had just blown the corporate demo and lost RobotsRUs's business. CorrectWebDesign was put in charge of the entire RobotsRUs site and got to work getting everything nailed down before the site launch later in the month. But you'll also remember that RadWebDesign decided to bone up on their HTML and CSS. They decided to rework the RobotsRUs site on their own, using proper HTML and stylesheets, just to get some experience under their belt before they took on another consulting job.

As fate would have it, just before RobotsRUs's big site launch, it happened again: RobotsRUs called CorrectWebDesign with an urgent message. "We're changing our corporate look and we need all the colors, backgrounds, and fonts changed on our site." At this point, the site consisted of almost 100 pages, so CorrectWebDesign responded that it would take them a few days to rework the site. "We don't have a few days!" the CEO said. Desperate, the CEO decided to call in RadWebDesign for help. "You flubbed up the demo last month, but we really need your help. Can you help the CorrectWebDesign guys convert the site over to the new look and feel?" RadWebDesign said they could do better than that; in fact, they could deliver the entire site to them in less than an hour.

How did RadWebDesign go from disgrace to web page superheroes? What allowed them to change the look and feel of 100 pages faster than a speeding bullet?

Uh, I think you forgot to style the elixirs and directions pages?

Getting the lounge style into the elixirs and directions pages

It's great that we've added all this style to "lounge.html", but what about "elixir.html" and "directions.html"? They need to have a look that is consistent with the main page. Easy enough…just copy the style element and all the rules into each file, right? *Not so fast*. If you did that, then whenever you needed to change the style of the site, you'd have to change *every single file*—not what you want. But luckily, there is a better way. Here's what you're going to do:

1 Take the rules in "lounge.html" and place them in a file called "lounge.css".

2 Create an **external link** to this file from your "lounge.html" file.

3 Create the same external links in "elixir.html" and "directions.html".

4 Give all three files a good test drive.

Creating the "lounge.css" file

You're going to create a file called "lounge.css" to contain the style rules
for all your Head First Lounge pages. To do that, create a new text file
named "lounge.css" in your text editor.

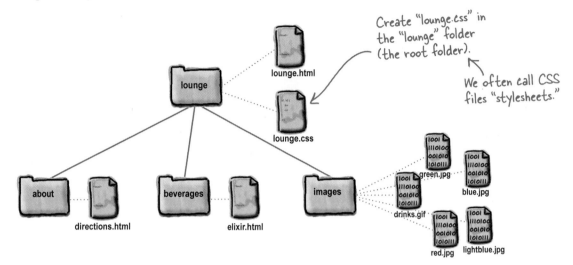

Create "lounge.css" in
the "lounge" folder
(the root folder).

We often call CSS
files "stylesheets."

Now type, or copy and paste from your "lounge.html" file, the CSS rules
into the "lounge.css" file. Delete the rules from your "lounge.html" file
while you're at it.

Note that you should not copy the `<style>` and `</style>` tags because
the "lounge.css" file contains only CSS, not HTML.

```
h1, h2 {
    font-family: sans-serif;
    color: gray;
}


h1 {
    border-bottom: 1px solid black;
}


p {
    color: maroon;
}
```

Your "lounge.css" file
should look like this.
Remember, no <style> tags!

Linking from "lounge.html" to the external stylesheet

Now we need a way to tell the browser that it should style this page with the styles in the external stylesheet. We can do that with the HTML `<link>` element. Here's how you use the `<link>` element in your HTML:

```
<!doctype html>
<html>
  <head>
    <meta charset="utf-8">
    <title>Head First Lounge</title>
    <link type="text/css" rel="stylesheet" href="lounge.css">
    <style>
    </style>
  </head>
  <body>
    <h1>Welcome to the Head First Lounge</h1>
    <p>
      <img src="drinks.gif" alt="Drinks">
    </p>
    .
    .
    .
    </p>
  </body>
</html>
```

Here's the HTML that links to the external stylesheet.

You don't need the <style> element anymore—just delete it.

The rest of the HTML is the same.

HTML Up Close

Let's take a closer look at the `<link>` element since you haven't seen it before:

Use the link element to "link in" external information.

The type of this information is "text/css"—in other words, a CSS stylesheet. As of HTML5, you don't need this anymore (it's optional), but you may see it on older pages.

And the stylesheet is located at this href (in this case, we're using a relative link, but it could be a full-blown URL).

```
<link type="text/css" rel="stylesheet" href="lounge.css">
```

The rel attribute specifies the relationship between the HTML file and the thing you're linking to. We're linking to a stylesheet, so we use the value "stylesheet".

<link> is a void element. It has no closing tag.

Linking from "elixir.html" and "directions.html" to the external stylesheet

Now you're going to link the "elixir.html" and "directions.html" files just as you did with "lounge.html". The only thing you need to remember is that "elixir.html" is in the "beverages" folder, and "directions.html" is in the "about" folder, so they both need to use the relative path "../lounge.css".

So, all you need to do is add the following `<link>` element to both files:

```
<!DOCTYPE html>
<html>
  <head>
    <meta charset="utf-8">
    <title>Head First Lounge Elixirs</title>
    <link type="text/css" rel="stylesheet" href="../lounge.css">
  </head>
  <body>
    .
    .
    .
  </body>
</html>
```

This is "elixir.html". Just add the <link> line.

```
<!DOCTYPE html>
<html>
  <head>
    <meta charset="utf-8">
    <title>Head First Lounge Directions</title>
    <link type="text/css" rel="stylesheet" href="../lounge.css">
  </head>
  <body>
    .
    .
    .
  </body>
</html>
```

Same for "directions.html". Add the <link> line here.

Test driving the entire lounge...

Save each of these files and then open "lounge.html" with the browser. You should see no changes in its style, even though the styles are now coming from an external file. Now click on the "elixirs" and "detailed directions" links.

Wow! We have a whole new style for the Elixirs and Directions pages with only a *one-line change* to the HTML in each file! Now you can really see the power of CSS.

Head First Lounge Elixirs

file:///chapter7/lounge/beverages/elixir.html

Our Elixirs

Green Tea Cooler

Chock full of vitamins and minerals, this elixir combines the healthful benefits of green tea with a twist of chamomile blossoms and ginger root.

Raspberry Ice Concentration

...combining raspberry juice with lemon grass, citrus peel and rosehips, this icy ...make your mind feel clear and crisp.

...erry Bliss Elixir

Head First Lounge

file:///chapter7/lounge/lounge.html

Welcome to the Head First Lounge

Join us any evening for refreshing elixirs, conversation and maybe a game or two of *Dance Dance Revolution*. Wireless access is always provided; BYOWS (Bring your own web server).

Directions

You'll find us right in the center of downtown Webville. If you need help finding us, check out our detailed directions. Come join us!

Head First Lounge Directions

file:///chapter7/lounge/about/directions.html

Directions

Take the 305 S exit to Webville - go 0.4 mi

Continue on 305 - go 12 mi

Turn right at Structure Ave N - go 0.6 mi

Turn right and head toward Structure Ave N - go 0.0 mi

Turn right at Structure Ave N - go 0.7 mi

Continue on Stucture Ave S - go 0.2 mi

Turn right at SW Presentation Way - go 0.0 mi

The Case of Brute Force Versus Style

So, how did RadWebDesign become web page superheroes? Or maybe we should first ask how the "do no wrong" CorrectWebDesign firm flubbed things up this time? The root of the problem was that CorrectWebDesign was creating the RobotsRUs pages using circa-1998 techniques. They were putting their style rules right in with their HTML (copying and pasting them each time), and, even worse, they were using a lot of old HTML elements like `<font>` and `<center>` that have now been deprecated (eliminated from HTML). So, when the call came to change the look and feel, that meant going into every web page and making changes to the CSS. Worse, it meant going through the HTML to change elements as well.

Compare that with what RadWebDesign did: they used HTML5, so they had no old presentation HTML in their pages, and they used an external stylesheet. The result? To change the style of the entire site, all they had to do was go into their external stylesheet and make a few changes to the CSS, which they easily did in minutes, not days. They even had time to try out multiple designs and have three different versions of the CSS ready for review before the site launch. Amazed, the RobotsRUs CEO not only promised RadWebDesign more business, but he also promised them the first robot that comes off the assembly line.

Five-Minute Mystery

Solved

Sharpen your pencil

Now that you've got one external style file (or "stylesheet"), use it to change all the paragraph fonts to "sans-serif" to match the headings. Remember, the property to change the font style is "font-family", and the value for sans-serif font is "sans-serif". You'll find the answer on the next page.

The headings use sans-serif fonts, which don't have serifs and have a very clean look.

The paragraphs still use the default serif fonts, which have serifs, and are often considered more difficult to read on a computer screen.

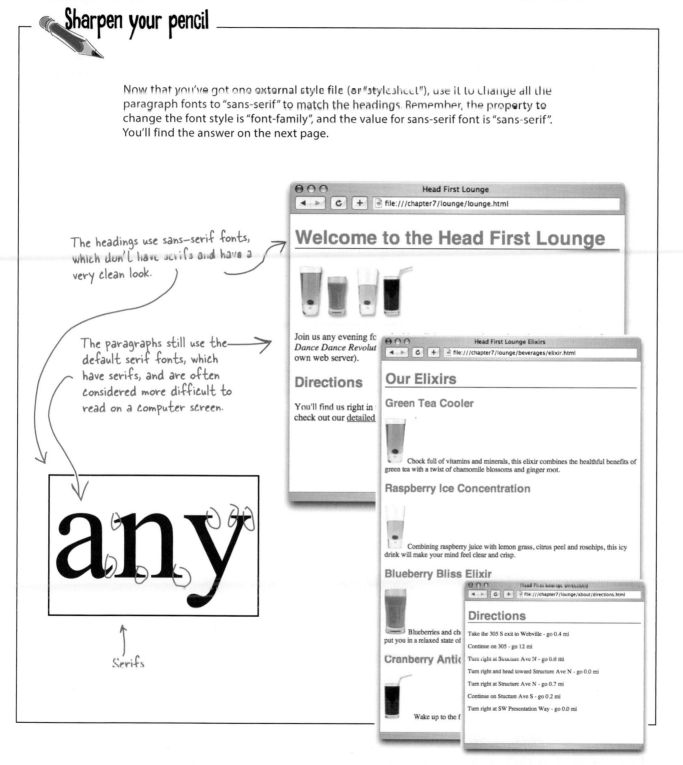

Serifs

Sharpen your pencil
Solution

Now that you've got one external style file (or "stylesheet"), use it to change all the paragraph fonts to "sans-serif" to match the headings. Remember, the property to change the font style is "font-family", and the value for sans-serif font is "sans-serif". Here's our solution.

```
h1, h2 {
      font-family:  sans-serif;
      color:        gray;
}

h1 {
      border-bottom: 1px solid black;
}

p {
      font-family:  sans-serif;
      color:        maroon;
}
```

Just add a font-family property to your paragraph rule in the "lounge.css" file.

I'm wondering if that is really the best solution. Why are we specifying the font-family for EACH element? What if someone added a <blockquote> to the page—would we have to then add a rule for that too? Can't we just tell the *whole* page to be sans-serif?

It's time to talk about your inheritance...

Did you notice when you added the `font-family` property to your p selector that it also affected the font family of the elements inside the `<p>` element? Let's take a closer look:

When you added the font-family property to your CSS p selector, it changed the font family of your `<p>` elements. But it also changed the font family of the two links and the emphasized text.

The elements inside the `<p>` element <u>inherit</u> the font-family style from `<p>`

Just like you can inherit your blue eyes or brown hair from your parents, elements can inherit styles from their parents. In this case, the `<a>` and `<em>` elements inherited the `font-family` style from the `<p>` element, which is their parent element. It makes sense that changing your paragraph style would change the style of the elements in the paragraph, doesn't it? After all, if it didn't, you'd have to go in and add CSS rules for every inline element in every paragraph in your whole site…which would definitely be so NOT fun.

Not every style is inherited. Just some are, like font-family.

Not to mention, error-prone, tedious, and time-consuming

Let's take a look at the HTML tree to see how inheritance works:

If we set the font-family of all the `<p>` elements, here are all the elements that would be affected.

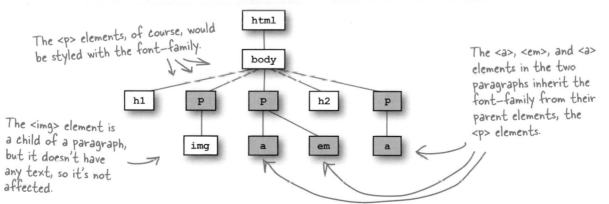

The `<p>` elements, of course, would be styled with the font-family.

The `<img>` element is a child of a paragraph, but it doesn't have any text, so it's not affected.

The `<a>`, `<em>`, and `<a>` elements in the two paragraphs inherit the font-family from their parent elements, the `<p>` elements.

What if we move the font up the family tree?

If most elements inherit the `font-family` property, what if we move it up to
the `<body>` element? That should have the effect of changing the font for all
the `<body>` element's children, and children's children.

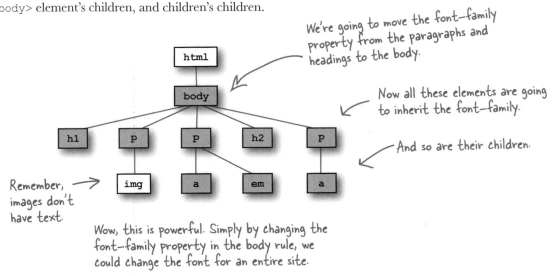

We're going to move the font-family property from the paragraphs and headings to the body.

Now all these elements are going to inherit the font-family.

And so are their children.

Remember, images don't have text.

Wow, this is powerful. Simply by changing the font-family property in the body rule, we could change the font for an entire site.

What are you waiting for...give it a try

Open your "lounge.css" file and add a new rule that selects the `<body>` element.
Then remove the `font-family` properties from the headings and paragraph
rules, because you're not going to need them anymore.

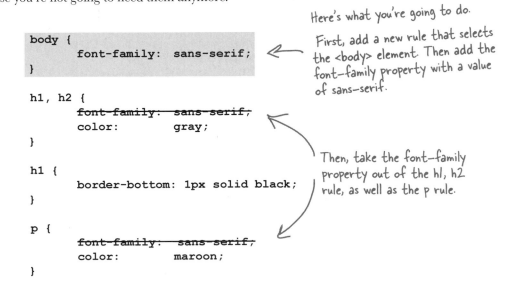

Here's what you're going to do.

First, add a new rule that selects the <body> element. Then add the font-family property with a value of sans-serif.

Then, take the font-family property out of the h1, h2 rule, as well as the p rule.

```
body {
        font-family:  sans-serif;
}

h1, h2 {
        font-family:  sans-serif;
        color:        gray;
}

h1 {
        border-bottom: 1px solid black;
}

p {
        font-family:  sans-serif;
        color:        maroon;
}
```

Test drive your new CSS

As usual, go ahead and make these changes in the "lounge.css" stylesheet, save, and reload the "lounge.html" page. You shouldn't expect any changes, because the style is the same. It's just coming from a different rule. But you should feel better about your CSS, because now you can add new elements to your pages and they'll automatically inherit the sans-serif font.

Surprise, surprise. This doesn't look any different at all, but that is exactly what we were expecting, isn't it? All you've done is move the sans-serif font up into the body rule and let all the other elements inherit that.

Okay, so now that the whole site is set to sans-serif with the body selector, what if I want *one* element to be a different font? Do I have to take the font-family out of the body and add rules for every element separately again?

Overriding inheritance

By moving the `font-family` property up into the body, you've set that
font style for the entire page. But what if you don't want the sans-serif
font on every element? For instance, you could decide that you want <em>
elements to use the serif font instead.

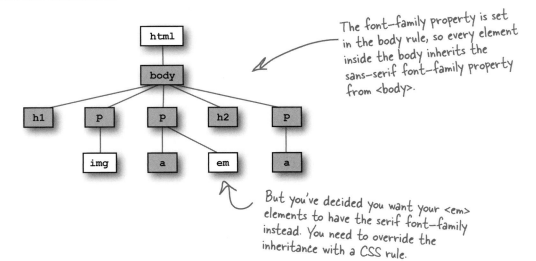

The font-family property is set
in the body rule, so every element
inside the body inherits the
sans-serif font-family property
from <body>.

But you've decided you want your <em>
elements to have the serif font-family
instead. You need to override the
inheritance with a CSS rule.

Well, then you can override the inheritance by supplying a
specific rule just for <em>. Here's how you add a rule for <em>
to override the `font-family` specified in the body:

```
body {
        font-family:  sans-serif;
}

h1, h2 {
        color:         gray;
}

h1 {
        border-bottom: 1px solid black;
}

p {
        color:         maroon;
}

em {
        font-family: serif;
}
```

To override the font-family property
inherited from body, add a new rule
selecting em with the font-family
property value set to serif.

Test drive

Add a rule for the `<em>` element to your CSS with a `font-family` property value of `serif`, and reload your "lounge.html" page:

> *Notice that the "Dance Dance Revolution" text, which is the text in the `<em>` element, is now a serif font.*

As a general rule, it's not a good idea to change fonts in the middle of a paragraph like this, so go ahead and change your CSS back to the way it was (without the em rule) when you're done testing.

Welcome to the Head First Lounge

Join us any evening for refreshing <u>elixirs</u>, conversation and maybe a game or two of *Dance Dance Revolution*. Wireless access is always provided; BYOWS (Bring your own web server).

Directions

You'll find us right in the center of downtown Webville. If you need help finding us, check out our <u>detailed directions</u>. Come join us!

---

there are no
Dumb Questions

Q: How does the browser know which rule to apply to `<em>` when I'm overriding the inherited value?

A: With CSS, the most specific rule is always used. So, if you have a rule for `<body>`, and a more specific rule for `<em>` elements, it is going to use the more specific rule. We'll talk more later about how you know which rules are most specific.

Q: How do I know which CSS properties are inherited and which are not?

A: This is where a good reference really comes in handy, like O'Reilly's *CSS Pocket Reference*. In general, all of the styles that affect the way your text looks, such as font color (the color property), the font-family, as you've just seen, and other font-related properties such as font-size, font-weight (for bold text), and font-style (for italics) are

inherited. Other properties, such as border, are not inherited, which makes sense, right? Just because you want a border on your `<body>` element doesn't mean you want it on *all* your elements. A lot of the time, you can follow your common sense (or just try it and see), and you'll get the hang of it as you become more familiar with the various properties and what they do.

Q: Can I always override a property that is being inherited when I don't want it?

A: Yes. You can always use a more specific selector to override a property from a parent.

Q: This stuff gets complicated. Is there any way I can add comments to remind myself what the rules do?

A: Yes. To write a comment in your CSS, just enclose it between /* and */. For instance:

```
/*  this rule selects all
paragraphs and colors them
blue */
```

Notice that a comment can span multiple lines. You can also put comments around CSS and browsers will ignore it, like this:

```
/* this rule will have no
effect because it's in a
comment

p { color: blue; }   */
```

Make sure you close your comments correctly; otherwise, your CSS won't work!

> I was thinking it would be cool to have the text below each elixir match the color of the elixir. Can you do that?

We're not sure we agree with the aesthetics of that suggestion, but hey, you're the customer.

Can you style each of these paragraphs separately so that the color of the text matches the drink? The problem is that using a rule with a p selector applies the style to *all* <p> elements. So, how can you select these paragraphs individually?

That's where *classes* come in. Using both HTML and CSS, we can define a class of elements, and then apply styles to any element that belongs to that class. So, what exactly is a class? Think of it like a club—someone starts a "greentea" club, and by joining you agree to all the rights and responsibilities of the club, like adhering to their style standards. Anyway, let's just create the class and you'll see how it works.

Creating a class takes two steps: first, we add the element to the class by adding a class attribute to the element in the HTML; second, we select that class in the CSS. Let's step through that...

Green
text →

Blue text →

Purple text →

Red text...oh, we
don't need to
change this one. →

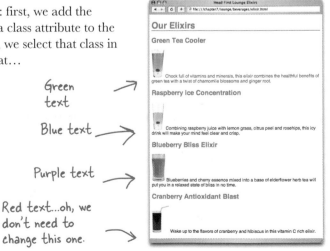

Adding an element to the greentea class

Open up the "elixir.html" file and locate the "Green Tea Cooler" paragraph. This is the text we want to change to green. All you're going to do is add the <p> element to a class called greentea. Here's how you do that:

```
<!DOCTYPE html>
<html>
  <head>
    <meta charset="utf-8">
    <title>Head First Lounge Elixirs</title>
    <link type="text/css" rel="stylesheet" href="../lounge.css">
  </head>
  <body>
    <h1>Our Elixirs</h1>
    <h2>Green Tea Cooler</h2>
    <p class="greentea">
            <img src="../images/green.jpg" alt="Green Tea">
            Chock full of vitamins and minerals, this elixir
            combines the healthful benefits of green tea with
            a twist of chamomile blossoms and ginger root.
    </p>
    <h2>Raspberry Ice Concentration</h2>
    <p>
            <img src="../images/lightblue.jpg" alt="Raspberry Ice">
            Combining raspberry juice with lemon grass,
            citrus peel and rosehips, this icy drink
            will make your mind feel clear and crisp.
    </p>
    <h2>Blueberry Bliss Elixir</h2>
    <p>
            <img src="../images/blue.jpg" alt="Blueberry Bliss">
            Blueberries and cherry essence mixed into a base
            of elderflower herb tea will put you in a relaxed
            state of bliss in no time.
    </p>
    <h2>Cranberry Antioxidant Blast</h2>
    <p>
            <img src="../images/red.jpg" alt="Cranberry Blast">
            Wake up to the flavors of cranberry and hibiscus
            in this vitamin C rich elixir.
    </p>
  </body>
</html>
```

To add an element to a class, just add the attribute "class" along with the name of the class, like "greentea".

Now that the green tea paragraph belongs to the greentea class, you just need to provide some rules to style that class of elements.

Creating a class selector

To create a class in CSS and select an element in that class, you write a *class selector*, like this:

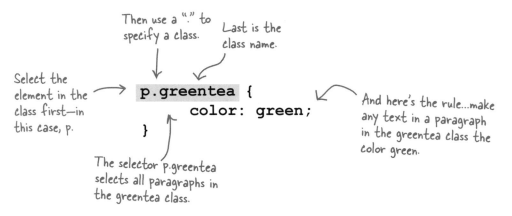

Then use a "." to specify a class.

Last is the class name.

Select the element in the class first—in this case, p.

```
p.greentea {
        color: green;
}
```

And here's the rule...make any text in a paragraph in the greentea class the color green.

The selector p.greentea selects all paragraphs in the greentea class.

So now you have a way of selecting <p> elements that belong to a certain class to style them. All you need to do is add the class attribute to any <p> elements you want to be green, and this rule will be applied. Give it a try: open your "lounge.css" file and add the p.greentea class selector to it.

```
body {
        font-family: sans-serif;
}

h1, h2 {
        color: gray;
}

h1 {
        border-bottom: 1px solid black;
}

p {
        color: maroon;
}

p.greentea {
        color: green;
}
```

A greentea test drive

Save and then reload to give your new class a test drive.

Here's the new greentea class applied to the paragraph. Now the font is green and matches the Green Tea Cooler. Maybe this styling wasn't such a bad idea after all.

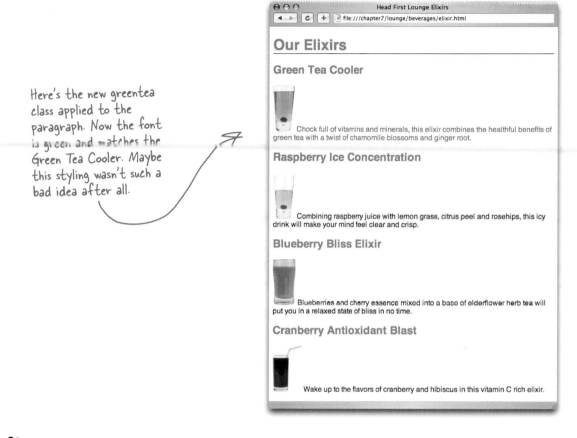

─── **Sharpen your pencil** ───────────────────────

Your turn: add two classes, "raspberry" and "blueberry", to the correct paragraphs in "elixir.html", and then write the styles to color the text blue and purple, respectively. The property value for raspberry is "blue" and for blueberry is "purple". Put these at the bottom of your CSS file, under the greentea rule: raspberry first, and then blueberry.

Yeah, we know you're probably thinking, how can a raspberry be blue? Well, if Raspberry Kool-Aid is blue, that's good enough for us. And seriously, when you blend up a bunch of blueberries, they really are more purple than blue. Work with us here.

Taking classes further...

You've already written one rule that uses the `greentea` class to change any
paragraph in the class to the color "green":

```
p.greentea {
        color: green;
}
```

But what if you wanted to do the same to all `<blockquote>`s?
Then you could do this:

```
blockquote.greentea, p.greentea {
        color: green;
}
```

Just add another selector to handle
`<blockquote>`s that are in the greentea
class. Now this rule will apply to `<p>`
and `<blockquote>` elements in the
greentea class.

And in your HTML you'd write:

```
<blockquote class="greentea">
```

So what if I want to
add `<h1>`, `<h2>`, `<h3>`, `<p>`, and
`<blockquote>` to the greentea
class? Do I have to write one
huge selector?

No, there's a better way. If you want all
elements that are in the `greentea` class to
have a style, then you can just write your
rule like this:

```
.greentea {
        color: green;
}
```

If you leave out all the element names,
and just use a period followed by a class
name, then the rule will apply to all
members of the class.

Cool! Yes, that works. One more question...you said being in a class is like being in a club. Well, I can join many clubs. So, can an element be in more than one class?

Yes, elements can be in more than one class.

It's easy to put an element into more than one class. Say you want to specify a <p> element that is in the greentea, raspberry, and blueberry classes. Here's how you would do that in the opening tag:

```
<p class="greentea raspberry blueberry">
```

Place each class name into the value of the class attribute, with a space in between each. The ordering doesn't matter.

So, for example, I could put an <h1> into my "products" class that defines a font size and weight, and also a "specials" class to change its color to red when something's on sale?

Exactly. Use multiple classes when you want an element to have styles you've defined in different classes. In this case, all your <h1> elements associated with products have a certain style, but not all your products are on sale at the same time. By putting your "specials" color in a separate class, you can simply add only those elements associated with products on sale to the "specials" class to add the red color you want.

Now you may be wondering what happens when an element belongs to multiple classes, all of which define the *same* property—like our <p> element up there. How do you know which style gets applied? You know each of these classes has a definition for the color property. So, will the paragraph be green, blue (raspberry), or purple?

We're going to talk about this in great detail after you've learned a bit more CSS, but on the next page you'll find a quick guide to hold you over.

The world's smallest and fastest guide to how styles are applied

Elements and document trees and style rules and classes…it can get downright confusing. How does all this stuff come together so that you know which styles are being applied to which elements? As we said, *to fully answer that* you're going to have to know a little more about CSS, and you'll be learning that in the next few chapters. But before you get there, let's just walk through some common-sense rules of thumb about how styles are applied.

First, do <u>any</u> selectors select your element?

Let's say you want to know the `font-family` property value for an element. The first thing to check is: is there a selector in your CSS file that selects your element? If there is, and it has a `font-family` property and value, then that's the value for your element.

What about inheritance?

If there are no selectors that match your element, then you rely on inheritance. So, look at the element's parents, and parents' parents, and so on, until you find the property defined. When and if you find it, that's the value.

Struck out again? Then use the default

If your element doesn't inherit the value from any of its ancestors, then you use the default value defined by the browser. In reality, this is a little more complicated than we're describing here, but we'll get to some of those details later in the book.

What if multiple selectors select an element?

Ah, this is the case we have with the paragraph that belongs to all three classes:

```
<p class="greentea raspberry blueberry">
```

There are multiple selectors that match this element and define the same `color` property. That's what we call a *conflict*. Which rule breaks the tie? Well, if one rule is more *specific* than the others, then it wins. But what does "more specific" mean? We'll come back in a later chapter and see *exactly* how to determine how specific a selector is, but for now, let's look at some rules and get a feel for it:

```
p { color: black;}
.greentea { color: green; }
p.greentea { color: green; }
p.raspberry { color: blue; }
p.blueberry { color: purple; }
```

Here's a rule that selects any old paragraph element.

This rule selects members of the greentea class. That's a little more specific.

And this rule selects only paragraphs that are in the greentea class, so that's even more specific.

These rules also select only paragraphs in a particular class. So they are about the same in specificity as the p.greentea rule.

And if we still don't have a clear winner?

So, if you had an element that belonged only to the greentea class, there would be an obvious winner: the p.greentea selector is the most specific, so the text would be green. But you have an element that belongs to *all three* classes: greentea, raspberry, and blueberry. So, p.greentea, p.raspberry, and p.blueberry all select the element, and are of equal specificity. What do you do now? You choose the one that is listed *last* in the CSS file. If you can't resolve a conflict because two selectors are equally specific, you use the ordering of the rules in your stylesheet file; that is, you use the rule listed last in the CSS file (nearest the bottom). And in this case, that would be the p.blueberry rule.

Exercise

In your "elixir.html" file, change the greentea paragraph to include all the classes, like this:

```
<p class="greentea raspberry blueberry">
```

Save and reload. What color is the Green Tea Cooler paragraph now? _purple_

Next, reorder the classes in your HTML:

```
<p class="raspberry blueberry greentea">
```

Save and reload. What color is the Green Tea Cooler paragraph now? _purple_

Next, open your CSS file and move the p.greentea rule to the bottom of the file.

Save and reload. What color is the Green Tea Cooler paragraph now? _green_

Finally, move the p.raspberry rule to the bottom of the file.

Save and reload. What color is the Green Tea Cooler paragraph now? _blue_

After you've finished, rewrite the green tea element to look like it did originally:

```
<p class="greentea">
```

Save and reload. What color is the Green Tea Cooler paragraph now? _green_

Fireside Chats

Tonight's talk: **CSS & HTML compare languages**

CSS:

HTML:

Did you see that? I'm like Houdini! I broke right out of your `<style>` element and into my own file. And you said in Chapter 1 that I'd never escape.

Don't get all excited; I still have to link you in for you to be at all useful.

Have to link me in? Come on; you know your pages wouldn't cut it without my styling.

Here we go again…while me and all my elements are trying to keep things structured, you're talking about hair highlights and nail color.

If you were paying attention in this chapter, you would have seen I'm downright powerful in what I can do.

Okay, okay, I admit it; using CSS sure makes my job easier. All those old deprecated styling elements were a pain in my side. I do like the fact that my elements can be styled without inserting a bunch of stuff in the HTML, other than maybe an occasional class attribute.

Well now, that's a little better. I like the new attitude.

But I still haven't forgotten how you mocked my syntax…<remember>?

CSS:

You have to admit HTML is kinda clunky, but that's what you get when you're related to an early '90s technology.

Are you kidding? I'm very expressive. I can select just the elements I want, and then describe exactly how I want them styled. And you've only just begun to see all the cool styling I can do.

Yup; just wait and see. I can style fonts and text in all kinds of interesting ways. I can even control how each element manages the space around it on the page.

Bwahahaha. And you thought you had me controlled between your `<style>` tags. You're going to see I can make your elements sit, bark, and roll over if I want to.

HTML:

I call it standing the test of time. And you think CSS is elegant? I mean, you're just a bunch of rules. How's that a language?

Oh yeah?

Hmmm…sounds as if you have a little too much power; I'm not sure I like the sound of that. After all, my elements want to have some control over their own lives.

Whoa now! Security…security?!

Who gets the inheritance?

Sniff, sniff; the <body> element has gone to that great browser in the sky. But he left behind a lot of descendants and a big inheritance of color "green". Below, you'll find his family tree. Mark all the descendants that inherit the <body> element's color green. Don't forget to look at the CSS below first.

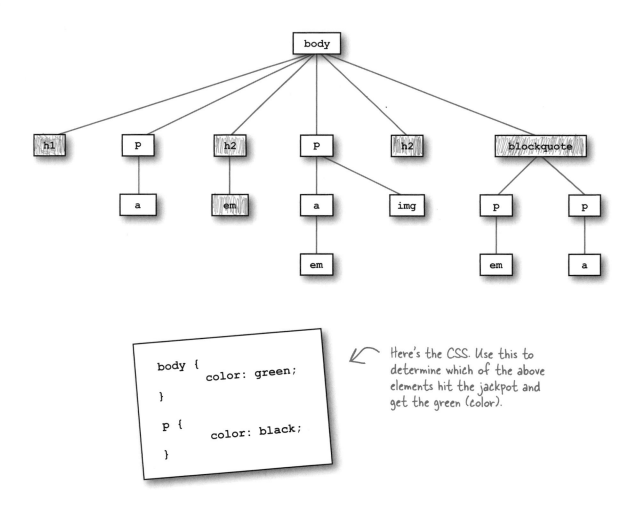

Here's the CSS. Use this to determine which of the above elements hit the jackpot and get the green (color).

```
body {
        color: green;
}

p {
        color: black;
}
```

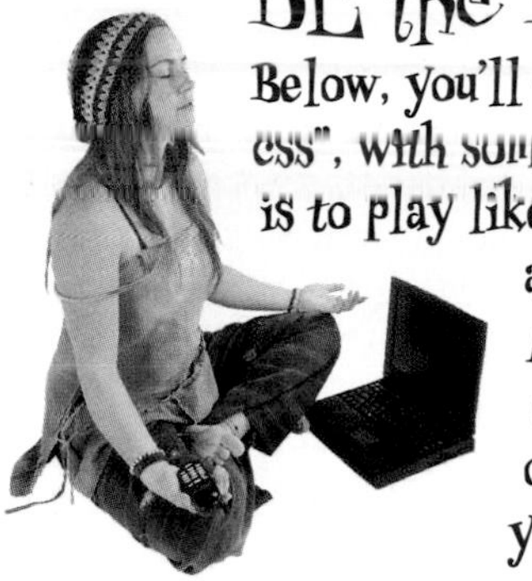

If you have errors in your CSS, usually what happens is all the rules below the error are ignored. So, get in the habit of looking for errors now, by doing this exercise.

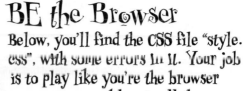

BE the Browser

Below, you'll find the CSS file "style. css", with some errors in it. Your job is to play like you're the browser and locate all the errors. After you've done the exercise, look at the end of the chapter to see if you caught all the errors.

The file "style.css"

```
<style>

body {
    background-color: white
                               missing
                               ; semicolon

missing closing brace

h1, {    missing selector
   color: gray;   missing color property
    font-family: sans-serif;
}

h2, p {
    color:    missing color value
}

                remove angle brackets
<em> {
    font-style: italic;
}

</style>
```

The exercise got me thinking...is there a way to validate CSS like there is with HTML?

Of course!

Those W3C boys and girls aren't just sitting around on their butts, they've been working hard. You can find their CSS validator at:

http://jigsaw.w3.org/css-validator/

Type that URL in your browser, and we think you'll feel quite at home when you get there. You're going to find a validator that works almost exactly like the HTML validator. To use the CSS version, just point the validator to your CSS URL, upload a file with your CSS in it (first tab), or just paste it into the form (second tab), and submit.

You shouldn't encounter any big surprises, like needing doctypes or character encodings with CSS. Go ahead, give it a try (like we're not going to make you do it on the next page, anyway).

Making sure the lounge CSS validates

Before you wrap up this chapter, wouldn't you feel a lot better if all that Head First Lounge CSS validated? Sure, you would. Use whichever method you want to get your CSS to the W3C. If you have your CSS on a server, type your URL into the form; otherwise, either upload your CSS file or just copy and paste the CSS into the form. (If you upload, make sure you're directing the form to your CSS file, not your HTML file.) Once you've done that, click on Check.

If your CSS didn't validate, check it with the CSS a few pages back and find any small mistakes you've made, then resubmit.

Yay! Our CSS validates as CSS 2.1 (the validator hasn't upgraded to CSS 3 yet, but if it has by the time you read this, it should still validate).

Here are some icons you can put on your web page if you want to show off that your CSS validates. (You can get similar icons for validated HTML, too.)

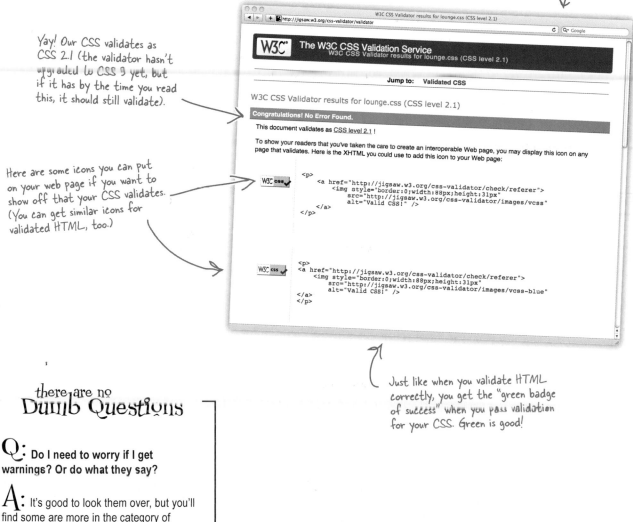

Just like when you validate HTML correctly, you get the "green badge of success" when you pass validation for your CSS. Green is good!

there are no Dumb Questions

Q: Do I need to worry if I get warnings? Or do what they say?

A: It's good to look them over, but you'll find some are more in the category of suggestions than "must do's." The validator can err on the side of being a little anal, so just keep that in mind.

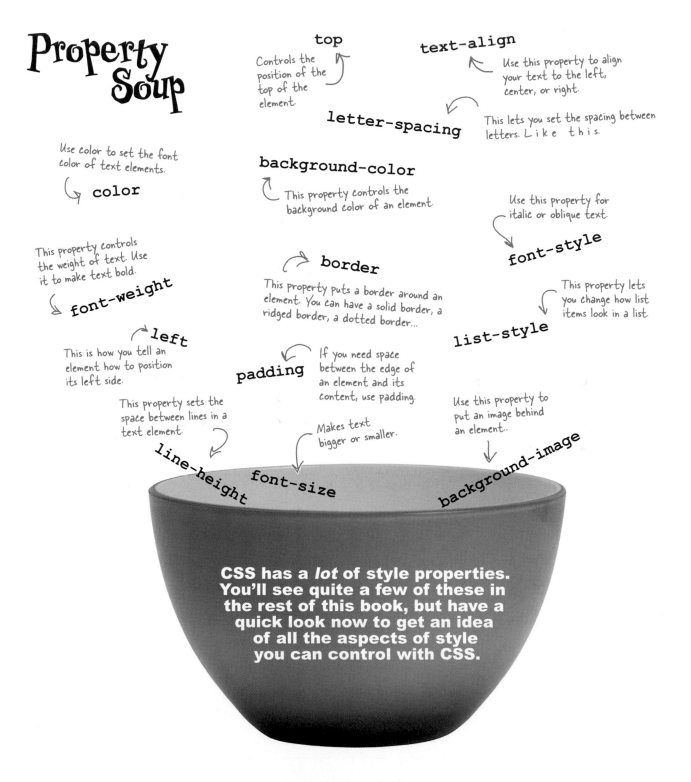

Property Soup

top
Controls the position of the top of the element.

text-align
Use this property to align your text to the left, center, or right.

letter-spacing
This lets you set the spacing between letters. L i k e   t h i s.

Use color to set the font color of text elements.
color

background-color
This property controls the background color of an element.

Use this property for italic or oblique text.
font-style

This property controls the weight of text. Use it to make text bold.
font-weight

border
This property puts a border around an element. You can have a solid border, a ridged border, a dotted border...

This property lets you change how list items look in a list.
list-style

left
This is how you tell an element how to position its left side.

padding
If you need space between the edge of an element and its content, use padding.

This property sets the space between lines in a text element.
line-height

Makes text bigger or smaller.
font-size

Use this property to put an image behind an element.
background-image

CSS has a *lot* of style properties. You'll see quite a few of these in the rest of this book, but have a quick look now to get an idea of all the aspects of style you can control with CSS.

It looks like you're getting the hang of this style stuff. We're looking forward to seeing what you come up with in the next couple of chapters.

BULLET POINTS

- CSS contains simple statements, called rules.

- Each rule provides the style for a selection of HTML elements.

- A typical rule consists of a selector along with one or more properties and values.

- The selector specifies which elements the rule applies to.

- Each property declaration ends with a semicolon.

- All properties and values in a rule go between { } braces.

- You can select any element using its name as the selector.

- By separating element names with commas, you can select multiple elements at once.

- One of the easiest ways to include a style in HTML is the <style> tag.

- For HTML and for sites of any complexity, you should link to an external stylesheet.

- The <link> element is used to include an external stylesheet.

- Many properties are inherited. For instance, if a property that is inherited is set for the <body> element, all the <body>'s child elements will inherit it.

- You can always override properties that are inherited by creating a more specific rule for the element you'd like to change.

- Use the class attribute to add elements to a class.

- Use a "." between the element name and the class name to select a specific element in that class.

- Use ".classname" to select any elements that belong to the class.

- You can specify that an element belongs to more than one class by placing multiple class names in the class attribute with spaces between the names.

- You can validate your CSS using the W3C validator, at http://jigsaw.w3.org/css-validator.

HTMLcross

Here are some clues with mental twist and turns that will help you burn alternative routes to CSS right into your brain!

Across

3. Styles are defined in these.
5. Selects an element.
8. Each rule defines a set of properties and _____.
10. Defines a group of elements.
11. Property that represents font color.
13. Ornamental part of some fonts.
14. How elements get properties from their parents.
15. Property for font type.

Down

1. Fonts without serifs.
2. You can place your CSS inside these tags in an HTML file.
4. An external style file is called this.
6. With inheritance, a property set on one element is also passed down to its _____.
7. Won this time because they used external stylesheets.
9. They really wanted some style.
12. Use this element to include an external stylesheet.

Markup Magnets Solution

Remember drawing the hierarchy diagram of HTML elements in Chapter 3? You did that again for the Lounge's main page. Here's our solution.

Like this →

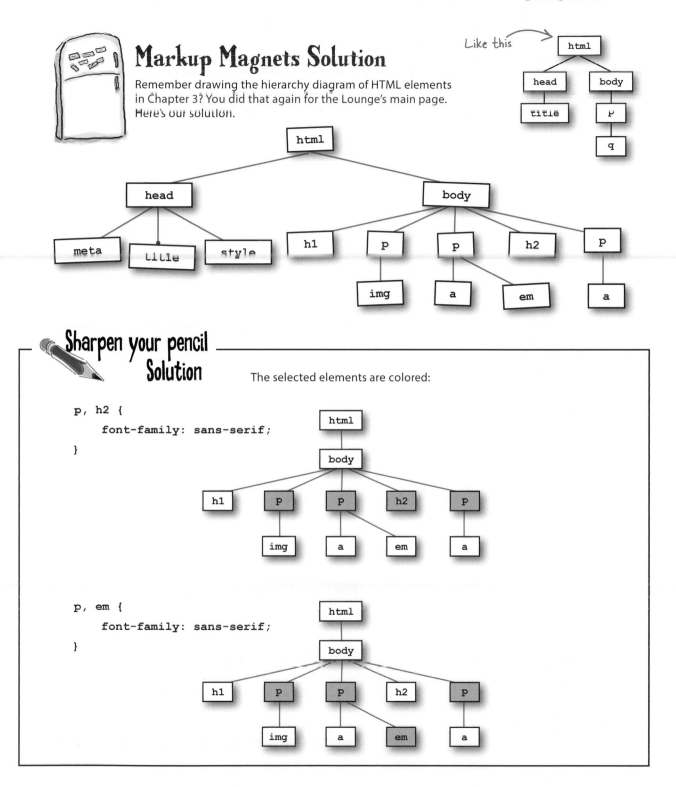

Sharpen your pencil Solution

The selected elements are colored:

```
p, h2 {
    font-family: sans-serif;
}
```

```
p, em {
    font-family: sans-serif;
}
```

Sharpen your pencil Solution

Your turn: add two classes, "raspberry" and "blueberry" to the correct paragraphs in "elixir.html" and then write the styles to color the text blue and purple, respectively. The property value for raspberry is "blue" and for blueberry is "purple".

```
body {
        font-family: sans-serif;
}

h1, h2 {
        color: gray;
}

h1 {
        border-bottom: 1px solid black;
}

p {
        color: maroon;
}

p.greentea {
        color: green;
}

p.raspberry {
        color: blue;
}

p.blueberry {
        color: purple;
}
```

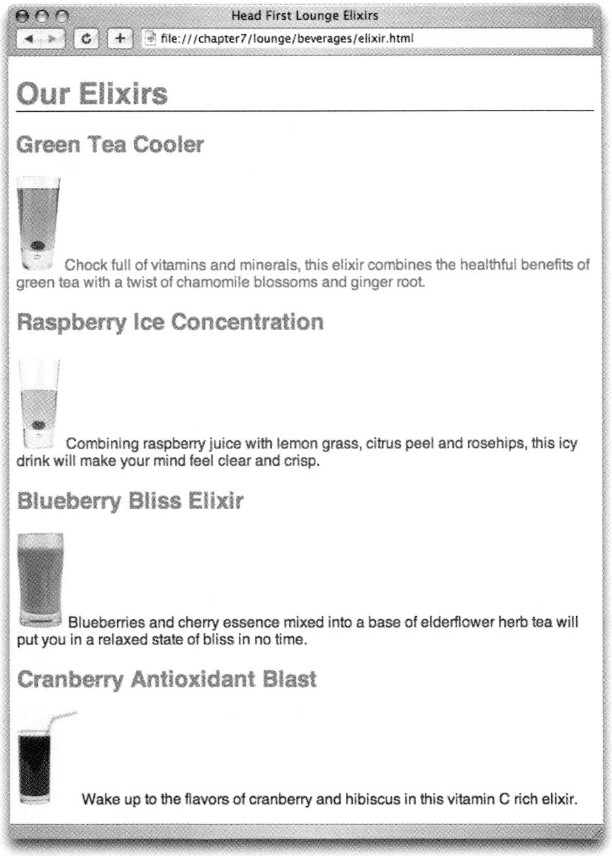

Head First Lounge Elixirs

file:///chapter7/lounge/beverages/elixir.html

Our Elixirs

Green Tea Cooler

Chock full of vitamins and minerals, this elixir combines the healthful benefits of green tea with a twist of chamomile blossoms and ginger root.

Raspberry Ice Concentration

Combining raspberry juice with lemon grass, citrus peel and rosehips, this icy drink will make your mind feel clear and crisp.

Blueberry Bliss Elixir

Blueberries and cherry essence mixed into a base of elderflower herb tea will put you in a relaxed state of bliss in no time.

Cranberry Antioxidant Blast

Wake up to the flavors of cranberry and hibiscus in this vitamin C rich elixir.

```
<!doctype html>
<html>
  <head>
    <meta charset="utf-8">
    <title>Head First Lounge Elixirs</title>
    <link type="text/css" rel="stylesheet" href="../lounge.css">
  </head>
  <body>
    <h1>Our Elixirs</h1>
    <h2>Green Tea Cooler</h2>
    <p class="greentea">
            <img src="../images/green.jpg" alt="Green Tea">
            Chock full of vitamins and minerals, this elixir
            combines the healthful benefits of green tea with
            a twist of chamomile blossoms and ginger root.
    </p>
    <h2>Raspberry Ice Concentration</h2>
    <p class="raspberry">
            <img src="../images/lightblue.jpg" alt="Raspberry Ice">
            Combining raspberry juice with lemon grass,
            citrus peel and rosehips, this icy drink
            will make your mind feel clear and crisp.
    </p>
    <h2>Blueberry Bliss Elixir</h2>
    <p class="blueberry">
            <img src="../images/blue.jpg" alt="Blueberry Bliss">
            Blueberries and cherry essence mixed into a base
            of elderflower herb tea will put you in a relaxed
            state of bliss in no time.
    </p>
    <h2>Cranberry Antioxidant Blast</h2>
    <p>
            <img src="../images/red.jpg" alt="Cranberry Blast">
            Wake up to the flavors of cranberry and hibiscus
            in this vitamin C rich elixir.
    </p>
  </body>
</html>
```

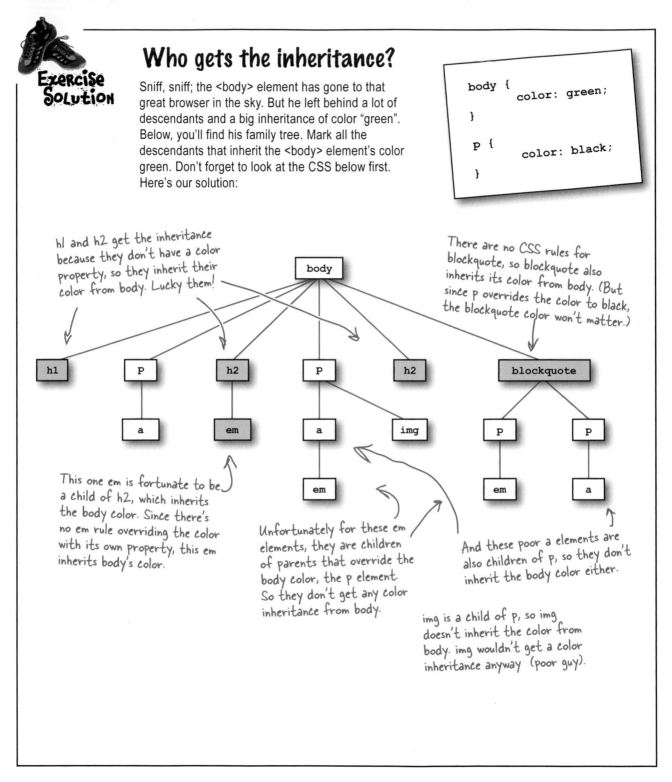

Who gets the inheritance?

Sniff, sniff; the <body> element has gone to that great browser in the sky. But he left behind a lot of descendants and a big inheritance of color "green". Below, you'll find his family tree. Mark all the descendants that inherit the <body> element's color green. Don't forget to look at the CSS below first. Here's our solution:

```
body {
        color: green;
}

p {
        color: black;
}
```

ExErcise SoLuTioN

h1 and h2 get the inheritance because they don't have a color property, so they inherit their color from body. Lucky them!

There are no CSS rules for blockquote, so blockquote also inherits its color from body. (But since p overrides the color to black, the blockquote color won't matter.)

This one em is fortunate to be a child of h2, which inherits the body color. Since there's no em rule overriding the color with its own property, this em inherits body's color.

Unfortunately for these em elements, they are children of parents that override the body color, the p element. So they don't get any color inheritance from body.

And these poor a elements are also children of p, so they don't inherit the body color either.

img is a child of p, so img doesn't inherit the color from body. img wouldn't get a color inheritance anyway (poor guy).

BE the Browser Solution

Below, you'll find the CSS file with some errors in it. Your job was to play like you're the browser and locate all the errors. Did you find them all?

```
<style>                    No HTML in your CSS! The
                           <style> tags are HTML and don't
                           work in a CSS stylesheet.

body {
                                              Missing semicolon
    background-color: white

                    — Missing }
   Extra comma
            h1, {

Missing property name      gray;
and colon
           font-family: sans-serif;

}


h2, p {     Missing property value and semicolon
    color:

}

                                Using the HTML tag instead of just the
                                element name. This should be em.
<em> {

    font-style: italic;

}
                    No </style> tags needed
                    in the CSS
</style>
```

Exercise Solution

In your "elixir.html" file, change the greentea paragraph to include all the classes, like this:

```
<p class="greentea raspberry blueberry">
```

Save and reload. What color is the Green Tea Cooler paragraph now?   <u>purple</u>

It's purple because the blueberry rule is last in the CSS file.

Next, reorder the classes in your HTML:

```
<p class="raspberry blueberry greentea">
```

Save and reload. What color is the Green Tea Cooler paragraph now?   <u>purple</u>

It's still purple because the ordering of the names in the class attribute doesn't matter.

Next, open your CSS file and move the p.greentea rule to the bottom of the file.

Save and reload. What color is the Green Tea Cooler paragraph now?   <u>green</u>

Now, it's green, because the greentea rule comes last in the CSS file.

Finally, move the p.raspberry rule to the bottom of the file.

Save and reload. What color is the Green Tea Cooler paragraph now?   <u>blue</u>

Now, it's blue, because the raspberry rule comes last in the CSS file.

After you've finished, rewrite the green tea element to look like it did originally:

```
<p class="greentea">
```

Save and reload. What color is the Green Tea Cooler paragraph now?   <u>green</u>

Okay, now the <p> element only belongs to one class, so we use the most specific rule, which is p.greentea.

HTMLcross Solution

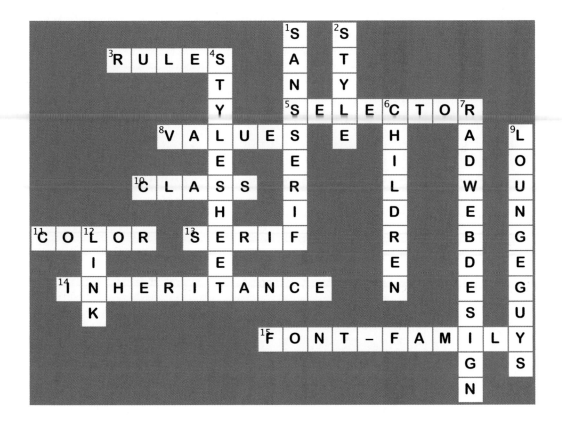

8 styling with fonts and colors

Expanding Your Vocabulary

Your CSS language lessons are coming along nicely. You already have the basics of CSS down, and you know how to create CSS rules to select and specify the style of an element. Now it's time to build your vocabulary, and that means picking up some new properties and learning what they can do for you. In this chapter we're going to work through some of the most common properties that affect the display of text. To do that, you'll need to learn a few things about fonts and color. You're going to see you don't have to be stuck with the fonts everyone else uses, or the clunky sizes and styles the browser uses as the defaults for paragraphs and headings. You're also going to see there is a lot more to color than meets the eye.

Text and fonts from 30,000 feet

A lot of CSS properties are dedicated to helping you style your text. Using CSS, you can control font, style, color, and even the decorations that are put on your text, and we're going to cover all these in this chapter. We'll start by exploring the actual fonts that are used to display your pages. You've already seen the `font-family` property, and in this chapter you're going to learn a lot more about specifying fonts.

Before we dive in, let's get the 30,000-foot view of some properties you can use to specify and change the look of your fonts. After that, we'll take the fonts one by one and learn the ins and outs of using each.

Andale Mono
Arial
Arial Black
Comic Sans
Courier New
Georgia
Impact
Times New Roman
Trebuchet MS
Verdana

Customize the fonts in your pages with the font-family property.

Fonts can have a dramatic effect on your page designs. In CSS, fonts are divided into "font families" from which you can specify the fonts you'd like used in each element of your page. Only certain fonts are commonly installed on most computers, so you need to be careful in your font choices. In this chapter we'll take you through everything you need to know to specify and make the best use of fonts.

Although we'll see in a bit how you can expand the fonts available to your browser.

```
body {
    font-family: Verdana, Geneva, Arial, sans-serif;
}
```

Control the size of your fonts with the font-size property.

Font size also has a big impact on the design and the readability of your web pages. There are several ways to specify font sizes with CSS, and in this chapter we'll cover each one, but we'll also teach you how to specify your fonts in a way that allows your users to increase the font size without affecting your designs.

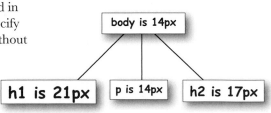

```
body {
    font-size: 14px;
}
```

Add color to your text with the color property.

You can change your text color with the color property. To do that, it helps to know a little about web colors, and we'll take you through all the ins and outs of color, including the mysterious color "hex codes."

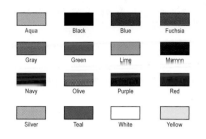

```
body {
    color: silver;
}
```

Affect the weight of your fonts with the font-weight property.

Why settle for boring, average fonts when you can give them some extra weight when needed? Or are your fonts looking too heavy? Slim them down to a normal weight. All this is easily done with the font-weight property.

```
body {
    font-weight: bold;
}
```

lighter

normal

bold

bolder

Add even more style to your text with the text-decoration property.

Using the text-decoration property, you can decorate your text with decorations including overlines, underlines, and line-throughs.

```
body {
    text-decoration: underline;
}
```

underline

overline

~~line-through~~

What is a font family anyway?

You've already come across the `font-family` property, and so far you've always specified a value of "sans-serif". You can get a lot more creative than that with the `font-family` property, but it helps to know what a font family is first. Here's a quick rundown…

Each font-family contains a set of fonts that share common characteristics. There are five font families: sans-serif, serif, monospace, cursive, and fantasy. Each family includes a large set of fonts, so on this page you'll see only a few examples of each.

Sans-serif family

Verdana **Arial Black**

Trebuchet MS   Arial

Geneva

The serif family includes fonts with serifs. A lot of people associate the look of these fonts with newspaper print.

Serifs are the decorative barbs and hooks on the ends of the letters.

The sans-serif family includes fonts without serifs. These fonts are usually considered more readable on computer screens than serif fonts.

Sans-serif means "without serifs."

Serif family

Times

Times New Roman

Georgia

Fonts aren't consistently available from one computer to another. In fact, the set of available fonts will vary depending on the operating system as well as what fonts and applications a user has installed. So keep in mind that the fonts on your machine may differ from what is available to your users. And, as we said, we'll show you how to extend the set of fonts in a bit…

Monospace family

Courier

Courier New

Andale Mono

← The monospace family is made up of fonts that have constant-width characters. For instance, the horizontal space an "i" takes up will be the same width that an "m" takes up. These fonts are primarily used to show software code examples.

The cursive family includes fonts that look handwritten. You'll sometimes see these fonts used in headings.

Take a good look at the font families: serif fonts have an elegant, traditional look, while sans-serif fonts have a very clean and readable look. Monospace fonts feel like they were typed on a typewriter. Cursive and fantasy fonts have a playful or stylized feel.

Cursive family

Comic Sans

Apple Chancery

Fantasy family

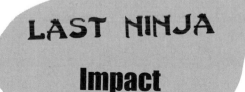

LAST NINJA

Impact

← The fantasy font family contains stylized decorative fonts.

Font Magnets

Your job is to help the fictional fonts below find their way home to their own font family. Move each fridge magnet on the left into the correct font family on the right. Check your answers before you move on. Review the font family descriptions on the previous pages if you need to.

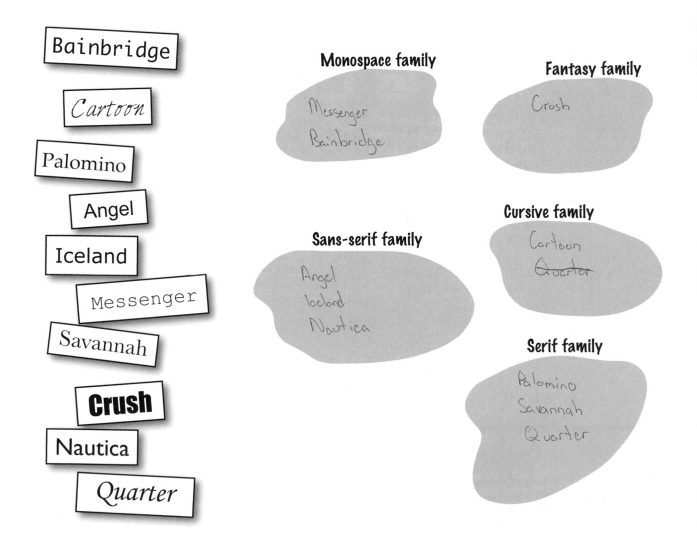

Bainbridge

Cartoon

Palomino

Angel

Iceland

Messenger

Savannah

Crush

Nautica

Quarter

Monospace family

Messenger
Bainbridge

Fantasy family

Crush

Sans-serif family

Angel
Iceland
Nautica

Cursive family

Cartoon
~~Quarter~~

Serif family

Palomino
Savannah
Quarter

Specifying font families using CSS

Okay, so there are a lot of good fonts out there from several font families. How do you get them in your pages? Well, you've already had a peek at the `font-family` property in the last chapter, when you specified a `font-family` of "sans-serif" for the lounge. Here's a more interesting example:

> Usually, your font-family specification contains a list of alternative fonts, all from the same family.

```
body {
        font-family: Verdana, Geneva, Arial, sans-serif;
}
```

You can specify more than one font using the font-family property. Just type the font names separated by commas.

Write font names as they are spelled, including upper- and lowercase letters.

Always put a generic font family name at the end, like "serif", "sans-serif", "cursive", or "monospace". You'll see what this does in a sec.

How font-family specifications work

Here's how the browser interprets the fonts listed in your `font-family` specification:

Check to see if the font Verdana is available on the user's computer and if so, use it as the font for this element (in this case, the <body> element).

If Verdana isn't available, then look for the font Geneva, and if it is available, use it for the body.

If Geneva isn't available, then look for the font Arial, and if it is available, use it for the body.

Finally, if none of the specific fonts can be found, just use whatever the browser considers its default "sans-serif" font.

```
body {
        font-family: Verdana, Geneva, Arial, sans-serif;
}
```

You don't have to specify four alternative fonts; you can have two, three, etc. In the last chapter, we only used one—the default sans-serif font—although we don't recommend that because it doesn't give you much control over the fonts you'd like used.

The `font-family` property gives you a way to create a list of preferred fonts. Hopefully, most browsers will have one of your first choices, but if not, you can at least be assured that the browser will provide a generic font from the same family.

Let's get some fonts into your pages…

Dusting off Tony's journal

Now that you know how to specify fonts, let's take another look at Tony's Segway'n USA page and give it a different look. We'll be making some small, incremental changes to the text styles in Tony's page, and while no single change is going to look dramatically different, by the end of the chapter we think you'll agree the site has a slick new look. Let's get an idea of where we might make some improvements and then let's give Tony a new `font-family`.

Remember that we haven't applied any styles to Tony's site, so his site is using a serif <u>font-family</u> for the entire page.

The default <u>size</u> of the heading fonts is also pretty large and doesn't make for an attractive page.

The quote is just indented. It would be nice to improve its look a bit by adding some <u>font-style</u>.

Except for the photos, this page is rather monochromatic, so we'll also add some font <u>color</u> to make it a little more interesting.

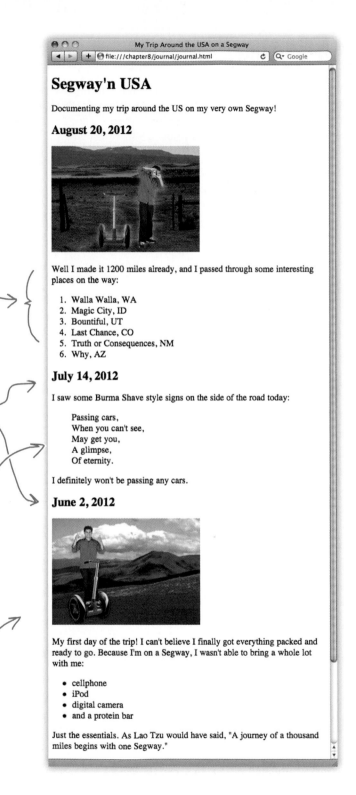

Getting Tony a new font-family

Let's get Tony set up with a `font-family`. We're going to start with
some clean sans-serif fonts. First, create a new file, "journal.css" in the
"chapter8/journal" folder and add this rule:

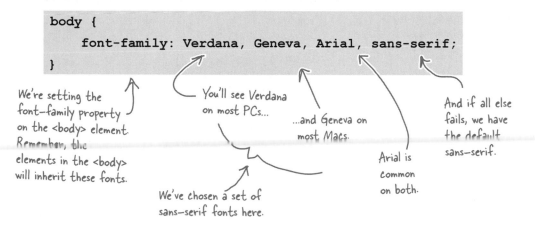

```
body {
    font-family: Verdana, Geneva, Arial, sans-serif;
}
```

We're setting the
font-family property
on the <body> element.
Remember, the
elements in the <body>
will inherit these fonts.

You'll see Verdana
on most PCs...

...and Geneva on
most Macs.

Arial is
common
on both.

And if all else
fails, we have
the default
sans-serif.

We've chosen a set of
sans-serif fonts here.

Now you need to link Tony's journal to the new stylesheet file. To do that, open the
file "journal.html" in the "chapter8/journal" folder. Add the `<link>` element to
link in the style in "journal.css", like we did below.

We've also gone ahead and updated Tony's
journal.html file to be official HTML5,
adding in the doctype and the <meta> tag.

```
<!doctype html>
<html>
    <head>
        <meta charset="utf-8">
        <link type="text/css" rel="stylesheet" href="journal.css">
        <title>My Trip Around the USA on a Segway</title>
    </head>
    <body>
        .
        .
        .
    </body>
</html>
```

Here's where we're
linking in the new
"journal.css" file.

After you've made this change, save the file, fire up your browser, and load the page.

Test driving Tony's new fonts

Open the page with the new CSS in the browser and you should see we've now got a nice set of sans-serif fonts. Let's check out the changes…

The font definitely gives Tony's web page a new look. The headings now have a cleaner look without the serifs on the letters, although they still look a tad large on the page.

The paragraph text is also clean and very readable.

Because font-family is an inherited property, all elements on the page are now using a sans-serif font, even the list elements...

...and the <blockquote>s.

And if the serif fonts were more your cup of tea, don't let us stop you. You can always redo the font-family declaration to use serif fonts.

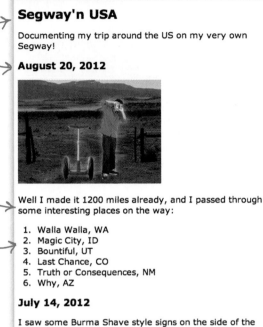

Segway'n USA

Documenting my trip around the US on my very own Segway!

August 20, 2012

Well I made it 1200 miles already, and I passed through some interesting places on the way:

1. Walla Walla, WA
2. Magic City, ID
3. Bountiful, UT
4. Last Chance, CO
5. Truth or Consequences, NM
6. Why, AZ

July 14, 2012

I saw some Burma Shave style signs on the side of the road today:

> Passing cars,
> When you can't see,
> May get you,
> A glimpse,
> Of eternity.

I definitely won't be passing any cars.

there are no Dumb Questions

Q: How do I specify a font with multiple words in the name, like Courier New?

A: Just put quotes around the name in your font-family declaration, like this:
`font-family: "Courier New", Courier;`

Q: So the font-family property is really a set of alternative fonts?

A: Yes. It's basically a priority list of fonts. The first is the font you'd like used, followed by a good substitute, followed by more substitutes, and so on. For the last font, you should specify the catch-all generic "sans-serif" or "serif", which should be in the same family as all the fonts in your list.

Q: Are "serif" and "sans-serif" real fonts?

A: "serif" and "sans-serif" are not the names of actual fonts. However, your browser will substitute a real font in place of "serif" or "sans-serif" if the other fonts before it in the font-family declaration can't be found. The font used in its place will be whatever the browser has defined as the default font in that family.

Q: How do I know which to use? Serif or sans-serif?

A: There are no rules. However, on a computer display, many people consider sans-serif the best for body text. You'll find plenty of designs that use serif for body text, or mix serif fonts with sans-serif fonts. So, it really is up to you and what kind of look you want your page to have.

How do I deal with everyone having different fonts?

The unfortunate thing about fonts is that you can't control what fonts are installed on your users' computers. Not only that, but they tend to differ across operating systems—what might be on your Mac may not be on your user's PC.

So, how do you deal with that? Well, the tried-and-true strategy is to create a list of fonts that are most appropriate for your pages and then hope the user has one of those fonts installed. If he doesn't, well, at least we can count on the browser to supply a generic font in the same font family.

Let's look at how to do that in a little more detail. What you need to do is ensure that your `font-family` declaration includes fonts that are likely to occur on both Windows and the Mac (as well as any other platforms your users might be using, like Linux or perhaps mobile devices), and that it also ends with a font family.

Here's an example:

These fonts are likely to be available on both Windows and Macintosh computers.

Andale Mono

Arial

Arial Black

Comic Sans

Courier New

Georgia

Impact

Times New Roman

Trebuchet MS

Verdana

These fonts are most likely to be found on Macintosh computers.

Geneva

Courier

Helvetica

Times

Let's take a look at our definition for Tony's pages again...

(1) We'd like for Verdana to be used, but...

(3) That's okay, because we can probably count on Arial to be on either Windows or Macs, but if it's not...

`font-family: Verdana, Geneva, Arial, sans-serif;`

(2) If it's not, Geneva would be nice, but this will probably only happen on Macs. But if it's not...

(4) Then that's still okay; we'll just let the browser choose a sans-serif font for us.

I get how we need to make sure we specify fonts that will be appropriate all across all my users' machines, but I was really hoping we could use this cool Emblema One font I found for my main heading. Can I just use that, and if the users don't have it they can use a fallback?

Yes, but there's a better way...

Your suggestion would work, but most likely for only a very small percentage of your users. If you just have to have that oh-so-cool font, or typography is important to your site design, you can actually deliver a font right to your user's browser using Web Fonts.

To do this, you're going to use a newer feature of CSS: the `@font-face` rule. This rule allows you to define the name and location of a font that can then be used in your page.

Let's see how this works...

How Web Fonts work

With Web Fonts you can take advantage of a new capability of modern browsers that allows you to deliver new fonts directly to your users. Once the font is delivered, the browser can then make use of the Web Font just like it can any other font, and you can even style your text with CSS. Let's look at how Web Fonts work in a little more detail:

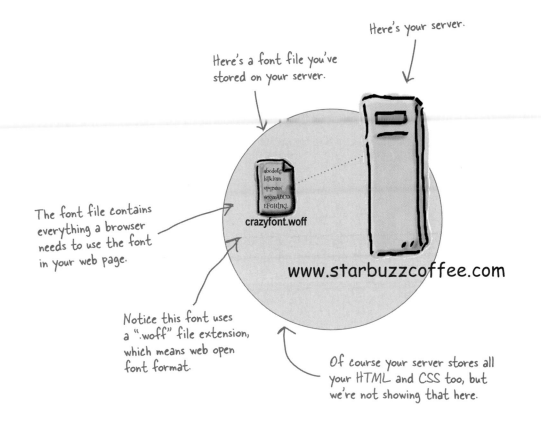

Here's your server.

Here's a font file you've stored on your server.

crazyfont.woff

www.starbuzzcoffee.com

The font file contains everything a browser needs to use the font in your web page.

Notice this font uses a ".woff" file extension, which means web open font format.

Of course your server stores all your HTML and CSS too, but we're not showing that here.

1 To make use of Web Fonts, the browser first retrieves an HTML page that references them.

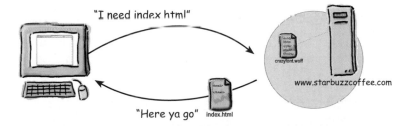

"I need index html"

"Here ya go"   index.html

crazyfont.woff

www.starbuzzcoffee.com

2 The browser then retrieves the Web Font files needed for the page.

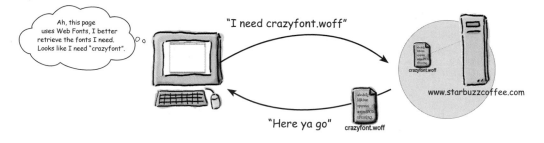

3 Now, with the font retrieved, the browser uses the font when it displays the page.

there are no
Dumb Questions

Q: What's the woff, or web open font format?

A: Woff is emerging as the standard font format for Web Fonts, and you'll see it supported today across all modern browsers. That said, there has previously been some lack of standardization in this area, with different browsers supporting different font formats. If you need to provide Web Fonts to browsers that may not support woff, you'll need to supply one or more of a few formats that are available as alternatives. Web Font hosting services can help a lot here.

Q: So to use a Web Font, I have to host the font files on a server?

A: If you're just testing fonts you can actually store and refer to them as local files on your own file system (just like you do with, say, an image). But if you want to deliver fonts to your users on the Web, you either have to host the files yourself on a server, or make use of a hosting service, such as Google's, which is free.

Q: If I use a Web Font, can I then count on it being there for my users?

A: As long as they have a modern browser (and discounting any network connectivity or server issues), for the most part, yes. However, if they are using old browsers or mobile devices that don't yet support Web Fonts, all bets are off and you still need to supply font alternatives (we'll see how in a sec).

How to add a Web Font to your page...

So you've got a special font you want to add to your page? Let's step through how to do that using Web Fonts and the `@font-face` rule in CSS.

Step one: Find a font

If you don't have a font, like Tony does, you'll want to visit the many sites out there that have both free and licensed fonts you can use in your pages (check out the appendix for more information). We're going to use Tony's suggestion, Emblema One, which is a free font.

Step two: Make sure you have all the formats of the font you need

Here's the good news on Web Fonts: the `@font-face` CSS rule is pretty much a standard across modern browsers. Here's the bad news: the actual format used to store the fonts isn't quite yet a standard (although we're getting there), and in fact there are several different formats (at the time of writing) supported across the browsers to varying degrees. Here are the common formats (and their respective file extensions):

TrueType fonts: .ttf   *TrueType and OpenType fonts are closely related; OpenType is built on top of TrueType (and is newer than TrueType).*

OpenType fonts: .otf

Embedded OpenType fonts: .eot   *Embedded OpenType (EOT) is a compact form of OpenType. It's proprietary (Microsoft), and supported only on IE.*

SVG fonts: .svg   *Scalable Vector Graphics, or SVG, is a general-purpose graphics format, and SVG fonts use this format to represent characters.*

Web open font format: .woff   *Web open font format is based on TrueType, and is being developed as a standard for Web Fonts. It's well supported on most modern browsers.*

The best supported format across most modern browsers is web open font format, so that's the one we recommend you use. You can offer an alternative for older browsers; we'll use TrueType as that's well supported across all browsers too (except IE).

Step three: Place your font files on the Web

You'll want to place your font files on the Web, so they are accessible to your user's browsers. Or you can use one of the many font services coming online that will host these files for you. In either case, you'll need the URL of your font files. Here are Tony's files, which we've placed on `wickedlysmart.com`:

```
http://wickedlysmart.com/hfhtmlcss/chapter8/journal/EmblemaOne-Regular.woff

http://wickedlysmart.com/hfhtmlcss/chapter8/journal/EmblemaOne-Regular.ttf
```

Step 4: Add the @font-face property to your CSS

You've got the URLs for the .woff and .ttf versions of the font named "Emblema One," so now you're ready to add a `@font-face` rule to your "journal.css" file. Add the rule to the *top* of the file, above the `body` rule:

> *Let's start the rule with @font-face.*

> *Unlike a normal rule that selects a set of elements and assigns style, the @font-face rule sets up a font, which is assigned to a font-family name for later use.*

> *In the @font-face rule, we create a name for our font using the font-family property. You can use any name you want, but it is best usually to just match the font name, like "Emblema One."*

```
@font-face {
    font-family: "Emblema One";
    src: url("http://wickedlysmart.com/hfhtmlcss/chapter8/journal/EmblemaOne-Regular.woff"),
         url("http://wickedlysmart.com/hfhtmlcss/chapter8/journal/EmblemaOne-Regular.ttf");
}
```

> *The src property tells the browser where to get the font. We need to specify a src value for every file the browser might recognize. In our case, we're going to supply both the .woff and .ttf types recognized by today's browsers.*

The `@font-face` rule tells the browser to load the font files at the `src` URLs. Browsers will attempt to load each `src` file until it finds one that it can support. Once loaded, the font is assigned the name you specify in the `font-family` property—in this case, "EmblemaOne." Now let's take that font and see how we can use it in the style of the page.

Step five: Use the font-family name in your CSS

> *Hint: you already know how to do this!*

Once you've loaded a font into the browser with the `@font-face` rule, you can use the font by referencing the name you gave it with the `font-family` property. Let's change the font of the `<h1>` heading in Tony's page to use the "Emblema One" font. To do that, we'll add a rule for `<h1>` like this::

```
h1 {
    font-family: "Emblema One", sans-serif;
}
```

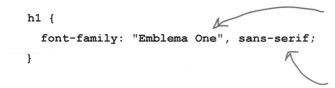

> *We specify the name of the font just like normal, only this time, it's a font we've loaded using @font-face! And just in case something goes wrong, we specify sans-serif as a fallback.*

Step six: Load the page!

That's it! You're ready to test your font. Reload Tony's journal page and check out the next page to see what we got...

Test drive the Web Font in Tony's journal

When you reload "journal.html", you should see the `<h1>` heading at the top of the page use the Emblema One. Not bad for just a few lines of CSS!

Now, the `<h1>` heading at the top of Tony's journal page is using font "Emblema One."

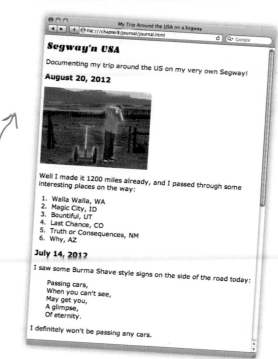

Watch it!

TTF and WOFF font formats don't work in IE8 and earlier.

If you want to support users with older IE browsers, you'll need to do a bit more work with Web Fonts, and use an EOT font.

---

there are no Dumb Questions

Q: The @font-face rule doesn't really look or act like a CSS rule, does it?

A: You're right; think of @font-face as a built-in CSS rule rather than a rule that acts like a selector. Instead of selecting an element, @font-face allows you to retrieve a Web Font, and assign it to a font-family name. The @ at the beginning is a good clue this isn't an ordinary CSS rule.

Q: Are there other built-in CSS rules I should know about?

A: There are. Two common built-in rules you'll see are @import, which allows you to import other CSS files (rather than a `<link>` in your HTML), and @media, which allows you to create CSS rules that are specific to certain "media" types, like a printed page versus a desktop screen versus a mobile phone. More on @media later.

Q: Web fonts seem great; are there any disadvantages to using them?

A: A few. First, it takes time to retrieve Web Fonts, and so your page performance might suffer the first time you have to retrieve them. Also, there's the pain of managing the multiple font files. Finally, you may find mobile and small devices that don't support them, so make sure you always allow for alternatives in your design.

Q: Can I use multiple custom fonts with @font-face?

A: Yes. If you're using @font-face to load the fonts, then for each font you want to use, make sure the font files are available on your server, and create a separate @font-face rule for each one, so you can give each a unique name.

For even more on Web Fonts, check out the appendix.

However, remember to make sure you only choose the fonts you really need in your web page; each extra font takes extra loading time for your page, so having multiple Web Fonts in your page will slow down your web page. If it gets too slow, you might have frustrated users on your hands!

Q: You mentioned services to help me with hosting Web Fonts. Can you say more?

A: Sure! FontSquirrel (http://www.fontsquirrel.com/) is a great place to find open source, free fonts that you can upload to your server. Their font kits make it easy to offer multiple formats of a given font. Google Web Font Service (http://www.google.com/webfonts) is a way you can let Google do all the hard work for managing the fonts and the CSS for you; in this case, you just link to the fonts you want on the Google service, and then use the names in your CSS. Easy!

Adjusting font sizes

Now that Tony has a new set of fonts, we need to work on those font sizes, as most people find the default sizes of the headings a bit large, at least aesthetically. To do that, you need to know how to specify font sizes, and there are actually a few ways to do this. Let's take a look at some ways to specify `font-size`, and then we'll talk about how best to specify font size so they are consistent and user friendly.

If you do things right, any user will be able to increase the font sizes on your web page for readability. You'll see how in a couple of pages.

px You can specify your font size in pixels, just like the pixel dimensions you used for images in Chapter 5. When you specify font size in pixels, you're telling the browser how many pixels tall the letters should be.

`font-size: 14px;`

In CSS, you specify pixels with a number followed by "px". This says that the font-size should be 14 pixels high.

The px must come right after the number of pixels. You can't have a space in between.

`h i p` } *14 pixels*

Here's how you'd specify font-size within a body rule.

```
body {
        font-size: 14px;
}
```

Setting a font to 14 pixels high means that there will be 14 pixels between the lowest part of the letters and the highest.

% Unlike pixels, which tell the font exactly how big it should be in pixels, a font size specified as a percentage tells the font how big it should be relative to another font size. So,

`font-size: 150%;`

says that the font size should be 150% of another font size. But which other font size? Well, since `font-size` is a property that is inherited from the parent element, when you specify a percentage font size, it is relative to the parent element. Let's check out how that works…

Here we've specified a body font size in pixels, and a level-one heading as 150%.

```
body {
        font-size: 14px;
}
h1 {
        font-size: 150%;
}
```

em

You can also specify font sizes using em, which, like percentage, is another relative unit of measure. With em, you don't specify a percentage; instead, you specify a scaling factor. Here's how you use em:

Don't mix this up with the <em> element!

```
font-size: 1.2em;
```

This says that the font size should be scaled by 1.2.

Say you use this measurement to specify the size of an <h2> heading. Your <h2> headings will be 1.2 times the font size of the parent element, which in this case is 1.2 times 14px, which is about 17px.

It's actually 16.8, but most browsers will round it up to 17.

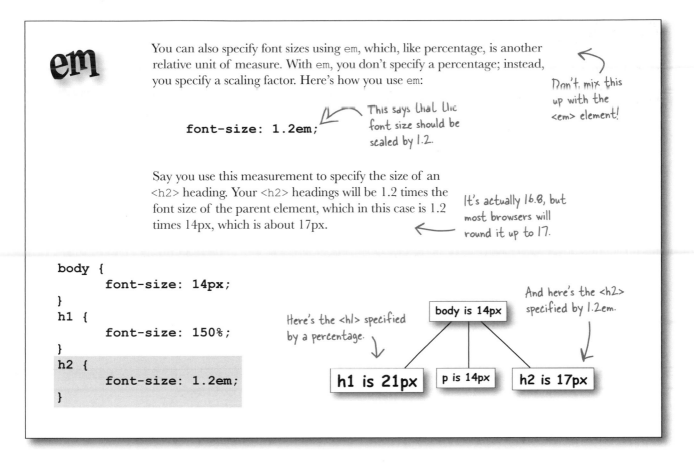

```
body {
        font-size: 14px;
}
h1 {
        font-size: 150%;
}
h2 {
        font-size: 1.2em;
}
```

Here's the <h1> specified by a percentage.

And here's the <h2> specified by 1.2em.

body is 14px

h1 is 21px   p is 14px   h2 is 17px

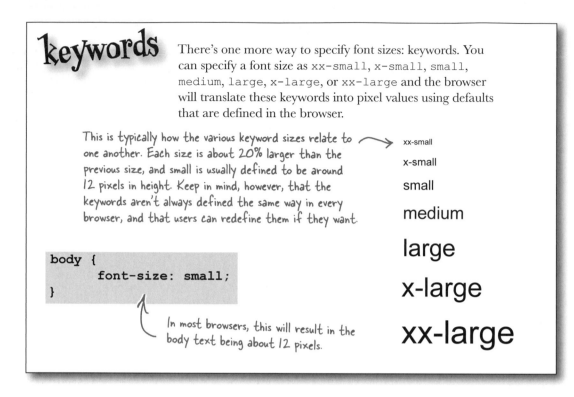

keywords There's one more way to specify font sizes: keywords. You can specify a font size as xx-small, x-small, small, medium, large, x-large, or xx-large and the browser will translate these keywords into pixel values using defaults that are defined in the browser.

This is typically how the various keyword sizes relate to one another. Each size is about 20% larger than the previous size, and small is usually defined to be around 12 pixels in height. Keep in mind, however, that the keywords aren't always defined the same way in every browser, and that users can redefine them if they want.

xx-small
x-small
small
medium
large
x-large
xx-large

```
body {
        font-size: small;
}
```

In most browsers, this will result in the body text being about 12 pixels.

So, how should I specify my font sizes?

You've got quite a few choices for specifying font sizes: px, em, percentages, and keywords. So, which do you use? Here's a recipe for specifying font sizes that will give you consistent results for most browsers.

 Choose a keyword (we recommend small or medium) and specify it as the font size in your body rule. This acts as the default size for your page.

 Specify the font sizes of your other elements relative to your body font size using either em or percentages (the choice between em and percentages is yours, as they are essentially two ways to do the same thing).

Nice recipe, but what's good about it? By defining your fonts relative to the body font size, it's really easy to change the font sizes in your web page simply by changing the body font size. Want to redesign the page to make the fonts larger? If your body font size value is small, simply change it to medium, and voilà—every other element will automatically get larger in proportion because you specified their font sizes relative to the body's font size. Better yet, say your users want to resize the fonts on the page. Again, no problem; using this recipe, all the fonts on the page will automatically readjust.

Let's look at how this all works. First, you set a size for your
<body> element. Then, you set all the other font sizes relative to
that size, like this:

```
body { font-size: small; }
h1 { font-size: 150%; }
h2 { font-size: 120%; }
```

That gives you a document tree that looks like this:

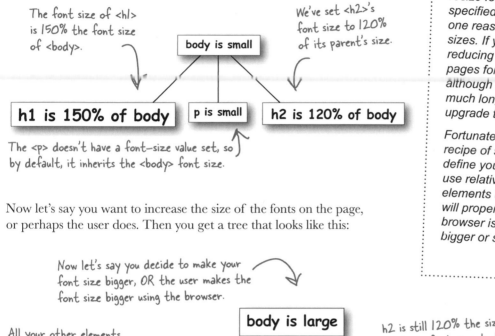

The font size of <h1>
is 150% the font size
of <body>.

We've set <h2>'s
font size to 120%
of its parent's size.

body is small

h1 is 150% of body

p is small

h2 is 120% of body

The <p> doesn't have a font-size value set, so
by default, it inherits the <body> font size.

Now let's say you want to increase the size of the fonts on the page,
or perhaps the user does. Then you get a tree that looks like this:

Now let's say you decide to make your
font size bigger, OR the user makes the
font size bigger using the browser.

body is large

h2 is still 120% the size of
the body font size. In this
case, it's 120% of "large."

All your other elements
automatically get bigger too,
without you having to do a thing.

h1 is 150% of body

p is large

h2 is 120% of body

Now the body font size has changed to large, and everything else has
changed too, in relation to the body font size. That's great, because
you didn't have to go through and change all your other font sizes;
all you had to do was change the body font size. And if you're a user,
everything happened behind the scenes. When you increased the text
size, all the text got bigger because all the elements are sized relative to
one another, so the page still looks good at a larger font size.

Let's make these changes to the font sizes in Tony's web page

It's time to try these font sizes in Tony's web page. Add the new properties to the "journal.css" file in the "chapter8/journal" folder. Once you've made the changes, reload the page in the browser and check out the differences in the font size. If you don't see a difference, check your CSS carefully for errors.

```css
@font-face {
    font-family: "Emblema One";
    src: url("http://wickedlysmart.com/hfhtmlcss/chapter8/journal/EmblemaOne-Regular.woff"),
         url("http://wickedlysmart.com/hfhtmlcss/chapter8/journal/EmblemaOne-Regular.ttf");
}
body {
    font-family: Verdana, Geneva, Arial, sans-serif;
    font-size: small;
}
h1 {
    font-family: "Emblema One", sans-serif;
    font-size: 220%;
}
h2 {
    font-size: 130%;
}
```

Following our recipe, we're using a font-size of small for the <body> element. This will act as the base font size.

And we'll set the other fonts relative to the body font size. In the case of <h1>, we'll try a font size that is 220% of the base font size.

We'll make the <h2> font size smaller than <h1>, or 130% of the body font size.

Sharpen your pencil

If you specified <h1> and <h2>'s font sizes using em rather than percentage, what would their values be?

h1 - 2.2em

h2 - 1.3em

Answer: <h1> would be 2.2em and <h2> 1.3em.

Test driving the font sizes

Here's the evolving journal, complete with new smaller fonts. Check out the differences…

Here's the new version with updated fonts. The design is starting to look a little less clunky!

Here's the previous version before the change in font sizes.

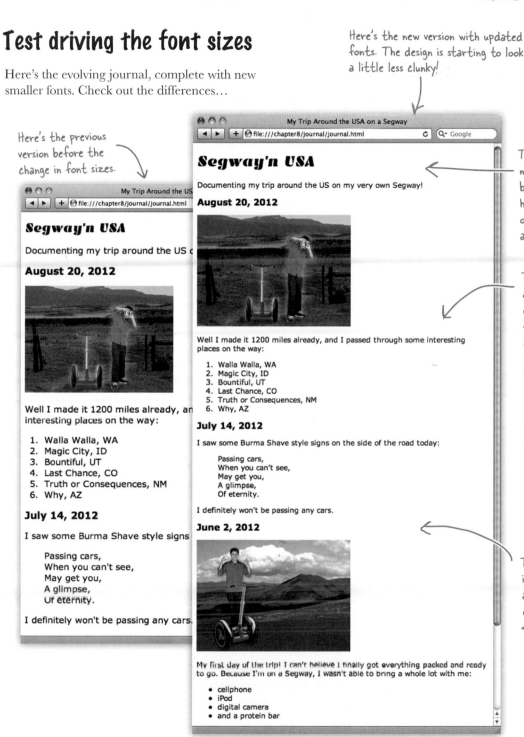

This <h1> heading looks much better now. It's bigger than the <h2> headings but doesn't overwhelm the body text and the page in size.

The body text is a tad smaller. The default body text font size is usually 16px, although it does depend on the browser. But it's still easily readable at the "small" size, which is probably about 12px.

The <h2> heading is a bit smaller too, and is a good size compared to the <h1> heading.

there are no
Dumb Questions

Q: So, by defining a font size in the `<body>` element, I'm somehow defining a default size for the page? How does that work?

A: Yes, that's right. By setting a font size in your `<body>` element, you can then define the other font sizes of your elements in relation to their parent. What's so great about that? Well, if you need to change the font size, then all you need to do is change the body font size, and everything else will change in proportion.

Q: Do we really need to worry about users resizing their browser fonts? I never do that.

A: Yes. Almost all browsers allow their users to make the text of a page bigger or smaller, and many users take advantage of this feature. If you define your fonts in a relative manner, then your users will have no trouble doing this. Just be careful not to use pixel sizes, because some browsers have problems resizing those.

Q: I like the idea of using pixels because then my page will look exactly like I specify it.

A: There is some truth to that—by using pixels for every element's font size, you are choosing the precise font size you want for each element. But you do that at the cost of giving some of your users (the ones using older versions of Internet Explorer) the flexibility to pick a font size that is appropriate for their display and eyesight.

You also are creating pages that are a little harder to maintain because if you suddenly want to increase the font sizes of all the elements in a page, you have a lot of changes to make.

Q: What's the difference between em and %? They seem like the same thing.

A: They are basically two different ways to achieve the same thing. Both give you a way to specify a size relative to the parent font size. A lot of people find percent easier to think about than em, and also easier to read in your CSS. But you should use whichever you want.

Q: If I don't specify any font sizes, do I just get the default font sizes?

A: Yes, and what those sizes are depends on your browser, and even the version of the browser you are running. But in most cases, the default body font size will be 16 pixels.

Q: And what are the default sizes for the headings?

A: Again, it depends on the browser, but in general, `<h1>` is 200% of the default body text font size, `<h2>` is 150%, `<h3>` is 120%, `<h4>` is 100%, `<h5>` is 90%, and `<h6>` is 60%. Notice that by default `<h4>` is the same font size as the body font size, and `<h5>` and `<h6>` are smaller.

Q: So rather than using the size keywords, can I use em or % in the body rule? If I use 90% for the font size of the body, what does that mean exactly? It's 90% of what?

A: Yes, you can do that. If you specify a font size of 90% in your body rule, then that would be 90% of the default font size, which we just said is usually 16 pixels, so 90% would be about 14 pixels. If you'd like a font size slightly different than the keywords provided, go ahead and use % or em.

Q: There seems to be so many differences between browsers: font-family, font-size, various default settings, and so on. How will I ever know if my design looks good on other browsers?

A: Great question. The easy answer is that if you follow the guidelines in this chapter, then most of your designs are going to look just fine in other browsers. However, you should know that they may look slightly different in different browsers—the fonts may be slightly bigger or smaller, spacing here and there may be different, etc. But all the differences should be very minor and should not affect the readability of your pages.

However, if you really care about having your pages looking almost identical in many browsers, then you really need to test them in lots of browsers. And to really take this to the extreme, you'll find a variety of CSS "hacks" to try to make different browsers behave the same. If you want to take it this far, there's nothing wrong with that, but just keep in mind a lot of these activities take time and have diminishing returns.

Changing a font's weight

The `font-weight` property allows you to control how bold the text looks. As you know, bold text looks darker than normal text and tends to be a bit fatter too. You can make any element use bold text by setting the `font-weight` property to `bold`, like this:

font-weight: bold;

You can also go the other way. If you have an element that is set to bold by default, or is inheriting bold from a parent, then you can remove the bold style like this:

font-weight: normal;

There are also two relative `font-weight` properties: `bolder` and `lighter`. These will make your text style a little bolder or a little lighter relative to its inherited value. These values are seldom used and because not many fonts allow for slight differences in the amount of boldness, in practice these two values often have no effect.

You can also set your `font-weight` property to a number between 100 and 900 (in multiples of 100), but again, this is not well supported across fonts and browsers and so is not often used.

font-weight: normal;

Starbuzz Coffee
Beverages

font-weight: bold;

**Starbuzz Coffee
Beverages**

Sharpen your pencil

Write the CSS to change the second-level headings in Tony's page from their default bold value to normal weight. Then, add the rule to your CSS and give it a test drive. You'll find the answer to this one on the next page.

Test drive the normal-weight headings

Here's what your CSS should look like after you make the change to use a normal `font-weight` for the `<h2>` headings:

```
@font-face {          ← We're leaving out the full @font-face
    ...                 definition to save some space.
}
body {
    font-family: Verdana, Geneva, Arial, sans-serif;
    font-size: small;
}
h1 {
    font-family: "Emblema One", sans-serif;
    font-size: 220%;
}
h2 {
    font-size: 130%;
    font-weight: normal;
}
```

Here we're changing the font-weight of the <h2> headings to normal.

And here are the results. The <h2> headings are now lighter looking. You can still tell they are headings because they are 130% the size of the body text.

Segway'n USA

Documenting my trip around the US on my very own Segway!

August 20, 2012

Well I made it 1200 miles already, and I passed through some interesting places on the way:

1. Walla Walla, WA
2. Magic City, ID
3. Bountiful, UT
4. Last Chance, CO
5. Truth or Consequences, NM
6. Why, AZ

July 14, 2012

I saw some Burma Shave style signs on the side of the road today:

Passing cars,
When you can't see,
May get you,
A glimpse,
Of eternity.

I definitely won't be passing any cars.

Adding style to your fonts

You're familiar with *italic* text, right? Italic text is slanted, and sometimes has extra curly serifs. For example, compare these two styles.

not italic
italic

← The italic text is slanted to the right and has extra curls on the serifs.

You can add an italic style to your text in CSS using the `font-style` property:

`font-style: italic;`

A common mistake is to write "italic" as "italics". If you do, you won't see italic text. So remember to check your spelling.

However, not all fonts support the italic style, so what you get instead is called *oblique* text. Oblique text is also slanted text, but rather than using a specially designed slanted set of characters in the font, the browser just applies a slant to the normal letters. Compare these non-oblique and oblique styles:

not oblique
oblique

← The regular letters are slanted to the right in the oblique style.

You can use the `font-style` property to get oblique text too, like this:

`font-style: oblique;`

In practice, you're going to find that, depending on your choice of font and browser, sometimes the two styles will look identical, and sometimes they won't. So, unless italic versus oblique is very important to you, choose one and move on. If it *is* important, you'll need to test your font and browser combination for the best effect.

Italic and oblique styles are two styles that give fonts a slanted appearance.

Unless you can control the fonts and browsers your visitors are using, you'll find that sometimes you get italic, and sometimes oblique, no matter which style you specify.

So just go with italic and don't worry about the differences (you probably can't control them anyway).

Styling Tony's quotes with a little italic

Now we're going to use the `font-style` property to add a little pizzazz to Tony's quotes. Remember the Burma Shave slogan in the `<blockquote>` element? We're going to change the slogan to italic style to set it off from the rest of the text. To do that, we just need to style the `<blockquote>` with a `font-style` of italic, like this:

```
blockquote {
        font-style: italic;
}
```

Add this new CSS rule to the CSS in your "journal.css" file, save it, and give the page a test drive. You should see the Burma Shave slogan change to italic; here's our test drive.

there are no Dumb Questions

Q: The text for the `<blockquote>` is actually inside a `<p>` that's inside the `<blockquote>`. So, how did this change the paragraph to italic?

A: Remember, by default most elements get their font styles from their parents, and the parent of this paragraph is the `<blockquote>` element. So the paragraph within the `<blockquote>` inherits the italic style.

Q: Why didn't we just put the text into an `<em>` element inside the `<blockquote>`? Wouldn't that do the same thing and make the `<blockquote>` italic?

A: Remember that `<em>` is for specifying structure. `<em>` says that a set of words should be emphasized. What we're doing is styling a `<blockquote>`, we are not indicating that the text in the `<blockquote>` should be emphasized. So, while you're right, on most browsers `<em>` is styled with italic, it's not the right way to style the text in the `<blockquote>`. Also, keep in mind that the style of `<em>` could change, so you shouldn't count on `<em>` always being italic.

Segway'n USA

Documenting my trip around the US on my very own Segway!

August 20, 2012

Well I made it 1200 miles already, and I passed through some interesting places on the way:

1. Walla Walla, WA
2. Magic City, ID
3. Bountiful, UT
4. Last Chance, CO
5. Truth or Consequences, NM
6. Why, AZ

July 14, 2012

I saw some Burma Shave style signs on the side of the road today:

> *Passing cars,*
> *When you can't see,*
> *May get you,*
> *A glimpse,*
> *Of eternity.*

I definitely won't be passing any cars.

June 2, 2012

Here's the new style on the Burma Shave slogan in Tony's page. We got slanted text, just like we wanted.

Cool. Love the new look. Hey, how about a little color in those fonts? Say, ummm...the color of my shirt? I love orange!

You'd think we could just tell you there was a color property and send you on your way to use it. But unlike font sizes or weights or text styles, you've got to understand a fair bit about color to be able to work with it and specify it in CSS.

So, over the next few pages, you're going to dive into color and learn everything you need to know to use it on your pages: how colors on the screen work, the various ways of describing color in CSS, what those mysterious hex codes are all about, whether you should be worried about "web-safe colors," and what's the easiest way to find and specify colors.

How do web colors work?

You're starting to see that there are lots of places you can add color to your pages: background colors, border colors, and soon, font colors as well. But how do colors on a computer actually work? Let's take a look.

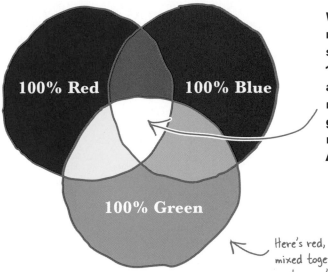

Web colors are specified in terms of how much red, green, and blue make up the color. You specify the amount of each color from 0 to 100% and then add them all together to arrive at a final color. For instance if you add 100% red, 100% green, and 100% blue together, you get white. Notice that on a computer screen, mixing together colors results in a lighter color. After all, this is light we're mixing!

Here's red, green, and blue being mixed together. If you look at the center you'll see how they all add up.

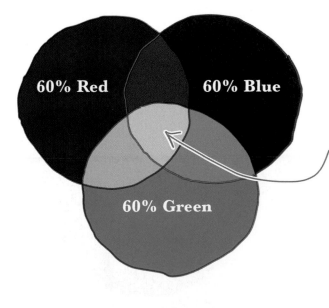

But if you add, say, only 60% of each component (red, green, and blue), then what would you expect? Less white, right? In other words, you get a gray color, because we're adding equal amounts of the three colors, but not as much light to the screen.

On a computer screen, if 0% blue is added, then blue doesn't add anything to the color.

Or, say you mix together **80% red and 40% green. You'd expect an orange color, right? Well, that's exactly what you'll get. Notice that if a color is contributing zero, then it doesn't affect the other two colors. Again, this is because there is no blue light being mixed with red and green.**

Mixing 80% red and 40% green, we get a nice orange color.

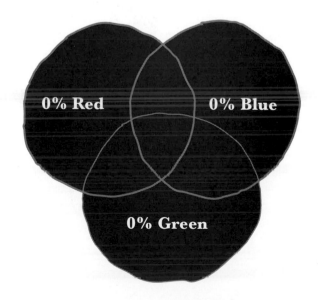

80% Red

0% Blue

40% Green

And what if you mix **0% of red, green, and blue, then what do you get? That means you're sending no light of any kind to the screen, so you get black.**

0% Red

0% Blue

0% Green

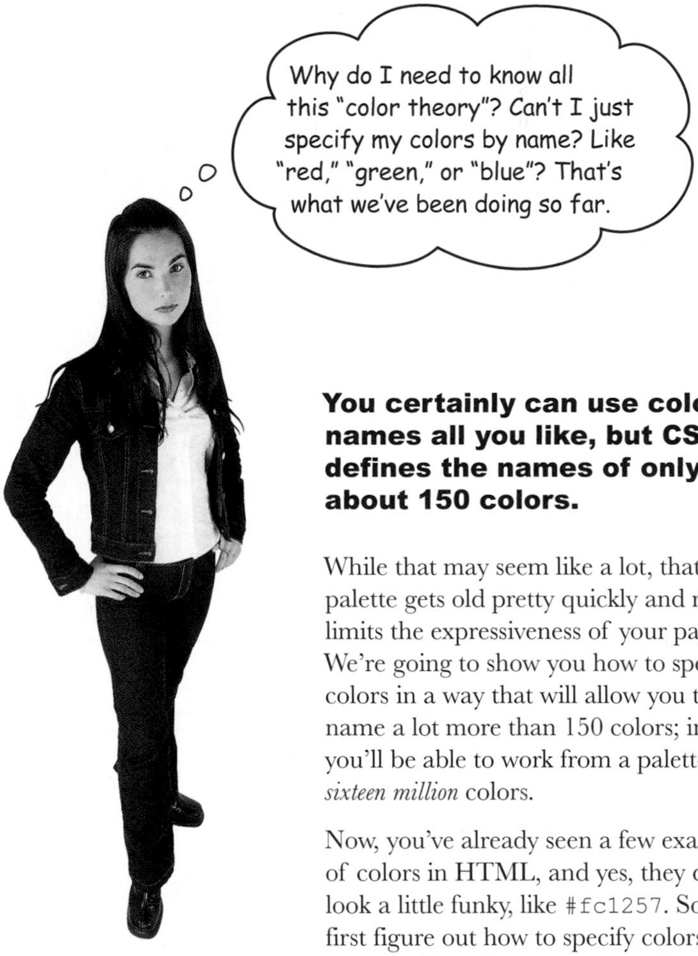

> Why do I need to know all this "color theory"? Can't I just specify my colors by name? Like "red," "green," or "blue"? That's what we've been doing so far.

You certainly can use color names all you like, but CSS defines the names of only about 150 colors.

While that may seem like a lot, that palette gets old pretty quickly and really limits the expressiveness of your pages. We're going to show you how to specify colors in a way that will allow you to name a lot more than 150 colors; in fact, you'll be able to work from a palette of *sixteen million* colors.

Now, you've already seen a few examples of colors in HTML, and yes, they do look a little funky, like `#fc1257`. So, let's first figure out how to specify colors and then you'll see how you can easily use color charts, online color pickers, or your photo editing application to pick your colors.

How do I specify web colors?
Let me count the ways...

CSS gives you a few ways to specify colors. You can specify the *name* of a color, specify a color in terms of its *relative percentages* in red, green, and blue, or you can specify your color using a *hex code*, which is shorthand for describing the red, green, and blue components of the color.

While you might think that the Web would have decided on one format by now, all these formats are commonly used, so it's good to know about them all. However, hex codes are by far the most common way of specifying web colors. But remember that all these ways of specifying color ultimately just tell the browser the amount of red, green, and blue that goes into a color.

Let's work through each method of specifying colors in CSS.

Specify color by name

The most straightforward way to describe a color in CSS is just to use its name. There are 16 basic colors and 150 extended colors that can be specified this way. Let's say you want to specify the color "silver" as the background color of a body element; here's how you write that in CSS:

```
body {
        background-color: silver;
}
```

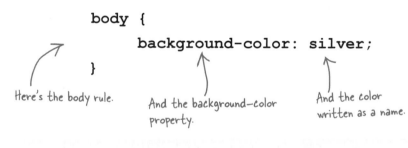

Here's the body rule.

And the background-color property.

And the color written as a name.

So, to specify a color by name, just type the color name as the value of the property. CSS color names are case-insensitive, so you can type silver, Silver, or SILVER, and all will work. Here are the 16 basic colors in CSS. Remember, these are just names for predefined amounts of red, green, and blue.

You can count on these 16 colors in any browser, but you might only find the 150 extended colors in newer browsers.

Aqua
Black
Blue
Fuchsia
Gray
Green
Lime
Maroon
Navy
Olive
Purple
Red
Silver
Teal
White
Yellow

Color in a book happens by light bouncing off the printed page. On a computer, the light is emitted by the screen, so these colors will look slightly different in your web pages.

Specify color in red, green, and blue values

You can also specify a color as the amount of red, green, and blue. So, say you wanted to specify the orange color we looked at a couple of pages back, which consisted of 80% red, 40% green, and 0% blue. Here's how you do that:

```
body {
        background-color: rgb(80%, 40%, 0%);
}
```

Begin with "rgb", short for red, green, blue.

And then specify the percentages for red, green, and blue within parentheses, and with a % sign after each one.

You can also specify the red, green, and blue values as a numeric value between 0 and 255. So, instead of 80% red, 40% green, and 0% blue, you can use 204 red, 102 green, and 0 blue.

Here's how you use straight numeric values to specify your color:

Where did these numbers come from?

80% of 255 is 204,

40% of 255 is 102, and

0% of 255 is 0.

```
body {
        background-color: rgb(204, 102, 0);
}
```

We still start with "rgb".

To specify numeric values and not percentages, just type in the value and don't use a %.

there are no Dumb Questions

Q: Why are there two different ways to specify rgb values? Don't percentages seem more straightforward?

A: Sometimes they are more straightforward, but there is some sanity to using numbers between 0 and 255. This number is related to the number of values that can be held in one byte of information. So, for historical and technical reasons, 255 is often used as a unit of measurement for specifying red, green, and blue values in a color. In fact, you might have noticed that photo editing applications often allow you to specify color values from 0 to 255 (if not, you'll see how to do that shortly).

Q: I never see anyone use rgb or actual color names in their CSS. It seems everyone uses the #00fc9a type of color codes.

A: Using rgb percents or numeric values is becoming more common, but you are right, "hex codes" are still the most widely used because people consider them a convenient way to specify color.

Q: Is it important that I be able to look at something like rgb(100, 50, 200) and know what color it is?

A: Not at all. The best way to know what rgb(100, 50, 200) looks like is to load it in your browser or use an online color picker or photo editing application to see it.

Specify color using hex codes

Now let's tackle those funky-looking hex codes. Here's the secret to them: each set of two digits of a hex code just represents the red, green, and blue component of the color. So the first two digits represent the red, the next two the green, and the last two represent the blue. Like this:

Always start a hex code with the # sign.

Then specify the red, green, and blue components, using two digits for each.

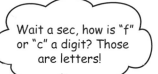

#cc6600
red green blue

Wait a sec, how is "f" or "c" a digit? Those are letters!

Believe it or not, they <u>are</u> digits, but they're written using a notation only a computer scientist could love.

Here's the second secret to reading hex codes: each set of two digits represents a number from 0 to 255. (Sound familiar?) The problem is that if we used numbers, we'd only be able to represent up to 99 in two digits, right? Well, not wanting to be constrained by something as simple as the digits 0–9, computer scientists decided they could represent all 256 values with the help of some letters too (A–F). This is the *hexadecimal* system of numbering, or "hex" for short.

Let's take a quick look at how hex codes really work, and then we'll show you how to get them from color charts or your photo editing application.

The two-minute guide to hex codes

The first thing you need to know about hex codes is that they aren't based on 10 digits (0 to 9); they're based on 16 digits (0 to F). Here's how hex digits work:

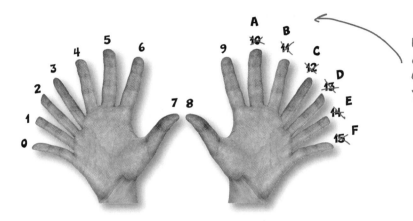

Using hex, you only need a single digit to count all the way from 0 to 15. When you get above 9, you start using letters.

So if you see a hex number like B, you know that just means 11. But what does BB, or E1, or FF mean? Let's disassemble a hex color and see what it actually represents. In fact, here's how you can do that for any hex color you might encounter.

Step one:

Separate the hex color into its three components.

Remember that each hex color is made up of a red, green, and blue component. The first thing you want to do is separate those.

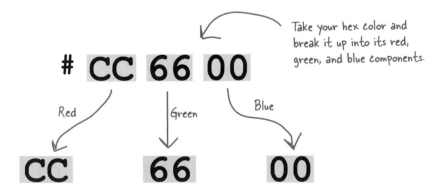

Take your hex color and break it up into its red, green, and blue components.

Step two:

Convert each hex number into its decimal equivalent.

Now that you have the components separated, you can compute the value for each from 0 to 255. Let's start with the hex number for the red component:

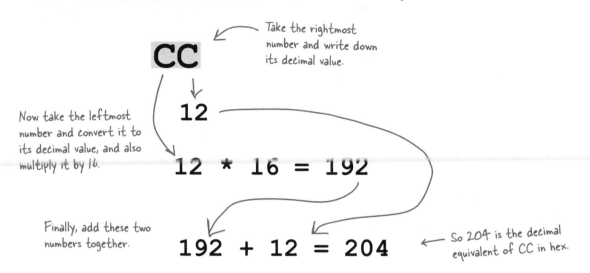

Take the rightmost number and write down its decimal value.

CC

12

Now take the leftmost number and convert it to its decimal value, and also multiply it by 16.

12 * 16 = 192

Finally, add these two numbers together.

192 + 12 = 204

So 204 is the decimal equivalent of CC in hex.

Step three:

Now do this for the other two values.

Repeat the same method on the other two values. Here's what you should get:

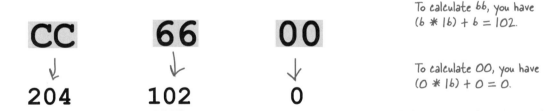

CC → 204   66 → 102   00 → 0

To calculate 66, you have (6 * 16) + 6 = 102.

To calculate 00, you have (0 * 16) + 0 = 0.

Step four:

There is no step four; you're done!

That's it. Now you've got the numbers for each component and you know exactly how much red, green, and blue go into the color. You can disassemble any hex color in exactly the same way. Now let's see how you'll usually determine web colors.

Putting it all together

You've now got a few different ways to specify colors. Take our orange color that is made up of 80% red, 40% green, and 0% blue. In CSS, we could specify this color in any of these ways:

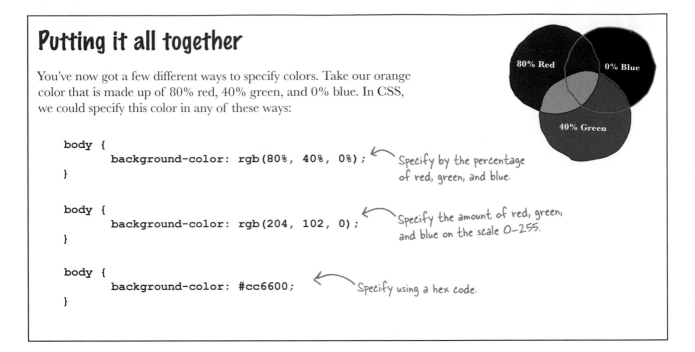

```
body {
        background-color: rgb(80%, 40%, 0%);
}
```
← Specify by the percentage of red, green, and blue.

```
body {
        background-color: rgb(204, 102, 0);
}
```
← Specify the amount of red, green, and blue on the scale 0-255.

```
body {
        background-color: #cc6600;
}
```
← Specify using a hex code.

How to find web colors

The two most common ways to find web colors are to use a color chart or an application like Photoshop Elements. You'll also find a number of web pages that allow you to choose web colors and translate between rgb and hex codes. Let's check out Photoshop Elements (most photo editing applications offer the same functionality).

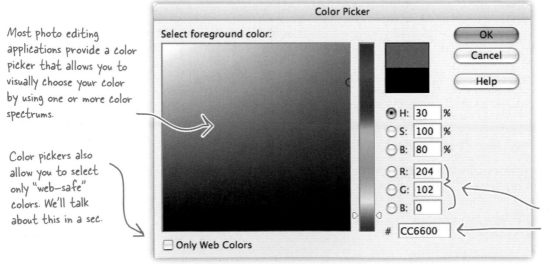

Most photo editing applications provide a color picker that allows you to visually choose your color by using one or more color spectrums.

Color pickers also allow you to select only "web-safe" colors. We'll talk about this in a sec.

Once you've picked a color, the color picker will show you the color as both rgb values and a hex code.

Using an online color chart

You'll also find some useful color charts on the Web. These charts typically display web colors that are arranged according to a number of different criteria with their corresponding hex code. Using these colors is as easy as choosing the colors you want in your page and copying the hex codes into your CSS.

This chart is maintained by Wikipedia at http://en.wikipedia.org/wiki/Web_colors. You'll also find many others by searching for "HTML color charts."

Try out the decorative name to see if it works across browsers. If it doesn't, then use the hex code instead.

there are no
Dumb Questions

Q: I heard that if I don't use web-safe colors, my pages will never look right on other browsers. Why haven't we talked about web-safe colors?

A: Back in the early days of web browsers, few people had computer screens that supported a lot of colors, so the web-safe palette of colors was created to ensure that pages looked consistent on most displays.

Today the picture has changed drastically and most web users have computer displays that support millions of colors. So, unless you have a special set of users that you know have limited color displays, you can pretty much count web-safe colors as a thing of the past.

Q: I know how to specify colors now, but how do I choose font colors that work well together?

A: It would take an entire book to answer that question properly, but there are some basic guidelines to selecting font colors. The most important is to use colors with high contrast for the text and the background to aid readability. For instance, black text on a white background has the highest contrast. You don't always have to stick with black and white, but do try to use a dark hue for the text, and a light hue for the background. Some colors, when used together, can create strange visual effects (like blue and orange, or red and green), so try your color combinations out on some friends before launching them on the world.

Q: I've seen hex codes like #cb0; what does that mean?

A: You're allowed to use shorthand if each two-digit pair shares the same numbers. So, for instance, #ccbb00 can be abbreviated #cb0, or #11eeaa as #1ea. However, if your hex code is something like #ccbb10, then you can't abbreviate it.

Crack the Safe Challenge

Dr. Evel's master plans have been locked away inside his personal safe and you've just received a tip that he encodes the combination in hex code. In fact, so he won't forget the combination, he makes the hex code the background color of his home page. Your job is to crack his hex code and discover the combination to the safe. To do that, simply convert his web color into its red, green, and blue decimal values, and you'll have the right-left-right numbers of his combination. Here's the background web color from his home page:

```
body {
        background-color: #b817e0;
}
```

Crack the code, and then write the combination here:

RIGHT 184   **LEFT** 23   **RIGHT** 224

Back to Tony's page...we're going to make the headings orange, and add an underline too

Now that you know all about color, it's time to add some color to Tony's web page. He wanted orange, and he's going to get orange. But rather than making all his text orange—which would probably be unattractive and hard to read against a white background—we're going to add a subtle splash of color in his headings. The orange is dark enough that there is good contrast between the text and the background, and by color-coordinating with the orange in the photos (Tony's shirt), we're creating a color relationship between the headings and the photos that should tie the images and text together. And just to make sure the headings stand out and create separation between the journal entries, we'll also add an underline to each heading. You haven't seen how to add an underline yet, but let's do it, and then we'll look at more about text decorations.

Here are all the changes in the CSS. Make these changes in your "journal.css" file.

```css
@font-face {
    font-family: "Emblema One";
    src: url("http://wickedlysmart.com/hfhtmlcss/chapter8/journal/EmblemaOne-Regular.woff"),
         url("http://wickedlysmart.com/hfhtmlcss/chapter8/journal/EmblemaOne-Regular.ttf");
}
body {
    font-family: Verdana, Geneva, Arial, sans-serif;
    font-size: small;
}

h1, h2 {
    color: #cc6600;
    text-decoration: underline;
}

h1 {
    font-family: "Emblema One", sans-serif;
    font-size: 220%;
}

h2 {
    font-weight: normal;
    font-size: 130%;
}

blockquote {
    font-style: italic;
}
```

We're going to make both <h1> and <h2> orange, so we're putting the color property in a shared rule.

Here's the hex code for the orange color Tony wants, otherwise known as rgb(80%, 40%, 0%).

And here's the way we create an underline. We use the text-decoration property and set it to underline.

Notice that we created one new rule for both the <h1> and <h2> headings. This is a good thing to do because it reduces duplication.

Test drive Tony's orange headings

Once you've made the changes to your "journal. css" file to add the color property to the `h1`, `h2` rule, reload the web page and check out the results.

Now both <h1> and <h2> headings are orange. This ties in nicely with Tony's orange theme and shirt.

The headings are also set off further with underlines. Hmmm...we thought this would be a good way to distinguish the headings, but actually they seem to look a little too much like clickable links, since people tend to think anything underlined in a web page is clickable.

So, underlines may have been a bad choice. Let's quickly look at some other text decorations, then we'll reconsider these underlines in the web page.

Segway'n USA

Documenting my trip around the US on my very own Segway!

August 20, 2012

Well I made it 1200 miles already, and I passed through some interesting places on the way:

1. Walla Walla, WA
2. Magic City, ID
3. Bountiful, UT
4. Last Chance, CO
5. Truth or Consequences, NM
6. Why, AZ

July 14, 2012

I saw some Burma Shave style signs on the side of the road today:

Passing cars,
When you can't see,
May get you,
A glimpse,
Of eternity.

I definitely won't be passing any cars.

June 2, 2012

Sharpen your pencil

What do all these colors have in common? Try each one in a web page, say as a font color, or use your photo editing application's color picker to determine what colors they are by entering the hex code into the dialog box directly.

#111111	#444444	#777777	#aaaaaa	#dddddd
#222222	#555555	#888888	#bbbbbb	#eeeeee
#333333	#666666	#999999	#cccccc	

Everything you ever wanted to know about text decorations in less than one page

Text decorations allow you to add decorative effects to your text like underlines, overlines, and linethroughs (also known as a strikethrough). To add a text decoration, just set the `text-decoration` property on an element, like this:

```
em {
        text-decoration: line-through;
}
```

This rule will cause the <em> element to have a line through the middle of the text.

You can set more than one decoration at a time. Say you want underline and overline at the same time—you specify your text decoration like this:

```
em {
        text-decoration: underline overline;
}
```

This rule results in the <em> element having an underline AND overline.

And if you have text that is inheriting text decoration you don't want, just use the value "none":

```
em {
        text-decoration: none;
}
```

With this rule, <em> elements will have no decoration.

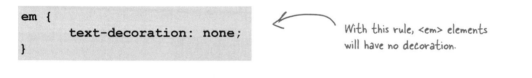

there are no Dumb Questions

Q: So if I have two different rules for an <em>, and one specifies overline and the other underline, will they be added together so I get both?

A: No. You need to combine the two values into one rule to get both text decorations. Only one rule is chosen for the text-decoration, and decorations in separate rules are not added together. Only the rule that is chosen for the text-decoration styling will determine the decoration used, so the only way to get two decorations is to specify them both in the same text-decoration declaration.

Q: I've been meaning to ask why the color property isn't called text-color?

A: The color property really controls the foreground color of an element, so it controls the text and the border color, although you can give the border its own color with the border-color property.

Q: I like the linethrough decoration. Can I use it on text I'm editing to indicate things that need to be deleted?

A: You could, but there's a better way. HTML has an element we haven't talked about called <del> that marks content in your HTML as content that should be deleted. There is a similar element called <ins> that marks content that should be inserted. Typically browsers will style these elements with a strikethrough and underline, respectively. And with CSS, you can style them any way you like. By using <del> and <ins>, you are marking the meaning of your content in addition to styling it.

Removing the underline...

Let's get rid of that confusing underline and instead add a nice bottom border like we did in the lounge. To do that, open your "journal.css" file and make these changes to the combined h1, h2 rule:

```css
h1, h2 {
    color: #cc6600;
    border-bottom: thin dotted #888888;
    text-decoration: underline;
}
```

Add a border on the bottom of the <h1> and <h2> elements. You can almost read this like English: "add a thin, dotted line with the color #888888 on the bottom border"...

In the next chapter, we are going to go into borders in detail. Hang on, we're almost there!

Delete the text decoration.

And here's how our new "underline" looks— definitely more stylish and less confusing than a text decoration underline.

Now we've got borders under the <h1> and <h2> element, not underlines.

Notice that borders extend all the way to the end of the page, rather than just under the text. Why? You'll find out in the next chapter.

My Trip Around the USA on
file:///chapter8/journal/journal.html

Segway'n USA

Documenting my trip around the US on my very own Segway!

August 20, 2012

Well I made it 1200 miles already, and I passed through some interesting places on the way:

1. Walla Walla, WA
2. Magic City, ID
3. Bountiful, UT
4. Last Chance, CO
5. Truth or Consequences, NM
6. Why, AZ

July 14, 2012

I saw some Burma Shave style signs on the side of the road today:

> *Passing cars,*
> *When you can't see,*
> *May get you,*
> *A glimpse,*
> *Of eternity.*

I definitely won't be passing any cars.

BULLET POINTS

- CSS gives you lots of control over the look of your fonts, including properties like font-family, font-weight, font-size, and font-style.

- A font-family is a set of fonts that share common characteristics.

- The font families for the Web are serif, sans-serif, monospace, cursive, and fantasy. Serif and sans-serif fonts are most common.

- The fonts that your visitors will see in your web page depend on the fonts they have installed on their own computers, unless you use Web Fonts.

- It's a good idea to specify font alternatives in your font-family CSS property in case your users don't have your preferred font installed.

- Always make the last font a generic font like serif or sans-serif, so that the browser can make an appropriate substitution if no other fonts are found.

- To use a font that your users may not have installed by default, use the @font-face rule in CSS.

- Font sizes are usually specified using px, em, %, or keywords.

- If you use pixels ("px") to specify your font size, you are telling the browser how many pixels tall to make your letters.

- em and % are relative font sizes, so specifying your font size using em and % means the size of the letters will be relative to the font size of the parent element.

- Using relative sizes for your fonts can make your pages more maintainable.

- Use the font size keywords to set the base font size in your body rule, so that all browsers can scale the font sizes if users want the text to be bigger or smaller.

- You can make your text bold using the font-weight CSS property.

- The font-style property is used to create italic or oblique text. Italic and oblique text is slanted.

- Web colors are created by mixing different amounts of red, green, and blue.

- If you mix 100% red, 100% green, and 100% blue, you will get white.

- If you mix 0% red, 0% green, and 0% blue, you will get black.

- CSS has 16 basic colors, including black, white, red, blue, and green, and 150 extended colors.

- You can specify which color you want using percentages of red, green, and blue, using numerical values of 0–255 for red, green, and blue, or using a color's hex code.

- An easy way to find the hex code of a color you want is to use a photo editing application's color picker or one of many online web tools.

- Hex codes representing colors have six digits, and each digit can be from 0–F. The first two digits represent the amount of red, the second two the amount of green, and the last two the amount of blue.

- You can use the text-decoration property to create an underline for text. Underlined text is often confused as linked text by users, so use this property carefully.

HTMLcross

You've absorbed a lot in this chapter: fonts, color, weights, and styles. It's time to do another crossword and let it all sink in.

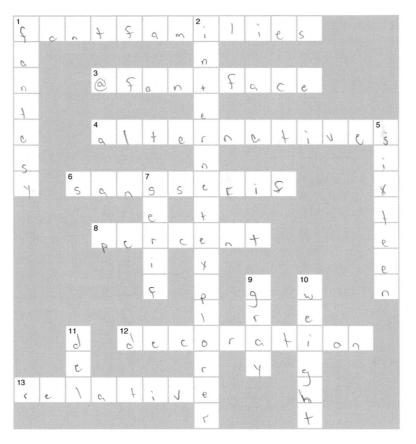

Across

1. Similar fonts are grouped into ____.
3. Use the ____ rule in CSS to load fonts from the Web.
4. When you specify fonts in the font-family property, you are specifying ____.
6. Considered cleaner and easier to read on a computer display.
8. You can specify fonts in terms of pixels, em, or ___.
12. Underline and linethrough are examples of text ___.
13. em and % are both this kind of size.

Down

1. Font family almost never used in web pages.
2. Browser that doesn't handle pixel font sizes well.
5. Hex codes use this many different digits.
7. Fonts with little barbs on them.
9. Colors like #111111 through #EEEEEE are all shades of ____.
10. Controls how bold a font looks.
11. Element that can be used to mark text for deletion.

Font Magnets Solution

Your job was to help the fictional fonts below find their way home to their own font family. You moved each fridge magnet into the correct font family. Check your answers before you move on. Here's the solution.

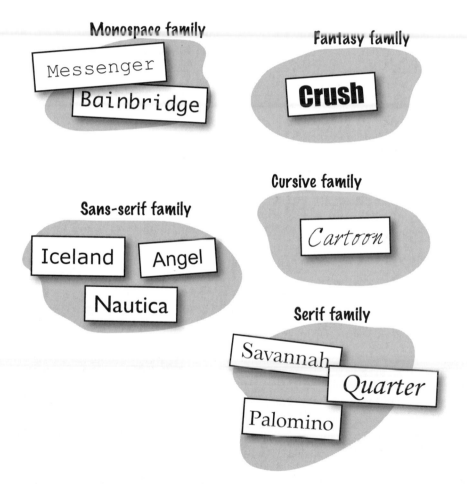

Monospace family

Messenger

Bainbridge

Fantasy family

Crush

Sans-serif family

Iceland   Angel

Nautica

Cursive family

Cartoon

Serif family

Savannah

Quarter

Palomino

Crack the Safe Challenge Solution

Dr. Evel's master plans have been locked away inside his personal safe and you've just received a tip that he encodes the combination in hex code. In fact, so he won't forget the combination, he makes the hex code the background color of his home page. Your job is to crack his hex code and discover the combination to the safe. To do that, simply convert his web color into its red, green, and blue decimal values, and you'll have the right-left-right numbers of his combination. Here's the background web color from his home page:

```
body {
        background-color: #b817e0;
}
```

Crack the code, and then write the combination here:

(11 * 16) + 8 =   (1 * 16) + 7 =   (14 * 16) + 0 =

RIGHT ....184....   **LEFT** ....23....   **RIGHT** ....224....

Sharpen your pencil
Solution

What do all these colors have in common? You can try each one in a web page, or use the color picker to determine what colors they are, by entering the hex code into the dialog box directly.

```
#111111
#222222
#333333
#444444
#555555
#666666
#777777
#888888
#999999
#aaaaaa
#bbbbbb
#cccccc
#dddddd
#eeeeee
```

All colors that use just one digit in their hex codes are grays, from very dark (almost black) to very light (almost white).

HTMLcross Solution

¹F	O	N	T	F	A	M	²I	L	I	E	S
A						N				
N			³@	F	O	N	T	F	A	C	E
T					E					
A			⁴A	L	T	E	R	N	A	T	I	V	E	⁵S
S					N					I
Y		⁶S	A	N	⁷S	S	E	R	I	F		X
			E		T					T
		⁸P	E	R	C	E	N	T			E
		I		X					E
		F		P		⁹G		¹⁰W		N
		L		R			E
¹¹D		¹²D	E	C	O	R	A	T	I	O	N
E			R		Y		G
¹³R	E	L	A	T	I	V	E			H
			R				T

9 the box model

Getting Intimate with Elements

> I think we'd be a little closer if it weren't for all the padding, margins, and this darn table.

To do advanced web construction, you really need to know your building materials. In this chapter we're going to take a close look at our building materials, the HTML elements. We're going to put block and inline elements right under the microscope and see what they're made of. You'll see how you can control just about every aspect of how an element is constructed with CSS. But we don't stop there—you'll also see how you can give elements unique identities. And, if that weren't enough, you're going to learn when and why you might want to use multiple stylesheets. So, turn the page and start getting intimate with elements.

The lounge gets an upgrade

You've come a long way in eight chapters, and so has the Head First Lounge. In fact, over the next two chapters, we're giving it a total upgrade with all new content for the main page and restyling it from scratch. And, just to entice you, we're going to give you a little sneak peek before we even get started. Check this out—on this page, you'll find the new unstyled lounge page with all the new content. On the next page, you'll find the stylized version that we're going to create by the end of the next chapter.

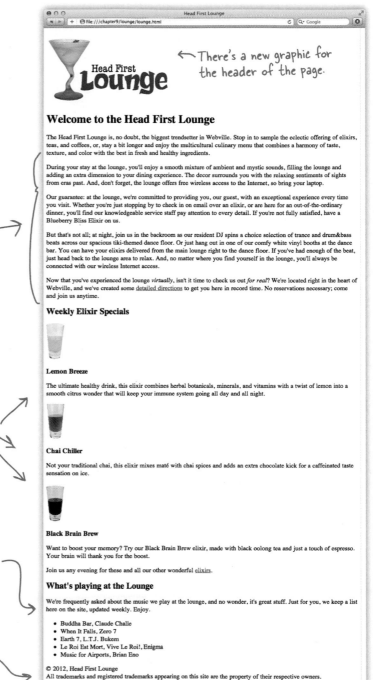

← There's a new graphic for the header of the page.

The lounge guys have supplied a lot of new text describing the lounge and what it offers.

They've included a set of elixir specials for the week.

And they even let visitors sample some of the music that is played in the lounge each week, a common request of customers.

Finally, they've got some legalese in the footer of the page with a copyright.

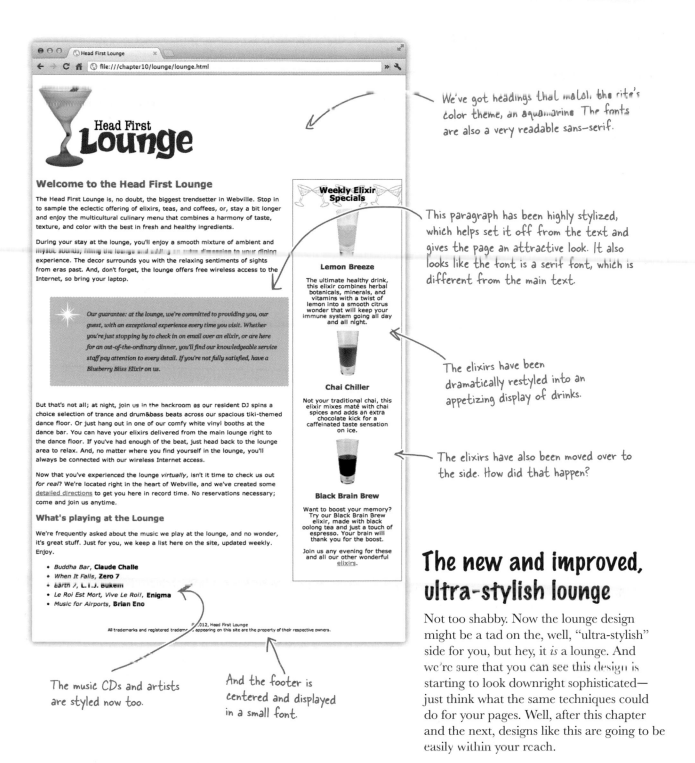

We've got headings that match the site's color theme, an aquamarine. The fonts are also a very readable sans-serif.

This paragraph has been highly stylized, which helps set it off from the text and gives the page an attractive look. It also looks like the font is a serif font, which is different from the main text.

The elixirs have been dramatically restyled into an appetizing display of drinks.

The elixirs have also been moved over to the side. How did that happen?

The music CDs and artists are styled now too.

And the footer is centered and displayed in a small font.

The new and improved, ultra-stylish lounge

Not too shabby. Now the lounge design might be a tad on the, well, "ultra-stylish" side for you, but hey, it *is* a lounge. And we're sure that you can see this design is starting to look downright sophisticated— just think what the same techniques could do for your pages. Well, after this chapter and the next, designs like this are going to be easily within your reach.

Setting up the new lounge

Before we start the major construction, let's get familiar with the new lounge.
Here's what you need to do:

1 Take a look at the "chapter9/lounge" folder and you'll find the file "lounge.html",
with all new content. Open the file in your editor and have a look around. Everything
should look familiar: head, paragraphs, a few images, and a list.

2 You're going to spend most of this chapter adding style to this HTML, so you need a
place for your CSS. You're going to create all new styles for the lounge in the stylesheet
file "lounge.css", so you'll find your `<link>` element in the `<head>` of "lounge.html" is
still there, but the previous version of "lounge.css" stylesheet is gone.

```
<link type="text/css" rel="stylesheet" href="lounge.css">
```

Remember, this `<link>` element tells the browser to look for an external stylesheet called
"lounge.css".

3 Next, you need to create the new "lounge.css" in the "chapter9/lounge" folder. This file is
going to hold all the new CSS for the new lounge.

Starting with a few simple upgrades

Now you're all ready to start styling the lounge. Let's add a few
rules to your CSS just to get some basics out of the way—like the
font family, size, and some color—that will immediately improve
the lounge (and give you a good review from the last chapter). So,
open your "lounge.css" file and add the following rules.

Here's the default font size for the page.

```
body {
        font-size:    small;
        font-family: Verdana, Helvetica, Arial, sans-serif;
}

h1, h2 {
        color: #007e7e;
}

h1 {
        font-size: 150%;
}

h2 {
        font-size: 130%;
}
```

We're going to go with a sans-serif font family for the lounge. We've picked a few font alternatives, and ended the declaration with the generic sans-serif font.

We're going to set the color of the <h1> and <h2> elements to an aquamarine to match the glass in the logo.

Now let's get some reasonable heading sizes for <h1> and <h2>. Since we're setting two different sizes for these, we need separate rules and can't add them to the combined rule for <h1> and <h2>.

A very quick test drive

Let's do a quick test drive just to see how these styles affect the page. Make sure you've made all the changes; then save and test.

Headings are now sans-serif and a color that matches the logo, creating a theme for the page.

Paragraph text is also sans-serif since every element inherits the <body>'s font-family property.

The <h2> heading is also styled with a new color and sans-serif, but a tad smaller.

We haven't applied any styles to the <h3>, so it just inherits the font-family property from <body>.

This link looks oddly out of place with its default blue color. We'll have to fix that (later).

One more adjustment

We're going to make one more adjustment to the lounge before we move on to start making some bigger changes. This adjustment involves a new property you haven't seen before, but at this point, you've got enough experience under your belt that we're not going to treat you with kid gloves every time a new property comes along. So, just jump in and give it a try.

Here's what we're going to do: we're going to adjust the line height of the text on the entire page so that there's more vertical space between each line. To do that, we add a `line-height` property in the body rule:

Increasing the line height of your text can improve readability. It also gives you another way to provide contrast between different parts of your page (you'll see how that works in a bit).

Here we're changing the space between each line to 1.6em— in other words, 1.6 times the font size.

```
body {

    font-size:    small;

    font-family: Verdana, Helvetica, Arial, sans-serif;

    line-height: 1.6em;

}
```

Checking out the new line height

As you might have guessed, the `line-height` property allows you to specify the amount of vertical space between each line of your text. Like other font-related properties, you can specify the line height in pixels, or using an em or percent value that's relative to the font size.

Let's see what the effect of the `line-height` property is on the lounge. Make sure you add the `line-height` property to your CSS file and then save. You should see the line height increase when you refresh.

Using the line-height property, we've increased the space between each line of text from the default to 1.6em.

Before
↓

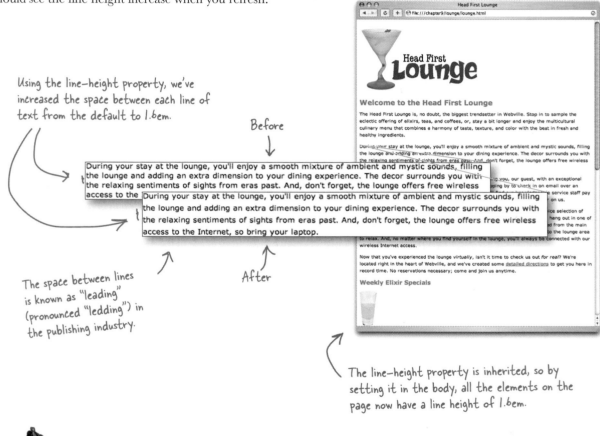

The space between lines is known as "leading" (pronounced "ledding") in the publishing industry.

After

The line-height property is inherited, so by setting it in the body, all the elements on the page now have a line height of 1.6em.

Exercise

Try a few different values for line-height, like 200%, .5em, and 20px to see the effect. Which looks the best? The worst? Which is most readable? When you're done, make sure you change the line-height back to 1.6em.

Getting ready for some major renovations

After only a few pages of this chapter, you already have a ton of text style on the new lounge. Congrats!

Now things are going to get really interesting. We're going to move from changing simple properties of elements, like size, color, and decorations, to really tweaking some fundamental aspects of how elements are displayed. This is where you move up to the big leagues.

But to move up to the big leagues, you've got to know *the box model*. What's that? It's how CSS sees elements. CSS treats every single element as if it were represented by a box. Let's see what that means.

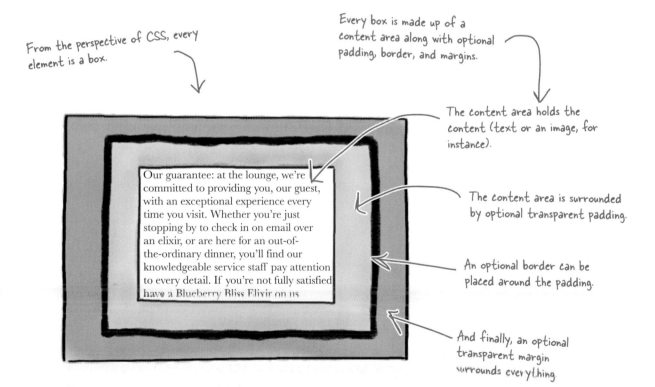

From the perspective of CSS, every element is a box.

Every box is made up of a content area along with optional padding, border, and margins.

The content area holds the content (text or an image, for instance).

Our guarantee: at the lounge, we're committed to providing you, our guest, with an exceptional experience every time you visit. Whether you're just stopping by to check in on email over an elixir, or are here for an out-of-the-ordinary dinner, you'll find our knowledgeable service staff pay attention to every detail. If you're not fully satisfied have a Blueberry Bliss Elixir on us.

The content area is surrounded by optional transparent padding.

An optional border can be placed around the padding.

And finally, an optional transparent margin surrounds everything.

All elements are treated as boxes: paragraphs, headings, block quotes, lists, list items, and so on. Even inline elements like <em> and links are treated by CSS as boxes.

A closer look at the box model

You're going to be able to control every aspect of the box with CSS: the size of the padding around the content, whether or not the element has a border (as well as what kind and how large), and how much margin there is between your element and other elements. Let's check out each part of the box and its role:

The content area holds the element's content. It's typically just big enough to hold the content.

What is the content area?

Every element starts with some content, like text or an image, and this content is placed inside a box that is just big enough to contain it. Notice that the content area has no whitespace between the content and the edge of this box.

We've drawn an edge around the content area just so you know how big it is. But in a browser, there is never a visible edge around the content area.

Our guarantee: at the lounge, we're committed to providing you, our guest, with an exceptional experience every time you visit. Whether you're just stopping by to check in on email over an elixir, or are here for an out-of-the-ordinary dinner, you'll find our knowledgeable service staff pay attention to every detail. If you're not fully satisfied have a Blueberry Bliss Elixir on us.

The browser adds optional padding around the content area.

What is the padding?

Any box can have a layer of padding around the content area. Padding is optional, so you don't have to have it, but you can use padding to create visual whitespace between the content and the border of the box. The padding is transparent and has no color or decoration of its own.

Our guarantee: at the lounge, we're committed to providing you, our guest, with an exceptional experience every time you visit. Whether you're just stopping by to check in on email over an elixir, or are here for an out-of-the-ordinary dinner, you'll find our knowledgeable service staff pay attention to every detail. If you're not fully satisfied have a Blueberry Bliss Elixir on us.

Using CSS, you're going to be able to control the width of the padding around the entire content area, or even control the padding on any one side (top, right, bottom, or left).

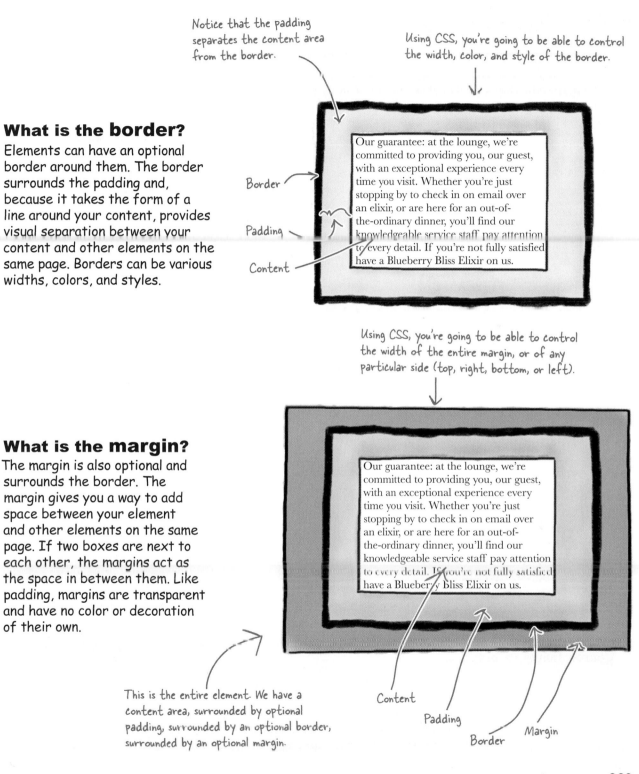

Notice that the padding separates the content area from the border.

Using CSS, you're going to be able to control the width, color, and style of the border.

What is the border?

Elements can have an optional border around them. The border surrounds the padding and, because it takes the form of a line around your content, provides visual separation between your content and other elements on the same page. Borders can be various widths, colors, and styles.

Border

Padding

Content

Our guarantee: at the lounge, we're committed to providing you, our guest, with an exceptional experience every time you visit. Whether you're just stopping by to check in on email over an elixir, or are here for an out-of-the-ordinary dinner, you'll find our knowledgeable service staff pay attention to every detail. If you're not fully satisfied, have a Blueberry Bliss Elixir on us.

Using CSS, you're going to be able to control the width of the entire margin, or of any particular side (top, right, bottom, or left).

What is the margin?

The margin is also optional and surrounds the border. The margin gives you a way to add space between your element and other elements on the same page. If two boxes are next to each other, the margins act as the space in between them. Like padding, margins are transparent and have no color or decoration of their own.

Our guarantee: at the lounge, we're committed to providing you, our guest, with an exceptional experience every time you visit. Whether you're just stopping by to check in on email over an elixir, or are here for an out-of-the-ordinary dinner, you'll find our knowledgeable service staff pay attention to every detail. If you're not fully satisfied, have a Blueberry Bliss Elixir on us.

This is the entire element. We have a content area, surrounded by optional padding, surrounded by an optional border, surrounded by an optional margin.

Content

Padding

Border

Margin

What you can do to boxes

The box model may look simple with just the content, some padding, a border, and margins. But when you combine these all together, there are endless ways you can determine the layout of an element with its internal spacing (padding) and the spacing around it (margins). Take a look at just a few examples of how you can vary your elements.

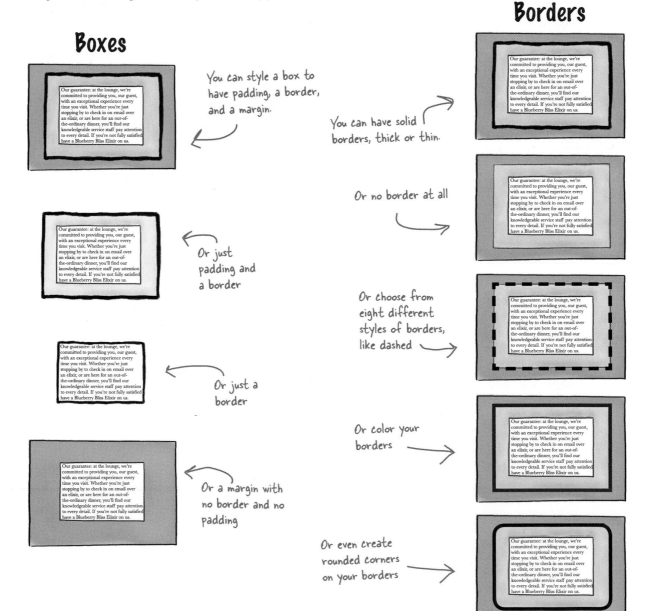

Boxes

You can style a box to have padding, a border, and a margin.

Or just padding and a border

Or just a border

Or a margin with no border and no padding

Borders

You can have solid borders, thick or thin.

Or no border at all

Or choose from eight different styles of borders, like dashed

Or color your borders

Or even create rounded corners on your borders

Padding

With CSS, you can control padding on any side of the content area. Here we've got a lot of left and right padding.

And here there's a lot of top and bottom padding.

And here the content is offset to the bottom right with padding on the top and left.

Margins

You have the same level of control over the margins. Here there's a lot of top and bottom margin.

And here's a lot of left and right margin.

And as with padding, you can specify all sides independently to create margins like this.

Content Area

You can even control width and height in a variety of ways. Here, the content area has been made wide.

And here the content area is tall but thin.

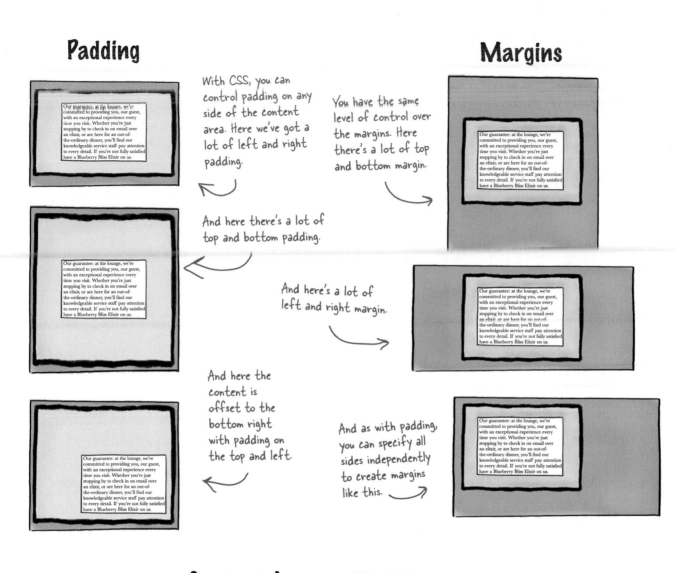
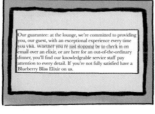

Q: It seems like knowing this box stuff would be important if I were someone creating the software for a web browser, but how is this going to help me make better web pages?

A: To go beyond simple web pages that use the browser's default layout, you need to be able to control how elements sit on the page, as well as the relative position of other elements. To do that, you alter various aspects of each element's padding and margins. So to create interesting web page designs, you definitely need to know something about the box model.

Q: What's the difference between padding and margin? They seem like the same thing.

A: The margin provides space between your element and other elements, while padding gives you extra space around your content. If you have a visual border, the padding is on the inside of the border and the margin on the outside. Think of padding as part of the element, while the margin surrounds your element and buffers it from the things around it.

Q: I know they are all optional, but do you need to have padding to have a border or a margin?

A: No, they are all totally optional and don't rely on each other. So you can have a border and no padding, or a margin and no border, and so on.

Q: I'm not sure I get how elements get laid out and how margins fit into that.

A: Hold that thought. While you're going to see a little of how margins interact with other elements in this chapter, we'll get way into this topic in Chapter 11 when we talk about positioning.

Q: So other than size, it sounds like I can't really style padding and margins?

A: That's basically right. Both are used to provide more visual space, and you can't give the padding or margin a direct color or any kind of decoration. But because they are transparent, they will take on the color of any background colors or background images. One difference between padding and margins is that the element's background color (or background image) will extend under the padding, but not the margin. You'll see how this works in a bit.

Q: Is the size of the content area determined solely by the size of the content in it?

A: Browsers use several rules to determine the width and height of the content area, and we'll be looking at that more in-depth later. The short answer is that while the content is the primary way the size of an element is determined, you can set the width and height yourself if you need control over the size of the element.

> Hey guys, love the shop talk, really do. But did you forget you were in the middle of renovating the lounge?

Meanwhile, back at the lounge...

We do have our work cut out for us on the lounge page, so let's get back to it. Did you notice the blue, stylized paragraph when you looked at the final version of the lounge page in the beginning of the chapter? This paragraph contains text with the lounge's guarantee to their customers, and obviously they want to really highlight their promise. Let's take a closer look at this paragraph, and then we'll build it.

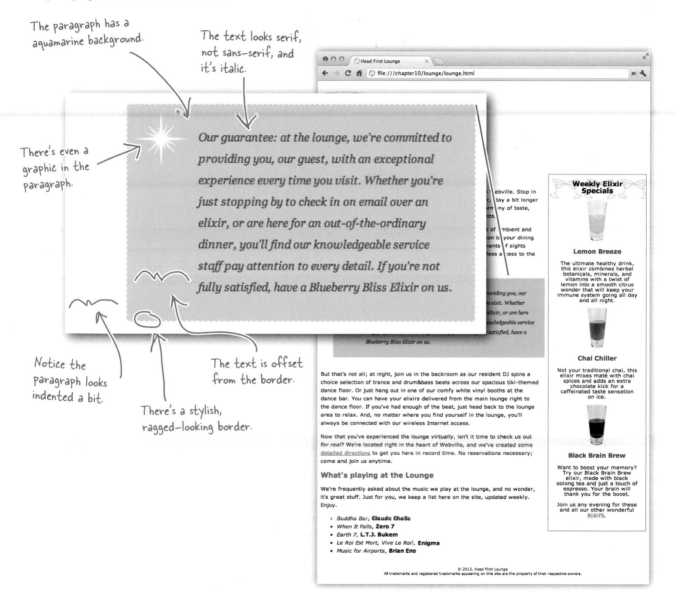

The paragraph has a aquamarine background.

The text looks serif, not sans-serif, and it's italic.

There's even a graphic in the paragraph.

Notice the paragraph looks indented a bit.

There's a stylish, ragged-looking border.

The text is offset from the border.

Sharpen your pencil

See if you can identify the padding, border, and margins of this paragraph. Mark all the padding and margins (left, right, top, and bottom):

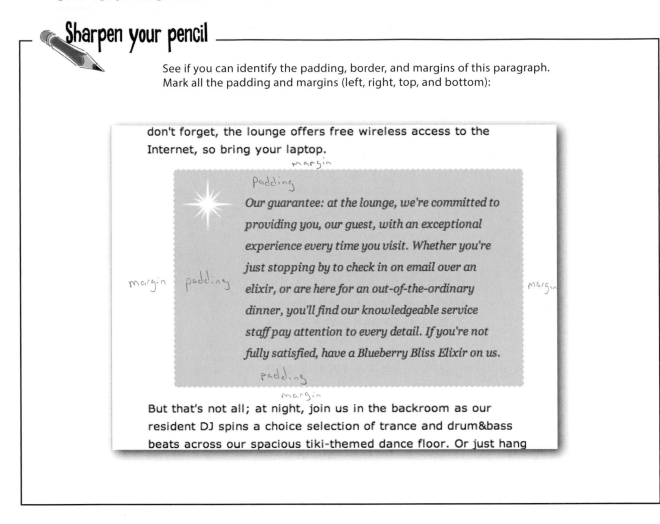

⚛ BRAIN POWER

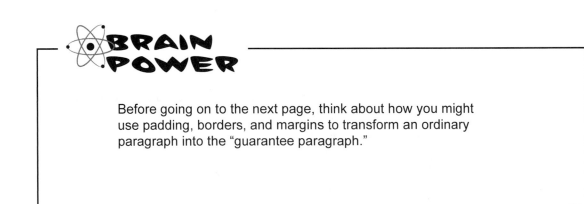

Before going on to the next page, think about how you might use padding, borders, and margins to transform an ordinary paragraph into the "guarantee paragraph."

Creating the guarantee style

Let's get started by making a few small changes to the style of the guarantee paragraph just to get a feel for how the paragraph's box is set up. To do that, you're going to add the paragraph to a class called quarantee so that you can create some custom styles for just this paragraph. You're then going to add a border along with a little background color, which will let you see exactly how the paragraph is a box. Then we'll get to work on the rest of the style. Here's what you need to do:

 Open your "lounge.html" file and locate the paragraph that starts "Our guarantee". Add a class attribute "guarantee" to the element like this:

> Add the class attribute with a value of "guarantee".
> Remember, a class will allow you to style this paragraph
> independently of the other paragraphs.

```
<p class="guarantee">
        Our guarantee: at the lounge, we're committed to providing
        you, our guest, with an exceptional experience every time you
        visit. Whether you're just stopping by to check in on email
        over an elixir, or are here for an out-of-the-ordinary dinner,
        you'll find our knowledgeable service staff pay attention to every
        detail. If you're not fully satisfied, have a Blueberry Bliss
        Elixir on us.
</p>
```

2 Save your "lounge.html" file and open the "lounge.css" file. You're going to add a border and background color to the guarantee paragraph. Add the following CSS to the bottom of your stylesheet and then save.

> The first three properties add a border to any
> element that is in the guarantee class. So far,
> that's just this paragraph.

```
.guarantee {
        border-color:      black;
        border-width:      1px;
        border-style:      solid;
        background-color: #a7cece;
}
```

> We're making the color of the border black...
>
> ...and one pixel thick...
>
> ...and solid.
>
> We're also giving the element a background color, which
> will help you see the difference between padding and
> margins, and make the guarantee look good.

A test drive of the paragraph border

Reload the page in your browser, and you'll now see the guarantee paragraph with an aquamarine background and a thin black border around it. Let's examine this a little more closely…

It doesn't look like the paragraph has any padding around the content—there is no space between the text and the border.

the lounge and adding an extra dimension to your dining experience. The decor surrounds you with the relaxing sentiments of sights from eras past. And, don't forget, the lounge offers free wireless access to the Internet, so bring your laptop.

Our guarantee: at the lounge, we're committed to providing you, our guest, with an exceptional experience every time you visit. Whether you're just stopping by to check in on email over an elixir, or are here for an out-of-the-ordinary dinner, you'll find our knowledgeable service staff pay attention to every detail. If you're not fully satisfied, have a Blueberry Bliss Elixir on us.

But that's not all; at night, join us in the backroom as our resident DJ spins a choice selection of trance and drum&bass beats across our spacious tiki-themed dance floor. Or just hang out in one of our comfy white vinyl booths at the dance bar. You can have your elixirs delivered from the main

But there does seem to be a margin on the top and bottom of the paragraph element.

There isn't a noticeable margin between the left and right edges of the paragraph and the browser window edges.

Here's what the paragraph would look like if we drew it as a box model diagram:

We've got a top and bottom margin.

Our guarantee: at the lounge, we're committed to providing you, our guest, with an exceptional experience every time you visit. Whether you're just stopping by to check in on email over an elixir, or are here for an out-of-the-ordinary dinner, you'll find our knowledgeable service staff pay attention to every detail. If you're not fully satisfied have a Blueberry Bliss Elixir on us.

But the left and right margins are very small.

And we have a border, but it's right up against the content, which means the padding is set very small, or there's no padding at all.

Padding, border, and margins for the guarantee

Now that you've seen how the padding, border, and margins are
currently set on the guarantee paragraph, let's think more about
how we'd actually like them to look.

We definitely need some padding
all around the content.

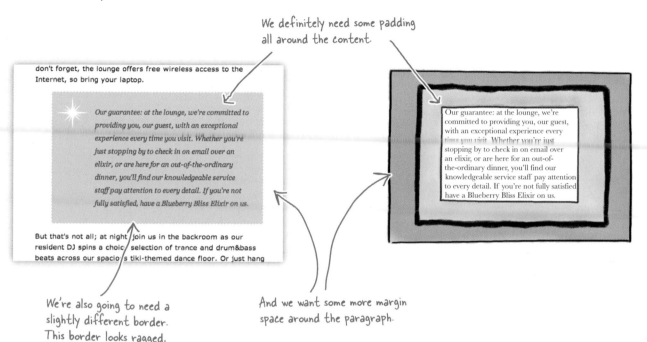

We're also going to need a
slightly different border.
This border looks ragged,
not like a solid line.

And we want some more margin
space around the paragraph.

Adding some padding

Let's start with the padding. CSS has a `padding` property that you can
use to set the same padding for all four sides of the content. You can
set this property either to a number of pixels or a percentage. We'll use
pixels and set the padding to 25 pixels.

```
.guarantee {
        border-color:       black;
        border-width:       1px;
        border-style:       solid;
        background-color:   #a7cece;
        padding:            25px;
}
```

We're adding 25 pixels of padding
to all sides of the content (top,
right, bottom, and left).

A test drive with some padding

When you reload the page in your browser, you'll notice the text in the guarantee paragraph has a little more breathing room on the sides now. There's some space between the text and the border, and it's much easier to read.

Now you can see 25 pixels of space between the edge of the text content and the border.

Notice that the background color is under both the content and the padding. But it doesn't extend into the margin.

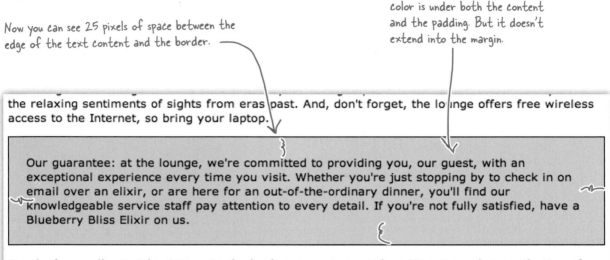

the relaxing sentiments of sights from eras past. And, don't forget, the lounge offers free wireless access to the Internet, so bring your laptop.

Our guarantee: at the lounge, we're committed to providing you, our guest, with an exceptional experience every time you visit. Whether you're just stopping by to check in on email over an elixir, or are here for an out-of-the-ordinary dinner, you'll find our knowledgeable service staff pay attention to every detail. If you're not fully satisfied, have a Blueberry Bliss Elixir on us.

But that's not all; at night, join us in the backroom as our resident DJ spins a choice selection of trance and drum&bass beats across our spacious tiki-themed dance floor. Or just hang out in one of

Now let's add some margin

Margins are easy to add using CSS. Like padding, you can specify the margin as a percentage or in pixels. You're going to add a 30-pixel margin around the entire guarantee paragraph. Here's how you do that:

```
.guarantee {
    border-color:      black;
    border-width:      1px;
    border-style:      solid;
    background-color:  #a7cece;
    padding:           25px;
    margin:            30px;
}
```

We're adding 30 pixels of margin to all sides of the content (top, right, bottom, and left).

A test drive with the margin

When you reload the lounge page, you'll see the paragraph is really beginning to stand out on the page. With the margins in place, the paragraph looks inset from the rest of the text, and that, combined with the background color, makes it look more like a "callout" than an ordinary paragraph. As you can see, with only a few lines of CSS, you're doing some powerful things.

Now we have 30 pixels of margin on all sides.

the relaxing sentiments of sights from eras past. And, don't forget, the lounge offers free wireless access to the Internet, so bring your laptop.

Our guarantee: at the lounge, we're committed to providing you, our guest, with an exceptional experience every time you visit. Whether you're just stopping by to check in on email over an elixir, or are here for an out-of-the-ordinary dinner, you'll find our knowledgeable service staff pay attention to every detail. If you're not fully satisfied, have a Blueberry Bliss Elixir on us.

But that's not all; at night, join us in the backroom as our resident DJ spins a choice selection of trance and drum&bass beats across our spacious tiki-themed dance floor. Or just hang out in one of

Exercise

If you look at the guarantee paragraph as it's supposed to look in its final form, it has an italic, serif font, a line height greater than the rest of the page, and (if you're looking really close) gray text. Write the CSS below to set the line height to 1.9em, the font style to italic, the color to #444444, and the font family to Georgia, "Times New Roman", Times, serif. Check your CSS with the answers in the back of the chapter, then type it in and test.

```
.guarantee {
    border-color: black;
    border-width: 1px;
    border-style: solid
    background-color: #a7cece;
    padding: 25px;
    margin: 30px;
    font-family: Georgia, "Time New Roman", Times, serif;
    font-style: italic;
    color: #444;
    line-height: 1.9em;
}
```

Adding a background image

You're almost there. What's left? We still need to get the white "guarantee star" graphic into the paragraph and work on the border, which is a solid, black line. Let's tackle the image first.

If you look in the "chapter9/lounge/images" folder, you'll find a GIF image called "background.gif" that looks like this:

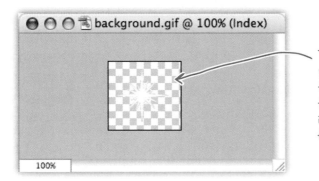

This image is a simple star–like pattern in white against a transparent background. Notice that it also has a matte around it that matches the color of the background.

Now you just need to get that image into your paragraph element, so you'll be using an `<img>` element, right? Not so fast. If you're adding an image to the background of an element, there is another way. Using CSS, you can add a background image to any element using the `background-image` property. Let's give it a try and see how it works:

Here are the properties you added in the exercise on the previous page.

```
.guarantee {
    line-height:      1.9em;
    font-style:       italic;
    font-family:      Georgia, "Times New Roman", Times, serif;
    color:            #444444;
    border-color:     black;
    border-width:     1px;
    border-style:     solid;
    background-color: #a7cece;
    padding:          25px;
    margin:           30px;
    background-image: url(images/background.gif);
}
```

Add this to your CSS, save, and reload your page.

Wait a sec, it seems like we have two ways to put images on a page. Is background-image a replacement for the <img> element?

No, the `background-image` property has a very specific purpose, which is to set the background image of an element. It isn't for placing images in a page—for that, you definitely want to use the `<img>` element.

Think about it this way: a background image is pure presentation, and the only reason you would use a `background-image` property is to improve the attractiveness of your element. An `<img>` element, on the other hand, is used to include an image that has a more substantial role in the page, like a photo or a logo.

Now, we could have just placed the image inside the paragraph, and we could probably get the same look and feel, but the guarantee star is pure decoration—it has no real meaning on the page, and it's only meant to make the element look better. So, `background-image` makes more sense.

Test driving the background image

Well, this is certainly an interesting test drive—we have a background image, but it appears to be repeated many times. Let's take a closer look at how to use CSS background images, and then you'll be able to fix this.

Here's the guarantee star image in the background. Notice that it sits on top of the background color, and because it has a transparent background, it lets the color show through.

Also notice that background images, like the background color, only show under the content area and padding, and not outside the border in the margin.

CSS Up Close

The background-image property places an image in the background of an element. Two other properties also affect the background image: background-position and background-repeat.

```
background-image: url(images/background.gif);
```

The background-image property is set to a URL, which can be a relative path or a full-blown URL (http://...).

Notice that no quotes are required around the URL.

Fixing the background image

By default, background images are repeated. Luckily, there is a `no-repeat` value for the `background-repeat` property. Also, by default, browsers position a background image in the top left of the element, which is where we want it, but let's also add a `background-position` property just to give it a try.

```
.guarantee {
        line-height:        1.9em;
        font-style:         italic;
        font-family:        Georgia, "Times New Roman", Times, serif;
        color:              #444444;
        border-color:       black;
        border-width:       1px;
        border-style:       solid;
        background-color:   #a7cece;
        padding:            25px;
        margin:             30px;
        background-image:   url(images/background.gif);
        background-repeat:  no-repeat;
        background-position: top left;
}
```

You've got two new properties to add.

We want the background image to not repeat.

And we want it in the top-left corner.

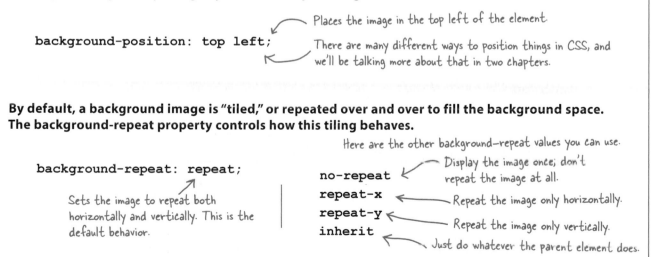

The background-position property sets the position of the image and can be specified in pixels, or as a percentage, or by using keywords like top, left, right, bottom, and center.

`background-position: top left;`

Places the image in the top left of the element.

There are many different ways to position things in CSS, and we'll be talking more about that in two chapters.

By default, a background image is "tiled," or repeated over and over to fill the background space. The background-repeat property controls how this tiling behaves.

`background-repeat: repeat;`

Sets the image to repeat both horizontally and vertically. This is the default behavior.

Here are the other background-repeat values you can use.

no-repeat — *Display the image once; don't repeat the image at all.*

repeat-x — *Repeat the image only horizontally.*

repeat-y — *Repeat the image only vertically.*

inherit — *Just do whatever the parent element does.*

Another test drive of the background image

Here we go again. This time, it looks like we're much closer to what we want. But since this is a background image, the text can sit on top of it. How do we fix this? That's exactly what padding is for! Padding allows you to add visual space around the content area. Let's increase the padding on the left and see if we can nail this down once and for all.

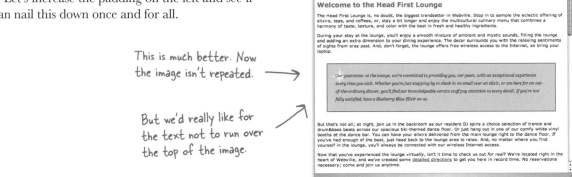

This is much better. Now the image isn't repeated. →

But we'd really like for the text not to run over the top of the image. →

How do you add padding only on the left?

For padding, margins, and even borders, CSS has a property for every direction: top, right, bottom, and left. To add padding on the left side, use the `padding-left` property, like this:

```
.guarantee {
    line-height:         1.9em;
    font-style:          italic;
    font-family:         Georgia, "Times New Roman", Times, serif;
    color:               #444444;
    border-color:        black;
    border-width:        1px;
    border-style:        solid;
    background-color:    #a7cece;
    padding:             25px;
    padding-left:        80px;
    margin:              30px;
    background-image:    url(images/background.gif);
    background-repeat:   no-repeat;
    background-position: top left;
}
```

We're using the padding-left property to increase the padding on the left.

Notice that we first set the padding on all sides to 25 pixels, and then we specify a property for the left side.

Order matters here—if you switch the order, then you'll set the padding for the left side first, and then the general padding property will set all sides back to 25 pixels, including the left side!

Are we there yet?

Make sure you save your changes and reload the page. You should see more padding on the left side of the paragraph, and the text is now positioned well with respect to the guarantee star. This is a great example of where you use padding instead of margins. If you need more visual space around the content area itself, use padding, as opposed to if you want space between elements or the sides of the page, in which case, use margin. In fact, we could actually use a little more margin on the right side to set the paragraph off even more. Let's do that, and then all we need to do is fix the border.

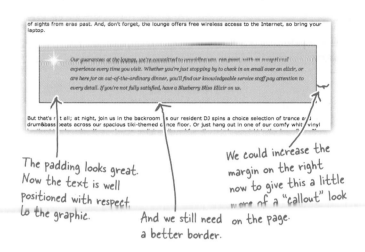

The padding looks great. Now the text is well positioned with respect to the graphic.

And we still need a better border.

We could increase the margin on the right now to give this a little more of a "callout" look on the page.

How do you increase the margin just on the right?

You do this just like you did with the padding: add another property, `margin-right`, to increase the right margin.

See the pattern? There's a property to control all sides together, and properties for each side if you want to set them individually.

```
.guarantee {
    line-height:          1.9em;
    font-style:           italic;
    font-family:          Georgia, "Times New Roman", Times, serif;
    color:                #444444;
    border-color:         black;
    border-width:         1px;
    border-style:         solid;
    background-color:     #a7cece;
    padding:              25px;
    padding-left:         80px;
    margin:               30px;
    margin-right:         250px;
    background-image:     url(images/background.gif);
    background-repeat:    no-repeat;
    background-position:  top left;
}
```

Remember, we're already setting the margins to be 30 pixels.

And now we're going to override that setting for the right side, and set it to 250 pixels.

Add the new `margin-right` property and reload. Now the paragraph should have 250 pixels of margin on the right side.

250 pixels

A two-minute guide to borders

There's only one thing left to do to perfect the guarantee paragraph: add a better border. Before you do, take a look at all the different ways you can control the border of an element.

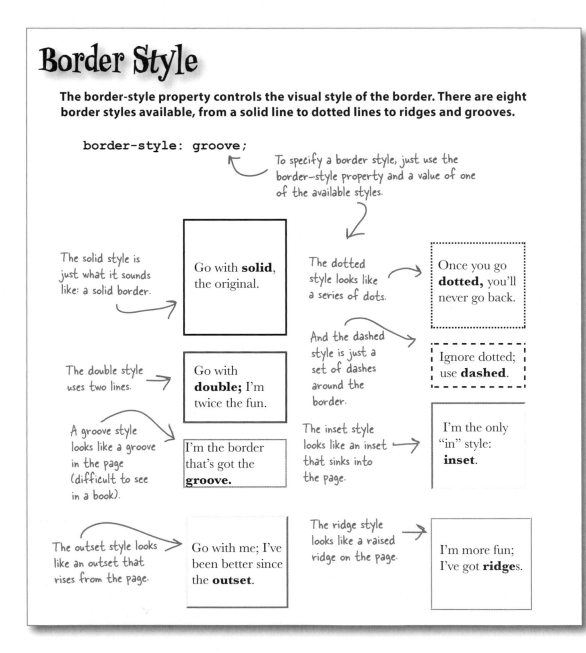

Border Style

The border-style property controls the visual style of the border. There are eight border styles available, from a solid line to dotted lines to ridges and grooves.

```
border-style: groove;
```

To specify a border style, just use the border-style property and a value of one of the available styles.

The solid style is just what it sounds like: a solid border.

Go with **solid**, the original.

The dotted style looks like a series of dots.

Once you go **dotted,** you'll never go back.

The double style uses two lines

Go with **double;** I'm twice the fun.

And the dashed style is just a set of dashes around the border.

Ignore dotted; use **dashed**.

A groove style looks like a groove in the page (difficult to see in a book).

I'm the border that's got the **groove.**

The inset style looks like an inset that sinks into the page.

I'm the only "in" style: **inset**.

The outset style looks like an outset that rises from the page.

Go with me; I've been better since the **outset**.

The ridge style looks like a raised ridge on the page.

I'm more fun; I've got **ridge**s.

Border Width

The border-width property controls the width of the border. You can use keywords or pixels to specify the width.

```
border-width: thin;
border-width: 5px;
```

You can specify widths using the keywords thin, medium, or thick, or by the number of pixels.

thin

medium

thick

1px
2px
3px
4px
5px
6px

Border Color

The border-color property sets the color of the border. This works just like setting font colors; you can use color names, rgb values, or hex codes to specify color.

```
border-color: red;
border-color: rgb(100%, 0%, 0%);
border-color: #ff0000;
```

Use border-color to specify the color of a border. You can use any of the common ways to specify color.

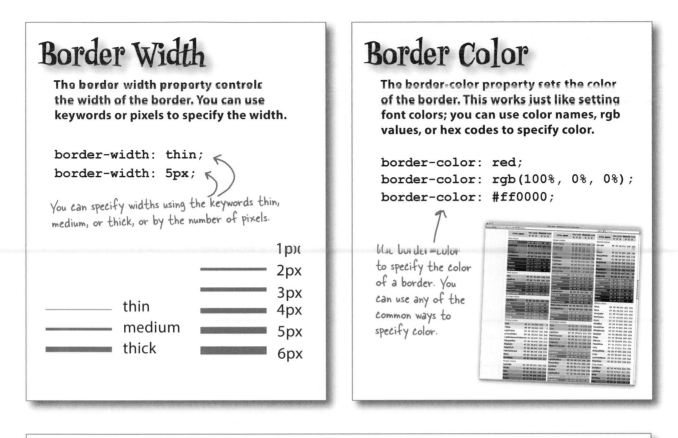

Specifying Border Sides

border-top-color
border-top-style
border-top-width

border-right-color
border-right-style
border-right-width

border-bottom-color
border-bottom-style
border-bottom-width

border-left-color
border-left-style
border-left-width

Just as with margins and padding, you can specify border style, width, or color on any side (top, right, bottom, or left):

```
border-top-color: black;
border-top-style: dashed;
border-top-width: thick;
```

These properties are for the top border only. You can specify each side of the border independently.

Specifying Border Corners

You can create rounded corners on all four corners, or just one corner, or any combination.

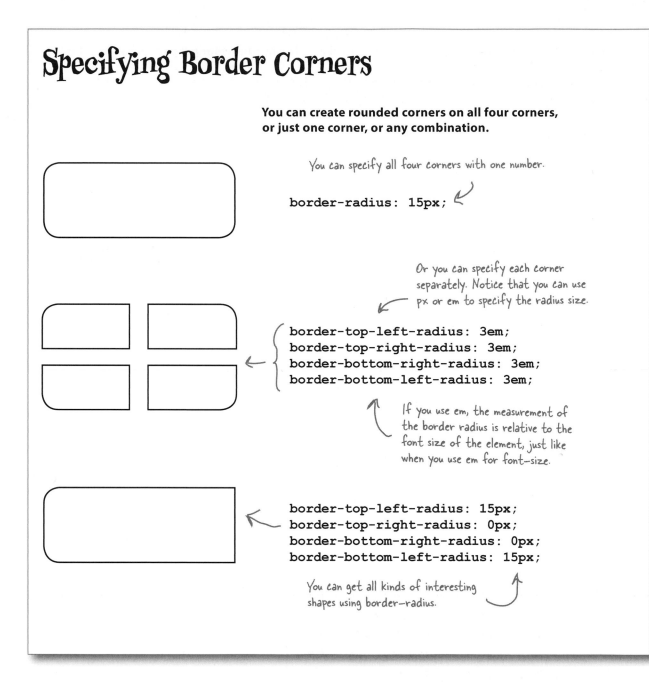

You can specify all four corners with one number.

```
border-radius: 15px;
```

Or you can specify each corner separately. Notice that you can use px or em to specify the radius size.

```
border-top-left-radius: 3em;
border-top-right-radius: 3em;
border-bottom-right-radius: 3em;
border-bottom-left-radius: 3em;
```

If you use em, the measurement of the border radius is relative to the font size of the element, just like when you use em for font-size.

```
border-top-left-radius: 15px;
border-top-right-radius: 0px;
border-bottom-right-radius: 0px;
border-bottom-left-radius: 15px;
```

You can get all kinds of interesting shapes using border-radius.

Border fit and finish

It's time to finish off the guarantee paragraph. All we need to do is give it a ragged-looking border. But which style is that? The available styles are solid, double, dotted, dashed, groove, ridge, inset, and outset. So how do we make it look ragged? It's actually just a trick: we're using a dashed border that has its color set to white (matching the background color of the page). Here's how you do it. Begin by just making the border dashed. Find the `border-style` property in your "lounge.css" and change it, like this:

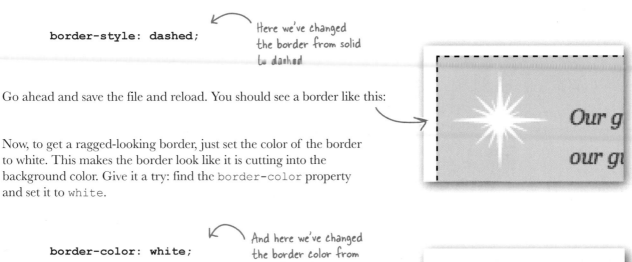

`border-style: dashed;`

Here we've changed the border from solid to dashed

Go ahead and save the file and reload. You should see a border like this:

Now, to get a ragged-looking border, just set the color of the border to white. This makes the border look like it is cutting into the background color. Give it a try: find the `border-color` property and set it to `white`.

`border-color: white;`

And here we've changed the border color from black to white.

Save the file and reload again. Now you should see the ragged border:

Watch it!

Browsers don't always agree on the size of thin, medium, and thick.

Browsers can have different default sizes for the keywords thin, medium, and thick, so if the size of your border is really important to you, consider using pixel sizes instead.

Nice! I can't wait to see the entire page remodeled. Take a break and have an iced chai on me!

Congratulations!

Bravo! You've taken an ordinary HTML paragraph and transformed it into something a lot more appealing and stylish using only 15 lines of CSS.

It was a long trip getting here, so at this point we encourage you to take a little break. Grab yourself an iced chai and take a little time to let things sink in—when you come back, we'll nail down a few more of the fine points of CSS.

Exercise

While you're drinking that iced chai, try your hand at adding a border-radius to the guarantee paragraph. We've got some examples below of the guarantee paragraph with a variety of border-radius values set. Write the CSS to create the border you see in the example. For each example, we've provided the size of the border-radius used to create the rounded corners in that example.

30px

Our guarantee: at the lounge, we're committed to providing you, our guest, with an exceptional experience every time you visit. Whether you're just stopping by to check in on email over an elixir, or are here for an out-of-the-ordinary dinner, you'll find our knowledgeable service staff pay attention to every detail. If you're not fully satisfied, have a Blueberry Bliss Elixir on us.

Write your CSS here.

border - left-radius: 30px.

40px

Our guarantee: at the lounge, we're committed to providing you, our guest, with an exceptional experience every time you visit. Whether you're just stopping by to check in on email over an elixir, or are here for an out-of-the-ordinary dinner, you'll find our knowledgeable service staff pay attention to every detail. If you're not fully satisfied, have a Blueberry Bliss Elixir on us.

border-radius: 40px;

40px

Our guarantee: at the lounge, we're committed to providing you, our guest, with an exceptional experience every time you visit. Whether you're just stopping by to check in on email over an elixir, or are here for an out-of-the-ordinary dinner, you'll find our knowledgeable service staff pay attention to every detail. If you're not fully satisfied, have a Blueberry Bliss Elixir on us.

border-top-left-radius: 0px; border-right-radius: 40px; border-bottom-left-radius: 40px;

2em

Our guarantee: at the lounge, we're committed to providing you, our guest, with an exceptional experience every time you visit. Whether you're just stopping by to check in on email over an elixir, or are here for an out of the-ordinary dinner, you'll find our knowledgeable service staff pay attention to every detail. If you're not fully satisfied, have a Blueberry Bliss Elixir on us.

border-bottom-left-radius: 2em; border-top-right-radius: 2em

Welcome back, and good timing. We're just about to listen in on an interview with a class...

The Class Exposed

**This week's interview:
Are classes always right?**

Head First: Hey, Class; you know we've been making good use of you, but we still don't know a lot about you.

Class: Well, there's not all that much to know. If you want to create a "group, " so to speak, that you can style, just come up with a class, put your elements in it, and then you can style all the elements in that class together.

Head First: So the class lets you take sets of elements and apply one or more style properties to them?

Class: Exactly. Say you have some holiday-themed areas in your page—one Halloween, one Christmas. You could add all Halloween elements to the halloween class and all Christmas elements to the christmas class. Then you can style those elements independently—say, orange for Halloween and red for Christmas—by writing rules that apply to each class.

Head First: That makes a lot of sense. We just saw a good example of that in this chapter, didn't we?

Class: I'm not sure; I was off working. You'll have to catch me up.

Head First: Well, we have a paragraph on the Head First Lounge page that contains a written guarantee from the owners, and they want this paragraph to stand out independently of the other paragraphs.

Class: So far, so good...but let me ask you this: are there a few of these paragraphs, or just the one?

Head First: Well, I don't think there is any reason to have multiple guarantee paragraphs, and I don't see the same style being applied anywhere else in the page, so just the one.

Class: Hmmm, I don't like the sound of that. You see, classes are meant to be used for styles that you want to reuse with multiple elements. If you've got one unique element that you need styled, that's not really what classes are for.

Head First: Wait a second—a class seemed to work perfectly...how can this be wrong?

Class: Whoa, now, don't freak out. All you need to do is switch your class attribute to an id attribute. It will only take you a minute.

Head First: An `id` attribute? I thought those were for those link destinations, like in Chapter 4?

Class: `id`s have lots of uses. They're really just unique identifiers for elements.

Head First: Can you tell us a little more about `id` attributes? This is all news to me. I mean, I just went through an entire chapter using `class` incorrectly!

Class: Hey, no worries; it's a common mistake. Basically, all you need to know is that you use a `class` when you might want to use a style with more than one element. And if what you need to style is unique and there's only one on your page, then use an `id`. The `id` attribute is strictly for naming unique elements.

Head First: Okay, I think I've got it, but why does it really matter? I mean, `class` worked just fine for us.

Class: Because there are some things you really want *only one* of on your page. The guarantee paragraph you mentioned is one example, but there are better examples, like the header or footer on your page, or a navigation bar. You're not going to have two of those on a page. Of course, you can use a class for just one element, but someone else could come along and add another element to the class, and then your element won't have a unique style anymore. It also becomes important when you are positioning HTML elements, which is something you haven't gotten to yet.

Head First: Well, okay, Class. This conversation has certainly been educational for us. It sounds like we definitely need to convert that paragraph from a `class` to an `id`. Thanks again for joining us.

Class: Any time, Head First!

BRAIN POWER

Choose whether you'd use class or id for the following elements:

id	class	
☑	☐	A paragraph containing the footer of a page.
☐	☑	A set of headings and paragraphs that contain company biographies.
☑	☐	An `<img>` element containing a "picture of the day."

id	class	
☐	☑	A set of `<p>` elements containing movie reviews.
☑	☐	An `<ol>` element containing your to-do list.
☐	☑	`<q>` elements containing *Buckaroo Banzai* quotes.

Answer: The footer, the picture of the day, and the to-do list are great candidates for using id.

The id attribute

Because you've already used ids on <a> elements, and because you already know how to use a class attribute, you're not going to have to learn much to use the id attribute. Say you have a footer on your page. There's usually only one footer on any page, so that sounds like the perfect candidate for an id. Here's how you'd add the identifier footer to a paragraph that contains the footer text:

Similar to a class; just add the attribute "id" and choose a unique id name.

Unlike a class, you can only have one element in your page with an id of "footer".

`<p id="footer">Please steal this page, it isn't copyrighted in any way</p>`

Each element can have only one id.

No spaces or special characters are allowed in id names.

Giving an element an id is similar to adding an element to a class. The only differences are that the attribute is called id, not class; an element can't have multiple ids; and you can't have more than one element on a page with the same id.

there are no Dumb Questions

Q: What's the big deal? Why do I need an id just to prove something is unique on the page? I could use a class exactly the same way, right?

A: Well, you can always "simulate" a unique id with a class, but there are many reasons not to. Say you're working on a web project with a team of people. One of your teammates is going to look at a class and think it can be reused with other elements. If, on the other hand, she sees an id, then she's going to know that's for a unique element. There are a couple of other reasons ids are important that you won't see for a few chapters. For instance, when you start positioning elements on a page, you'll need each element you want to position to have a unique id.

Q: Can an element have an id and also belong to a class?

A: Yes, it can. Think about it this way: an id is just a unique identifier for an element, but that doesn't prevent it from belonging to one or more classes (just like having a unique name doesn't prevent you from joining one or more clubs).

But how do I use id in CSS?

You select an element with an id almost exactly like you select an element with a class. To quickly review: If you have a class called specials, there are a couple of ways you can select elements using this class. You could select just certain elements in the class, like this:

```
p.specials {
        color: red;
}
```

 This selects <u>only paragraphs</u> that are in the specials class.

Or you can select all the elements that belong to the specials class, like this:

```
.specials {
        color: red;
}
```

 This selects <u>all elements</u> in the specials class.

Using an id selector is very similar. To select an element by its id, you use a # (hash mark) character in front of the id (compare this to class, where you use a . [dot] in front of the class name). Say you want to select any element with the id footer:

```
#footer {
        color: red;
}
```

 This selects <u>any element</u> that has the id "footer".

Or you could select only a <p> element with the id footer, like this:

```
p#footer {
        color: red;
}
```

 This selects <u>a <p> element</u> if it has the id "footer".

The other difference between class and id is that an id selector should match *only one* element in a page.

Using an id in the lounge

Our guarantee paragraph really should have an id since it's
intended to be used just once in the page. While we should have
designed it that way from the beginning, making the change is
going to be quite simple.

Step one: Change the class attribute to an id in your "lounge.html" file

Just change the class
attribute to an id.

```
<p id="guarantee">
        Our guarantee: at the lounge, we're committed to providing
        you, our guest, with an exceptional experience every time you
        visit. Whether you're just stopping by to check in on email
        over an elixir, or are here for an out-of-the-ordinary dinner,
        you'll find our knowledgeable service staff pay attention to every
        detail. If you're not fully satisfied, have a Blueberry Bliss Elixir
        on us.
</p>
```

Step two: Change the ".guarantee" class selector in "lounge.css" to an id selector

Just change the . to a
 # in the selector.

```
#guarantee {
        line-height:        1.9em;
        font-style:         italic;
        font-family:        Georgia, "Times New Roman", Times, serif;
        color:              #444444;
        border-color:       white;
        border-width:       1px;
        border-style:       dashed;
        background-color:   #a7cece;
        padding:            25px;
        padding-left:       80px;
        margin:             30px;
        margin-right:       250px;
        background-image:   url(images/background.gif);
        background-repeat:  no-repeat;
        background-position: top left;
}
```

Step three: Save your changes and reload the page

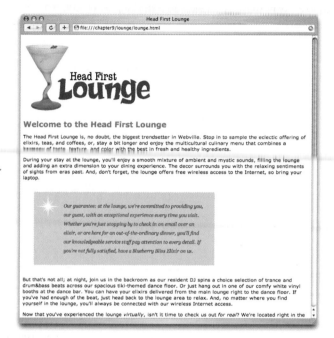

Well, everything should look EXACTLY the same. But don't you feel much better now that everything is as it should be?

there are no
Dumb Questions

Q: So why did you make the selector #guarantee rather than p#guarantee?

A: We could have done either, and they both would select the same thing. On this page, we know that we will always have a paragraph assigned to the id, so it doesn't really matter (and #guarantee is simpler). However, on a more complex set of pages, you might have some pages where the unique id is assigned to, say, a paragraph, and on others it's assigned to a list or block quote. So you might want several rules for the id, like p#someid, and blockquote#someid, depending on which kind of element is on the page.

Q: Should I always start with a class, and then change it to an id when I know it's going to be unique?

A: No. You'll often know when you design your pages if an element is going to be unique or not. We only did things this way in the chapter because, well, you didn't know about id when we started. But don't you think we tied id into the story rather nicely? ☺

Q: What are the rules for class and id names?

A: Class names should begin with a letter, but id names can start with a number or a letter. Both id and class names can contain letters and numbers as well as the _ character, but no spaces. So "number1" works, as does "main_content", but not "header content". Just remember, ids must be unique!

Remixing stylesheets

Before we wind this chapter down, let's have a little fun remixing some stylesheets. So far, you've been using only one stylesheet. Well, who ever said you can't use more than one stylesheet? You can specify a whole set of stylesheets to be used with any HTML. But you may be wondering why anyone would want to. There are a couple of good reasons. Here's the first one…

Imagine that the Head First Lounge takes off, gets franchised, does the IPO, and so on (all thanks to you and your terrific web work, of course). Then there would be a whole corporate website with hundreds of pages, and obviously you'd want to style those pages with external CSS stylesheets. There would be various company divisions, and they might want to tweak the styles in individual ways. And the lounge franchises also might want some control over style. Here's how that might look:

> We use all the corporate colors and fonts, but we add in a few special touches of our own, like a different line height.

> We've set up all the main styles to be used by the company websites—fonts, colors, and so on.

> We've got a young, hip clientele. We tweak the colors a bit and add a little edge, but overall we use the division's main styles.

Corporate

Beverage Division

Seattle Lounge
(part of the Beverage Division)

Using multiple stylesheets

So how do you start with a corporate style and then allow the division and the lounge franchises to override and make changes to the styles? You use several stylesheets, like this:

```
<!DOCTYPE html>
<html>
  <head>
    <meta charset="utf-8">
    <title>Head First Lounge</title>
      <link type="text/css" href="corporate.css" rel="stylesheet">
      <link type="text/css" href="beverage-division.css" rel="stylesheet">
      <link type="text/css" href="lounge-seattle.css" rel="stylesheet">
  </head>
  <body>
    .
    .
    .
  </body>
</html>
```

In your HTML, you can specify more than one stylesheet. Here, we've got three.

One stylesheet for the entire corporation.

The beverage division can add to the corporate style a little, or even override some of the corporate styles.

And the lounge in Seattle has its own tweaks in its stylesheet.

Order matters! A stylesheet can override the styles in the stylesheets linked above it.

there are no Dumb Questions

Q: So the order of the stylesheets matters?

A: Yes, they go top to bottom, with the stylesheets on the bottom taking precedence. So if you have, say, a font-family property on the <body> element in both the corporate and the division stylesheets, the division's takes precedence, since it's the last one linked in the HTML.

Q: Do I ever need this for a simple site?

A: You'd be surprised. Sometimes there's a stylesheet you want to base your page on, and rather than changing that stylesheet, you just link to it, and then supply your own stylesheet below that to specify what you want to change.

Q: Can you say more about how the style for a specific element is decided?

A: We talked a little about that in Chapter 7. And for now, just add to that knowledge that the ordering of the stylesheets linked into your file matters. In the next chapter, after you've learned a few other CSS details, we're going to go through exactly how the browser knows which style goes with which element.

Stylesheets—they're not just for desktop browsers anymore...

There's actually another reason you might want to have multiple style files: let's say you want to tailor your page's style to the type of device your page is being displayed on (desktops, laptops, tablets, smartphones, or even printed versions of your pages). Well, to do that there is a `media` attribute you can add to the `<link>` element that lets you use only the style files that are appropriate for your device. Let's look at an example:

> The media attribute allows you to specify the type of device this stylesheet is for.

> You specify the type of device by creating a "media query," which is matched with the device.

```
<link href="lounge-mobile.css" rel="stylesheet" media="screen and (max-device-width: 480px)">
```

> Here our query specifies anything with a screen (as opposed to, say, a printer, or 3D glasses, or a braille reader)...

> ...and any device that has a width of at most 480 pixels.

Likewise, we could create a query that matches the device if it is a printer, like this:

```
<link href="lounge-print.css" rel="stylesheet" media="print">
```

> The lounge-print.css file is only going to be used if...

> ...the media type is "print", which means we're viewing it on a printer.

There are a variety of propeties you can use in your queries, like `min-device-width`, `max-device-width` (which we just used), and the `orientation` of the display (landscape or portrait), to name just a few. And keep in mind you can add as many `<link>` tags to your HTML as necessary to cover all the devices you need to.

Add media queries right into your CSS

There's another way to target your CSS to devices with specific properties: rather than using media queries in link tags, you can also use them right in your CSS Here's an example:

Use the @media rule...   *...followed by your query.*

And then put all the rules that apply to devices matching this query within curly braces.

```
@media screen and (min-device-width: 481px) {
    #guarantee {
        margin-right: 250px;
    }
}
```

So, these rules will be used if the screen is wider than 480px.

```
@media screen and (max-device-width: 480px) {
    #guarantee {
        margin-right: 30px;
    }
}
```

...these rules will be used if the screen is 480px or less...

```
@media print {
    body {
        font-family: Times, "Times New Roman", serif;
    }
}
```

...and these rules will be used if you're printing the page.

```
p.specials {
        color: red;
}
```

All other rules apply to all pages because they aren't contained within a @media rule.

So, the way this works, only the CSS rules that are specific to a media type are included in an @media rule. All the rules that are common to all the media types are included in the CSS file below the @media rules, so that way you don't have any unnecessarily repeated rules. And, when a browser loads the page, it determines through the media queries the rules that are appropriate for the page, and ignores any that don't match.

Media queries are an area of active development by the standards groups, so keep your eyes on evolving best practices for targeting devices.

Media queries are not supported by IE8 and earlier.

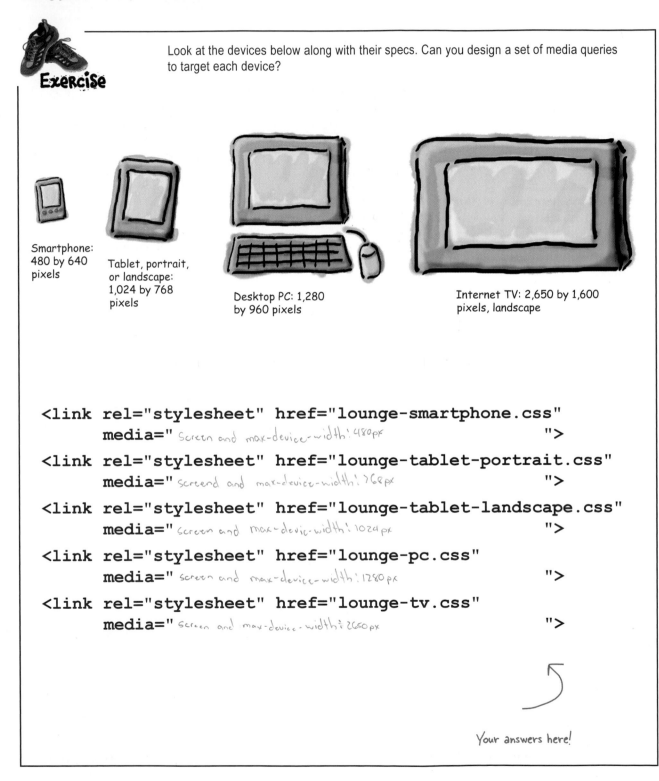

Exercise

Look at the devices below along with their specs. Can you design a set of media queries to target each device?

Smartphone: 480 by 640 pixels

Tablet, portrait, or landscape: 1,024 by 768 pixels

Desktop PC: 1,280 by 960 pixels

Internet TV: 2,650 by 1,600 pixels, landscape

```
<link rel="stylesheet" href="lounge-smartphone.css"
    media=" screen and max-device-width: 480px           ">
<link rel="stylesheet" href="lounge-tablet-portrait.css"
    media=" screend and max-device-width: 768px           ">
<link rel="stylesheet" href="lounge-tablet-landscape.css"
    media=" screen and max-device-width: 1024px           ">
<link rel="stylesheet" href="lounge-pc.css"
    media=" screen and max-device-width: 1280px           ">
<link rel="stylesheet" href="lounge-tv.css"
    media=" screen and max-device-width: 2650px           ">
```

Your answers here!

there are no
Dumb Questions

Q: That's pretty cool. So I can set up different stylesheets for different devices?

A: Yes, you can set up several stylesheets and then link to them all in your HTML. It's the browser's job to use the right stylesheet based on the media type and the characteristics you specify in your media query.

Q: Are there other media properties besides max-device-width and min-device-width?

A: Yes, there are quite a few, including max and min width (different from device-width, as you'll see shortly), max and min height, orientation, color, aspect ratio, and more. Check out the CSS3 Media Queries specification for all the details (http://www.w3.org/TR/css3-mediaqueries/), and *Head First Mobile Web* for examples.

Q: Is it better to use <link> or @media to specify different CSS rules for different media types and characteristics?

A: Either one will work. But notice that if you put all your rules in one file and split them up using @media rules, your CSS could get pretty big. By using different <link> elements for different media types, you can keep your CSS organized in different files depending on the media type. So, if your CSS files are fairly large, we recommend using <link> elements to specify different stylesheets.

Exercise

In your "chapter9/lounge" folder, you'll find "lounge-print.css". Open up "lounge.html" in the "chapter9/lounge" folder and add a new link to this stylesheet for the media type "print". Make sure you also add the attribute media="screen" to the <link> element that links to "lounge.css", so you have one stylesheet for the screen, and one for the printer. Then save, reload the page, and choose your browser's Print option. Run to the printer to see the result!

```
<link type="text/css" href="lounge-print.css"
      rel="stylesheet" media="print">
```

Here's the new link you need to add to your "lounge.html" file.

Here's the printed version. You've totally changed how the page looks when it's printed, using CSS. That structure versus presentation thing is really paying off.

OPTIONAL PRINTER REQUIRED, NOT INCLUDED WITH BOOK.

Exercise

The max-device-width and min-device-width media characteristics are dependent on the actual screen size of the device (*not* the width of your browser window). What if you are more concerned with the size of the browser? Well, you can use the **max-width** and **min-width** properties instead, which represent the maximum and minimum width of the browser window itself (not the screen size). Let's see how this works: In your "chapter9/lounge" folder, you'll find "lounge-mobile.css". Open up your lounge.html file again, and change the <link> elements in the <head> of the document to look like this:

```
<link type="text/css" rel="stylesheet" href="lounge.css"
      media="screen and (min-width: 481px)">

<link type="text/css" href="lounge-mobile.css" rel="stylesheet"
      media="screen and (max-width: 480px)">

<link type="text/css" href="lounge-print.css" rel="stylesheet" media="print">
```

Now, reload the "lounge.html" page in your browser. Make sure the browser window is nice and big. You should see the lounge page as normal.

Next, make your browser window narrow (less than 480 pixels). What happens to the lounge page? Do you notice a difference? Describe below what happens when you make the web page narrow and load the page. Why is this version of the page better for mobile browsers?

Make sure you're using a modern browser! If you're using IE, that means IE9+.

BULLET POINTS

- CSS uses a box model to control how elements are displayed.

- Boxes consist of the content area and optional padding, border, and margin.

- The content area contains the content of the element.

- The padding is used to create visual space around the content area.

- The border surrounds the padding and content and provides a way to visually separate the content.

- The margin surrounds the border, padding, and content, and allows space to be added between the element and other elements.

- Padding, border, and margin are all optional.

- An element's background will show under the content and the padding, but not under the margin.

- Padding and margin size can be set in pixels or percentages.

- Border width can be set in pixels or by using the keywords thin, medium, and thick.

- There are eight different styles for borders, including solid, dashed, dotted, and ridge.

- For margins, padding, or the border, CSS provides properties for setting all the sides (top, right, bottom, left) at once, or it allows them to be set independently.

- Use the border-radius property to create rounded corners on an element with a border.

- Use the line-height property to add space between lines of text.

- You can place an image in the background of an element with the background-image property.

- Use the background-position and background-repeat properties to set the position and tiling behavior of the background image.

- Use the class attribute for elements that you want to style together, as a group.

- Use the id attribute to give an element a unique name. You can also use the id attribute to provide a unique style for an element.

- There should only be one element in a page with a given id.

- You can select elements by their id using the id selector; for example, #myfavoriteid.

- An element can have only one id, but it can belong to many classes.

- You can use more than one stylesheet in your HTML.

- If two stylesheets have conflicting property definitions, the stylesheet that is last in the HTML file will receive preference.

- You can target devices by using media queries in your <link> element or the @media rule in your CSS.

HTMLcross

You're really expanding your HTML and CSS skills. Strengthen those neural connections by doing a crossword. All the answers come from this chapter.

The crossword grid is filled in with the following answers:

- 1 Across: repeat
- 4 Across: dashed
- 6 Across: optional
- 9 Across: blueberrybliss
- 10 Across: border
- 13 Across: guarantee
- 14 Across: media

Across

1. By default, background images do this.
4. To create a "ragged" border, use the _____ border style.
6. Padding, borders, and margins are all _____.
9. Which kind of elixir do you get if you're not fully satisfed?
10. Between padding and margin.
13. We changed the _____ class to an id.
14. To use a different style for different devices, use _____ queries.

Down

2. The space between the content and the border.
3. If you want your element to have a unique style, use this kind of selector.
5. Property used to increase the space between lines of text.
7. Publishing term for the space between lines.
8. The preferred font used in the guarantee paragraph.
10. CSS sees every element as a _____.
11. Style of border we used on the guarantee paragraph.
12. Optional <link> attribute for other kinds of _____.

Sharpen your pencil
Solution

See if you can identify the padding, border, and margins of this paragraph. Mark all the padding and margins (left, right, top, and bottom):

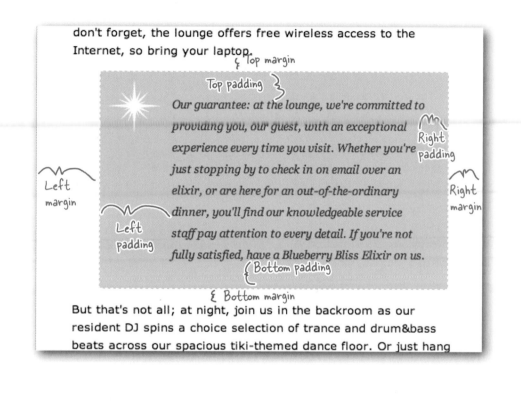

don't forget, the lounge offers free wireless access to the Internet, so bring your laptop.

Top margin

Top padding

Right padding

Left margin

Right margin

Left padding

Our guarantee: at the lounge, we're committed to providing you, our guest, with an exceptional experience every time you visit. Whether you're just stopping by to check in on email over an elixir, or are here for an out-of-the-ordinary dinner, you'll find our knowledgeable service staff pay attention to every detail. If you're not fully satisfied, have a Blueberry Bliss Elixir on us.

Bottom padding

Bottom margin

But that's not all; at night, join us in the backroom as our resident DJ spins a choice selection of trance and drum&bass beats across our spacious tiki-themed dance floor. Or just hang

Exercise Solution

If you look at the guarantee paragraph as it's supposed to look in its final form, it has an italic, serif font, a greater line height than the rest of the page, and (if you're looking really close) gray text. Write the CSS below to set the line height to 1.9em, the font style to italic, the color to #444444, and the font family to Georgia, "Times New Roman", Times, serif. Here's the solution...did you test it?

You can add the new properties anywhere in the rule. We added them at the top.

```
.guarantee {
        line-height:      1.9em;
        font-style:       italic;
        font-family:      Georgia, "Times New Roman", Times, serif;
        color:            #444444;
        border-color:     black;
        border-width:     1px;
        border-style:     solid;
        background-color: #a7cece;
        padding:          25px;
        margin:           30px;
}
```

Notice that if a font name has spaces in it, you should surround it with quotes.

of sights from eras past. And, don't forget, the lounge offers free wireless access to the Internet, so bring your laptop.

Increased line height

An italic, serif font

Our guarantee: at the lounge, we're committed to providing you, our guest, with an exceptional experience every time you visit. Whether you're just stopping by to check in on email over an elixir, or are here for an out-of-the-ordinary dinner, you'll find our knowledgeable service staff pay attention to every detail. If you're not fully satisfied, have a Blueberry Bliss Elixir on us.

Gray color gives the text a softer look.

But that's not all; at night, join us in the backroom as our resident DJ spins a choice selection of trance and drum&bass beats across our spacious tiki-themed dance floor. Or just hang out in one of our comfy white vinyl

 HTMLcross Solution

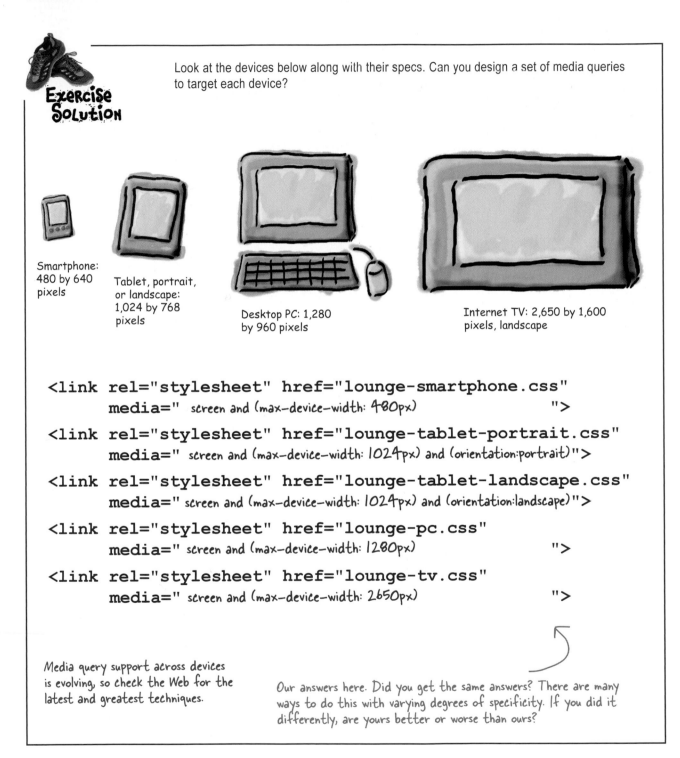

Look at the devices below along with their specs. Can you design a set of media queries to target each device?

Exercise
Solution

Smartphone:
480 by 640
pixels

Tablet, portrait,
or landscape:
1,024 by 768
pixels

Desktop PC: 1,280
by 960 pixels

Internet TV: 2,650 by 1,600
pixels, landscape

```
<link rel="stylesheet" href="lounge-smartphone.css"
    media=" screen and (max-device-width: 480px)                    ">

<link rel="stylesheet" href="lounge-tablet-portrait.css"
    media=" screen and (max-device-width: 1024px) and (orientation:portrait)">

<link rel="stylesheet" href="lounge-tablet-landscape.css"
    media=" screen and (max-device-width: 1024px) and (orientation:landscape)">

<link rel="stylesheet" href="lounge-pc.css"
    media=" screen and (max-device-width: 1280px)                    ">

<link rel="stylesheet" href="lounge-tv.css"
    media=" screen and (max-device-width: 2650px)                    ">
```

Media query support across devices
is evolving, so check the Web for the
latest and greatest techniques.

Our answers here. Did you get the same answers? There are many
ways to do this with varying degrees of specificity. If you did it
differently, are yours better or worse than ours?

While you're drinking that iced chai, try your hand at adding a border-radius to the guarantee paragraph. We've got some examples below of the guarantee paragraph with a variety of border radius values set. Write the CSS to create the border you see in the example. For each example, we've provided the size of the border-radius used to create the rounded corners in that example.

Write your CSS here.

30px

> *Our guarantee: at the lounge, we're committed to providing you, our guest, with an exceptional experience every time you visit. Whether you're just stopping by to check in on email over an elixir, or are here for an out-of-the-ordinary dinner, you'll find our knowledgeable service staff pay attention to every detail. If you're not fully satisfied, have a Blueberry Bliss Elixir on us.*

```
border-top-left-radius: 30px;
border-top-right-radius: 0px;
border-bottom-right-radius: 0px;
border-bottom-left-radius: 30px;
```

40px

> *Our guarantee: at the lounge, we're committed to providing you, our guest, with an exceptional experience every time you visit. Whether you're just stopping by to check in on email over an elixir, or are here for an out-of-the-ordinary dinner, you'll find our knowledgeable service staff pay attention to every detail. If you're not fully satisfied, have a Blueberry Bliss Elixir on us.*

```
border-top-left-radius: 40px;
border-top-right-radius: 40px;
border-bottom-right-radius: 40px;
border-bottom-left-radius: 40px;
```

40px

> *Our guarantee: at the lounge, we're committed to providing you, our guest, with an exceptional experience every time you visit. Whether you're just stopping by to check in on email over an elixir, or are here for an out-of-the-ordinary dinner, you'll find our knowledgeable service staff pay attention to every detail. If you're not fully satisfied, have a Blueberry Bliss Elixir on us.*

```
border-top-left-radius: 0px;
border-top-right-radius: 40px;
border-bottom-right-radius: 40px;
border-bottom-left-radius: 40px;
```

2em

> *Our guarantee: at the lounge, we're committed to providing you, our guest, with an exceptional experience every time you visit. Whether you're just stopping by to check in on email over an elixir, or are here for an out-of-the-ordinary dinner, you'll find our knowledgeable service staff pay attention to every detail. If you're not fully satisfied, have a Blueberry Bliss Elixir on us.*

```
border-top-left-radius: 0em;
border-top-right-radius: 2em;
border-bottom-right-radius: 0em;
border-bottom-left-radius: 2em;
```

Exercise

The max-device-width and min-device-width media characteristics are dependent on the actual screen size of the device (*not* the width of your browser window). What if you are more concerned with the size of the browser? Well, you can use the **max-width** and **min-width** properties instead, which represent the maximum and minimum width of the browser window itself (not the screen size). Let's see how this works: In your "chapter9/lounge" folder, you'll find "lounge-mobile.css". Open up your lounge.html file again, and change the <link> elements in the <head> of the document to look like this:

```
<link type="text/css" rel="stylesheet" href="lounge.css"
      media="screen and (min-width: 481px)">
<link type="text/css" href="lounge-mobile.css" rel="stylesheet"
      media="screen and (max-width: 480px)">
<link type="text/css" href="lounge-print.css" rel="stylesheet" media="print">
```

Now, reload the "lounge.html" page in your browser. Make sure the browser window is nice and big. You should see the lounge page as normal.

Next, make your browser window narrow (less than 480 pixels). What happens to the lounge page? Do you notice a difference? Describe below what happens when you make the web page narrow and load the page. Why is this version of the page better for mobile browsers?

When we make the lounge page narrower than 480 pixels, the guarantee paragraph changes style. The right margin gets reduced from 250px to 30px (to match the rest of the margin); the background star image disappears, and the extra padding on the left goes away too.

This version will work better for mobile browsers because the guarantee paragraph gets too narrow with the CSS that's designed for wider screens. By removing the background image and the extra margin and padding, the paragraph is easier to read. And it's really the content that matters at the end of the day, right?

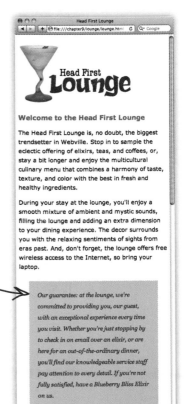

Make sure you're using a modern browser! If you're using IE, that means IE9+.

10 divs and spans

Advanced Web Construction

> Some builders say,
> "measure twice, cut once."
> I say, "plan, div, and span."

It's time to get ready for heavy construction. In this chapter we're going to roll out two new HTML elements: <div> and <span>. These are no simple "two by fours"; these are full blown steel beams. With <div> and <span>, you're going to build some serious supporting structures, and once you've got those structures in place, you're going to be able to style them all in new and powerful ways. Now, we couldn't help but notice that your CSS toolbelt is really starting to fill up, so it's time to show you a few shortcuts that will make specifying all these properties a lot easier. And we've also got some special guests in this chapter, the *pseudo-classes*, which are going to allow you to create some very interesting selectors. (If you're thinking that "pseudo-classes" would make a great name for your next band, too late; we beat you to it.)

You know, we'd love it if you could make the elixir specials a little more attractive on the web page. Could you make it look just like our handout menu?

The elixir mixer, Alice

Here's the handout menu with the elixir specials. Wow, the design is a lot different than the rest of the page: it's thin, the text is centered, and there are red headings, an aquamarine border around the whole thing, and even some cocktail graphics at the top.

Weekly Elixir Specials

Lemon Breeze

The ultimate healthy drink, this elixir combines herbal botanicals, minerals, and vitamins with a twist of lemon into a smooth citrus wonder that will keep your immune system going all day and all night.

Chai Chiller

Not your traditional chai, this elixir mixes maté with chai spices and adds an extra chocolate kick for a caffeinated taste sensation on ice.

Black Brain Brew

Want to boost your memory? Try our Black Brain Brew elixir, made with black oolong tea and just a touch of espresso. Your brain will thank you for the boost.

Join us any evening for these and all our wonderful elixirs.

A close look at the elixirs HTML

Alice sure has asked for a tall order, hasn't she? She wants us to take the existing lounge HTML and make it look like the handout menu. Hmmm…that looks challenging, but *we do have* CSS on our side, so let's give it a try. But before we jump right into styling, let's get an overview of the existing HTML. Here's just the HTML snippet for the elixir specials; you'll find it in "lounge.html" in the "chapter10/lounge" folder:

We have three elixirs, each with the same structure.

The elixir specials section begins with an <h2> heading.

```
<h2>Weekly Elixir Specials</h2>
<p>
        <img src="images/yellow.gif" alt="Lemon Breeze Elixir">
</p>
<h3>Lemon Breeze</h3>
<p>
        The ultimate healthy drink, this elixir combines
        herbal botanicals, minerals, and vitamins with
        a twist of lemon into a smooth citrus wonder
        that will keep your immune system going all
        day and all night.
</p>

<p>
        <img src="images/chai.gif" alt="Chai Chiller Elixir">
</p>
<h3>Chai Chiller</h3>
<p>
        Not your traditional chai, this elixir mixes mat&eacute;
        with chai spices and adds an extra chocolate kick for
        a caffeinated taste sensation on ice.
</p>

<p>
        <img src="images/black.gif" alt="Black Brain Brew Elixir">
</p>
<h3>Black Brain Brew</h3>
<p>
        Want to boost your memory? Try our Black Brain Brew
        elixir, made with black oolong tea and just a touch
        of espresso. Your brain will thank you for the boost.
</p>

<p>
        Join us any evening for these and all our
        other wonderful
        <a href="beverages/elixir.html"
           title="Head First Lounge Elixirs">elixirs</a>.
</p>
```

Each elixir has an image in a <p> element.

…a name, in an <h3> heading…

…and a description, also in a paragraph.

And this structure is repeated for each elixir.

And, finally, at the bottom, there is another paragraph, with some text and a link to the real elixirs page.

This looks tough, guys. There are a lot of style changes we've got to make, and the elixirs style doesn't really match the rest of the page.

Jim

Frank

Joe

Jim: Come on, Frank, you know we can just create a class or two and then style all the elixir elements separately from the rest of the page.

Frank: That's true. Maybe this isn't so bad. I'm sure there is a simple property to make text align to the center. And we know how to handle the colored text.

Jim: Wait a sec, what about that border around everything?

Frank: Piece of cake. We just learned how to make borders. Remember, every element can have one.

Joe: Hmm, I don't think so. If you look at the HTML, this is a bunch of `<h2>`, `<h3>`, and `<p>` elements. If we put separate borders on every element, they'll just look like separate boxes.

Frank: You're right, Joe. What we need is an element to nest all these other elements inside, so we can put a border on that. Then we'll have one border around everything in the elixirs section of the page.

Jim: Well, I see why you get paid the big bucks, Frank. Could we nest the elixir stuff inside a `<p>` element, or a `<blockquote>`?

Frank: Well, that would ruin the structure and meaning of the page, an elixir menu isn't a paragraph or a block quote. Feels like a hack to me…

Frank: …actually, I don't think we're that far off. I've been reading a *certain book* on HTML and CSS, and I'm just up to a section on a new element called `<div>`. I think it might be the tool we need.

Joe: `<div>`—what's that? It sounds like it's for math.

Frank: That's not far off, because a `<div>` lets you *divide* your page into logical sections or groupings.

Jim: Hey, that sounds like exactly what we need!

Frank: Yup. Let me show you guys how to divide a page into logical sections, and then I'll show you what I know about `<div>`…

Let's explore how we can divide a page into logical sections

Take a look at the web page to the right: it's a web page for PetStorz.com, and we're going to spend a few pages looking at how we might add some more structure to it by identifying some logical sections and then enclosing those inside a `<div>` element.

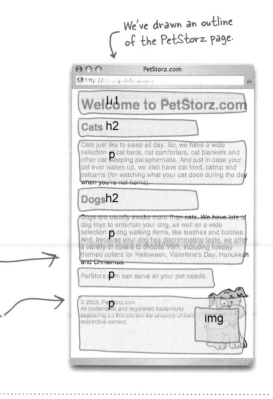

We've drawn an outline of the PetStorz page.

This is a pretty normal-looking page: lots of headings, paragraphs, and an image in there.

But by just focusing on the *structure* of the page, you can't really tell a whole lot about the page. What elements make up the header? Is there a footer on the page? What are the content areas?

Identifying your logical sections

Okay, so our job is to locate "logical sections" in this page. What's a logical section? It's just a group of elements that are all related on the page. For instance, in the PetStorz.com web page, there are some elements that are used for the cats area on the page, and some that are used for dogs. Let's check it out.

The PetStorz page has two main content areas, one for cats, and one for dogs. It has some other areas too, but we'll come back to those.

In this case, both the cats and dogs sections consist of two elements, a heading and a paragraph. But often these groupings can contain many more elements.

Cats

Dogs

h1

h2

p

h2

p

p

p

img

Using <divs to mark sections

Now that you know which elements belong in each section, you can add some HTML to mark up this structure. The common way to do this is to place <div> opening and closing tags around the elements that belong to a logical section. Let's first do this pictorially, and then we'll come back to the real markup in a couple of pages.

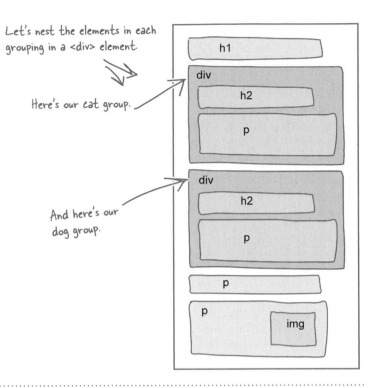

Let's nest the elements in each grouping in a <div> element.

Here's our cat group.

And here's our dog group.

Labeling the <divs

Just by nesting your elements in <div>s, you've indicated that all those elements belong to the same group. But you haven't given them any kind of label that says what the grouping means, right?

A good way to do that is to use an id attribute to provide a unique label for the <div>. For instance, let's give the cats <div> an id of "cats" and the dogs <div> an id of "dogs".

Here we've added an id of "cats" to the first <div> to indicate what the logical section is for.

And likewise for dogs

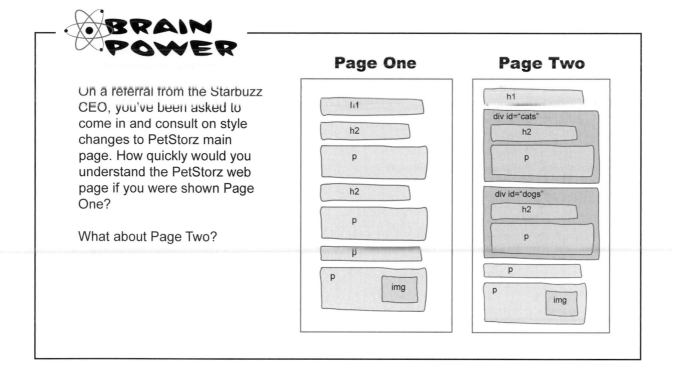

On a referral from the Starbuzz CEO, you've been asked to come in and consult on style changes to PetStorz main page. How quickly would you understand the PetStorz web page if you were shown Page One?

What about Page Two?

Adding some style

Okay, so you've added some logical structure to the PetStorz page, and you've also labeled that structure by giving each `<div>` a unique id. That's all you need to start styling the group of elements contained in the `<div>`.

Now the `<div>`s have a little style.

By setting the background on the `<div>`, it also shows through the elements contained in the `<div>`.

The elements in the `<div>` will also inherit some properties from the `<div>`, just as any child element does (like font-size, color, etc).

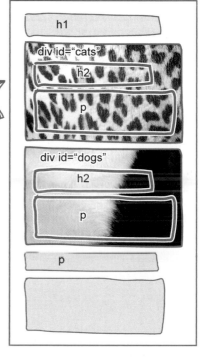

Here we have two rules, one for each `<div>`. Each `<div>` is selected by an id selector.

Each rule sets the background-image property. For cats we have a leopard image, and for dogs we have a mutt image.

```css
#cats {
    background-image: url(leopard.jpg);
}

#dogs {
    background-image: url(mutt.jpg);
}
```

Exposing even more structure

There are a couple of reasons you might
want to add more structure to your
pages with <div>s. First, you may want
to further expose the underlying logical
structure of your pages, which can help
others understand them, and also help
in maintaining them. Second, there are
times when you need the structure so
that you have a way to apply style to a
section. Often, you'll want to add the
structure for both reasons.

So, in the case of PetStorz, we could
take this to the next level and add a few
more <div>s…

*Now we've added
another <div> with an
id indicating this is the
header of the page.*

*And another indicating
the footer of the page.*

*Adding this structure through <div>s
can even help you think through your
page design. For instance, does this
lone <p> really need to be here?*

Adding structure on structure

And you don't have to stop there. It is
common to nest structure, too. For instance,
in the PetStorz page, we have a cat section
and a dog section, and the two together are
logically the "pets" section of the page. So,
we could place both the "cats" and "dogs"
<div>s into a "pets" <div>.

*Now we've marked up this HTML so that we
know there is a logical section in the page
with "pets" content in it. Further, that "pets"
section has two logical subsections, one for
"cats" and one for "dogs".*

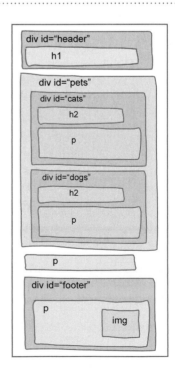

Q: So, a <div> acts like a container that you can put elements into to keep them all together?

A: It sure does. In fact, we often describe <div>s as "containers." Not only do they act as logical containers that you can use to hold a bunch of related elements (like the "cat" elements) together, but when we start styling <div>s and using them for positioning in the next chapter, you'll see they act as graphical containers, too.

Q: Beyond the structure I'm already putting into my pages with headings and paragraphs and so on, should I also be adding a higher level of structure with <div>s?

A: Yes and no. You want to add structure where it has a real purpose, but don't add structure for structure's sake. Always keep your structure as simple as possible to get the job done. For instance,

if it is helpful to add a "pets" section that contains both "cats" and "dogs" to the PetStorz page, by all means add it. However, if it provides no real benefit, then it just complicates your page. After working with <div>s for a while, you'll start to get a feel for when and how much to use them.

Q: Do you ever put a <div> in a class instead of giving it an id?

A: Well, remember that an element can have an id *and* be in one or more classes at the same time, so the choice isn't mutually exclusive. And, yes, there are many times you create <div>s and place them into classes. Say you have a bunch of album sections in a page of music playlists; you might put all the elements that make up the album into a <div> and then put them all in an "albums" class. That identifies where the albums are, and they can all be styled together with the class. At the same time, you might give each album an id so that it can have additional style applied separately.

Q: I was having a little trouble following the <div> within <div> stuff, with the "pets" and "cats" and "dogs". Could you explain that a little more?

A: Sure. You're used to elements being nested in other elements, right? Like a <p> nested in a <body> nested in an <html> element. You've even seen lists nested within lists. The <div> is really no different; you're just nesting an element inside another element, and, in the case of PetStorz, we're using it to show larger chunks of structure (a "cats" and "dogs" nested in a "pets" section). Or, you might use <div>s to have a beer section nested in a beverages section nested in a menu section.

But the best way to understand why you'd want something like a <div> within a <div> is by using them and encountering a situation where they mean something to you. Put this in the back of your mind, and you'll see an example soon enough where we need one.

Use, don't abuse, <div>s in your pages. Add more structure where it helps you separate a page into logical sections for clarity and styling. Adding <div>s just for the sake of creating a lot of structure in your pages complicates them with no real benefit.

Meanwhile, back at the lounge...

Enough "theory" about <div>s—let's get one into the lounge page. Remember, we're trying to get all the elixir elements into a group and then we're going to style it to make it look like the elixir handout. So, open up your "lounge.html" file in the "chapter10/lounge" folder, locate the elixir elements, and then insert opening and closing <div> tags around them.

Here's the opening tag, and we've given it an id of "elixirs" to identify it.

Remember, we're just showing a snippet of HTML from the entire file. When you open "lounge.html", you'll see all the markup for the page.

```
<div id="elixirs">
    <h2>Weekly Elixir Specials</h2>

    <p>
        <img src="images/yellow.gif" alt="Lemon Breeze Elixir">
    </p>
    <h3>Lemon Breeze</h3>
    <p>
        The ultimate healthy drink, this elixir combines
        herbal botanicals, minerals, and vitamins with
        a twist of lemon into a smooth citrus wonder
        that will keep your immune system going all
        day and all night.
    </p>

    <p>
        <img src="images/chai.gif" alt="Chai Chiller Elixir">
    </p>

    <h3>Chai Chiller</h3>
    <p>
        Not your traditional chai, this elixir mixes mat&eacute;
        with chai spices and adds an extra chocolate kick for
        a caffeinated taste sensation on ice.
    </p>

    <p>
        <img src="images/black.gif" alt="Black Brain Brew Elixir">
    </p>

    <h3>Black Brain Brew</h3>
    <p>
        Want to boost your memory? Try our Black Brain Brew
        elixir, made with black oolong tea and just a touch
        of espresso. Your brain will thank you for the boost.
    </p>

    <p>
        Join us any evening for these and all our
        other wonderful
        <a href="beverages/elixir.html"
           title="Head First Lounge Elixirs">elixirs</a>.
    </p>
</div>
```

And here's the closing tag.

Taking the <div> for a test drive

That was easy, wasn't it? Now that we've got a more structured page, let's fire up the browser and see how it looks...

Hmmm...no change at all! But that's okay: the <div> is pure structure, and it doesn't have any "look" or default style in the page.

That said, a <div> is just a block element, and you can apply any styles you want to it. So, once you know how to style a block element (and you do), you know how to style a <div>.

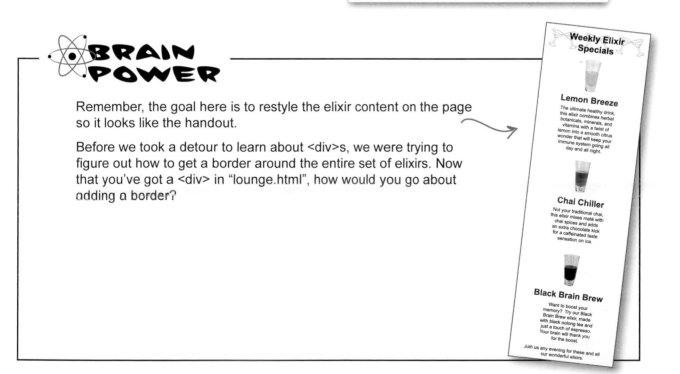

BRAIN POWER

Remember, the goal here is to restyle the elixir content on the page so it looks like the handout.

Before we took a detour to learn about <div>s, we were trying to figure out how to get a border around the entire set of elixirs. Now that you've got a <div> in "lounge.html", how would you go about adding a border?

Adding a border

Now that you have a `<div>` around all the elements in the elixirs section, the fun begins: *you can style it.*

The first thing we want to reproduce in the elixirs handout is a border that wraps around *all* the elements in the elixirs section, right? Well, now that you actually have a `<div>` element that wraps around the elixirs section, you can style it and add a border. Let's try that now.

You'll need a new rule in the lounge's CSS to select the `<div>` element using its id. Open up your "lounge.css" file in the "chapter10/lounge" folder, and add this rule at the end:

```
#elixirs {
    border-width: thin;
    border-style: solid;
    border-color: #007e7e;
}
```

Add this at the end of your CSS file. It selects the elixirs `<div>` element using its id, and adds a thin, solid border in our favorite aquamarine color.

An over-the-border test drive

After you've added the CSS, save it and then reload your "lounge.html" file.

Here's the border that you just added to the elixirs `<div>` element.

You added a visible border to this `<div>`, but it still has no padding and no margin. We'll need to add that too.

Notice that the border goes around all the elements inside the `<div>` element. The `<div>` is a box like every other element, so when you add a border, the border goes around the content, which is all the elements in the `<div>`.

Adding some real style to the elixirs section

So far, so good. We've found a way to get that border around the entire section. Now you're going to see how to use the `<div>` to customize the styling of the entire elixirs section independent of the rest of the page.

We obviously have some padding issues to deal with, because the border is right up against the content. But there's a lot of other style we need to work out, too. Let's take a look at everything we need to take care of…

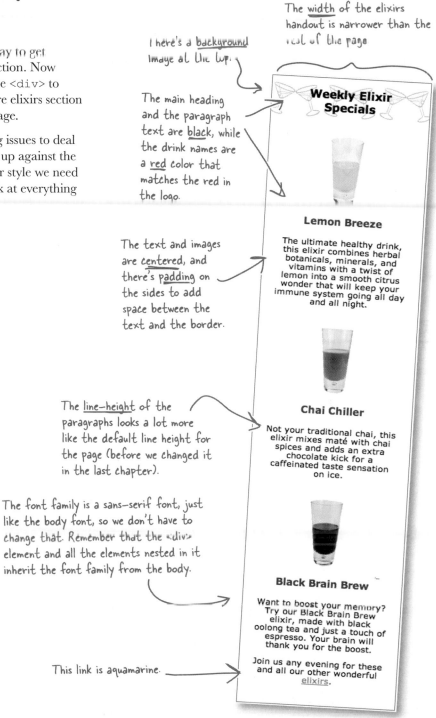

There's a background image at the top.

The width of the elixirs handout is narrower than the rest of the page.

The main heading and the paragraph text are black, while the drink names are a red color that matches the red in the logo.

The text and images are centered, and there's padding on the sides to add space between the text and the border.

The line-height of the paragraphs looks a lot more like the default line height for the page (before we changed it in the last chapter).

The font family is a sans-serif font, just like the body font, so we don't have to change that. Remember that the `<div>` element and all the elements nested in it inherit the font family from the body.

This link is aquamarine.

The game plan

That's a lot of new style, so let's get a game plan together before attacking it. Here's what we need to do:

☐ First, we're going to change the width of the elixirs `<div>` to make it narrower.

☐ Next, we'll knock out some of the styles you're already familiar with, like padding and the background image. We'll also play with the text alignment, which you haven't seen before.

☐ Then all we've got left are the text line heights and the heading colors. You're going to see that you need to upgrade your CSS selector skills just a bit to get those changed.

That's a lot to do, so let's get started.

Working on the elixir width

We'd like the elixirs to be quite narrow, so it looks like the narrow handout menu at the lounge; about 1/4 the width of a typical browser window should be about right. So, let's say you set your browser to 800 pixels wide; that would be about 200 pixels. You've set the widths of padding, borders, and margins, but you've never set the width of an element before. To do that, you use the `width` property, like this:

```
#elixirs {
        border-width: thin;
        border-style: solid;
        border-color: #007e7e;
        width: 200px;
}
```

The width property lets you specify the width of the element's content area. Here, we're specifying that the content width be 200 pixels.

We're setting this on the elixirs <div>. So the content in the elixirs <div> will be 200 pixels wide, and the browser's layout rules will work to fit all the elements nested in the <div> within that width.

Give this a try. Open your "lounge.css" and add this rule to the bottom.

Test driving the width

Next, save the CSS and then reload the "lounge.html" file. You'll see the elixirs section get much skinnier, thanks to the width you gave it. The width of the content in the `<div>` is now exactly 200 pixels. There's also some interesting behavior you should check out...

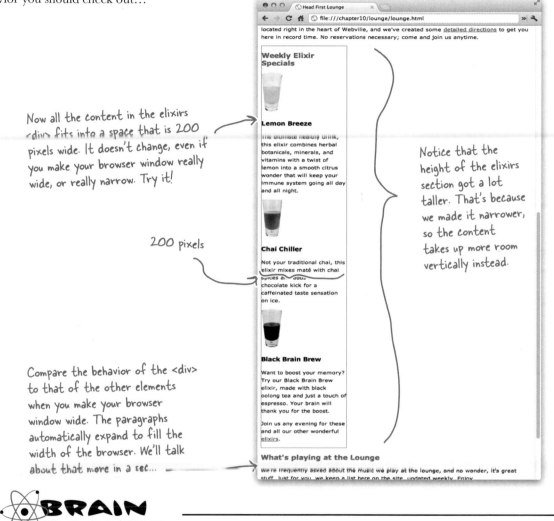

Now all the content in the elixirs `<div>` fits into a space that is 200 pixels wide. It doesn't change, even if you make your browser window really wide, or really narrow. Try it!

200 pixels

Notice that the height of the elixirs section got a lot taller. That's because we made it narrower, so the content takes up more room vertically instead.

Compare the behavior of the `<div>` to that of the other elements when you make your browser window wide. The paragraphs automatically expand to fill the width of the browser. We'll talk about that more in a sec...

I was wondering how the width property relates to padding and margins. Is this the width of the content itself? Or the entire box, including the padding and margin?

The width property specifies the width for the content area only.

To figure out the width of the entire box, you need to add the width of the content area to the width of the left and right margins, the left and right padding, and the border width. Don't forget that you have to include *twice* the border width, because there is a border on the left and the right.

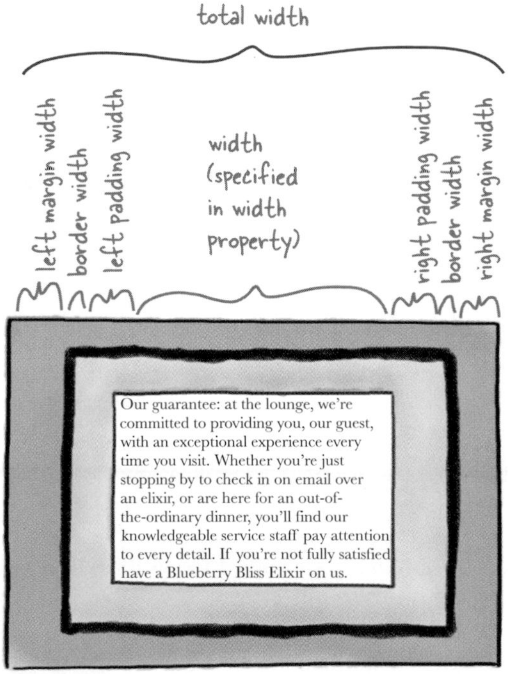

total width

left margin width
border width
left padding width

width
(specified
in width
property)

right padding width
border width
right margin width

Our guarantee: at the lounge, we're committed to providing you, our guest, with an exceptional experience every time you visit. Whether you're just stopping by to check in on email over an elixir, or are here for an out-of-the-ordinary dinner, you'll find our knowledgeable service staff pay attention to every detail. If you're not fully satisfied, have a Blueberry Bliss Elixir on us.

Well, then how do we specify the width of the entire element?

You don't. You specify the width of the content area, the padding, the border, and the margin. All of that added together is the width of the entire element.

Say you set the content area width to be 300 pixels using the `width` property in a CSS rule.

And let's say you've set the margins to 20 pixels and the padding to 10 pixels, and you have a 1-pixel border. What's the width of your element's box? Well, it's the width of the content area added to the width of the left and right margins, the left and right padding, and the left and right border width. Let' see how to calculate that…

(1) The content area is 300 pixels.

300 pixels

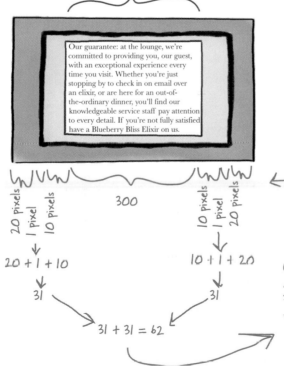

Our guarantee: at the lounge, we're committed to providing you, our guest, with an exceptional experience every time you visit. Whether you're just stopping by to check in on email over an elixir, or are here for an out-of-the-ordinary dinner, you'll find our knowledgeable service staff pay attention to every detail. If you're not fully satisfied have a Blueberry Bliss Elixir on us.

(2) Figure out how much is taken up by the margins, padding, and border.

20 pixels / 1 pixel / 10 pixels   300   10 pixels / 1 pixel / 20 pixels

20 + 1 + 10   10 + 1 + 20

31   31

(3) It looks like 62 pixels are taken up, so add that to the content area's width of 300 pixels, and we have 300 + 62 = 362 pixels for the entire box.

31 + 31 = 62

there are no
Dumb Questions

Q: If I don't set the width of an element, then where does the width come from?

A: The default width for a block element is "auto", which means that it will expand to fill whatever space is available. If you think about any of the web pages we've been building, each block element can expand to the entire width of the browser, and that's exactly what it does. Now, hold this thought, because we're going to go into this in detail in the next chapter. Just remember that "auto" allows the content to fill whatever space is available (after taking padding, border, and margin into account).

Q: What if I don't have any margin, padding, or borders?

A: Then your content gets to use the *entire* width of the box. If the width of the content area is 300 pixels, and you have no padding, border, or margin, then the width of the entire box would also be 300 pixels.

Q: What are the different ways I can specify widths?

A: You can specify an actual size—usually in pixels—or you can specify a percentage. If you use a percentage, then the width is calculated as a percentage of the width of the container the element is in (which could be the <body>, a <div>, etc.).

Q: What about the height?

A: In general, the height of an element is left at the default, which is auto, and the browser expands the content area vertically so all of the content is visible. Take a look at the elixirs section after we set the width to 200 pixels, and you'll see the <div> got a lot taller.

You can explicitly set a height, but you risk having the bottom of your content overflow into other elements if your height isn't big enough to contain it. In general, leave your element heights unspecified so they default to auto.

Sharpen your pencil

Here's a box that has all the widths labeled. What is the width of the entire box?

Your answer here

269 pixels

Our guarantee: at the lounge, we're committed to providing you, our guest, with an exceptional experience every time you visit. Whether you're just stopping by to check in on email over an elixir, or are here for an out-of-the-ordinary dinner, you'll find our knowledgeable service staff pay attention to every detail. If you're not fully satisfied, have a Blueberry Bliss Elixir on us.

30 pixels
2 pixels
5 pixels

200 pixels

10 pixels
2 pixels
20 pixels

Adding the basic styles to the elixirs

We've got the width out of the way. What's left to do?

☑ First, we're going to change the width of the elixirs `<div>` to make it narrower.

☐ Next, we'll knock out some of the styles you're already familiar with, like padding, text alignment, and the background image. ← *We're doing this step next.*

☐ Then all we've got left are the text line heights and the heading colors. You're going to see that you need to upgrade your CSS selector skills just a bit to get those changed.

Now we're going to concentrate on some of the basic styles, like the padding, the text alignment, and also getting that background image of the cocktail glasses in the elixirs `<div>`. You're already familiar with how most of this works, so let's take a quick look at the CSS:

Remember, we're going to apply all this style to the elixirs <div> so that it only affects the <div> and the elements it contains, not the entire page.

The default padding on a <div> is 0 pixels, so we're going to add some padding to provide a bit of space for the content. Notice that we're not adding any padding at the top because there's already plenty of room there, thanks to the default margin on the <h2> heading (look back at the last test drive and you'll see there's plenty of room above the <h2>). But we do need it on the right, bottom, and left.

```
#elixirs {
    border-width:       thin;
    border-style:       solid;
    border-color:       #007e7e;
    width:              200px;

    padding-right:      20px;
    padding-bottom:     20px;
    padding-left:       20px;

    margin-left:        20px;

    text-align:         center;

    background-image:   url(images/cocktail.gif);
    background-repeat:  repeat-x;
}
```

We're adding some margin on the left to indent the elixirs from the rest of the page a bit. This is going to come in handy later...

Use text-align on block elements to align the text they contain. Here, we're going to center-align the text.

And finally we're specifying an image to use in the background, in this case the cocktail image. We're setting the background-repeat property to repeat-x, which will tile the image only in the horizontal direction.

Test driving the new styles

Now it's time to add those new properties to your "lounge.css" file and reload the page. Let's check out the changes: the headings, the images, and the text are all centered in the `<div>` and have a little more breathing room now that there's some padding in place. We've also got a little decoration at the top with the tiled cocktail image.

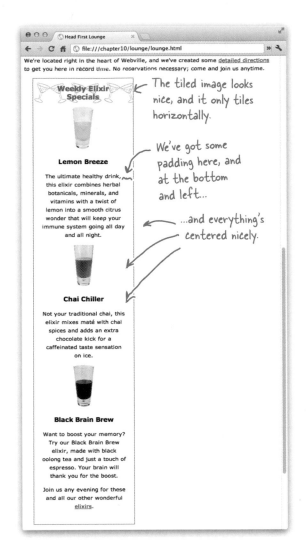

The tiled image looks nice, and it only tiles horizontally.

We've got some padding here, and at the bottom and left...

...and everything's centered nicely.

> Wait just a sec...why does the *text*-align property affect the alignment of the images? Shouldn't it align only *text*? Seems like it should be called something else if it aligns images too.

Good point...it doesn't seem right, does it? But the truth is that `text-align` will align *all the inline content* in a block element. So in this case, we're setting the property on the `<div>` block element, and all its inline content is nicely centered as a result. Just remember that `text-align`, despite its name, works on any kind of inline element. One other thing to keep in mind: the `text-align` property should be set on block elements only. It has no effect if it's used directly on inline elements (like `<img>`).

That's interesting because I noticed the text inside the <div> is all inside other block elements, like <h2>, <h3>, and <p>. So, if text-align is aligning *inline* elements in the <div> block element, how is the text in these nested block elements getting aligned?

Good catch. All the text inside the <div> element is in nested block elements, but it is all aligned now. That's because these block elements *inherit* the text-align property from the <div>. So here's the difference: rather than the <div> itself aligning the text in the headings and the paragraphs (which it won't do because these are block elements), the headings and paragraphs are inheriting the text-align value of "center", and then aligning *their own content* to center.

So what? Well, if you think about it, this gives you a lot of leverage when you use a <div>, because you can wrap a section of content in a <div> and then apply styles to the <div> rather than each individual element. Of course, keep in mind that not all properties are inherited by default, so this won't work for all properties.

Sharpen your pencil

So now that you understand widths, what's the total width of the elixirs box? To start with, we know the content area is 200 pixels. We've also set some left and right padding that affects the width, as well as a border that's set to "thin". Just assume a thin border is 1 pixel thick, like it is on most browsers. And what about margins? We set a left margin value, but no right margin value, so the right margin is 0 pixels by default.

Here are all the properties that relate to width. Your job is to figure out the total width of the elixirs <div>.

```
border-width:    thin;          1 + 1 = 2 px

width:           200px;         200 px

padding-right:   20px;
padding-left:    20px;

margin-left:     20px;

                 262 px
```

Weekly Elixir Specials

Lemon Breeze

The ultimate healthy drink, this elixir combines herbal botanicals, minerals, and vitamins with a twist of lemon into a smooth citrus wonder that will keep your immune system going all day and all night.

Chai Chiller

Not your traditional chai, this elixir mixes maté with chai spices and adds an extra chocolate kick for a caffeinated taste sensation on ice.

Black Brain Brew

Want to boost your memory? Try our Black Brain Brew elixir, made with black oolong tea and just a touch of espresso. Your brain will thank you for the boost.

Join us any evening for these and all our wonderful elixirs.

We're almost there...

We're close to having the elixirs done. What's left?

☑ First, we're going to change the width of the elixirs `<div>` to make it narrower.

☑ Next, we'll knock out some of the styles you're already familiar with, like padding, text alignment, and the background image.

☐ Then all we've got left are the text line heights and the heading colors. You're going to see that you need to upgrade your CSS selector skills just a bit to get those changed.

← We're on the last step.

Sounds pretty easy, right? After all, you've done all this before. In fact, given that you know you can just set styles on the `<div>` and they will be inherited, you can take care of this real fast.

> We've almost got this done; we just need to change the header colors and also the line height.

Frank: Yeah, this is interesting. The main elixirs heading, which is an `<h2>`, has the aquamarine color because there is already an `<h2>` rule in the CSS. But we need for that to be black. Then we've got the `<h3>`s in the elixirs, which need to be red.

Jim: Yeah, no problem, we'll just add a few more rules.

Frank: But wait a sec…if we change the `<h2>` rule, or add an `<h3>` rule, then we're going to change the heading colors on the entire page. We just want these colors in the elixirs section.

Jim: Oh, good point. Hmmm…Well, we could use two classes.

Frank: That would work, although it's a bit messy. Anytime you add a new heading to the elixirs `<div>`, you'll have to remember to add it to the class.

Jim: Yeah, well, c'est la vie.

Frank: Actually Jim, before you use classes, go check out descendant selectors. I think they'll work better here.

Jim: Descendant selectors?

Frank: Right, they're just a way of specifying a selector like "select an `<h2>` element, but only if it's inside an elixirs `<div>`."

Joe: I'm not following.

Frank: Okay, let's step through this…

Frank

Jim

What are we trying to do?

Let's take a quick look at what we're trying to do to the heading colors.

What we have now

Here's just the main heading elements in the lounge HTML.

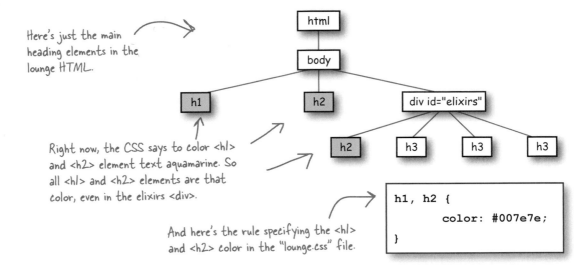

Right now, the CSS says to color <h1> and <h2> element text aquamarine. So all <h1> and <h2> elements are that color, even in the elixirs <div>.

And here's the rule specifying the <h1> and <h2> color in the "lounge.css" file.

```
h1, h2 {
        color: #007e7e;
}
```

What we want

We want the <h1> and <h2> in the main page to stay aquamarine.

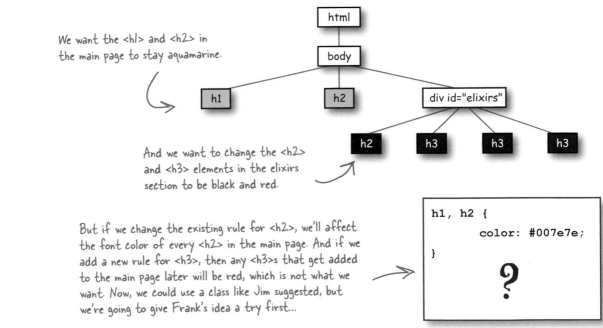

And we want to change the <h2> and <h3> elements in the elixirs section to be black and red.

But if we change the existing rule for <h2>, we'll affect the font color of every <h2> in the main page. And if we add a new rule for <h3>, then any <h3>s that get added to the main page later will be red, which is not what we want. Now, we could use a class like Jim suggested, but we're going to give Frank's idea a try first...

```
h1, h2 {
        color: #007e7e;
}
?
```

What we need is a way to select descendants

What we're really missing is a way to tell CSS that we want to only select elements that *descend* from certain elements, which is kinda like specifying that you only want your inheritance to go to the children of one daughter or son. Here's how you write a descendant selector:

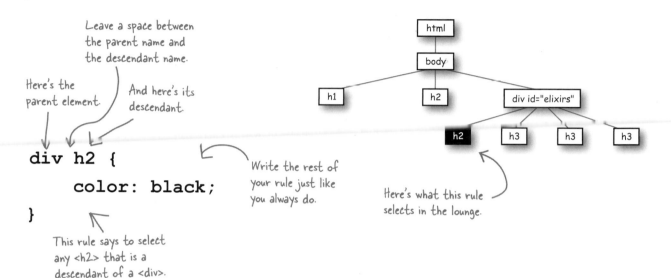

Leave a space between the parent name and the descendant name.

Here's the parent element.

And here's its descendant.

```
div h2 {
        color: black;
}
```

Write the rest of your rule just like you always do.

Here's what this rule selects in the lounge.

This rule says to select any <h2> that is a descendant of a <div>.

Now the only problem with this rule is that if someone created another <div> in the "lounge.html" file, she'd get black <h2> text, even if she didn't want it. But we've got an `id` on the elixirs <div>, so let's use it to be more specific about which descendants we want:

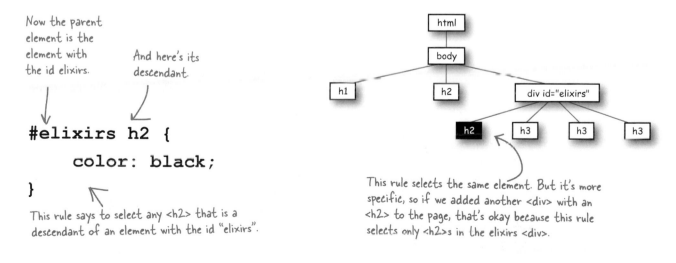

Now the parent element is the element with the id elixirs.

And here's its descendant.

```
#elixirs h2 {
        color: black;
}
```

This rule says to select any <h2> that is a descendant of an element with the id "elixirs".

This rule selects the same element. But it's more specific, so if we added another <div> with an <h2> to the page, that's okay because this rule selects only <h2>s in the elixirs <div>.

Sharpen your pencil

Your turn. Write the selector that selects only <h3> elements inside the elixirs <div>.
In your rule, set the color property to #d12c47. Also label the elements in the graph
below that are selected.

Write your CSS rule here.

```
#elixirs h3 {
    color: #d12c47;
}
```

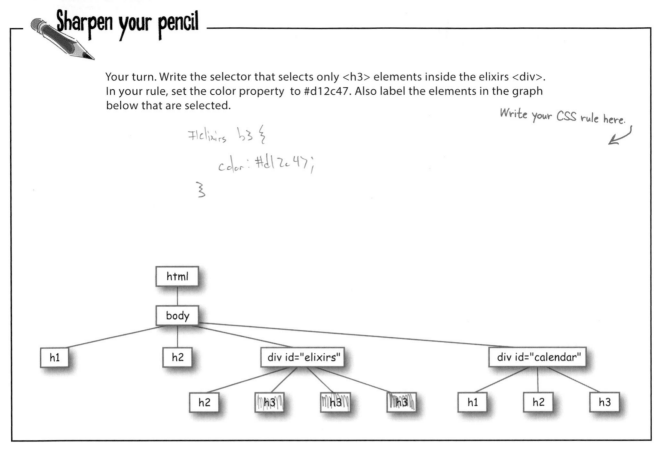

there are no
Dumb Questions

Q: **Descendant usually means child, grandchild, great-grandchild. Here, we're just selecting the child descendants, right?**

A: That's a really good point. The selector "#elixirs h2" means ANY descendant of elixirs, so the <h2> could be a direct child of the <div> or nested down inside a <blockquote> or another nested <div> (making it a grandchild) and so on. So a descendant selector selects any <h2> nested inside an element, no matter how deeply it is nested.

Q: **Well, is there a way to select a direct child?**

A: Yes. For example, you could use "#elixirs > h2" to select <h2> only if it is the direct child of an element with an id of "elixirs".

Q: **What if I need something more complex, like an <h2> that is the child of a <blockquote> that is in elixirs?**

A: It works the same way. Just use more descendants, like this:

```
#elixirs blockquote h2 {
    color: blue;
}
```

This selects any <h2> elements that descend from <blockquote>s that descend from an element with an id of "elixirs".

Changing the color of the elixir headings

Now that you know about descendant selectors, let's set the <h2> heading to black and the <h3> headings to red in the elixirs. Here's how you do that:

```
#elixirs h2 {
    color: black;
}

#elixirs h3 {
    color: #d12c47;
}
```

 Here, we're using the descendant selectors to target just the <h2> and <h3> elements in the elixirs <div>. We're setting <h2> to black, and <h3> to a red color, using a hex code.

A quick test drive...

Go ahead and add these new properties to the bottom of your "lounge.css" file, save, and reload "lounge.html".

We've got black and red headings in the elixirs section, and we haven't affected the aquamarine color being used for <h2> headings in the main page.

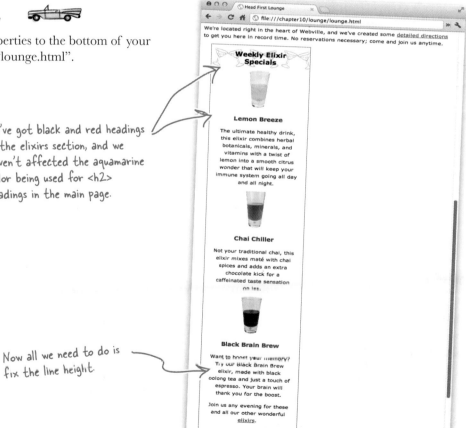

Now all we need to do is fix the line height.

Fixing the line height

Recall that in the last chapter, we made the line height of the text in the lounge a little taller than normal. This looks great, but in the elixirs we want our text to be a normal, single-spaced line height to match the handout. Sounds easy enough, right? Just set the `line-height` property on the `<div>` and everything will be fine, because line height is inherited. The only problem is that the headings will also inherit the line height, and we'll end up with something like this.

```
#elixirs {
    line-height: 1em;
}
```

If you set the line-height property on the entire <div>, then it will be inherited by all elements in the <div>, including the headings. Notice that the line height in the heading is too small and the two lines are starting to run together.

The reason that the line height for the elixirs heading is too small is because every element in the elixirs `<div>` inherits the line height of 1em, or "1 times the font size of the elixirs element," which in this case is "small", or about 12 pixels (depending on your browser). Remember, the elixirs `<div>` is inheriting its font size from the `<body>` element, which we set to "small".

What we really want is for all the elements in the elixirs `<div>` to have a line height that's based not on the font size of the elixirs `<div>`, but rather the font size of each element itself. We want the `<h2>` heading to have a line height that is 1 times its font size (which is 120% of "small"), and the `<p>` should also have a line height of 1 times its font size (which is "small"). How can you do this? Well, the `line-height` property is a bit special because you can use *just a number* instead of a relative measure—like em or %—for it. When you use just the number 1, you're telling each element in the elixirs `<div>` to have a line height of 1 times its *own* font size, rather than the font size of the elixirs `<div>`. Give it a try; set the line height of the elixirs `<div>` to 1, and you'll see that it fixes the heading.

```
#elixirs {
    line-height: 1;
}
```

Add a line-height of 1 to the elixirs <div> to change the line-height of each element in it.

Here are the font sizes of the elements. We set body to "small", so that's inherited by elixirs.

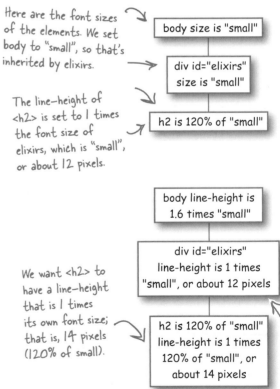

The line-height of <h2> is set to 1 times the font size of elixirs, which is "small", or about 12 pixels.

> body size is "small"

> div id="elixirs" size is "small"

> h2 is 120% of "small"

We want <h2> to have a line-height that is 1 times its own font size; that is, 14 pixels (120% of small).

> body line-height is 1.6 times "small"

> div id="elixirs" line-height is 1 times "small", or about 12 pixels

> h2 is 120% of "small" line-height is 1 times 120% of "small", or about 14 pixels

The font-size of the p element is "small" (p inherits its font-size from the elixirs <div>), so it will have a line-height of 12 pixels, which is what we want.

Look what you've accomplished...

Take a look at the elixirs section now. You've completely transformed it, and now it looks just like the handout. And, other than adding a `<div>` and an `id` attribute to your HTML, you were able to do this with just a few CSS rules and properties.

By now, you should be realizing just how powerful CSS is, and how flexible your web pages are when you separate your structure (HTML) from your presentation (CSS). You can give your HTML a whole new look, simply by changing the CSS.

Remember, this is how the elixirs section looked when we started...

...and here's what it looks like now.

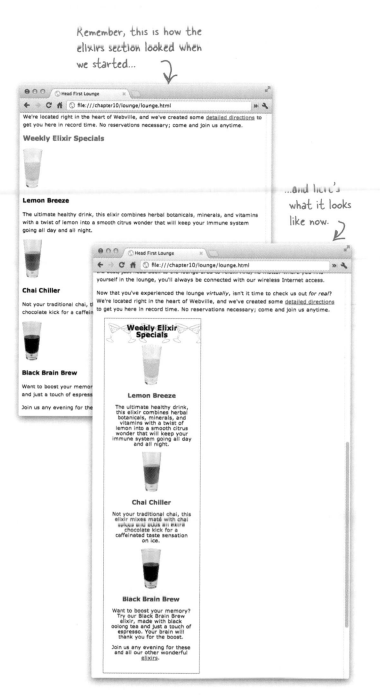

> Wow, that's fantastic! You were able to make the elixirs section on the website look like the handout, with just a little CSS.

It's time to take a little shortcut

You've probably noticed that there are quite a few CSS properties that seem to go together. For instance, `padding-left`, `padding-right`, `padding-bottom`, and `padding-top`. Margin properties are the same way. How about `background-image`, `background-color`, and `background-repeat`? Those all set different property values on the background of an element. Have you also noticed it gets a little tedious typing all those in? There are better things to spend your time on than typing all this, right?

```
padding-top:     0px;
padding-right:   20px;
padding-bottom:  30px;
padding-left:    10px;
```

 That's a lot of typing just to specify four numbers.

Well, here's a special bonus for this chapter. You're going to learn how to specify all those values without risking carpal tunnel. Here's how:

Here's the old-school way of specifying your padding.

⬇

```
padding-top:     0px;
padding-right:   20px;
padding-bottom:  30px;
padding-left:    10px;
```

And here's the new and improved way to write them as a shorthand.

```
padding: 0px 20px 30px 10px;
```
top   *right*   *bottom*   *left*

You can use the same sort of shorthand with margins:

```
margin-top:     0px;
margin-right:   20px;
margin-bottom:  30px;
margin-left:    10px;
```

```
margin: 0px 20px 30px 10px;
```
top   *right*   *bottom*   *left*

Just like padding, you can use a shorthand to specify all your margin values with one property.

If your padding or margins are the same value on all sides, you can make the shorthand *really* short:

```
padding-top:     20px;
padding-right:   20px;
padding-bottom:  20px;
padding-left:    20px;
```

```
padding: 20px;
```

This says that the padding should be 20 pixels on every side of the box.

If all your padding values are the same, then you can write it like this.

But there's more...

Here's another common way to abbreviate margins (or padding):

```
margin-top:      0px;
margin-right:    20px;
margin-bottom:   0px;
margin-left:     20px;
```

top and bottom are the same.

right and left are the same.

If the top and bottom, as well as the right and left, margins are the same, then you can use a shorthand.

```
margin:  0px 20px;
```

top and bottom   *right and left*

And what about the border properties we mentioned? You can use a shorthand for those too.

```
border-width:    thin;
border-style:    solid;
border-color:    #007e7e;
```

Rewrite border properties as one property. These can be in any order you like.

```
border:  thin solid #007e7e;
```

The border shorthand is even more flexible than margins or padding because you can specify them in any order you like.

```
border: solid thin #007e7e;

border: #007e7e solid thin;
```

```
border: solid thin;

border: #007e7e solid;

border: solid;
```

These are all perfectly valid border shorthands.

...and don't forget the shorthand for backgrounds

You can also use shorthand for backgrounds:

```
background-color:  white;
background-image:  url(images/cocktail.gif);
background-repeat: repeat-x;
```

Like border, values can go in any order in this shorthand. There are also a few other values you can specify in the shorthand, like background-position.

```
background: white url(images/cocktail.gif) repeat-x;
```

And even more shorthands

No description of shorthands would be complete without mentioning font shorthands. Check out all the properties we need for fonts: `font-family`, `font-style`, `font-weight`, `font-size`, `font-variant`, and don't forget `line-height`. Well, there's a shorthand that wraps all these into one. Here's how it works:

Here are the properties that go into the font shorthand. Ordering matters here unless we say otherwise...

You must specify font size.

Finally, you need to add your font families. You only need to specify one font, but alternatives are highly encouraged.

`font:` ***font-style font-variant font-weight font-size/line-height font-family***

These values are all optional. You can specify any combination of them, but they need to come before the font-size property.

The line-height property is optional. If you want to specify one, just put a / right after the font-size property and add your line height.

Use commas between your font-family names.

So let's give this a try. Here are the font properties for the lounge body:

```
font-size: small;
font-family: Verdana, Helvetica, Arial, sans-serif;
line-height: 1.6em;
```

Now let's map those to the shorthand:

We're not using any of these, but that's okay—they're all optional.

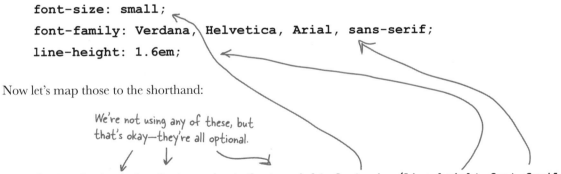

`font:` ***font-style font-variant font-weight font-size/line-height font-family***

And now let's write the shorthand:

```
font: small/1.6em Verdana, Helvetica, Arial, sans-serif;
```

And here's the shorthand version. Wow, that's quite a shorthand, huh? You're going to be able to double your time at the slopes (or on the beach) now.

there are no
Dumb Questions

Q: Should I always use shorthand?

A: Not necessarily. Some people find the long form more readable. Shorthands do have the advantage of reducing the size of your CSS files, and certainly they are more quickly entered because they require less typing. However, when there is a problem, they are a little more difficult to "debug" if you have incorrect values or the wrong order. So, you should use whichever form is more comfortable because they are both perfectly valid.

Q: Shorthands are more complex because I have to remember the ordering and what is and isn't optional. How do I memorize it all?

A: Well, you'll be surprised how quickly it becomes second nature, but those of us in the "biz" have a little secret we like to call a "reference manual." Just pick one up, and should you need to quickly look up property names or the syntax of a property,

just grab your handy reference manual and look it up. We're particularly fond of the *CSS Pocket Reference* by Eric Meyer. It's tiny and makes a great reference.

Make It Stick

To remember the ordering of the padding and margin shorthand values, think of a clock labeled with top, right, bottom, and left. Then, always go in a clockwise direction: top to right to bottom to left.

margin: 0px 20px 30px 10px;
top right bottom left

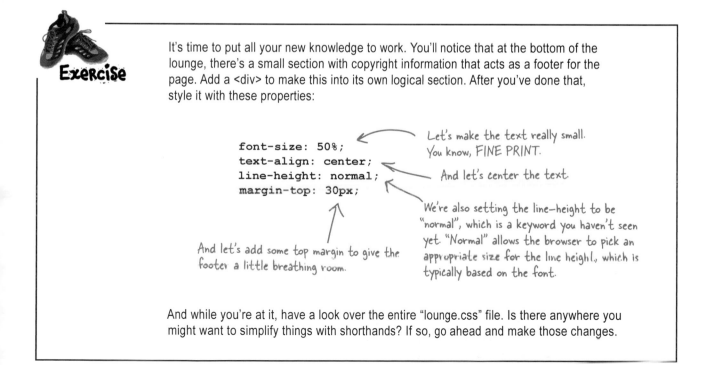

Exercise

It's time to put all your new knowledge to work. You'll notice that at the bottom of the lounge, there's a small section with copyright information that acts as a footer for the page. Add a <div> to make this into its own logical section. After you've done that, style it with these properties:

```
font-size: 50%;
text-align: center;
line-height: normal;
margin-top: 30px;
```

Let's make the text really small. You know, FINE PRINT.

And let's center the text.

We're also setting the line-height to be "normal", which is a keyword you haven't seen yet. "Normal" allows the browser to pick an appropriate size for the line height, which is typically based on the font.

And let's add some top margin to give the footer a little breathing room.

And while you're at it, have a look over the entire "lounge.css" file. Is there anywhere you might want to simplify things with shorthands? If so, go ahead and make those changes.

I saw the nice job you did on the elixirs. Can you give us a hand with the music recommendations on the site? We don't need much, just some simple styling.

The lounge's resident DJ

What's playing at the Lounge

We're frequently asked about the music we play at the lounge, and no wonder, it's great stuff. Just for you, we keep a list here on the site, updated weekly. Enjoy.

- *Buddha Bar*, **Claude Challe**
- *When It Falls*, **Zero 7**
- *Earth 7*, **L.T.J. Bukem**
- *Le Roi Est Mort, Vive Le Roi!*, **Enigma**
- *Music for Airports*, **Brian Eno**

All the CD titles are in an italic font style.

And all the artists are in bold.

BRAIN POWER

What do you think is the best way to style the CD and artists in the "What's playing at the Lounge" section?

> I was thinking we could just wrap <em> and <strong> elements around the CDs and artists. On most browsers, that's going to give us italic and bold.

Jim

Frank

Frank: Yeah, but that's kind of like using a <blockquote> just to indent text. What I mean is that we don't really want to emphasize and strongly emphasize the CD and artists. We just want italic and bold. Plus, what if someone changes the style for <em> and <strong>? That would show up on the CDs and artists too.

Jim: Well, I actually thought about that, but I couldn't think of any other way to do it. I mean, this is just text in the same list item. It's not like we have any way to style it.

Frank: What do you mean?

Jim: We can only style elements, and here we just have a bit of text, like, "Music for Airports, Brian Eno". We'd need an element around each piece of text to be able to style them differently.

Frank: Oh, right, right. I see what you mean.

Jim: I suppose we could use something like:

```
<div class="cd">Music for Airports</div>
<div class="artist">Brian Eno</div>.
```

But that's a block element, so that is going to cause linebreaks.

Frank: Ahhh, I think you're on to something, Jim. There's another element like <div> that is for inline elements. It's called a <span>. That could work out perfectly.

Jim: I'm game. How does it work?

Frank: Well, a <span> gives you a way to create a grouping of inline characters and elements. Here, let's just give it a try…

Adding <span>s in three easy steps

<span> elements give you a way to logically separate inline content in the same way that <div>s allow you to create logical separation for block-level content. To see how this works, we're going to style the music recommendations by first adding <span> elements around the CDs and artists, and then we'll write two CSS rules to style the <span>s. Here's exactly what you're going to do:

 You're going to nest the CDs and artists in separate <span> elements.

 You're going to add one <span> to the "cd" class and the other to the "artist" class.

3 You're going to create a rule to style the "cd" class with italic, and the "artist" class with bold.

Steps one and two: Adding the <span>s

Open your "lounge.html" file and locate the "What's playing at the Lounge" heading. Just below that, you'll see the unordered list of recommendations. Here's what it looks like:

Each list item consists of a CD title, a comma, and then the music artist.

```
<ul>
<li>Buddha Bar, Claude Challe</li>
<li>When It Falls, Zero 7</li>
<li>Earth 7, L.T.J. Bukem</li>
<li>Le Roi Est Mort, Vive Le Roi!, Enigma</li>
<li>Music for Airports, Brian Eno</li>
</ul>
```

Let's try adding <span>s to the first CD and artist:

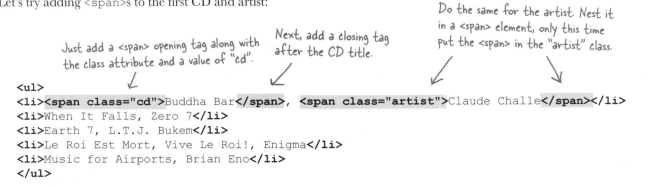

Just add a <span> opening tag along with the class attribute and a value of "cd".

Next, add a closing tag after the CD title.

Do the same for the artist. Nest it in a <span> element, only this time put the <span> in the "artist" class.

```
<ul>
<li><span class="cd">Buddha Bar</span>, <span class="artist">Claude Challe</span></li>
<li>When It Falls, Zero 7</li>
<li>Earth 7, L.T.J. Bukem</li>
<li>Le Roi Est Mort, Vive Le Roi!, Enigma</li>
<li>Music for Airports, Brian Eno</li>
</ul>
```

Step three: Styling the <span>s

Before we move on, save the file and reload it in your browser. Like a <div>, by default a <span> has no effect on style, so you should see no changes.

Now let's add some style. Add these two rules to the bottom of your "lounge.css" file:

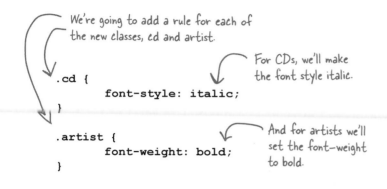

We're going to add a rule for each of the new classes, cd and artist.

For CDs, we'll make the font style italic.

```
.cd {
        font-style: italic;
}

.artist {
        font-weight: bold;
}
```

And for artists we'll set the font-weight to bold.

Test driving the spans

That's it. Save and reload. Here's what you'll see:

Now the first music recommendation has the correct styling.

Nice job. This next one's for you.

Sharpen your pencil

You need to finish the job. Add <span> elements to the rest of the music recommendations and test your page. You'll find the solution in the back of the chapter.

```
<ul>
<li><span class="cd">Buddha Bar</span>, <span class="artist">Claude Challe</span></li>
<li>When It Falls, Zero 7</li>
<li>Earth 7, L.T.J. Bukem</li>
<li>Le Roi Est Mort, Vive Le Roi!, Enigma</li>
<li>Music for Airports, Brian Eno</li>
</ul>
```

there are no Dumb Questions

Q: When do I use a <span> rather than another inline element like <em> or <strong>?

A: As always, you want to mark up your content with the element that most closely matches the meaning of your content. So, if you are emphasizing words, use <em>; if you're trying to make a big point, use <strong>. But if what you really want is to change the style of certain words—say, the names of albums or music artists on a fan site web page—then you should use a <span> and put your <span> elements into appropriate classes to group them and style them.

Q: Can I set properties like width on <span> elements? Actually, what about inline elements in general?

A: You can set the width of inline elements like <span>, <em>, and <strong>, but you won't notice any effect until you position them (which you'll learn how to do in the next chapter). You can also add margin and padding to these elements, as well as a border. Margins and padding on inline elements work a little differently from block elements—if you add a margin on all sides of an inline element, you'll only see space added to the left and right. You can add padding to the top and bottom of an inline element, but the padding doesn't affect the spacing of the other inline elements around it, so the padding will overlap other inline elements.

Images are a little different from other inline elements. The width, padding, and margin properties all behave more like they do for a block element. Remember from Chapter 5: if you set the width of an image using either the width attribute in the <img> element or the width property in CSS, the browser scales the image to fit the width you specify. This can sometimes be handy if you can't edit the image yourself to change the dimensions, and you want the image to appear bigger or smaller on the page. But remember, if you rely on the browser to scale your image, you may be downloading more data than you need (if the image is larger than you need).

Hey, I know you think you're about done, but you forgot to style the links. They're still that default blue color, which kinda clashes with our site.

⚛ BRAIN POWER

Think about the <a> element. Is there something about its style that seems different from other elements?

The <a> element and its multiple personalities

Have you noticed that links act a little differently when it comes to style? Links are chameleons of the element world because, depending on the circumstance, they can change their style at a moment's notice. Let's take a closer look:

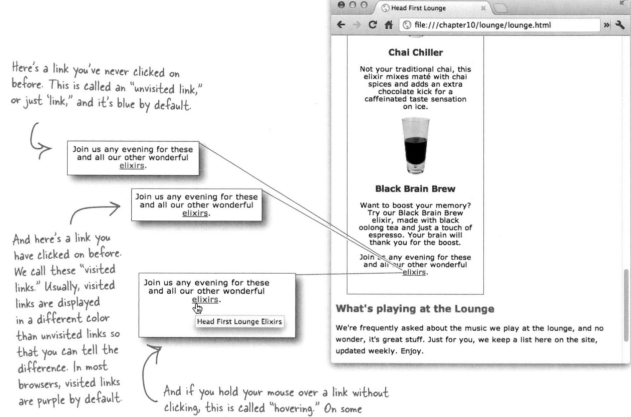

Here's a link you've never clicked on before. This is called an "unvisited link," or just 'link,' and it's blue by default.

And here's a link you have clicked on before. We call these "visited links." Usually, visited links are displayed in a different color than unvisited links so that you can tell the difference. In most browsers, visited links are purple by default.

And if you hold your mouse over a link without clicking, this is called "hovering." On some browsers you'll see a tool tip that displays the text of the "title" attribute. And if you pay close attention, on some web pages, you'll see a different style as you hover.

Unlike other elements, the style of an <a> element changes depending on its *state*. If the link has never been clicked on, it has one style, and if it has been clicked on, another. And if you hover over a link, it can have yet another style. Perhaps there's more to styling <a> elements than meets the eye? You betcha…let's take a look.

How can you style elements based on their state?

A link can be in a few states: it can be unvisited, visited, or in the hover state (and a couple of other states too). So, how do you take advantage of all those states? For instance, it would be nice to be able to specify what the visited and unvisited colors are. Or maybe highlight the link when the user is hovering over it. If only there were a way…

Well, of course there is, but if we told you it involves using *pseudo-classes* you'd probably just decide you've read enough for the night, and close the book. Right? But hold on! Pretend we never said the word *pseudo-class*, and let's just look at how you can style your links:

Notice we have the element <a>, followed by a : (colon), followed by the state we want to select. Make sure you don't have any spaces in these selectors (e.g., a : link won't work!)

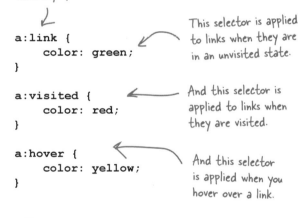

```
a:link {
    color: green;
}
```
This selector is applied to links when they are in an unvisited state.

```
a:visited {
    color: red;
}
```
And this selector is applied to links when they are visited.

```
a:hover {
    color: yellow;
}
```
And this selector is applied when you hover over a link.

Exercise

Add these rules to the bottom of your "lounge.css" file and then save and reload "lounge.html". Play around with the links to see them in each state. Note that you might have to clear your browser history to see the unvisited color (green).

there are no
Dumb Questions

Q: What happens if I just style the <a> element like a normal element? Like:

```
a {  color: red; }
```

A: You certainly can do that, but then your links will look the same in all states, which makes your links less user-friendly because you can't tell which ones you've visited and which ones you haven't.

Q: What are the other link states you mentioned?

A: There are two others: focus and active. The focus state occurs when the browser focuses on your link. What does that mean? Some browsers allow you to press your Tab key to rotate through all the links on your page. When the browser comes to a link, that link has the "focus." Setting a value for the focus pseudo-class is helpful for accessibility because those who need to use a keyboard to access a link (as opposed to a mouse) will know when they've got the right link selected. The active state occurs when the user first clicks on a link.

Q: Can't my links be in multiple states at the same time? For instance, my link could be visited, have the mouse hovering over it, and the user could be actively clicking on it all at once.

A: They sure can. You determine which style is applied by the ordering of your rules. So, the right ordering is generally considered to be: link, visited, hover, focus, and then active. If you use that ordering, you'll get the results you expect.

Q: Okay, I give. What's a pseudo-class?

A: Only one of the most confusing words in the CSS language. But as you've seen, styling links is pretty straightforward. So, let's talk about pseudo-classes…

The Pseudo-class Exposed

This week's interview:
Getting to know the pseudo-class.

Head First: Welcome, Pseudo-class. It's a pleasure to have you here. I must confess that when they first asked me to do this interview, I drew a blank. Pseudo-class? The only thing that came to mind was that '80s Phil Collins song.

Pseudo-class: Uh, that would be *Sussudio*. My name is *Pseudo*.

Head First: Oops. Honest mistake. Maybe we could start there. Can you tell us a little about where Pseudo came from?

Pseudo-class: Pseudo usually means something that looks like the real thing, but isn't.

Head First: And the last name? Class?

Pseudo-class: Everyone knows what a CSS class is. It's a grouping you create to place elements in so you can style them together. Put "pseudo" and "class" together and you have a pseudo-class: it acts like a class, but it isn't a real class.

Head First: What's not real about it if it acts like a class?

Pseudo-class: Okay, open up an HTML file and look for the class `:visited`, or `:link`, or `:hover`. Let me know when you find one.

Head First: I don't see any.

Pseudo-class: And yet, `a:link`, `a:visited`, and even `a:hover` all allow you to specify style, just like they were classes. So, those are pseudo-classes. In other words, you can style pseudo-classes, but no one ever types them into their HTML.

Head First: Well then, how do they work?

Pseudo-class: You can thank your browser for that. The browser goes through and adds all your `<a>` elements to the right pseudo-classes. If a link's been visited, no problem; it goes into the `:visited` pseudo-class. Is the user hovering over a link? No problem, the browser throws it in the `:hover` pseudo-class. Oh, now the user isn't hovering? The browser yanks it out of the "hover" pseudo-class.

Head First: Wow, I never knew. So there are all these classes out there that the browser is adding and removing elements from behind the scenes.

Pseudo-class: That's right, and it's damned important to know about; otherwise, how would you give your links style that adapted to what state the link was in?

Head First: So, Pseudo, do you just do links?

Pseudo-class: No, I do other elements too. Modern browsers already support pseudo-classes like `:hover` on other types of elements. And there are some other pseudo-classes, too. For instance, the pseudo-class `:first-child` is assigned to the first child of any element, like the first paragraph in a `<blockquote>`. And you can even select the last paragraph of a `<blockquote>` with the `:last-child` pseudo-class. I'm quite versatile, really.

Head First: Well, I've certainly learned something in this interview. Who knew that song was actually called "Sussudio"?! Thanks for being here, Pseudo-class.

Putting those pseudo-classes to work

Okay, let's be honest. You've probably just learned the most important thing in this book: pseudo-classes. Why? No, no, not because they allow you to style elements based on various "classes" your browser decides they belong to, like :link or :first-child. And, no, not because they give you really powerful ways to style elements based on things that happen while your visitors are using your page, like :hover. It's because the next time you're in that design meeting and you start talking about pseudo-classes with a real understanding, you're going to move to the *head of the class*. We're talking promotions and bonuses...at a minimum, the awe and respect of your fellow web buddies.

So, let's put those pseudo-classes to good use. You've already added some pseudo-class rules to your "lounge.css" and they had a dramatic impact on the look of the links, but they're probably not quite right for the lounge. So let's rework the style a little.

Okay, big change here. We're using a descendant selector combined with a pseudo-class. The first selector says to select any unvisited <a> element that is nested in an element with the id "elixirs". So we're styling JUST the links inside elixirs.

```
#elixirs a:link {
    color: #007e7e;
}

#elixirs a:visited {
    color: #333333;
}

#elixirs a:hover {
    background: #f88396;
    color: #0d5353;
}
```

On these two, we're setting the color. For unvisited links, a nice aquamarine...

...and for visited links we're using a dark gray.

Now for the really interesting rule. When the user is hovering over the link, we're changing the background to red. This makes the link loo highlighted when you pass the mouse over it. Give it a try!

Exercise

Open up your "lounge.css" and rework your a:link, a:visited, and a:hover rules to use the new descendant selector and the new style definitions. Save, reload, and turn the page.

Test drive the links

When you reload, you should see some new style in the elixirs section. Keep in mind, to see the unvisited links you may have to clear your browser's history; otherwise, the browser will know you've visited these links before.

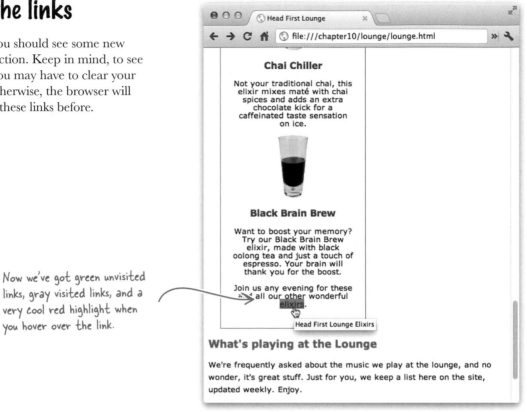

Now we've got green unvisited links, gray visited links, and a very cool red highlight when you hover over the link.

Sharpen your pencil

Your job is to give the "detailed directions" link in the lounge some style. Just like the elixirs link, we want all unvisited links to be aquamarine, and all visited links to be gray. However, we don't want the other links in the lounge to have any hover style...that's unique to the elixirs. So, how would you do it? Fill in the blanks to give the "detailed directions" link, and any other links you might add to the lounge later, this style. Check your answer in the back of the chapter and then make the changes in your lounge files.

a:link   {   color   : #007e7e; }
a:visited   {   color   : #333333; }

Isn't it about time we talk about the "cascade"?

Well, well, we're quite far into this book (457 pages to be exact) and we still haven't told you what the "Cascade" in *Cascading Style Sheets* is all about. Truth be told, you have to know a lot about CSS to fully understand the cascade. But guess what, you're almost there, so wait no more.

Here's just one last piece of information you need to understand the cascade. You already know about using multiple stylesheets to either better organize your styles or to support different types of devices. But there are actually some other stylesheets hanging around when your users visit your pages. Let's take a look:

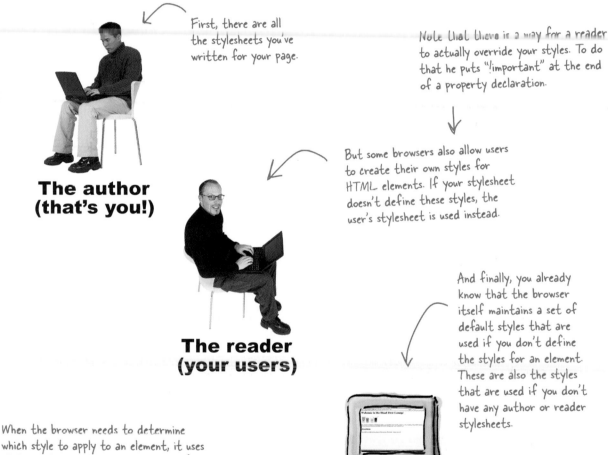

First, there are all the stylesheets you've written for your page.

The author (that's you!)

Note that there is a way for a reader to actually override your styles. To do that he puts "!important" at the end of a property declaration.

But some browsers also allow users to create their own styles for HTML elements. If your stylesheet doesn't define these styles, the user's stylesheet is used instead.

The reader (your users)

And finally, you already know that the browser itself maintains a set of default styles that are used if you don't define the styles for an element. These are also the styles that are used if you don't have any author or reader stylesheets.

When the browser needs to determine which style to apply to an element, it uses all these stylesheets. Priority is given first to the author's styles (that is, your styles), then to the reader's styles, and then finally to the browser's default styles.

The browser

So, to review, as the page authors, we can use multiple stylesheets with our HTML. And the user might also supply his own styles, and then the browser has its default styles, too. And on top of all that, we might have multiple selectors that apply to the same element. How do we figure out which styles an element gets?

That's actually another way of asking what cascade does. The cascade is the way the browser decides, given a bunch of styles in a bunch of stylesheets, which style is going to be used. To answer that question, we need to bring everything together—all the various stylesheets hanging around, the rules, and the individual property declarations in those rules.

In the next two pages, we're going to step through the nitty-gritty details of how all this works. The details involve a lot of sorting and various details of determining which rules are the most specific with respect to an element. But here's the payoff: after going through the next two pages, you'll be able to get to the bottom of any styles that don't seem to be applied in the way you expect, and further, you're going to understand more about the cascade than 99% of web page developers out there (we're not kidding).

The cascade

For this exercise, you need to "be the browser." Let's say you've got an <h1> element on a page and you want to know the font-size property for it. Here's how you do it:

Step one:

Gather all your stylesheets together.

For this step you need *all* the stylesheets: the stylesheets the web page author has written, any stylesheets that the reader has added to the mix, and the browser's default styles. (Remember, *you're* the browser now, so you have access to all this stuff!)

Step two:

Find all the declarations that match.

We're looking specifically for the font-size property, so look at all the declarations for font-size that have a selector that could possibly select the <h1> element. Go through all the stylesheets and pull out any rules that match <h1> and also have a font-size property.

Step three:

Now take all your matches, and sort them.

Now that you've got all the matching rules together, sort them in the order of author, reader, browser. In other words, if you wrote them as the author of the page, then they are more important than if the reader wrote them. And, in turn, the reader's styles are more important than the browser's default styles.

> Remember we mentioned that the reader could put !important on his CSS properties, and if he does that, those properties come first when you sort.

Step four:

Now sort all the declarations by how specific they are.

Remember, we talked about this a little, way back in Chapter 7. You can intuitively think about a rule being more specific if it more accurately selects an element; for instance, the descendant selector "blockquote h1" is more specific than just the "h1" selector because it only selects <h1>s inside of <blockquote>s. But there is a little recipe you can follow to calculate exactly how specific a selector is, and we'll do that on the next page.

Step five:

Finally, sort any conflicting rules in the order they appear in their individual stylesheets.

Now you just need to take the list, and order any conflicting rules so that the ones appearing later (closer to the bottom) of their respective stylesheets are more important. That way, if you put a new rule in your stylesheet, it can override any rules before it.

That's it! The first rule in the sorted list is the winner, and its font-size property is the one to use. Now let's see how you determine how specific a selector is.

Welcome to the "What's my specificity?" game

To calculate the specificity, you start with a set of three numbers, like this:

0 0 0

And then we just tally up various things from the selector, like this:

Does the selector have any ids? One point each.

Does the selector have any classes or pseudo-classes? One point each.

Does the selector have any element names? One point for each.

0 0 0

For instance, the selector "h1" has one element in it, so you get:

Read this as the number one.

0 0 1

Both "h1" and "h1.blue" have one element, so they both get a 1 in the rightmost number column.

As another example, the selector "h1.blue" has one element and one class, so you'd get:

Read this as the number eleven.

0 1 1

"h1.blue" also has one class, so it gets a 1 in the middle number column.

Neither has ids in its selector, so they both get a 0 in the left number column

After you've tallied up all the ids, classes, and elements, the bigger the specificity number, the more specific the rule. So, since "h1.blue" has a specificity of 11, it is more specific than "h1", which has a specificity of 1.

Sharpen your pencil

Try your hand at calculating the specificity of these selectors using the rules above:

h1.greentea	0 1 1	ol li p	0 0 3	em	0 0 1
p img	0 0 2	.green	0 1 0	span.cd	0 1 1
a:link	0 1 1	#elixirs h1	1 0 1	#sidebar	1 0 0

Q: What makes a specificity number bigger than another?

A: Just read them like real numbers: 100 (one hundred) is bigger than 010 (ten) which is bigger than 001 (one), and so on.

Q: What about a rule like "h1, h2"; what is its specificity?

A: Think of that as two separate rules: an "h1" rule, which has a specificity of "001" and an "h2" rule that also has a specificity of "001".

Q: Can you say more about the !important thing?

A: The reader can override a style by putting an "!important" on the end of his property declarations like this:

```
h1 {
    font-size: 200% !important;
}
```

and this will override any author styles.

Q: I can't get the reader's stylesheet, so how can I ever figure out the way the cascade works?

A: You can't, but look at it this way: if the reader overrides your styles, then that is really beyond your control. So just make your pages look like you want them to using your styles. If the reader chooses to override them, then he'll get what he asks for (for better or for worse).

Putting it all together

Woo hoo! It's time for an example. Say you want to know the `color` property for this `<h1>` element:

```
<h1 class="blueberry">Blueberry Bliss Elixir</h1>
```

Let's take this through all the cascade steps:

Remember, you're the browser, because you're trying to figure out how to display this <h1> element.

Step one:

Gather all your stylesheets together.

```
h1 {
    color: black;
}
```

The browser

That's you (for now).

```
h1 {
    color: #efefef;
}

h1.blueberry {
    color: blue;
}
```

Usually, you're the author (the person writing the CSS). But right now, you're the browser.

The author

```
body h1 {
    color: #cccccc;
}
```

The reader

The person using the browser

Step two:

Find all the declarations that match.

Here are all the rules that could possibly match the <h1> element and that contain the color property.

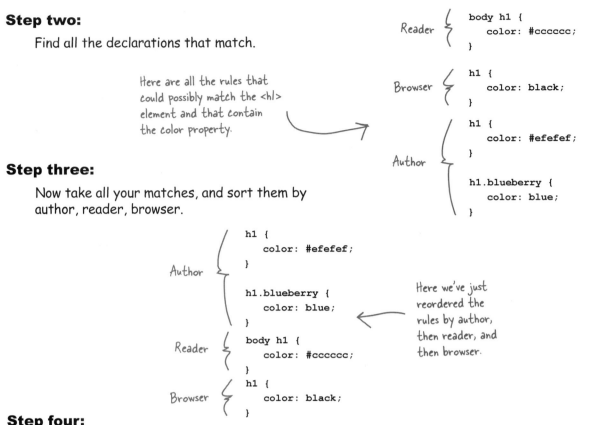

```
Reader    body h1 {
              color: #cccccc;
          }

Browser   h1 {
              color: black;
          }

Author    h1 {
              color: #efefef;
          }

          h1.blueberry {
              color: blue;
          }
```

Step three:

Now take all your matches, and sort them by author, reader, browser.

```
Author    h1 {
              color: #efefef;
          }

          h1.blueberry {
              color: blue;
          }

Reader    body h1 {
              color: #cccccc;
          }

Browser   h1 {
              color: black;
          }
```

Here we've just reordered the rules by author, then reader, and then browser.

Step four:

Now sort the declarations by how specific they are. To do that, we need to first calculate each specificity score, and then reorder the rules.

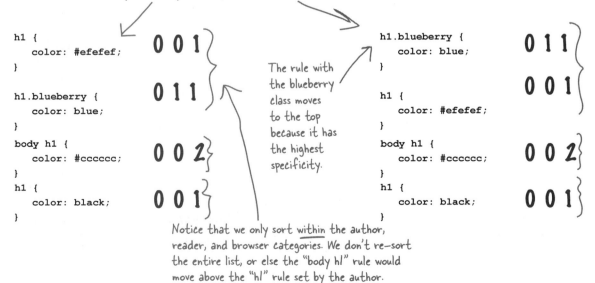

```
h1 {
    color: #efefef;
}

h1.blueberry {
    color: blue;
}

body h1 {
    color: #cccccc;
}

h1 {
    color: black;
}
```

0 0 1

0 1 1

0 0 2

0 0 1

The rule with the blueberry class moves to the top because it has the highest specificity.

```
h1.blueberry {
    color: blue;
}

h1 {
    color: #efefef;
}

body h1 {
    color: #cccccc;
}

h1 {
    color: black;
}
```

0 1 1

0 0 1

0 0 2

0 0 1

Notice that we only sort *within* the author, reader, and browser categories. We don't re-sort the entire list, or else the "body h1" rule would move above the "h1" rule set by the author.

Step five:

Finally, sort any conflicting rules in the order that they appear in their individual stylesheets.

We're okay here, because we don't have any conflicting rules at this point. The blueberry, with a score of 11, is the clear winner. If there had been two rules with a score of 011, then the rule appearing latest would be the winner.

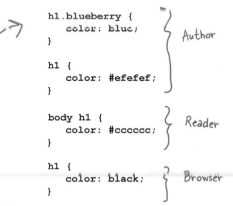

```
h1.blueberry {
    color: blue;
}

h1 {
    color: #efefef;
}
```
Author

```
body h1 {
    color: #cccccc;
}
```
Reader

```
h1 {
    color: black;
}
```
Browser

We have a winner...

After sweating through the first choice of elements, the sorting, more sorting, and being judged on specificity, the "h1.blueberry" rule has risen to the top. So the color property in the <h1> element will be blue.

there are no
Dumb Questions

Q: So, one more time: I get that the lower in the CSS file, the higher the precedence, but how does having multiple links to stylesheets in my HTML work?

A: It's always top to bottom, whether it is in the same CSS file or not. Just pretend that you inserted the CSS all together right into your file in the order the files are linked. That's the order that counts.

Q: So when you sort for specificity, you don't re-sort everything?

A: No. Think of each time you sort as refining what you've done before. So first you sort for author, reader, browser. Then, within each of those sortings, you sort for specificity. And then, for any elements that have the same specificity, you sort again based on the ordering in the stylesheets.

Q: Do readers really make their own stylesheets?

A: By and large, no. But there are cases where people with visual impairments do, and of course you've always got the crowd that just has to tinker with everything. But since each reader is controlling only how she sees things, it really shouldn't factor into your designs.

Q: How much of this do I really need to remember?

A: You're going to develop some intuition for how all these stylesheets fit together, and on a day-to-day basis that intuition will get you a long way. Every once in a while, though, you'll see a style popping up in your pages that just boggles your mind, and that's when you fall back on your training. You'll be able to work through the cascade, and before you know it, you'll know exactly what's happening in your page.

So, what happens if, after all this, I still don't have any rules with a property declaration for the property value I'm trying to figure out?

Ah, good question. We actually talked about this a little in Chapter 7. If you don't find a match for the property in any rules in the cascade, then you try to use inheritance. Remember that not all properties are inherited, like border properties, for instance. But for the properties that *are* inherited (like `color`, `font-family`, `line-height`, and so on), the browser looks at the ancestors of the element, starting with its parent, and tries to find a value for the property. If it does, there's your property value.

Got it. Hey, but what if the property isn't inherited or I can't find a value in the ancestor's rules? Then what?

Then the only thing left to do is fall back on the default values that are set in the browser's stylesheets, and all browsers should have default styles for every element.

Oh, and why is this called the "cascade" anyway?

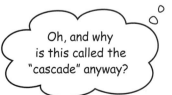

The name "cascade" was chosen because of the way that styles coming from multiple stylesheets can all "cascade" down into the page, with the most specific styling being applied to each element. (If that doesn't clear things right up for you about why it's called cascade, don't feel bad. It didn't make it any clearer for us, either. Just call it "CSS" and move on.)

STOP! Do this exercise before
going on to the next chapter!

SUPER BRAIN POWER

This is a special brain power—so special that we're going
to let you think about it between chapters. Here's what
you need to do:

1 Open the file "lounge.html" and locate the elixirs <div>.

2 Move the entire elixirs <div> section to the top of the
file so it's just below the paragraph that contains the
lounge logo.

3 Save and reload your page. What changed?

4 Open the file "lounge.css".

5 Locate the "#elixirs" rule.

6 Add this declaration at the bottom of the rule:

```
float: right;
```

7 Save your file, and reload the page in your browser.

What changed? What do you think this property does?

BULLET POINTS

- <div> elements are used to group related elements together into logical sections.

- Creating logical sections can help you identify the main content areas, header, and footer of your page.

- You can use <div> elements to group elements together that need a common style.

- Use nested <div> elements to add further structure to your files for clarity or styling. But don't add structure unless you really need it.

- Once you have grouped together sections of content with <div> elements, you can style the <div>s just like you would any other block element. For example, you can add a border around a group of elements using the border property on the <div> they are nested in.

- The width property sets the width of the content area of an element.

- The total width of an element is the width of the content area, plus the width of any padding, border, and margins you add.

- Once you set the width of an element, it no longer expands to fit the entire width of the browser window.

- Text-align is a property for block elements that aligns all inline content in the block element, to the center, left or right. It is inherited by any nested block elements.

- You can use descendant selectors to select elements nested within other elements. For instance, the descendant selector

      div h2 {...}
  selects all <h2>s nested in <div> elements (including children, grandchildren, etc.).

- You can use shortcuts for related properties. For instance, padding-top, padding-right, padding-bottom, and padding-left are all related to padding, and can be specified with one shortcut rule, padding.

- Padding, margin, border, background, and font properties can all be specified with shortcuts.

- The <span> inline element is similar to the <div> element: it is used to group together related inline elements and text.

- Just like with <div>, you can add <span> elements to classes (or give <span> elements unique ids) to style them.

- The <a> element is an example of an element with different states. The main <a> element states are unvisited, visited, and hover.

- You can style each of these states separately with pseudo-classes. The pseudo-classes used most often with the <a> element are :link, for unvisited links; :visited, for visited links; and :hover, for the hover state.

- Pseudo-classes can be used with other elements too, not just <a>.

- Additional pseudo-classes are the :hover, :active, :focus, :first-child, and last-child pseudo-classes, among others.

HTMLcross on Vacation

Since you've got a Super Brain Power to work on, we gave the HTMLcross a vacation in this chapter. Don't worry; he'll be back in the next one.

Sharpen your pencil
Solution

Here's a box that has all the widths labeled. Your job was to figure out the width of an entire box. Here's the solution.

$$30 + 2 + 5 + 200 + 10 + 2 + 20 = 269 \text{ pixels}$$

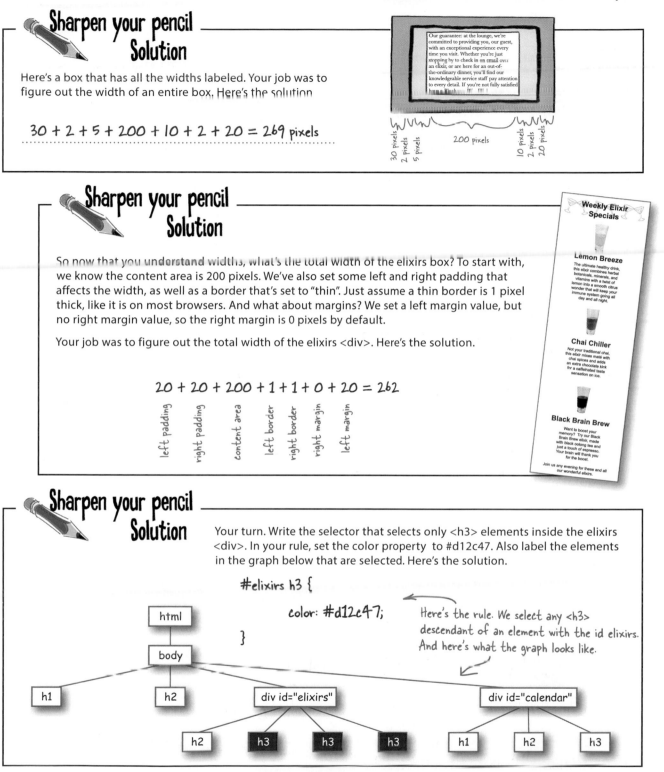

30 pixels · 2 pixels · 5 pixels · 200 pixels · 10 pixels · 2 pixels · 20 pixels

Sharpen your pencil
Solution

So now that you understand widths, what's the total width of the elixirs box? To start with, we know the content area is 200 pixels. We've also set some left and right padding that affects the width, as well as a border that's set to "thin". Just assume a thin border is 1 pixel thick, like it is on most browsers. And what about margins? We set a left margin value, but no right margin value, so the right margin is 0 pixels by default.

Your job was to figure out the total width of the elixirs <div>. Here's the solution.

$$20 + 20 + 200 + 1 + 1 + 0 + 20 = 262$$

left padding · right padding · content area · left border · right border · right margin · left margin

Sharpen your pencil
Solution

Your turn. Write the selector that selects only <h3> elements inside the elixirs <div>. In your rule, set the color property to #d12c47. Also label the elements in the graph below that are selected. Here's the solution.

```
#elixirs h3 {

    color: #d12c47;

}
```

Here's the rule. We select any <h3> descendant of an element with the id elixirs. And here's what the graph looks like.

html → body → h1, h2, div id="elixirs", div id="calendar"

div id="elixirs" → h2, **h3**, **h3**, **h3**

div id="calendar" → h1, h2, h3

Exercise Solution

It's time to put all your new knowledge to work. You'll notice that at the bottom of the lounge, there's a small section with copyright information that acts as a footer for the page. Add a <div> to make this into its own logical section. After you've done that, style it with these properties:

```
font-size: 50%;
text-align: center;
line-height: normal;
margin-top: 30px;
```

Let's make the text really small. You know, FINE PRINT.

And let's center the text.

We're also setting the line-height to be "normal".

And let's add some top margin to give the footer a little breathing room.

Place <div> tags around the copyright information.

And give it an id named "footer".

```
<div id="footer">
  <p>
  &copy; 2012, Head First Lounge<br>
  All trademarks and registered trademarks appearing on
  this site are the property of their respective owners.
  </p>
</div>
```

An even better solution would be to change <p> to <small>, which is an element designed specifically for "small print." Try it!

And here's the CSS for the footer.

```
#footer {
    font-size: 50%;
    text-align: center;
    line-height: normal;
    margin-top: 30px;
}
```

Sharpen your pencil
Solution

Your job was to finish adding the <span> elements to the rest of the music recommendations and test your page. Here's the solution:

```html
<ul>
<li><span class="cd">Buddha Bar</span>,
    <span class="artist">Claude Challe</span></li>
<li><span class="cd">When It Falls</span>,
    <span class="artist">Zero 7</span></li>
<li><span class="cd">Earth 7</span>,
    <span class="artist">L.T.J. Bukem</span></li>
<li><span class="cd">Le Roi Est Mort, Vive Le Roi!</span>,
    <span class="artist">Enigma</span></li>
<li><span class="cd">Music for Airports</span>
    <span class="artist">Brian Eno</span></li>
</ul>
```

What's playing at the Lounge

We're frequently asked about the music we play at the lounge, and no wonder, it's great stuff. Just for you, we keep a list here on the site, updated weekly. Enjoy.

- *Buddha Bar*, **Claude Challe**
- *When It Falls*, **Zero 7**
- *Earth 7*, **L.T.J. Bukem**
- *Le Roi Est Mort, Vive Le Roi!*, **Enigma**
- *Music for Airports*, **Brian Eno**

exercise solutions

Sharpen your pencil
Solution

Your job is to give the "detailed directions" link in the lounge some style. Just like the elixirs link, we want all unvisited links to be aquamarine, and all visited links to be gray. However, we don't want the other links in the lounge to have any hover style…that's unique to the elixirs. So, how would you do it? Fill in the blanks to give the "detailed directions" link, and any other links you might add to the lounge later, this style. Here's the solution.

| a:link | { | color | : #007e7e; } |
| a:visited | { | color | : #333333; } |

Sharpen your pencil
Solution

Try your hand at calculating the specificity of these selectors using the cascade rules. Here's the solution.

h1.greentea	0 1 1	ol li p	0 0 3	em	0 0 1
p img	0 0 2	.green	0 1 0	span.cd	0 1 1
a:link	0 1 1	#elixirs h1	1 0 1	#sidebar	1 0 0

11 layout and positioning

Arranging Elements

You can bet all my divs and spans are in the right place.

It's time to teach your HTML elements new tricks. We're not going to let those HTML elements just sit there anymore—it's about time they get up and help us create some pages with real *layouts*. How? Well, you've got a good feel for the <div> and <span> structural elements and you know all about how the box model works, right? So, now it's time to use all that knowledge to craft some real designs. No, we're not just talking about more background and font colors—we're talking about full-blown professional designs using multicolumn layouts. This is the chapter where everything you've learned comes together.

Did you do the Super Brain Power?

If you didn't do the **SUPER BRAIN POWER** at the end of the last chapter, then march right back there and do it. It's required.

Okay, now that we have that out of the way, at the end of the last chapter, we left you with a bit of a cliff-hanger. We asked you to move the elixirs `<div>` up under the logo, and then add one little property to the elixirs rule in your CSS, like this:

```
float: right;
```

And, wow, what a difference one property can make! All of a sudden, the page has gone from a fairly ordinary-looking web page to a great-looking web page with two columns. It's immediately more readable and pleasant to the eye.

So what's the magic? How did this seemingly innocent little property produce such big effects? And can we use this property to do even more interesting things with our pages? Well, of course, but first, you're going to need to learn how a browser lays out elements on a page. Once you know that, we can talk about all kinds of ways you can alter how it does that layout, and also how you can start to position your elements on the page.

Here's the good news: you already know about block elements and inline elements, and you even know about the box model. These are the real foundations of how the browser puts a page together. Now all you need to know is exactly how the browser takes all the elements in a page and decides where they go.

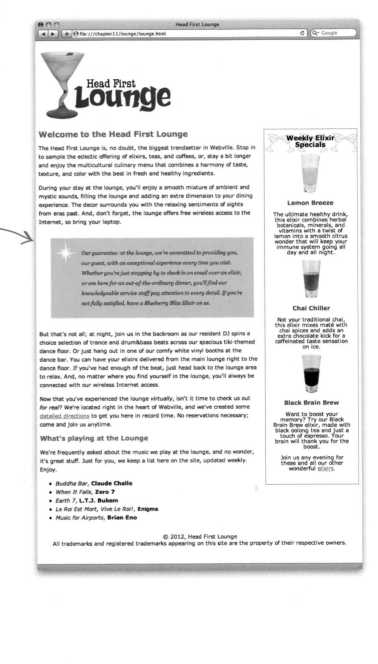

Use the Flow, Luke

The Flow is what gives a CSS master his power. It's an energy field created by all living things. It surrounds us and penetrates us. It binds the galaxy together... oh, sorry.

Flow is actually what the browser uses to lay out a page of HTML elements. The browser starts at the top of any HTML file and follows the flow of elements from top to bottom, displaying each element it encounters. And, just considering the block elements for a moment, it puts a linebreak between each one. So the first element in a document is displayed first, then a linebreak, followed by the second element, then a linebreak, and so on, from the top of your file to the bottom. That's flow.

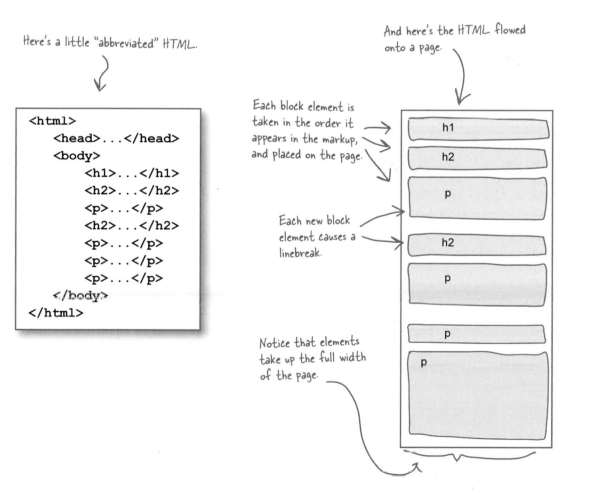

Here's a little "abbreviated" HTML.

```
<html>
    <head>...</head>
    <body>
        <h1>...</h1>
        <h2>...</h2>
        <p>...</p>
        <h2>...</h2>
        <p>...</p>
        <p>...</p>
        <p>...</p>
    </body>
</html>
```

And here's the HTML flowed onto a page.

Each block element is taken in the order it appears in the markup, and placed on the page.

Each new block element causes a linebreak.

Notice that elements take up the full width of the page.

Here's your page. Flow the block elements in "lounge.html" here.

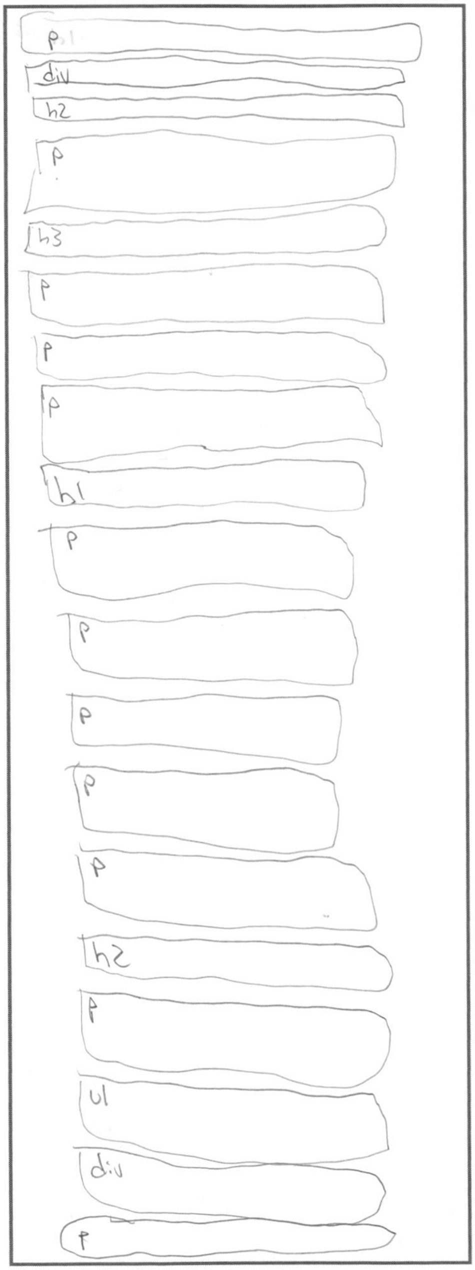

BE the Browser

Open your "lounge.html" file and locate all the block elements. Flow each one on to the page to the left. Just concentrate on the block elements nested directly inside the body element. You can also ignore the "float" property in your CSS because you don't know what it does yet. Check your answer before moving on.

p

div

h2

p

h3

p

p

p

h1

p

p

p

p

p

h2

p

ul

div

p

Here are all the block elements you'll need to complete the job.

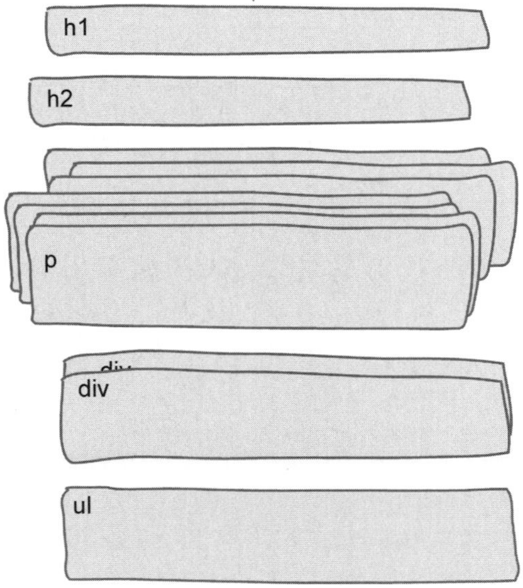

h1

h2

p

div

ul

What about inline elements?

So you know that block elements flow top to bottom, with a linebreak in between each element. Easy enough. What about the inline elements?

Inline elements are flowed next to each other, horizontally, from top left to bottom right. Here's how that works.

Here's another little snippet of HTML.

```
<p>
Join us <em>any evening</em> for
these and all our other wonderful
<a href="beverages/elixir.
html" title="Head First Lounge
Elixirs">elixirs</a>.
</p>
```

If we take the inline content of this <p> element and flow it onto the page, we start at the top left.

The inline elements are laid next to one another horizontally, as long as there is room on the right to place them.

p
| text | em | text | a |

Here, there's room to fit all the inline elements horizontally. Notice that text is a special case of an inline element. The browser breaks it into inline elements that are the right size to fit the space.

So what if we make the browser window a little thinner, or we reduce the size of the content area with the width property? Then there's less room to place the inline elements in. Let's see how this works.

Now the content has been flowed left to right until there's no more room, and then the content is placed on the next line. Notice the browser had to break the text up a little differently to make it fit nicely.

p
| text | em | text |
| text | a |

And if we make the content area even thinner, look what happens. The browser uses as many lines as necessary to flow the content into the space.

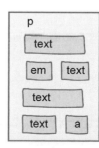

How it all works together

Now that you know how block and inline elements are flowed, let's put them together. We'll use a typical page with headings, paragraphs, and a few inline elements like spans, some emphasis elements, and even images. And we can't forget inline text.

We're starting with a browser window that's been resized to a fairly wide width.

Each block element is flowed top to bottom as you'd expect, with a linebreak in between each.

Here, we've resized the browser window, squeezing all the content into a smaller horizontal size.

Things flow the same way, although in some places, the inline elements take up more vertical lines to fit.

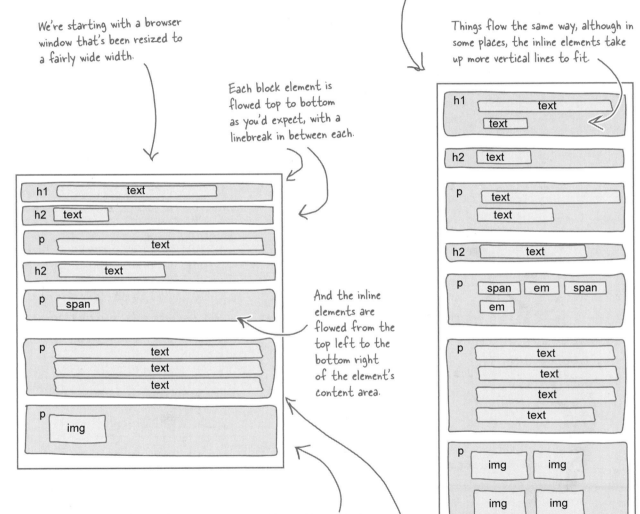

And the inline elements are flowed from the top left to the bottom right of the element's content area.

If the inline content of each block fits the width of the content area, then it's placed there; otherwise, more vertical room is made for the content and it's continued on the next line.

Now the block elements take up more vertical room because the inline content has to fit into a smaller horizontal space.

One more thing you should know about flow and boxes

Let's zoom in just a bit and look at one more aspect of how the browser lays out block and inline elements. It turns out that the browser treats margins differently depending on which type of element is being placed on the page.

When the browser is placing two inline elements next to each other...

When the browser has the task of placing two inline elements side by side, and those elements have margins, then the browser does what you might expect. It creates enough space between the elements to account for both margins. So, if the left element has a margin of 10 pixels and the right has a margin of 20 pixels, then there will be 30 pixels of space between the two elements.

margin   margin

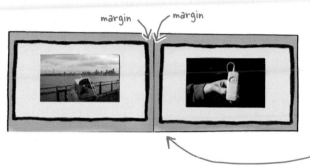

Here we've got two images side by side, and images are displayed as inline elements by default. So, the browser uses both of their margins to calculate the space that goes between them.

When the browser is placing two block elements on top of each other...

Here's where things get more interesting. When the browser places two block elements on top of each other, it collapses their shared margins together. The height of the collapsed margin is the height of the largest margin.

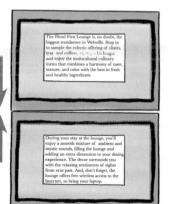

When the browser places two block elements on top of each other, it collapses their margins.

Their shared margin is the size of the larger of the two margins. Say the top element's bottom margin is 10 pixels, and the bottom element's top margin is 20 pixels. Then the collapsed margin will be 20 pixels.

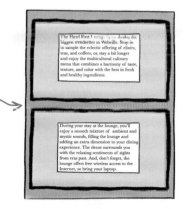

there are no
Dumb Questions

Q: So if I have a block element with a zero margin, and a block element below it with a top margin of 20, the margin between them would end up being 20?

A: Right. If one of the margins is bigger, then the margin becomes the larger of the two, even if one margin is zero. But if the margins are the same, say, 10 pixels, then they just get collapsed together to 10 pixels total.

Q: Can inline elements really have margins?

A: They sure can, although you'll find that you often don't set the margins of inline elements. The one exception is images. It is very common to not only set margins but also borders and padding on images. And while we aren't going to be setting any inline element margins in this chapter, we will be setting the border on one a little later.

Q: What if I have one element nested inside another and they both have margins? Can they collapse?

A: Yes, that can happen. Here's how to figure out when they will: whenever you have two vertical margins touching, they will collapse, even if one element is nested inside the other. Notice that if the outer element has a border, the margins will never touch, so they won't collapse. But if you remove the border, they will. This is sometimes puzzling when you first see it happen, so put it in the back of your mind for when it occurs.

Q: So how exactly does text work as an inline element since its content is not an element?

A: Even if text is content, the browser needs to flow it onto the page, right? So the browser figures out how much text fits on a given line, and then treats that line of text as if it were an inline element. The browser even creates a little box around it. As you've seen, if you resize the page, then all those blocks may change as the text is refit within the content area.

> We've been through seven pages of "flow." When are you going to explain that one little property we put into our CSS file? You know, the
>
> **float: right;**

To understand float, you have to understand flow.

It might be one little property, but the way it works is closely tied to how the browser flows elements and content onto the page. But hey, you know that now, so we can explain float.

Here's the short answer: the float property first takes an element and *floats* it as far left or right as it can (based on the value of float). It then flows all the content below it around the element. Of course there are a few more details, so let's take a look…

How to float an element

Let's step through an example of how you get an element to float, and then we'll look at what it does to the flow of the page when you do.

First, give it an identity

Let's take one of these paragraphs and give it an id. We'd like to call it the "amazing floating paragraph," but we'll just call it "amazing" for short.

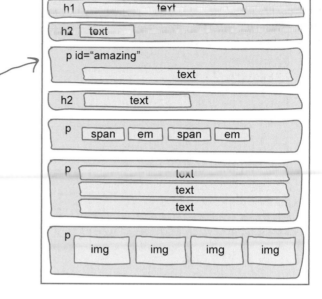

Now give it a width

A requirement for any floating element is that it have a width. We'll make this paragraph 200 pixels wide. Here's the rule:

```
#amazing {
    width: 200px;
}
```

Now the paragraph is 200 pixels wide, and the inline content contained in it has adjusted to that width. Keep in mind, the paragraph is a block element, so no elements are going to move up beside it because all block elements have linebreaks before and after them.

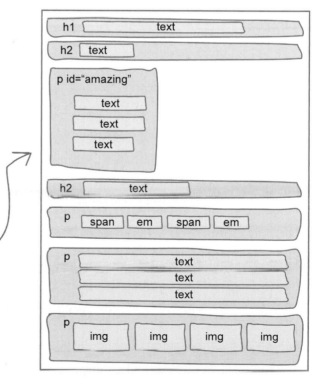

Now float it

Now let's add the `float` property. The `float` property can be set to either left or right. Let's stick with right:

```
#amazing {
    width: 200px;
    float: right;
}
```

Now that we've floated the "amazing" paragraph, let's step through how the browser flows it and everything else on the page.

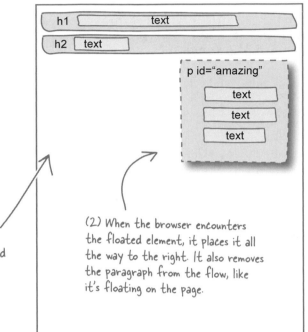

(1) First, the browser flows the elements on the page as usual, starting at the top of the file and moving toward the bottom.

(2) When the browser encounters the floated element, it places it all the way to the right. It also removes the paragraph from the flow, like it's floating on the page.

(3) Because the floated paragraph has been <u>removed from</u> the normal flow, the block elements are filled in, like the paragraph isn't even there.

(4) But when the <u>inline elements</u> are positioned, they respect the boundaries of the floated element. So they are flowed around it.

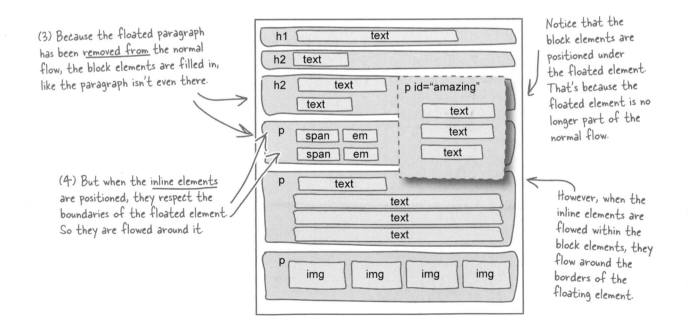

Notice that the block elements are positioned under the floated element. That's because the floated element is no longer part of the normal flow.

However, when the inline elements are flowed within the block elements, they flow around the borders of the floating element.

Behind the scenes at the lounge

Now you know all about flow and how floated elements are placed on the page. Let's look back at the lounge and see how this all fits together.

Remember, in addition to setting the elixirs <div> to float right, we also moved the elixirs <div> up just below the logo at the top of the page.

Moving the <div> allowed us to float it to the right and then have the entire page flow around it. If we had left the elixirs <div> below the music recommendations, then the elixirs would have been floated right after most of the page had been placed.

All these elements follow the elixirs in the HTML, so they are flowed around it.

Remember that the elixirs <div> is floating on top of the page. All the other elements are underneath it, but the inline content respects the elixirs' boundaries when they are flowing into the page.

Also notice that the text wraps around the bottom of the elixirs, because the text is contained in a block element that is the width of the page. If yours doesn't wrap, try narrowing your browser window until the text wraps underneath the elixirs.

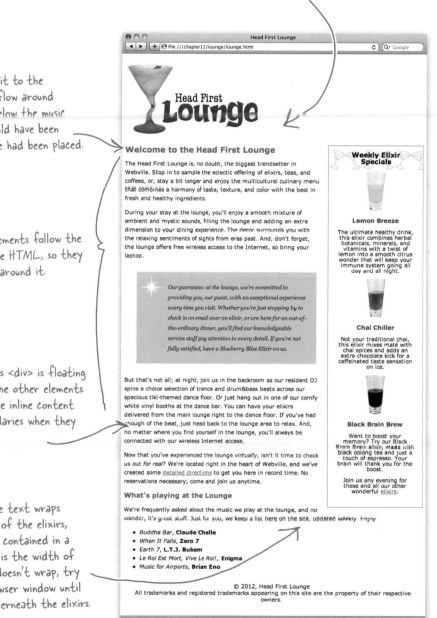

Exercise

Move the elixirs <div> back to its original place below the main content, then save and reload the page. Where does the element float now? Check your answer in the back and then put your elixirs <div> back underneath the header.

Nice stuff. Do you think I'm going to watch these fantastic lounge designs and not want you to improve Starbuzz? You've got a blank check...take Starbuzz to the next level.

It looks like we've got a new assignment. Starbuzz really could use some improvement. Sure, you've done a great job of creating the typical top-to-bottom page, but now that you know flow, you should be able to give Starbuzz Coffee a slick new look that is more user-friendly than the last design.

We do have a little secret though...we've been working on this one a bit already. We've created an updated version of the site. Your job is going to be to provide all the layout. Don't worry, we'll bring you up to speed on everything we've done so far—it's nothing you haven't seen before.

The new Starbuzz

Let's take a quick look at what we've got so far, starting with the page as it looks now. Then we'll take a peek at the markup and the CSS that's styling it.

We've got a header now with a new spiffy Starbuzz logo and the company mission statement. This is actually just a GIF image.

We've got four sections: the header, a main content section, a section advertising something new called the "Bean Machine," and a footer.

Each section is a <div> that can be styled independently.

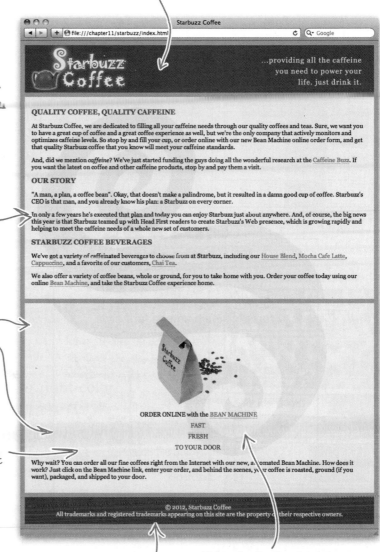

It looks like we've got one background color for the page as a whole, and then each <div> is using an image as a background.

Here's the "Bean Machine" area. This links to a new area of Starbuzz Coffee where you can order your coffee beans online. This link doesn't work just yet because you're going to build the Bean Machine in an upcoming chapter.

Here's the footer. It doesn't use a background image, just a background color.

Notice that we've styled the links in an interesting way, with dotted underlines...

A look at the markup

Now let's take a look at the new Starbuzz markup. We've taken each of the logical sections and placed it into a `<div>`, each with its own `id`. Beyond the `<div>`s and `<span>`s, there's really nothing here that you hadn't already seen by about Chapter 5. So, take a quick look and get familiar with the structure, and then turn the page to check out the CSS style.

Here's all the usual HTML administravia...

...followed by a <div> for the header and a <div> for the main content area.

```
<!DOCTYPE html>
<html>
<head>
    <meta charset="utf-8">
    <title>Starbuzz Coffee</title>
    <link type="text/css" rel="stylesheet" href="starbuzz.css">
</head>
<body>
```

```
<div id="header">
    <img src="images/header.gif" alt="Starbuzz Coffee header image">
</div>
```

```
<div id="main">
    <h1>QUALITY COFFEE, QUALITY CAFFEINE</h1>
    <p>
        At Starbuzz Coffee, we are dedicated to filling all your caffeine needs through our
        quality coffees and teas. Sure, we want you to have a great cup of coffee and a great
        coffee experience as well, but we're the only company that actively monitors and
        optimizes caffeine levels. So stop by and fill your cup, or order online with our new Bean
        Machine online order form, and get that quality Starbuzz coffee that you know will meet
        your caffeine standards.
    </p>
    <p>
        And, did we mention <em>caffeine</em>? We've just started funding the guys doing all
        the wonderful research at the <a href="http://buzz.wickedlysmart.com"
        title="Read all about caffeine on the Buzz">Caffeine Buzz</a>.
        If you want the latest on coffee and other caffeine products,
        stop by and pay them a visit.
    </p>
    <h1>OUR STORY</h1>
    <p>
        "A man, a plan, a coffee bean". Okay, that doesn't make a palindrome, but it resulted
        in a damn good cup of coffee. Starbuzz's CEO is that man, and you already know his
        plan: a Starbuzz on every corner.
    </p>
    <p>
        In only a few years he's executed that plan and today
        you can enjoy Starbuzz just about anywhere. And, of course, the big news this year
        is that Starbuzz teamed up with Head First readers to create Starbuzz's Web presence,
        which is growing rapidly and helping to meet the caffeine needs of a whole new set of
        customers.
    </p>
    <h1>STARBUZZ COFFEE BEVERAGES</h1>
    <p>
        We've got a variety of caffeinated beverages to choose
        from at Starbuzz, including our
```

This is more of the main content
area continued over here.

```
                <a href="beverages.html#house" title="House Blend">House Blend</a>,
                <a href="beverages.html#mocha" title="Mocha Cafe Latte">Mocha Cafe Latte</a>,
                <a href="beverages.html#cappuccino" title="Cappuccino">Cappuccino</a>,
                and a favorite of our customers,
                <a href="beverages.html#chai" title="Chai Tea">Chai Tea</a>.
        </p>
        <p>
                We also offer a variety of coffee beans, whole or ground, for you to
                take home with you. Order your coffee today using our online
                <a href="form.html" title="The Bean Machine">Bean Machine</a>,
                 and take the Starbuzz Coffee experience home.
        </p>

</div>
```

```
<div id="sidebar">
        <p class="beanheading">
                <img src="images/bag.gif" alt="Bean Machine bag">
                <br>
                ORDER ONLINE
                with the
                <a href="form.html">BEAN MACHINE</a>
                <br>
                <br>
                <span class="slogan">
                        FAST <br>
                        FRESH <br>
                        TO YOUR DOOR <br>
                </span>
        </p>
        <p>
                Why wait? You can order all our fine coffees right from the Internet with our new,
                automated Bean Machine. How does it work? Just click on the Bean Machine link,
                enter your order, and behind the scenes, your coffee is roasted, ground
                (if you want), packaged, and shipped to your door.
        </p>
</div>
```

Here's the <div> for the Bean Machine.
We've given it an id of "sidebar". Hmm,
wonder what that could mean?

```
<div id="footer">
        &copy; 2012, Starbuzz Coffee
        <br>
        All trademarks and registered trademarks appearing on
        this site are the property of their respective owners.
</div>
```

```
</body>
</html>
```

And finally, we have the <div> that
makes up the footer of the page.

And a look at the style

Let's get a good look at the CSS that styles the new Starbuzz page. Step through
the CSS rules carefully. While the new Starbuzz page may look a little advanced,
you'll see it's all just simple CSS that you already know.

```
body {
        background-color: #b5a789;
        font-family:      Georgia, "Times New Roman", Times, serif;
        font-size:        small;
        margin:           0px;
}

#header {
        background-color: #675c47;
        margin:           10px;
        height:           108px;
}

#main {
        background:       #efe5d0 url(images/background.gif) top left;
        font-size:        105%;
        padding:          15px;
        margin:           0px 10px 10px 10px;
}

#sidebar {
        background:       #efe5d0 url(images/background.gif) bottom right;
        font-size:        105%;
        padding:          15px;
        margin:           0px 10px 10px 10px;
}

#footer {
        background-color: #675c47;
        color:            #efe5d0;
        text-align:       center;
        padding:          15px;
        margin:           10px;
        font-size:        90%;
}

h1 {
        font-size:        120%;
        color:            #954b4b;
}

.slogan { color:          #954b4b;}

.beanheading {
        text-align:       center;
        line-height:      1.8em;
}
```

First, we just set up
some basics in the body:
a background color and
fonts, and we also set the
margin of the body to 0.
This makes sure there's no
extra room around the
edges of the page.

Next, we have a rule for
each logical section. In
each, we're tweaking the
font size, adding padding
and margins and also—in
the case of main and
the sidebar—specifying a
background image.

Next, we set up the fonts and
colors on the headings.

And then some colors on the class
called slogan, which is used in the
sidebar <div>, and likewise with
the beanheading class, which is
used there as well.

```
a:link {
    color:              #b76666;
    text-decoration:    none;
    border-bottom:      thin dotted #b76666;
}
a:visited {
    color:              #675c47;
    text-decoration:    none;
    border-bottom:      thin dotted #675c47;
}
```

For the last two rules in the Starbuzz CSS, we use the a:link and a:visited pseudo-classes to style the links.

We're removing the default underline that links get by setting text-decoration to none. Instead...

...we're getting a nice dotted underline effect on the links by using a dotted bottom border instead of an underline. This is a great example of using the border property on an inline element.

We're setting the border-bottom only for this <a> element.

Let's take Starbuzz to the next level

Here's the goal: to turn Starbuzz Coffee into the site on the right. To do that, we need to move the Bean Machine sidebar over to the right so we've got a nice two-column page. Well, you've done this once already with the lounge, right? So, based on that, here's what you need to do:

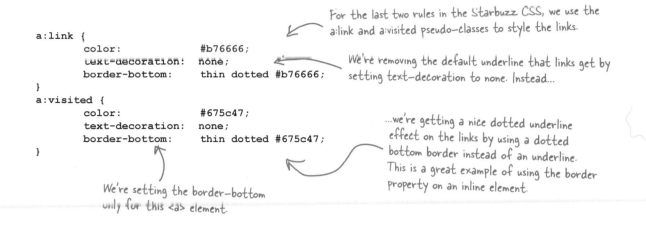

 Give the element you're going to float a unique name using an `id`. That's already done.

 Make sure the element's HTML is just below the element you want it to float under—in this case, the Starbuzz header.

❸ Set a width on the element.

❹ Float the element to the left or the right. It looks like you want to float it right.

Let's get started. In a few simple steps, we should have the Starbuzz CEO sending a few Chai Teas over on the house.

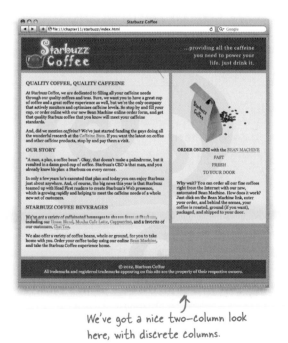

We've got a nice two-column look here, with discrete columns.

Move the sidebar just below the header

It's a fact of life that when you float an element, you need to move the HTML for the element directly below the element that you want it to follow. In this case, the sidebar needs to come under the header. So, go ahead and locate the sidebar `<div>` in your editor and move the entire `<div>` to just below the header `<div>`. You'll find the HTML in the file "index.html" in the "chapter11/starbuzz" folder. After you've done that and saved, reload the page.

Now the sidebar should be on top of the main content area.

Set the width of the sidebar and float it

Let's set the width of the sidebar to 280 pixels. And to float the sidebar, add a float property to "chapter11/starbuzz.css", like this:

We're using an id selector to select the element with the id "sidebar", which we know is the `<div>` for the sidebar.

```
#sidebar {
        background:  #efe5d0 url(images/background.gif) bottom right;
        font-size:   105%;
        padding:     15px;
        margin:      0px 10px 10px 10px;
        width:       280px;
        float:       right;
}
```

We're setting the width of the content area to 280 pixels.

And then we're floating the sidebar to the right. Remember, this moves the sidebar as far right as possible below the header, and it also removes the sidebar from the normal flow. Everything else below the sidebar in the HTML is going to move up and wrap around it.

I have an idea. In the future, why don't we float the main content to the left, rather than the sidebar to the right? Since the main content is already at the top, we wouldn't have to move things around, and we get the same effect.

That's actually a great idea, but there are a couple of issues.

On paper, this looks like a great idea. What we do is set a width on the main content `<div>` and float it to the left, and then let the rest of the page flow around it. That way, we get to keep the ordering of the page and we also get two columns.

The only problem is, this doesn't result in a very nice page. Here's why: remember, you have to set a width on the element that you are going to float, and if you set a width on the content area, then its width is going to remain fixed while the rest of the page resizes along with the width of the browser. Typically, sidebars are designed to be narrower than the main content area, and often look terrible when they expand. So, in most designs, you want the main content area to expand, not the sidebar.

But we are going to look at a way to use this idea that works great. So hang on to this idea. We'll also talk a little more about why you'd even care what order your sections are in.

Test driving Starbuzz

Make sure you add the new sidebar properties to the "starbuzz.css" file in the "chapter11/starbuzz" folder, and then reload the Starbuzz page. Let's see what we've got…

Hmm, this looks pretty good, but if you flip back three pages, you'll see we're not quite where we want to be.

The main content and the sidebar are on the left and the right, but they don't really look like two columns yet.

Look at how the background images of the two sections just run together. There's no separation between the columns.

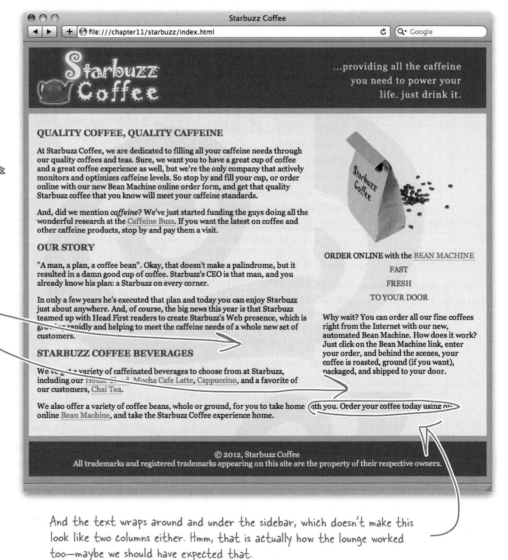

And the text wraps around and under the sidebar, which doesn't make this look like two columns either. Hmm, that is actually how the lounge worked too—maybe we should have expected that.

Fixing the two-column problem

At this point, you might be realizing that page layout is a bit of an art—we've got a set of techniques for laying out block elements, but none of them is perfect. So, what we're going to do is solve our problem using a common technique that is widely used. It's not perfect, as you'll see, but in most cases it gives you good results. And after this, you're going to see a few other ways to approach the same two-column problem, each with its own advantages. What's important here is that you understand the techniques and why they work, so you can apply them to your own problems and even adapt them where necessary.

The first thing to remember is that the sidebar is floating on the page. The main content area extends all the way under it.

So, what if we give the main content area a right margin that is at least as big as the sidebar? Then its content will extend almost to the sidebar, but not all the way.

Then we'll have separation between the two, and since margins are transparent and don't show the background image, the background color of the page itself should show through. And that's what we're looking for (flip back a few pages and you'll see).

Let's make the margin as wide as the sidebar.

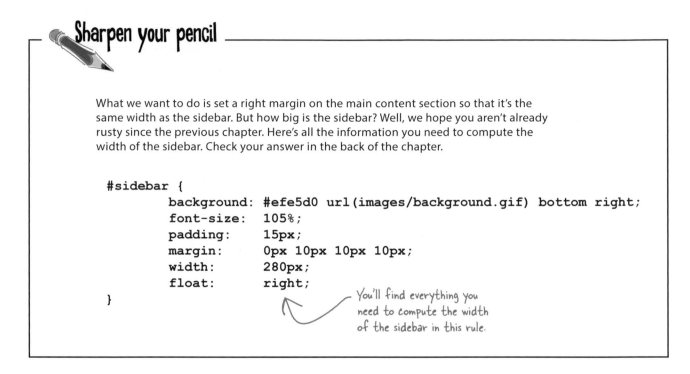

Sharpen your pencil

What we want to do is set a right margin on the main content section so that it's the same width as the sidebar. But how big is the sidebar? Well, we hope you aren't already rusty since the previous chapter. Here's all the information you need to compute the width of the sidebar. Check your answer in the back of the chapter.

```
#sidebar {
        background:  #efe5d0 url(images/background.gif) bottom right;
        font-size:   105%;
        padding:     15px;
        margin:      0px 10px 10px 10px;
        width:       280px;
        float:       right;
}
```

You'll find everything you need to compute the width of the sidebar in this rule.

Setting the margin on the main section

The width of the sidebar is 330 pixels, and that includes 10 pixels of left margin on the sidebar, which will provide the separation we need between the two columns (what the publishing world calls a "gutter"). Add the 330-pixel right margin to the #main rule in your "starbuzz.css" file, like we've done below:

```
#main {
        background:  #efe5d0 url(images/background.gif) top left;
        font-size:   105%;
        padding:     15px;
        margin:      0px 330px 10px 10px;
}
```

We're changing the right margin to 330 pixels to match the size of the sidebar.

Test drive

As usual, save your "starbuzz.css" file and then reload "index.html". You should now see a nice gutter between the two columns. Let's think through how this is working one more time. The sidebar is floating right, so it's been moved as far to the right as possible, and the whole <div> has been removed from the normal flow and is floating on top of the page. Now the main content <div> is still taking up the width of the browser (because that's what block elements do), but we've given it a margin as wide as the sidebar to reduce the width of the content area. The result is a nice two-column look. You know the box of the main <div> still goes under the sidebar, but we won't tell anyone if you don't.

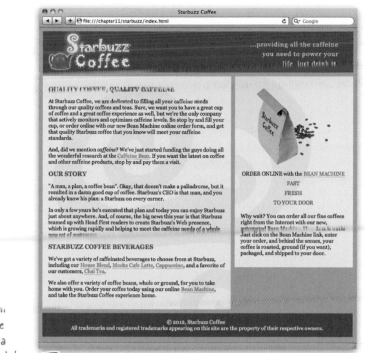

By expanding the margin of the main <div>, we're creating the illusion of a two-column layout, complete with a gutter in between.

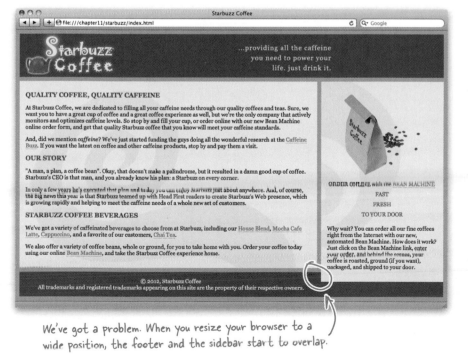

We've got a problem. When you resize your browser to a wide position, the footer and the sidebar start to overlap.

Uh oh, we have another problem

As you were test driving the page, you might have noticed a little problem. If you resize the browser to a wide position, the footer comes up underneath the sidebar. Why? Well, remember, the sidebar is not in the flow, so the footer pretty much ignores it, and when the content area is too short, the footer moves right up. We could use the same margin trick on the footer, but then the footer would only be under the content area, not the whole page. Geez. So, what now?

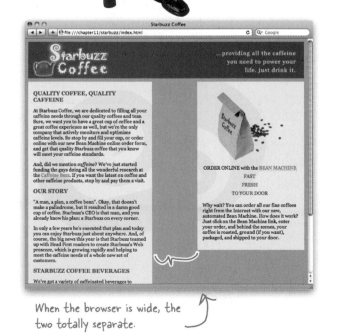

Wait a sec. Before you get way into solving that problem, I have to ask, why did we have to go to all this trouble of using a margin? Why don't we just set the width of the main area? Wouldn't that do the same thing?

That sounds good...until you try it.

The problem with setting a width on both the content area and the sidebar is that this doesn't allow the page to expand and contract correctly because both have fixed widths. Check the screen-shots below that show how it works (or rather, doesn't work).

But this is good. You're thinking in the right ways, and a little later in the chapter we're going to come back to this idea when we talk about "liquid versus frozen" layouts. There are ways to make your idea work if we lock a few other things down first.

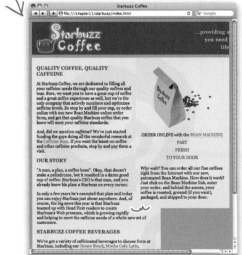

And when the browser window is made small, the two start to overlap.

When the browser is wide, the two totally separate.

Solving the overlap problem

To fix our overlapping problem, we're going to use another CSS property that you haven't seen yet; the `clear` property, and here's how it works...

Here's what we've got now. The "main" <div> is short enough that the footer <div> is coming right up and overlapping with the sidebar <div>.

This happens because the sidebar has been pulled out of the flow. So, the browser just lays out the main and footer <div>s like it normally would, ignoring the sidebar (although remember that when the browser flows inline elements, it will respect the borders of the sidebar and wrap inline elements around it).

You can use the CSS `clear` property on an element to request that as the element is being flowed onto the page, no floating content is allowed on the left, right, or both sides of the element. Let's give it a try...

```css
#footer {
        background-color:  #675c47;
        color:             #efe5d0;
        text-align:        center;
        padding:           15px;
        margin:            10px;
        font-size:         90%;
        clear:             right;
}
```

Here we're adding a property to the footer rule, which says that no floating content is allowed on the right of the footer.

Now when the browser places the elements on the page, it looks to see if there is a floating element to the right side of the footer, and if there is, it moves the footer down until there is nothing on its right. Now, no matter how wide you open the browser, the footer will always be below the sidebar.

Don't even think about putting a floating element to the right of me.

Now the footer is placed below the sidebar so that there are no floating elements to its right.

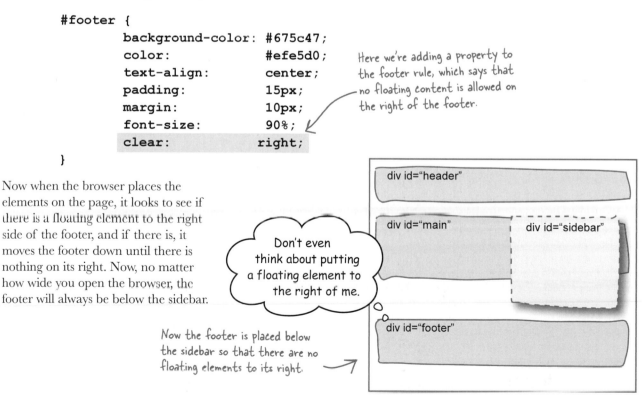

Test drive

Go ahead and add the clear property to your "starbuzz.css" file in the footer rule, and then reload "index.html". You'll see that when the screen is wide, the footer now stays below the sidebar. Not bad!

Now, at this point the page is looking pretty good, but there are still a few improvements we can make. For instance, we'd like each column to come down to meet the footer so they are even—notice, as it is now, there is a gap either between the main content and the footer (if the browser window is set wide), or the sidebar and the footer (if the browser is set to a normal width). But fixing this isn't that easy using float, so instead, we're going to move on and look at a few more ways to lay out these pages using other CSS techniques. As you're going to see, there are many ways to do things in CSS, and each method has its own strengths and weaknesses.

What's important to you is that you understand the techniques so that you can apply them when and where you need to.

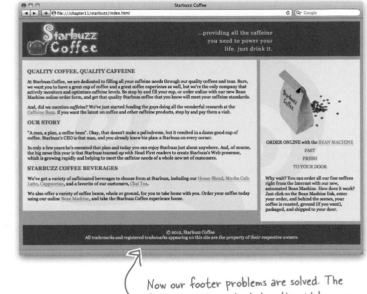

Now our footer problems are solved. The footer will always be below the sidebar, no matter how narrow or wide the browser.

---

there are no Dumb Questions

Q: Can I float to the center?

A: No, CSS only allows you to float an element to the left or right. But if you think about it, if you were to float to the center, then the inline content under the floated element would have to be flowed around both sides of your element, which would be quite tricky to get to work in a browser. But one of the new layout solutions that will be coming in future versions of CSS may provide a way to do it—we'll have to wait and see.

Q: Do margins collapse on floated elements?

A: No, they don't, and it's pretty easy to see why. Unlike block elements that are flowed on the page, floated elements are just, well, floating. In other words, the margins of floated elements aren't actually touching the margins of the elements in the normal flow, so they can't be collapsed.

But this raises a good point, and identifies a common error in layouts. If you have a main content area and a sidebar, it is common to set a top margin on each. Then, if you float the sidebar, it still has a margin, and that margin won't be collapsed with whatever is above it anymore. So you can easily end up having different margins on the sidebar and on the main content if you don't remember that floated elements don't collapse margins.

Q: Can I float an inline element?

A: Yes, you sure can. The best example —and a common one—is to float images. Give it a try—float an image left or right in a paragraph and you'll see your text flow around it. Don't forget to add padding to give the image a little room, and possibly a border. You can also float any other inline element you like, but it's not commonly done.

Q: Is it correct to think about floated elements as elements that are ignored by block elements, while inline elements know they are there?

A: Yes, that's a good way of thinking about it. Inline content nested inside a block element always flows around a floated element, observing the boundaries of the floated element, while block elements are flowed onto the page as normal. The exception is when you set the clear property on a block element, which causes a block element to move down until there are no floating elements next to it on the right, left, or both sides, depending on the value of clear.

> The only thing I don't like about this design is that when I view the web page on my smartphone, it puts the sidebar content above the main content, so I have to scroll through it.

Right. That happens because of the way we ordered the <div>s.

This is one of the disadvantages of the way we've designed this page—because we need the sidebar to be located just under the header and before the main content, anyone using a browser with limited capabilities (PDAs, small mobile devices, screen readers, and so on) will see the page in the order it is written, with the sidebar first. However, most people would rather see your main content before any kind of sidebar or navigation.

So, let's look at another way of doing this, which goes back to your idea of using float "left" on the main content.

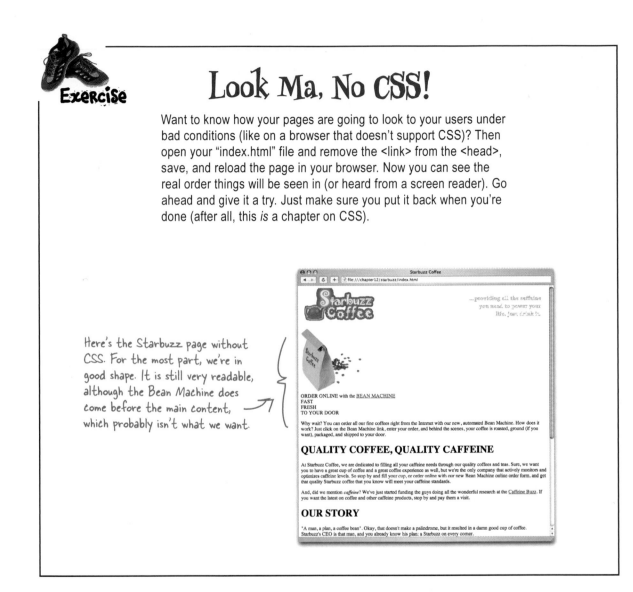

Look Ma, No CSS!

Want to know how your pages are going to look to your users under bad conditions (like on a browser that doesn't support CSS)? Then open your "index.html" file and remove the <link> from the <head>, save, and reload the page in your browser. Now you can see the real order things will be seen in (or heard from a screen reader). Go ahead and give it a try. Just make sure you put it back when you're done (after all, this *is* a chapter on CSS).

Here's the Starbuzz page without CSS. For the most part, we're in good shape. It is still very readable, although the Bean Machine does come before the main content, which probably isn't what we want.

Righty tighty, lefty loosey

Let's get the Starbuzz page switched over so that the main content is floating left. You're going to see that the mnemonic righty tighty, lefty loosey holds true in the CSS world too…well, for our sidebar, anyway. Here's how we convert the page over…just a few simple steps.

Step one: Start with the sidebar

We're basically swapping the roles of the sidebar and the main content area. The content area is going to have a fixed width and float, while the sidebar is going to wrap around the content. We're also going to use the same margin technique to keep the two visually separate. But before we start changing CSS, go to your "index.html" file and move the "sidebar" `<div>` down below the "main" `<div>`. After you've done that, here are the changes you need to make to the sidebar CSS rule:

```
#sidebar {
        background:    #efe5d0 url(images/background.gif) bottom right;
        font-size:     105%;
        padding:       15px;
        margin:        0px 10px 10px 470px;
        width:         280px;
        float:         right;
}
```

Because the sidebar is now going to flow under the main content, we need to move the large margin to the sidebar. The total width of the main content area is 470 pixels. (Go ahead and compute that yourself in all that free time you have. Compute it in the same way as you did for the sidebar. You should know that we're going to set the width of the main content area to 420 pixels.)

We're setting a fixed width on the main content `<div>`, so delete the sidebar width property along with the float.

Step two: Take care of the main content

Now we need to float the main `<div>`. Here's how to do it:

```
#main {
        background: #efe5d0 url(images/background.gif) top left;
        font-size:     105%;
        padding:       15px;
        margin:        0px 10px 10px 10px;
        width:         420px;
        float:         left;
}
```

We're changing the right margin from 330 pixels back to 10 pixels.

We need to set an explicit width because we're going to float this element. Let's use 420 pixels.

We're going to float the main `<div>` to the left.

Step three: Take care of the footer

Now we just need to adjust the footer to clear everything to the left, rather than the right.

```
#footer {
        background-color: #675c47;
        color:            #efe5d0;
        text-align:       center;
        padding:          15px;
        margin:           10px;
        font-size:        90%;
        clear:            left;
}
```

Change the clear property to have a value of left, rather than right. That way, the footer will stay clear of the main content area.

A quick test drive

We've already said there might be a few problems with this method of floating the content to the left. Do a quick test drive before you move on just to see how this is all working. Go ahead and make the changes to your "starbuzz.css" file and then reload "index.html" in your browser. Get a good feel for how the page performs when it is resized to narrow, normal, and wide.

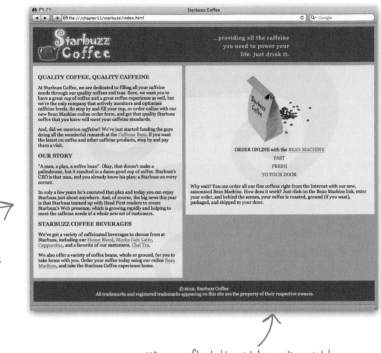

Actually, this looks pretty good, and we have the <div>s in the right order now. But it's not great that the sidebar expands; it looks a lot better fixed. Sidebars are often used for navigation, and they don't look very good when expanded.

When we float the sidebar <div> right, then the design stays nice and tight, allowing the content to expand, but if we float the main content to the left, the design feels too loose, allowing the sidebar to expand.

BRAIN POWER

Design-wise, the first design worked better, while information-wise, the second works better (because of the placement of the <div>s). Is there a way we can have the best of both worlds: have the sidebar at a fixed width, but the main <div> still first in the HTML? What design tradeoffs could we make to get there?

Liquid and frozen designs

All the designs we've been playing with so far are called *liquid layouts* because they expand to fill whatever width we resize the browser to. These layouts are useful because, by expanding, they fill the space available and allow users to make good use of their screen space. Sometimes, however, it is more important to have your layout locked down so that when a user resizes the screen, your design still looks as it should. These are called *frozen layouts*. Frozen layouts lock the elements down, frozen to the page, so they can't move at all, and so we avoid a lot of issues that are caused by the window expanding. Let's give a frozen layout a try.

Refreshing Frozen CSS Designs

Going from your current page to a frozen page only requires one addition to your HTML, and one new rule in your CSS.

HTML changes

In your HTML you're going to add a new `<div>` element with the id "allcontent". Like its name suggests, this `<div>` is going to go around all the content in your page. So place the opening `<div>` tag before the header `<div>` and the closing tag below the footer `<div>`.

```
<body>
    <div id="allcontent">
        <div id="header">
         ...rest of the HTML goes here...
        </div>
    </div>
</body>
```

Add a new <div> with the id of "allcontent" around all the other elements in the <body>.

This <div> closes the footer <div>.

CSS changes

Now we're going to use this `<div>` to constrain the size of all the elements and content in the "allcontent" `<div>` to a fixed width of 800 pixels. Here's the CSS rule to do that:

We're going to set the width of "allcontent" to 800 pixels. This will have the effect of constraining everything in it to fit within 800 pixels.

```
#allcontent {
    width:              800px;
    padding-top:        5px;
    padding-bottom:     5px;
    background-color:   #675c47;
}
```

While we're at it, since this is the first time we're styling this <div>, let's add some padding and give it its own background color. You'll see this helps to tie the whole page together.

The outer "allcontent" <div> is always 800 pixels, even when the browser is resized, so we've effectively frozen the <div> to the page, along with everything inside it.

A frozen test drive

Go ahead and add this rule to the bottom of "starbuzz.css", and then reload "index.html". Now you can see why we call it a frozen layout. It doesn't move when the browser is resized.

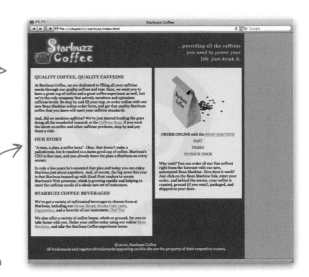

Now the "allcontent" <div> is 800 pixels in width, no matter how you resize the browser. And, because all the other <div>s are inside "allcontent", they will fit into the 800-pixel space as well. So, the page is basically frozen to 800 pixels.

This certainly solves the problem of the sidebar expanding, and it looks pretty nice. It is a little strange when the browser is very wide, though, because of all the empty space on the right side.

But we're not done yet; we've got a little room for improvement.

What's the state between liquid and frozen? Jello, of course!

The frozen layout has some benefits, but it also just plain looks bad when you widen the browser. But we've got a fix, and it's a common design you'll see on the Web. This design is between frozen and liquid, and it has a name to match: *Jello*. Jello layouts lock down the width of the content area in the page, but center it in the browser. It's actually easier to change the layout to a jello layout and let you play with it than to explain how it behaves, so let's just do it:

```
#allcontent {
        width: 800px;
        padding-top:    5px;
        padding-bottom: 5px;
        background-color: #675c47;
        margin-left:   auto;
        margin-right:  auto;
}
```

Rather than having fixed left and right margins on the "allcontent" <div>, we're setting the margins to "auto".

If you remember, when we talked about giving a content area a width of "auto", the browser expanded the content area as much as it needed to. With "auto" margins, the browser figures out what the correct margins are, but also makes sure the left and right margins are the same, so that the content is centered.

Test driving with a tank of jello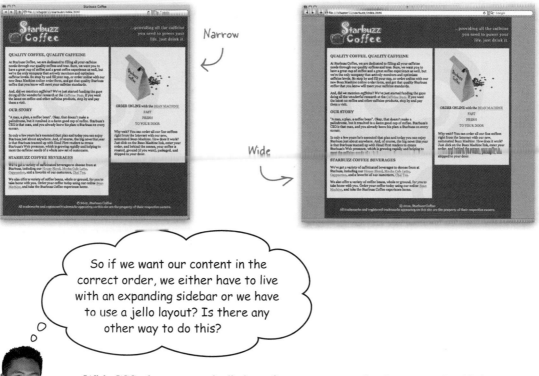

Add the two margin properties to your "starbuzz.css" file, and then reload the page. Now play with the size of the browser. Pretty nice, huh?

Narrow

Wide

> So if we want our content in the correct order, we either have to live with an expanding sidebar or we have to use a jello layout? Is there any other way to do this?

With CSS, there are typically lots of ways to approach a layout, each with its own strengths and weaknesses. Actually, we're just about to look at another common technique for creating a two-column layout that keeps the content in the correct order, and avoids some of the problems of the liquid layouts. But as you'll see, there are some tradeoffs.

With this new technique, we're not going to float elements at all. Instead, we're going to use a feature of CSS that allows you to precisely *position* elements on the page. It's called *absolute positioning*. You can also use absolute positioning for some nice effects beyond just multicolumn layouts, and we'll look at an example of that, too.

To do all this, we're going to step back to the original HTML and CSS we started with in the beginning of this chapter. You can find a fresh copy of these files in the "chapter11/absolute" folder. Be sure and take another look at these files so you remember what they originally looked like. Recall that we've got a bunch of `<div>`s: one for the header, one for main, one for the footer, and also a sidebar. Also remember that in the original HTML, the sidebar `<div>` is below the main content area, where we'd optimally like to have it.

How absolute positioning works

Let's start by getting an idea of what absolute positioning does, and how it works. Here's a little CSS to position the sidebar <div> with absolute positioning. Don't type this in just yet; right now we just want you to get a feel for how this works:

The first thing we do is use the position property to specify that the element will be positioned absolutely.

```
#sidebar {
    position: absolute;
    top:    100px;
    right: 200px;
    width: 280px;
}
```

Next we set top and right properties.

And we also give the <div> a width.

What the CSS does

Now let's look at what this CSS does. When an element is absolutely positioned, the first thing the browser does is remove it completely from the flow. The browser then places the element in the position indicated by the `top` and `right` properties (you can use `bottom` and `left` as well). In this case, the sidebar is going to be 100 pixels from the top of the page, and 200 pixels from the right side of the page. We're also setting a width on the <div>, just like we did when it was floated.

The sidebar is positioned 200 pixels from the right of the page.

Because sidebar is now absolutely positioned, it is removed from the flow and positioned according to any top, left, right, or bottom properties that are specified.

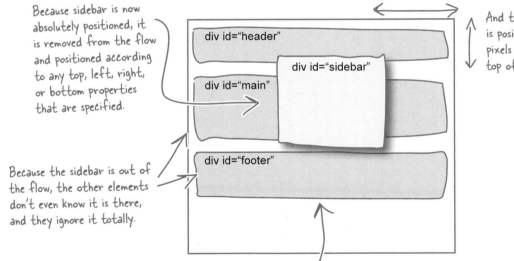

And the sidebar is positioned 100 pixels from the top of the page.

Because the sidebar is out of the flow, the other elements don't even know it is there, and they ignore it totally.

Elements that are in the flow don't even wrap their inline content around an absolutely positioned element. They are totally oblivious to it being on the page.

Another example of absolute positioning

Let's look at another example. Say we have another `<div>` with the id "annoyingad". We could position it like this:

```
#annoyingad {
    position: absolute;
    top:    150px;
    left:   100px;
    width:  400px;
}
```

The annoying ad is being positioned 100 pixels from the left, and 150 pixels from the top. It's also a bit wider than the sidebar, at 400 pixels.

Just like with the sidebar, we've placed the "annoying ad" `<div>` at a precise position on the page. Any elements underneath that are in the normal flow of the page don't have a clue about the absolutely positioned elements layered overhead. This is a little different from floating an element, because elements that were in the flow adjusted their inline content to respect the boundaries of the floated element. But absolutely positioned elements have no effect whatsoever on the other elements.

Now we have a second `<div>`, positioned absolutely, 100 pixels from the left and 150 pixels from the top.

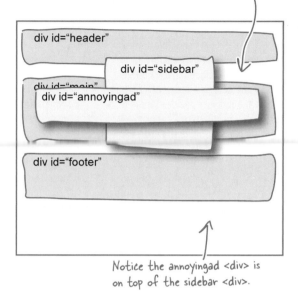

Notice the annoyingad `<div>` is on top of the sidebar `<div>`.

Who's on top?

Another interesting thing about absolutely positioned elements is that you can layer them on top of each other. But if you've got a few absolutely positioned elements at the same position in a page, how do you know the layering? In other words, who's on top?

Each positioned element has a property called a `z-index` that specifies its placement on an imaginary z-axis (items on top are "closer" to you, and have a bigger z-index).

The sidebar and annoyingad `<div>`s are layered on the page, with the annoyingad having a greater z-index than the sidebar, so it's on top.

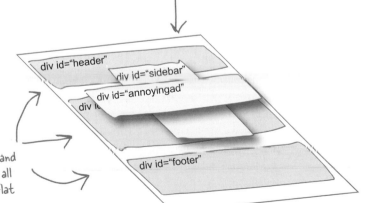

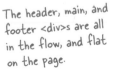

The header, main, and footer `<div>`s are all in the flow, and flat on the page.

there are no
Dumb Questions

Q: What is the position property set to by default?

A: The default value for positioning is "static". With static positioning, the element is placed in the normal document flow and isn't positioned by you—the browser decides where it goes. You can use the float property to take an element out of the flow, and you can say it should float left or right, but the browser is still ultimately deciding where it goes. Compare this to the "absolute" value for the position property. With absolute positioning, you're telling the browser exactly where to position elements.

Q: Can I only position <div>s?

A: You can absolutely position any element, block or inline. Just remember that when an element is absolutely positioned, it is removed from the normal flow of the page.

Q: So, I can position an inline element?

A: Yes, you sure can. For instance, it's common to position the <img> element. You can position <em>s, <span>s, and so on as well, but it isn't common to do so.

Q: Are there position property values other than static and absolute?

A: There are actually four: static, absolute, fixed, and relative. You've already heard about static and absolute. Fixed positioning places an element in a location that is relative to the browser window (rather than the page), so fixed elements never move. You'll see an example of fixed positioning in a few pages. Relative positioning takes an element and flows it on the page just like normal, but then offsets it before displaying it on the page. Relative positioning is commonly used for more advanced positioning and special effects.

Q: Do I have to specify a width for an absolutely positioned element just like the floated elements?

A: No, you don't have to specify a width for absolutely positioned elements. But if you don't, by default, the block element will take up the entire width of the browser, minus any offset you specify from the left or right. This might be exactly what you want, or it might not. So set the value of the width property if you want to change this default behavior.

Q: Do I have to use pixels for positioning?

A: No—another common way to position elements is using percentages. If you use percentages, the positions of your elements may appear to change as you change the width of your browser. So, for example, if your browser is 800 pixels wide, and your element's left position is set to 10%, then your element will be 80 pixels from the left of the browser window. But if your browser is resized to 400 pixels wide, then the width will be reduced to 10% of 400 pixels, or 40 pixels from the left of the browser window.

Another common use for percentages is in specifying widths. If you don't need specific widths for your elements or margins, then you can use percentages to make both your main content area and your sidebars flexible in size. You'll see this done a lot in two- and three-column layouts.

Q: Do I have to know how to use z-indexes to use absolute positioning?

A: No, z-indexes tend to be used most often for various advanced uses of CSS, especially when web page scripting is involved, so they're a little beyond the scope of this book. But they are a part of how absolute positioning works, so it's good to know about z-index (we'll come back to touch on z-index again in just a bit).

Using absolute positioning

We're now going to create a two-column Starbuzz page using techniques similar to those we used with the float version of the page; however, this time we'll use absolute positioning. Here's what we're going to do:

 First we're going to make the sidebar <div> absolutely positioned. In fact, we're going to position it in exactly the same place that we floated it to before.

 Next, we're going to give the main content another big margin so that the sidebar can sit on top of the margin space.

 Finally, we're going to give this a good testing and see how it compares to the float version.

Changing the Starbuzz CSS

Our HTML is all ready to go, and the sidebar <div> is right where we want it (below the important main content). All we need to do is make a few CSS changes and we'll have a sidebar that is absolutely positioned. Open your "starbuzz.css" file and let's make a few changes to the sidebar:

> Remember, we are going back to the original versions of the files, which you can find in the "chapter11/absolute" folder.

> You can work out of the "absolute" folder, or copy the files "index.html" and "starbuzz.css" into the "starbuzz" folder and work from there, like we did.

```
#sidebar {
    background:  #efe5d0 url(images/background.gif) bottom right;
    font-size:   105%;
    padding:     15px;
    margin:      0px 10px 10px 10px;
    position:    absolute;
    top:         128px;
    right:       0px;
    width:       280px;
}
```

> Okay, now we're going to specify that the sidebar is absolutely positioned 128 pixels from the top, and 0 pixels from the right of the page. We also want the sidebar to have a width, so let's make it the same as the float version: 280 pixels.

> You'll see where the 128 came from in a sec...

> Zero pixels from the right will make sure that the sidebar sticks to the right side of the browser.

Now we just need to rework the main <div>

Actually, there's not much reworking to be done. We're just adding a
margin like we did with the float version. So, change the right margin
of the main <div> to be 330 pixels, like you did last time.

```
#main {
    background:  #efe5d0 url(images/background.gif) top left;
    font-size:   105%;
    padding:     15px;
    margin:      0px 330px 10px 10px;
}
```

We're going to give the sidebar some space to be positioned over by giving the main <div> a
big margin. This is really the same technique we used with the float. The only difference is
the way the sidebar <div> is being placed over the margin.

All you need to do is make that change to your margin, and then save.
But before we take this for a test drive, let's think about how this is going
to work with the absolutely positioned sidebar.

We're positioning the sidebar to be 128 pixels from
the top, and up against the right side of the page.
Keep in mind, the sidebar has 10 pixels of margin
on the right, so the background color will show
through that like before.

The main <div> is flowed
just below the header,
so it will align with the
top of the sidebar. Also,
it has a right margin
that is the same size
as the sidebar, so all
its inline content will
be to the left of the
sidebar. Remember that
the flowed elements
don't know about the
absolutely positioned
elements at all, so
the inline content in
the flowed elements
doesn't wrap around the
absolutely positioned
elements.

10-pixel top margin

108 pixels for the header. You can
see this height set in the CSS.

10-pixel bottom margin

The sidebar needs to be
128 pixels from the top
because that's exactly
how much room the
header takes up, including
margins.

div id="header"

div id="main"

div id="sidebar"

div id="footer"

You might want to think about what happens to the
footer. Because flowed elements don't know about
absolute elements, we can't use "clear" anymore.

Time for the absolute test drive

Make sure you've saved the new CSS and then reload "index.html" in your browser. Let's check out the results:

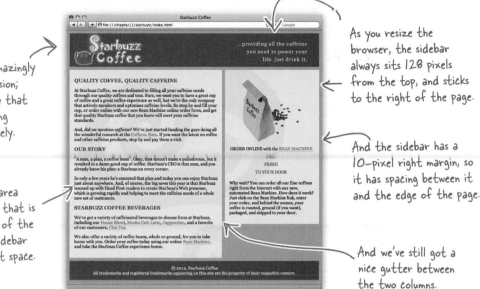

Wow, this looks amazingly like the float version; however, you know that the sidebar is being positioned absolutely.

As you resize the browser, the sidebar always sits 128 pixels from the top, and sticks to the right of the page.

And the sidebar has a 10-pixel right margin, so it has spacing between it and the edge of the page.

The main content area has a right margin that is exactly the width of the sidebar, and the sidebar sits on top of that space.

And we've still got a nice gutter between the two columns.

But we are now back to having a problem with the footer. When the browser gets wide enough, the absolutely positioned sidebar comes down over the top of the footer. Unfortunately, we can't fall back on the `clear` property this time, because flowed elements ignore the presence of absolutely positioned elements.

When the browser is wide, the vertical space of the main content area is reduced, and the sidebar can come down over the footer.

Okay, enough already, all we're trying to do is create two columns...why can't I just write some HTML or CSS that easily creates two columns?

Well, actually, you can...

And to do that, you have to use a fairly new capability of modern browsers: the *CSS table display*. What's that? CSS table display allows you to display block elements in a table with rows and columns (you'll see how in just a sec), and, by putting your content in a CSS table, you can easily create multicolumn designs with HTML and CSS.

At this point, all modern browsers support this.

Now if you are thinking "why didn't you tell us about this before?" well, it was important for you to understand how browsers flow and display content (because not every design task is going to look like two-column display). But now that you understand layouts, we can rework the page using CSS table display.

Like all the other layout solutions, even table display has its advantages and disadvantages.

How CSS table display works

You can think of a table like a spreadsheet—a table has *columns* and *rows*, and at the intersection of each column and row we have a *cell*. In a spreadsheet table, you can put a value, like a number or some text, in each cell. With CSS table display, each cell contains an HTML block element instead.

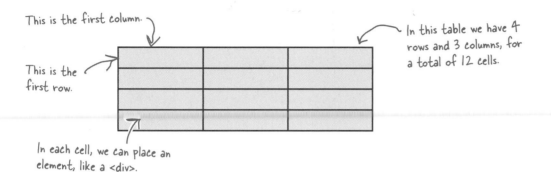

This is the first column.

This is the first row.

In this table we have 4 rows and 3 columns, for a total of 12 cells.

In each cell, we can place an element, like a <div>.

Let's say you've got a page with three images and three paragraphs, and you want to lay them out in two columns with three rows. Here's how you'd do that conceptually, using a table:

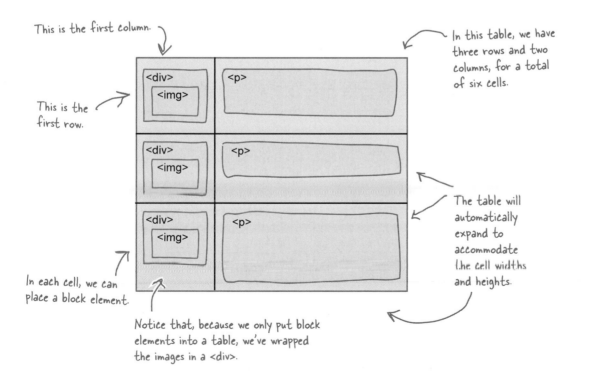

This is the first column.

This is the first row.

In this table, we have three rows and two columns, for a total of six cells.

The table will automatically expand to accommodate the cell widths and heights.

In each cell, we can place a block element.

Notice that, because we only put block elements into a table, we've wrapped the images in a <div>.

Sharpen your pencil

Given what you know about CSS table displays, sketch out how the two columns from the Starbuzz page, "main" and "sidebar", would fit into a table. Check the answer at the end of the chapter before moving on…

<div id="main">

<div id="sidebar">

Draw your table here.

How to create the CSS and HTML for a table display

As you can imagine, we're going to need to add some CSS to tell the browser to display our columns like a table, but we also need to add some HTML. Why? We need to add a bit of structure that represents the columns and rows of the table, and the structure of the enclosing table as well.

Doing this is straightforward—all we need to do is create a `<div>` for the entire table and then one `<div>` per row. And for each column, we just need a block-level element that is placed within the row `<div>`. Let's see how the HTML is going to work, and then we'll come back to the CSS we need.

Adding HTML structure for the table display

Let's step through how we're going to add structure to support the CSS table display using HTML:

1 First, we'll create a <div> that represents the entire table, and nest the columns and rows within that <div>.

Table

Row

Column

<div id="main">

<div id="sidebar">

2 Next, for each row in the table, we'll create another <div> that will contain the row content. For Starbuzz, we have only one row.

3 And, for each column, we just need a block element to act as that column. We already have two block elements we can use: the "main" <div> and the "sidebar" <div>.

Sharpen your pencil

Now it's your turn: go ahead and write the HTML you'll need for the table structure for Starbuzz below.

Write the HTML we'll need for the Starbuzz table display layout here.

```
<div id="table">
    <div id="row">
        <div id="main">
        </div>
        <div ="sidebar">
        </div>
    </div>
</div>
```

Sharpen your pencil
Solution

Now it's your turn: go ahead and write the HTML you'll need for the table structure for Starbuzz below.

Here's our answer!

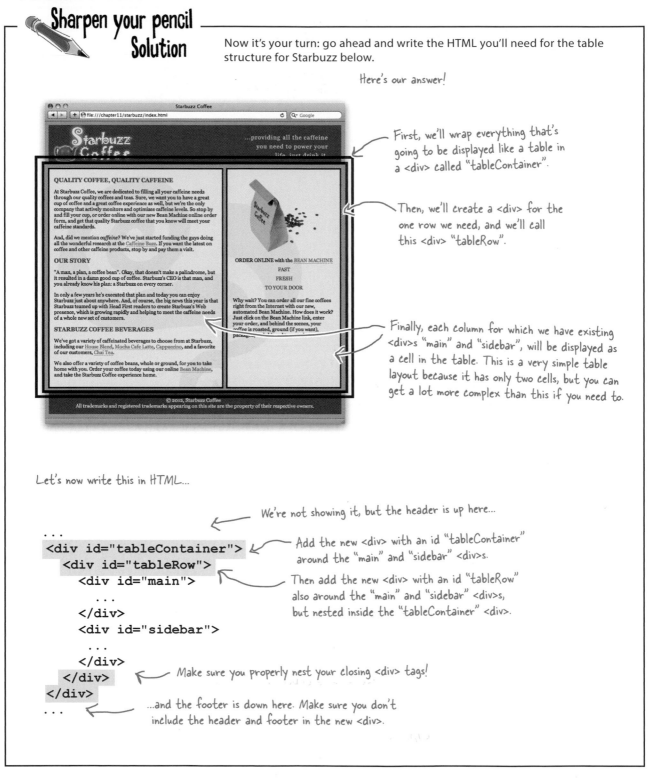

First, we'll wrap everything that's going to be displayed like a table in a <div> called "tableContainer".

Then, we'll create a <div> for the one row we need, and we'll call this <div> "tableRow".

Finally, each column for which we have existing <div>s "main" and "sidebar", will be displayed as a cell in the table. This is a very simple table layout because it has only two cells, but you can get a lot more complex than this if you need to.

Let's now write this in HTML...

We're not showing it, but the header is up here...

```
...
<div id="tableContainer">
  <div id="tableRow">
    <div id="main">
      ...
    </div>
    <div id="sidebar">
      ...
    </div>
  </div>
</div>
...
```

Add the new <div> with an id "tableContainer" around the "main" and "sidebar" <div>s.

Then add the new <div> with an id "tableRow" also around the "main" and "sidebar" <div>s, but nested inside the "tableContainer" <div>.

Make sure you properly nest your closing <div> tags!

...and the footer is down here. Make sure you don't include the header and footer in the new <div>.

How to use CSS to create table displays

Now that you know how to add the HTML structure to support the CSS table display, let's look at how we specify the CSS for each element to create the table display.

1 First, we added a <div> for the table with the id "tableContainer". This <div> contains the rows and columns. We style the "tableContainer" <div> like this:

```
div#tableContainer {
    display: table;
}
```

The "tableContainer" is the outermost <div> and represents the entire table structure.

2 Next, we added a <div> for the row, with the id "tableRow". We have only one row, with two cells, so we need just one <div>. If we had multiple rows, we'd need multiple <div>s. We style the row <div> like this:

```
div#tableRow {
    display: table-row;
}
```

The "tableRow" <div> represents a row in the table. We have one row in our table, so we just need this one rule. If you have multiple rows, consider using a class instead (e.g., div.tableRow) so you can use one rule to style all the rows.

3 Finally, we used our existing "main" and "sidebar" <div>s for the cells corresponding to each column in the row. We style these <div>s like this:

```
#main {
    display: table-cell;
    background: #efe5d0 url(images/background.gif) top left;
    font-size: 105%;
    padding: 15px;
    margin: 0px 10px 10px 10px;
}
#sidebar {
    display: table-cell;
    background: #efe5d0 url(images/background.gif) bottom right;
    font-size: 105%;
    padding: 15px;
    margin: 0px 10px 10px 10px;
}
```

The "main" and "sidebar" <div>s are the columns in our table, so they each get displayed as table cells.

Meanwhile, back at Starbuzz...

It's time to add table display into Starbuzz to see how those columns are going to look. To do that, we're going to roll back to the Starbuzz HTML and CSS we created at the beginning of the chapter, so open "chapter11/tabledisplay" to get fresh copies of the HTML and CSS. Edit "index.html", and add the two `<div>`s around both the "main" `<div>` and the "sidebar" `<div>`— the outer one called "tableContainer" and the inner one called "tableRow". Next, open your "starbuzz.css" file and let's add the following to the CSS:

Refer back a couple of pages to see the HTML if you need to.

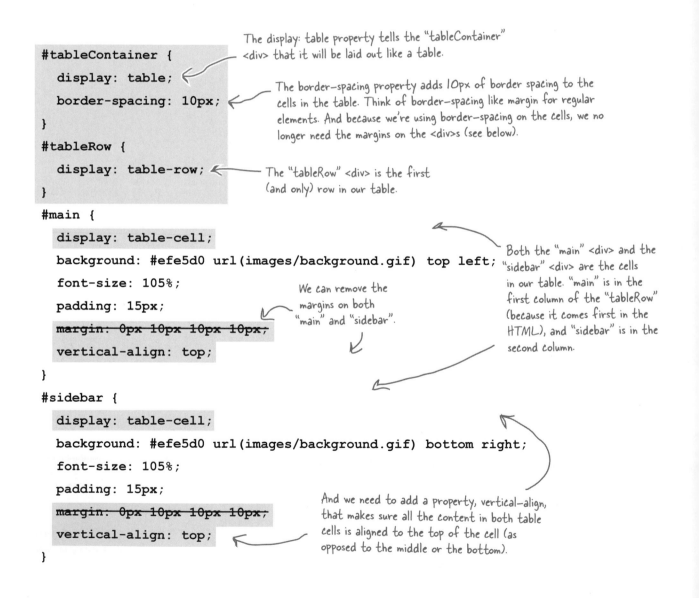

The display: table property tells the "tableContainer" `<div>` that it will be laid out like a table.

```
#tableContainer {
  display: table;
  border-spacing: 10px;
}
```

The border-spacing property adds 10px of border spacing to the cells in the table. Think of border-spacing like margin for regular elements. And because we're using border-spacing on the cells, we no longer need the margins on the `<div>`s (see below).

```
#tableRow {
  display: table-row;
}
```

The "tableRow" `<div>` is the first (and only) row in our table.

```
#main {
  display: table-cell;
  background: #efe5d0 url(images/background.gif) top left;
  font-size: 105%;
  padding: 15px;
  margin: 0px 10px 10px 10px;
  vertical-align: top;
}
```

We can remove the margins on both "main" and "sidebar".

Both the "main" `<div>` and the "sidebar" `<div>` are the cells in our table. "main" is in the first column of the "tableRow" (because it comes first in the HTML), and "sidebar" is in the second column.

```
#sidebar {
  display: table-cell;
  background: #efe5d0 url(images/background.gif) bottom right;
  font-size: 105%;
  padding: 15px;
  margin: 0px 10px 10px 10px;
  vertical-align: top;
}
```

And we need to add a property, vertical-align, that makes sure all the content in both table cells is aligned to the top of the cell (as opposed to the middle or the bottom).

A quick test drive...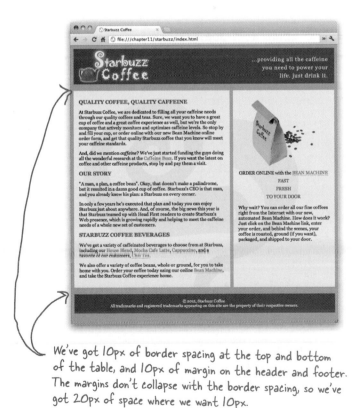

This is great! Our two columns look (almost) perfect. Try making the browser wider, and then narrower. Notice that both columns are always equal in height and we no longer have the problem with a column overlapping the footer. And we've got our content in the correct order for mobile users!

There's only one tiny little problem, which is easily fixed: notice that the spacing between the header and the columns, as well as the footer and the columns, is just a bit too large…

Almost perfect! The only remaining issue is the extra space here…

…and here.

What's the problem with the spacing?

We currently have a 10px bottom margin on the "header" `<div>`, and a 10px top margin on the "footer" `<div>`. Before we added the table layout, we were specifying the margins of both the "main" and "sidebar" `<div>` to have a 0px top margin, so the total margin between them and the "header" is 10px, and a 10px bottom margin. Now, remember that the vertical margin's block elements sitting next to each other collapse—meaning that even though we had 10px of margin on the bottom of the columns and 10px of margin on the footer, this margin collapses into 10px, so the total space between the columns and footer is also 10px.

When we removed the margins from the "main" and "sidebar" `<div>`s, we created the 10px of spacing using the `border-spacing` property in the "tableContainer" `<div>` instead. This adds 10px of space between cells, as well as 10px of space around the edges.

But the space created by `border-spacing` and a margin does *not* collapse! So we ended up with 20px of space between the header and the columns, as well as 20px of space between the columns and the footer. Fortunately, it's really easy to fix.

We've got 10px of border spacing at the top and bottom of the table, and 10px of margin on the header and footer. The margins don't collapse with the border spacing, so we've got 20px of space where we want 10px.

Fix the spacing

To fix the spacing between the header and the columns, and the footer and the columns, all we have to do is change the bottom margin of the header to be 0px and the top margin of the footer to be 0px. We currently specify all four sides of margin with the shortcut rule `margin: 10px` in the rules for both the header and the footer, so instead, we'll expand that margin property to specify each side separately so we can specify 10px for all sides except the one next to the columns. Like this:

```
#header {
  background-color: #675c47;
  margin: 10px;
  margin: 10px 10px 0px 10px;
  height: 108px;
}

#footer {
  background-color: #675c47;
  color: #efe5d0;
  text-align: center;
  padding: 15px;
  margin: 10px;
  margin:  0px 10px 10px 10px;
  font-size: 90%;
}
```

Instead of having 10px on all sides of the header, we now have 10px on all sides except the bottom side, which has 0px.

Likewise, we now have 10px of margin on all sides of the footer except the top.

A final test drive of our table display

With this change, our columns are now perfect! We have 10px of spacing between all the pieces and the columns line up evenly, even if you expand or narrow the browser window.

While `display: table` won't always be the right tool for your layout needs, in this case, it's the best solution to get two even columns of content in the Starbuzz page.

Perfect!

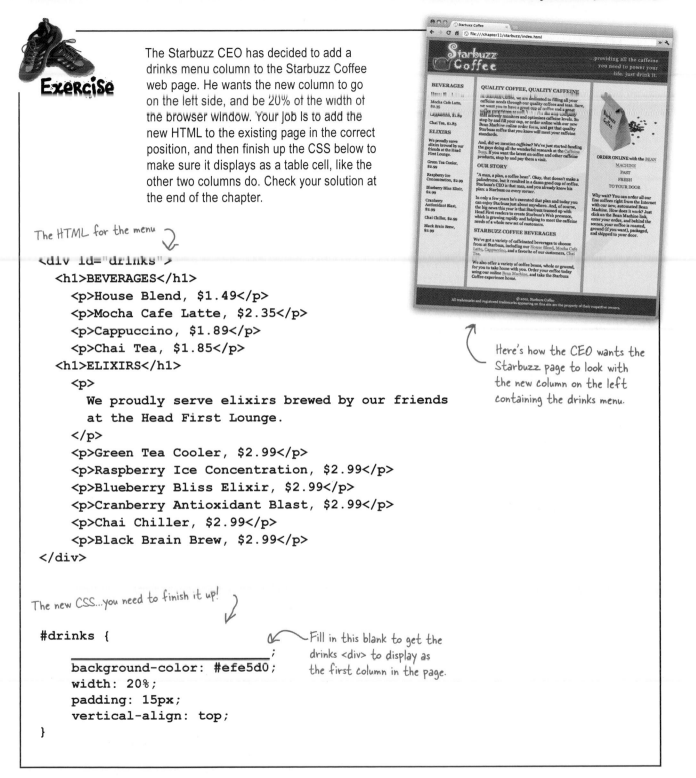

The Starbuzz CEO has decided to add a drinks menu column to the Starbuzz Coffee web page. He wants the new column to go on the left side, and be 20% of the width of the browser window. Your job is to add the new HTML to the existing page in the correct position, and then finish up the CSS below to make sure it displays as a table cell, like the other two columns do. Check your solution at the end of the chapter.

Here's how the CEO wants the Starbuzz page to look with the new column on the left containing the drinks menu.

The HTML for the menu

```html
<div id="drinks">
  <h1>BEVERAGES</h1>
    <p>House Blend, $1.49</p>
    <p>Mocha Cafe Latte, $2.35</p>
    <p>Cappuccino, $1.89</p>
    <p>Chai Tea, $1.85</p>
  <h1>ELIXIRS</h1>
    <p>
      We proudly serve elixirs brewed by our friends
      at the Head First Lounge.
    </p>
    <p>Green Tea Cooler, $2.99</p>
    <p>Raspberry Ice Concentration, $2.99</p>
    <p>Blueberry Bliss Elixir, $2.99</p>
    <p>Cranberry Antioxidant Blast, $2.99</p>
    <p>Chai Chiller, $2.99</p>
    <p>Black Brain Brew, $2.99</p>
</div>
```

The new CSS...you need to finish it up!

```css
#drinks {
    _____;
    background-color: #efe5d0;
    width: 20%;
    padding: 15px;
    vertical-align: top;
}
```

Fill in this blank to get the drinks <div> to display as the first column in the page.

there are no Dumb Questions

Q: So, I know we're not covering HTML tables until later in the book, but is the CSS display: table similar to using HTML tables?

A: It is similar in the sense that you're creating structure in your HTML that you can map to the rows and columns of a table. But unlike HTML tables, CSS display-table is all about presenting the content in that structure using a table-like layout. HTML tables are for *tabular data*: data that should be structured as a table. So, using CSS display-table is a way of creating a certain kind of presentation layout, while HTML tables are all about structuring your data. You'll learn all about HTML tables in Chapter 13.

Q: What do I do if I need more than one row in my table display?

A: If you need to display content in multiple rows, then you just add more HTML structure to support that. If you take a look at the Starbuzz HTML, you'll see we have two columns (or three, after you add the Beverages column) in one row. To add another row, you'd add another <div> similar to the "tableRow" <div>, nested inside the "tableContainer" <div>, and containing the same number of columns as the first row. You can keep adding rows by adding more <divs> like this.

Q: Why did we add the vertical alignment to each cell in the CSS with vertical-align: top?

A: We added vertical-align: top to each table cell to make sure that all the content aligns with the top of the cell. If each cell is aligned this way, then the content in each of our Starbuzz page columns should align at the top, which makes for a more professional-looking presentation. If you don't add a vertical alignment, you may find the default alignment in your browser is set to middle instead. In some cases, that might be what you want, of course! You can set the vertical alignment to top, middle, or bottom.

Q: Does it matter how much content I put in a cell?

A: Not really. You'll probably want to make sure that no one column has so much more content than other columns that your page looks unbalanced, but ultimately, it's up to you and how you want your page to look.

Q: Can we control the width of the columns?

A: Yes, you have some control over the width of the columns with the width property. In the exercise to add the Beverages column that you just did, you probably noticed that we set the width of the column to 20%. You can set the width of each column like this (and it's a good idea to make sure the widths add up to 100%!). By using percentages, your table will still expand and contract appropriately as you resize the browser window.

Strategies for your CSS layout toolbox

As you've seen, there are a variety of methods you can use to lay out your pages using HTML and CSS. And we didn't have to change the HTML much to change the layout of the page; other than moving a piece of content around (for handling the floating sidebar), and adding a couple of <div>s (for the table display layout), you handle the *presentation* of your content entirely with your CSS. That's really the idea: your HTML should be all about *structuring* your content, and the CSS is what handles the layout. Which method you choose for doing that layout is up to you and is going to depend on the kind of layout you choose and how flexible you want it to be.

Let's review.

The Floating Layout

We used **float** to lay out the lounge page and float the elixirs <div> to the right of the main content in the page. In this case, float was perfect because we wanted the main content to flow around the elixirs <div>, which it did just beautifully. We haven't used it this way yet, but float also works great for floating images within a paragraph of text, and having the text flow around the image.

We then used float to float the sidebar <div> in the Starbuzz page, and used clear to make sure that the floating sidebar didn't overlap with the footer.

The big downside is that we have to move the entire <div> we're floating above the main content of the page, which isn't always optimal if that ordering doesn't reflect the relative importance of the content in the page. Another potential downside is that it's impossible to create two equal columns of content with float, so if that's your goal, you'll need another solution.

Float works great for the lounge page; it's okay for Starbuzz, but we'd like to keep the sidebar content below the main content and have equal columns.

The Jello Layout

Next we created a **frozen** layout by wrapping a fixed-size <div> around all the content in the page, and then we made it **jello** by allowing the margins to expand with the auto property value. This makes for a great-looking layout, and lots of pages on the Web use this design; for instance, you'll see a lot of blogs set up this way. This also solved the problem of our content ordering. The disadvantage here is that the content doesn't expand to fill the entire browser window (which many people don't find to be a disadvantage at all).

Jello gives you a nicely centered, fixed-size area of content with expandable margins.

Strategies for your CSS layout toolbox (continued)

Absolute gives you a nice liquid main content area with a fixed sidebar.

The Absolute Layout

We then used **absolute positioning** to get back to a liquid layout, and this also allows us to keep our content in the order we want. By setting the sidebar to a specific width, and positioning it to the right of the main content, we have a main content area that expands and contracts with the size of the page, and a sidebar that stays fixed in size and is anchored to the right side of the browser window. This is a great choice for layouts when you want one part of your page to be fixed in size and one part to expand and contract, or when you need an element to be located at a precise location (we'll see how to do that shortly!).

The downside for the Starbuzz page, however, is that the sidebar overlaps the footer again when the browser is wide. So we continued in our quest for two perfect columns, and moved on to…

The Table Display Layout

With table display, we got the even columns we wanted.

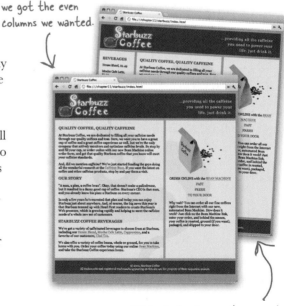

With the **table display** layout, we hit the jackpot of layouts for Starbuzz. We did have to add a couple of `<div>`s to our HTML structure to get it to work right, but that paid off with two perfectly aligned columns that expand and contract beautifully with the size of the browser window.

In this case, the structure we added to the page was purely in support of the layout; it didn't add any meaning to the page. You'll find that `<div>` is often used that way (and in fact, when you get to the next chapter, you'll see this is even more true today than it was just a few years ago). But don't go `<div>` crazy; you want to pick the best layout for your needs and add as few `<div>`s as necessary to get the layout you want.

Table display layout isn't always the right choice for layout, but for Starbuzz, it works perfectly and even let us easily expand to add a third column for the Beverages menu. Nice!

Table display is easy to expand to more columns (or rows!).

There are as many page designs on the Web as there are designers, but many of those designs are based on the layouts you've learned about here (or some variation of these). You now have several strategies in your layout toolbox to choose from, so you're in good shape to handle just about any layout job your boss might throw at you!

Hey, the site is looking great, and I really like the CSS table layout, but I noticed that the header at the top with the logo and the slogan doesn't expand with the page. I mean, it feels like the slogan should move to the right if I expand my browser window.

Yup, we agree.

Except for the header, the Starbuzz page expands nicely as you make your browser window wider. Thanks to the CSS table layout, the columns expand proportionally as you expand the window, and because the footer text is centered, the footer always looks like it's in the middle of the page, whether the page is wide or narrow. But the header doesn't expand as nicely. The background color does, but the Starbuzz slogan always seems stuck in the same place, while you might expect that it would be anchored to the right side of the window.

The reason the header isn't expanding with the rest of the page is because the header is *one* image with both the Starbuzz logo and the slogan in it. And that image is exactly 800px wide. If your browser window is opened wider than 800px, you see a lot of extra space over on the right. And likewise, if your browser window is narrower than 800px, you'll see the image fall off the side of the browser window.

Can we fix it?

Problems with the header

Go ahead and play with the page a bit by opening your browser window wider than the header image, and then narrower than the header image. You'll see that the header isn't working quite like we'd like it to yet.

When the browser window is more than 800px wide, you get all this extra space over here to the right.

And when the browser is narrower than 800px wide, the slogan part of the header image falls off the edge of the browser window!

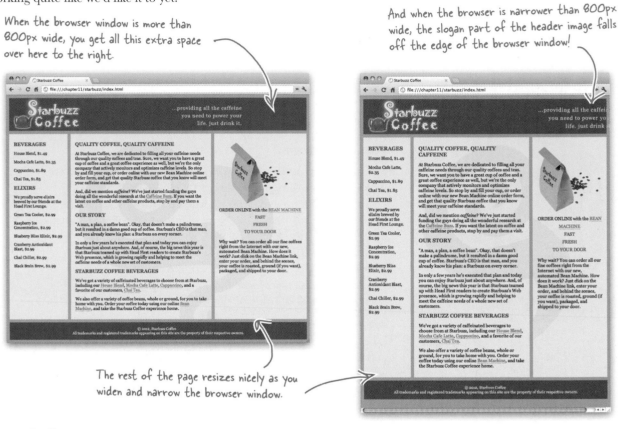

The rest of the page resizes nicely as you widen and narrow the browser window.

BRAIN POWER

If we split the header image into two different images, one with the logo and one with the slogan, can you think of ways you might lay out the two images in the `<div id="header">` element so they are positioned correctly (that is, the logo stays on the left of the header, while the slogan is always anchored to the right part of the header, even if you open up your browser window)?

We can easily split the header into two gif images (they both have a transparent background with a matte that works perfectly with our coffee-colored background color in the header).

...providing all the caffeine you need to power your life. just drink it.

Fixing the header images with float

It's often true that there are multiple strategies to solving a layout problem with CSS, and that's certainly the case here. The way we're going to solve it is to use `float`. You already used `float` once, to lay out part of the Starbuzz page, before we switched to using the CSS table layout. But there's no reason you can't mix and match different strategies, like table display with `float` in the same page; in fact, it's very common. So let's take a look at how we're going to do this.

❶ Split the header image into two images

headerLogo.gif

We already did this for you; you'll find the images "headerLogo.gif" and "headerSlogan.gif" in the "chapter11/starbuzz/images" folder.

headerSlogan.gif

...providing all the caffeine you need to power your life. just drink it.

❷ Update your HTML to use these images

Next, you need to update your HTML to replace the existing header image, which is one big 800-pixel-wide image, with the two images we created in Step 1. We'll go ahead and give each image an id that we'll use to select each of them in our CSS.

```
<div id="header">
    <img src="images/header.gif" alt="Starbuzz Coffee header image">
    <img id="headerLogo"
        src="images/headerLogo.gif" alt="Starbuzz Coffee logo image">
    <img id="headerSlogan"
        src="images/headerSlogan.gif"
        alt="Providing all the caffeine you need to power your life.">
</div>
```

❸ Fix the images with CSS

Finally, you need to get the images laid out in the header correctly. If you load the page now, you'll see both images in the header, right next to each other over on the left side of the page.

The logo image looks okay where it is...

But now, the slogan image is right next to the logo image. We need to move it over here with CSS.

Exercise

This CSS is so easy you could probably do it in your sleep, after all the layout experience you've had in this chapter already. Go ahead and write the CSS to fix the images in the header. You know you're going to use float; fill in the blanks below with the rest of the rule you need to get the images into the right place. Check your answer at the end of the chapter before you go on.

```
_____ {
       float: _____;
}
```

Test drive your float

Get your CSS updated in "starbuzz.css" and reload the Starbuzz page. You should see the header slogan image all the way over on the right side of the page, just where it should be, and, better yet, it stays over on the right even if you open your browser really wide. Success!

Now the slogan image is all the way over on the right, and it stays there, even if you change the browser window size.

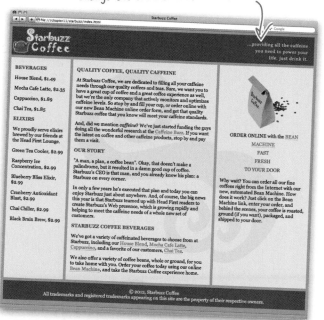

How float works in the header

Remember the steps for how to float an element from earlier in the chapter:

Give the element an identity. We gave the image we wanted to float the id "headerSlogan". Check.

Give the element a width. We didn't actually have to do that explicitly this time (although you could). Why? Because an image element has a specific width by default: it's the width of the image itself. CSS recognizes that the image has a width, so we don't have to specify it ourselves.

Float the element. Check, we floated it. The `<img>` is nested in the "header" `<div>`, so it floats up to the top right of the `<div>`. But remember, we set the height of the header to be exactly the same as the height of our two images. And, as we explained before, the other inline content in the page will flow around the floated element. In this case, the other inline content in the header is the logo image, which happens to also be exactly the same height as the slogan image and the header. So the two images line up perfectly!

there are no
Dumb Questions

Q: Why didn't we have to add "clear: right" to the "tableContainer" <div> below the header?

A: Because the image we floated is the same exact height—108px—as the other image in the header, so there's no room for the other content in the page to move up and flow around the floated image. Both images take up the exact same amount of vertical space, so the other elements in the page stay firmly in their places.

Q: What if I float an image that's in a paragraph of text?

A: Then the text will flow around the image. It works just like when we floated the elixirs <div> in the lounge; remember how the text in the rest of the page flowed around that <div>? Same thing if you float an image.

Q: Could we have positioned the header images using one of the other layout strategies we talked about?

A: Yes, indeed. There is usually more than one way of doing things in CSS. Another strategy might have been to use absolute positioning. We'll look at how to absolutely position an image next.

Hey guys! Starbuzz just won the Roaster of the Year Award. This is huge. Can we get it on the page front and center? All our customers need to see this. Top priority; make it happen!

The award

Well, we could just throw this as an image into any old paragraph on the page, but the CEO really wants this to be noticeable on the page. What if we could place the award on the page like this?

Not only does that look great, but it's exactly what the CEO wants. But how? Is this another situation for using float? Or are we going to need another strategy?

Adding the award

Notice that the award is sitting in a position that overlaps both the header and the main part of the page. It would be pretty tricky to get a floated image into this position. Not only that, but we know the award shouldn't affect the flow of any other elements in the page.

This sounds like a job for absolute positioning. After all, by using absolute positioning you can place it anywhere you want on the page, and since it isn't in the flow it won't affect any other element on the page. Seems like an easy addition to make to the page without disrupting what's already there.

Let's give it a try. Start by adding a new `<div>`, just below the header (the CEO thinks this is pretty important, so it should be up high in the order of content). Here's the `<div>`:

```
<div id="award">
    <img src="images/award.gif"
        alt="Roaster of the Year award">
</div>
```

The `<div>` contains the image of the award.

Positioning the award

We want the award to sit just about in the middle of the page when the browser's open to 800 pixels (a typical size for browser widths) and just overlapping the main content `<div>`.

So we're going to use the `top` and `left` properties to position the award 30 pixels from the top, and 365 pixels from the left.

```
#award {
    position:  absolute;
    top:       30px;
    left:      365px;
}
```

We're using an absolute position for the award `<div>` that is 30 pixels from the top and 365 pixels from the left.

Add this CSS to your "starbuzz.css" file, save, and reload the web page. You'll see the award image appear like magic, right where we want it. Make sure you resize the browser to see how the award displays.

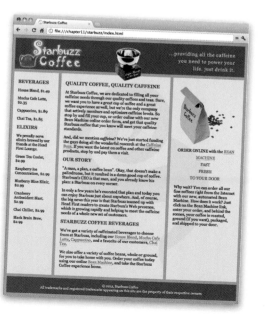

there are no
Dumb Questions

Q: Seems like absolute positioning is better than float because I have more control over where the elements go. Should I prefer absolute positioning over floating?

A: Not really; it just depends on what you need. If you really need an element to appear at a precise position in the page, then absolute positioning is the way to go. But if you want to, say, have text flow around an image, you can't easily do that with absolute positioning; in that case, you'll definitely want to use float. You'll find uses for both fairly regularly.

Q: I was playing with a couple of absolutely positioned <div> elements, and one always is displayed on top of the other. Is there a way I can change which one is on top?

A: Yes, every positioned element has what is called a "z-index," which is the ordering of the elements on an imaginary z-axis (think of it as pointing out of your screen). You use it like this:

```
#div1 {
    position: absolute;
    top:      30px;
    left:     30px;
    z-index:  0;
}
#div2 {
    position: absolute;
    top:      30px;
    left:     30px;
    z-index:  1;
}
```

Those rules would place the element with id "div2" on top of the element with an id "div1".

Q: How do I know what z-index each element on the page is by default?

A: You don't really, unless you inspect the CSS the browser computes for each element in the page with developer tools. But most of the time you won't care about the z-index of elements unless you are specifically layering them or you run into a situation like we did with the award. Usually just setting the z-index to 1 is good enough to make sure an element is above other elements in the page, but if you have multiple elements you are positioning and layering yourself, you'll have to be a little more deliberate about the z-index values.

Q: Is there a maximum z-index value?

A: Yes, but it's a very large number, and practically, you'll never need your z-index values to go that high.

Q: What about negative z-index values, can you have z-index values of, say, –1?

A: Yes, you can! The same rules apply (that is, the more positive and larger the value, the higher the layer, and the closer it is to you on the screen).

Q: Can any element have a z-index?

A: No, only elements that have been positioned with CSS using absolute, relative, or fixed positioning. You'll see an example of fixed positioning next!

Hey, can we get a coupon on the site and put it right in customers' faces so they can't miss it? I'd like to offer one free coffee to everyone who clicks on the coupon—for a limited time, of course.

Just the words we've been waiting for: "right in the customer's face."

Why? Because it's going to give us the opportunity to try a little *fixed* positioning. This is the last kind of positioning we're going to use in the chapter, so let's make it fun. What we're going to do is put a coupon on the page that always stays on the screen, even if you scroll. Is this a great technique to make your users happy? Probably not, but work with us here…it is going to be a fun way to play with fixed positioning.

ONE FREE COFFEE 151332

How does fixed positioning work?

Compared to absolute positioning, fixed positioning is pretty straightforward. With fixed positioning, you specify the position of an element just like you do with absolute positioning, but the position is an offset from the edge of the browser's *window* rather than the *page*. The interesting effect this has is that once you've placed content with fixed positioning, it stays right where you put it and doesn't move, even if you scroll the page.

So, say you have a <div> with an id of "coupon". You can position the <div> fixed to a spot 300 pixels from the top of the viewport, and 100 pixels from the left side, like this:

> Impress friends and coworkers by referring to the browser window as the *viewport*. Try it—it works, and the W3C will nod approvingly.

Here's the id selector for the coupon <div>.

We're using fixed positioning.

```
#coupon {
    position: fixed;
    top:     300px;
    left:    100px;
}
```

Position the coupon 300 pixels from the top, and 100 pixels from the left. You can also use right and bottom, just like with absolute positioning.

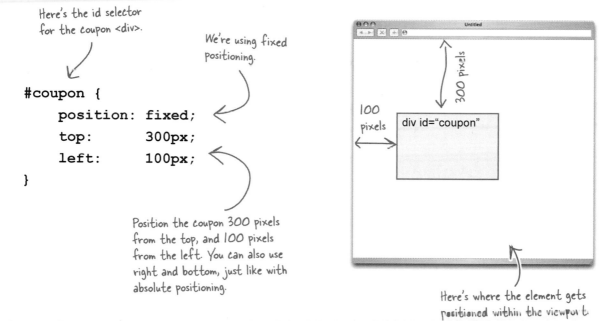

Here's where the element gets positioned within the viewport.

Once you've got an element positioned, then comes the fun: scroll around...it doesn't move. Resize the window...it doesn't move. Pick up your monitor and shake it...it doesn't move. Okay, just kidding on the last one. But the point is, fixed-position elements don't move; they are there for good as long as the page is displayed.

Now, we're sure you're already thinking of fun things to do with fixed positioning, but you've got a job to do. So let's get that coupon on the Starbuzz page.

Putting the coupon on the page

Now we're going to get the Free Coffee Coupon on the page.
Let's start by creating a `<div>` for the coupon to go into:

Here's the `<div>` with an id of "coupon".

Inside we've got an image of the coupon, which you'll find in the "chapter11/starbuzz/images" folder.

```
<div id="coupon">
    <a href="freecoffee.html" title="Click here to get your free coffee">
        <img src="images/ticket.gif" alt="Starbuzz coupon ticket">
    </a>
</div>
```

And we've wrapped the image in an `<a>` element so that users can click on the image to be taken to a page with a coupon they can print.

Go ahead and add this `<div>` at the bottom of your "index.html" file, just
above the footer. Because we're going to position it, the placement in the
HTML will only matter to browsers that don't support positioning, and the
coupon isn't important enough to have at the top.

Now let's write the CSS to position the coupon:

```
#coupon {
    position: fixed;
    top: 350px;
    left: 0px;
}

#coupon a, img {
    border: none;
}
```

We're setting the coupon to fixed positioning, 350 pixels from the top of the viewport, and let's put the left side right up against the edge of the viewport. So we need to specify 0 pixels from the left.

We need to style the image and the links, too; otherwise, we may have borders popping up on the image because it is clickable. So, let's set the border on the image to none, and do the same on the links. We're using the same property for both, so we can combine the rules into one.

Remember that we have a rule in the CSS that says to turn off text-decoration, and use a border to underline links instead. Here, we're overriding that rule for the link in the coupon `<div>` and saying we don't want any border on the link. Go back and look at the original CSS if you need to remind yourself of the other rules for the links.

Putting the coupon on the page

Add the new coupon rules to your "starbuzz.css" file, save, and then reload the page. You may need to make the browser smaller to be able to see that the coupon stays put even when you scroll. Clicking on the coupon should take you to the "freecoffee.html" page.

You know, this looks great, but it might just be even more snazzy if the coupon was offset to the left, so it looks like it's coming out of the side of the viewport. Now, we *could* get into our photo editing software and cut off the left side of the image to create that effect. Or we could just use a negative offset so that the left side of the image is positioned to the left of the edge of the viewport. That's right, *you can do that.*

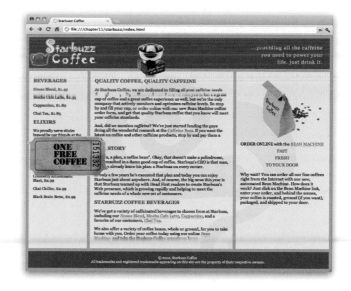

Using a negative left property value

Specify a negative property value just like you do a positive one: just put a minus sign in front. Like this:

```
#coupon {
    position: fixed;
    top: 350px;
    left: -90px;
}
```

By specifying –90 pixels, we're telling the browser to position the image 90 pixels to the left of the edge of the viewport.

–90 pixels

350 pixels

div id="coupon"

The browser will gladly position the image to the left of the viewport for you, and only the part of the image that is still on the screen will be viewable.

A rather positive, negative test drive

Make sure you've put in the negative left property value, save, and reload the page. Doesn't that look slick? Congrats, you've just achieved your first CSS special effect. Watch out, George Lucas!

Just remember, using fixed positioning to cover up your content is not the most user-friendly thing to do, but it is FUN.

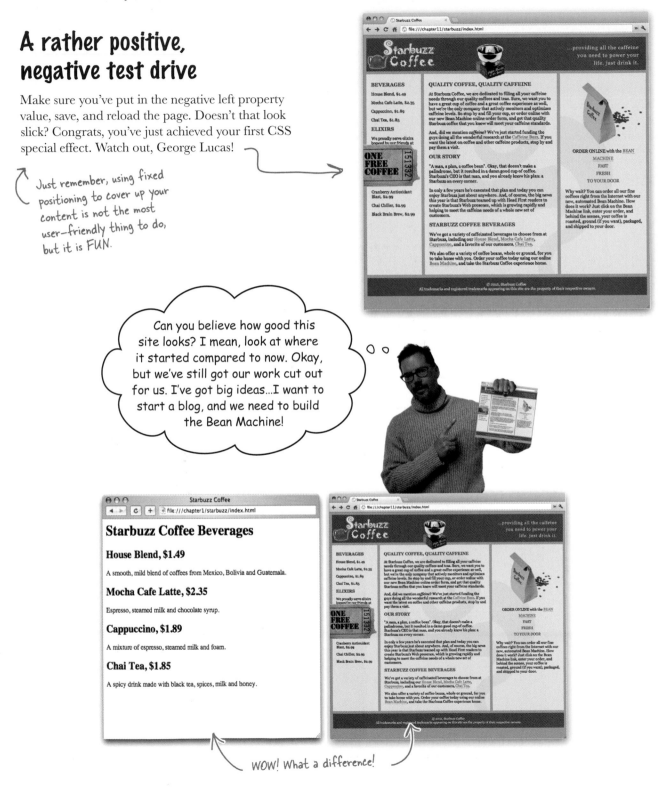

Can you believe how good this site looks? I mean, look at where it started compared to now. Okay, but we've still got our work cut out for us. I've got big ideas...I want to start a blog, and we need to build the Bean Machine!

WOW! What a difference!

Sharpen your pencil

Time to put all this knowledge about floating and absolute positioning to the test! Take a look at the web page below. There are four elements with an id. Your job is to correctly match each of these elements with the CSS rules on the right, and fill in the correct id selector for each one. Check your answers at the end of the chapter.

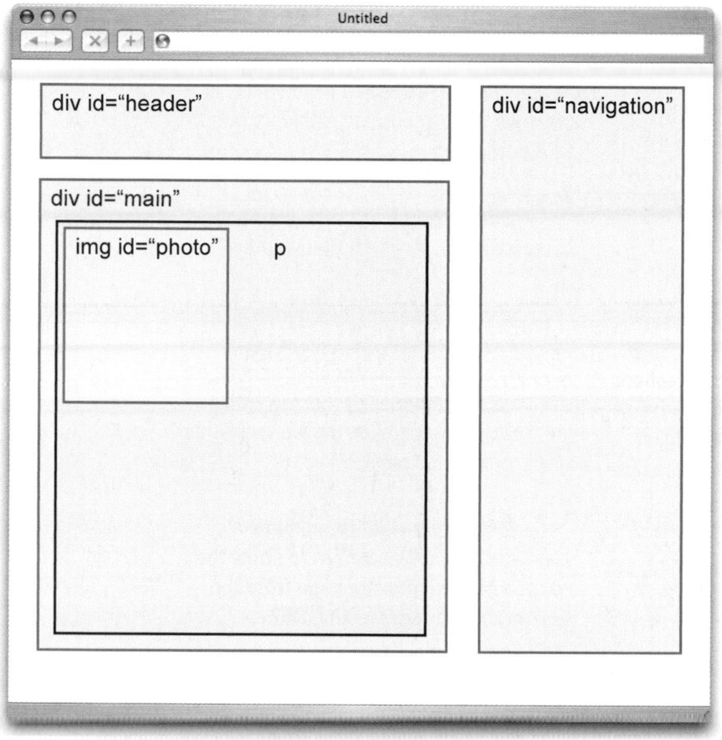

Fill in the selectors to complete the CSS.

```
div id="header"

div id="navigation"

div id="main"

    img id="photo"      p
```

.....main.................   {
    margin-top: 140px;
    margin-left: 20px;
    width: 500px;
}

.....navigation...........   {
    position: absolute;
    top: 20px;
    left: 550px;
    width: 200px;
}

.....photo................   {
    float: left;
}

.....header...............   {
    position: absolute;
    top: 20px;
    left: 20px;
    width: 500px;
    height: 100px;
}

there are no
Dumb Questions

Q: **The fixed coupon is cool, but kind of annoying. Is there another way we could position it so it doesn't overlap content, say at the bottom of the Beverages column?**

A: Sure. You could position the coupon at the bottom of the Beverages column using something called *relative* positioning. We didn't cover this kind of positioning, but it's similar to absolute except that the element is left in the flow of the page (where it would normally be), and then shifted by the amount you specify. You can shift the element using top, left, bottom, or right, just like with absolutely positioned elements. So, let's say you wanted the coupon below the drinks in the Beverages column: you'd move the coupon so it's nested in the "drinks" <div> at the bottom, and then set the position property to relative. After that, it's up to you to put the coupon precisely where you want it; you could position it 20px below the drinks with top: 20px, and hanging off the left side of the page with left: –90px (just like we did with fixed).

Q: **So the four kinds of positioning are static, absolute, fixed, and relative?**

A: That's right. *Static* is what you get by default if you don't specify any positioning. It leaves everything to flow as normal into the page. *Absolute* takes an element completely out of the flow of the page and allows you to position it at an absolute position relative to the closest positioned parent element (which is <html> unless you specify one yourself); *fixed* positions an element at a specific, fixed position relative to the browser window; and *relative* positions an element relative to its containing element by leaving it in the normal flow, and then shifting it over by an amount you specify.

You can also use these positioning techniques together. For instance, remember how we said the absolutely positioned elements are positioned relative to the closest positioned parent? You could absolutely position a <div> within another <div> by positioning the outer <div> with relative (leaving it in the flow), and then positioning the inner <div> with absolute, allowing you to position it relative to the parent <div>.

As you can see, there is a huge variety in the ways you can position elements with CSS positioning.

Q: **Could you position an element completely off screen if you wanted?**

A: Yes! For instance, the coupon image is 283 pixels wide, so if you set the left position to –283px, the coupon would disappear. It's still there on the page; it's just not visible in the viewport. Remember, the viewport is the visible area of the page.

Q: **What if we want to animate elements, like if we wanted to show the coupon sliding into the page from the left? Is that possible with CSS?**

A: Actually, it is, and we're glad you asked. It's beyond the scope of this book to get into CSS animation, but CSS3 introduced basic animation for elements with the transform and transition features, which is exciting for us web geeks. It's fairly limited, but you can do some pretty cool things with CSS animation. If you want more than what you can do with CSS, you'll have to use JavaScript, and that's a whole other topic. We give you a brief introduction to CSS transforms and transitions in the appendix just to whet your appetite.

BULLET POINTS

- Browsers place elements in a page using flow.

- Block elements flow from the top down, with a linebreak between elements. By default, each block element takes up the entire width of the browser window.

- Inline elements flow inside a block element from the top left to the bottom right. If more than one line is needed, the browser creates a new line, and expands the containing block element vertically to contain the inline elements.

- The top and bottom adjacent margins of two block elements in the normal page flow collapse to the size of the larger margin, or to the size of one margin if they are the same size.

- Floated elements are taken out of the normal flow and placed to the left or right.

- Floated elements sit on top of block elements and don't affect their flow. However, the inline content respects the boundaries of a floated element and flows around it.

- The clear property is used to specify that no floated elements can be on the left or right (or both) of a block element. A block element with clear set will move down until it is free of the block element on its side.

- A floated element must have a specific width set to a value other than auto.

- A liquid layout is one in which the content of the page expands to fit the page when you expand the browser window.

- A frozen layout is one in which the width of the content is fixed, and it doesn't expand or shrink with the browser window. This has the advantage of providing you more control over your design, but at the cost of not using the browser width as efficiently.

- A jello layout is one in which the content width is fixed, but the margins expand and shrink with the browser window. A jello layout usually places the content in the center of the page. This has the same advantages as the frozen layout, but is often more attractive.

- There are four values the position property can be set to: static, absolute, fixed, and relative.

- Static positioning is the default, and places an element in the normal flow of the page.

- Absolute positioning lets you place elements anywhere in the page. By default, absolutely positioned elements are placed relative to the sides of the page.

- If an absolutely positioned element is nested within another positioned element, then its position is relative to the containing element that is positioned.

- The properties top, right, bottom, and left are used to position elements for absolute, fixed, and relative positioning.

- Absolutely positioned elements can be layered on top of one another using the z-index property. A larger z-index value indicates it is higher in the stack (closer to you on the screen).

- Fixed-position elements are always positioned relative to the browser window and do not move when the page is scrolled. Other content in the page scrolls underneath these elements.

- Relatively positioned elements are first flowed into the page as normal, and then offset by the specified amount, leaving empty the space where they would normally sit.

- With relative positioning, left, right, top, and bottom refer to the amount of offset from the element's position in the normal flow.

- CSS table display allows you to lay out your elements in a table-like layout.

- To create a CSS table display, use a block element for the table, block elements for the rows, and block elements for the cells. Typically, these will be <div> elements.

- Table display is a good layout strategy for multicolumn layouts where even columns of content are needed.

HTMLcross

This has been a turbo-charged chapter, with lots to learn. Help it all sink in by doing this crossword. All the answers come from the chapter.

Across

4. State between liquid and frozen.
6. Method browser uses to position static elements on the page.
7. This kind of offset was used on the coupon for a special effect.
10. Usually used to identify an element that is going to be positioned.
11. When boxes are placed on top of each other, these collapse.
12. When you place two inline elements next to each other, their margins don't _____.
15. Absolute positioning is relative to the positioned _____ block.
16. Inline elements are flowed from the top _____.
17. A positioning type that keeps elements in the flow.

Down

1. Special inline elements that get grouped together into boxes as the page is laid out.
2. Use _____ to create space between cells in a table display.
3. Block elements are flowed top to _____.
5. Type of positioning that is relative to the viewport.
6. Removes element from the flow, and sets it to one side.
8. In general, _____ is a better technique for column layouts.
9. Another name for the browser window.
12. Property used to fix footer overlap problems.
13. Inline content flows around _____ elements.
14. Property that describes the layering behavior of positioned elements.

Here's your page. Flow the block elements in "lounge.html" here.

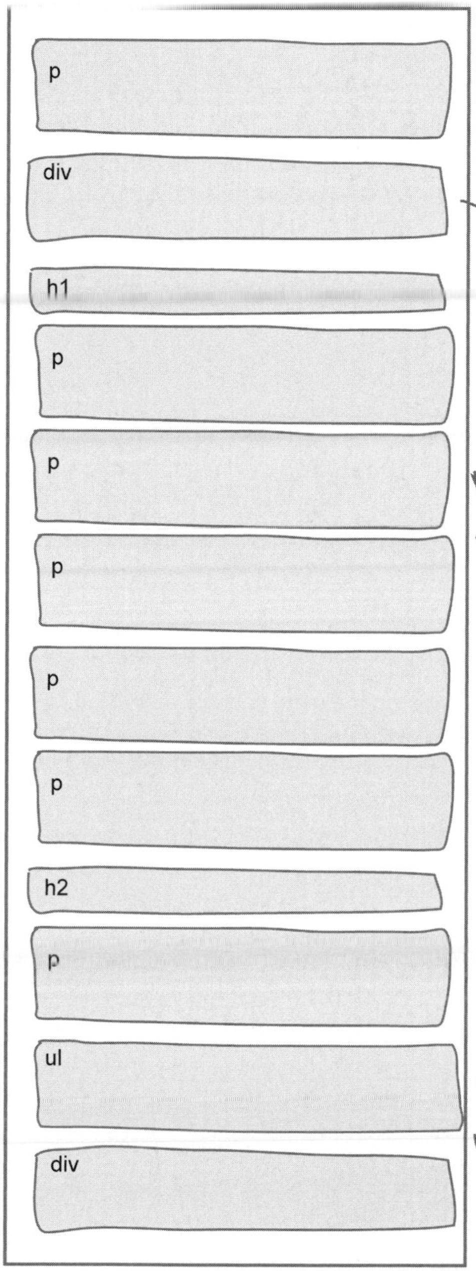

BE the Browser Solution

Open your "lounge.html" file and locate all the block elements. Flow each one on to the page below. Just concentrate on the block elements nested directly inside the body element. You can also ignore the "float" property in your CSS because you still don't know what it does. Here's the solution.

p

div

h1

p

p

p

p

p

p

Each block element in your "lounge. html" file is flowed from top to bottom, with a linebreak in between.

div
- h2
- p
- h3
- p
- p
- h3
- p
- p
- h3
- p
- p

h2

p

ul

div

Some of these elements have nested block elements in them, like the <ul>, the elixirs <div>, and the footer <div>.

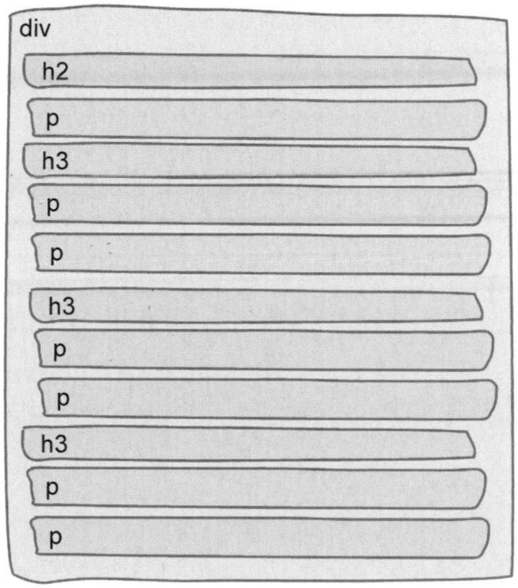

We didn't ask you to, but if you went the extra mile, here's how the elements in the elixirs <div> get flowed.

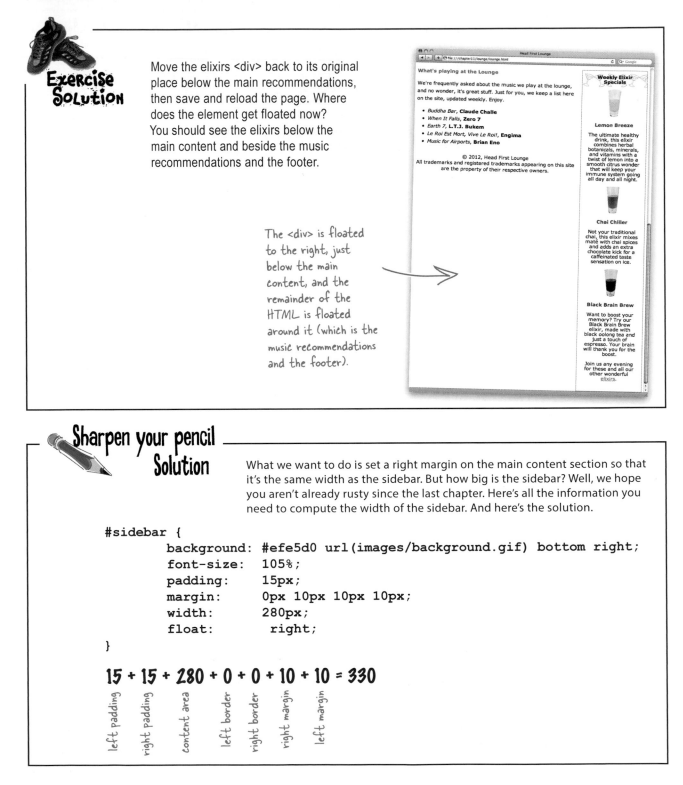

Exercise Solution

Move the elixirs <div> back to its original place below the main recommendations, then save and reload the page. Where does the element get floated now? You should see the elixirs below the main content and beside the music recommendations and the footer.

The <div> is floated to the right, just below the main content, and the remainder of the HTML is floated around it (which is the music recommendations and the footer).

Sharpen your pencil Solution

What we want to do is set a right margin on the main content section so that it's the same width as the sidebar. But how big is the sidebar? Well, we hope you aren't already rusty since the last chapter. Here's all the information you need to compute the width of the sidebar. And here's the solution.

```
#sidebar {
        background:  #efe5d0 url(images/background.gif) bottom right;
        font-size:   105%;
        padding:     15px;
        margin:      0px 10px 10px 10px;
        width:       280px;
        float:        right;
}
```

15 + 15 + 280 + 0 + 0 + 10 + 10 = 330

left padding   right padding   content area   left border   right border   right margin   left margin

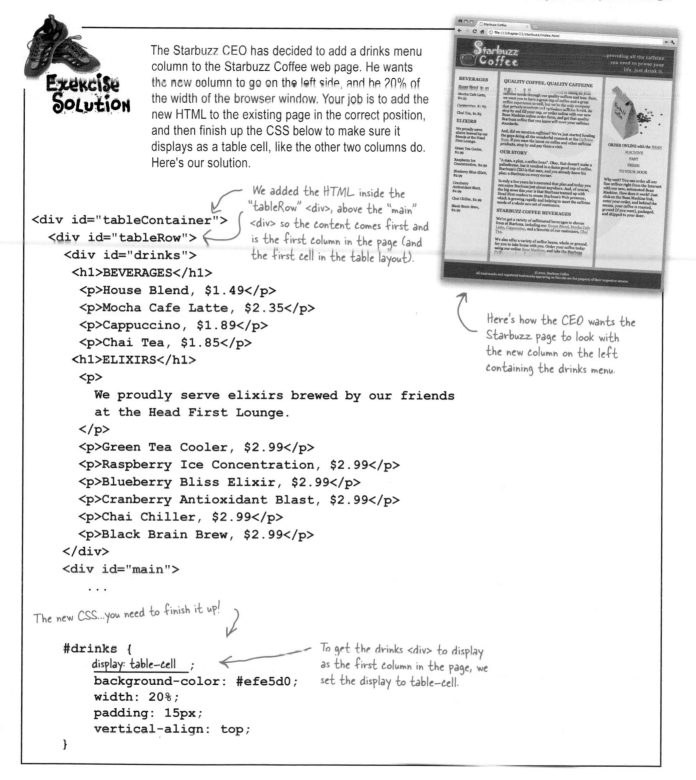

Exercise Solution

The Starbuzz CEO has decided to add a drinks menu column to the Starbuzz Coffee web page. He wants the new column to go on the left side, and be 20% of the width of the browser window. Your job is to add the new HTML to the existing page in the correct position, and then finish up the CSS below to make sure it displays as a table cell, like the other two columns do. Here's our solution.

We added the HTML inside the "tableRow" <div>, above the "main" <div> so the content comes first and is the first column in the page (and the first cell in the table layout).

```
<div id="tableContainer">
  <div id="tableRow">
    <div id="drinks">
     <h1>BEVERAGES</h1>
      <p>House Blend, $1.49</p>
      <p>Mocha Cafe Latte, $2.35</p>
      <p>Cappuccino, $1.89</p>
      <p>Chai Tea, $1.85</p>
     <h1>ELIXIRS</h1>
      <p>
        We proudly serve elixirs brewed by our friends
        at the Head First Lounge.
      </p>
      <p>Green Tea Cooler, $2.99</p>
      <p>Raspberry Ice Concentration, $2.99</p>
      <p>Blueberry Bliss Elixir, $2.99</p>
      <p>Cranberry Antioxidant Blast, $2.99</p>
      <p>Chai Chiller, $2.99</p>
      <p>Black Brain Brew, $2.99</p>
    </div>
    <div id="main">
        . . .
```

Here's how the CEO wants the Starbuzz page to look with the new column on the left containing the drinks menu.

The new CSS...you need to finish it up!

```
    #drinks {
        display: table-cell   ;
        background-color: #efe5d0;
        width: 20%;
        padding: 15px;
        vertical-align: top;
    }
```

To get the drinks <div> to display as the first column in the page, we set the display to table-cell.

Sharpen your pencil
Solution

Time to put all this knowledge about floating and positioning to the test! Take a look at the web page below. There are four elements with an id. Your job was to correctly match each of those elements with the CSS rules on the right, and fill in the correct id selector for each one. Here's the solution. Did you get them all correct?

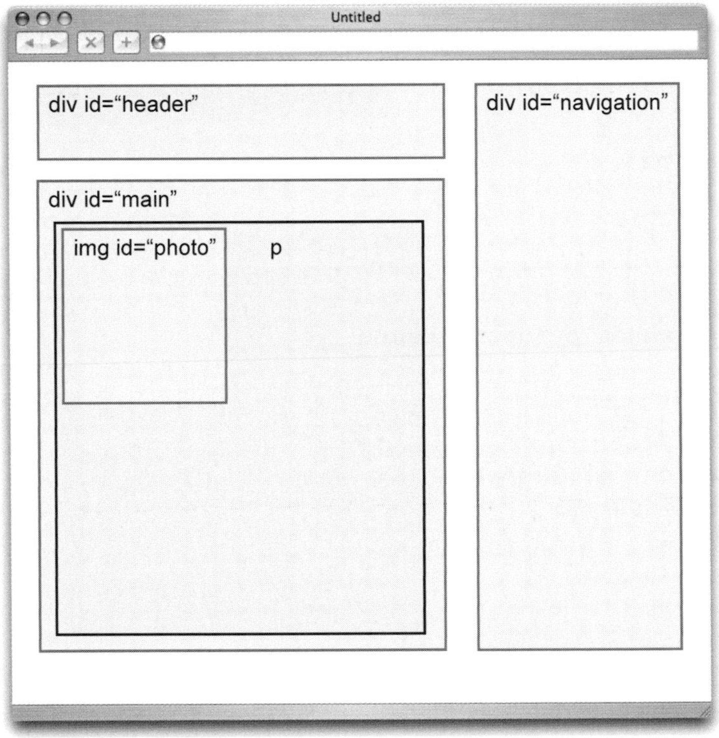

```
div id="header"

div id="navigation"

div id="main"

img id="photo"      p
```

Fill in the selectors to complete the CSS.

```
#main              {
    margin-top:    140px;
    margin-left:   20px;
    width:         500px;
}

#navigation        {
    position: absolute;
    top:      20px;
    left:     550px;
    width:    200px;
}

#photo             {
    float: left;
}

#header            {
    position: absolute;
    top:      20px;
    left:     20px;
    width:    500px;
    height:   100px;
}
```

This CSS is so easy you could probably do it in your sleep, after all the layout experience you've had in this chapter already. Go ahead and write the CSS to fix the images in the header. You know you're going to use float; fill in the blanks below with the rest of the rule you need to get the images into the right place. Here's our solution.

#header img#headerSlogan {

float: __right__;

}

You could also just use #headerSlogan here as the selector if you want.

HTMLcross Solution

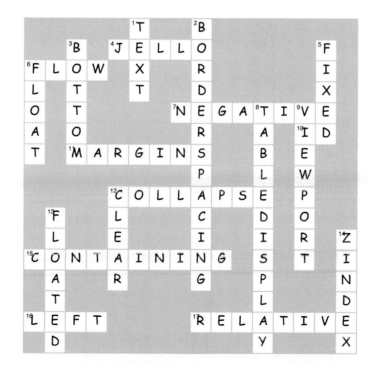

Sharpen your pencil Solution

Given what you know about CSS table displays, sketch out how our two columns from the Starbuzz page would fit into a table. Check the answer at the end of the chapter before moving on…

This is the first column.

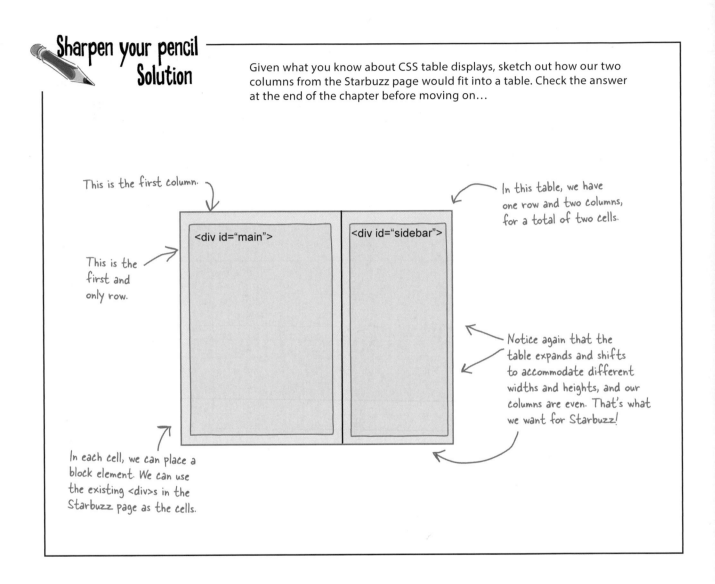

<div id="main">

<div id="sidebar">

This is the first and only row.

In this table, we have one row and two columns, for a total of two cells.

Notice again that the table expands and shifts to accommodate different widths and heights, and our columns are even. That's what we want for Starbuzz!

In each cell, we can place a block element. We can use the existing <div>s in the Starbuzz page as the cells.

12 html5 markup

Modern HTML

We're the first on the block to move up to HTML5...the salesman told us it was more refined and shinier than HTML4.01.

So, we're sure you've heard the hype around HTML5. And, given how far along you are in this book, you're probably wondering if you made the right purchase. Now, one thing to be clear about, up front, is that everything you've learned in this book has been HTML, and more specifically has met the HTML5 standard. But there are some new aspects of HTML markup that were added with the HTML5 standard that we haven't covered yet, and that's what we're going to do in this chapter. Most of these additions are evolutionary, and you're going to find you are quite comfortable with them given all the hard work you've already done in this book. There's some revolutionary stuff too (like video), and we'll talk about that in this chapter as well. So, let's dive in and take a look at these new additions!

Rethinking HTML structure

Before we learn even more markup, let's step back for a second…we've talked a lot about structure, but are <div>s really good structure? After all, the browser doesn't really know your <div id="footer"> is a footer, it just knows it is a <div>, right? That seems rather unsatisfying, doesn't it?

Much of the new HTML5 markup is aimed at recognizing how people structure their pages with <div>s and providing markup that is more specific, and better suited for certain kinds of structure. You see, when the browser (or search engines, or screen readers) see id="navigation" in your page, they have no idea your <div> is for navigation. It might as well say id="goobledygoop".

So, the standards bodies actually took a look at how <div> elements were being used—for headers, navigation, footers, articles, and so on—and they added new elements to represent those things. That means with HTML5 we can rework our pages a bit and replace our <div>s with elements that more specifically identify the kind of content contained in them.

Think about the way you've seen <div>s used. Also, check out a few web pages and see how they are using <div>s. Let's say you wanted to take the most common patterns and change the <div>s into real HTML elements. For instance, you could change all the <div id="footer"> elements to just <footer> elements. Make a list of all the new elements you'd add to HTML. Of course, you won't want to add too many, just enough to cover the most common uses. Also note any advantages (or disadvantages) of adding these new elements:

WHO DOES WHAT?

Sure, we could just tell you about the new HTML5 elements, but wouldn't it be more fun to figure them out? Below, you'll find the new elements to the left (these aren't *all* the new elements, but you'll find the more important ones here); for each element, match it with its description to the right:

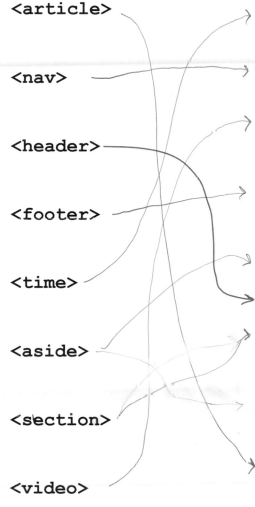

<article> — Can contain a date or time or both.

<nav> — Contains content meant for navigation links in the page.

<header> — Used to add video media to your page

<footer> — Content that goes at the bottom of the page, or the bottom of a section of the page.

<time> — Contains content that is supplemental to the page content, like a callout or sidebar.

<aside> — Content that goes at the top of the page, or the top of a section of the page.

<section> — A thematic grouping of content, typically with a header and possibly a footer.

<video> — Represents a self-contained composition in a page, like a blog post, user forum post, or newspaper article.

Modern Starbuzz

Starbuzz Coffee is a modern, hip company, so shouldn't they be using the latest and greatest markup in their pages? Let's take a look at where they might be missing out on opportunities to use HTML5:

Could we use a header element here to make the structure more obvious?

Starbuzz uses a <div> with id="header" for the heading.

They use a <div> with an id="main" for the main, center column.

We can definitely think of that as the main content area of the page, or maybe we should say, a main section.

Here's a <div> with an id="drinks" for this left column.

This content is all related; is there a better way?

And the main content area is made up of a set of, well, almost articles about various aspects of Starbuzz

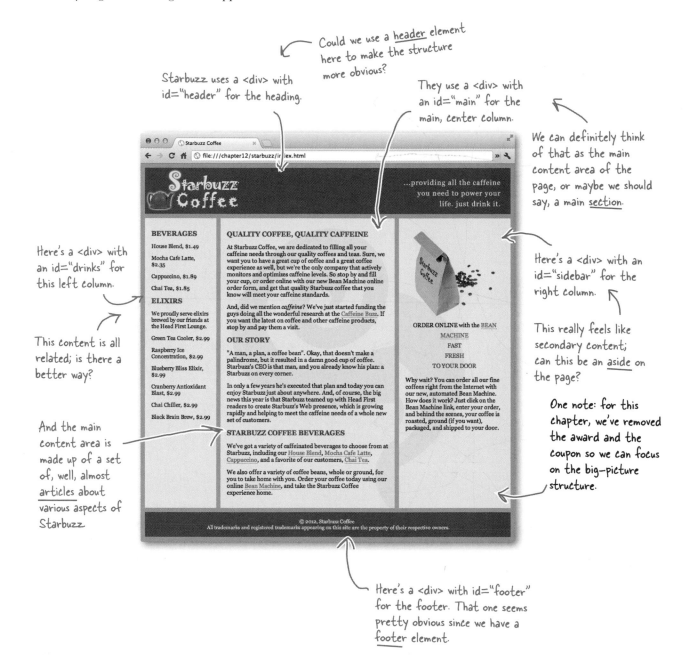

Here's a <div> with an id="sidebar" for the right column.

This really feels like secondary content; can this be an aside on the page?

One note: for this chapter, we've removed the award and the coupon so we can focus on the big-picture structure.

Here's a <div> with id="footer" for the footer. That one seems pretty obvious since we have a footer element.

Using everything you know so far about the new HTML5 elements, see if you can rework the Starbuzz page to make use of them. Go ahead and just mark out and scribble on this page.

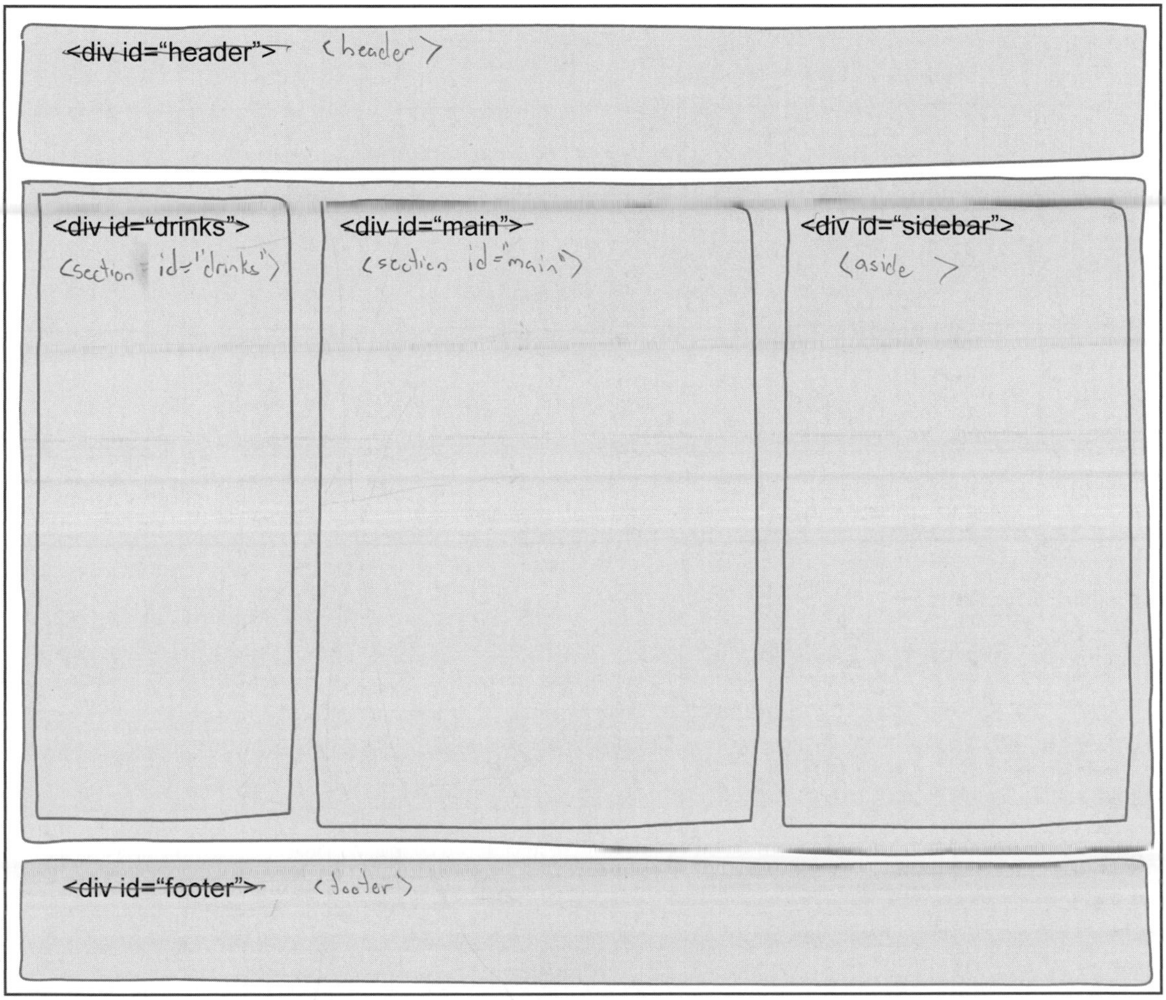

Exercise

<div id="header"> ⟨header⟩

<div id="drinks"> ⟨section id="drinks"⟩

<div id="main"> ⟨section id="main"⟩

<div id="sidebar"> ⟨aside⟩

<div id="footer"> ⟨footer⟩

We're not showing the super-detailed structure of the page, so for now just focus on this large-grained structure.

Exercise Solution

Using everything you know so far about the new HTML5 elements, see if you can rework the Starbuzz page to make use of them. Go ahead and just mark out and scribble on this page.

We can use the <header> element for our header <div>; that's pretty straightforward!

<header>

<section id="drinks">   <section id="main">   <aside>

Each of these "sections" groups together a set of related content; that's just what the <section> element is for.

The sidebar is really peripheral content; we can place that in an aside element, given that's exactly what the <aside> is for.

<footer>

And we can use the <footer> element for our footer.

Update your Starbuzz HTML

Let's go ahead and add these new elements to your Starbuzz HTML, starting with the `<header>`, `<footer>`, and `<aside>` elements. We'll come back and look at the `<section>` element in a bit, but for now you can just leave the drinks and main content `<div>`s as they are. Go ahead and open up the Starbuzz "index.html" file and make the following changes:

 Add the `<header>` element

Start by replacing the `<div id="header">` with a `<header>` element. Like this:

```
<div id="header">
<header>
<img id="headerLogo"
     src="images/headerLogo.gif" alt="Starbuzz Coffee logo image">
<img id="headerSlogan"
     src="images/headerSlogan.gif" alt="Providing all the...">
</header>
</div>
```

Remove the `<div>` tags and replace them with `<header>` tags.

 Add the `<footer>` element

Do the same for the `<div id="footer">`, only replace it with a `<footer>` element:

```
<div id="footer">
<footer>
    &copy; 2012, Starbuzz Coffee
    <br>
    All trademarks and registered trademarks appearing on
    this site are the property of their respective owners.
</footer>
</div>
```

 Change the sidebar to an `<aside>`

Now let's change the "sidebar" `<div>` to an `<aside>` element:

```
<div id="sidebar">
<aside>
    <p class="beanheading">
        <img src="images/bag.gif" alt="Bean Machine bag">
        . . .
    </p>
    <p>
        . . .
    </p>
</aside>
</div>
```

We decided to save a few trees (or bits) by abbreviating the content a little; just make sure you keep all the original content in the page and change the `<div>` tags to `<aside>` tags.

Test driving the new ride

We've got a bit more to rework, but doesn't your HTML already feel somehow newer, cleaner, more modern? Go ahead and do a test drive by loading your page in your browser.

Uh oh...looks like things didn't work so well.

> *What happened? You had me all talked into this HTML5 stuff. That page doesn't look so good.*

No worries; we just got ahead of ourselves. The page doesn't look right because we changed the HTML, but we never reworked the CSS. Think about it like this: we had a bunch of `<div>`s with ids that the CSS was relying on and some of those `<div>`s aren't there anymore. So, we need to rewrite the CSS to target the new elements instead of those old `<div>`s. Let's do that now.

Before you continue...

Watch it!

Older browsers do not support the new elements in HTML5 you'll be using in this chapter.

The elements we're using in this chapter are new to HTML5 and aren't well supported in older browsers (such as IE8 and earlier, Safari 3 and earlier, etc). If you are concerned that your web page might be used by people who are still using these old browsers, then don't use these new elements yet.

Mobile browsers in smartphones, like Android and iPhone, support these new elements, so if your primary audience target is mobile users, you're good to go!

Check http://caniuse.com/#search=new%20elements for updates on browser support of the elements in this chapter.

How to update your CSS for the new elements

Let's update the CSS to reflect our new elements. Don't worry; we've already got all the basics correct in the CSS file. All we need to do is change the selectors a bit:

```
body {
  background-color: #b5a789;
  font-family:      Georgia, "Times New Roman", Times, serif;
  font-size:        small;
  margin:           0px;
}
#header {
header {
  background-color: #675c47;
  margin: 10px 10px 0px 10px;
  height:           108px;
}
#header img#headerSlogan {
header img#headerSlogan {
  float: right;
}

...

#sidebar {
aside {
  display:          table-cell;
  background:       #efe5d0 url(images/background.gif) bottom right;
  font-size:        105%;
  padding:          15px;
  vertical-align:   top;
}
#footer {
footer {
  background-color: #675c47;
  color:            #efe5d0;
  text-align:       center;
  padding:          15px;
  margin: 0px 10px 10px 10px;
  font-size:        90%;
}
...
```

First, remove the # mark from the header rules. We're going from targeting a <div> with an id of "header" to an element named header.

Saving some trees...just imagine the rest of the CSS here.

Here we need to change this from targeting an element with an id of "sidebar" to an aside element.

Finally, we need to select the footer element.

Test drive #2

Ahh...much better.

All right, that's all we need to do; let's give it another try, and this time you should see the page is back to normal. In fact, it should look exactly like it did before we add the HTML5 markup.

Fireside Chats

Tonight's talk: **HTML5 and HTML4.01 mix it up**

HTML5	HTML4.01
Ah, my old pal, HTML4.01. You had a good run, but now I'm here.	
	A good run? Take a look at the Web; it is still a sea of HTML4.01.
I'm just getting started.	
	Yeah? And how are those new elements going? I haven't seen many of them out there.
Sure, people are beginning to use them. Remember, they aren't going to change the world, they just make explicit what web developers have been doing all along.	
	How is <p> not explicit? Hello? That's a paragraph. Can't get more explicit than that.
I'm thinking more about <div> here…	
	There's nothing wrong with <div>. Leave him alone.
I'm not talking about getting rid of <div>. Yeah, he's great for grouping content together for styling and stuff, but what if you want to, say, identify some content as an article on your page? Or break your page into sections?	
	You know as well as I do that everyone is confused about how to use those elements, and you can do both those things with a <div>.

HTML5

Yes, you can do it with a `<div>`, but with, say, an `<article>` element, the browser, search engines, screen readers, and your fellow web developers all know for sure that's an article.

Remember, we use the right element for the job, right? That way we can communicate the most explict structure we can, and all our tools can do the right thing.

See, that is just exactly where you are wrong. Take the `<aside>` element, which is for marking up supplementary content on a page. Now on a mobile phone with limited screen space, if the browser knows that content is an `<aside>`, you might see that content pushed to the bottom so that you see more important content first. If the content is in `<div>` instead, then any number of things can happen depending on where in the HTML file the content is.

Now the browser can know the difference between the main content in the page and an `<aside>`. So it can treat the content in the `<aside>` differently. For instance, a search engine might prioritize the main content in the page over the content in an `<aside>`.

No, no, this applies to all the new HTML markup: header, footer, sections, articles, time, and so on.

CENSORED

HTML4.01

So? It still looks the same.

Right thing? Like what? Display it exactly the same?

I still don't see what the big deal is.

Great, so with HTML5 we know how to deal with asides.

Well, I think it is about time you take that footer of yours and stuff it in

CENS **CENSORED**

Note to editor: they got out of hand—can we get them back to redo the end of the chat?

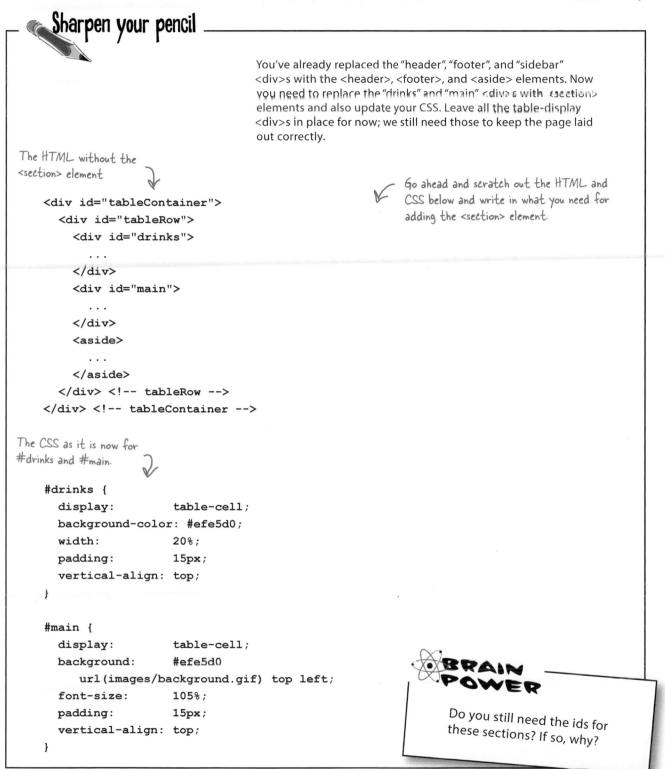

Sharpen your pencil

You've already replaced the "header", "footer", and "sidebar" <div>s with the <header>, <footer>, and <aside> elements. Now you need to replace the "drinks" and "main" <div>s with <section> elements and also update your CSS. Leave all the table-display <div>s in place for now; we still need those to keep the page laid out correctly.

The HTML without the <section> element

Go ahead and scratch out the HTML and CSS below and write in what you need for adding the <section> element.

```
<div id="tableContainer">
  <div id="tableRow">
    <div id="drinks">
      ...
    </div>
    <div id="main">
      ...
    </div>
    <aside>
      ...
    </aside>
  </div> <!-- tableRow -->
</div> <!-- tableContainer -->
```

The CSS as it is now for #drinks and #main.

```
#drinks {
  display:          table-cell;
  background-color: #efe5d0;
  width:            20%;
  padding:          15px;
  vertical-align:   top;
}

#main {
  display:          table-cell;
  background:       #efe5d0
    url(images/background.gif) top left;
  font-size:        105%;
  padding:          15px;
  vertical-align:   top;
}
```

✦ BRAIN POWER

Do you still need the ids for these sections? If so, why?

Sharpen your pencil
Solution

You've already replaced the "header", "footer", and "sidebar" <div>s with the <header>, <footer>, and <aside> elements. Now you need to replace the "drinks" and "main" <div>s with <section> elements and also update your CSS. Leave all the table-display <div>s in place for now; we still need those to keep the page laid out correctly.

Here's our solution:

The HTML with the <section> element

```
<div id="tableContainer">
  <div id="tableRow">
    <section id="drinks">
      ...
    </section>
    <section id="main">
      ...
    </section>
    <aside>
      ...
    </aside>
  </div> <!-- tableRow -->
</div> <!-- tableContainer -->
```

All we did was replace <div>s with <section>s for "drinks" and "main".

We left the ids there because we need to be able to uniquely identify each <section> to style it.

The CSS updated for the two sections

```
section#drinks {
  display:           table-cell;
  background-color: #efe5d0;
  width:             20%;
  padding:           15px;
  vertical-align:   top;
}
```

We could have left the CSS exactly as it was! Because we are using ids, the same two elements would have been targeted with the existing rules. We went ahead and added the tag name in front of the id selector just to make it clear we're using <section>s here.

```
section#main {
  display:          table-cell;
  background:       #efe5d0 url(images/background.gif) top left;
  font-size:        105%;
  padding:          15px;
  vertical-align:  top;
}
```

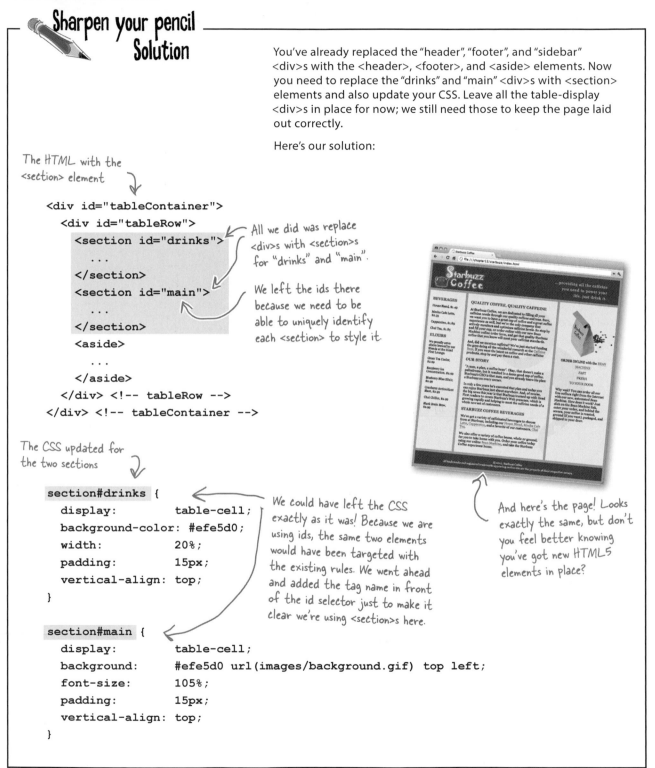

And here's the page! Looks exactly the same, but don't you feel better knowing you've got new HTML5 elements in place?

Hey, I'm starting a blog. Can we use any of these new HTML5 elements to build it? I want to make sure I'm using the latest and greatest stuff...it's going to be super popular, just like our coffee.

Interesting you should ask, because many of the new HTML5 elements are perfect for creating a blog. Before we get into the actual markup, though, let's think about what a blog might look like, making sure we keep it consistent with the current Starbuzz design. To do that, we'll create a new page with the same "drinks" `<section>` on the left, and the same `<aside>` on the right, and all we'll change is the content in the middle to be the blog. Let's check it out:

Here's what the finished blog page will look like.

We've got a nice navigation menu below the header...

And the main content area now has several blog posts in it.

The rest of the page is the same.

Exercise

Your job is to choose the elements you think will work the best for the new blog. Fill in the blanks in the diagram below to show which elements you would choose. Note that each blog post will have a heading and at least one paragraph of text.

Choose your elements from the list below:

`<header>`	`<aside>`
`<footer>`	`<section>`
`<article>`	`<div>`
`<nav>`	`<h1>`
`<time>`	`<p>`

The new blog page. It's like the home page, except the middle section is now blog posts and we have a navigation menu below the header.

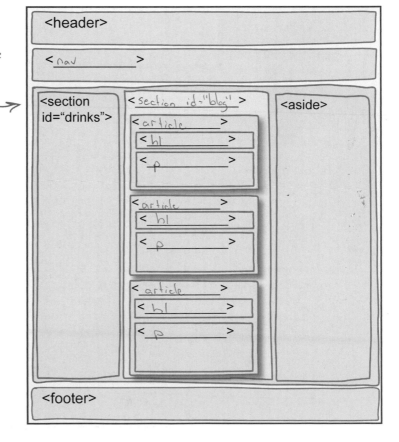

Your job is to choose the elements you think will work the best for the new blog. Fill in the blanks in the diagram below to show which elements you would choose. Note that each blog post will have a heading and at least one paragraph of text.

Choose your elements from the list below:

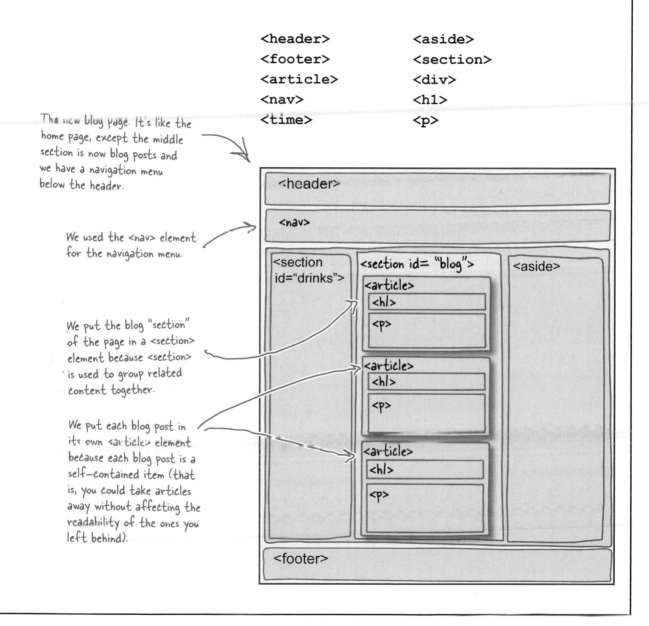

The new blog page. It's like the home page, except the middle section is now blog posts and we have a navigation menu below the header.

We used the <nav> element for the navigation menu.

We put the blog "section" of the page in a <section> element because <section> is used to group related content together.

We put each blog post in its own <article> element because each blog post is a self-contained item (that is, you could take articles away without affecting the readability of the ones you left behind).

<header>

<nav>

<section id="drinks">   <section id="blog">   <aside>
   <article>
      <h1>
      <p>
   <article>
      <h1>
      <p>
   <article>
      <h1>
      <p>

<footer>

Building the Starbuzz blog page

From the previous exercise, you know that we're using a `<section>` element for the blog section (in the middle column) and an `<article>` element for each blog post. Let's get started doing that, and we'll come back to navigation in a bit. We've already created the "blog.html" file for you by making a copy of the file "index.html", and replacing the "main" `<section>` with a "blog" `<section>`. You can get the complete "blog.html" from the code downloads for the book; here's part of it:

```
<section id="blog">

  <article>

    <h1>Starbuzz meets social media</h1>

    <p>

    Here at Starbuzz we're embracing the social media craze. In fact,
we're going further than any of our competitors and we're very close…

    </p>

    <p>

    Sound like science fiction? It's not; I'm already testing our final
prototype social network cup as I write this…

    </p>

    <p>

    So, keep your eyes out for this amazing new cup. And I'll be
releasing a video teaser soon to tell you all about this new invention,
straight from Starbuzz Coffee.

    </p>

  </article>

  <article>

    <h1>Starbuzz uses computer science</h1>

    <p>

      ...

    </p>

  </article>

  <article>

    <h1>Most unique patron of the month</h1>

    <p>

      ...

    </p>

  </article>

</section>
```

We're using a `<section>` element for the middle column, just like we did for "main" in the index.html file.

We're only showing part of each blog post here.

Each blog post gets its own `<article>` element.

And within each `<article>`, we use `<h1>` for the heading, and `<p>` for the paragraphs of text. Pretty simple! But more meaningful than a bunch of `<div>`s, right?

Get the full blog post text from the "blog.html" file you downloaded from wickedlysmart.com.

Setting up the CSS for the blog page

You might have noticed that both the "index.html" file and the "blog.html" file link to the same CSS file, "starbuzz.css". Let's take a quick look at "blog.html":

```
<!DOCTYPE html>
<html>
  <head>
    <meta charset="utf-8">
    <title>Starbuzz Coffee - Blog</title>
    <link rel="stylesheet" type="text/css" href="starbuzz.css">
  </head>
```

Here's the link to the CSS...

...and while we're here, go ahead and update the title of the page.

Now, we haven't yet added any CSS to target our new section with an id of "blog", so let's do that now. We know we want the "blog" `<section>` to be styled exactly like the "main" `<section>` on the home page, so we can just reuse the same rule by adding the rule for the blog section to the existing rule for the main section, like this:

```
section#main, section#blog {
  display:          table-cell;
  background:       #efe5d0 url(images/background.gif) top left;
  font-size:        105%;
  padding:          15px;
  vertical-align:   top;
}
```

We can use the same rule for both `<section>` elements by using the two selectors separated by a comma. This says, apply all these properties to both of the selected elements.

Even though the two elements, the "main" `<section>` and the "blog" `<section>`, are on two different pages, this will work because both pages link to the same CSS file.

That's it! All the other styling we need for the "blog" `<section>` of the page is already in the CSS, and we're not adding any special styling for `<article>`. So it's time to…

Test drive the blog page

With the creation of a new blog page, and those quick tweaks to the page (that is, adding the `<section>` and `<article>` elements), let's save the page and load it in the browser.

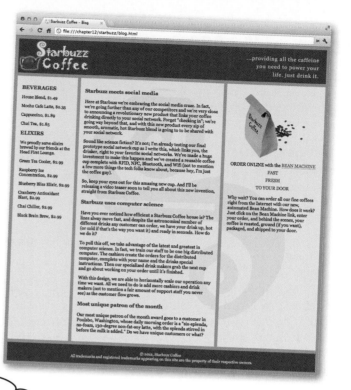

As you can see, elements like `<section>`, `<article>`, and `<aside>` have a similar default style to `<div>`; that is, not much! But they do add information about the meaning of the content in your page.

> What's the difference between a section and an article?

Yes, it can be confusing. We'll tell you right up front that there is no crystal-clear answer to this; in fact, there are many ways to use `<article>` and `<section>`. But here is a general way to think about them: use `<section>` to group together related content, and use `<article>` to enclose a self-contained piece of content like a news article, a blog post, or a short report.

In the Starbuzz page, each column contains related content, so we've treated each column as a section of the page. We've also taken the individual blog posts and made those articles because they are self-contained (you could even imagine taking one and reposting it on another site or blog).

Your mileage may vary, but in general, stick to grouping related content together with `<section>`, and for self-contained content, use `<article>`. And if you need to group content together that doesn't feel as related, you always have `<div>` to fall back on.

We still need to add a date to the blog...

Did you notice in our blog design that we added a date to every blog post? Before HTML5, dates were created in an ad hoc way—you might have just added the date without marking it up at all, or used a `<span>` or even a `<p>` to mark it up. But now, we have an element that's perfect for the job: the `<time>` element.

A two-minute guide to the `<time>` element

Let's take a closer look at the `<time>` element. It has an important attribute, datetime, and the element's kind of picky about the values you use in this attribute, so it's worth going over some of the details.

If you're using the datetime attribute to specify a date and/or a time, then you can write whatever you want as the content for the element. Most often, that will be some date- or time-related text, like "February 18, 2012" or even "yesterday" or "now".

The datetime attribute is required if the content of the element isn't written using the official Internet date/time format.

```
<time datetime="2012-02-18">2/18/2012</time>
```

This is the official Internet format for specifying dates with a day, month, and year.

Here are some other ways to express dates and times using the official format.

2012-02 ← You can specify just a year and month, or even just a year.

2012

2012-02-18 09:00 ← You can add on a time, in 24-hour format.

2012-02-18 18:00

05:00 ← You can specify just a time.

2012-02-18 05:00Z ← If you use a "Z" after the date and time, then it means UTC time. (UTC = GMT)

Adding the <time> element to your blog

Edit your "blog.html" file, and add the following dates below each article heading:

```
<article>
  <h1>Starbuzz meets social media</h1>
  <time datetime="2012-03-12">3/12/2012</time>
  ...
</article>
<article>
  <h1>Starbuzz uses computer science</h1>
  <time datetime="2012-03-10">3/10/2012</time>
  ...
</article>
<article>
  <h1>Most unique patron of the month</h1>
  <time datetime="2012-02-18">2/18/2012</time>
  ...
</article>
```

Below each heading, we've added a <time> element.

The content of the time element is the date of the blog post (written American style, with the month first). You could also write March 10, 2012 if you want.

We're using the datetime attribute of the <time> element to specify the precise date using the official Internet date/time format for dates.

Test drive the blog

Test drive the blog again, and you should see the date of the blog post show up underneath each blog post heading.

Now we have a date below each blog posting.

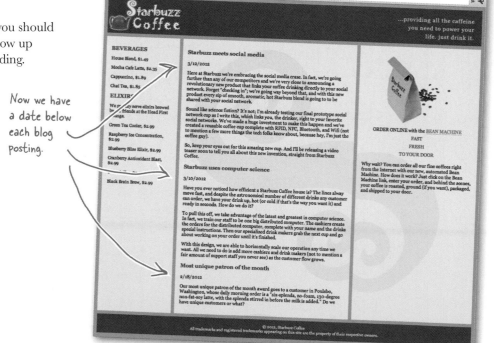

It seems like semantically each article has its own little header, with a heading and date. I assume we could even add things like a byline with the author's name and location. Is that the right way to be using article?

It sure is. Again, think of an article as a self-contained piece of content—something you could even take out and syndicate to another web page somewhere. And if you did that, you'd definitely want to add something like a byline with who wrote it, when, and maybe where.

We can take this even further, because the <header> element isn't meant just for your main header; you can use it whenever you want to group together items into a header. For instance, you can add the <header> element to an <article>, a <section>, or even an <aside>.

To see how this works, let's go back and add some more <header> elements to the Starbuzz articles.

Note that the footer can be used within sections, articles, and asides as well. We're not going to do that on Starbuzz, but many sites do create headers and footers for these elements.

How to add more <header> elements

Adding <header> elements is straightforward. Within each
<article> element, we'll place a <header> to contain the
heading and time. To do that, find the <article> elements
within the blog section and add an opening and closing
<header> tag to each one.

```
    . . .
<section id="blog">
<article>
  <header>
      <h1>Starbuzz meets social media</h1>
      <time datetime="2012-03-12">3/12/2012</time>
  </header>
  <p>...</p>
</article>

<article>
  <header>
      <h1>Starbuzz uses computer science</h1>
      <time datetime="2012-03-10">3/10/2012</time>
  </header>
  <p>...</p>
</article>

<article>
  <header>
      <h1>Most unique patron of the month</h1>
      <time datetime="2012-02-18">2/18/2012</time>
  </header>
  <p>...</p>
</article>
</section>
    . . .
```

Place your <header> element here, around the heading and the time elements.

Make sure you add a <header> to each article in the blog section.

BRAIN POWER

Feel free to add an author byline to the header as well. Hmm, there isn't an <author> element.
Any idea how you might mark up an author byline?

Testing the header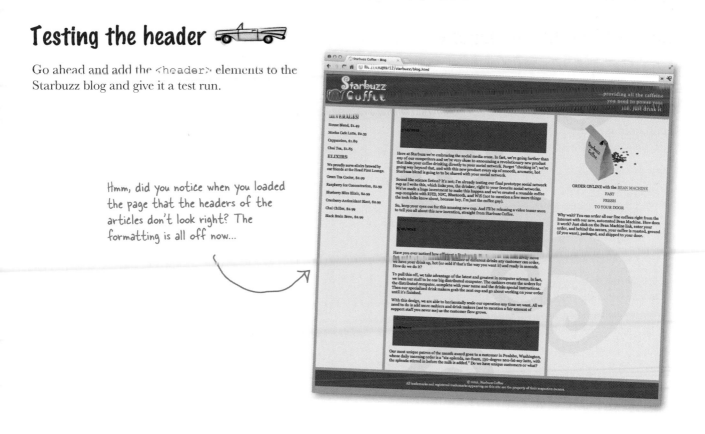

Go ahead and add the <header> elements to the Starbuzz blog and give it a test run.

Hmm, did you notice when you loaded the page that the headers of the articles don't look right? The formatting is all off now...

Sharpen your pencil

Now that we've added the <header> elements, the spacing and formatting is off; did you notice we've got way too much space below the article heading and below the date, and the background color is all wrong? Any idea why? Write your ideas about why this might be happening below.

Hint: take a look at your CSS and see if there are any other <header> rules that might be affecting the new article headers you just added.

. We are using the style for the
header at the top of the page.
We need to specify the header for articles

So, what's wrong with the header anyway?

Clearly, we've messed up the formatting a bit by adding the `<header>` elements. Why? Let's take another look at the "starbuzz.css" file and check out the rule for the `<header>` element:

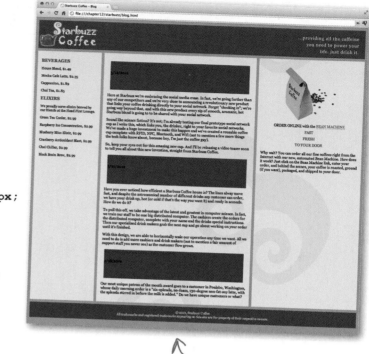

```css
header {
    background-color: #675c47;
    margin:          10px 10px 0px 10px;
    height:          108px;
}
```

This header rule height property causes the background color to be set and space to be added to ALL headers in the page, not just the main header. And the margin isn't helping either.

We can fix this by creating a class just for the `<header>` at the top of the page. We might have several `<header>` elements in sections and articles throughout the site, and in our case, for Starbuzz Coffee, the `<header>` at the top of the page will always be treated differently from these other headers because it has a special graphical look. So, first find the top `<header>` element in your "blog.html" file and add a class named "top" to the element:

The rule for styling the header works great for the main header but looks terrible for the headers in the articles.

Add the class "top" to the first `<header>` element in the page.

```html
<body>
    <header class="top">
        <img id="headerLogo"
            src="images/headerLogo.gif" alt="Starbuzz Coffee header logo image">
        <img id="headerSlogan"
            src="images/headerSlogan.gif" alt="Starbuzz Coffee header slogan image">
    </header>
...
```

Add the "top" class to the top `<header>` in your "index.html" file, too.

Once you've added the "top" class to both your "blog.html" and "index.html" files, then all you have to do is update your CSS to use the class in the selector in the rules for the header.

> *We've added the .top class selector to the header rule in the CSS.*

```css
header.top {
  background-color: #675c47;
  margin:           10px 10px 0px 10px;
  height:           108px;
}

header.top img#headerSlogan {
  float:            right;
}
```

> *We added it to this rule too—while we don't need to for the selector to work correctly, it does make it more clear in the CSS exactly which headerSlogan we're selecting. Just a little best-practice work.*

A final test drive for the headers

Once you've made all the changes to your "blog.html", "index.html", and "starbuzz.css" files, reload the blog page.

Notice that now the `<header>` rules apply only to the `<header>` at the very top of the page, which is just what we want. Meanwhile, the article `<header>`s get the default style, which will work fine as well.

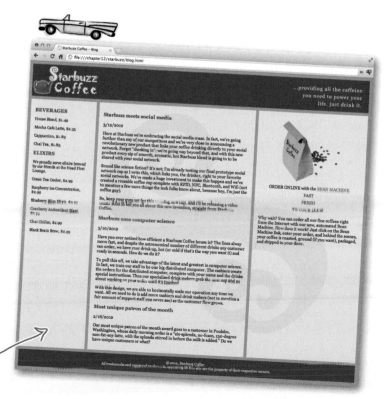

> *Now the headers in the articles are formatted correctly!*

there are no
Dumb Questions

Q: We are doing a lot of work to add elements to the page, and it looks exactly the same as it did before! Tell me again what all this is getting me?

A: We've replaced a few elements and added a few elements, and in the process, we've added a lot of meaning to our pages. The browser, search engines, and applications for building web pages, can—if they want—be a lot smarter about how they handle different parts of your page. And your page is easier for you, and other web developers, to read. Even though your page looks the same, it's a lot more meaningful under the covers.

Q: What's the difference between a <section> and an <article> again? They seem similar to me.

A: It is easy to get confused about which element to use, so we're glad you asked. The <section> element is more generic than <article>, but it's not as generic as <div>. For instance, if you're just adding an element so you can style the page, then use a <div>. If you're adding an element to mark up content that forms a well-defined section of related content, then use <section>. And if you have some content that can be reused or distributed independently from the rest of the content on the page, then use <article>.

Q: Should every <section> and every <article> always have a <header>?

A: Most of the time, your <section>s and <article>s will have a <header>, or at least a heading (like <h1>). Think about it: content within an <article> element can be reused elsewhere, so chances are, that content will

need a header for descriptive or introduction purposes. Likewise, content with a <section> element is a group of related content in your page, so it will typically have some kind of header to separate and introduce that section of content.

Q: Should we use <header> only when we've got more than one thing to put in it? What if we've only got one heading and nothing else?

A: You can use <header> even if you have only one heading to put in it. The <header> element provides extra semantic meaning that separates the header of a page, a section, or an article from the rest of the content. However, it's not required that you always put your heading content in a <header> element (that is, the page will validate if you don't).

A quick interview with <div>
<div>'s feeling a bit left out...

Head First: Hey <div>, we heard you've been feeling really down lately. What's up?

<div>: In case you haven't noticed, I'm being made mostly redundant! They're replacing me all over the place with these new elements, <section>, <nav>, <aside>...

Head First: Hey, Element-up; after all, I still see you in Starbuzz handling the "tableContainer" and the "tableRow".

<div>: They haven't gotten rid of me completely yet, but if they keep inventing new elements, it won't be long before it's game over, man.

Head First: The last time I looked, you were still in the HTML specification. Web developers have all sorts of special needs for adding structure to their pages and the standards guys (and gals) have no interest in inventing zillions of new elements.

<div>: That's true, and I haven't seen any new elements

come along that are simply for creating generic structure.

Head First: Right! All these other new elements are specifically for adding semantic meaning to pages, and you're much more general purpose. You're what everyone falls back on when they need table layout, for instance.

<div>: That's so true!

Head First: If you ask us, you were way overworked before these new elements came along...isn't it time you start enjoying your reduced workload?

<div>: You know, you make a good point. Maybe I should close down shop for a while and see the world; after all, I racked up a lot of frequent flyer mileage flying around the Internet.

Head First: Hold on now, you can't just disappear; most of the Web is relying on you...

Head First: Hello? <div>?

> Being a forward-thinking CEO, I feel better knowing we're making the page as semantically sound as we can. But don't we need some navigation? How do I get from the home page to the blog? And back?

We agree! Having multiple pages isn't going to do us much good if readers can't navigate between them.

And to create navigation for these pages, we're going to use some of the tools we already know about; namely, a list and some anchor tags. Let's see how that works.

First, create a set of links for our navigation:

```html
<a href="index.html">HOME</a>
<a href="blog.html">BLOG</a>
<a href="">INVENTIONS</a>
<a href="">RECIPES</a>
<a href="">LOCATIONS</a>
```

We're leaving these three links blank because we won't be adding these pages, but you should feel free to create these pages!

Now, wrap up those anchors in an unordered list so we can treat them as a group of items. We haven't done this before, but watch how this works, and see how lists are perfect for navigation items:

Notice that each link is now an item in an unordered list. This may not look much like navigation, but it will when we apply some style.

```html
<ul>
    <li><a href="index.html">HOME</a></li>
    <li class="selected"><a href="blog.html">BLOG</a></li>
    <li><a href="">INVENTIONS</a></li>
    <li><a href="">RECIPES</a></li>
    <li><a href="">LOCATIONS</a></li>
</ul>
```

Notice also that we are identifying one item as the selected one, by using a class.

Completing the navigation

Now place the navigation right into your HTML. Do that by inserting it just below the header in the "blog.html" file:

```html
<body>
  <header class="top">
    <img id="headerLogo"
         src="images/headerLogo.gif" alt="Starbuzz Coffee header logo image">
    <img id="headerSlogan"
         src="images/headerSlogan.gif" alt="Providing all the caffeine...">
  </header>
  <ul>
      <li><a href="index.html">HOME</a></li>
      <li class="selected"><a href="blog.html">BLOG</a></li>
      <li><a href="">INVENTIONS</a></li>
      <li><a href="">RECIPES</a></li>
      <li><a href="">LOCATIONS</a></li>
  </ul>
  ...
</body>
```

Adding the navigation CSS

You can try that HTML if you want, but you won't be satisfied that it feels anything like "navigation." So, before you try it, let's add some CSS:

Make sure and add this CSS to the BOTTOM of your starbuzz.css file.

```css
ul {
    background-color: #efe5d0;
    margin: 10px 10px 0px 10px;
    list-style-type: none;
    padding: 5px 0px 5px 0px;
}
```

We're adding a background color, and some margins and padding. Notice that the bottom margin is 0 because the table display already has a 10px border-spacing at the top.

Also notice that we've removed the bullets from the list items.

```css
ul li {
    display: inline;
    padding: 5px 10px 5px 10px;
}
```

Here, we're changing the display of each list item from "block" to "inline", so now the list items won't have a carriage return before and after; they'll all flow into one line on the page like regular inline elements do.

```css
ul li a:link, ul li a:visited {
    color: #954b4b;
    border-bottom: none;
    font-weight: bold;
}
```

We want the links in the navigation list to look a bit different from the rest of the links in the page, so we override the other rules for <a> (above this rule in the CSS) with a rule that sets properties for both the links and the visited state of the links (so they look the same).

```css
ul li.selected {
    background-color: #c8b99c;
}
```

And finally, we're setting the background of the <li> element with the class "selected" so the navigation item corresponding to the page we're on looks different from the rest.

Who needs GPS? Giving the navigation a test drive

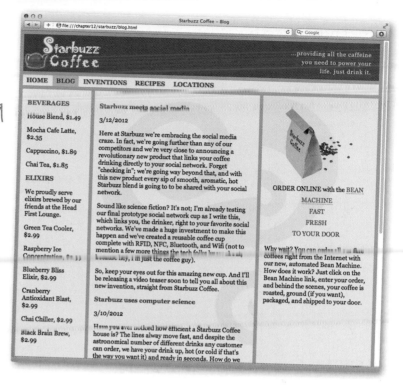

Let's give this a try. Go ahead and get the CSS typed into the bottom of your CSS file, and then load it in your browser.

Hey, not bad for a first try. We've got a nice navigation bar that even has the page we're on—the blog page—highlighted.

But…can we take this even further? After all, you're in the "modern HTML" chapter and we haven't used a new element from HTML5 for the navigation yet. As you've probably guessed, we can improve this by adding a `<nav>` element to the HTML file. Doing so will give everyone (browser, search engines, screen readers, your fellow web developers) a bit more information about what this list really is…

Adding a <nav> element...

As you already know, there is a `<nav>` element, and using it is as simple as wrapping your navigation list with `<nav>` opening and closing tags, like this:

Here's the <nav> starting tag, and we're enclosing the entire navigation list within a <nav> element.

```
<nav>
    <ul>
        <li><a href="index.html">HOME</a></li>
        <li class="selected"><a href="blog.html">BLOG</a></li>
        <li><a href="">INVENTIONS</a></li>
        <li><a href="">RECIPES</a></li>
        <li><a href="">LOCATIONS</a></li>
    </ul>
</nav>
```

We should really talk about best practices. You see, right now your CSS assumes that every unordered list is a navigational menu. So, what happens when the Starbuzz CEO needs to add a list of new cafes he's going to open in the blog? Disaster—he'll probably get a navigation list right in the middle of his blog because it will be styled just like the navigation list we just added to the page.

But no worries; to fix this potential problem, we just need to be more specific about targeting the navigation list items, and that's not hard because the only navigation list items we want to target are the ones contained within a <nav> element.

Before moving on, think through how you'd change the CSS to specifically target the navigation items, and no other unordered lists.

Making our CSS more specific...

Okay, let's use the fact that we have a `<nav>` element in the HTML and make the selectors more specific. That way, we ensure that future changes to the HTML (such as adding a innocent `<ul>` element to somewhere else in the page down the road), don't result in any unexpected styling. Here's how we do that…but notice that we do have to make a few adjustments to the margins of the `<nav>` element so it behaves correctly.

```css
nav {
    background-color: #efe5d0;
    margin: 10px 10px 0px 10px;
}
nav ul {
    margin: 0px;
    list-style-type: none;
    padding: 5px 0px 5px 0px;
}
nav ul li {
    display: inline;
    padding: 5px 10px 5px 10px;
}
nav ul li a:link, nav ul li a:visited {
    color: #954b4b;
    border-bottom: none;
    font-weight: bold;
}
nav ul li.selected {
    background-color: #c8b99c;
}
```

We've added a new rule for the `<nav>` element, and moved the properties for setting the background color and margin into this rule, so everything in the `<nav>` element gets styled with these properties.

And we've added a property to set the margin of the `<ul>` element to 0, so it fits snugly within the `<nav>` element (by default, `<ul>` elements have a margin that will cause the `<ul>` to be shifted over a bit if we don't set it to 0).

Finally, for ALL these rules, we've added the selector "nav" in front of them so the rules affect ONLY `<ul>` elements that appear within a `<nav>` element. That way, we can be sure that if the CEO adds a `<ul>` to his blog in the future, it won't get styled like a navigation list!

Notice, we added "nav" to <u>both</u> rules in this rule with two selectors!

Ta-da! Look at that navigation!

Get these changes into the CSS and give it a try. Not bad, huh? And now we can rest assured that any future `<ul>` elements won't be affected by the navigation CSS. Remember, when possible, add the most specific rule you can to style your elements.

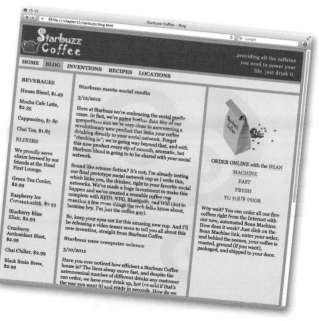

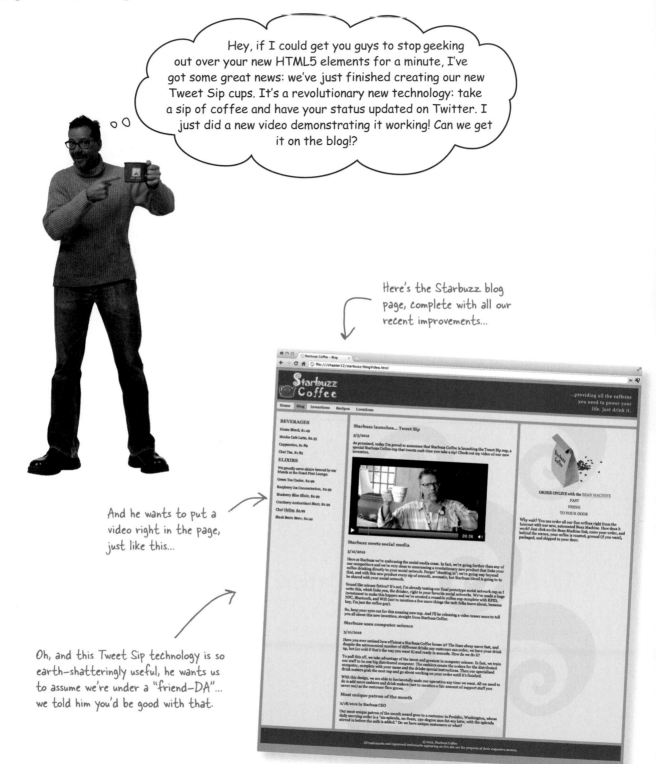

Hey, if I could get you guys to stop geeking out over your new HTML5 elements for a minute, I've got some great news: we've just finished creating our new Tweet Sip cups. It's a revolutionary new technology: take a sip of coffee and have your status updated on Twitter. I just did a new video demonstrating it working! Can we get it on the blog!?

Here's the Starbuzz blog page, complete with all our recent improvements...

And he wants to put a video right in the page, just like this...

Oh, and this Tweet Sip technology is so earth-shatteringly useful, he wants us to assume we're under a "friend-DA"... we told him you'd be good with that.

Now we're going to have to add video to the Starbuzz page. It doesn't seem like a big deal, but aren't we going to need a Flash developer?

Jim: Well, we used to need Flash for video, but with HTML5 we now have a `<video>` element we can use.

Frank: Wait, isn't Flash still better? It's been around a long time.

Jim: I could see some short-term arguments for that on the desktop, but what are you going to do on certain mobile devices that don't support Flash? Think of how many mobile users Starbuzz has; some of those customers are going to be in the dark if we use Flash.

Frank: Got it. So how do we go about using an element to do video?

Jim: Think of video like the `<img>` element; we supply a src attribute that references the video, which is placed in the page at the location of the `<video>` element.

Frank: That sounds easy enough. This is going to be a piece of cake.

Jim: Well, let's not promise anything too quickly. Like most media types, video can get complicated, especially when it comes to dealing with the encodings for video.

Frank: Encodings?

Jim: The format used to encode the video and the audio of a video clip.

Frank: That's a big deal?

Jim: It is because the browser makers haven't agreed on a common standard for video encodings. But let's come back to all that. For now, let's get a `<video>` element in our page and see what all we can do with it.

Frank: Sounds good; lead the way!

Jim

Frank

Creating the new blog entry

Let's get started by adding a new blog entry, which in HTML-speak, should be a new `<article>` element. Go ahead and add this HTML just under the `<section>` element, above the other articles:

```
<article>
    <header>
        <h1>Starbuzz launches...Tweet Sip</h1>
        <time datetime="2012-05-03">5/3/2012</time>
    </header>
    <p>
        As promised, today I'm proud to announce that Starbuzz
        Coffee is launching the Tweet Sip cup, a special Starbuzz
        Coffee cup that tweets each time you take a sip! Check
        out my video of our new invention.
    </p>

</article>
```

Add this in the "blog" `<section>` at the top...

We're going to add the video right here, below the paragraph in the blog entry.

And now, introducing the `<video>` element

At first blush, the `<video>` element really is similar to the `<img>` element. In the chapter downloads, you'll find a file named "tweetsip.mp4" in the "video" folder. Make sure the "video" folder is at the *same* level as your "blog.html" file. Then add this markup to your page right below the closing `</p>` tag and before the closing `</article>` tag:

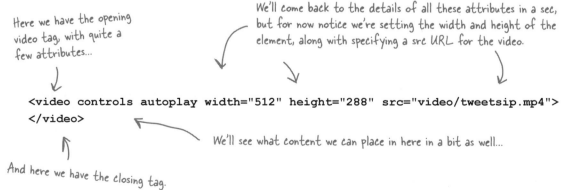

Here we have the opening video tag, with quite a few attributes...

We'll come back to the details of all these attributes in a sec, but for now notice we're setting the width and height of the element, along with specifying a src URL for the video.

```
<video controls autoplay width="512" height="288" src="video/tweetsip.mp4">
</video>
```

We'll see what content we can place in here in a bit as well...

And here we have the closing tag.

Lights, camera, action...

Get this new markup in and give it a try! Hopefully you'll see what we do here, *but if you don't, keep reading — you'll soon know how to fix it.*

Here's our video embedded in the page right where we put it with the correct width and height.

Did you notice the video started autoplaying? That's because we supplied an "autoplay" attribute. Just remove it, and the user will have to click play to see the video.

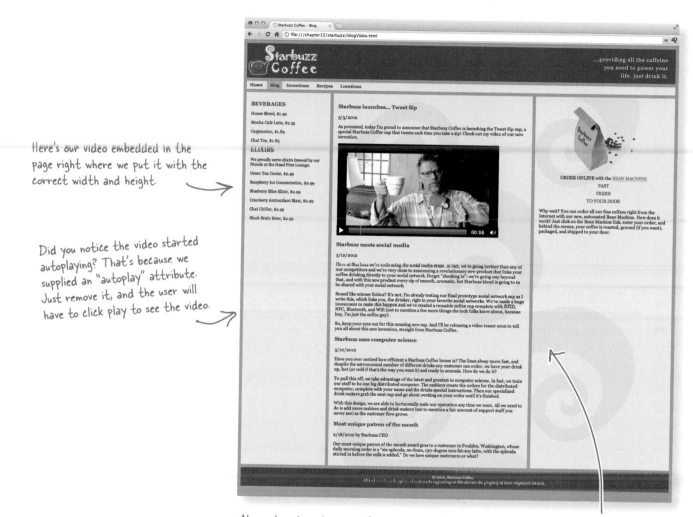

Also notice there's a set of controls for playing, pausing, controlling volume, and so on. These are supplied if you place a "controls" attribute in your <video> element.

Not bad for a couple lines of markup, huh? But don't rest too easy (especially if you aren't seeing video yet); we still have a lot to learn about the <video> element. Let's get started...

> I'm not seeing any video. I've triple-checked the code and I have the video in the right folder. Any ideas?

Yes, it's probably the video format.

While the browser makers have agreed on what the `<video>` element and API look like in HTML5, not everyone can agree on the *actual format* of the video files themselves. For instance, if you are on Safari, H.264 format is favored; if you're on Chrome, WebM is favored; and so on.

In the code we just wrote, we're assuming H.264 as a format, which works in Safari, Mobile Safari, and IE9+. If you're using another browser, then look in your "video" folder and you'll see three different types of video, with three different file extensions: .mp4, .ogv, and .webm (we'll talk more about what these mean in a bit).

For Safari, you should already be using .mp4 (which contains H.264).

For Google Chrome, use the .webm format by replacing your `src` attribute with:

```
src="video/tweetsip.webm"
```

If you're using Firefox or Opera, then replace your `src` attribute with:

```
src="video/tweetsip.ogv"
```

And if you're using IE8 or earlier, you're out of luck—wait a sec; this is Chapter 12! How could you still be using IE8 or earlier? Upgrade! But if you need to know how to supply fallback content for your IE8 users, hang on; we're getting to that.

By the time you read this, these formats could be more widely supported across all browsers. So if your video's working, great. Always check the Web to see the latest on this unfolding topic. And we'll come back for more on this topic shortly.

Give this a try to get you going; we're coming back to all this in a bit.

How does the ‹video› element work?

At this point, you've got a video up and playing on your page, but before we move on, let's step back and look at the ‹video› element and its attributes;

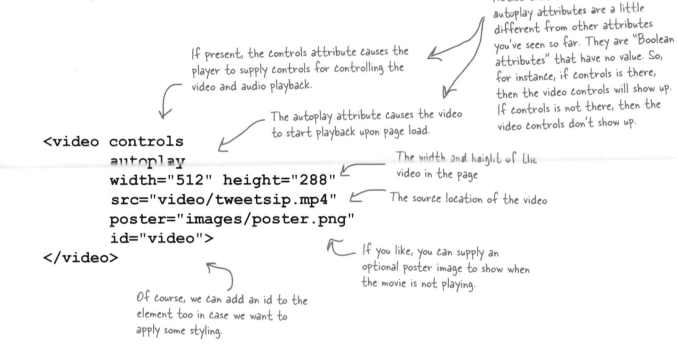

Notice that the controls and autoplay attributes are a little different from other attributes you've seen so far. They are "Boolean attributes" that have no value. So, for instance, if controls is there, then the video controls will show up. If controls is not there, then the video controls don't show up.

If present, the controls attribute causes the player to supply controls for controlling the video and audio playback.

The autoplay attribute causes the video to start playback upon page load.

The width and height of the video in the page

The source location of the video

```
<video controls
       autoplay
       width="512" height="288"
       src="video/tweetsip.mp4"
       poster="images/poster.png"
       id="video">
</video>
```

If you like, you can supply an optional poster image to show when the movie is not playing.

Of course, we can add an id to the element too in case we want to apply some styling.

A little Webville good video etiquette: the autoplay attribute

While autoplay may be the best thing for sites like YouTube and Vimeo (or WebvilleTV, for that matter), think twice before setting it in your ‹video› element. Often, users want to participate in the decision of whether or not video is played when they load your page.

Closely inspecting the video attributes...

Let's look more closely at some of the more important video attributes:

controls

The controls attribute is a **Boolean** attribute. It's either there or it's not. If it is there, then the browser will add its built-in controls to the video display. The controls vary by browser, so check out each browser to see what they look like. Here's what they look like in Safari.

src

The src attribute is just like the <img> element's src—it is a URL that tells the video element where to find the source file. In this case, the source is "video/tweetsip.mp4". (If you downloaded the code for this chapter, you'll find this video and two others in the "video" directory).

src is what video file is used here.

height

width

The video player

preload

The attribute preload is typically used for fine-grained control over how video loads for optimization purposes. Most of the time, the browser chooses how much video to load, based on things like whether autoplay is set and the user's bandwidth. You can override this by setting preload to "none" (none of the video is downloaded until the user "plays" it), "metadata" (the video metadata is downloaded, but no video content), or "auto" to let the browser make the decision.

autoplay

The autoplay Boolean attribute tells the browser to start playing the video as soon as it has enough data. For the videos we're demoing with, you'll probably see them start to play almost immediately.

poster

The browser will typically display one frame of the video as a "poster" image to represent the video. If you remove the autoplay attribute, you'll see this image displayed before you click play. It's up to the browser to pick which frame to show; often, the browser will just show the first frame of the video...which is often black. If you want to show a specific image, then it's up to you to create an image to display, and specify it by using the poster attribute.

loop

Another Boolean attribute, loop automatically restarts the video after it finishes playing.

width, height

The width and height attributes set the width and height of the video display area (also known as the "viewport"). If you specify a poster, the poster image will be scaled to the width and height you specify. The video will also be scaled, but will maintain its aspect ratio (e.g., 4:3 or 16:9), so if there's extra room on the sides, or the top and bottom, the video will be letter-boxed or pillar-boxed to fit into the display area size. You should try to match the native dimensions of the video if you want the best performance (so the browser doesn't have to scale in real time).

Pillar-boxing

Letter-boxing

I was testing on different browsers, and the controls look different on each one. At least with solutions like Flash, I had consistent-looking controls.

Yes, the controls in each browser are different with HTML video.

The look and feel of your controls is dictated by those who implement the browsers. They do tend to look different in different browsers and operating systems. In some cases, for instance, on a tablet, they have to look and behave differently because the device just works differently (and it's a good thing that's already taken care of for you). That said, we understand; across, say, desktop browsers, it would be nice to have consistent controls, but that isn't a formal part of the HTML5 spec, and in some cases, a method that works on one OS might clash with another OS's user interface guidelines. So, just know that the controls may differ, and if you really feel motivated, you can implement custom controls for your apps.

We do this in Head First HTML5 Programming. Come join us there; JavaScript is fun!

What you need to know about video formats

We wish everything were as neat and tidy as the `<video>` element and its attributes, but as it turns out, video formats are a bit of a mess on the Web. What's a video format? Think about it this way: a video file contains two parts, a video part and an audio part, and each part is encoded (to reduce size and to allow it to be played back more efficiently) using a specific encoding type. That encoding, for the most part, is what no one can agree on—some browser makers are enamored with H.264 encodings, others really like VP8, and yet others like the open source alternative, Theora. And to make all this *even more* complicated, the file that holds the video and audio encoding (which is known as a *container*) has its own format with its own name. So we're really talking buzzword soup here.

Anyway, while it might be a big, happy world if all browser makers agreed on a single format to use across the Web, well, that just doesn't seem to be in the cards for a number of technical, political, and philosophical reasons. But rather than open that debate here, we're just going to make sure you're reasonably educated on the topic so you can make your own decisions about how to support your audience.

Let's take a look at the popular encodings out there; right now, there are three contenders trying to rule the (Web) world…

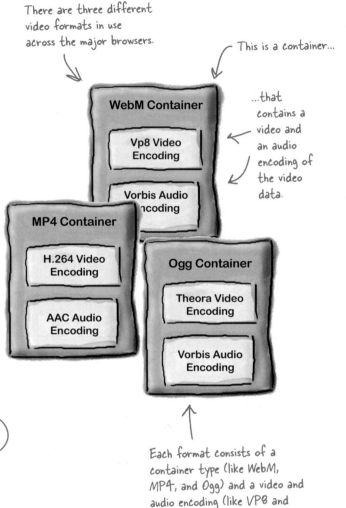

There are three different video formats in use across the major browsers.

This is a container...

...that contains a video and an audio encoding of the video data.

Your mileage may vary by the time you read this book, as favored encodings tend to change over time.

Each format consists of a container type (like WebM, MP4, and Ogg) and a video and audio encoding (like VP8 and Vorbis).

The HTML5 specification allows for any video format. It is the browser implementation that determines what formats are actually supported.

The video format contenders

The reality is, if you're going to be serving content to a wide spectrum of users, you're going to have to supply more than one format. On the other hand, if all you care about is, say, the Apple iPad, you may be able to get away with just one. Today we have three main contenders—let's have a look at them:

MP4 container with H.264 video and AAC audio

H.264 is licensed by the MPEG-LA group.

There is more than one kind of H.264; each is known as a "profile."

MP4/H.264 is supported by Safari and IE9+. You may find support in some versions of Chrome.

WebM container with VP8 video and Vorbis audio

WebM was designed by Google to work with VP8-encoded videos.

WebM/VP8 is supported by Firefox, Chrome, and Opera.

You'll find WebM-formatted videos with the .webm extension.

Ogg container with Theora video and Vorbis audio

Theora is an open source codec.

Video encoded with Theora is usually contained in an Ogg file, with the .ogv file extension.

Ogg/Theora is supported by Firefox, Chrome, and Opera.

H.264 is the industry darling, but not the reigning champ...

Theora is the open source alternative.

VP8, the contender, is backed by Google, supported by others, and coming on strong...

YOUR MISSION:
VIDEO RECONNAISSANCE

GO OUT AND DETERMINE ████████████ THE CURRENT LEVEL OF SUPPORT FOR VIDEO IN EACH BROWSER
████████████████ THE CURRENT LEVEL OF SUPPORT FOR VIDEO IN EACH BROWSER
BELOW (HINT, HERE ARE A FEW SITES THAT KEEP UP WITH SUCH THINGS: █████████████
http://en.wikipedia.org/wiki/HTML5_video, ████████████████
http://caniuse.com/#search=video). ASSUME THE LATEST VERSION OF THE
BROWSER. FOR EACH BROWSER/FEATURE PUT A CHECKMARK IF IT IS SUPPORTED.
UPON YOUR RETURN, REPORT BACK FOR YOUR NEXT ASSIGNMENT!

TOP SECRET

CASE FILE: VIDEO

iOS and Android devices (among others)

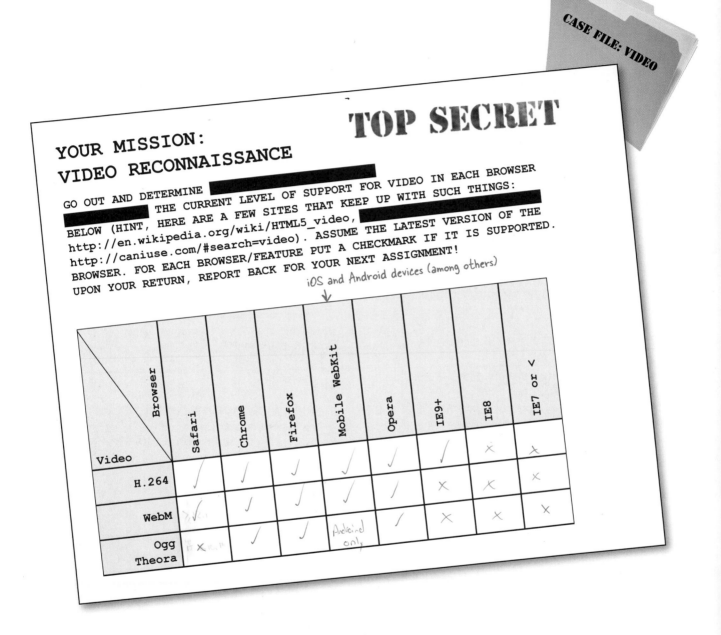

Video Browser	Safari	Chrome	Firefox	Mobile WebKit	Opera	IE9+	IE8	IE7 or ∨
H.264	✓	✓	✓	✓	✓	✓	✗	✗
WebM	✓	✓	✓	✓	✓	✗	✗	✗
Ogg Theora	✓	✓	✓	Android only	✓	✗	✗	✗

How to juggle all those formats...

So we know it's a messy world with respect to video format, but what to do? Depending on your audience, you may decide to provide just one format of your video, or several. In either case, you can use one `<source>` element (not to be confused with the *src attribute*) per format inside a `<video>` element to provide a set of videos, each with its own format, and let the browser pick the first one it supports. Like this:

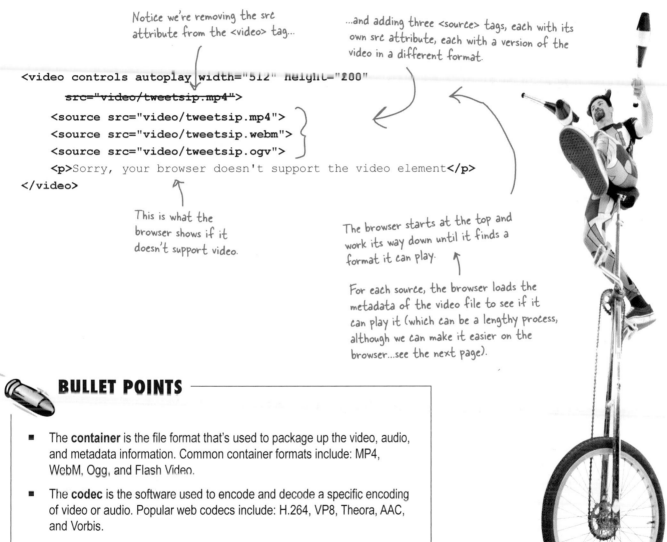

Notice we're removing the src attribute from the `<video>` tag...

...and adding three `<source>` tags, each with its own src attribute, each with a version of the video in a different format.

```
<video controls autoplay width="512" height="200"
    src="video/tweetsip.mp4">
  <source src="video/tweetsip.mp4">
  <source src="video/tweetsip.webm">
  <source src="video/tweetsip.ogv">
  <p>Sorry, your browser doesn't support the video element</p>
</video>
```

This is what the browser shows if it doesn't support video.

The browser starts at the top and work its way down until it finds a format it can play.

For each source, the browser loads the metadata of the video file to see if it can play it (which can be a lengthy process, although we can make it easier on the browser...see the next page).

BULLET POINTS

- The **container** is the file format that's used to package up the video, audio, and metadata information. Common container formats include: MP4, WebM, Ogg, and Flash Video.

- The **codec** is the software used to encode and decode a specific encoding of video or audio. Popular web codecs include: H.264, VP8, Theora, AAC, and Vorbis.

- The browser decides what video it can decode. Not all browser makers agree, so if you want to support everyone, you need multiple encodings.

Take 2: lights, camera, action...

Okay, if you were having trouble seeing video, add the markup on the previous page, and even if you weren't having trouble, add it anyway. Give the video another try. Try it in a few different browsers, as well.

Now the video should be working cross-browser! ⟶

How to be even more specific with your video formats

Telling the browser the location of your source files gives it a selection of different versions to choose from; however, the browser has to do some detective work before it can truly determine if a file is playable. You can help your browser even more by giving it more information about the MIME type and (optionally) codecs of your video files:

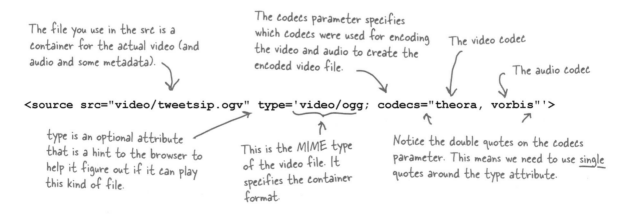

The file you use in the src is a container for the actual video (and audio and some metadata).

The codecs parameter specifies which codecs were used for encoding the video and audio to create the encoded video file.

The video codec

The audio codec

```
<source src="video/tweetsip.ogv" type='video/ogg; codecs="theora, vorbis"'>
```

type is an optional attribute that is a hint to the browser to help it figure out if it can play this kind of file.

This is the MIME type of the video file. It specifies the container format.

Notice the double quotes on the codecs parameter. This means we need to use single quotes around the type attribute.

Next, you'll update your `<source>` elements to include the type information for all three types of video we have.

Update and test drive

Update your <source> elements like below, and give your page a test drive:

```
<video controls autoplay width="512" height="288" >
    <source src="video/tweetsip.mp4" type='video/mp4; codecs="avc1.42E01E, mp4a.40.2"'>
    <source src="video/tweetsip.webm" type='video/webm; codecs="vp8, vorbis"'>
    <source src="video/tweetsip.ogv" type='video/ogg; codecs="theora, vorbis"'>
    <p>Sorry, your browser doesn't support the video element</p>
</video>
```

If you don't know the codecs parameters, then you can leave them off and just use the MIME type. It will be a little less efficient, but most of the time, that's okay.

The codecs for mp4 are more complicated than the other two because h.264 supports various "profiles," different encodings for different uses (like high bandwidth vs. low bandwidth). So, to get those right, you'll need to know more details about how your video was encoded.

Most likely, your video will play as before, but you'll know that behind the scenes you're helping the browser with the additional type and codec information. If and when you do your own video encoding, you'll need to know more about the various options for the type parameters to use in your source element. You can get a lot more information on type parameters at http://wiki.whatwg.org/wiki/Video_type_parameters.

there are no Dumb Questions

Q: Is there any hope of getting to one container format or codec type in the next few years? Isn't this why we have standards?

A: There probably won't be one encoding to rule them all anytime soon—as we said earlier, this topic intersects with a whole host of issues, including companies wanting to control their own destiny in the video space to a complex set of intellectual property issues. The HTML5 standards committee recognized this and decided not to specify the video format in the HTML5 specification. So, while in principle HTML5 supports (or is at least agnostic to) all of these formats, it is really up to the browser makers to decide what they do and don't support.

Keep an eye on this topic if video is important to you; It will surely be an interesting one to watch over the next few years as this is all sorted out. And, as always, keep in mind what your audience needs and make sure you're doing what you can to support them.

Q: If I want to encode my own video, where do I start?

A: There are a variety of video capture and encoding programs out there, and which one you choose is really going to depend on what kind of video you're capturing and how you want to use the end result. Entire books have been written on video encoding, so be prepared to enter a world of all new acronyms and technology. You can start simple with programs like iMovie or Adobe Premiere Elements, which include the ability to encode your video for the Web. If you're getting into serious video work with Final Cut Pro or Adobe Premiere, these software programs include their own production tools.

And, finally, if you are delivering your videos from a content delivery network (CDN), many CDN companies also offer encoding services. So you've got a wide variety of choices depending on your needs.

Q: Can I play my video back fullscreen?

A: That functionality hasn't yet been standardized, although you'll find ways to do it with some of the browsers if you search the Web. Some of the browsers supply a fullscreen control (for instance, on tablets) that give the video element this capability. Also note that once you've got a way to go fullscreen, what you can do with the video, other than basic playback, may be limited for security reasons (just as it is with plug-in video solutions today).

> I think Flash video is still important, and I want to make sure I have a fallback if my users' browsers don't support HTML5 video.

No problem.

There are techniques for falling back to another video player if your preferred one (whether that be HTML5 or Flash or another) isn't supported.

Below, you'll find an example of how to insert your Flash video as a fallback for HTML5 video, assuming the browser doesn't know how to play HTML5 video. Obviously, this is an area that is changing fast, so please take a look on the Web (which is updated a lot more often than a book) to make sure you're using the latest and greatest techniques. You'll also find ways to make HTML5 the fallback rather than Flash if you prefer to give Flash video priority.

```
<video poster="video.jpg" controls>
        <source src="video.mp4">
        <source src="video.webm">
        <source src="video.ogv">
        <object>...</object>
</video>
```

For Flash video, you need an <object> element. Insert the <object> element inside the <video> element below the <source> tags. If the browser doesn't know about the <video> element, the <object> will be used, and you'll see Flash video playing.

I just wanted to say nice job! The site is totally new and improved, and now we can do video anytime we need to. Umm, about that Tweet Sip cup...well, if you watched the video, then I guess you know we're back to the drawing board. But don't worry—we're already working on a new coffee mug with social networking, gamification, digital scrapbooking, auto-checkin, and analytics built right in! This one is going to be a winner, I promise!

Would you believe we're really just getting started with video? That's right: markup is just the first step. With HTML5, you can also create interactive experiences around video by using JavaScript.

Now, that's far beyond the scope of this book (unless you want to carry around a 1,400-page book), so after you've finished this book, pick up **Head First HTML5 Programming** (by your all-time favorite Head First authors, of course), and take this all to the next level.

Element Soup

<progress>

Need to show progress on a task? Like 90% done? Use this element.

<section>

Use this element to define the major sections of your document.

Use this element for content that's aside from the main content, like a sidebar or a pullquote.

<aside>

<footer>

This element defines the footer of a section or a whole document.

<header>

Use this for sections with headers, or the header of the whole document.

This element is for highlighting bits of text. Almost as good as that ink highlighter!

<mark>

<meter>

Need to display a measurement in a range? Like a thermometer that goes from 0 to 212, and shows it's 90 degrees outside? Hot!

Want a video in your page? You need this element.

<video>

Use this element to group together links that are used for navigation in your site.

<nav>

Use this for including sound content in your page.

<audio>

<article>

For marking up content like news articles or blog posts that are self-contained content.

The time element is a time, a date, or a date-time (like January 21st at 2am).

This is used to display graphics and animations drawn with JavaScript in your page.

This element is to define self-contained content like a photo, a diagram or even a code listing.

<time>

<canvas>

<figure>

Here are a bunch of elements you know, and a few you don't, that are all new in HTML5.

Remember, half the fun of HTML is experimenting! So make some files of your own and try these out.

BULLET POINTS

- HTML5 added several new elements to HTML.

- <section>, <article>, <aside>, <nav>, <header>, and <footer> are all new elements to help you structure your page, and add more meaning than if you use <div>.

- <section> is for grouping related content.

- <article> is for self-contained content like blog posts, forum posts, and news articles.

- <aside> is for content that is not central to the main content of the page, such as callouts and sidebars.

- <nav> is for grouping site navigation links.

- <header> groups content such as headings, logos, and bylines that typically go at the top of a page or section.

- <footer> groups content such as document information, legalese, and copyright that typically go at the bottom of a page or section.

- <time> is also a new element in HTML5. It is used to mark up times and dates.

- <div> is still used for structure. It is often used to group elements together for styling purposes or to create structure for content that doesn't fit into one of the new structure-related elements in HTML5.

- Older browsers don't support new HTML5 elements, so be sure you know the browsers your primary audience will be using to access your web page, and don't use the new elements until you're sure they will work for your audience.

- <video> is a new HTML element for adding video to your page.

- A video codec is the encoding used to create the video file. Popular codecs include h.264, Vp8, and Theora.

- A video container file contains video, audio, and metadata. Popular container formats include MP4, OGG, and WebM.

- Provide multiple video source files to be sure your audience can view your video files in their browsers.

HTMLcross

There are lots of new ideas and new elements in this chapter. Do the crossword to help make it all stick. All the answers come from the chapter.

Across

3. A _____ attribute is one that doesn't have a specified value.

6. The TweetSip cup measures coffee in _____.

7. The design of the Starbuzz page has a main content _____.

8. Specify a date in the _____ attribute of the <time> element.

11. The _____ in the Starbuzz blog had the wrong style until we added the "top" class.

12. A browser doesn't know that <div id="footer"> means _____.

13. Use _____ selectors in your CSS to make sure you don't get unintended styling.

14. The <section> element is used to group _____ content.

Down

1. The Starbuzz CEO made a video about the _____ cup.

2. Browser makers can't agree on video _____.

4. A section can have a header and a _____.

5. You'd probably use this element for a sidebar.

9. Your local newspaper might use this kind of element to mark up its news articles.

10. The _____ tag is used for specifying multiple video files.

11. You can use a _____ at the top of the page, or at the top of a section or article.

WHO DOES WHAT?
SOLUTION

Sure, we could just tell you about the new HTML5 elements, but wouldn't it be more fun to figure them out? Below, you'll find the new elements to the left (these aren't *all* the new elements, but you'll find the more important ones here); for each element, match it with its description to the right:

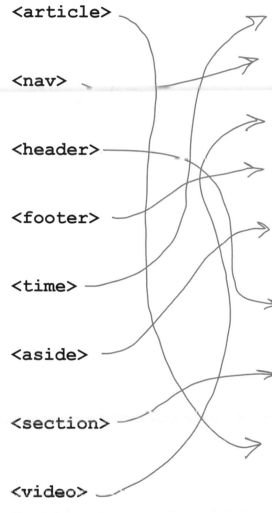

`<article>`

`<nav>`

`<header>`

`<footer>`

`<time>`

`<aside>`

`<section>`

`<video>`

Can contain a date or time or both.

Contains content meant for navigation links in the page.

Used to add video media to your page.

Content that goes at the bottom of the page, or the bottom of a section of the page.

Contains content that is supplemental to the page content, like a callout or sidebar.

Content that goes at the top of the page, or the top of a section of the page.

A thematic grouping of content, typically with a header and possibly a footer.

Represents a self-contained composition in a page, like a blog post, user forum post, or newspaper article.

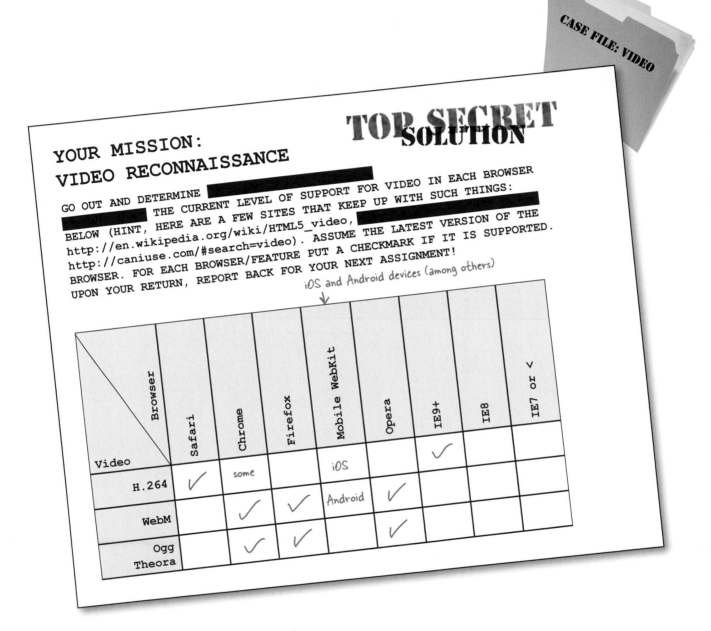

CASE FILE: VIDEO

YOUR MISSION:
VIDEO RECONNAISSANCE

TOP SECRET SOLUTION

GO OUT AND DETERMINE ███████████ THE CURRENT LEVEL OF SUPPORT FOR VIDEO IN EACH BROWSER
BELOW (HINT, HERE ARE A FEW SITES THAT KEEP UP WITH SUCH THINGS:
http://en.wikipedia.org/wiki/HTML5_video, ███████████ ASSUME THE LATEST VERSION OF THE
http://caniuse.com/#search=video). ASSUME THE LATEST VERSION OF THE
BROWSER. FOR EACH BROWSER/FEATURE PUT A CHECKMARK IF IT IS SUPPORTED.
UPON YOUR RETURN, REPORT BACK FOR YOUR NEXT ASSIGNMENT!

iOS and Android devices (among others)

Browser / Video	Safari	Chrome	Firefox	Mobile WebKit	Opera	IE9+	IE8	IE7 or <
H.264	✓	some		iOS		✓		
WebM		✓	✓	Android	✓			
Ogg Theora		✓	✓		✓			

HTMLcross Solution

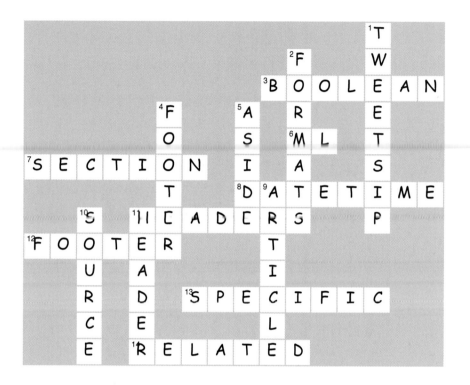

13 tables and more lists

Getting Tabular

If it walks like a table and talks like a table... There comes a time in life when we have to deal with the dreaded *tabular data*. Whether you need to create a page representing your company's inventory over the last year or a catalog of your vinylmation collection (don't worry, we won't tell), you know you need to do it in HTML, but how? Well, have we got a deal for you: order now, and in a single chapter we'll reveal the secrets that will allow you to put your very own data right inside HTML tables. But there's more: with every order we'll throw in our exclusive guide to styling HTML tables. And, if you act now, as a special bonus, we'll throw in our guide to styling HTML lists. Don't hesitate; call now!

Hey guys, I just created this little table of the cities in my journal. I was going to put it on the website, but I couldn't find a good way to do it with headings or blockquotes or paragraphs. Can you help?

City	Date	Temperature	Altitude	Population	Diner Rating
Walla Walla, WA	June 15	75	1,204 ft	29,686	4/5
Magic City, ID	June 25	74	5,312 ft	50	3/5
Bountiful, UT	July 10	91	4,226 ft	41,173	4/5
Last Chance, CO	July 23	102	4,780 ft	265	3/5
Truth or Consequences, NM	August 9	93	4,242 ft	7,289	5/5
Why, AZ	August 18	104	860 ft	480	3/5

How do you make tables with HTML?

Tony's right; you really haven't seen a good way of using HTML to represent his table data, at least not yet. You do know there's a way to use CSS and `<div>`s to create a table-like layout (with CSS table display), but that's for layout (presentation) purposes, and isn't related to the content itself. Here, we've got *tabular data* that we want to mark up with HTML. Luckily, HTML has a `<table>` element to take care of marking up tabular data. Before we dive into the `<table>` element, let's first get an idea of what goes into a table:

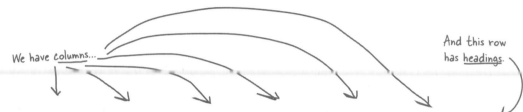

We have columns...

And this row has <u>headings</u>.

And we have <u>rows</u>...

City	Date	Temp	Altitude	Population	Diner Rating
Walla Walla, WA	June 15th	75	1,204 ft	29,686	4/5
Magic City, ID	June 25th	74	5,312 ft	50	3/5
Bountiful, UT	July 10th	91	4,226 ft	41,173	4/5
Last Chance, CO	July 23rd	102	4,780 ft	265	3/5
Truth or Consequences, NM	August 9th	93	4,242 ft	7,289	5/5
Why, AZ	August 18th	104	860 ft	480	3/5

We call each piece of data a <u>cell</u>, or sometimes just <u>table data</u>.

BRAIN POWER

If they put you in charge of HTML, how would you design one or more elements that could be used to specify a table, including headings, rows, columns, and the actual table data?

Creating a table with HTML

Before we pull out Tony's site and start making changes, let's get the table working like we want it in a separate HTML file. We've started the table and already entered the headings and the first three rows of the table into an HTML file called "table.html" in the "chapter13/journal/" folder. Check it out:

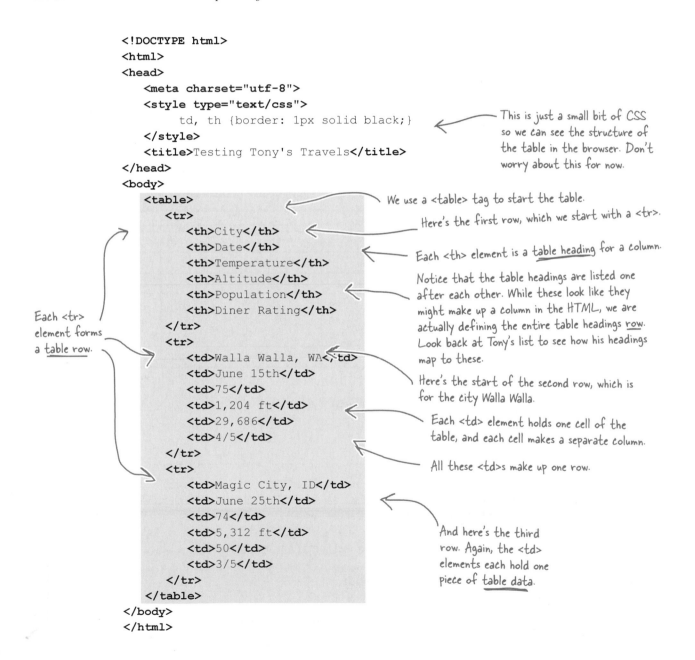

```
<!DOCTYPE html>
<html>
<head>
    <meta charset="utf-8">
    <style type="text/css">
        td, th {border: 1px solid black;}
    </style>
    <title>Testing Tony's Travels</title>
</head>
<body>
    <table>
        <tr>
            <th>City</th>
            <th>Date</th>
            <th>Temperature</th>
            <th>Altitude</th>
            <th>Population</th>
            <th>Diner Rating</th>
        </tr>
        <tr>
            <td>Walla Walla, WA</td>
            <td>June 15th</td>
            <td>75</td>
            <td>1,204 ft</td>
            <td>29,686</td>
            <td>4/5</td>
        </tr>
        <tr>
            <td>Magic City, ID</td>
            <td>June 25th</td>
            <td>74</td>
            <td>5,312 ft</td>
            <td>50</td>
            <td>3/5</td>
        </tr>
    </table>
</body>
</html>
```

This is just a small bit of CSS so we can see the structure of the table in the browser. Don't worry about this for now.

We use a <table> tag to start the table.

Here's the first row, which we start with a <tr>.

Each <th> element is a table heading for a column.

Notice that the table headings are listed one after each other. While these look like they might make up a column in the HTML, we are actually defining the entire table headings row. Look back at Tony's list to see how his headings map to these.

Each <tr> element forms a table row.

Here's the start of the second row, which is for the city Walla Walla.

Each <td> element holds one cell of the table, and each cell makes a separate column.

All these <td>s make up one row.

And here's the third row. Again, the <td> elements each hold one piece of table data.

What the browser creates

Let's take a look at how the browser displays this HTML table. We'll warn you now: this isn't going to be the *best-looking* table, but it *will* look like a table. We'll worry about how it looks shortly; for now, let's make sure you've got the basics down.

Here's how the browser displays the table HTML.

We've got three rows total, including the headings...

City	Date	Temperature	Altitude	Population	Diner Rating
Walla Walla, WA	June 15th	75	1,204 ft	29,686	4/5
Magic City, ID	June 25th	74	5,312 ft	50	3/5

Testing Tony's Travels

file:///chapter13/journal/table.html

...and six columns, just what we expected.

Each <td> is in its own cell...

...and each <th> is in a cell as well. It looks like the browser displays headings in bold by default.

Exercise

Finishing typing in the "Testing Tony's Table" HTML from the previous page (we started it in "table.html", but you need to finish it). Typing this in, while tedious, will help get the structure of the <table>, <tr>, <th>, and <td> tags in your head. When you finish, give it a quick test, and then add the remaining items from Tony's table. Test that too.

Tables dissected

You've seen four elements used to create a single table: <table>, <tr>, <th>, and <td>. Let's take a closer look at each one to see exactly what role it plays in the table.

The <th> element contains one cell in the heading of your table. It must be inside a table row.

The <table> tag starts the whole thing off. When you want a table, start here.

The </tr> tag ends a row of the table.

<th>Date</th>

<table>

City	Date	Temp	Altitude	Population	Diner Rating
Walla Walla, WA	June 15th	75	1,204 ft	29,686	4/5
Magic City, ID	June 25th	74	5,312 ft	50	3/5
Bountiful, UT	July 10th	91	4,226 ft	41,173	4/5
Last Chance, CO	July 23rd	102	4,780 ft	265	3/5
Truth or Consequences, NM	August 9th	93	4,242 ft	7,289	5/5
Why, AZ	August 18th	104	860 ft	480	3/5

<tr> … **</tr>**

Each <tr> element specifies a table row. So, all the table data that goes in a row is nested inside the <tr> element.

<td>August 9th</td>

The <td> element contains one data cell in your table. It must be inside a table row.

</table>

The </table> tag ends the table.

there are no
Dumb Questions

Q: Why isn't there a table column element? That seems pretty important

A: The designers of HTML decided to let you specify tables by row, rather than by column. But notice that by specifying each row's <td> elements, you are implicitly specifying each column anyway.

Q: What happens if I have a row that doesn't have enough elements? In other words, I've got fewer things than the number of columns in the table?

A: The easiest way to deal with that is to just leave the content of the data cell empty; in other words, you write <td></td>. If you leave out the data cell, then the table won't line up properly, so all the data cells have to be there, even if they are empty.

Q: What if I want my table headings to be down the left side of the table, instead of across the top; can I do that?

A: Yes, you certainly can. You just need to put your table heading elements in each row instead of all in the first row. If your <th> element is the first item in each row, then the first column will consist of all table headings.

Q: My friend showed me a cool trick where he did all his page layout right within a table. He didn't even have to use CSS!

A: Go straight to CSS jail. Do not pass go; do not collect $200.

Using tables for layout was commonly done in the HTML era before CSS, when, frankly, there was no better way to do complex layouts. However, it is a poor way to do your layouts today. Using tables for layout is notoriously hard to get right and difficult to maintain. Instead, it's much better to use CSS table display to get the benefits of a table layout without actually creating an HTML table (this is how we styled the Starbuzz page in Chapter 11). Tell your friend that his technique is old school, and he needs to get up to speed with the right way to do layout: CSS with HTML.

Q: Isn't a table all about presentation? What happened to presentation versus structure?

A: Not really. With tables, you are specifying the relationships between tabular data items. We'll use CSS to alter the presentation of the table.

Q: How do HTML tables relate to CSS table display?

A: HTML tables allow you to specify the structure of a table using markup while CSS table display gives you a way to display block-level elements in a table-like presentation. Think about it this way, when you really need to create tabular data in your page, use tables (and we'll see how to style these in a bit); however, when you just need to make use of a table-like presentation with other types of content, then you can use a CSS table display layout.

Q: Can we use CSS table display to style HTML tables?

A: Well, you don't really need to. Why? Because you're already creating a tabular structure with HTML, so, as you'll see, you can use simple CSS to style the table however you like.

Tables give you a way to specify tabular data in your HTML.

Tables consist of data cells within rows. Columns are implicitly defined within the rows.

The number of columns in your table will be the number of data cells you have in a row.

In general, tables are not meant to be used for presentation; that's the job of CSS.

```
<table><tr><th>Artist</th>

<th>Album</th></tr><tr>

<td>Enigma</td><td>Le Roi Est Mort,
Vive Le Roi!</td></tr> <tr><td>LTJ
Bukem</td>

<td>Progression Sessions 6</td>

</tr><tr>

<td>Timo Maas</td>

<td>Pictures</td></tr></table>
```

BE the Browser

On the left, you'll find the HTML for a table. Your job is to play like you're the browser displaying the table. After you've done the exercise, look at the end of the chapter to see if you got it right.

Here's just the table HTML.

Argh! Someone needs to learn how to format her HTML.

Draw the table here.

Artist	Album
Enigma	Le Roi Est Mort, Vive Le Roi!
LTJ Bukem	Progression Sessions 6
Timo Maas	Pictures

Adding a caption

You can improve your table right off the bat by adding a caption.

```
<table>
    <caption>
        The cities I visited on my
        Segway'n USA travels
    </caption>
    <tr>
        <th>City</th>
        <th>Date</th>
        <th>Temperature</th>
        <th>Altitude</th>
        <th>Population</th>
        <th>Diner Rating</th>
    </tr>
    <tr>
        <td>Walla Walla, WA</td>
        <td>June 15th</td>
        <td>75</td>
        <td>1,204 ft</td>
        <td>29,686</td>
        <td>4/5</td>
    </tr>
    <tr>
        <td>Magic City, ID</td>
        <td>June 25th</td>
        <td>74</td>
        <td>5,312 ft</td>
        <td>50</td>
        <td>3/5</td>
    </tr>
    .
    .
    .
</table>
```

The caption is displayed in the browser. By default, most browsers display this above the table.

If you don't like the default location of the caption, you can use CSS to reposition it (we'll give that a try in a sec). Keep in mind that older browsers don't fully support repositioning the caption.

You should always put the caption at the top of your table in the HTML, and use CSS to reposition it to the bottom, if that's where you want it.

The rest of the table rows go here.

Test drive...and start thinking about style

Add the caption to your table. Save and reload.

> The caption is at the top of the table. It'll probably look better on the bottom.

```
○ ○ ○                        Tony's Table
◀  ▶   C   +    📄 file:///chapter13/journal/table.html
```

The cities I visited on my Segway'n USA travels

City	Date	Temperature	Altitude	Population	Diner Rating
Walla Walla, WA	June 15th	75	1,204 ft	29,686	4/5
Magic City, ID	June 25th	74	5,312 ft	50	3/5
Bountiful, UT	July 10th	91	4,226 ft	41,173	4/5
Last Chance, CO	July 23rd	102	4,780 ft	265	3/5
Truth or Consequences, NM	August 9th	93	4,242 ft	7,289	5/5
Why, AZ	August 18th	104	860 ft	480	3/5

> We really need to add some padding to the table data cells, to make them easier to read...

> ...and the border lines are really "heavy" visually. We could use much "lighter" borders in the table cells, although it would be nice to have a dark border around the whole table...

> ...and a splash of orange to match Tony's site could really pull the whole thing together.

Before we start styling, let's get the table into Tony's page

Before we start adding style to Tony's new table, we should really get the table into his main page. Remember that Tony's main page already has set a `font-family`, `font-size`, and other styles that the table is going to inherit. So without putting the table into his page, we won't really know what the table looks like.

Start by opening "journal.html" in the "chapter13/journal" folder, locate the August 20th entry, and make the following changes. When you've finished, move on to the next page before reloading.

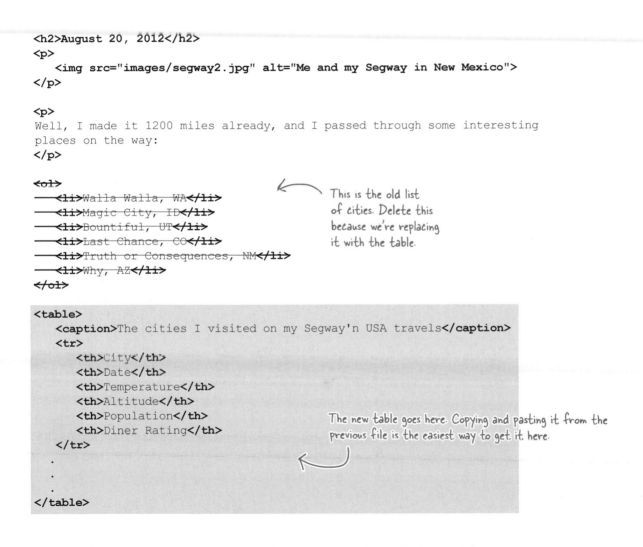

```
<h2>August 20, 2012</h2>
<p>
    <img src="images/segway2.jpg" alt="Me and my Segway in New Mexico">
</p>


<p>
Well, I made it 1200 miles already, and I passed through some interesting
places on the way:
</p>

<ol>
    <li>Walla Walla, WA</li>
    <li>Magic City, ID</li>
    <li>Bountiful, UT</li>
    <li>Last Chance, CO</li>
    <li>Truth or Consequences, NM</li>
    <li>Why, AZ</li>
</ol>
```

This is the old list of cities. Delete this because we're replacing it with the table.

```
<table>
    <caption>The cities I visited on my Segway'n USA travels</caption>
    <tr>
        <th>City</th>
        <th>Date</th>
        <th>Temperature</th>
        <th>Altitude</th>
        <th>Population</th>
        <th>Diner Rating</th>
    </tr>
    .
    .
    .
</table>
```

The new table goes here. Copying and pasting it from the previous file is the easiest way to get it here.

Now let's style the table

Add the new style highlighted below at the bottom of the "journal.css" stylesheet file.

```css
@font-face {
    font-family: "Emblema One";
    src: url("http://wickedlysmart.com/hfhtmlcss/chapter8/journal/EmblemaOne-Regular.woff"),
         url("http://wickedlysmart.com/hfhtmlcss/chapter8/journal/EmblemaOne-Regular.ttf");
}
body {
    font-family:      Verdana, Geneva, Arial, sans-serif;
    font-size:        small;
}
h1, h2 {
    color:            #cc6600;
    border-bottom:    thin dotted #888888;
}
h1 {
    font-family:      "Emblema One", sans-serif;
    font-size:        220%;
}
h2 {
    font-size:        130%;
    font-weight:      normal;
}
blockquote {
    font-style:       italic;
}
```

At the top here is all the style that's currently in Tony's web page. We added all this in Chapter 8. We're going to add the new style for the tables below it.

```css
table {
    margin-left: 20px;
    margin-right: 20px;
    border: thin solid black;
    caption-side: bottom;
}

td, th {
    border: thin dotted gray;
    padding: 5px;
}

caption {
    font-style: italic;
    padding-top: 8px;
}
```

First, we'll style the table. We're going to add a margin on the left and right, and a thin, black border to the table.

And we're going to move that caption to the bottom of the table.

Let's also change the border on the table data cells to be a much lighter, dotted border in gray.

And let's add some padding to the data cells so there's some space between the data content and the border.

This rule styles the caption. We're changing the font-style to italic and adding some top padding.

Taking the styled tables for a test drive

That's a lot of changes at once. Make sure you save them, and you should validate as well. Then load "journal.html" into your browser.

The table looks quite different now that you've styled it. We're also inheriting a few styles that were already in Tony's journal.

All the fonts are now sans-serif and a smaller size. We picked that up from the previous styles already in the file.

Now we've got a dark border and dotted lines.

And we've got some margin on the table and some padding in each table cell.

Those dotted lines are looking really busy and distracting, though. It doesn't help that they are duplicated between each pair of table cells.

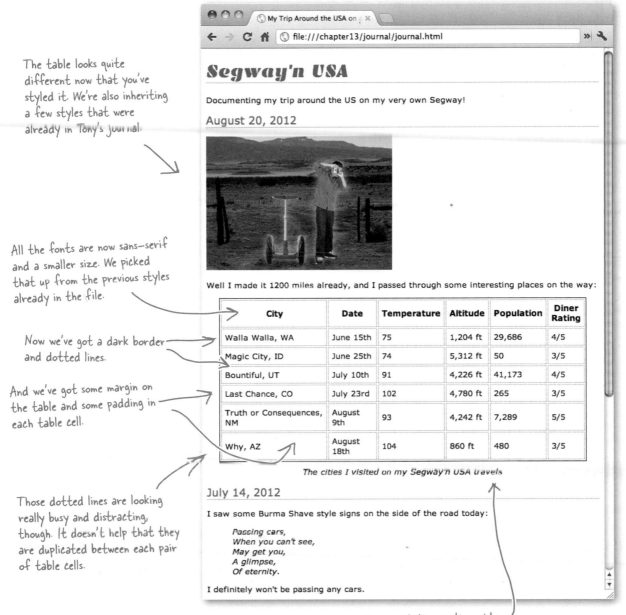

Segway'n USA

Documenting my trip around the US on my very own Segway!

August 20, 2012

Well I made it 1200 miles already, and I passed through some interesting places on the way:

City	Date	Temperature	Altitude	Population	Diner Rating
Walla Walla, WA	June 15th	75	1,204 ft	29,686	4/5
Magic City, ID	June 25th	74	5,312 ft	50	3/5
Bountiful, UT	July 10th	91	4,226 ft	41,173	4/5
Last Chance, CO	July 23rd	102	4,780 ft	265	3/5
Truth or Consequences, NM	August 9th	93	4,242 ft	7,289	5/5
Why, AZ	August 18th	104	860 ft	480	3/5

The cities I visited on my Segway'n USA travels

July 14, 2012

I saw some Burma Shave style signs on the side of the road today:

Passing cars,
When you can't see,
May get you,
A glimpse,
Of eternity.

I definitely won't be passing any cars.

Remember, in browsers that don't support the caption-side property, the caption will still be at the top of the table.

> Table cells look like they just use the box model too...they've got padding and a border. Do they also have a margin?

Table cells do have padding and a border—just like you've seen in the box model—but they are a little different when it comes to margins.

The box model is a good way to think about table cells, but they do differ when it comes to margins. Let's take a look at one of the cells in Tony's table:

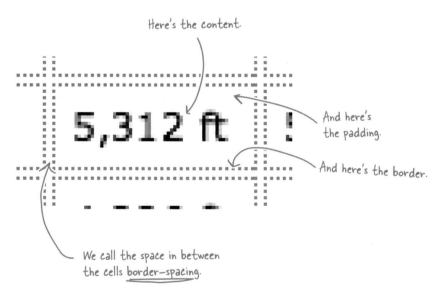

Here's the content.

And here's the padding.

And here's the border.

We call the space in between the cells border-spacing.

This is just like the border-spacing property we used in the CSS table display layout for Starbuzz

So instead of a margin, we have a border-spacing property, which is defined over the entire table. In other words, you can't set the "margin" of an individual table cell; rather, you set a common spacing around all cells.

Sharpen your pencil

The double dotted lines are giving Tony's table a busy and distracting look. It would be much better, and wouldn't detract from the table, if we could just have one border around each table cell. Can you think of a way to do that with styling given what you've just learned? Give it a try and check your answer in the back of the chapter.

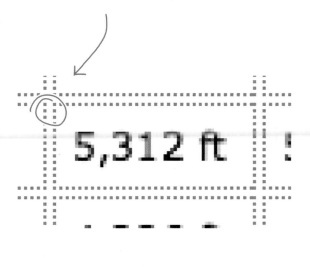

there are no Dumb Questions

Q: You said border spacing is defined for the entire table, so I can't set a margin for an individual table cell?

A: Right. Table cells don't have margins; what they have is spacing around their borders, and this spacing is set for the entire table. You can't control the border spacing of each table cell separately.

Q: Well, is there any way to have different border spacing on the vertical than I have on the horizontal? That seems useful.

A: You sure can. You can specify your border spacing like this:

```
border-spacing: 10px 30px;
```

That sets 10 pixels of horizontal border space and 30 pixels of vertical border space.

Q: The border-spacing property doesn't seem to work in my browser.

A: Are you using an old version of Internet Explorer? We're sorry to report that IE version 6 doesn't support border-spacing. But seriously, isn't it time you upgraded your browser?

Getting those borders to collapse

There is another way to solve the border dilemma, besides the `border-spacing` property. You can use a CSS property called `border-collapse` to collapse the borders so that there is no border spacing at all. When you do this, your browser will ignore any border spacing you have set on the table. It will also combine two borders that are right next to each other into one border. This "collapses" two borders into one.

Here's how you can set the `border-collapse` property. Follow along and make this change in your "journal.css" file:

```
table {
    margin-left: 20px;
    margin-right: 20px;
    border: thin solid black;
    caption-side: bottom;
    border-collapse: collapse;
}
```

Add a border-collapse property and set its value to "collapse".

Save the file and reload; then check out the changes in the border.

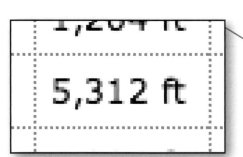

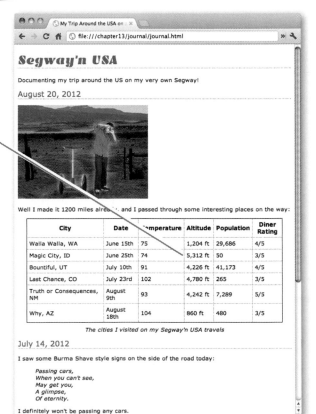

Now you just have one single border around all the table cells. Just what we wanted, and don't you agree that the table looks much cleaner now?

Well I made it 1200 miles already, and I passed through some interesting places on the way:

City	Date	Temperature	Altitude	Population	Diner Rating
Walla Walla, WA	June 15th	75	1,204 ft	29,686	4/5
Magic City, ID	June 25th	74	5,312 ft	50	3/5
Bountiful, UT	July 10th	91	4,226 ft	41,173	4/5
Last Chance, CO	July 23rd	102	4,780 ft	265	3/5
Truth or Consequences, NM	August 9th	93	4,242 ft	7,289	5/5
Why, AZ	August 18th	104	860 ft	480	3/5

The cities I visited on my Segway'n USA travels

July 14, 2012

I saw some Burma Shave style signs on the side of the road today:

> Passing cars,
> When you can't see,
> May get you,
> A glimpse,
> Of eternity.

I definitely won't be passing any cars.

Sharpen your pencil

You're becoming quite the pro at HTML and CSS, so we don't mind giving you a little more to play with in these exercises. How about this: we'd like to spruce this table up even a little more, starting with some text alignment issues. Let's say we want the date, temperature, and diner rating to be center-aligned. And how about right alignment on the altitude and population? How would you do that?

Here's a hint: create two classes, one for center-aligned and one for right-aligned. Then just use the text-align property in each. Finally, add the appropriate class to the correct <td> elements.

This may sound tough, but take it step by step; you already know everything you need to finish this one. And, of course, you can find the answer in the back of the chapter, but give yourself the time to solve it before you peek.

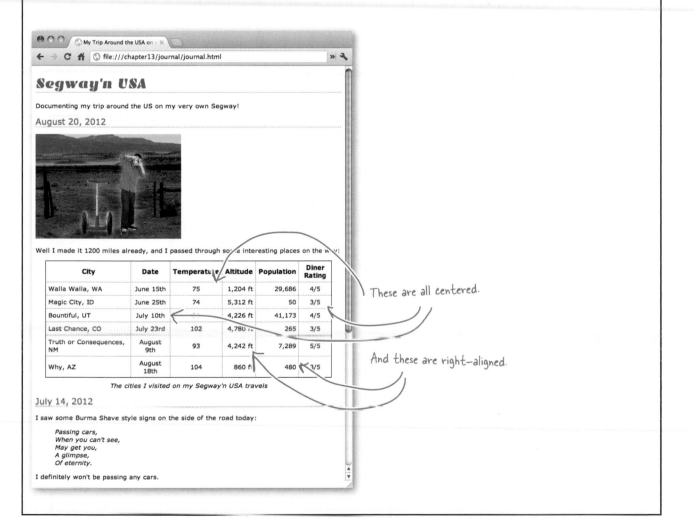

How about some color?

You know Tony loves his signature color and there's no reason not to add a splash of orange to his table; not only will it look great, but we can actually improve the readability of the table by adding some color. Just like for any other element, all you need to do is set the `background-color` property on a table cell to change its color (notice how everything you've learned about HTML and CSS is starting to come together!). Here's how you do that:

```css
th {
    background-color: #cc6600;
}
```

Add this new rule to your "journal.css" file and reload. Here's what you'll see:

How about some color in the table rows?

So far, the color is looking pretty nice. Let's take it to the next level. A common way to color tables is to give rows an alternating color, which allows you to more easily see each row without getting confused about which column goes with which row. Check it out:

Difficult to do in CSS? Nope. Here's how you can do this. First define a new class—let's call it "cellcolor":

```css
.cellcolor {
    background-color: #fcba7a;
}
```

and then add this class attribute to each row you'd like to color. So in this case, you find the `<tr>` opening tags for Magic City, Last Chance, and Why, and add `class="cellcolor"` to each one.

Exercise

Your turn. Add the class "cellcolor" to your CSS in "journal.css", and then, in your HTML, add class="cellcolor" to each of the `<tr>` opening tags needed to make the rows alternating colors. Check your answers before moving on.

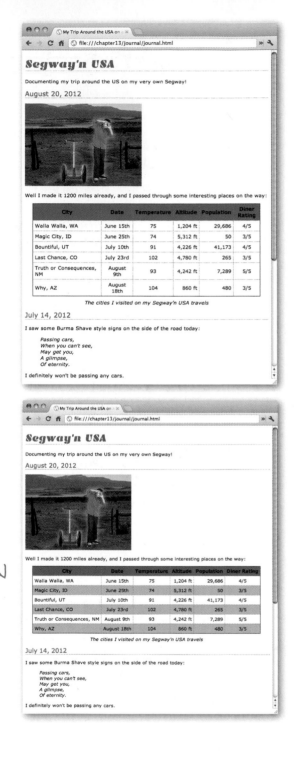

Some Serious CSS

Want to see another, more advanced way to add color to every other row of a table? It's called the **nth-child pseudo-class**. Remember, pseudo-classes are used to style elements based on their state (like the `a:hover` pseudo-class we used in Head First Lounge, which styles a link if the user is hovering the mouse over the link).

For the nth-child pseudo-class, that state is the numerical order of an element in relation to its sibling elements. Let's look at an example of what that means:

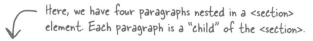
Here, we have four paragraphs nested in a <section> element. Each paragraph is a "child" of the <section>.

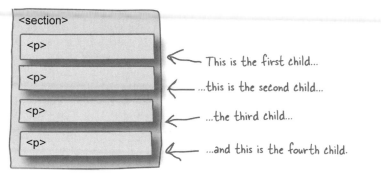

This is the first child...

...this is the second child...

...the third child...

...and this is the fourth child.

Let's say you want to select the even paragraphs (that is, paragraphs 2 and 4) so they have a red background color, and the odd paragraphs so they have a green background color. You do that like this:

```
p:nth-child(even) {
    background-color: red;        Paragraphs 2 and 4 will be red...
}
p:nth-child(odd) {
    background-color: green;      ...and paragraphs 1 and 3 will be green.
}
```

As you might guess from the name "nth-child", this pseudo-class is even more flexible than just selecting odd and even items nested in an element. You can also specify simple expressions that use the number **n** to give you a wide variety of options in selecting elements. For instance, you can also select the even and odd paragraphs like this:

```
                        Selects even-
p:nth-child(2n) {       numbered <p>s
    background-color: red;
}
                        Selects odd-
p:nth-child(2n+1) {     numbered <p>s
    background-color: green;
}
```

If $n=0$, then $2n=0$ (no paragraph), and $2n+1$ is 1, which is the first paragraph.

If $n=1$, then $2n=2$, the second paragraph, and $2n+1=3$, the third paragraph.

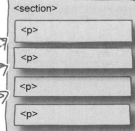

A Serious Exercise

Why don't you try your hand using the nth-child pseudo-class? Complete the CSS rule below using the nth-child pseudo-class to color the odd rows light orange.

Write your pseudo-class selector here.

```
tr:nth-child(even)    {
    background-color: #fcba7a;
}
```

Comment out your .cellcolor class like this:

```
/* .cellcolor {
    background-color: #fcba7a;
} */
```

If you want to try this for real, first comment out your .cellcolor class so it doesn't take effect anymore. Next, place the new tr pseudo-class rule *above* the rule for setting the background color of the <th> row (so the <th> row stays dark orange). Make sure you're using a modern browser (IE9+!), and reload the page. Did it work? Go ahead and remove this new rule, and uncomment the .cellcolor rule before moving on.

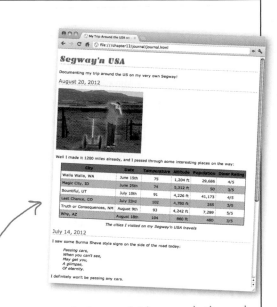

Rows 1, 3, 5, and 7 all have a light-orange background color. But the rule for th will override the rule for the "odd" rows, so it will stay dark orange.

Did we mention that Tony made an interesting discovery in Truth or Consequences, New Mexico?

Tess

It's fair to say Tony found something interesting about Truth or Consequences, New Mexico; in fact, he found *her* so interesting that after going to Arizona, he turned around and came right back.

We're glad for Tony, but he's really given us a conundrum with the table. While we could just add a new row for Truth or Consequences, we'd really like to do it in a more elegant way. What are we talking about? Look on the next page to find out.

Another look at Tony's table

Based on his return trip to New Mexico, Tony's added a new entry for August 27th, just below the original Truth or Consequences entry. He's also reused a couple of cells where the information didn't change (a great technique for reducing the amount of information in a table). You can see that when he added the new row, all he needed to do was list the things that were different the second time around (the date, the temperature, and that he revisited the diner).

Here are both of Tony's visits to Truth or Consequences.

City	Date	Temp	Altitude	Population	Diner Rating
Walla Walla, WA	June 15th	75	1,204 ft	29,686	4/5
Magic City, ID	June 25th	74	5,312 ft	50	3/5
Bountiful, UT	July 10th	91	4,226 ft	41,173	4/5
Last Chance, CO	July 23rd	102	4,780 ft	265	3/5
Truth or Consequences, NM	August 9th	93	4,242 ft	7,289	5/5
	August 27th	98			4/5
Why, AZ	August 18th	104	860 ft	480	3/5

These table data cells span TWO rows now.

But where does this leave you with HTML? It seems like you'd have to add an entirely new row and just duplicate the city, altitude, and population, right? Well, not so fast. We have the technology…using HTML tables, you can have cells span more than one row (or more than one column). Let's see how this works…

How to tell cells to span more than one row

What does it mean for a cell to span more than one row? Let's look at the entries for Truth or Consequences, NM, in Tony's table again. The data cells for city, altitude, and population span *two rows*, not one, while the date, temp, and diner rating span one row, which is the normal, default behavior for data cells.

City	Date	Temp	Altitude	Population	Diner Rating
Walla Walla, WA	June 15th	75	1,204 ft	29,686	4/5
Magic City, ID	June 25th	74	5,312 ft	50	3/5
Bountiful, UT	July 10th	91	4,226 ft	41,173	4/5
Last Chance, CO	July 23rd	102	4,780 ft	265	3/5
Truth or Consequences, NM	August 9th	93	4,242 ft	7,289	5/5
	August 27th	98			4/5
Why, AZ	August 18th	104	860 ft	480	3/5

These cells span two rows.

While the date, temp, and diner rating cells take up just one.

So, how do you do that in HTML? It's easier than you might think: you use the `rowspan` attribute to specify how many rows a table data cell should take up, and then remove the corresponding table data elements from the other rows that the cell spans over. Have a look—it's easier to see than describe:

```
<tr>
    <td rowspan="2">Truth or Consequences, NM</td>
    <td class="center">August 9th</td>
    <td class="center">93</td>
    <td rowspan="2" class="right">4,242 ft</td>
    <td rowspan="2" class="right">7,289</td>
    <td class="center">5/5</td>
</tr>
<tr>

    <td class="center">August 27th</td>
    <td class="center">98</td>

    <td class="center">4/5</td>
</tr>
```

Here are the two table rows that have the New Mexico data.

The city is not needed because of the rowspan.

For the data cells that don't change on the second visit (city, altitude, and population), we add a rowspan attribute indicating that the table data spans two rows.

Same with altitude and population

Then in the second row, we specify just the columns we need (date, temp, and a new rating).

WHO DOES WHAT?

Just to make sure you've got this down, fill in each cell in the table with the data from the correct <td> table cell. We've done one for you to get you started. Check your answers before moving on.

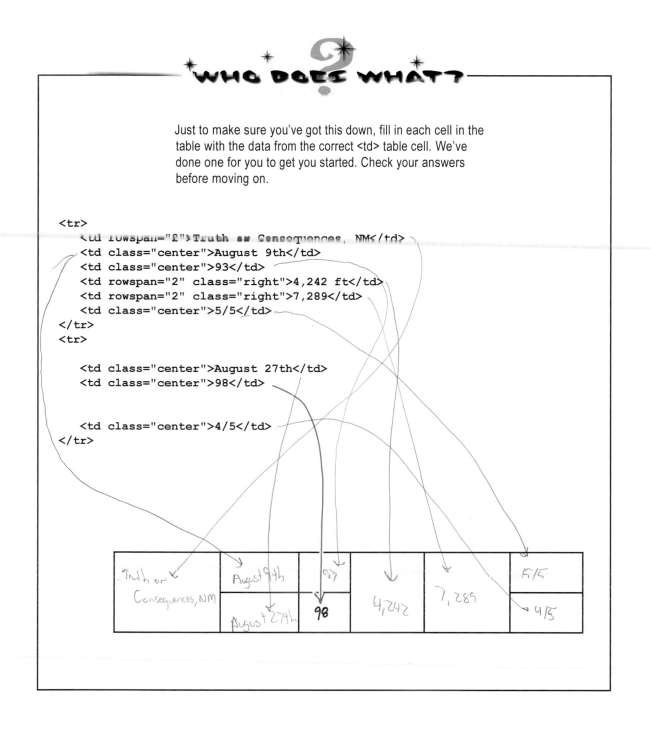

```
<tr>
   <td rowspan="2">Truth or Consequences, NM</td>
   <td class="center">August 9th</td>
   <td class="center">93</td>
   <td rowspan="2" class="right">4,242 ft</td>
   <td rowspan="2" class="right">7,289</td>
   <td class="center">5/5</td>
</tr>
<tr>

   <td class="center">August 27th</td>
   <td class="center">98</td>


   <td class="center">4/5</td>
</tr>
```

Test drive the table

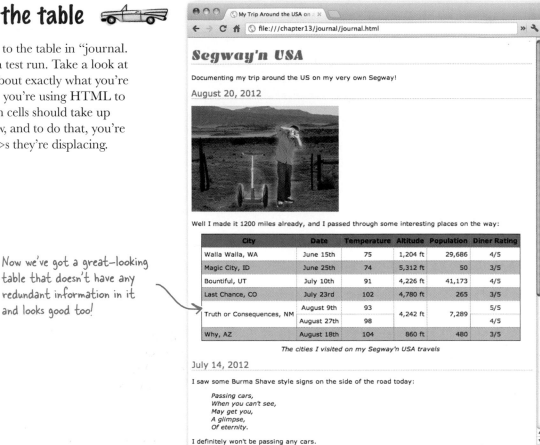

Make the changes to the table in "journal. html" and give it a test run. Take a look at the table. Think about exactly what you're doing to the table: you're using HTML to specify that certain cells should take up more than one row, and to do that, you're removing the `<td>`s they're displacing.

Now we've got a great-looking table that doesn't have any redundant information in it and looks good too!

---

there are no
Dumb Questions

Q: **You said you can have table data span columns too?**

A: You sure can. Just add a colspan attribute to your `<td>` element and specify the number of columns. Unlike the rowspan, when you span columns, you remove table data elements that are in the *same* row (since you are spanning columns, not rows).

Q: **Can I have a colspan and rowspan in the same `<td>`?**

A: You sure can. Just make sure you adjust the other `<td>`s in the table to account for both the row and column spans. In other words, you'll need to remove the corresponding number of `<td>`s from the same row, *and* from the column.

Q: **Do you really think these rowspans look better?**

A: Well, they certainly reduce the amount of information in the table, which is usually a good thing. And, if you look at a few tables out there in the real world, you'll find that rowspans and colspans are quite common, so it's great to be able to do them in HTML. But if you liked the table better before, feel free to change your HTML and go back to the previous version.

Four out of five stars? I know my diners, and that was a solid five-star rating! You better change that in the table.

Trouble in paradise?

It looks like we've got a disagreement on the diner rating for August 27th, and while we could ask Tony and Tess to come to a consensus, why should we? We've got tables, and we should be able to get another rating in there. But how? We don't really want to add yet another entry just for Tess's review. Hmmm…why don't we do it like this?

City	Date	Temp	Altitude	Population	Diner Rating
Walla Walla, WA	June 15th	75	1,204 ft	29,686	4/5
Magic City, ID	June 25th	74	5,312 ft	50	3/5
Bountiful, UT	July 10th	91	4,226 ft	41,173	4/5
Last Chance, CO	July 23rd	102	4,780 ft	265	3/5
Truth or Consequences, NM	August 9th	93	4,242 ft	7,289	5/5
	August 27th	98			Tess 5/5 Tony 4/5
Why, AZ	August 18th	104	860 ft	480	3/5

Why not put both their ratings in the table? That way, we get more accurate information.

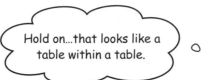

Hold on...that looks like a
table within a table.

That's because it is. But nested tables in
HTML are straightforward. All you need
to do is put another <table> element
inside a <td>. How do you do that? You
create a simple table to represent both
Tony's and Tess's ratings together, and
when you have that working, put it inside
the table cell that now holds Tony's 4/5
rating. Let's give it a try…

```
<tr>
    <td rowspan="2">Truth or Consequences, NM</td>
    <td class="center">August 9th</td>
    <td class="center">93</td>
    <td rowspan="2" class="right">4,242 ft</td>
    <td rowspan="2" class="right">7,289</td>
    <td class="center">5/5</td>
</tr>
<tr>
    <td class="center">August 27th</td>
    <td class="center">98</td>
    <td>
        4/5
        <table>
            <tr>
                <th>Tess</th>
                <td>5/5</td>
            </tr>
            <tr>
                <th>Tony</th>
                <td>4/5</td>
            </tr>
        </table>
    </td>
</tr>
```

First, delete the old rating
that represented Tony's rating...

...and put a table in its place. This table holds
two diner ratings: one for Tess and one for
Tony. We're using table headings for their
names, and data cells for their ratings.

Test driving the nested table

Go ahead and type in the new table. Tables are easy to mistype, so make sure you validate and then reload your page. You should see the new, nested table.

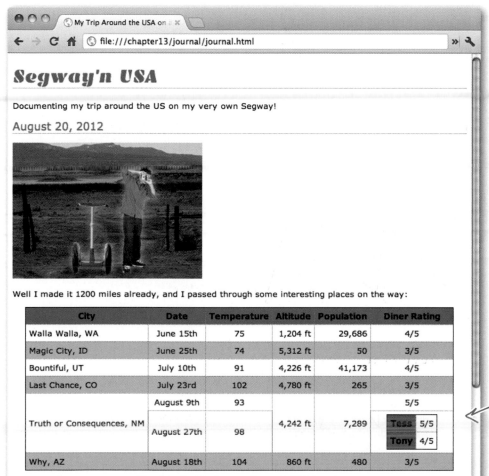

Wow, looking nice. Only that background really is a bit much for a nested table. Let's keep the names bold, but take off the background color.

BRAIN BARBELL

It's time to fall back on all that training you've done. What you need to do is change the table heading background color for just Tony and Tess, and do it without changing the background of the main table headings. How? You need to find a selector that selects only the nested table headings.

City	Date	Temperature	Altitude	Population	Diner Rating
Walla Walla, WA	June 15th	75	1,204 ft	29,686	4/5
Magic City, ID	June 25th	74	5,312 ft	50	3/5
Bountiful, UT	July 10th	91	4,226 ft	41,173	4/5
Last Chance, CO	July 23rd	102	4,780 ft	265	3/5
Truth or Consequences, NM	August 9th	93			5/5
	August 27th	98	4,242 ft	7,289	**Tess** 5/5 **Tony** 4/5
Why, AZ	August 18th	104	860 ft	480	3/5

The cities I visited on my Segway'n USA travels

We want to change the background color of the nested table headers to white.

```
table table th {
    background-color: white;
}
```

Determine the selector to select only the nested table heading elements.

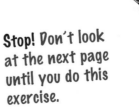

Stop! Don't look at the next page until you do this exercise.

Overriding the CSS for the nested table headings

You can target just the `<th>` elements in the nested table using a descendant selector. Add a new rule to your CSS that uses the "table table th" selector to change the background color of the nested table headers to white:

```css
table table th {
    background-color: white;
}
```

Now save the changes to your "journal.css" file and reload.

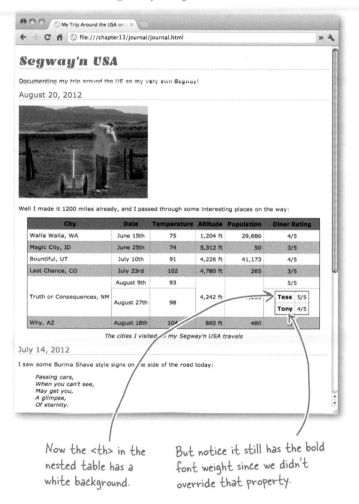

Now the `<th>` in the nested table has a white background.

But notice it still has the bold font weight since we didn't override that property.

there are no Dumb Questions

Q: I used a class to solve the Brain Barbell. I created a class called "nestedtable" and assigned each table heading to it. Then I created a rule like this:

```css
.nestedtable {
    background-color: white;
}
```

Is that an okay solution too?

A: There are lots of different ways to solve problems using CSS, and certainly your solution is an effective and perfectly valid way to use CSS. We'll just point out that by using the descendant selector instead, we didn't have to make any changes to our HTML. What if Tony and Tess keep adding reviews for diners? Then for every review, you'd have to make sure and add the class to each `<th>`. With our solution, the styling happens automatically.

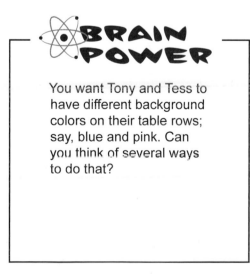

BRAIN POWER

You want Tony and Tess to have different background colors on their table rows; say, blue and pink. Can you think of several ways to do that?

Giving Tony's site the final polish

Tony's page is really looking nice, but there's one more area we haven't spent any time styling yet: the list that contains the set of items he was preparing for his trip. You'll find this list in his June 2nd entry; check it out below:

We're looking at just the HTML snippet from the June 2nd entry.

```
<h2>June 2, 2012</h2>

<p>
    <img src="images/segway1.jpg"
         alt="The first day of the trip" />
</p>

<p>
    My first day of the trip! I can't
    believe I finally got everything
    packed and ready to go. Because
    I'm on a Segway, I wasn't able
    to bring a whole lot with me:
</p>
<ul>
    <li>cellphone</li>
    <li>iPod</li>
    <li>digital camera</li>
    <li>a protein bar</li>
</ul>
<p>
    Just the essentials. As Lao Tzu
    would have said, <q>A journey of
    a thousand miles begins with
    one Segway.</q>
</p>
</body>
</html>
```

Here's the bottom of Tony's journal, "journal.html". Remember his packing list in his first journal entry?

June 2, 2012

My first day of the trip! I can't believe I finally got everything packed and ready to go. Because I'm on a Segway, I wasn't able to bring a whole lot with me:

- cellphone
- iPod
- digital camera
- and a protein bar

Just the essentials. As Lao Tzu would have said, "A journey of a thousand miles begins with one Segway."

Here's what the list looks like now.

Giving the list some style

You already know that once you know the basic CSS font, text, color, and other properties, you can style just about anything, including lists. You've already seen a little list styling (Chapter 12), and it turns out there are only a couple properties that are specific to lists, so there's not too much more to learn. The main list property is called `list-style-type`, and it allows you to control the bullets (or *markers*, as they are called) used in your lists. Here are a few ways you can do that:

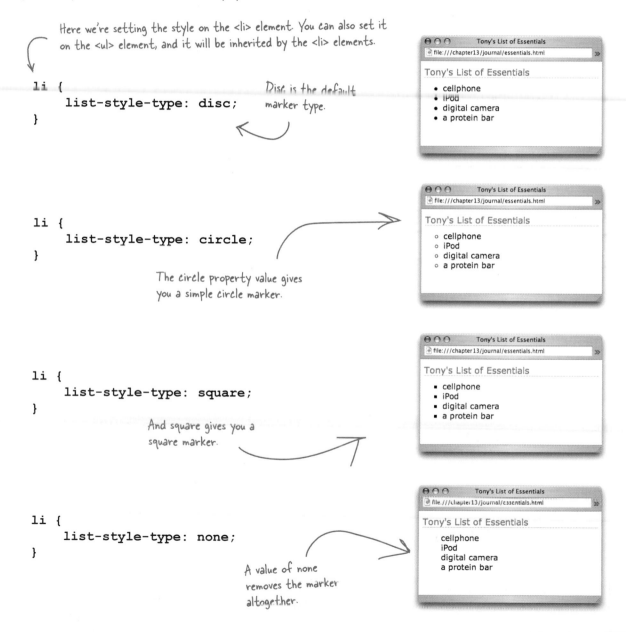

Here we're setting the style on the <li> element. You can also set it on the <ul> element, and it will be inherited by the <li> elements.

```
li {
    list-style-type: disc;
}
```

Disc is the default marker type.

```
li {
    list-style-type: circle;
}
```

The circle property value gives you a simple circle marker.

```
li {
    list-style-type: square;
}
```

And square gives you a square marker.

```
li {
    list-style-type: none;
}
```

A value of none removes the marker altogether.

What if you want a custom marker?

Do you really think Tony would want anything less than his own custom marker? Well, luckily CSS has a property called `list-style-image` that lets you set an image to be the marker for a list. Let's give it a try on Tony's list:

Here's the list-style-image property, which we're setting to a URL.

```
li {
    list-style-image: url(images/backpack.gif);
    padding-top: 5px;
    margin-left: 20px;
}
```

The image "backpack.gif" is a small version of this backpack. Seems fitting, doesn't it? And in Tony's signature color, too.

We're adding some margin to add space on the left of the list items, and also a little top padding to give each list item a bit of headroom.

And, the final test drive...

This is it: your last change to Tony's site. Add the rule for the list item to your CSS and then reload.

Here's the list with the marker replaced with an image and some extra margin and padding spacing.

there are no
Dumb Questions

Q: What about ordered lists? What can I do to change their style?

A: You style ordered and unordered lists in the same way. Of course, an ordered list has a sequence of numbers or letters for markers, not bullets. Using CSS, you can control whether an ordered list's markers are decimal numbers, roman numerals, or alphabetic letters (like a, b, c) with the list-style-type property. Common values are decimal, upper-alpha, lower-alpha, upper-roman, and lower-roman. Consult a CSS reference for more options (there are many).

Q: How can I control the text wrap on lists? In other words, how can I control whether text wraps underneath the marker or just underneath the text?

A: There's a property called list-style-position. If you set this property to "inside", then your text will wrap under the marker. If you set it to "outside", then it will wrap just under the text above it.

Q: Are you sure that's right? That seems backward.

A: Yes, and here's what inside and outside *really* mean: if you set your list-style-position to "inside", then the *marker is inside* your list item and so text will wrap under it. If you set it to "outside", then the *marker is outside* your list item and so text will just wrap under itself. And by "inside your item," we mean inside the border of the list item's box.

Wow, who would have known we could take my site this far when we started?

We're going to get Tess a Segway of her own so she can go with me on the rest of my Segway'n USA trip. See ya somewhere...and we'll BOTH be updating the web page. Thanks for everything!

BULLET POINTS

- HTML tables are used to structure tabular data.

- Use the HTML table elements <table>, <tr>, <th>, and <td> together to create a table.

- The <table> element defines and surrounds the entire table.

- Tables are defined in rows, using the <tr> element.

- Each row contains one or more data cells, defined with the <td> element.

- Use the <th> element for data cells that are row or column headings.

- Tables are laid out in a grid. Each row corresponds to a <tr>...</tr> row in your HTML, and each column corresponds to the <td>...</td> content within the rows.

- You can provide additional information about your tables with the <caption> element.

- Tables have border-spacing, which is the space between cells.

- Table data cells can also have padding and borders.

- Just like you can control the padding, borders, and margins of elements, you can control the padding, borders, and border-spacing of table cells with CSS.

- border-collapse is a special CSS property for tables that allows you to combine cell borders into one border for a cleaner look.

- You can change the alignment of the data in your table cells with the text-align and vertical-align CSS properties.

- You can add color to your tables with the background-color property. Background color can be added to the entire table, to each row, or to a single data cell.

- Use the CSS nth-child pseudo-class to add background color to every other row of a table.

- If you have no data for a data cell, put no content into the <td> element. You need to use a <td>...</td> element to maintain the alignment of the table, however.

- If your data cell needs to span multiple rows or columns, you can use the rowspan or colspan attributes of the <td> element.

- You can nest tables within tables by placing the <table> element and all its content inside a data cell.

- Tables should be used for tabular data, not for laying out your pages. Use CSS table display to create multicolumn page layouts as we described in Chapter 11.

- Lists can be styled with CSS just like any other element. There are a few CSS properties specific to lists, such as list-style-type and list-style-image.

- list-style-type allows you to change the type of the marker used in your list.

- list-style-image allows you to specify an image for your list marker.

HTMLcross

That crossword looks a bit like a table, doesn't it? Give your left brain a
workout and solve this crossword. All the words are from this chapter.

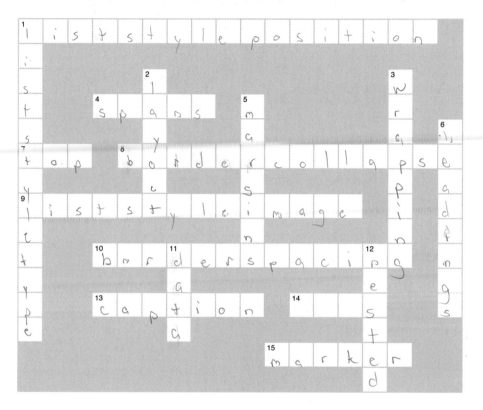

Across

1. Used to control whether the marker is inside or outside the
list items border.
4. What a data cell does when it uses more than one row or
column.
7. Default position of the caption.
8. Used to merge borders.
9. Use this property to use an image instead of a built-in
marker in your lists.
10. Area between borders.
13. Adds a short description that is displayed with the table.
14. You specify HTML tables by ____, not columns.
15. We call bullets a type of list _____.

Down

1. Use this property to change your list marker.
2. Don't use tables for this.
3. list-style-position can be used to control the behavior of
text ____.
5. Table cells have padding and borders, but no _____.
6. <th> is used for these.
11. <td> is for this.
12. One table inside another is called _____.

Exercise Solution

First, type in the "Testing Tony's Table" HTML. Typing this in, while tedious, will help get the structure of the `<table>`, `<tr>`, `<th>`, and `<td>` tags in your head. When you finish, give it a quick test, and then add the remaining items from Tony's table. Test that too.

```html
<!DOCTYPE html>
<html>
<head>
    <meta charset="utf-8">
    <style type="text/css">
        td, th {border: 1px solid black;}
    </style>
    <title>Testing Tony's Table</title>
</head>
<body>
    <table>
        <tr>
            <th>City</th>
            <th>Date</th>
            <th>Temperature</th>
            <th>Altitude</th>
            <th>Population</th>
            <th>Diner Rating</th>
        </tr>
        <tr>
            <td>Walla Walla, WA</td>
            <td>June 15th</td>
            <td>75</td>
            <td>1,204 ft</td>
            <td>29,686</td>
            <td>4/5</td>
        </tr>
        <tr>
            <td>Magic City, ID</td>
            <td>June 25th</td>
            <td>74</td>
            <td>5,312 ft</td>
            <td>50</td>
            <td>3/5</td>
        </tr>
        <tr>
            <td>Bountiful, UT</td>
            <td>July 10th</td>
            <td>91</td>
            <td>4,226 ft</td>
            <td>41,173</td>
            <td>4/5</td>
        </tr>
        <tr>
            <td>Last Chance, CO</td>
            <td>July 23rd</td>
            <td>102</td>
            <td>4,780 ft</td>
            <td>265</td>
            <td>3/5</td>
        </tr>
```

Continues over the page ⟶

Exercise
Solution
Continued

```
        <tr>
            <td>Truth or Consequences, NM</td>
            <td>August 9th</td>
            <td>93</td>
            <td>4,242 ft</td>
            <td>7,289</td>
            <td>5/5</td>
        </tr>
        <tr>
            <td>Why, AZ</td>
            <td>August 18th</td>
            <td>104</td>
            <td>860 ft</td>
            <td>480</td>
            <td>3/5</td>
        </tr>
    </table>
</body>
</html>
```

Testing Tony's Table

file:///chapter13/journal/table.html

City	Date	Temperature	Altitude	Population	Diner Rating
Walla Walla, WA	June 15th	75	1,204 ft	29,686	4/5
Magic City, ID	June 25th	74	5,312 ft	50	3/5
Bountiful, UT	July 10th	91	4,226 ft	41,173	4/5
Last Chance, CO	July 23rd	102	4,780 ft	265	3/5
Truth or Consequences, NM	August 9th	93	4,242 ft	7,289	5/5
Why, AZ	August 18th	104	860 ft	480	3/5

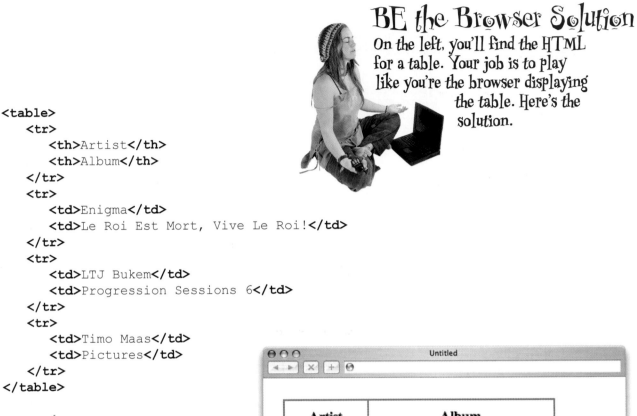

BE the Browser Solution

On the left, you'll find the HTML for a table. Your job is to play like you're the browser displaying the table. Here's the solution.

```html
<table>
    <tr>
        <th>Artist</th>
        <th>Album</th>
    </tr>
    <tr>
        <td>Enigma</td>
        <td>Le Roi Est Mort, Vive Le Roi!</td>
    </tr>
    <tr>
        <td>LTJ Bukem</td>
        <td>Progression Sessions 6</td>
    </tr>
    <tr>
        <td>Timo Maas</td>
        <td>Pictures</td>
    </tr>
</table>
```

We formatted the HTML so that it's easier to read if you happen to be a human.

Artist	Album
Enigma	Le Roi Est Mort, Vive Le Roi!
LTJ Bukem	Progression Sessions 6
Timo Maas	Pictures

Sharpen your pencil
Solution

The double dotted lines are giving Tony's table a busy and distracting look. It would be much better, and wouldn't detract from the table, if we could just have one border around each table cell. Can you think of a way to do that with styling given that you've just learned? You can set the border-spacing property to 0 to remove the space between the borders.

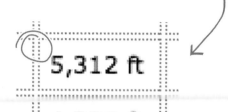

We could use border-spacing to set spacing to 0; then the two lines would be right next to each other.

```
table {
    margin-left: 20px;
    margin-right: 20px;
    border: thin solid black;
    caption-side: bottom;
    border-spacing: 0px;
}
```

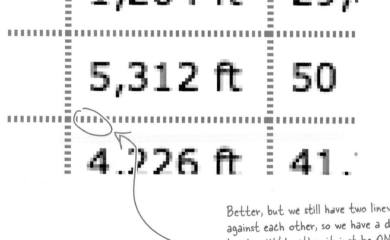

Better, but we still have two lines and they're right up against each other, so we have a double, thick, dotted border. We'd rather it just be ONE border between the cells. Wouldn't we?

Sharpen your pencil
Solution

Let's say we want the date, temperature, and diner rating to be center-aligned. And how about right alignment on the altitude and population? Here's how you would do that:

```
.center {
    text-align: center;
}
.right {
    text-align: right;
}
```

Here are the two classes, one for center and one for right alignment.

```
<table >
  <caption>The cities I visited on my Segway'n USA travels</caption>
    <tr>
        <th>City</th>
        <th>Date</th>
        <th>Temperature</th>
        <th>Altitude</th>
        <th>Population</th>
        <th>Diner Rating</th>
    </tr>
    <tr>
        <td>Walla Walla, WA</td>
        <td class="center">June 15th</td>
        <td class="center">75</td>
        <td class="right">1,204 ft</td>
        <td class="right">29,686</td>
        <td class="center">4/5</td>
    </tr>
    <tr>
        <td>Magic City, ID</td>
        <td class="center">June 25th</td>
        <td class="center">74</td>
        <td class="right">5,312 ft</td>
        <td class="right">50</td>
        <td class="center">3/5</td>
    </tr>
    .
    .
    .
</table>
```

And here you just add each <td> to the appropriate class!

Exercise Solution

To create alternating colors in the Magic City, Last Chance, and Why table rows with a class, add the class="cellcolor" attribute to the opening <tr> tags in the table rows, like this:

```
<tr class="cellcolor">
  <td>Magic City, ID</td>
  ...
</tr>
```

City	Date	Temperature	Altitude	Population	Diner Rating
Walla Walla, WA	June 15th	75	1,204 ft	29,686	4/5
Magic City, ID	June 25th	74	5,312 ft	50	3/5
Bountiful, UT	July 10th	91	4,226 ft	41,173	4/5
Last Chance, CO	July 23rd	102	4,780 ft	265	3/5
Truth or Consequences, NM	August 9th	93	4,242 ft	7,289	5/5
Why, AZ	August 18th	104	860 ft	480	3/5

WHO DOES WHAT?
SOLUTION

Just to make sure you've got this down, draw an arrow from each <td> element to its corresponding cell in the table. Here are the answers.

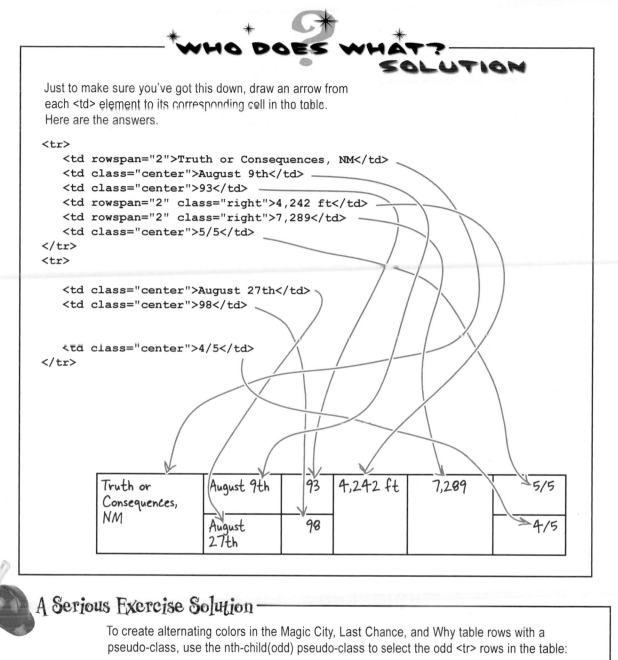

```
<tr>
    <td rowspan="2">Truth or Consequences, NM</td>
    <td class="center">August 9th</td>
    <td class="center">93</td>
    <td rowspan="2" class="right">4,242 ft</td>
    <td rowspan="2" class="right">7,289</td>
    <td class="center">5/5</td>
</tr>
<tr>

    <td class="center">August 27th</td>
    <td class="center">98</td>


    <td class="center">4/5</td>
</tr>
```

A Serious Exercise Solution

To create alternating colors in the Magic City, Last Chance, and Why table rows with a pseudo-class, use the nth-child(odd) pseudo-class to select the odd <tr> rows in the table:

```
tr:nth-child(odd) {
    background-color: #fcba7a;
}
```

City	Date	Temperature	Altitude	Population	Diner Rating
Walla Walla, WA	June 15th	75	1,204 ft	29,686	4/5
Magic City, ID	June 25th	74	5,312 ft	50	3/5
Bountiful, UT	July 10th	91	4,226 ft	41,173	4/5
Last Chance, CO	July 23rd	102	4,780 ft	265	3/5
Truth or Consequences, NM	August 9th	93	4,242 ft	7,289	5/5
Why, AZ	August 18th	104	860 ft	480	3/5

BRAIN BARBELL SOLUTION

It's time to fall back on all that training you've done. What you need to do is change the table heading background color for just Tony and Tess, and do it without changing the background of the main table headings. How? You need to find a selector that selects only the nested table headings.

We can use a descendant selector to select just the nested table header. Here's how you can do that:

(1) Start by selecting the outer table...

City	Date	Temperature	Altitude	Population	Diner Rating
Walla Walla, WA	June 15th	75	1,204 ft	29,686	4/5
Magic City, ID	June 25th	74	5,312 ft	50	3/5
Bountiful, UT	July 10th	91	4,226 ft	41,173	4/5
Last Chance, CO	July 23rd	102	4,780 ft	265	3/5
Truth or Consequences, NM	August 9th	93	4,242 ft	7,289	5/5 · Tess 5/5 · Tony 4/5
	August 27th	98			
Why, AZ	August 18th	104	860 ft	480	/5

(2) Then select the inner table...

(3) Then select the table heading.

```
     (1)     (2)    (3)
table table th {
     background-color: white;
}
```

Determine the selector to select only the nested table heading elements.

HTMLcross Solution

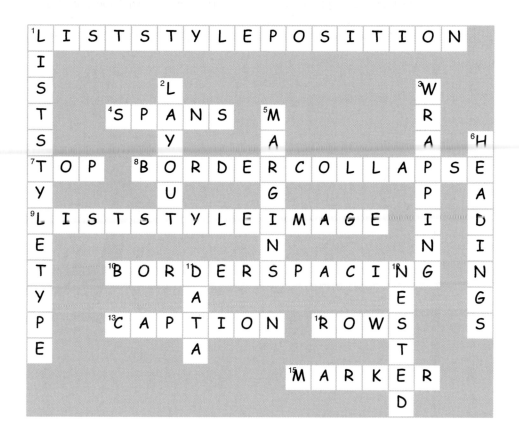

14 html forms

Getting Interactive

Yeah, just got your form. We're checking it with the server now, and then we'll get a response right back to you.

So far all your web communication has been one-way: from your page to your visitors. Golly, wouldn't it be nice if your visitors could talk back? That's where HTML forms come in: once you enable your pages with forms (along with a little help from a web server), your pages are going to be able to gather customer feedback, take an online order, get the next move in an online game, or collect the votes in a "hot or not" contest. In this chapter you're going to meet a whole team of HTML elements that work together to create web forms. You'll also learn a bit about what goes on behind the scenes in the server to support forms, and we'll even talk about keeping those forms stylish.

How forms work

If you use the Web at all, then you know what a form is. But you might not have really thought about what they have to do with HTML. A form is basically a web page with input fields that allows you to enter information. When the form is *submitted*, that information is packaged up and sent off to a web server to be processed by a server script. When the processing is done, what do you get? Another web page, of course, as a response. Let's take a closer look at how this works:

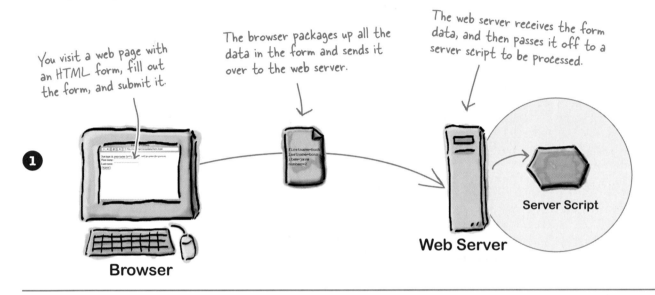

You visit a web page with an HTML form, fill out the form, and submit it.

The browser packages up all the data in the form and sends it over to the web server.

The web server receives the form data, and then passes it off to a server script to be processed.

Browser

Web Server

Server Script

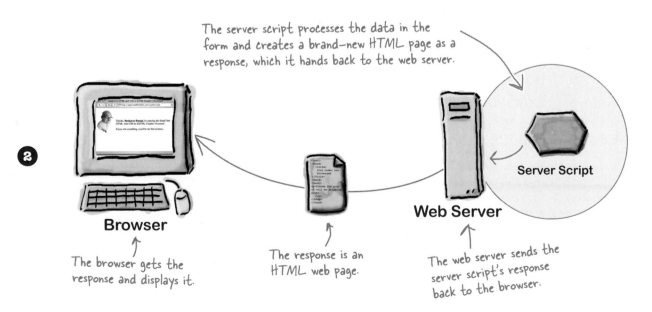

The server script processes the data in the form and creates a brand-new HTML page as a response, which it hands back to the web server.

Browser

Web Server

Server Script

The browser gets the response and displays it.

The response is an HTML web page.

The web server sends the server script's response back to the browser.

How forms work in the browser

To a browser, a form is just a bit of HTML in a page. You'll see that you can easily create forms in your pages by adding a few new elements. Here's how a form works from the browser's perspective:

The browser loads the page

The browser loads the HTML for a page like it always does, and when it encounters form elements, it creates *controls* on the page that allow you to input various kinds of data. A control is just something like a button or a text input box or a drop-down menu—basically something that allows you to input data.

You enter data

You use the controls to enter data. Depending on the type of control, this happens in different ways. You can type a single line of text into a text control, or you might click one option of many in a checkbox control. We'll look at the different kinds of controls shortly.

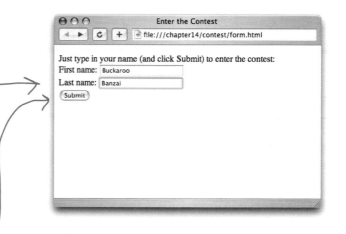

You submit the form

You *submit* the form by clicking on a submit button control. That's the browser's cue that it needs to package up all the data and send that data off to the server.

The server responds

Once the server has the form data, it passes it off to the appropriate server script for processing. This processing results in a brand-new HTML page that is returned to the browser, and since it's just HTML, the browser displays it for you.

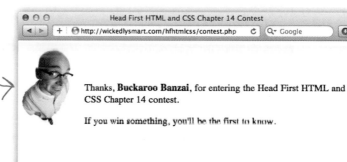

What you write in HTML

There's no deep mystery to creating forms with HTML. In fact, in this chapter you're going to meet a whole new set of HTML elements that all work together to create forms. The best way to get a feel for forms is to look at a little HTML and then to give it a try. Check out this form:

```
<!DOCTYPE html>
<html>
    <head>
        <meta charset="utf-8">
        <title>Enter the Contest</title>
    </head>
    <body>
```

This stuff is all old hat for you now.

Here's the form.

```
        <form action="http://wickedlysmart.com/hfhtmlcss/contest.php"
              method="POST">
 (A)        <p>Just type in your name (and click Submit) to
              enter the contest: <br>

 (B)        First name: <input type="text" name="firstname" value=""> <br>
 (C)        Last name: <input type="text" name="lastname" value=""> <br>
 (D)        <input type="submit">

        </p>
        </form>
```

We've got the <form> element itself...

...and a bunch of elements nested inside it.

```
    </body>
</html>
```

Relax

For now, just take a good look at the form and what's in it; we'll be going into all the details throughout the chapter.

What the browser creates

Big surprise; to create a form, you use a `<form>` element. Now, just about any block-level element can go inside the `<form>` element, but there's a whole new set of elements that are made especially for forms. Each of these form elements provides a different way for you to enter information: text boxes, checkboxes, menus of options, and more. We'll examine all these elements, but first take another look back at the HTML on the previous page and see how the elements and content inside the `<form>` element are displayed in the page below:

Here's just normal paragraph text in a form.

And here are two text controls for entering a first and last name. In HTML you use the `<input>` element to create these.

And here's the submit button. (Your button might say "Submit Query" instead.)

Enter the Contest

file:///chapter14/contest/form.html

(A) Just type in your name (and click Submit) to enter the contest:
(B) First name: _____
(C) Last name: _____
(D) [Submit]

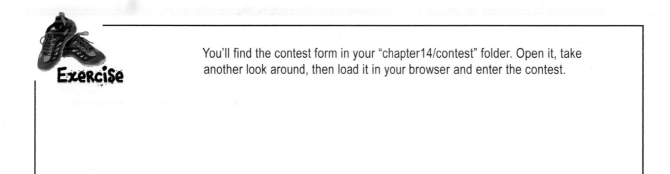

Exercise

You'll find the contest form in your "chapter14/contest" folder. Open it, take another look around, then load it in your browser and enter the contest.

How the `<form>` element works

Let's take a closer look at the `<form>` element—not only does it hold all the elements that make up the form, but it also tells the browser where to send your form data when you submit the form (and the method the browser should use to send it).

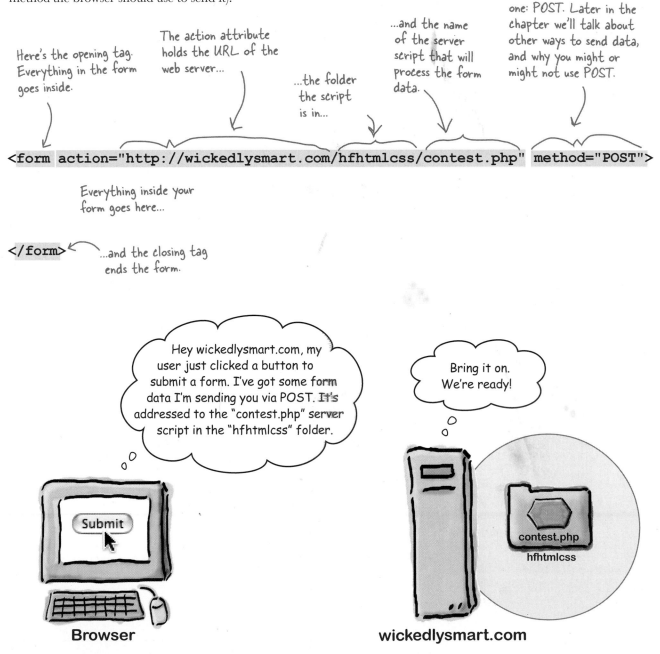

Here's the opening tag. Everything in the form goes inside.

The action attribute holds the URL of the web server...

...the folder the script is in...

...and the name of the server script that will process the form data.

The method attribute determines how the form data will be sent to the server. We're going to use the most common one: POST. Later in the chapter we'll talk about other ways to send data, and why you might or might not use POST.

`<form action="http://wickedlysmart.com/hfhtmlcss/contest.php" method="POST">`

Everything inside your form goes here...

`</form>`

...and the closing tag ends the form.

Hey wickedlysmart.com, my user just clicked a button to submit a form. I've got some form data I'm sending you via POST. It's addressed to the "contest.php" server script in the "hfhtmlcss" folder.

Bring it on. We're ready!

Submit

Browser

contest.php

hfhtmlcss

wickedlysmart.com

Okay, so I have an HTML form—that seems like the easy part. But where do I get a server script, or how do I make one?

Good question.

Creating server scripts is a whole topic unto itself and far beyond what we cover in this book. Well, we tried to cover them, but the book ended up weighing more than you do (not good). So, anyway…

To create server scripts, you need to know a scripting or programming language, and one that is supported by your hosting company. Most hosting companies support languages like PHP, Ruby on Rails, Perl, Python, Node.js, and Java (to name a few), and if you're interested, you'll definitely want to pick up a book specifically for creating server scripts (also known as server-side programs). Check with your hosting company; they sometimes provide simple scripts to their customers, which takes the work out of developing these scripts yourself.

As for this chapter, we've already developed the server scripts you'll need. All you'll need to do is put the URL of the script in the `action` attribute of your `<form>` element.

What can go in a form?

You can put just about any element into a form, but that's not what we really care about right now; we're interested in the *form elements that create controls in the browser*. Here's a quick rundown of all the commonly used form elements. We're going to start with the `<input>` form element, which plays many roles in the form's world.

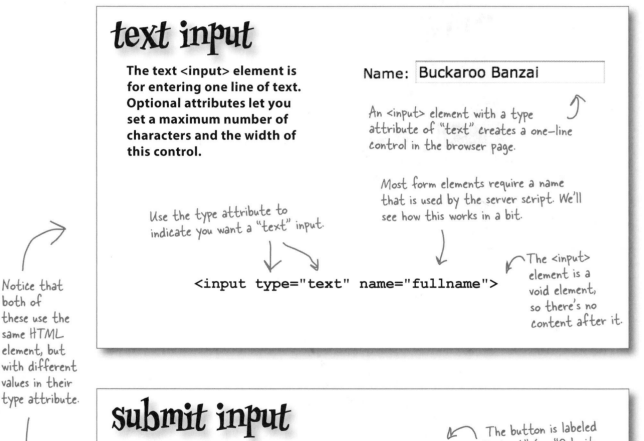

text input

The text `<input>` element is for entering one line of text. Optional attributes let you set a maximum number of characters and the width of this control.

Name: Buckaroo Banzai

An `<input>` element with a type attribute of "text" creates a one-line control in the browser page.

Most form elements require a name that is used by the server script. We'll see how this works in a bit.

Use the type attribute to indicate you want a "text" input.

```
<input type="text" name="fullname">
```

The `<input>` element is a void element, so there's no content after it.

Notice that both of these use the same HTML element, but with different values in their type attribute.

submit input

The submit `<input>` element creates a button that allows you to submit a form. When you click this button, the browser sends the form to the server script for processing.

Submit

The button is labeled "Submit" (or "Submit Query") by default, although you can change that (we'll show you how later).

```
<input type="submit">
```

For a submit button, specify "submit" as the `<input>` element's type.

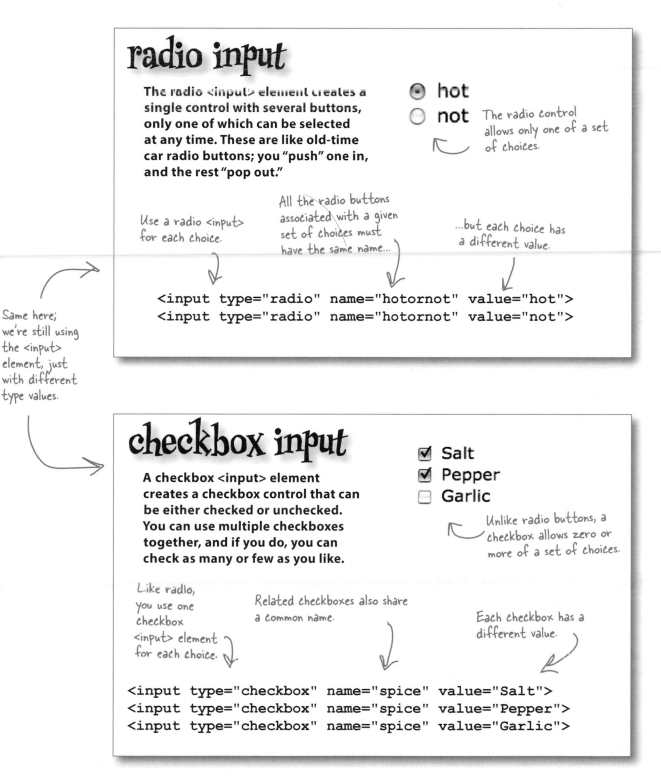

radio input

The radio <input> element creates a single control with several buttons, only one of which can be selected at any time. These are like old-time car radio buttons; you "push" one in, and the rest "pop out."

hot
not

The radio control allows only one of a set of choices.

Use a radio <input> for each choice.

All the radio buttons associated with a given set of choices must have the same name...

...but each choice has a different value.

```
<input type="radio" name="hotornot" value="hot">
<input type="radio" name="hotornot" value="not">
```

Same here; we're still using the <input> element, just with different type values.

checkbox input

A checkbox <input> element creates a checkbox control that can be either checked or unchecked. You can use multiple checkboxes together, and if you do, you can check as many or few as you like.

☑ Salt
☑ Pepper
☐ Garlic

Unlike radio buttons, a checkbox allows zero or more of a set of choices.

Like radio, you use one checkbox <input> element for each choice.

Related checkboxes also share a common name.

Each checkbox has a different value.

```
<input type="checkbox" name="spice" value="Salt">
<input type="checkbox" name="spice" value="Pepper">
<input type="checkbox" name="spice" value="Garlic">
```

What can go in a form? (part 2)

Okay, not every form element is an `<input>` element. There are a few others, like `<select>` for menus and `<textarea>` for typing in more than one line of text. So, why don't you get familiar with these as well before moving on? Oh, and by the way, once you do that, you'll know 90% of the form elements (and 99% of the form elements that are commonly used).

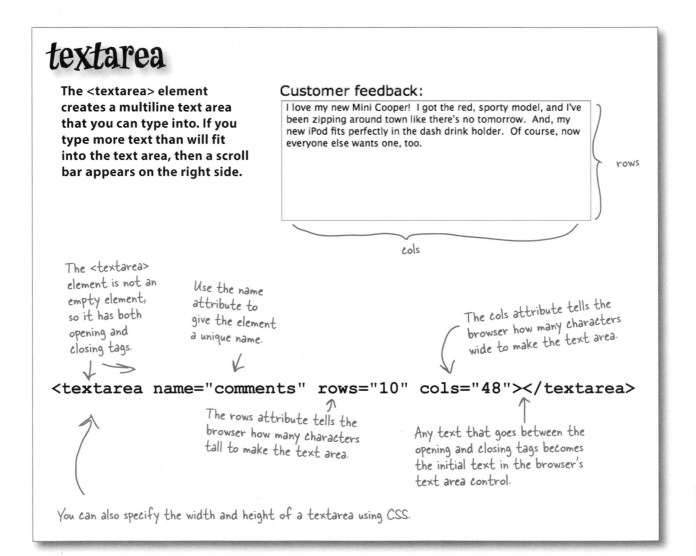

textarea

The `<textarea>` element creates a multiline text area that you can type into. If you type more text than will fit into the text area, then a scroll bar appears on the right side.

Customer feedback:

I love my new Mini Cooper! I got the red, sporty model, and I've been zipping around town like there's no tomorrow. And, my new iPod fits perfectly in the dash drink holder. Of course, now everyone else wants one, too.

rows

cols

The `<textarea>` element is not an empty element, so it has both opening and closing tags.

Use the name attribute to give the element a unique name.

The cols attribute tells the browser how many characters wide to make the text area.

`<textarea name="comments" rows="10" cols="48"></textarea>`

The rows attribute tells the browser how many characters tall to make the text area.

Any text that goes between the opening and closing tags becomes the initial text in the browser's text area control.

You can also specify the width and height of a textarea using CSS.

select

The <select> element creates a menu control in the web page. The menu provides a way to choose between a set of choices. The <select> element works in combination with the <option> element below to create a menu.

Buckaroo Banzai ⬍

The select element creates a menu that looks like this (although the look will vary depending on the browser you're using).

The <select> element goes around all the menu options to group them into one menu.

Just like the other form elements, give the select element a unique name using the name attribute.

```html
<select name="characters">
    <option value="Buckaroo">Buckaroo Banzai</option>
    <option value="Tommy">Perfect Tommy</option>
    <option value="Penny">Penny Priddy</option>
    <option value="Jersey">New Jersey</option>
    <option value="John">John Parker</option>
</select>
```

option

The <option> element works with the <select> element to create a menu. Use an <option> element for each menu item.

After clicking on the menu, the menu items drop down.

✓ Buckaroo Banzai
  Perfect Tommy
  Penny Priddy
  New Jersey
  John Parker

```html
<select name="characters">
    <option value="Buckaroo">Buckaroo Banzai</option>
    <option value="Tommy">Perfect Tommy</option>
    <option value="Penny">Penny Priddy</option>
    <option value="Jersey">New Jersey</option>
    <option value="John">John Parker</option>
</select>
```

The content of the <option> element is used for the menu items' description. Each menu option also includes a value representing the menu item.

Oh, even more can go in a form!

Ah yes, we can't forget all the new fun stuff. With HTML5, we've got even more specialized input forms. Let's take a look:

> Wait, HTML5 adds even more great input types! Don't forget those!

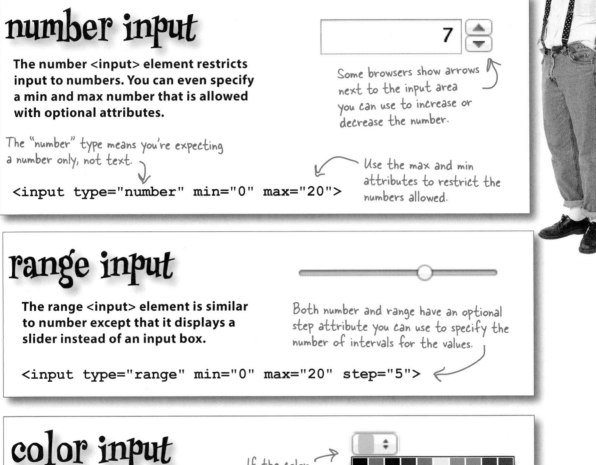

number input

The number <input> element restricts input to numbers. You can even specify a min and max number that is allowed with optional attributes.

Some browsers show arrows next to the input area you can use to increase or decrease the number.

The "number" type means you're expecting a number only, not text.

Use the max and min attributes to restrict the numbers allowed.

`<input type="number" min="0" max="20">`

range input

The range <input> element is similar to number except that it displays a slider instead of an input box.

Both number and range have an optional step attribute you can use to specify the number of intervals for the values.

`<input type="range" min="0" max="20" step="5">`

color input

Use the color <input> to specify a color. When you click on the control, a color picker pops up that allows you to select a color rather than having to type in the color name or value.

If the color input is not supported by the browser, you'll just get a regular text input instead.

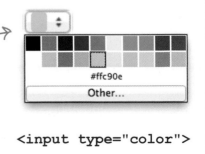

`<input type="color">`

date input

Use the date <input> element to specify a date, with a date picker control. The control creates a valid date format string to send to the server script.

`<input type="date">`

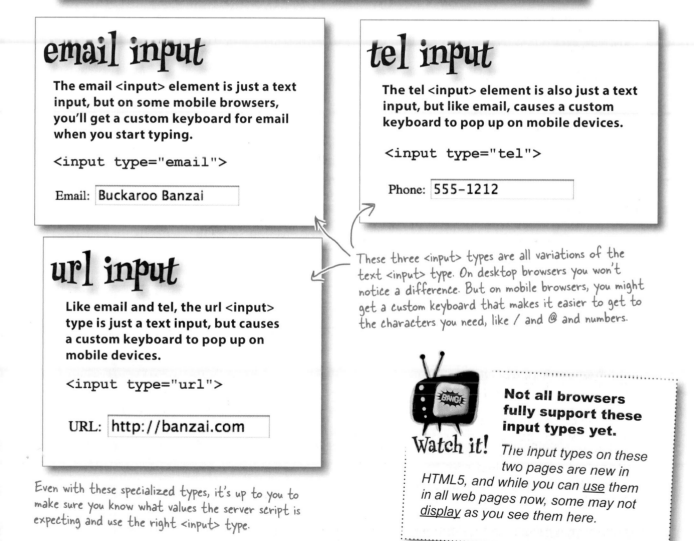

Like with color, if the date input isn't supported by the browser yet, you'll get a regular text input instead.

email input

The email <input> element is just a text input, but on some mobile browsers, you'll get a custom keyboard for email when you start typing.

`<input type="email">`

Email: Buckaroo Banzai

tel input

The tel <input> element is also just a text input, but like email, causes a custom keyboard to pop up on mobile devices.

`<input type="tel">`

Phone: 555-1212

These three <input> types are all variations of the text <input> type. On desktop browsers you won't notice a difference. But on mobile browsers, you might get a custom keyboard that makes it easier to get to the characters you need, like / and @ and numbers.

url input

Like email and tel, the url <input> type is just a text input, but causes a custom keyboard to pop up on mobile devices.

`<input type="url">`

URL: http://banzai.com

Even with these specialized types, it's up to you to make sure you know what values the server script is expecting and use the right <input> type.

Not all browsers fully support these input types yet.

Watch it! The input types on these two pages are new in HTML5, and while you can _use_ them in all web pages now, some may not _display_ as you see them here.

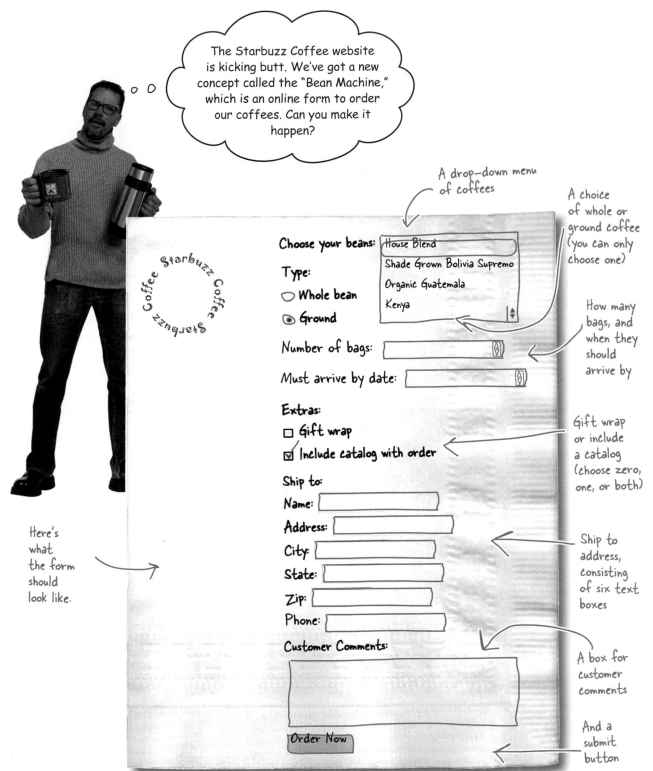

The Starbuzz Coffee website is kicking butt. We've got a new concept called the "Bean Machine," which is an online form to order our coffees. Can you make it happen?

Starbuzz Coffee Coffee Starbuzz Coffee

Here's what the form should look like.

A drop-down menu of coffees

Choose your beans: House Blend
Type: Shade Grown Bolivia Supremo
  Whole bean   Organic Guatemala
  Ground   Kenya

A choice of whole or ground coffee (you can only choose one)

Number of bags:

Must arrive by date:

How many bags, and when they should arrive by

Extras:
  ☐ Gift wrap
  ☑ Include catalog with order

Gift wrap or include a catalog (choose zero, one, or both)

Ship to:
Name:
Address:
City:
State:
Zip:
Phone:

Ship to address, consisting of six text boxes

Customer Comments:

A box for customer comments

Order Now

And a submit button

Markup Magnets

Your job is to take the form element magnets and lay them on top of the corresponding controls in the sketch. You won't need all the magnets below to complete the job; some will be left over. Check your answer in the back of the chapter before moving on.

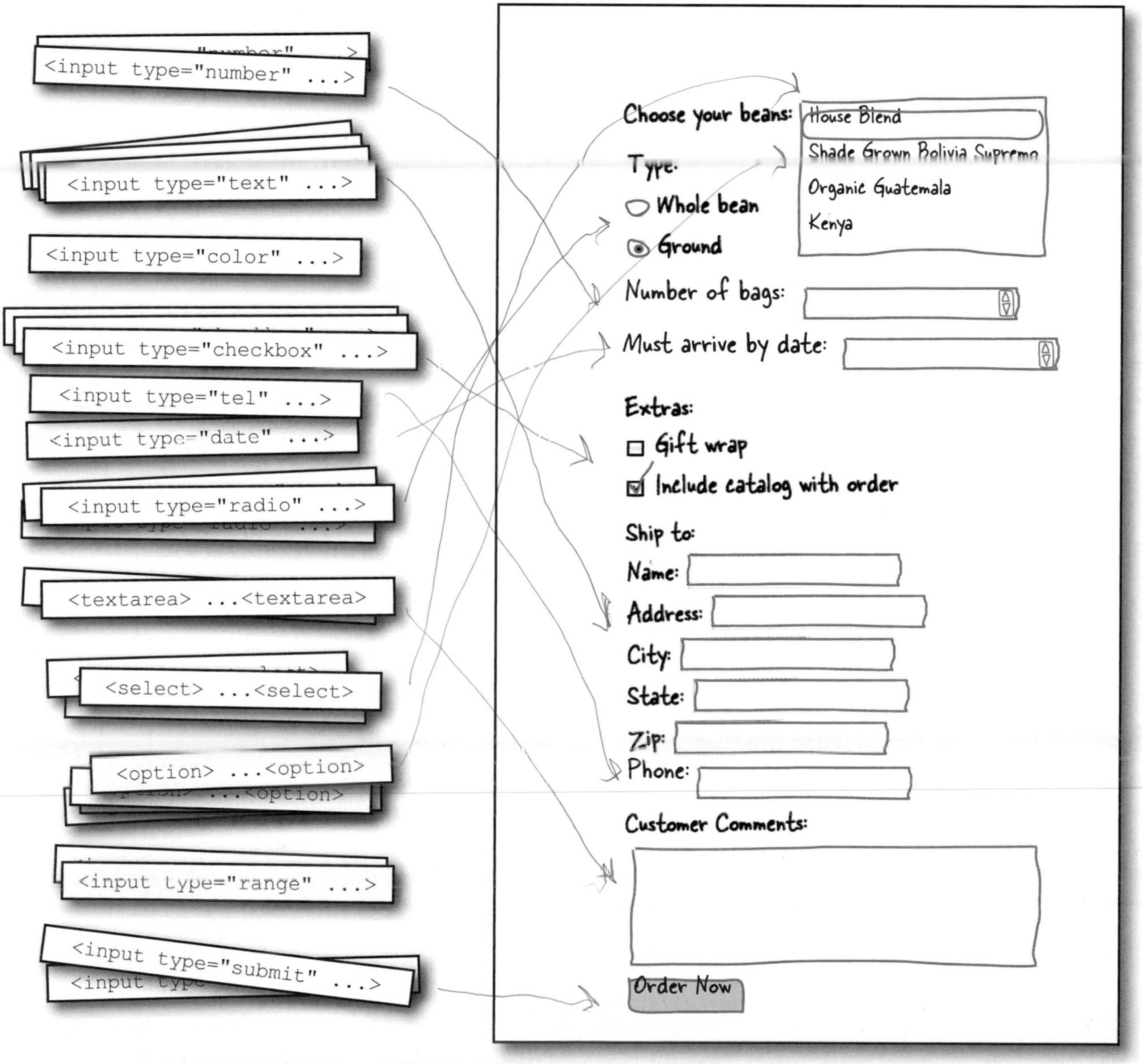

`<input type="number" ...>`

`<input type="text" ...>`

`<input type="color" ...>`

`<input type="checkbox" ...>`

`<input type="tel" ...>`

`<input type="date" ...>`

`<input type="radio" ...>`

`<textarea> ...<textarea>`

`<select> ...<select>`

`<option> ...<option>`

`<input type="range" ...>`

`<input type="submit" ...>`

Choose your beans:
House Blend
Shade Grown Bolivia Supremo
Organic Guatemala
Kenya

Type:
◯ Whole bean
◉ Ground

Number of bags:

Must arrive by date:

Extras:
☐ Gift wrap
☑ Include catalog with order

Ship to:
Name:
Address:
City:
State:
Zip:
Phone:

Customer Comments:

Order Now

Getting ready to build the Bean Machine form

Before we start building that form, take a look inside the "chapter14/starbuzz" folder, and you'll find the file "form.html". Open it and have a look around. All this file has in it are the HTML basics:

```
<!DOCTYPE html>
<html>
    <head>
        <meta charset="utf-8">
        <title>The Starbuzz Bean Machine</title>
    </head>
    <body>

        <h1>The Starbuzz Bean Machine</h1>
        <h2>Fill out the form below and click "order now" to order</h2>



    </body>
</html>
```

The form is going to go here.

All we've got so far is a heading identifying the page, along with instructions.

For now, we're going to build these forms without all the style we've been using on the Starbuzz site. That way, we can concentrate on the form HTML. We'll add the style in later.

Figuring out what goes in the form element

It's time to add your very first `<form>` element. The first thing you have to know when creating a `<form>` element is the URL of the server script that is going to process your form data. We've already taken care of that for you; you'll find the server script that processes Starbuzz orders here:

http://starbuzzcoffee.com/processorder.php

This URL points to the Starbuzz Coffee website...

...and to the processorder.php server script that's on the server there. This server script already knows how to take orders from the form we're going to build.

Adding the <form> element

Once you know the URL of the server script that will process your form, all you need
to do is plug it into the `action` attribute of your `<form>` element, like this (follow
along and type the changes into your HTML):

```
<!DOCTYPE html>
<html>
    <head>
        <meta charset="utf-8">
        <title>The Starbuzz Bean Machine</title>
    </head>
    <body>
        <h1>The Starbuzz Bean Machine</h1>
        <h2>Fill out the form below and click "order now" to order</h2>
        <form action="http://starbuzzcoffee.com/processorder.php" method="POST">



        </form>
    </body>
</html>
```

Here's the
form element.

The action attribute contains the
URL of the server script.

And remember we're using
the POST method to deliver
the form data to the server.
More on this later.

Go ahead and add the
form closing tag too.

So far, so good, but an empty `<form>` element isn't going to get you very far. Looking back
at the sketch of the form, there's a lot there to add, but we're going to start simple and get
the "Ship to" part of the form done first, which consists of a bunch of text inputs and a
number input. You already know a little about text inputs, but let's take a closer look. Here's
what the text inputs for the Starbuzz form look like:

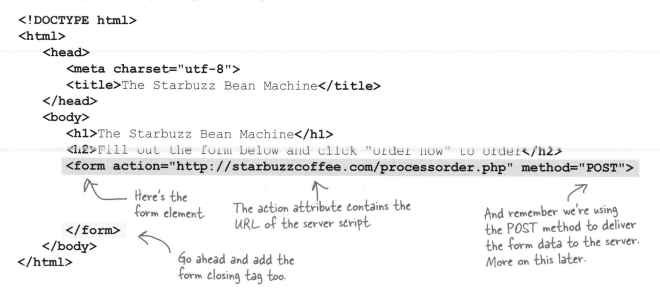

Here the type is "text" because this
is going to be a text input control.

We use the <input>
element for a few
different controls.
The type attribute
determines what kind
of control it is.

```
<input type="text" name="name">
<input type="text" name="address">
<input type="text" name="city">
<input type="text" name="state">
<input type="text" name="zip">
<input type="tel" name="phone">
```

We've got one text
input for each input
area in the form:
Name, Address, City,
State, Zip, and Phone.

Here the type is "tel" because we're expecting
a telephone number for the value.

The name attribute acts as an identifier for the
data the user types in. Notice how each one is set to
a different value. Let's see how this works...

How form element names work

Here's the thing to know about the name attribute: it acts as the glue between your form and the server script that processes it. Here's how this works:

Each input control in your form has a name attribute:

When you type the elements for a form into your HTML file, you give them unique names. You saw this with the text and tel inputs:

```
<input type="text" name="name">
<input type="text" name="address">
<input type="text" name="city">
<input type="text" name="state">
<input type="text" name="zip">
<input type="tel" name="phone">
```

Notice here we've got an element whose name is "name" (which is perfectly fine).

Each <input> element gets its own name.

When you submit a form, the browser packages up all the data using the unique names:

Say you type your name, address, city, state, zip, and phone into the form and click Submit. The browser takes each of these pieces of data and labels them with your unique name attribute values. The browser then sends the names and values to the server. Like this:

What you enter into the form.

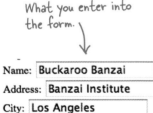

Name: Buckaroo Banzai
Address: Banzai Institute
City: Los Angeles
State: CA
Zip: 90050
Phone: 310-555-1212

The unique names for each form element

```
name = Buckaroo Banzai
address = Banzai Institute
city = Los Angeles
state = CA
zip = 90050
phone = 310-555-1212
```

Each unique name gets a value from the data you type into the form.

processorder.php

www.starbuzzcoffee.com

What the browser packages up for the server

The server script needs the form data to be labeled so it can tell what is what.

there are no
Dumb Questions

Q: What's the difference between a text <input> and a <textarea>?

A: You want to use a text <input> for entering text that is just a single line, like a name or zip code, and a <textarea> for longer, multiline text.

Q: Can I make the submit button say something other than "Submit"?

A: Yes, just put a value attribute in the element and give it a value like "Order Now". You can also use the value attribute of text input to give that input some default text.

Q: Is there a limit to how much text I can type into a text <input> or a <textarea>?

A: Browsers do place a limit on the amount of text you can type into either a text <input> or a <textarea>; however, it's usually way more than you'd ever need to type. If you'd like to limit how much your users can type into a text <input>, you can use the maxlength attribute and set it to a specific number of characters. For example, maxlength="100" would limit users to typing at most 100 characters. However, for a <textarea>, there is no way with HTML to limit how much your users can type.

Q: The "tel", "email", and "url" look just like text inputs. Is there really a difference?

A: The "tel", "email", and "url" type inputs all send text strings to the server script, so in that way, they are basically the same as a text type input. However, because the browser knows that the type is "tel", for instance, it can be a bit smarter about the user interface it provides to the user. So, on some mobile browsers, the browser may display a numeric phone keypad.

Q: I still don't get how the names get matched up with the form data.

A: Okay, you know each form element has a unique name, and you also know that the element has a corresponding value. When you click the Submit button, the browser takes all the names along with their values and sends them to the server. For instance, when you type the zip code "90050" into a text <input> element with the name "zip", the browser sends "zip = 90050" to the server when the form is submitted.

Q: How does the server script know the names I'm going to use in my form? In other words, how do I pick the names for my form elements?

A: Good question. It really works the other way around: you have to know what form names your server script is expecting and write your form to match it. If you're using a server script that someone else wrote, he'll have to tell you what names to use, or provide that information in the documentation for the script. A good place to start is to ask your hosting company for help.

Q: Why doesn't the <option> element have a name attribute? Every other form element does.

A: Good catch. All <option> elements are actually part of the menu that is created by the <select> element. So, we only really need one name for the entire menu, and that is already specified in the <select> element. In other words, <option> elements don't need a name attribute because the <select> has already specified the name for the entire menu. Keep in mind that when the form is submitted, only the value of the currently selected option is sent along with this name to the server.

Q: Didn't you say that the name for each form element needs to be unique? But the radio <input> elements all have the same name.

A: Right. Radio buttons come as a set. Think about it: if you push one button in, the rest pop out. So, for the browser to know the radio buttons belong together, you use the same name. Say you have a set of radio buttons named "color" with values of "red", "green", and "blue". They're all colors, and only one color can be selected at a time, so a single name for the set makes sense.

Q: What about checkboxes? Do they work like radio buttons?

A: Yes; the only difference is that you are allowed to select more than one choice with a checkbox.

When the browser sends the form data to the server, it combines all the checkbox values into one value and sends them along with the checkbox name. So, say you had "spice" checkboxes for "salt", "pepper", and "garlic", and you checked them all; then the browser would send "spice = salt&pepper&garlic" to the server.

Q: Geez, do I really need to know all this stuff about how data gets to the server?

A: All you need to know is the names and types of the form elements your server script is expecting. Beyond that, knowing how it all works sometimes helps, but, no, you don't need to know all the gory behind-the-scenes details of what is being sent to the server.

Back to getting those <input> elements into your HTML

Now we've got to get those <input> elements inside the form. Check out the additions below, and then make the changes in your "form.html" file.

We're going to start by putting everything inside a <p> element.

Nest elements directly inside a form.

Here's JUST the form snippet from "form.html". Hey, we've got to save a few trees here!

```
<form action="http://starbuzzcoffee.com/processorder.php" method="POST">
    <p>Ship to: <br>
        Name: <input type="text" name="name"> <br>
        Address: <input type="text" name="address"> <br>
        City: <input type="text" name="city"> <br>
        State: <input type="text" name="state"> <br>
        Zip: <input type="text" name="zip"> <br>
        Phone: <input type="tel" name="phone"> <br>
    </p>
    <p>
        <input type="submit" value="Order Now">
    </p>
</form>
```

Here are all the <input> elements: one for each input in the "Ship to" section of the form.

We've added a label for each input so the user knows what goes in the text input.

*And you should also know that <input> is an inline element, so if you want some linebreaks between the <input> elements, you have to add
s. That's also why you need to nest them all inside a paragraph.*

Finally, don't forget that users need a submit button to submit the form. So add a submit button by inserting an <input> at the bottom with a type of "submit". Also add a value of "Order Now", which will change the text of the button from "Submit" to "Order Now".

After you've made all these changes, save your "form.html" file and let's give this a whirl.

Don't forget to validate your HTML. Form elements need validation too!

A form-al test drive 🚗

Reload the page, fill in the text inputs, and submit the form. When you do that, the browser will package up the data and send it to the URL in the `action` attribute, which is at `starbuzzcoffee.com`.

You don't think we'd give you a toy example that doesn't really work, do you? Seriously, starbuzzcoffee.com is all ready to take your form submission. Go for it!

Notice the change in the URL of your address bar after you submit the form (you'll see the URL in the form's action attribute in the address bar).

Here's the form.

```
● ○ ○              The Starbuzz Bean Machine
◄ ► + ⊕ file:///chapter14/starbuzz/form.html    ⊘ Q▾ Google    ⊘ ⊕
```

The Starbuzz Bean Machine

Fill out the form below and click "order now" to order

Ship to:
Name: `Buckaroo Banzai`
Address: `Banzai Institute`
City: `Los Angeles`
State: `CA`
Zip: `90050`
Phone: `310-555-1212`

`Order Now`

And here's the response after submitting the form.

```
● ○ ○              The Starbuzz Bean Machine
◄ ► + ⊕ http://starbuzzcoffee.com/processorder.php    ⊘ Q▾ Google    ⊘ ⊕
```

The Starbuzz Bean Machine

Thanks, **Buckaroo Banzai**, for your order... But we didn't get your choice of beans or whether they are whole or ground. You might want to click the back button to go back and try again, otherwise, we won't be able to make your Bean Machine order, and that would suck.

Here's what we received from you so far:

Number of bags: 1
Name: Buckaroo Banzai
Address: Banzai Institute
City: Los Angeles
State: CA
Zip: 90050
Phone: 310-555-1212

Here's the server script's response. It looks like the script got what we submitted, but we haven't given it everything it needs.

Adding some more input elements to your form

It looks like the server script isn't going to let us get very far without telling it the beans we want, as well as the bean type (ground or whole). Let's add the bean selection first by adding a `<select>` element to the form. Remember that the `<select>` element contains a list of options, each of which becomes a choice in a drop-down menu. Also, associated with each choice is a value; when the form is submitted, the value of the chosen menu option is sent to the server. Turn the page and let's add the `<select>` element.

Adding the <select> element

```
<form action="http://starbuzzcoffee.com/processorder.php" method="post">
```

```
<p>
  Choose your beans:
  <select name="beans">
    <option value="House Blend">House Blend</option>
    <option value="Bolivia">Shade Grown Bolivia Supremo</option>
    <option value="Guatemala">Organic Guatemala</option>
    <option value="Kenya">Kenya</option>
  </select>
</p>
```

Here's our brand-new <select> element. It gets a unique name too.

Inside, we put each <option> element, one per choice of coffee.

```
  <p>
    Ship to: <br>
    Name: <input type="text" name="name" value=""><br>
    Address: <input type="text" name="address" value=""><br>
    City: <input type="text" name="city" value=""><br>
    State: <input type="text" name="state" value=""><br>
    Zip: <input type="text" name="zip" value=""><br>
    Phone: <input type="tel" name="phone" value=""><br>
  </p>
  <p>
    <input type="submit" value="Order Now">
  </p>
</form>
```

HTML Up Close

Let's take a closer look at the <option> element.

Each option has a value.

The content of the element is used as the label in the drop-down menu.

```
<option value="Guatemala">Organic Guatemala</option>
```

When the browser packages up the names and values of the form elements, it uses the name of the <select> element along with the value of the chosen option.

In this case, the browser would send the server beans = "Guatemala".

Test driving the <select> element 🚗

Let's give the <select> element a spin now. Reload your page, and
you should have a nice new menu waiting for you. Choose your
favorite coffee, fill in the rest of the form, and submit your order.

```
⊙ ○ ○                  The Starbuzz Bean Machine
◀ ▶  +  file:///chapter14/starbuzz/form.html     Q▾ Google

The Starbuzz Bean Machine

Fill out the for┌─────────────────────────────┐ der now" to order
               │  House Blend                │
               │  Shade Grown Bolivia Supremo│
Choose your beans:│✓ Organic Guatemala       │
               │  Kenya                      │
Ship to:       └─────────────────────────────┘
Name:  Buckaroo Banzai
Address:  Banzai Institute
City:  Los Angeles
State:  CA
Zip:  90050
Phone:  310-555-1212

Order Now
```

*Here's the form, complete with
a <select> element. Notice all
the options are there.*

```
⊙ ○ ○                  The Starbuzz Bean Machine
◀ ▶  +  http://starbuzzcoffee.com/processorder.php    Q▾ Google

The Starbuzz Bean Machine

Thanks, **Buckaroo Banzai**, for your order... But we didn't get your choice of
whole or ground beans. You might want to click the back button to go back and
try again, otherwise, we won't be able to make your Bean Machine order, and
that would suck.

Here's what we received from you so far:

**Beans:** Guatemala
**Number of bags:** 1
**Name:** Buckaroo Banzai
**Address:** Banzai Institute
**City:** Los Angeles
**State:** CA
**Zip:** 90050
**Phone:** 310-555-1212
```

*We still haven't given the server
script everything it needs, but
the script is getting everything
in the form so far.*

*Here's the result of
the <select> choice.*

*Here are all the
text inputs and
the tel input.*

*Looks like Starbuzz
assumes we want 1 bag of
coffee if we don't specify.*

Change the <select> element name attribute to "thembeans". Reload the form and resubmit your order. How does this affect the results you get back from the server script?

Make sure you change the name back to "beans" when you're done with this exercise.

Give the customer a choice of whole or ground beans

The customer needs to be able to choose whole or ground beans for her order. For those, we're going to use radio buttons. Radio buttons are like the buttons on old car radios—you can push only one in at a time. The way they work in HTML is that you create one <input> of type "radio" for each button, so in this case you need two buttons: one for whole beans and one for ground. Here's what that looks like:

There are two radio buttons here: one for whole beans, and one for ground.

```
<p>Type: <br>

   <input type="radio" name="beantype" value="whole"> Whole bean <br>
   <input type="radio" name="beantype" value="ground"> Ground

</p>
```

We're using the <input> element for this, with its type set to "radio".

Here's the unique name. All radio buttons in the same group share the same name.

And here's the value that will be sent to the server script. Only one of these will be sent (the one that is selected when the form is submitted).

Notice that we often label radio buttons on the righthand side of the element.

Punching the radio buttons

Take the radio button HTML on the previous page and insert it into your HTML just below the paragraph containing the `<select>` element. Make sure you reload the page, and then submit it again.

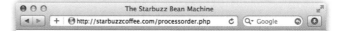

Depending on your browser, you may have noticed that no radio button was pressed when you reloaded the page.

Wow! Starbuzz took our order, and we're not even done with it yet. We've still got to add the number of bags, the ship by date, the gift options, and an area for customer comments.

How could the order work without all the elements being in the form? Well, it all depends on how the server script is programmed. In this case, it is programmed to process the order even if the gift wrap, catalog options, and the customer comments are not submitted with the rest of the form data. The only way you can know if a server script requires certain form elements is to talk to the person who developed it, or to read the documentation.

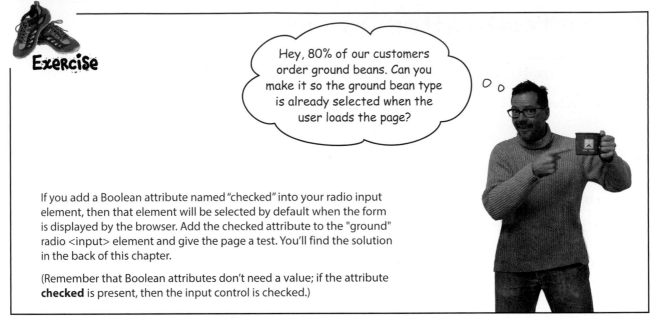

Exercise

Hey, 80% of our customers order ground beans. Can you make it so the ground bean type is already selected when the user loads the page?

If you add a Boolean attribute named "checked" into your radio input element, then that element will be selected by default when the form is displayed by the browser. Add the checked attribute to the "ground" radio <input> element and give the page a test. You'll find the solution in the back of this chapter.

(Remember that Boolean attributes don't need a value; if the attribute **checked** is present, then the input control is checked.)

Using more input types

Next, we need to get the number of bags of coffee the customer wants to purchase, and the arrive by date. Both of these are <input> elements, but rather than just using basic text inputs, we can be more specific about the exact type of content we want in these <input> elements by using the "number" type for the number of bags, and the "date" type for the arrive by date.

For the number of bags, we can get even more specific, by specifying both a minimum and maximum number of bags allowed:

By using the "number" type and specifying the min and max number of bags, we can restrict the input to a value that works for us (we don't want customers ordering more than 10 bags of one kind of coffee at a time!)

```
Number of bags: <input type="number" name="bags" min="1" max="10">
```

And by using the "date" type here, browsers that support this type will help out the customer by popping up a date picker control.

```
Must arrive by date: <input type="date" name="date">
```

You'll get an error message if you try to enter more (or less) than the allowed max or min.

Now, if you try to enter more than 10 bags or fewer than 1 bag, in browsers that support the "number" <input> type, you'll get an error message when you try to submit the form indicating that the value you've entered is not correct.

Number of bags: 24

⚠ Value must be less than or equal to 10.

Adding the number and date input types

Go ahead and add the two new `<input>` elements to your "form.html" file, below the bean type `<input>`s and above the Ship To fields, and give your new code a test drive.

```
<form action="http://starbuzzcoffee.com/processorder.php" method="post">
    <p>
        Choose your beans:
        <select name="beans">
            <option value="House Blend">House Blend</option>
            <option value="Bolivia">Shade Grown Bolivia Supremo</option>
            <option value="Guatemala">Organic Guatemala</option>
            <option value="Kenya">Kenya</option>
        </select>
    </p>
    <p>
        Type:<br>
            <input type="radio" name="beantype" value="whole">Whole bean<br>
            <input type="radio" name="beantype" value="ground" checked>Ground
    </p>

    <p>
        Number of bags: <input type="number" name="bags" min="1" max="10">
    </p>
    <p>
        Must arrive by date: <input type="date" name="date">
    </p>

    <p>
        Ship to: <br>
        Name: <input type="text" name="name" value=""><br>
        Address: <input type="text" name="address" value=""><br>
        City: <input type="text" name="city" value=""><br>
        State: <input type="text" name="state" value=""><br>
        Zip: <input type="text" name="zip" value=""><br>
        Phone: <input type="tel" name="phone" value=""><br>
    </p>
    <p>
        <input type="submit" value="Order Now">
    </p>
</form>
```

We've added the new code here. Remember that browsers may display these differently, depending on which browser you're using. Try more than one browser!

Turn the page to see the results of our test drive…

Test driving the number and date <input> elements

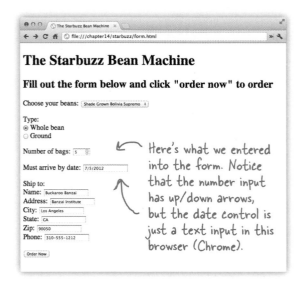

Here's what we entered into the form. Notice that the number input has up/down arrows, but the date control is just a text input in this browser (Chrome).

And here's what the Bean Machine returns. Looks like we ordered 5 bags of coffee!

Completing the form

You're almost there. You've got just two controls to add to the form: the "Extras" control with two checkboxes and the customer comment control. You're really getting the hang of forms, so we're going to add them both at the same time.

The Extras section consists of two checkboxes, one for gift wrap and another to include a catalog.

It looks like the "Include catalog" option should be checked by default.

The Customer Comments section is just a <textarea>.

Adding the checkboxes and text area

You know the drill: look over the new HTML and add it to your "form.html".

```html
<form action="http://starbuzzcoffee.com/processorder.php" method="post">
    <p>
        Choose your beans:
        <select name="beans">
            <option value="House Blend">House Blend</option>
            <option value="Bolivia">Shade Grown Bolivia Supremo</option>
            <option value="Guatemala">Organic Guatemala</option>
            <option value="Kenya">Kenya</option>
        </select>
    </p>
    <p>
        Type:<br>
            <input type="radio" name="beantype" value="whole">Whole bean<br>
            <input type="radio" name="beantype" value="ground" checked>Ground
    </p>
    <p>Number of bags: <input type="number" name="bags" min="1" max="10"></p>
    <p>Must arrive by date: <input type="date" name="date"></p>
```

Here we've added a checkbox for each option. Notice that these share the same name, "extras[]"... ...but have different values.

```html
    <p>
        Extras:<br>
        <input type="checkbox" name="extras[]" value="giftwrap">Gift wrap<br>
        <input type="checkbox" name="extras[]" value="catalog" checked>Include catalog
            with order
    </p>
```

We're using the checked attribute to specify that the catalog option should be checked by default. You can add a checked attribute to more than one checkbox.

As with the radio buttons, we've put these labels to the right of the checkboxes.

```html
    <p>
        Ship to: <br>
        Name: <input type="text" name="name" value=""><br>
        Address: <input type="text" name="address" value=""><br>
        City: <input type="text" name="city" value=""><br>
        State: <input type="text" name="state" value=""><br>
        Zip: <input type="text" name="zip" value=""><br>
        Phone: <input type="tel" name="phone" value=""><br>
    </p>

    <p>Customer Comments:<br>
        <textarea name="comments"></textarea>
    </p>
```

Here's the text area.

```html
    <p>
        <input type="submit" value="Order Now">
    </p>
</form>
```

The final form test drive 🚗

Save your changes, reload, and check out the new form.
Don't you think it's looking quite nice?

Here's what you get when you submit.
The server script has received all
the form data on the page and has
incorporated it into the response
page. See if you can locate all the
form data you submitted.

Here's our brand-new
checkboxes, with the catalog
checkbox already checked.

And a nice new
text area as well

Be sure and try out all the
various combinations of sending
this form (with/without gift
wrap, with/without a catalog,
different coffees, and so on)
and see how it all works.

Stop right there. Do you think I didn't see the way you slipped in that element name of "extras[]"? What's with those square brackets! You have to explain that.

Believe it or not, "extras[]" is a perfectly valid name for a form element.

But even if it's *valid*, it doesn't exactly look *normal*, does it? Here's the deal: from the perspective of HTML, this is a normal form element name; it doesn't have any effect on the browser at all if it has square brackets in the name.

So why did we use them? It turns out that the scripting language that the "processorder.php" server script is written in (PHP) likes a little hint that a form variable may have multiple values in it. The way you give it this hint is to add "[ ]" on the end of the name.

So, from the perspective of learning HTML, you can pretty much forget about all this, but you might just tuck this into the back of your mind in case you ever write a form that uses a PHP server script in the future.

BE the Browser

Below, you'll find an HTML form, and on the right the data a user entered into the form. Your job is to play like you're the browser and match each form element name with the values the user entered. After you've done the exercise, look at the end of the chapter to see if you matched up the form names with the values correctly.

```
<form action="http://www.chooseyourmini.com/choice.php" method="POST">
    <p>Your information: <br>

        Name: <input type="text" name="name"><br>
        Zip: <input type="text" name="zip"><br>

    </p>
    <p>Which model do you want? <br>
        <select name="model">
            <option value="cooper">Mini Cooper</option>
            <option value="cooperS">Mini Cooper S</option>
            <option value="convertible">Mini Cooper Convertible</option>
        </select>
    </p>
    <p>Which color do you want? <br>
        <input type="radio" name="color" value="chilired"> Chili Red   <br>
        <input type="radio" name="color" value="hyperblue"> Hyper Blue
    </p>
    <p>Which options do you want? <br>
        <input type="checkbox" name="caroptions[]" value="stripes"> Racing Stripes
        <br>
        <input type="checkbox" name="caroptions[]" value="sportseats"> Sport Seats
    </p>

    <p>
        <input type="submit" value="Order Now">
    </p>

</form>
```

Here's the form.

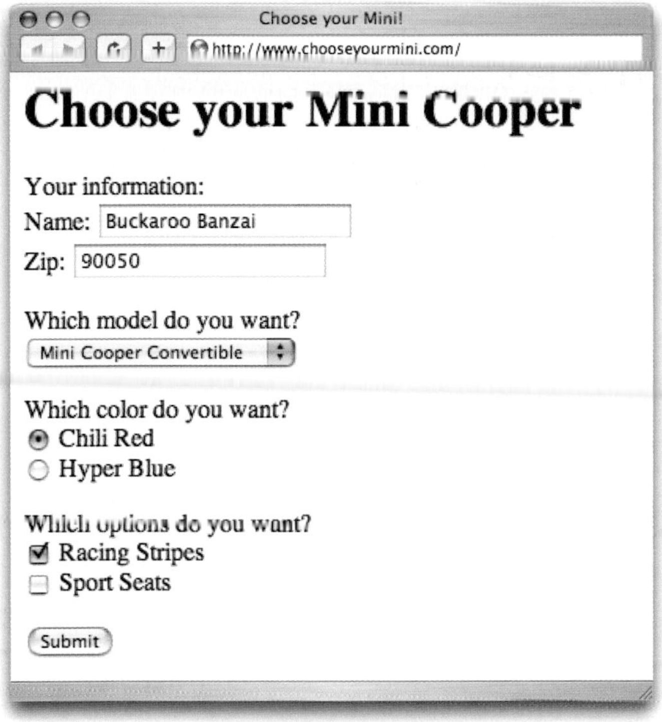

Choose your Mini Cooper

Your information:

Name: Buckaroo Banzai

Zip: 90050

Which model do you want?

Mini Cooper Convertible

Which color do you want?
- ⦿ Chili Red
- ○ Hyper Blue

Which options do you want?
- ☑ Racing Stripes
- ☐ Sport Seats

[Submit]

And here's the form filled out.

Match each piece of form data with its form name and put your answers here.

```
name = "Buckaroo Banzai"

zip = 90050

model = convertible

color = chilired

caroptions[] = stripes
```

Extra credit...

Now that we've got the form finished, can we talk about the method the browser uses to send this data to the server? We've been using POST, but you said there are other methods, too.

There are two primary methods the browser uses: POST and GET.

POST and **GET** accomplish the same thing—getting your form data from the browser to a server—but in two different ways. **POST** packages up your form variables and sends them behind the scenes to your server, while **GET** also packages up your form variables, but appends them on the end of the URL before it sends a request to the server.

With POST, all the form data is sent as part of the request and is invisible to the user.

POST

`http://wickedlysmart.com/hfhtmlcss/contest.php`

The user just sees the server script's URL in her browser address bar.

With GET, the form data is added to the URL itself, so the user sees the form data.

GET

Notice the form data added on to the end of the URL. This is what the user sees in the address bar.

`http://wickedlysmart.com/hfhtmlcss/contest.php?firstname=buckaroo&lastname=banzai`

Watching GET in action

There's no better way to understand GET than to see it in action.
Open up your "form.html" file and make the following small change:

Just change the method from "POST" to "GET".

```
<form action="http://starbuzzcoffee.com/processorder.php" method="GET">
```

Save and reload the page; then fill out the form and submit it. You
should see something like this:

You'll see this URL in your browser.

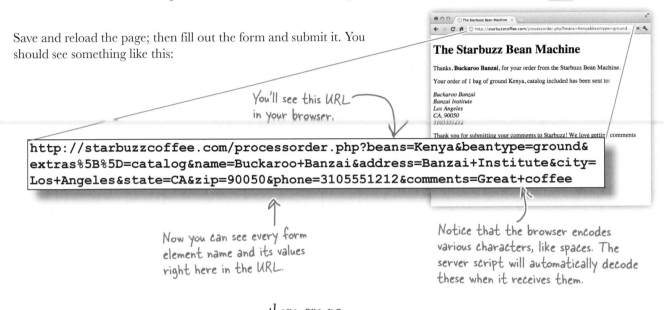

The Starbuzz Bean Machine

Thanks, **Buckaroo Banzai**, for your order from the Starbuzz Bean Machine.

Your order of 1 bag of ground Kenya, catalog included has been sent to:

Buckaroo Banzai
Banzai Institute
Los Angeles
CA, 90050
3105551212

Thank you for submitting your comments to Starbuzz! We love gettin comments

```
http://starbuzzcoffee.com/processorder.php?beans=Kenya&beantype=ground&
extras%5B%5D=catalog&name=Buckaroo+Banzai&address=Banzai+Institute&city=
Los+Angeles&state=CA&zip=90050&phone=3105551212&comments=Great+coffee
```

Now you can see every form element name and its values right here in the URL.

Notice that the browser encodes various characters, like spaces. The server script will automatically decode these when it receives them.

there are no Dumb Questions

Q: Why is it called GET if we're sending something to the server?

A: Good question. What's the main job of a browser? To get web pages from a server. And when you are using GET, the browser is just going about getting a web page in the normal way it always does, except that, in the case of a form, it has appended some more data to the end of the URL. Other than that, the browser just acts like it's a normal request.

With POST, on the other hand, the browser actually creates a little data package and sends it to the server.

Q: So why would I use POST over GET, or vice versa?

A: There are a couple of big differences that really matter. If you want users to be able to bookmark pages that are the result of submitting a form, then you have to use GET, because there is no way to bookmark a page that has been returned as a result of a POST. When would you want to do that? Say you have a server script that returns a list of search results; you might want users to be able to bookmark those results so they can see them again without having to fill out a form.

On the other hand, if you have a server script that processes orders, then you

wouldn't want users to be able to bookmark the page. (Otherwise, every time they returned to the bookmark, the order would be resubmitted.)

A situation when you'd *never* want to use a GET is when the data in your form is private, like a credit card or a password. Because the URL is in plain view, the private information is easily found by others if they look through your browser history or if the GET somehow gets bookmarked.

Finally, if you use a <textarea>, you should use POST, because you're probably sending a lot of data. Both GET and POST requests have a limit on the amount of data you can send, but the limit on a POST request is usually much larger.

Sharpen your pencil

GET or POST

For each description, circle either GET or POST depending on which method would be more appropriate. If you think it could be either, circle both. But be prepared to defend your answers...

GET ~~POST~~   *A form for typing in a username and password.*

GET ~~POST~~   *A form for ordering CDs.*

~~GET~~ POST   *A form for looking up current events.*

GET POST   *A form to post book reviews.*

GET ~~POST~~   *A form for retrieving benefits by your government ID number.*

GET ~~POST~~   *A form to send customer feedback.*

I've been meaning to say, great job on the Bean Machine! This is really going to boost our coffee bean sales. All you need to do is give this a little style, and we're ready to launch 11 for our customers.

The Starbuzz Bean Machine

Fill out the form below and click "order now" to order

Choose your beans: [Shade Grown Bolivia Supremo ⬍]

Type:
⦿ Whole bean
◯ Ground

Number of bags: [3 ⬍]

Must arrive by date: [8/1/2012]

Extras:
☑ Gift wrap
☑ Include catalog with order

Ship to:
Name: [Buckaroo Banzai]
Address: [Banzai Institute]
City: [Los Angeles]
State: [CA]
Zip: [90050]
Phone: [310-555-1212]

Customer Comments:
[Send me samples if you have any available.]

[Order Now]

⚛ BRAIN POWER

Given everything you know about HTML and CSS, how would you approach styling this form?

Sharpen your pencil

Forms are usually tabular in their layout, so you'll probably find that using a CSS table display layout works well for designing your form's presentation…and that's what we'll use to lay out the Bean Machine form. With this table display layout, the page will look like a real form rather than a ragged collection of input elements, and it will be easier to read.

Before we do that, let's figure out the table structure that is inherent in this form. Starting with the sketch below, fit the elements into a table (hint: we found it fits nicely into 2 columns and 14 rows), so each row is represented with a block element, and each cell is also represented with a block element. Notice you may have to add some structure to the HTML to make this work.

No peeking at the next page before you do the exercise. Really! Cover it up or something.

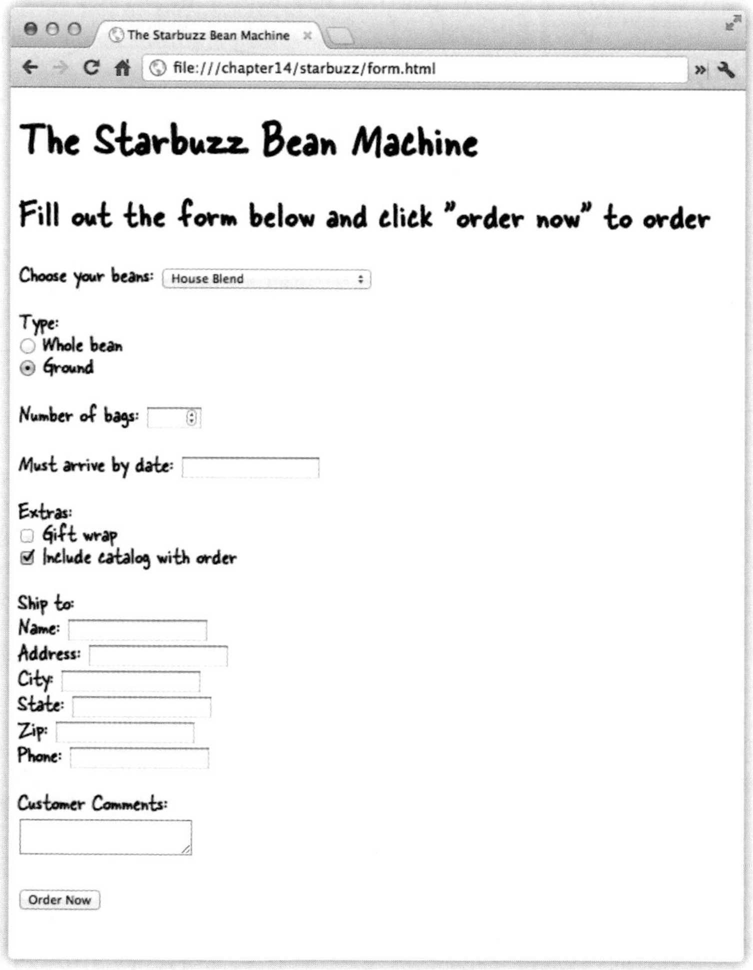

Sharpen your pencil
Solution

Forms are usually tabular in their layout, so you'll probably find that using a CSS table display layout works well for designing your form's presentation...and that's what we'll use to lay out the Bean Machine form. With this table display layout, the page will look like a real form rather than a ragged collection of input elements, and it will be easier to read.

Before we do that, let's figure out the table structure that is inherent in this form. Starting with the sketch below, fit the elements into a table (hint: we found it fits nicely into 2 columns and 14 rows), so each row is represented with a block element, and each cell is also represented with a block element. Notice you may have to add some structure to the HTML to make this work.

Here's what we came up with...compare to your solution before moving on!

Here's the sketch of the table. It's a simple table display layout, with 2 columns and 14 rows—1 row for each main part of the form.

The labels for each form element go in the left column.

The cell values are all aligned vertically to the top.

The cell on the right of "Ship to" is empty; there's no control here.

The cell on the left of the submit button is empty. There's no label to put here.

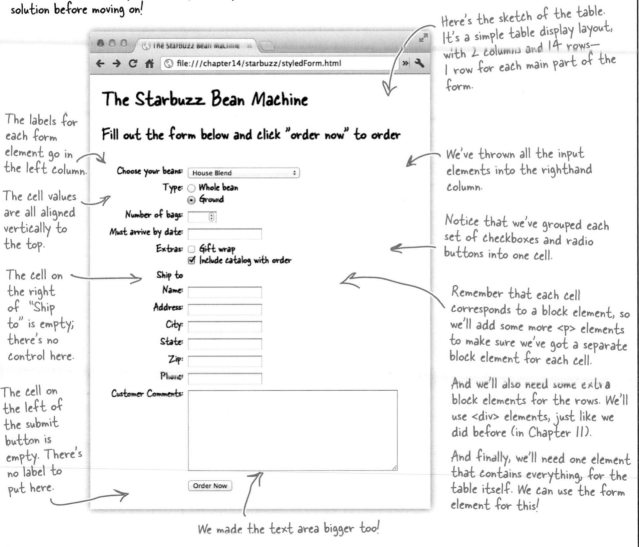

We've thrown all the input elements into the righthand column.

Notice that we've grouped each set of checkboxes and radio buttons into one cell.

Remember that each cell corresponds to a block element, so we'll add some more <p> elements to make sure we've got a separate block element for each cell.

And we'll also need some extra block elements for the rows. We'll use <div> elements, just like we did before (in Chapter 11).

And finally, we'll need one element that contains everything, for the table itself. We can use the form element for this!

We made the text area bigger too!

Getting the form elements into HTML structure for table display layout

Ready Bake HTML

Now that you know how to organize the form elements in a table display layout, you need to put your HTML writing skills to the test. So get typing!

Just kidding. We wouldn't make you type all this…after all, this chapter is really about forms, not table display layout. We already typed this in for you; it's in the file "styledform.html" in the "chapter14/starbuzz" folder. Even though it looks complicated, it's really not that bad. We've added a few annotations below to point out the main parts.

Here's the <form> element; we're going to use this element for the "table" part of the display.

```html
<form action="http://starbuzzcoffee.com/processorder.php" method="post">
    <div class="tableRow">
        <p>
            Choose your beans:
        </p>
        <p>
            <select name="beans">
                <option value="House Blend">House Blend</option>
                <option value="Bolivia">Shade Grown Bolivia Supremo</option>
                <option value="Guatemala">Organic Guatemala</option>
                <option value="Kenya">Kenya</option>
            </select>
        </p>
    </div>
    <div class="tableRow">
        <p> Type: </p>
        <p>
            <input type="radio" name="beantype" value="whole"> Whole bean<br>
            <input type="radio" name="beantype" value="ground" checked> Ground
        </p>
    </div>
    <div class="tableRow">
        <p> Number of bags: </p>
        <p> <input type="number" name="bags" min="1" max="10"> </p>
    </div>
    <div class="tableRow label">
        <p> Must arrive by date: </p>
        <p> <input type="date" name="date"> </p>
    </div>
    <div class="tableRow">
        <p> Extras: </p>
        <p>
            <input type="checkbox" name="extras[]" value="giftwrap"> Gift wrap<br>
            <input type="checkbox" name="extras[]" value="catalog" checked>
            Include catalog with order
        </p>
    </div>
```

We're using a <div> with the class "tableRow" for each row in the table.

And the content for each cell is nested inside a <p> element.

For the bean selection menu, the "beantype" radio buttons, and the "extras" checkboxes, we put all the form elements for each menu in one data cell.

Code continues on the next page.

For the row containing just the label "Ship to", we've added a class "heading" to the <p> so we can bold this text.

```
<div class="tableRow">
    <p class="heading"> Ship to </p>
    <p></p>
</div>
```

Notice that we've also got an empty cell in the right column, so we can just put an empty <p> element here.

```
<div class="tableRow">
    <p> Name: </p>
    <p> <input type="text" name="name" value=""> </p>
</div>
<div class="tableRow">
    <p> Address: </p>
    <p> <input type="text" name="address" value=""> </p>
</div>
<div class="tableRow">
    <p> City: </p>
    <p> <input type="text" name="city" value=""> </p>
</div>
<div class="tableRow">
    <p> State: </p>
    <p> <input type="text" name="state" value=""> </p>
</div>
<div class="tableRow">
    <p> Zip: </p>
    <p> <input type="text" name="zip" value=""> </p>
</div>
<div class="tableRow">
    <p> Phone: </p>
    <p> <input type="tel" name="phone" value=""> </p>
</div>
<div class="tableRow">
    <p> Customer Comments: </p>
    <p>
        <textarea name="comments" rows="10" cols="48"></textarea>
    </p>
</div>
<div class="tableRow">
    <p></p>
    <p> <input type="submit" value="Order Now"> </p>
</div>
</form>
```

All the rows are straightforward: a "tableRow" <div> for the row, and each cell in a <p>.

And for the last row, we've got an empty cell in the left column, so again, we can use an empty <p> element for that.

Styling the form with CSS

We've got all the structure we need, so now we just need to add a few styling rules and we'll be done. Because this form is part of the Starbuzz site, we're going to reuse some of the style in the "starbuzz.css" stylesheet, and create a new stylesheet, "styledform.css", to add new style rules for the Bean Machine form. All of this CSS should be familiar to you now. We're not using any rules unique to forms; it's all just the same stuff you've been using in the last few chapters.

You'll find this CSS in the file "styledform.css" in the folder "chapter14/starbuzz".

We're going to rely on the Starbuzz CSS for some of our style, but we're adding the Starbuzz background image, and a margin to the body.

```css
body {
    background: #efe5d0 url(images/background.gif) top left;
    margin: 20px;
}
```

```css
form {
    display: table;
    padding: 10px;
    border: thin dotted #7e7e7e;
    background-color: #e1ceb8;
}
```

We're using the form to represent the table in the table display...

...and adding a border around the form, and some padding between the form content and the border, and a background color to offset it from the background.

```css
form textarea {
    width: 500px;
    height: 200px;
}
```

We're making the textarea control in the form bigger, so there's more room for comments by setting its width and height.

```css
div.tableRow {
    display: table-row;
}
```

Each "tableRow" <div> acts as a row in the table display layout.

```css
div.tableRow p {
    display: table-cell;
    vertical-align: top;
    padding: 3px;
}
```

Each <p> element that is nested in a "tableRow" <div> is a table cell. We vertically align the content in each <p> so the content in each row lines up at the top of the cells. And we're adding a bit of padding here too, to add space between the rows.

```css
div.tableRow p:first-child {
    text-align: right;
}
```

This rule uses the first-child pseudo-element on the selector for <p> elements nested inside "tableRow" <div>s. This means the first <p> element in each row is aligned to the right, so they all line up vertically against the right side of the column.

```css
p.heading {
    font-weight: bold;
}
```

And for any <p> elements with the class "heading", we bold the text so it looks like a heading. We use this in the "Ship to" cell.

Test drive the styled form

You're going to add *two* `<link>` elements to the `<head>` of your HTML in "styledform.html", linking in the Starbuzz stylesheet from Chapter 12, "starbuzz.css", and your new stylesheet, "styledform.css". Make sure you get the order correct: link the "starbuzz.css" file first, then the "styledform.css". Once you've got the two stylesheets linked, save and reload your page. You should see the snazzy, styled version of the Starbuzz Bean Machine in your browser.

Wow, what a difference a little style makes!

If you want to stretch your HTML and CSS skills a bit, see if you can add the Starbuzz header and footer to the Bean Machine page and make the Bean Machine look really nice with those elements.

The Bean Machine form now matches the rest of the Starbuzz site better.

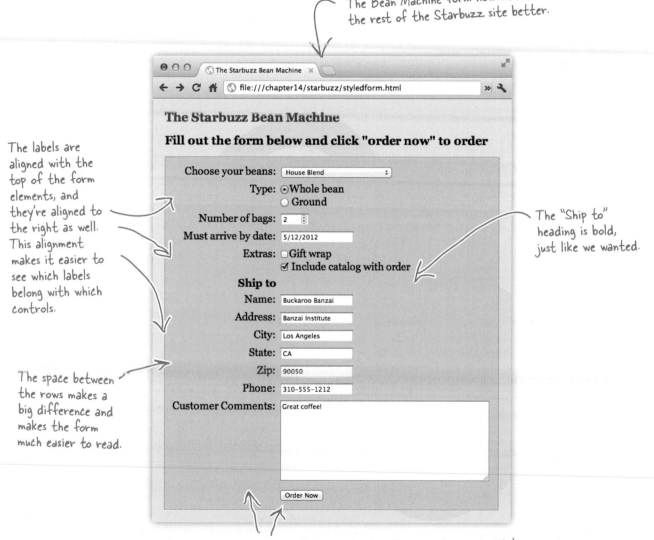

The labels are aligned with the top of the form elements, and they're aligned to the right as well. This alignment makes it easier to see which labels belong with which controls.

The space between the rows makes a big difference and makes the form much easier to read.

The "Ship to" heading is bold, just like we wanted.

We've got two columns and all the content in the rows lines up nicely!

A word about accessibility

So far we've been labeling our form elements with simple text, but we should really be using the `<label>` element to mark up these labels. The `<label>` element provides further information about the structure of your page, allows you to style your labels using CSS more easily, and helps screen readers for the visually impaired to correctly identify form elements.

We've created a complete version of the Bean Machine with labels, and updated the CSS to go with it. Check out accessform.html and accessform.css in the code downloads.

To use a <label> element, first add an id attribute to your form element.

```
<input type="radio" name="hotornot" value="hot" id="hot">
<label for="hot">hot</label>

<input type="radio" name="hotornot" value="not" id="not">
<label for="not">not</label>
```

Then add a <label> and set its "for" attribute to the corresponding id.

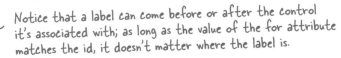

Now the text next to these radio buttons is a label.

By default, labels don't look any different from just normal text. However, they can make a big difference when it comes to accessibility. You can use the `<label>` element with any form control, so we can add a label to each part of our Bean Machine form. For instance, we could add a label to the number input for the number of bags like this:

```
<label for="bags">Number of bags:</label>
<input type="number" id="bags" name="bags" min="1" max="10">
```

We've added the id "bags" to the <input> element.

It's okay to have the name and id attributes use the same value, in this case, "bags".

When you add labels to radio or checkbox controls, remember that the id of each control needs to be unique, even though the name of all the controls in a group is the same. So, to add labels to the "beantype" radio control in the Bean Machine, create unique ids for both the whole and ground options:

The name of both controls is "beantype", so they are grouped together when you submit the form to the server script.

But each id needs to be unique.

```
<input type="radio" id="whole_beantype" name="beantype" value="whole">
    <label for="whole_beantype">Whole bean</label><br>
<input type="radio" id="ground_beantype" name="beantype" value="ground" checked>
    <label for="ground_beantype">Ground</label>
```

Notice that a label can come before or after the control it's associated with; as long as the value of the for attribute matches the id, it doesn't matter where the label is.

What more could possibly go into a form?

We've covered just about everything you'll regularly use in your forms, but there are a few more items you might want to consider adding to your form répertoire. We're including them here just in case you want to take your own form studies even further.

Fieldsets and legends

When your forms start getting large, it can be helpful to visually group elements together. While you might use `<div>`s and CSS to do this, HTML also provides a `<fieldset>` element that can be used to group together common elements. `<fieldset>` makes use of a second element, called `<legend>`. Here's how they work together:

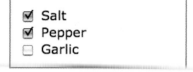

The `<fieldset>` element surrounds a set of input elements.

The `<legend>` provides a label for the group.

Here's how the fieldset and legend look in one browser. You'll find that browsers display them differently.

```
<fieldset>
    <legend>Condiments</legend>
        <input type="checkbox" name="spice" value="salt">
            Salt   <br>
        <input type="checkbox" name="spice" value="pepper">
            Pepper <br>
        <input type="checkbox" name="spice" value="garlic">
            Garlic
</fieldset>
```

Passwords

The password `<input>` element works just like the text `<input>` element, except that the text you type is masked. This is useful for forms that require you to type in a password, a secret code, or other sensitive information that you may not want other people to see as you type. Keep in mind, however, that the form data is *not* sent from the browser to the server script in a secure way, unless you make it secure. For more on security, contact your hosting company.

```
<input type="password" name="secret">
```

The password `<input>` element works exactly like the text `<input>` element, except the text you type is masked.

More things that can go in a form

File input

Here's a whole new input element we haven't talked about. If you need to send an entire file to a server script, you'll once again use the `<input>` element, but this time set its type to "file". When you do that, the `<input>` element creates a control that allows you to select a file and—when the form is submitted—the contents of the file are sent with the rest of your form data to the server. Remember, your server script will need to be expecting a file upload, and also note that you must use the POST method to use this element.

Here's what the file input element looks like in a couple of different browsers.

```
<input type="file" name="doc">
```

To create a file input element, just set the type of the `<input>` element to "file".

Multiple selection

This isn't an element, but rather a new way to use an element you already know. If you add the Boolean attribute `multiple` to your `<select>` element, you turn your single-choice menu into a multiple-choice menu. Instead of a pop-down menu, you'll get a multiple-choice menu that shows all the options on the screen (with a scroll bar if there are a lot of them); you can choose more than one by holding down the Ctrl (Windows) or Command (Mac) key as you select.

With multiple selection, you can choose more than one option at a time.

```
<select name="characters" multiple>
    <option value="Buckaroo">Buckaroo Banzai</option>
    <option value="Tommy">Perfect Tommy</option>
    <option value="Penny Priddy">Penny</option>
    <option value="New Jersey">Jersey</option>
    <option value="John Parker">John</option>
</select>
```

Just add the attribute multiple to turn a single selection menu into a multiple selection menu.

Placeholder

You can use the `placeholder` attribute with most of the `<input>` types in a form to give the person who's filling out the form a hint about the kind of content you expect him to enter into the control. For instance, if you have a text field that expects a first and last name, you can provide a sample first and last name using the `placeholder` attribute. The value in the attribute is shown in the control, but is fainter than normal content that you add to a control, and as soon as you click into the text field, the placeholder text will disappear so it doesn't get in the way of what you're typing.

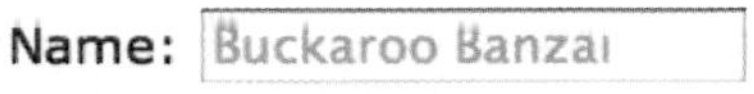

If you leave this field blank and submit the form, the placeholder content is NOT submitted as the value for the control!

```
<input type="text" placeholder="Buckaroo Banzai">
```

The placeholder attribute allows you to provide a hint about the kind of content you're expecting in this part of the form.

Required

This is an attribute you can use with any form control; it indicates that a field is required, so you shouldn't submit the form without specifying a value for the controls that have this attribute set. In browsers that support this attribute, if you try to submit the form without specifying a value for a `required` field, you'll get an error message and the form will not be submitted to the server.

Notice that this attribute is another *Boolean* attribute, like we saw in the `<video>` element. That just means that the value of the attribute is simply "there" or "not there." That is, if the attribute's there, then it's set, and if the attribute's not there, then it's not set. So in this example, `required` is there, so that means the attribute is set and the field is required to submit the form.

This is a screenshot from Chrome. As of this writing, not all browsers support required, but you can put it there anyway. You'll be able to submit the form, but then of course, the server script will complain that you haven't filled in the field.

required is a Boolean attribute, so if it's in the form control, that means the field must have a value for the form to submit correctly.

```
<input type="text" placeholder="Buckaroo Banzai" required>
```

BRAIN POWER

Edit your "styledform.html" file and add placeholders to each of the text `<input>`s and the tel `<input>`. Choose values that will give the customer a good hint about what kind of content is expected in each field.

Next, edit the same file and add the required attribute to each form field that is required by the Starbuzz Bean Machine (all the "Ship to" fields). Because beans and beantype have default values, do you really need required on those fields? What happens if you remove the checked attribute from beantype; do you need required then? Experiment with different browsers and see which browsers support placeholder and required.

BULLET POINTS

- The <form> element defines the form, and all form input elements are nested inside it.

- The action attribute contains the URL of the server script.

- The method attribute contains the method of sending the form data: either POST or GET.

- A POST packages form data and sends it as part of the request.

- A GET packages form data and appends it to the URL.

- Use POST when the form data should be private, or when it is large, such as when a <textarea> or file <input> element is used.

- Use GET for requests that might be bookmarked.

- The <input> element can act as many different input controls on the web page, depending on the value of its "type" attribute.

- A type of "text" creates a single-line text input.

- A type of "submit" creates a submit button.

- A type of "radio" creates one radio button. All radio buttons with the same name make up a group of mutually exclusive buttons.

- A type of "checkbox" creates one checkbox control. You can create a set of choices by giving multiple checkboxes the same name.

- A type of "number" creates a single-line text input that expects numeric characters only.

- A type of "range" creates a slider control for numeric input.

- A "color" type creates a color picker in browsers that support this type (and a text input otherwise).

- A "date" type creates a date picker in browsers that support this type (and a text input otherwise).

- The "email", "url", and "tel" types create single-line text inputs that cause custom keyboards to appear on some mobile browsers for easier data entry.

- A <textarea> element creates a multiline text input area.

- A <select> element creates a menu, which contains one or more <option> elements. <option> elements define the items in the menu.

- If you put text into the content of a <textarea> element, it will become the default text in a text area control on the web page.

- The value attribute in the text <input> element can be used to give a single-line text input an initial value.

- Setting the value attribute on a submit button changes the text of the button.

- When a web form is submitted, the form data values are paired with their corresponding names, and all names and values are sent to the server.

- CSS table display is often used to lay out forms, given that forms have a tabular structure. CSS can also be used to style the form's color, font styles, borders, and more.

- HTML allows form elements to be organized with the <fieldset> element.

- The <label> element can be used to attach labels to form elements in a way that aids accessibility.

- Use the placeholder attribute to give the form user a hint about the kind of content you expect in a field.

- The required attribute indicates a field is required for the form to be submitted correctly. Some browsers will force you to enter data into these fields before submitting the form.

Markup Magnets Solution

Your job was to take the form element magnets and lay them on top of the corresponding controls in the sketch. You didn't need all the magnets below to complete the job; some were left over. Here's our solution.

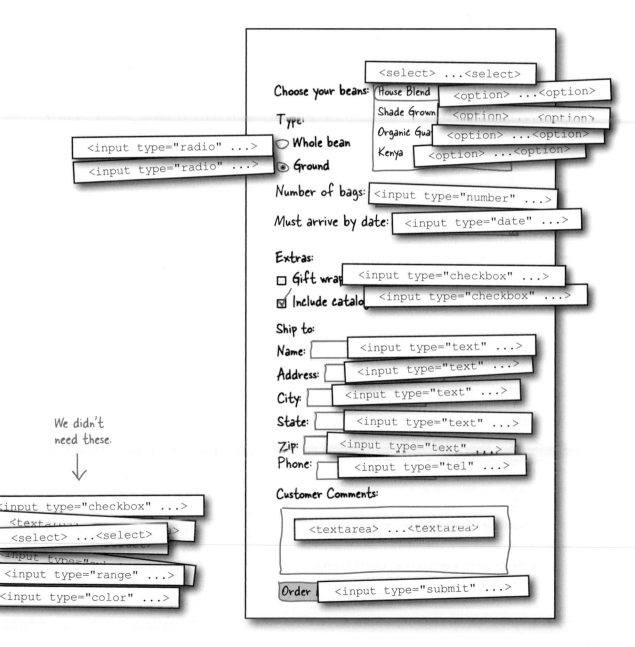

Choose your beans: `<select> ...<select>`

House Blend `<option> ...<option>`
Shade Grown `<option> ... <option>`
Organic Gua `<option> ...<option>`
Kenya `<option> ...<option>`

Type:
`<input type="radio" ...>`
`<input type="radio" ...>`
○ Whole bean
◉ Ground

Number of bags: `<input type="number" ...>`

Must arrive by date: `<input type="date" ...>`

Extras:
☐ Gift wrap `<input type="checkbox" ...>`
☑ Include catalo `<input type="checkbox" ...>`

Ship to:
Name: `<input type="text" ...>`
Address: `<input type="text" ...>`
City: `<input type="text" ...>`
State: `<input type="text" ...>`
Zip: `<input type="text" ...>`
Phone: `<input type="tel" ...>`

Customer Comments:

`<textarea> ...<textarea>`

Order `<input type="submit" ...>`

We didn't need these.
↓

`<input type="checkbox" ...>`
`<textarea ...>`
`<select> ...<select>`
`<input type="..."`
`<input type="range" ...>`
`<input type="color" ...>`

BE the Browser Solution

name = "Buckaroo Banzai"

zip = "90050"

model = "convertible"

color = "chilired"

caroptions[] = "stripes"

Sharpen your pencil Solution

GET or POST

For each description, circle either GET or POST depending on which method would be more appropriate. If you think it could be either, circle both. But be prepared to defend your answers...

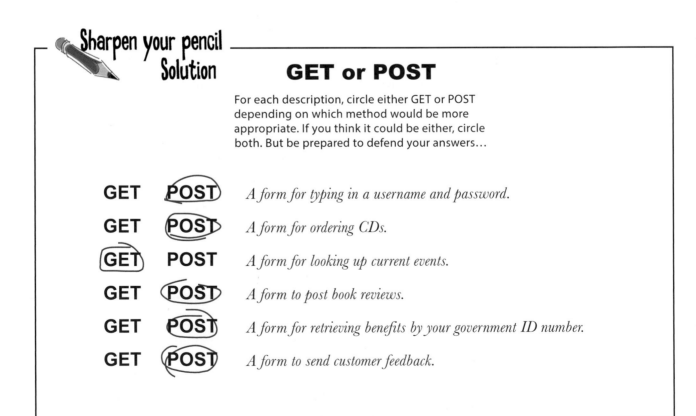

GET **(POST)**   *A form for typing in a username and password.*

GET **(POST)**   *A form for ordering CDs.*

(GET) POST   *A form for looking up current events.*

GET **(POST)**   *A form to post book reviews.*

GET **(POST)**   *A form for retrieving benefits by your government ID number.*

GET **(POST)**   *A form to send customer feedback.*

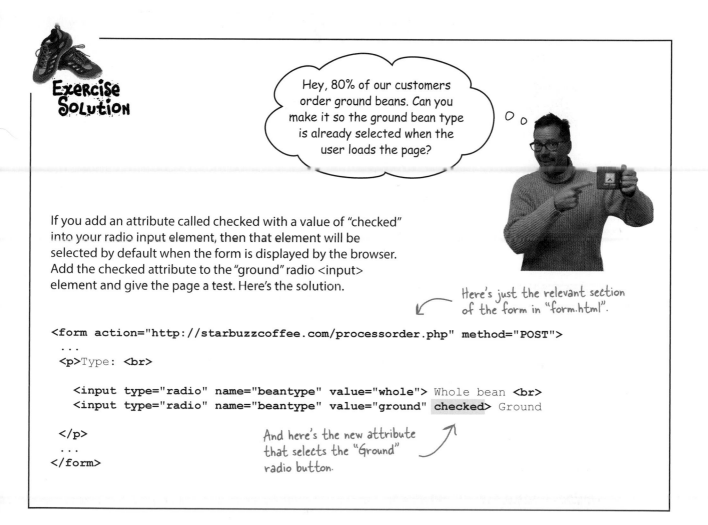

EXERCISE SOLUTION

Hey, 80% of our customers order ground beans. Can you make it so the ground bean type is already selected when the user loads the page?

If you add an attribute called checked with a value of "checked" into your radio input element, then that element will be selected by default when the form is displayed by the browser. Add the checked attribute to the "ground" radio <input> element and give the page a test. Here's the solution.

Here's just the relevant section of the form in "form.html".

```
<form action="http://starbuzzcoffee.com/processorder.php" method="POST">
  ...
  <p>Type: <br>

    <input type="radio" name="beantype" value="whole"> Whole bean <br>
    <input type="radio" name="beantype" value="ground" checked> Ground

  </p>
  ...
</form>
```

And here's the new attribute that selects the "Ground" radio button.

Congratulations!
You made it to the end.

Of course, there's still an appendix.

And the index.

And the colophon.

And then there's the website...

There's no escape, really.

Appendix: leftovers

The Top Ten Topics (We Didn't Cover)

We covered a lot of ground, and you're almost finished with this book. We'll miss you, but before we let you go, we wouldn't feel right about sending you out into the world without a little more preparation. We can't possibly fit everything you'll need to know into this relatively short chapter. Actually, we *did* originally include everything you need to know about HTML and CSS (not already covered by the other chapters), by reducing the type point size to .00004. It all fit, but nobody could read it. So, we threw most of it away, and kept the best bits for this Top Ten appendix.

#1 More CSS selectors

While you've already learned the most common selectors, here are a few more you might want to know about…

Pseudo-elements

You know all about pseudo-classes, and pseudo-elements are similar. Pseudo-elements can be used to select parts of an element that you can't conveniently wrap in a `<div>` or a `<span>` or select in other ways. For example, the `:first-letter` pseudo-element can be used to select the first letter of the text in a block element, allowing you to create effects like initial caps and drop caps. You can use the `:first-line` pseudo-element to select the first line of a paragraph. Here's how you'd use both to select the first letter and line of a `<p>` element:

```
p:first-letter {
        font-size: 3em;
}
p:first-line {
        font-style: italic;
}
```

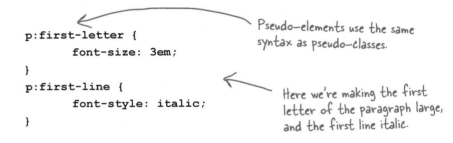

Pseudo-elements use the same syntax as pseudo-classes.

Here we're making the first letter of the paragraph large, and the first line italic.

Attribute selectors

Attribute selectors are exactly what they sound like: selectors that allow you to select elements based on attribute values. You use them like this:

This selector selects all images that have a width attribute in their HTML.

```
img[width] { border: black thin solid; }
img[height="300"] { border: red thin solid; }
image[alt~="flowers"] { border: #ccc thin solid; }
```

This selector selects all images that have an alt attribute that includes the word "flowers".

This selector selects all images that have a height attribute with a value of 300.

Selecting by siblings

You can also select elements based on their preceding sibling. For example, say you want to select only paragraphs that have an `<h1>` element preceding them, then you'd use this selector:

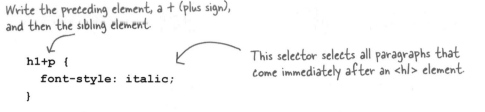

Write the preceding element, a + (plus sign), and then the sibling element.

```
h1+p {
    font-style: italic;
}
```

This selector selects all paragraphs that come immediately after an `<h1>` element.

Combining selectors

You've already seen examples of how selectors can be combined in this book. For instance, you can take a class selector and use it as part of a descendant selector, like this:

```
.blueberry p { color: purple; }
```

Here we're selecting all paragraphs that are descendants of an element in the blueberry class.

There's a pattern here that you can use to construct quite complex selectors. Let's step through how this pattern works:

1 Start by defining the context for the element you want to select, like this:

```
div#greentea > blockquote
```

Here we're using a descendant selector where a `<div>` with an id "greentea" must be the parent of the `<blockquote>`.

2 Then supply the element you want to select:

```
div#greentea > blockquote p
```
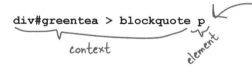
context   element

Next, we add the `<p>` element as the element we want to select in the context of the `<blockquote>`. The `<p>` element must be a descendant of `<blockquote>`, which must be a child of a `<div>` with an id of "greentea".

3 Then specify any pseudo-classes or pseudo-elements:

```
div#greentea > blockquote p:first-line { font-style: italic; }
```
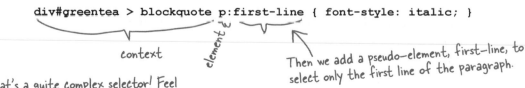
context   element

Then we add a pseudo-element, first-line, to select only the first line of the paragraph.

That's a quite complex selector! Feel free to construct your own selectors using this same method.

#2 Vendor-specific CSS properties

The browser makers (in other words, vendors like Microsoft, Mozilla, the folks behind WebKit, and so on) often add new functionality to their browsers to test new features, or to implement CSS extensions that are being considered, but aren't yet approved by the standards bodies. In these cases, vendors create CSS properties that look like this:

Start with a dash "–"   Another dash "–"

```
-moz-transform
```

The vendor identifier; here, it's "moz" for Mozilla

The property

You should feel free to make use of these vendor-specific properties, but they aren't necessarily intended for use in shipping products—the property may never be approved as a legit standard, or the vendor may change the implementation of the property at any time. That said, many of us need to be able to create pages that use the latest and greatest technology, but do so knowing that you're using properties that may change.

If you're going to make use of these properties, then often you'll create CSS that looks like this:

First, we list the general property in case it is supported, or gets supported in the future.

```
div {
    transform: rotate(45deg);
    -webkit-transform: rotate(45deg);     Safari & Chrome
    -moz-transform: rotate(45deg);        Mozilla
    -o-transform: rotate(45deg);          Opera
    -ms-transform: rotate(45deg);         IE
}
```

Then we list the known vendor-specific versions.

You can typically find these vendor-specific properties in the developer documentation and release notes for each browser, or by participating in the forums associated with each browser's development process.

And, if you're wondering what the transform property really does, check out the "#3 CSS transforms and transitions" section on the next page.

#3 CSS transforms and transitions

Using CSS, you can now do full-blown 2D and 3D transformations on elements. Rather than talk about it, let's look at an example (type this one in; it's worth it!).

```
<!doctype html>
<html>
<head>
    <meta charset="utf-8">
    <title>CSS Transforms and Transitions</title>
    <style>
        #box {
            position: absolute;
            top: 100px;
            left: 100px;
            width: 200px;
            height: 200px;
            background-color: red;
        }
        #box:hover {
            transform: rotate(45deg);
            -webkit-transform: rotate(45deg);
            -moz-transform: rotate(45deg);
            -o-transform: rotate(45deg);
            -ms-transform: rotate(45deg);
        }
    </style>
</head>
<body>
    <div id="box"></div>
</body>
</html>
```

Here's the basic style for the "box" <div> below...

The position is absolute (aren't you glad you stuck with us all through that positioning chapter?).

And let's give the <div> a position and size...

...and make it red.

This style rule applies ONLY if the <div> is in the hover state...yes, you can hover over <div>s too!

When you're hovering your mouse over the <div>, we transform the element by rotating it 45 degrees.

We still need browser-specific extensions for these.

This will only work in IE9+.

Here's the <div> we're transforming

Go ahead and type this in and then give it a test drive. When you pass our mouse over the "box" `<div>`, you should see it transform so that it is rotated by 45 degrees. Now, what if we want to make that transformation smooth with a nice animation? That's where transitions come in…so, turn the page.

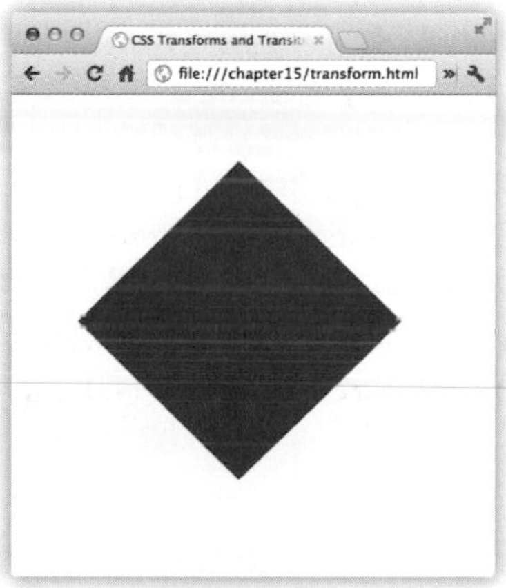

Mouse over the <div> to see it rotate!

We can add the `transition` property to the "box" `<div>` rule to have it transform to its new state over two seconds. Here's how we do that:

```
#box {
    position: absolute;
    top: 100px;
    left: 100px;
    width: 200px;
    height: 200px;
    background-color: red;
    transition: transform 2s;
    -webkit-transition: -webkit-transform 2s;
    -moz-transition: -moz-transform 2s;
    -o-transition: -o-transform 2s;
}
#box:hover {
    transform: rotate(45deg);
    -webkit-transform: rotate(45deg);
    -moz-transform: rotate(45deg);
    -o-transform: rotate(45deg);
    -ms-transform: rotate(45deg);
}
```

The transition property says: "If the value of the transform property changes, transition from the current value of transform to the new value of transform over the specified duration."

The default value of transform is nothing; that is, there is no transform.

But when you hover your mouse over the box, the value of transform is changed to a 45-degree rotation. So the transition from no transform to a 45-degree rotation transform happens over two seconds.

The value of the `transition` property is another property, in this case `transform`, and a duration, in this case two seconds. When the value of the specified property changes, the transition causes that change to happen over the specified duration, which creates an animation effect. You can transition other CSS properties too, like `width` or `opacity`.

IE currently (as of version 9) has no support for transition, but may in version 10. So you won't see the animation if you're using IE.

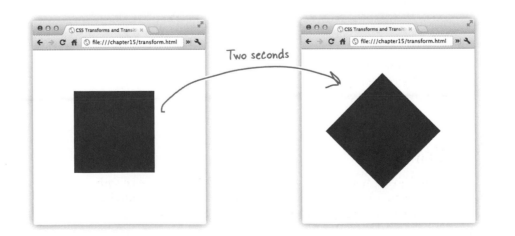

Two seconds

#4 Interactivity

HTML pages don't have to be passive documents; they can also have content that is *executable*. Executable content gives your pages behavior. You create executable content by writing programs or scripts using a scripting language called JavaScript. Here's a little taste of what it means to put executable content into your pages.

Here's a new HTML element, `<script>`, which allows you to place code right inside of HTML.

We're using the id of the form to get a handle to the form in JavaScript so we can do things with it, like define what happens when a button is clicked.

```
<script>
    window.onload = init;
    function init() {
        var submitButton = document.getElementById("submitButton");
        submitButton.onclick = validBid;
    }
    function validBid() {
        if (document.getElementById("bid").value > 0) {
            document.getElementById("theForm").submit();
        } else {
            return false;
        }
    }
</script>
```

And here's a bit of JavaScript that checks a user's bid to make sure it's not zero dollars or less.

If the bid is greater than 0, we submit the form; otherwise, we don't because it's an error.

Then in HTML, you can create a form that uses this script to check the bid before the form is submitted. If the bid is more than zero, the form gets submitted.

```
<form id="theForm" method="post" action="contest.php">
    <input type="number" id="bid" value="0"><br>
    <input type="button" id="submitButton" value="Bid!"><br>
</form>
```

In JavaScript, we can define what happens when the submitButton is clicked, and get the value of the input with the id of "bid".

What else can scripting do?

Form input validation, like we did above, is a common and useful task that is often done with JavaScript (and the types of validation you can do go far beyond this example). But that's just the beginning of what you can do with JavaScript...as you'll see on the next page.

#5 HTML5 APIs and web apps

In addition to the elements that HTML5 adds, HTML5 comes with a whole new set of application programming interfaces (APIs for short) that are accessible through JavaScript. These APIs open up a whole new universe of expression and functionality to your web pages. Let's look at just a few things you might do with them…

Interact with your pages in new ways that work for the desktop and mobile devices.

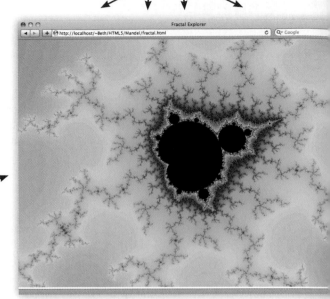

With HTML5 APIs and JavaScript, you can create a 2D drawable surface right in your page; no plug-ins required.

Make your pages location-aware to know where your users are, show them what's nearby, take them on a scavenger hunt, give them directions, to bring people with common interests together in the same area.

Use web workers to turbo-charge your JavaScript code and do some serious computation or make your app more responsive. You can even make better use of your user's multicore processor!

Access any web service and bring that data back to your app, in near real time.

Cache data locally using browser storage to speed up mobile apps.

No need for special plug-ins to play video.

Create your own video playback controls using HTML and JavaScript.

Integrate your pages with Google Maps and even let your users track their movement in real time.

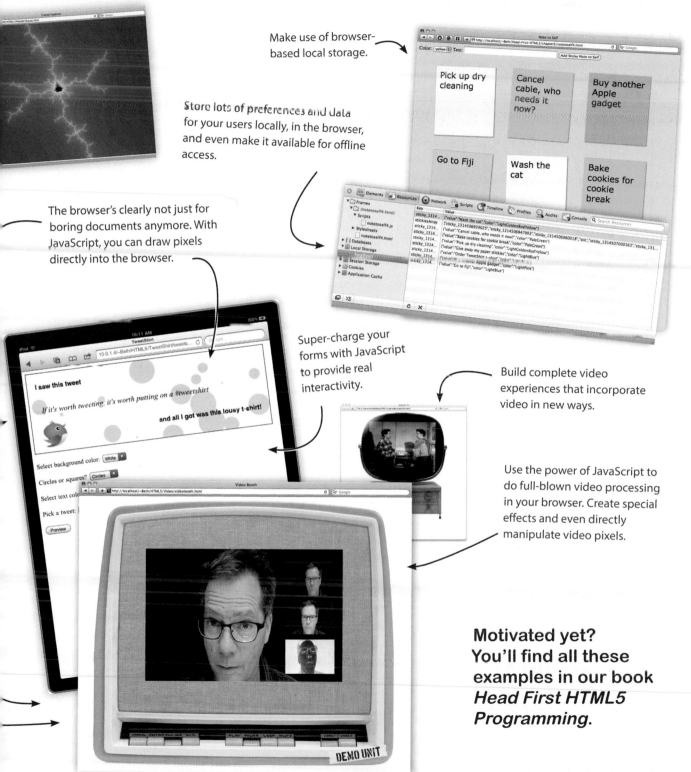

Make use of browser-based local storage.

Store lots of preferences and data for your users locally, in the browser, and even make it available for offline access.

The browser's clearly not just for boring documents anymore. With JavaScript, you can draw pixels directly into the browser.

Super-charge your forms with JavaScript to provide real interactivity.

Build complete video experiences that incorporate video in new ways.

Use the power of JavaScript to do full-blown video processing in your browser. Create special effects and even directly manipulate video pixels.

**Motivated yet?
You'll find all these
examples in our book
*Head First HTML5
Programming*.**

#6 More on Web Fonts

We would have liked to have spent a lot more time on Web Fonts, so they ended up making our "10 things we didn't cover," even though we did cover them. If you're using Web Fonts, there are a few more things you should know and investigate, so we've put together a top 10 of things you should know about Web Fonts:

1. There are services that help take the pain out of using Web Fonts, like Google Web Fonts (`http://www.google.com/webfonts`), Fonts.com (`http://www.fonts.com/web-fonts`), and Extensis (`http://www.extensis.com/`).

2. Browsers behave differently while they download your fonts. Some browsers display a backup font, while others wait for the font to be downloaded before rendering the text.

3. Once you've downloaded a font, it is cached by your browser and not retrieved again the next time you encounter a page that uses it.

4. All modern browsers (IE9+) support the Web Open Font Format (WOFF), which is likely to become the Web Font standard. However, Internet Explorer up through version 8 supports a font standard different from all other modern browsers (.eot), and has a bug that prevents the browser from loading multiple fonts (so you can't just list more than one font in your `@font-face` rule). If you need to support Web Fonts on IE8 and earlier, the services mentioned above can insulate you from having to worry about these cross-browser compatibility issues.

5. There are many free fonts out there. Look for "open source fonts" to find fonts you can include in your web page for free.

6. Because Web Fonts are real fonts, you can apply any styling to them just like you can to conventional fonts.

7. Using Web Fonts can have some impact on the performance of your page, but is considered a better practice and will typically provide better performance than using custom graphic images for typography.

8. Limit the fonts in your `@font-face` rule to only the fonts used on a particular page.

9. If you have existing font licenses, check with your vendor; they may allow web usage.

10. As with conventional fonts, always include a fallback font in case your page's font isn't available or an error is encountered retrieving or decoding it.

#7 Tools for creating web pages

Now that you know HTML and CSS, you're in a good position to decide if tools like Dreamweaver, Expression Web, or Coda are for you. Some of these applications give you much richer editors with features like code coloring and built-in preview to make creating and editing your HTML and CSS easier. Some of these applications provide what-you-see-is-what-you-get (WYSIWYG) tools for creating web pages; we're sure you know enough about HTML and browser support to know that this goal, while worthwhile, also comes up short from time to time. But that said, these tools also provide some very handy features, even if you're writing a lot of the HTML yourself:

- A "code" window for entering HTML and CSS with syntax checking to catch common mistakes and suggest common names and attributes as you type.

- A preview-and-publish functionality that allows you to test pages before making them "live" on the Web.

- A site manager that allows you to organize your site, and also keeps your local changes in synch with your website on the server. Note that this usually takes care of all the FTP work for you.

- Some provide built-in validation, so you know your page is valid as you develop it.

These tools are also not without their downsides:

- Sometimes these tools lag behind standards in terms of support, so to keep your HTML and CSS current, you may need to write (or edit) the HTML yourself.

- Not all of these tools enforce strict standards, and may allow you to get sloppy with your HTML and CSS, so don't forget to validate if the tool doesn't provide built-in validation.

Keep in mind that you can use a combination of simple editors along with these more sophisticated tools; one solution doesn't have to fit all your needs. So use a page creation tool when it makes sense.

Some tools to consider

- Dreamweaver (Adobe)
- Hype (Tumult)
- Coda (Panic)
- Microsoft Expression Web
- Flux (The Escapers)
- Amaya (Open source, developed by the W3C)
- Eclipse (by the Eclipse Foundation)

← The latest and greatest in web editors is always in flux, so be sure to check the Web for all the options for tools.

#8 XHTML5

We were pretty tough on XHTML in this book, with the whole
"XHTML is over" thing. The truth is, when it comes to XHTML, it is
only XHTML 2 and later that has died, and in fact, you can write your
HTML5 using XHTML style if you want to. Why would you want
to? Well, you might need to validate or transform your documents as
XML, or you might want to support XML technologies, like SVG (you'll
probably know if you do), that work with HTML.

Let's look at a simple XHTML document and then step through the high
points (we couldn't possibly cover everything you need to know on this
topic; as with all things XML, it gets complicated fast).

```
<!doctype html>                    ←—— Same doctype!
<html xmlns="http://www.w3.org/1999/xhtml">    This is XML; we need to add what is
                                               known as a namespace.
    <head>
        <title>You Rock!</title>
        <meta charset="UTF-8" />       All elements have to be extremely well formed; note the
                                       trailing /> here to close this void element. That's XML's
    </head>                            format for closing a void tag.
    <body>
        <p>I'm kinda liking this XHTML!</p>
        <svg xmlns="http://www.w3.org/2000/svg">        As an example, we're using
                                                        SVG to draw a rectangle
            <rect stroke="black" fill="blue" x="45px" y="45px"    into our page. The details
                  width="200px" height="100px" stroke-width="2" />  aren't important; what is
                                                        important is that this is
        </svg>                                          an XML format that lives
    </body>          We can embed XML right in the      inside XML, not HTML.
                     page! Kinda cool.
</html>
```

Now here's a few things you need to consider for your XHTML pages:

- Your page must be well-formed XML.

- Your page should be served with the `application/xhtml+xml`
  MIME type; for this, you'll need to make sure your server is serving
  this type (either read up on this or contact your server administrator).

- Make sure to include the XHTML namespace in your `<html>`
  element (which we've done above).

Closing all your elements, quotes around attribute values, valid nesting of elements, and all that

Like we said, with XML there's a lot more to know and lots of things to
watch out for. And, as always with XML, may the force be with you…

#9 Server-side scripting

Many web pages are generated by applications running on a server. For example, think about an online order system where a server is generating pages as you step through the order process, or an online forum, where there's a server generating pages based on forum messages that are stored in a database somewhere. We used a server application to process the form you created in Chapter 14 for the Starbuzz Bean Machine.

Many hosting companies will let you create your own server applications by writing server-side scripts and programs. Here's a few things server-side scripting will allow you to do:

- Build an online store complete with products, a shopping cart, and an order system.

- Personalize your pages for each user based on his or her preferences.

- Deliver up-to-date news, events, and information.

- Allow users to search your site.

- Allow users to help build the content of your site.

To create server applications, you'll need to know a server-side scripting or programming language. There are a lot of competing languages for web development, and you're likely to get differing opinions on which language is best depending on who you ask. In fact, web languages are a little like automobiles: you can drive anything from a Prius to a Hummer, and each has its own strengths and weaknesses (cost, ease of use, size, economy, and so on).

Web languages are constantly evolving; PHP, Python, Perl, Node.js, Ruby on Rails, and JavaServer Pages (JSPs) are all commonly used. If you're new to programming, PHP may be the easiest language to start with, and there are millions of PHP-driven web pages, so you'd be in good company. If you have some programming experience, you may want to try JSPs or Python. If you're more aligned with the Microsoft technologies, then you'll want to look at VB.NET and ASP.NET as a server-side solution. And, if JavaScript is your gig, then check out Node.js for a whole new approach.

#10 Audio

HTML gives you a standard way to play audio in your pages, without a plug-in, with the `<audio>` element. You'll find this element quite similar to the `<video>` element:

```
<audio src="song.mp3" id="boombox" controls>
  Sorry but audio is not supported in your browser.
</audio>
```

Look familiar? Yes, audio supports similar functionality as video (minus the video, obviously).

Also like video, each browser implements its own look and feel for player controls (which typically consist of a progress bar with play, pause, and volume controls).

Sadly, like video, there is no standard encoding for audio. Three formats are popular: MP3, WAV, and Ogg Vorbis. You'll find that support for these formats varies across the browser landscape (as of this writing, Chrome is the only browser that supports all three formats).

Despite its simple functionality, the `<audio>` element and its JavaScript API give you lots of control. Using the element with JavaScript, you can create interesting web experiences by hiding the controls and managing the audio playback in your code. And with HTML5, you can now do this without the overhead of having to use (and learn) a plug-in (like Adobe Flash).

Index

C

floating
    elements, 525–529
    float property, 472, 478–482, 487–490
    inline elements, 497
    layouts, 521, 525–526
flowing block/inline elements, 473–478
flow of elements, 537
:focus pseudo-class, 453
folders
    organizing files/images in, 56–59
    for thumbnails, 192
fonts (CSS)
    changing weight of, 335–336
    colors, background vs. font, 349
    families of, 355
    @font-face rule, 322–325
    font-family property, 279–280
    for Mac/Windows, 321
    properties, 312–313
    shorthand for, 444
    sizing, 328–334
    styling, 337–339
    Web Fonts, 325–327, 706
footers
    <footer> element (HTML5), 551, 595
    laying out, 493–496, 499
formats
    image, 167
    video, 586–591
forms, HTML
    action attribute, 650, 661, 665, 692
    adding checkboxes/text area to, 673–674
    adding fieldsets/legends to, 689
    adding <input> elements to, 664–666, 671–675
    adding <label> elements for accessibility, 688
    adding password <input> element to, 689
    basics, 646–649
    commonly used elements, 652–657
    file <input> element, 690
    <form> element, 649–651, 660–663, 692
    GET vs. POST methods, 678–680

    laying out with CSS table display, 682–685
    multiple choice menus, 690
    name attribute, 662
    placeholder attribute, 691
    required attribute, 691
    server scripts, 646–647, 650–652, 660, 663
    styling with CSS, 686–687
frozen layouts, 501–502, 537
FTP (File Transfer Protocol), 129–132, 159

G

get <filename> command, 131
GET method, 678–680, 692
GIF image format, 167–168, 172, 211
Google Web Fonts, 325–327, 706
Guide, HTML, 245–246

H

<h1> element (headings), 22
<h2> element (subheadings), 8, 22
<head> element, 8, 23–24, 36
<header> elements, 551, 568–571, 572–573, 595
header images, 523–524
Head First HTML5 Programming, 6, 52, 231, 593, 705
Head First learning principles, xxviii
Head First Lounge project, 4–5
Head First Mobile Web, 403
headings
    changing color of, 439
    levels of, 6
height properties
    attribute, 174, 584
    CSS box model and, 366, 371
    of elements, 430
    property, 570
hex code (colors), 32, 345–347, 349, 355
"Hide extensions for known file types" option, 15
hosting companies, 125, 159

Colophon

All interior layouts were designed by Eric Freeman and Elisabeth Robson.

The book's look and feel was based and extended from the original design by Kathy Sierra and Bert Bates The book was produced using Adobe InDesign CS5 and Adobe Photoshop CS. The book was typeset using Uncle Stinky, Mister Frisky (you think we're kidding), Ann Satellite, Baskerville, Comic Sans (can you believe it?), Myriad Pro, Skippy Sharp, Savoye LET, Jokerman LET, Courier New, and Woodrow typefaces.

Interior design and production all happened on two Mac Pros and two MacBook Airs.

Writing locations included: Bainbridge Island, Washington; Portland, Oregon; Seaside, Florida; Lexington, Kentucky. Long days of writing were powered by zero caffeine and Brew Dr. Kombucha, and the sounds of Foster the People, B-52s, Duran Duran, David Bowie, William Shatner, Elvis Presley, Pink Floyd, Genesis, Simple Minds, Ratt, Skid Row, Men without Hats, Men at Work, Berlin, Steve Roach, Tom Waits, Beyman Brothers, and a heck of a lot more 80s music than you'd care to know about.

This isn't goodbye

Bring your brain over to
wickedlysmart.com

Have it your way.

Get even more for your money.

Join the O'Reilly Community, and register the O'Reilly books you own. It's free, and you'll get:

- $4.99 ebook upgrade offer
- 40% upgrade offer on O'Reilly print books
- Membership discounts on books and events
- Free lifetime updates to ebooks and videos
- Multiple ebook formats, DRM FREE
- Participation in the O'Reilly community
- Newsletters
- Account management
- 100% Satisfaction Guarantee

Signing up is easy:

1. Go to: oreilly.com/go/register
2. Create an O'Reilly login.
3. Provide your address.
4. Register your books.

Note: English-language books only

To order books online:

oreilly.com/store

For questions about products or an order:

orders@oreilly.com

To sign up to get topic-specific email announcements and/or news about upcoming books, conferences, special offers, and new technologies:

elists@oreilly.com

For technical questions about book content:

booktech@oreilly.com

To submit new book proposals to our editors:

proposals@oreilly.com

O'Reilly books are available in multiple DRM-free ebook formats. For more information:

oreilly.com/ebooks

O'REILLY®

Spreading the knowledge of innovators | oreilly.com